Mc Graw Hill **Custom Publishing**

Finance

MG101 – Finance Part

Prepared by:

Dr. Elisabetta Bertero

The London School of Economics and Political Science

ISBN 13:   9781121778979

The **McGraw·Hill** Companies

McGraw-Hill Custom Publishing

www.mcgrawhillcreate.co.uk

Published by McGraw-Hill Education (UK) Ltd an imprint of the
McGraw-Hill Companies, Inc., 1221 Avenue of the Americas, New
York NY 10020.

ISBN: 9781121778979

Finance

Contents

Credits

Chapters from:
Fundamentals of Corporate
Finance, European Edition
by Hillier-Clacher-Ross-
Westerfield-Jordan

CHAPTER

1

Introduction to Corporate Finance

LEARNING OBJECTIVES

After studying this chapter, you should understand:

LO1 The basic types of financial management decision, and the role of the financial manager.
LO2 The goal of financial management.
LO3 How financial markets work and the reason they exist.

RECENT YEARS HAVE SEEN corporate finance and financial events displace other newsworthy events from the front pages of newspapers. In 2007 financial markets and the world economy nearly imploded after banks were unable or unwilling to lend money to other companies. This led to a worldwide recession in 2008 and 2009, which saw job losses on an unprecedented scale, massive corporate bankruptcies, and governments spending billions to shore up their own economies.

While the corporate world was experiencing major difficulties, the financial markets performed exceptionally well, with some stock exchanges reporting their best performance on record. For example, while the United Kingdom underwent its longest and deepest recession on record, the London Stock Exchange FTSE 100 index (representing the combined value of its largest companies) grew by just under 50 per cent!

Does this make sense? Understanding the decisions facing corporations, the impact of these decisions, how they affect firm value, and the role of investors is the goal of this text. This takes us into issues involving corporate goals and firm valuation, all of which we introduce in this chapter.

To begin our study of modern corporate finance we need to address two central issues. First, what is corporate finance, and what is the role of the financial manager in the corporation? Second, what is the goal of financial management? For many companies, share price valuation is an exceptionally important issue, and so we also take a brief look at the financial markets and their impact on corporate decision-making.

1.1 Corporate Finance and the Financial Manager

In this section we discuss where the financial manager fits in the corporation. We start by defining *corporate finance* and the financial manager's job.

Chapter 1 Introduction to Corporate Finance

What Is Corporate Finance?

Imagine that you were to start your own business. No matter what type you started, you would have to answer the following three questions in some form or another:

1 What long-term investments should you make? That is, what lines of business will you be in, and what sorts of buildings, machinery and equipment will you need?

2 Where will you get the long-term financing to pay for your investment? Will you bring in other owners, or will you borrow the money?

3 How will you manage your everyday financial activities, such as collecting from customers and paying suppliers?

These are not the only questions by any means, but they are among the most important. Corporate finance, broadly speaking, is the study of ways to answer these three questions. Accordingly, we'll be looking at each of them in the chapters ahead.

The Financial Manager

A striking feature of large corporations is that the owners (the shareholders) are not usually directly involved in making business decisions, particularly on a day-to-day basis. Instead, the corporation employs managers to represent the owners' interests and make decisions on their behalf. In a large corporation the financial manager would be in charge of answering the three questions we raised in the preceding section.

The financial management function is usually associated with a top officer of the firm, such as a finance director (FD) or chief financial officer (CFO). Figure 1.1 is a simplified organizational chart that highlights the finance activity in a large firm. As shown, the finance director co-ordinates the activities of the treasurer and the controller. The controller's office handles cost and financial accounting, tax payments, and management information systems. The treasurer's office is responsible for managing the firm's cash and credit, its financial planning, and its capital expenditures.

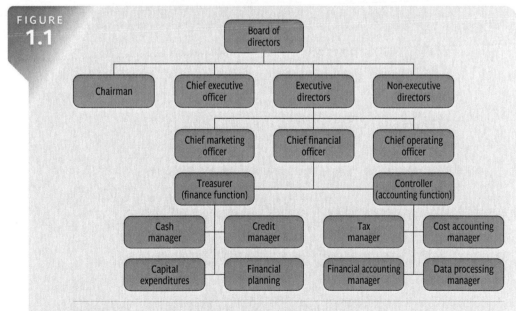

FIGURE
1.1

Figure 1.1 A sample simplified organizational chart

You may be wondering what the difference is between the finance and accounting functions in a firm. The accounting function takes all the financial information and data that arises as a result of ongoing business activities, and presents this in ways that allow management to assess the performance and risk of their firm (financial accounting) and make informed decisions on future corporate activity (management accounting). To ensure that all firms provide comparable information, there are generally accepted accounting standards. In the European Union all firms that are listed on a stock exchange must follow International Accounting Standards (IAS), as set by the International Accounting Standards Board (IASB).

The finance function of the firm is related to the three general questions raised earlier, and the chapters ahead deal primarily with these issues. However, although our study bears mostly on activities associated with the finance function, we also discuss the accounting function whenever it is required to better understand the decisions made by corporations.

Financial Management Decisions

As the preceding discussion suggests, the financial manager must be concerned with three basic types of question. We consider these in greater detail next.

Capital Budgeting The first question concerns the firm's long-term investments. The process of planning and managing a firm's long-term investments is called **capital budgeting**. In capital budgeting the financial manager tries to identify investment opportunities that are worth more to the firm than they cost to acquire. Loosely speaking, this means that the value of the cash flow generated by an asset exceeds the cost of that asset.

> **capital budgeting**
> The process of planning and managing a firm's long-term investments.

The types of investment opportunity that would typically be considered depend in part on the nature of the firm's business. For example, for a large retailer such as Tesco, deciding whether to open another store would be an important capital budgeting decision. Similarly, for a software company such as Microsoft, the decision to develop and market a new spreadsheet program would be a major capital budgeting decision. Some decisions, such as what type of computer system to purchase, might not depend so much on a particular line of business.

Regardless of the specific nature of an opportunity under consideration, financial managers must be concerned not only with how much cash they expect to receive, but also with when they expect to receive it, and how likely they are to receive it. Evaluating the *size*, *timing* and *risk* of future cash flows is the essence of capital budgeting. In fact, as we shall see in the chapters ahead, whenever we evaluate a business decision, the size, timing and risk of the cash flows will be by far the most important things we shall consider.

> **capital structure**
> The mixture of long-term debt and equity maintained by a firm.

Capital Structure The second question for the financial manager concerns ways in which the firm obtains and manages the long-term financing it needs to support its long-term investments. A firm's **capital structure** (or financial structure) is the specific mixture of **long-term debt** and **equity** the firm uses to finance its operations. The financial manager has two concerns in this area. First, how much should the firm borrow? That is, what mixture of debt and equity is best? The mixture chosen will affect both the risk and the value of the firm. Second, what are the least expensive sources of funds for the firm?

> **long-term debt**
> Long-term borrowing by the firm (longer than one year) to finance its long-term investments.

If we picture the firm as a pie, then the firm's capital structure determines how that pie is sliced – in other words, what percentage of the firm's cash flow goes to creditors and what percentage goes to shareholders. Firms have a great deal of flexibility in choosing a financial structure. The question of whether one structure is better than any other for a particular firm is the heart of the capital structure issue.

> **equity**
> The amount of money raised by the firm that comes from the owners' (shareholders') investment.

In addition to deciding on the financing mix, the financial manager has to decide exactly how and where to raise the money. The expenses associated with raising long-term financing can be considerable, so different possibilities must be carefully evaluated. Also, corporations borrow money from a variety of lenders in a number of different, and sometimes exotic, ways. Choosing among lenders and among loan types is another job handled by the financial manager.

> **working capital**
> A firm's short-term assets and liabilities.

Working Capital Management   The third question concerns **working capital** management. The term *working capital* refers to a firm's short-term assets, such as inventory, and its short-term liabilities, such as money owed to suppliers. Managing the firm's working capital is a day-to-day activity which ensures that the firm has sufficient resources to continue its operations and avoid costly interruptions. This involves a number of activities related to the firm's receipt and disbursement of cash.

Some questions about working capital that must be answered are the following:

1   How much cash and inventory should we keep on hand?

2   Should we sell on credit? If so, what terms will we offer, and to whom will we extend them?

3   How will we obtain any needed short-term financing? Will we purchase on credit, or will we borrow in the short term and pay cash? If we borrow in the short term, how and where should we do it?

These are just a small sample of the issues that arise in managing a firm's working capital.

Conclusion   The three areas of corporate financial management we have described – capital budgeting, capital structure, and working capital management – are very broad categories. Each includes a rich variety of topics, and we have indicated only a few questions that arise in the different areas. The chapters ahead contain greater detail.

CONCEPT QUESTIONS

1.1a   What is the capital budgeting decision?

1.1b   What do you call the specific mixture of long-term debt and equity that a firm chooses to use?

1.1c   Into what category of financial management does cash management fall?

1.2   The Goal of Financial Management

Assuming that we restrict ourselves to for-profit businesses, the main goal of financial management is to make money or add value for the owners. This goal is a little vague, of course, so we examine some different ways of formulating it to come up with a more precise definition. Such a definition is important, because it leads to an objective basis for making and evaluating financial decisions.

Possible Goals

If we were to consider possible financial goals, we might come up with some ideas like the following:

- Survive.
- Avoid financial distress and bankruptcy.
- Beat the competition.
- Maximize sales or market share.
- Minimize costs.
- Maximize profits.
- Maintain steady earnings growth.

These are only a few of the goals we could list. Furthermore, each of these possibilities presents problems as a goal for the financial manager.

1.3 Financial Markets and the Corporation

In most countries the financial markets play a fundamental role in the operations of large corporations. Even if a firm is not traded on a stock exchange, the stock market is important, because it can inform management of the performance of their competitors, suppliers, customers and the economy as a whole. The primary advantage of financial markets is that they facilitate the flow of money from those that have surplus cash to those that need financing.

Cash Flows To and From the Firm

The interplay between the corporation and the financial markets is illustrated in Fig. 1.2. The arrows in the figure trace the passage of cash from the financial markets to the firm, and from the firm back to the financial markets. Suppose we start with the firm selling shares of equity and borrowing money to raise cash. Cash flows to the firm from the financial markets (A). The firm invests the cash in assets (B). These can be short-term (current) or long-term (non-current), and they generate cash (C), some of which goes to pay corporate taxes (D). After taxes are paid, some of this cash flow is reinvested in the firm (E). The rest goes back to the financial markets as cash paid to creditors and shareholders (F).

The financial markets are not funded just by corporations paying cash to creditors or shareholders. The savings of households (G) also find their way into the financial markets. For example, whenever your salary goes into your bank account, whenever you pay insurance on your car, house or computers, and every time you pay your pension premium, this money will end up in the financial markets. This happens because the financial institutions (H) you pay your money to use it to invest in the financial markets. The difference between what financial institutions earn in the financial markets and what they have to pay you (in terms of monthly interest, random insurance payouts, and pensions) is their profit.

A financial market, like any market, is just a way of bringing buyers and sellers together. In financial markets it is debt and equity securities that are bought and sold. Financial markets differ in detail, however. The most important differences concern the types of security that are traded, how trading is conducted, and who the buyers and sellers are. Some of these differences are discussed next.

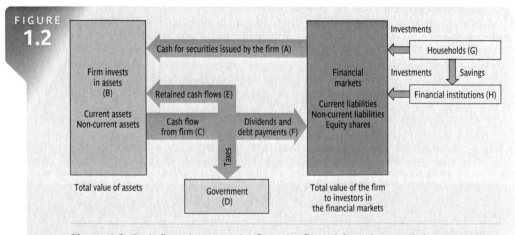

Figure 1.2 Cash flows between the firm, the financial markets, and the economy

Chapter 1 Introduction to Corporate Finance

Primary versus Secondary Markets

Financial markets function as both primary and secondary markets for debt and equity securities. The term *primary market* refers to the original sale of securities by governments and corporations. The *secondary markets* are those in which these securities are bought and sold after the original sale. Equities are, of course, issued solely by corporations. Debt securities are issued by both governments and corporations. In the discussion that follows, we focus on corporate securities only.

Primary Markets In a primary market transaction the corporation is the seller, and the transaction raises money for the corporation. Corporations engage in two types of primary market transaction: public offerings and private placements. A public offering, as the name suggests, involves selling securities to the general public, whereas a private placement is a negotiated sale involving a specific buyer.

By law, public offerings of debt and equity must be registered with the securities regulator in the country where the offerings are made. For example, in the UK this is the Financial Services Authority, and in the Netherlands it is the Authority for Financial Markets (Autoriteit Financiële Markten). Registration requires the firm to disclose a great deal of information before selling any securities. The accounting, legal and selling costs of public offerings can be considerable.

Partly to avoid the various regulatory requirements and the expense of public offerings, debt and equity are often sold privately to large financial institutions such as life insurance companies or mutual funds. Such private placements do not normally have to be registered with securities regulators, and do not require the involvement of underwriters (investment banks that specialize in selling securities to the public).

Secondary Markets A secondary market transaction involves one owner or creditor selling to another. Therefore the secondary markets provide the means for transferring ownership of corporate securities. Although a corporation is directly involved only in a primary market transaction (when it sells securities to raise cash), the secondary markets are still critical to large corporations. The reason is that investors are much more willing to purchase securities in a primary market transaction when they know that those securities can later be resold if desired.

Dealer versus Auction Markets There are two kinds of secondary market: *auction* markets and *dealer* markets. Generally speaking, dealers buy and sell for themselves, at their own risk. A car dealer, for example, buys and sells automobiles. In contrast, brokers and agents match buyers and sellers, but they do not actually own the commodity that is bought or sold. A real estate agent, for example, does not normally buy and sell houses.

Dealer markets in equities and long-term debt are called *over-the-counter* (OTC) markets. Most trading in debt securities takes place over the counter. The expression *over the counter* refers to days of old when securities were literally bought and sold at counters in offices around the country. Today, a significant fraction of the market for equities and almost all of the market for long-term debt have no central location; the many dealers are connected electronically.

Auction markets differ from dealer markets in two ways. First, an auction market or exchange has a physical location (such as Paternoster Square for the London Stock Exchange). Second, in a dealer market, most of the buying and selling is done by the dealer. The primary purpose of an auction market, on the other hand, is to match those who wish to sell with those who wish to buy. Dealers play a limited role.

Trading in Corporate Securities The equity shares of most large European firms trade in organized auction markets. The largest such market is Euronext, very closely followed by the London Stock Exchange. Other European exchanges include the Deutsche Börse, the BME Spanish Exchanges, the SIX Swiss Exchange, and the NASDAQ OMX Nordic Exchange.

There are many large and important financial markets outside Europe, of course, and European corporations often look to these markets to raise cash. The New York Stock Exchange, NASDAQ (US) and the Tokyo Stock Exchange are three well-known examples.

than the search engines that existed in 1996. Armed only with this idea and a few working algorithms, they approached several potential investors and successfully attracted $100,000 from one of the founders of Sun Microsystems to develop their business concept. Within a year they had received a further $25 million from venture capitalists. To receive this financing, Brin and Page would have used accounting and finance information to create a business plan and cash flow forecast, from which potential investors were able to arrive at a valuation of the future company. Valuation of companies and projects is covered in Part Two of this text.

The Google Share Issue

By 2004 Google had been so successful with its business model that it needed significant injections of cash to capture the emerging business opportunities that were becoming available. The company had two basic options. It could borrow the money (through a bank loan or public debt markets) or issue equity (through the equity markets). In the end, it chose to raise all the money in the form of equity financing. Google actually has no long-term debt. There are a number of reasons for this, and there are many factors to take into consideration when a firm chooses its own debt-to-equity mix, which is also known as its capital structure. Capital structure is covered in Part Three of the textbook.

The Google share issue was highly unusual in that it was organized wholly over the Internet. However, several fundamental issues had to be decided. First, what should the value of the new shares be? How risky are the shares? These questions are of huge importance to investors who are planning to invest their cash in any new investment. Assessing the risk of investments is covered in Part Four, and the process of issuing new securities is reviewed in Part Five.

Google as a Business

Although Google is known as an Internet search firm, its success and size make it quite similar to other large firms in more capital-intensive industries. At the beginning of 2010 Google had approximately $5 billion invested in property, and 20,000 employees. Like all other firms, Google needs to ensure it has enough liquidity and cash available to pay off its creditors. Short-term financial planning is therefore crucial to its continued existence. This is covered in Part Six of the text.

Finally, Google has undertaken over 60 acquisitions since 2001. Most notably, it bought YouTube ($1.65 billion) in 2006, DoubleClick ($3.1 billion) in 2007, and AdMob ($750 million) in 2009. Its operations span many countries, making its global reach enormous. It is one of the biggest companies in the world, and will continue to evolve and develop in the future. The final part of this textbook deals with international corporate finance, and the salient decisions that are involved in this area. These are extremely important to all companies, and not just Google.

So What Is Corporate Finance?

Many people who think of corporate finance tend to consider valuation as being most important. Others think of risk assessment, while many think that capital structure should be emphasized. Hopefully, this section shows that, for a business to be truly successful, the management of a firm and its shareholders must have a solid understanding of all corporate finance areas, and not just one or two topics. Google was a success, not just because it had a fantastic business idea, but also because it understands the fundamental basis of good business and corporate finance.

Summary and Conclusions

This chapter introduced you to some of the basic ideas in corporate finance:

1 Corporate finance has three main areas of concern:

   (a) Capital budgeting: what long-term investments should the firm take?

   (b) Capital structure: where will the firm get the long-term financing to pay for its investments? In other words, what mixture of debt and equity should the firm use to fund operations?

   (c) Working capital management: how should the firm manage its everyday financial activities?

2 The goal of financial management in a for-profit business is to make decisions that increase the market value of the equity.

3 The advantages of the corporate form are enhanced by the existence of financial markets. Financial markets function as both primary and secondary markets for corporate securities, and can be organized as either dealer or auction markets.

Of the topics we've discussed thus far, the most important is the goal of financial management: maximizing the value of the equity. Throughout the text we shall be analysing many different financial decisions, but we shall always ask the same question: how does the decision under consideration affect the value of the company's equity?

Concepts Review and Critical Thinking Questions

1 The Financial Management Decision Process [LO1] What are the three types of financial management decision? For each type of decision, give an example of a business transaction that would be relevant.

2 Goal of Financial Management [LO2] What goal should always motivate the actions of a firm's financial manager?

3 Primary versus Secondary Markets [LO3] You've probably noticed coverage in the financial press of an initial public offering (IPO) of a company's securities. Is an IPO a primary market transaction or a secondary market transaction?

4 Auction versus Dealer Markets [LO3] What does it mean when we say that Euronext is an auction market? How are auction markets different from dealer markets? What kind of market is the London Stock Exchange?

5 Not-for-Profit Firm Goals [LO2] Suppose you were the financial manager of a not-for-profit business (a not-for-profit hospital, perhaps). What kinds of goal do you think would be appropriate?

6 Goal of the Firm [LO2] Evaluate the following statement: Managers should not focus on the current equity value because doing so will lead to an overemphasis on short-term profits at the expense of long-term profits.

7 Ethics and Firm Goals [LO2] Can our goal of maximizing equity value conflict with other goals, such as avoiding unethical or illegal behaviour? In particular, do you think issues such as customer and employee safety, the environment, and the general good of society fit in this framework, or are they essentially ignored? Think of some specific examples to illustrate your answer.

8 International Firm Goal [LO2] Would our goal of maximizing equity value be different if we were thinking about financial management in a foreign country? Why or why not?

9   **Corporate Finance [LO1]**   Your grandmother sees you reading a fantastic book called *Fundamentals of Corporate Finance*. She asks you, 'What does corporate finance mean?' Explain to her in a way that doesn't put her to sleep.

10   **Financing Goals [LO2]**   Small firms tend to raise funds from private investors and venture capitalists. As these firms grow larger, they focus more on raising capital from the organized capital markets. Explain why this occurs.

11   **Financial Management Goals [LO2]**   You have read the first chapter of this textbook and have taken over a company that you now discover is losing £100,000 a week. At the rate things are going, the company won't have any cash left in 6 months to pay its creditors. What are your goals as a financial manager? Is this consistent with what you have read in this chapter? Explain.

12   **Financial Management Goals [LO2]**   If you are in charge of a private firm and it doesn't have a share price, what should be your goal as a financial manager? Explain.

13   **Financial Management Goals [LO2]**   You have been manager of a small company for 20 years and have become great friends with your employees. In the last month, new Norwegian owners have bought out the company's founding owner and have told you that they need to cut costs in order to maximize the value of the company. One of the things they suggest is to lay off 40 per cent of the workforce. However, you believe that the workforce is the company's greatest asset. On what basis do you argue against the new owners' opinions?

14   **Dealer versus Auction Markets [LO3]**   Explain the difference between dealer and auction markets. Why do you think both types of market exist? Is there one type of market that is the best? Explain.

15   **Financial Market Regulators [LO3]**   The UK's Financial Services Authority states that its objectives are to promote efficient, orderly and fair markets, help retail consumers achieve a fair deal, and improve the country's business capacity and effectiveness. The German financial markets regulator, BaFin, states that 'The objective of securities supervision is to ensure the transparency and integrity of the financial market and the protection of investors.' Are the British and German objectives consistent with each other? Explain.

MINI CASE   **Corporate Finance Information on the Web**

A skill any financial manager must have is to be able to find and understand financial information. Visit the websites of the German firms Adidas, BASF and Commerzbank. Download their financial accounts for the most recent year. At first you may find it difficult to locate these, but persevere, because the information *is* there.

QUESTIONS

1   For each firm, find the value of each company's total assets. Which firm is the biggest?

2   Visit the Yahoo! Finance website and find the share price of each firm. What does the share price history tell you about each company?

3   Find the market capitalization of each company. Which firm is the biggest?

4   On Yahoo! Finance read the news for each company. What does the news tell you about the fortunes of each company?

5   Combining all the information, which company do you think is the best investment? Explain.

CHAPTER

2

Corporate Governance

LEARNING OBJECTIVES

After studying this chapter, you should understand:

LO1   The financial implications of the different forms of business organization.
LO2   The conflicts of interest that can arise between managers and owners.
LO3   The institutional governance factors that influence corporate behaviour.

CORPORATE GOVERNANCE is concerned with how firms manage themselves, and the way in which this performance is monitored. When shareholders hire professional managers to run their company, it is important to ensure that business decisions are made that maximize the wealth of shareholders, and not the personal wealth of managers. Some ways in which this can be encouraged are by reducing the power of board members, appointing experienced independent non-executive directors to the company's board, and creating independent subcommittees to deal with executive remuneration, auditing and senior appointments.

Prior to 2007 the banking sector in Europe and the US led the world in providing financial services and products to companies and individuals. Commensurate with their importance to the global economy, all large Western banks followed their country's codes of corporate governance and also the principles of good governance as laid out by the Organization for Economic Co-operation and Development (OECD).

Even with excellent governance structures, banks were able to adopt exceptionally risky business strategies to maximize their growth rates and profits. Recent history has shown that this was a recipe for catastrophe, which led to a near-global financial meltdown, and pushed Western economies into deep recession.

Why, when banks were so well governed, did this come to pass? Does it mean that corporate governance is irrelevant? Does it mean that the corporate governance principles that Western companies follow are wrong? Over just a brief period, corporate governance has become one of the most important issues in corporate finance, and this chapter will explore some of the issues relating to the area.

To begin our study of corporate governance, it is important to understand the different ways in which companies are structured, and the pressures that management face in making business decisions.

2.1   Forms of Business Organization

Large European firms, such as BP, Renault and Vodafone, are almost all organized as corporations. We examine the three different legal forms of business organization – sole proprietorship, partnership and corporation – to see why this is so. Each form has distinct advantages and disadvantages for the life of the business, the ability of the business to raise cash, and how it is taxed. A key observation is that, as a firm grows, the advantages of the corporate form may come to outweigh the disadvantages.

Sole Proprietorship

A **sole proprietorship** is a business owned by one person. This is the simplest type of business to start, and is the least regulated form of organization. Depending on where you live, you might be able to start a proprietorship by doing little more than getting a business licence and opening your doors. For this reason, there are substantially more sole proprietorships than any other type of business, and many businesses that later become large corporations start out as small proprietorships.

> **sole proprietorship**
> A business owned by a single individual.

The owner of a sole proprietorship keeps all the profits. That's the good news. The bad news is that the owner has *unlimited liability* for business debts. This means that creditors can look beyond business assets to the proprietor's personal assets for payment. Similarly, there is no distinction between personal and business income, so all business income is taxed as personal income.

The life of a sole proprietorship is limited to the owner's lifespan, and the amount of equity that can be raised is limited to the amount of the proprietor's personal wealth. This limitation often means that the business is unable to exploit new opportunities, because of insufficient capital. Ownership of a sole proprietorship may be difficult to transfer, because this transfer requires the sale of the entire business to a new owner.

Sole proprietorships tend to be exceptionally small, and these firms are normally called *micro companies* (between one and nine employees). Although tiny, they are by far the dominant business form in Europe, with over 18 million micro businesses, constituting nearly 92 per cent of all firms in the region (source: Eurostat).

Partnership

A **partnership** is similar to a proprietorship except that there are two or more owners (partners). In a *general partnership*, all the partners share in gains or losses, and all have unlimited liability for *all* partnership debts, not just some particular share. The way partnership gains (and losses) are divided is described in the *partnership agreement*. This agreement can be an informal oral agreement, such as 'Let's start a lawnmowing business', or a lengthy, formal written document.

> **partnership**
> A business formed by two or more individuals or entities.

In a *limited partnership* one or more *general partners* will run the business and have unlimited liability, but there will be one or more *limited partners* who will not actively participate in the business. A limited partner's liability for business debts is limited to the amount that partner contributes to the partnership. This form of organization is common in law and accounting firms.

The advantages and disadvantages of a partnership are basically the same as those of a sole proprietorship. Partnerships based on a relatively informal agreement are easy and inexpensive to form. General partners have unlimited liability for partnership debts, and the partnership terminates when a general partner wishes to sell out or dies. All income is taxed as personal income to the partners, and the amount of equity that can be raised is limited to the partners' combined wealth. Ownership of a general partnership is not easily transferred, because a transfer requires that a new partnership be formed. A limited partner's interest can be sold without dissolving the partnership, but it may be difficult to find a buyer.

Because a partner in a general partnership can be held responsible for all partnership debts, it is very important to have a written agreement. Failure to spell out the rights and duties of the partners frequently leads to misunderstandings later on. Also, if you are a limited partner, you must not become deeply involved in business decisions unless you are willing to assume the obligations of a general partner. The reason is that, if things go badly, you may be deemed to be a general partner even though you say you are a limited partner.

Chapter 2 Corporate Governance

There are notable differences in the definition of partnerships across Europe. The UK has a limited liability partnership (LLP), whereby the partnership is deemed to be an independent corporate body that can continue to exist if one or more partners leave the firm. Partners can also sign a partnership agreement that collectively takes on the responsibility for the overall firm, but bear no liability for any other partners' actions. The German Partnerschaftsgesellschaft (PartG) is similar to a limited liability partnership except that it is not a corporate entity. However, it owns property under its own name, and can sue or be sued.

Based on our discussion, the primary disadvantages of sole proprietorships and partnerships as forms of business organization are:

1   Unlimited liability for business debts on the part of the owners

2   Limited life of the business

3   Difficulty of transferring ownership

These three disadvantages add up to a single, central problem: the ability of such businesses to grow can be seriously limited by an inability to raise cash for investment.

Corporation

> **corporation**
> A business created as a distinct legal entity composed of one or more individuals or entities.

The **corporation** is the most important form (in terms of size) of business organization in the world. A corporation is a legal 'person' separate and distinct from its owners, and it has many of the rights, duties and privileges of an actual person. Corporations can borrow money and own property, can sue and be sued, and can enter into contracts. A corporation can even be a general partner or a limited partner in a partnership, and a corporation can own equity in another corporation.

Not surprisingly, starting a corporation is somewhat more complicated than starting the other forms of business organization. Forming a corporation involves preparing *articles of incorporation* (or a charter) and a *memorandum of association*. The articles of incorporation must contain a number of things, including the corporation's name, its intended life (which can be for ever), its business purpose, and the number of shares that can be issued. This information must normally be supplied to the country in which the firm will be incorporated. For most legal purposes the corporation is a 'resident' of that country.

The memorandum of association consists of rules describing how the corporation regulates its existence. For example, the memorandum describes how directors are elected. This may be a simple statement of a few rules and procedures, or it may be quite extensive for a large corporation. The memorandum may be amended or extended from time to time by the shareholders.

In a large corporation the shareholders and managers are usually separate groups. In Europe there are two main ways in which directors of a company are elected. In single-tier board countries, such as the United Kingdom, Ireland and Sweden (and also the US), the shareholders elect the board of directors, who then select the managers. In two-tier board countries, such as Denmark, Germany and the Netherlands, there are two boards. The executive board manages the day-to-day operations of the company, and they report to the supervisory board who monitors their performance. The supervisory board will normally consist of representatives of major shareholders, creditors and employee groups. In both systems managers are charged with running the corporation's affairs in the shareholders' interests. In principle, shareholders control the corporation, because they elect the directors either directly or through a supervisory board.

As a result of the separation of ownership and management, the corporate form has several advantages. Ownership (represented by shares of equity) can be readily transferred, and the life of the corporation is therefore not limited. The corporation borrows money in its own name. As a result, the shareholders in a corporation have limited liability for corporate debts. The most they can lose is what they have invested.

The relative ease of transferring ownership, the limited liability for business debts, and the unlimited life of the business are why the corporate form is superior for raising cash. If a corporation needs new equity, for example, it can sell new shares and attract new investors. Apple is an example. Apple was a pioneer in the personal computer business. As demand for its products exploded, Apple had to convert to a corporation to raise the capital needed to fund growth and new product development. The number of owners can be huge: larger corporations have many thousands or even millions of shareholders. For example, in 2011 Royal Dutch Shell plc had several million shareholders and about 6 billion shares outstanding. In such cases ownership can change continuously without affecting the continuity of the business.

The corporate form has a significant disadvantage. Because a corporation is a legal person, it must pay taxes. Moreover, money paid out to shareholders in the form of dividends is taxed again as income to those shareholders. This is *double taxation*, meaning that corporate profits are taxed twice: at the corporate level when they are earned, and again at the personal level when they are paid out. Fortunately, in many countries, including the UK, shareholders are given a partial or full tax credit, which they can offset against the double tax that is levied on their dividends.

As the discussion in this section illustrates, the need of large businesses for outside investors and creditors is such that the corporate form will generally be the best for such firms. We focus on corporations in the chapters ahead because of the importance of the corporate form in the European and world economies. Also, a few important financial management issues, such as dividend policy, are unique to corporations. However, businesses of all types and sizes need financial management, so the majority of the subjects we discuss bear on any form of business.

A Corporation by Any Other Name . . .

The corporate form of organization has many variations around the world. The exact laws and regulations differ from country to country, of course, but the essential features of public ownership and limited liability remain. These firms are often called *joint stock companies*, *public limited companies*, or *limited liability companies*, depending on the specific nature of the firm and the country of origin.

Table 2.1 gives the names of a number of corporate abbreviations, the countries in which they are used, a translation of the abbreviation, and a description of its meaning

CONCEPT QUESTIONS	
2.1a	What are the three forms of business organization?
2.1b	What are the primary advantages and disadvantages of sole proprietorships and partnerships?
2.1c	What is the difference between a general and a limited partnership?
2.1d	Why is the corporate form superior when it comes to raising cash?

2.2 The Agency Problem and Control of the Corporation

We've seen that the financial manager acts in the best interests of the shareholders by taking actions that increase the value of the company's equity. However, in many large corporations, particularly in the UK, Ireland and the US, ownership can be spread over a huge number of shareholders. This dispersion of ownership arguably means that management effectively controls the firm. In this case, will management necessarily act in the best interests of the shareholders? Put another way, might not management pursue its own goals at the shareholders' expense?

TABLE
2.1

Type of corporation	Country of origin	In original language	Description
Pty Ltd	Australia	Proprietary Limited	Private limited
Limited	Australia	Limited	Publicly listed
AG	Austria, Germany	Aktiengesellschaft	Publicly listed
GmbH	Austria, Germany	Gesellschaft mit Beschränkter Haftung	Private limited
NV	Belgium, Netherlands	Naamloze Venootschap	Private/public
SA	Belgium, France, Luxembourg, Portugal, Spain	Société Anonyme/ Sociedade Anónima	Publicly listed
股份有限公司	China Mainland	股份有限公司	Publicly listed
有限公司	China Mainland	有限公司	Private limited
ApS	Denmark	Anpartsselkab	Private limited
A/S	Denmark	Aktieselskab	Publicly listed
SE	European Union	Societas Europaea	Publicly listed
Oy, AB	Finland, Sweden	Osakeyhtiö (Fin), Aktiebolag (Swe)	Private limited
Oyj, Abp	Finland, Sweden	Julkinen Osakeyhtiö (Fin), Publikt Aktiebolag (Swe)	Publicly listed
SARL	France, Luxembourg	Société à Responsibilité Limitée	Private limited
Pvt. Ltd	India	Private Limited Company	Private limited
Plc	India, Ireland, Thailand, UK	Public Limited Company	Publicly listed
Srl	Italy	Società a Responsabilità Limitata	Private limited
SpA	Italy	Società per Azioni	Publicly listed
AS	Norway	Aksjeselskap	Private limited
ASA	Norway	Allmennaksjeselskap	Publicly listed
(Pty) Ltd	South Africa	Privaat Maatskappy	Private limited
LTD	South Africa	Publieke Maatskappy	Publicly listed
SL	Spain	Sociedad Limitada	Private limited
Ltd	Ireland, UK, US	Limited	Private limited
Inc., Corp.	US	Incorporated, Corporation	Publicly listed

Table 2.1 International corporations

A different type of problem exists in many European firms. Whereas large British and American firms have a dispersed ownership structure, many businesses in Europe have a dominant shareholder with a very large ownership stake. Primarily, these shareholders are family groups, banks, or governments. In firms with a dominant shareholder it is possible that corporate objectives will be directed by only one individual or group at the expense of other, smaller, shareholders. In this case, managers are acting in the interests of only a subset of the company's owners.

The issues we have discussed above are caused by what we call *agency relationships*. In the following pages we briefly consider some of the arguments relating to this issue.

Type I Agency Relationships

The relationship between shareholders and management is called a *type I agency relationship*. Such a relationship exists whenever someone (the principal) hires another (the agent) to represent his or her interests. For example, you might hire someone (an agent) to sell a car you own while you are away at university. In all such relationships, there is a possibility there may be a conflict of interest between the principal and the agent. Such a conflict is called a **type I agency problem**.

> **type I agency problem**
> The possibility of conflict of interest between the shareholders and management of a firm.

Suppose you hire someone to sell your car, and agree to pay that person a flat fee when he or she sells the car. The agent's incentive in this case is to make the sale, not necessarily to get you the best price. If you offer a commission of, say, 10 per cent of the sales price instead of a flat fee, then this problem might not exist. This example illustrates that the way in which an agent is compensated is one factor that affects agency problems.

Management Goals

To see how management and shareholder interests might differ, imagine that the firm is considering a new investment. The new investment is expected to impact favourably on the share value, but it is also a relatively risky venture. The owners of the firm will wish to make the investment (because the share value will rise), but management may not, because there is the possibility that things will turn out badly, and management jobs will be lost. If management do not make the investment, then the shareholders may lose a valuable opportunity. This is one example of a type I agency cost.

In general, the term *agency cost* refers to the cost of the conflict of interest between shareholders and management (we shall consider later another agency relationship between controlling and minority shareholders). These costs can be indirect or direct. An indirect agency cost is a lost opportunity, such as the one we have just described.

Direct agency costs come in two forms. The first type is a corporate expenditure that benefits management but costs the shareholders. Perhaps the purchase of a luxurious and unneeded corporate jet would fall under this heading. The second type of direct agency cost is an expense that comes from the need to monitor management actions. Paying outside auditors to assess the accuracy of financial statement information could be one example.

It is sometimes argued that, left to themselves, managers would tend to maximize the amount of resources over which they have control or, more generally, corporate power or wealth. This goal could lead to an overemphasis on corporate size or growth. For example, cases in which management are accused of overpaying to buy up another company just to increase the business size or to demonstrate corporate power are not uncommon. Obviously, if overpayment does take place, such a purchase does not benefit the shareholders of the purchasing company.

Our discussion indicates that management may tend to overemphasize organizational survival to protect job security. Also, management may dislike outside interference, so independence and corporate self-sufficiency may be important goals.

Do Managers Act in the Shareholders' Interests?

Whether managers will, in fact, act in the best interests of shareholders depends on two factors. First, how closely are management goals aligned with shareholder goals? This question relates, at least in part, to the way managers are compensated. Second, can managers be replaced if they do not pursue shareholder goals? This issue relates to control of the firm. As we shall discuss, there are a number of reasons to think that, even in the largest firms, management has a significant incentive to act in the interests of shareholders.

Managerial Compensation Management will frequently have a significant economic incentive to increase share value, for two reasons. First, managerial compensation, particularly at the top, is usually tied to financial performance in general, and often to share value in particular. For example, managers are frequently given the option to buy equity at a bargain price. The more the equity is worth, the more valuable this option is. In fact, options are often used to motivate employees of all types, not just top managers. For example, in 2007 Google announced that it was issuing new share options to all of its 16,000 employees, thereby giving its workforce a significant stake in its share price, and achieving a better alignment of employee and shareholder interests. Many other corporations, large and small, have similar policies.

The second incentive managers have relates to job prospects. Better performers within the firm will tend to get promoted. More generally, managers who are successful in pursuing shareholder goals will be in greater demand in the labour market, and thus command higher salaries.

In fact, managers who are successful in pursuing shareholder goals can reap enormous rewards. For example, the best-paid executive in 2008 was Stephen Schwarzman, the CEO of Blackstone Group: according to *CNN* he made about £456 million (€523 million). By way of comparison, Schwarzman made quite a bit more than Larry Ellison of Oracle (£362 million/€415 million), Oprah Winfrey (£178 million/€205 million), and Lionel Messi (£30 million/€34 million). Information about executive compensation, along with lots of other information, can be easily found on the Web for almost any public company or even celebrity. Our nearby *Work the Web* box shows you how to get started.

Work the Web

A great skill to develop is to be able to find company information easily on the Internet. In Chapter 1 you gained some experience with using a financial data provider, Yahoo! Finance, to find out information on share prices and other financial characteristics. In this chapter we shall look at a company's annual report.

Go to the Vodafone website (www.vodafone.com) and download the company's annual report for the most recent year. Click on the 'Investor Relations' tab and then 'Annual Report'. In this chapter we shall focus on the corporate governance of Vodafone. Take your time and read through the section on Governance. There's a lot of information here, and many links for you to explore.

QUESTIONS

1 How many people are on the board of Vodafone? Who is the chairman, and who is the chief executive officer? How many non-executive directors and executive directors are there on the board of Vodafone?

2 How does the board of Vodafone evaluate its own performance?

3 How much did the chief executive of Vodafone earn in the most recent year?

Control of the Firm Control of the firm ultimately rests with shareholders. They elect the board of directors, who in turn hire and fire managers. The fact that shareholders control the corporation was made abundantly clear by Steve Jobs's experience at Apple. Even though he was a founder of the corporation, and was largely responsible for its most successful products, there came a time when shareholders, through their elected directors, decided that Apple would be better off without him, so out he went. Of course, he was later rehired and helped turn Apple around with great new products such as the iPod, iPhone and iPad.

Shareholder Rights   The conceptual structure of the corporation assumes that shareholders elect directors, who in turn hire managers to carry out their directives. Shareholders therefore control the corporation through the right to elect the directors. In countries with single-tier boards only shareholders have this right, and in two-tier board countries the supervisory board undertakes this task.

In two-tier board systems the supervisory board (which consists of the main shareholder representatives, major creditors, and employee representatives) chooses the executive board of directors. In companies with single-tier boards directors are elected each year at an annual meeting. Although there are exceptions (discussed next), the general idea is 'one share, one vote' (*not* one *shareholder*, one vote). Directors are elected at an annual shareholders' meeting by a vote of the holders of a majority of shares who are present and entitled to vote. However, the exact mechanism for electing directors differs across companies. The most important difference is whether shares must be voted cumulatively or voted straight.

To illustrate the two different voting procedures, imagine that a corporation has two shareholders: Smith with 20 shares and Jones with 80 shares. Both want to be a director. Jones does not want Smith, however. We assume there are a total of four directors to be elected.

The effect of **cumulative voting** is to permit minority participation. If cumulative voting is permitted, the total number of votes that each shareholder may cast is determined first. This is usually calculated as the number of shares (owned or controlled) multiplied by the number of directors to be elected.

> **cumulative voting**
> A procedure in which a shareholder may cast all votes for one member of the board of directors.

With cumulative voting the directors are elected all at once. In our example this means that the top four vote-getters will be the new directors. A shareholder can distribute votes however he or she wishes.

Will Smith get a seat on the board? If we ignore the possibility of a five-way tie, then the answer is yes. Smith will cast $20 \times 4 = 80$ votes, and Jones will cast $80 \times 4 = 320$ votes. If Smith gives all his votes to himself, he is assured of a directorship. The reason is that Jones can't divide 320 votes among four candidates in such a way as to give all of them more than 80 votes, so Smith will finish fourth at worst.

In general, if there are N directors up for election, then $1/(N + 1)$ per cent of the shares plus one share will guarantee you a seat. In our current example this is $1/(4 + 1) = 20\%$. So the more seats that are up for election at one time, the easier (and cheaper) it is to win one.

> **straight voting**
> A procedure in which a shareholder may cast all votes for each member of the board of directors.

With **straight voting** the directors are elected one at a time. Each time, Smith can cast 20 votes and Jones can cast 80. As a consequence, Jones will elect all of the candidates. The only way to guarantee a seat is to own 50 per cent plus one share. This also guarantees that you will win every seat, so it's really all or nothing.

EXAMPLE 2.1

Buying the Election

Shares in Sole SpA sell for €20 each, and feature cumulative voting. There are 10,000 shares outstanding. If three directors are up for election, how much does it cost to ensure yourself a seat on the board?

The question here is how many shares of equity it will take to get a seat. The answer is 2,501, so the cost is $2,501 \times €20 = €50,020$. Why 2,501? Because there is no way the remaining 7,499 votes can be divided among three people to give all of them more than 2,501 votes. For example, suppose two people receive 2,502 votes and the first two seats. A third person can receive at most $10,000 - 2,502 - 2,502 - 2,501 = 2,495$, so the third seat is yours.

As we've illustrated, straight voting can 'freeze out' minority shareholders: that is why many companies have mandatory cumulative voting. In companies where cumulative voting is mandatory, devices have been worked out to minimize its impact.

Chapter 2 Corporate Governance

One such device is to stagger the voting for the board of directors. With staggered elections, only a fraction of the directorships are up for election at a particular time. Thus if only two directors are up for election at any one time, it will take $1/(2 + 1) = 33.33$ per cent of the equity plus one share to guarantee a seat.

Overall, staggering has two basic effects:

1   Staggering makes it more difficult for a minority to elect a director when there is cumulative voting, because there are fewer directors to be elected at one time.

2   Staggering makes takeover attempts less likely to be successful, because it makes it more difficult to vote in a majority of new directors.

We should note that staggering may serve a beneficial purpose. It provides 'institutional memory' – that is, continuity on the board of directors. This may be important for corporations with significant long-range plans and projects.

proxy
A grant of authority by a shareholder allowing another individual to vote his or her shares.

Proxy Voting   A **proxy** is the grant of authority by a shareholder to someone else to vote his or her shares. For convenience, much of the voting in large public corporations is actually done by proxy.

As we have seen, with straight voting each share of equity has one vote. The owner of 10,000 shares has 10,000 votes. Large companies have hundreds of thousands or even millions of shareholders. In single-tier board environments shareholders can come to the annual meeting and vote in person, or they can transfer their right to vote to another party.

Obviously, management always tries to get as many proxies as possible transferred to it. However, if shareholders are not satisfied with management, an 'outside' group of shareholders can try to obtain votes via proxy. They can vote by proxy in an attempt to replace management by electing enough directors. The resulting battle is called a *proxy fight*.

Classes of Shares   Some firms have more than one class of ordinary equity. Often the classes are created with unequal voting rights. Google, for example, has two classes of shares. The co-founders, Larry Page and Sergey Brin, own Class B shares, which have 10 votes for each share. Other shareholders have Class A shares, which are entitled to one vote per share. So, although the founders only own 5.7 per cent of Google, they have 57 per cent of the voting power.

A primary reason for creating dual or multiple classes of equity has to do with control of the firm. If such shares exist, management of a firm can raise equity capital by issuing non-voting or limited-voting shares while maintaining control.

The subject of unequal voting rights is controversial, and the idea of one share, one vote has a strong following and a long history. Interestingly, however, shares with unequal voting rights are quite common in the United Kingdom and elsewhere around the world.

Other Rights   The value of a share of equity in a corporation is directly related to the general rights of shareholders. In addition to the right to vote for directors, shareholders usually have the following rights:

1   The right to share proportionally in dividends paid.

2   The right to share proportionally in assets remaining after liabilities have been paid in a liquidation.

3   The right to vote on shareholder matters of great importance, such as a merger. Voting is usually done at the annual meeting or a special meeting.

In addition, shareholders sometimes have the right to share proportionally in any new equity sold. This is called the *pre-emptive right*.

Essentially, a pre-emptive right means that a company that wishes to sell equity must first offer it to the existing shareholders before offering it to the general public. The purpose is to give shareholders the opportunity to protect their proportionate ownership in the corporation.

Dividends   A distinctive feature of corporations is that they have shares of equity on which they are authorized by law to pay dividends to their shareholders. **Dividends** paid to shareholders represent a return on the capital directly or indirectly contributed to the corporation by the shareholders. The payment of dividends is at the discretion of the board of directors.

> **dividends**
> Payments by a corporation to shareholders, made in either cash or shares.

Some important characteristics of dividends include the following:

- Unless a dividend is declared by the board of directors of a corporation, it is not a liability of the corporation. A corporation cannot default on an undeclared dividend. As a consequence, corporations cannot become bankrupt because of non-payment of dividends. The amount of the dividend and even whether it is paid are decisions based on the business judgement of the board of directors.

- The payment of dividends by the corporation is not a business expense. Dividends are not deductible for corporate tax purposes. In short, dividends are paid out of the corporation's after-tax profits.

- Dividends received by individual shareholders are taxable.

There is a common belief that shareholders prefer companies to issue dividends, because it imposes a form of discipline on incumbent managers. If a company has high levels of cash, managers may invest in projects that will not normally be chosen simply because they can. By transferring the company's cash to shareholders through dividends, managers have less scope to squander resources.

The discussion so far has concerned the agency relationship between professional managers and outside shareholders. We shall now discuss a different type of agency relationship, which is more subtle and complex, and is known as a Type II agency relationship. A Type II agency relationship exists between shareholders who own a significant amount of a company's shares (controlling shareholders) and other shareholders who own only a small proportional amount (minority shareholders).

Type II Agency Relationships

The relationship between a dominant or controlling shareholder and other shareholders who have a small proportional ownership stake is known as a *Type II agency relationship*. Such a relationship exists whenever a company has a concentrated ownership structure, which is common in many countries. When an investor owns a large percentage of a company's shares, they have the ability to remove or install a board of directors through their voting power. This means that, indirectly, they can make the firm's objectives aligned to their own personal objectives, which may not be the same as that of other shareholders with a smaller proportionate stake. This is the **Type II agency problem**.

> **Type II agency problem**
> The possibility of conflict of interest between controlling and minority shareholders.

It may seem strange that one set of shareholders can have a different objective from that of a different set of shareholders in the same company. Surely, all shareholders want to maximize the value of their firm? Agency theory recognizes that everyone has personal objectives, and these may not be congruent with other groups in an organization. Thus, for example, a dominant shareholder may benefit more from having one of her firms trading at advantageous prices with another firm she owns. This is known as a *related party transaction*.

Alternatively, a controlling shareholder may need cash for an investment in, for example, company A, and wish to take the cash from company B through an extraordinary dividend. This will obviously not be in the interests of company B's other shareholders, but in aggregate the action may be more profitable for the controlling shareholder of company B if it stands to make more money from an investment in company A.

> **EXAMPLE 2.2**
>
> # Ownership Structure of Fiat SpA
>
> The ownership structure of Italian automaker Fiat as of 2009 is presented below.
>
>
> The dominant or controlling shareholder of Fiat SpA is Exor SpA, which owns 30.5 per cent of the company's outstanding shares. The next question is who owns Exor SpA? Exor is 100 per cent owned by *Giovanni Agnelli e C. S.a.p.az*, which is the investment company of the Agnelli family in Italy. Thus, indirectly, the Agnelli family is the dominant shareholder of Fiat.

Conclusion

The available theory and evidence are consistent with the view that shareholders control the firm, and that shareholder wealth maximization is the relevant goal of the corporation. Even so, there will undoubtedly be times when management goals are pursued at the expense of some or all shareholders, at least temporarily.

Stakeholders

> **stakeholder**
> Someone, other than a shareholder or creditor, who potentially has a claim on the cash flows of the firm.

Our discussion thus far implies that management and shareholders are the only parties with an interest in the firm's decisions. This is an oversimplification, of course. Employees, customers, suppliers, and even the government all have a financial interest in the firm.

Taken together, these various groups are called **stakeholders**. In general, a stakeholder is someone, other than a shareholder or creditor, who potentially has a claim on the cash flows of the firm. Such groups will also attempt to exert control over the firm, perhaps to the detriment of the owners.

> **CONCEPT QUESTIONS**
>
> 2.2a What is an agency relationship?
> 2.2b What are agency problems, and how do they come about? What are agency costs?
> 2.2c What incentives do managers in large corporations have to maximize share value?

2.3 International Corporate Governance

Variations in economic, social and religious culture can lead to differences in the way that companies are run. While corporate differences are to be expected across geographical regions, you may be surprised to learn that the corporate environment within Europe is very varied. Although monetary union has been enacted across much of the continent, the legal, institutional and governance structures in member countries are markedly different. In this section we shall discuss some differences in international corporate governance, and how they may impact upon the business decisions of corporations.

Investor Protection: The Legal Environment

The legal environment in which a corporation does business can have a big impact on its decisions. In a common law system the law evolves as a result of the judgment decisions of courts, whereas in a civil law system judges interpret the law; they cannot change it. With respect to commercial decisions, the UK and Ireland follow a common law system, whereas the rest of Europe follows civil law.

The third form of legal system is based on religious principles: Canon Law for Christianity, Halakha for Judaism, and Sharia for Islam. Under religious law, specific religious principles form the basis of legal decisions. This can have a considerable impact on business activity, especially when religion forbids specific activities. For example, Islam forbids the use of interest in any economic transaction, and so financial loans are not allowed.

Figure 2.1 presents a snapshot of countries that follow different legal systems. Many countries do not follow one system alone, and the exact legal environment can be a hybrid of two systems. For example, India's legal system is based on common law, but personal laws are driven by religious law depending on an individual's religion. Scotland has a different legal system from the rest of the UK, with most laws based on continental or Roman civil law. Commercial law is an exception, and it is similar to the rest of the United Kingdom in this regard.

Because the corporate environment must respond quickly to different economic events, common law systems are able to adapt faster to these changes. For example, if a company can identify a loophole in the law that allows it to legally expropriate wealth from

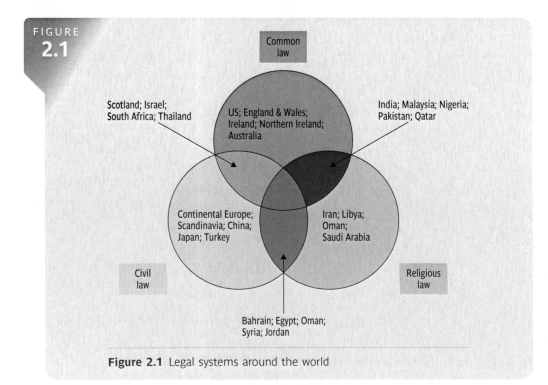

Figure 2.1 Legal systems around the world

Chapter 2 Corporate Governance

TABLE
2.2

Country	Corruption perceptions index	Country	Corruption perceptions index
Denmark	9.3	Portugal	5.8
Singapore, Sweden	9.2	Taiwan	5.6
Switzerland	9.0	Oman, South Korea	5.5
Finland, Netherlands	8.9	Bahrain	5.1
Australia, Canada, Iceland	8.7	South Africa	4.7
Norway	8.6	Malaysia	4.5
Hong Kong, Luxembourg	8.2	Turkey	4.4
Germany, Ireland	8.0	Italy	4.3
Austria	7.9	Greece	3.8
UK, Japan	7.7	China	3.6
US	7.5	India, Thailand	3.4
Belgium	7.1	Tanzania	2.6
Qatar	7.0	Nigeria	2.5
France	6.9	Pakistan	2.4
UAE	6.5	Kenya, Russia	2.2
Spain, Israel	6.1	Iran	1.8

Source: **Transparency International.**

Table 2.2 Transparency International Corruption Perceptions Index 2009

shareholders, a common law system can quickly close this loophole through the courts. In a civil law system any changes in regulation must be enacted through government statute, which can take a much longer time to process.

The inherent flexibility of common law legal environments ensures that shareholders and outside stakeholders are better protected than in civil law countries. This constrains the activities of corporate managers, and as a result they are held more accountable to shareholders. In addition, because investor protection is better in common law environments, it would be expected that raising capital through the equity markets would be more popular in countries that follow this system.

The type of legal system is not the only factor that affects corporate investors. Adherence to the rule of law and efficiency of law enforcement can have a major impact on corporate decision-making and regulatory compliance. Clearly, a country can have very comprehensive laws, but if they are not enforced then their effect is meaningless. Even in Europe, law enforcement and corruption are exceptionally varied. Table 2.2 presents the 2009 Corruption Perceptions Index as presented by Transparency International. The index is graded between 1 and 10, with a score of 1 indicating that a country is exceptionally corrupt. Scandinavian countries have very little corruption, and this tends to get worse as one goes further south through Europe. Consistent with their lack of economic development, emerging markets tend to have more corruption than developed countries.

The Financial System: Bank-Based and Market-Based Countries

In a bank-based financial system, banks play a major role in facilitating the flow of money between investors with surplus cash and organizations that require funding. In market-based

TABLE 2.3 Country	Domestic bank deposits/ Stock market capitalization	Country	Domestic bank deposits/ Stock market capitalization	Country	Domestic bank deposits/ Stock market capitalization
South Africa	0.40	Denmark	1.40	Finland	2.71
Malaysia	0.41	Thailand	1.44	Israel	2.76
Singapore	0.70	Netherlands	1.63	Greece	2.78
Hong Kong	0.76	Japan	1.66	France	3.11
Sweden	0.86	New Zealand	1.73	Belgium	3.31
United States	0.91	Kenya	1.80	Cyprus	3.73
United Kingdom	1.03	Switzerland	1.80	Italy	4.45
Australia	1.08	Nigeria	1.88	Iceland	4.50
Canada	1.12	Pakistan	2.17	Germany	5.01
India	1.24	Indonesia	2.67	Portugal	5.84
Turkey	1.35	Norway	2.69	Egypt	6.10
Ireland	1.36	Spain	3.20	Austria	10.24

Source: A. Demirguc-Kunt and R. Levine, 'Bank-based and market-based financial systems: cross-country comparisons', World Bank Working Paper.

Table 2.3 Bank-based versus market-based financial systems

systems, financial markets take on the role of the main financial intermediary. Corporations in countries with very well-developed financial markets find it easier to raise money by issuing debt and equity to the public than through bank borrowing. Countries with bank-based systems have very strong banks that actively monitor corporations and are often involved in long-term strategic decisions.

It has been argued that corporations in market-based countries have a shorter-term focus than in bank-based countries, because of the emphasis on share price and market performance. When banks are the major source of funding to a company, managers may have longer investment horizons and be less willing to take risks. On the other hand, market-based systems have been argued to be more efficient at funding companies than bank systems. There are many ways in which a country's financial system can be classified as bank or market-based. Table 2.3 shows, for a number of countries, the level of domestic deposits in banks divided by stock market size. A country with a high ratio would be regarded as a bank-based financial system.

Ownership Structure

Another factor that can affect business decision-making and corporate objectives is the ownership structure of companies. This is the make-up and constitution of shareholdings in a firm. In the UK and US most large companies are widely held, which means that no single investor has a large ownership stake in a firm. In such environments, Type I agency relationships dominate. The rest of the world is characterized by closely held firms, where governments, families and banks are the main shareholders in firms. Type II agency relationships are more important in closely held firms, and their corporate governance structure should reflect this.

Table 2.4 presents a breakdown of the ownership structure of the 20 largest corporations in a number of selected companies across the world. It is very clear from the table that no two countries are the exact same. For example, the UK is characterized by a widely held ownership structure, whereas most of the large firms in Greece are run by families.

TABLE
2.4

Country	Widely held (%)	Family (%)	State (%)	Other (%)	Country	Widely held (%)	Family (%)	State (%)	Other (%)
Austria	5	15	70	10	Japan	90	5	5	0
Belgium	5	50	5	40	Netherlands	30	20	5	45
Denmark	40	35	15	10	Norway	25	25	35	15
Finland	35	10	35	20	Portugal	10	45	25	20
France	60	20	15	5	Spain	35	15	30	20
Germany	50	10	25	15	Sweden	25	45	10	20
Greece	10	50	30	10	Switzerland	60	30	0	10
Italy	20	15	40	25	UK	100	0	0	0
Ireland	65	10	0	25	US	80	20	0	0

Source: R. La Porta, F. Lopez-de-Silanes, A. Shleifer and R.W. Vishny, 'Law and finance', *Journal of Political Economy* (1998), vol. 106, pp. 1113–1155.
The table presents the percentage of firms in a country that have a controlling shareholder with a greater than 20 per cent stake in the company. If no controlling shareholder exists, the firm is deemed to be widely held.

Table 2.4 Ownership structure of 20 largest companies in each country

Governments have a major role to play in many European countries, with the Austrian government being the most involved in firms.

Ownership structure has a massive impact on corporate objectives. Whereas all shareholders wish to maximize the value of their investment, how value is assessed differs according to the individual. For example, if a firm is widely held in a market-based economy, such as the UK, corporate objectives are likely to be focused on maximizing share price performance. Family firms have slightly different objectives, because managers have to consider not only current shareholders but also the descendants of those shareholders. This would suggest that managers of family firms would have a longer-term perspective than other firms, which would influence the types of investment and funding they choose. Firms with a government as a major shareholder would have to consider political objectives, in addition to maximizing share value. A good example is the banking sector, which was bailed out by governments in 2008 and 2009. Although banks did not feel it appropriate to increase lending significantly under the economic conditions at the time, state shareholders insisted that lending be focused on first-time house buyers and small businesses.

2.4   Bringing It All Together

The basis of all good corporate finance decisions is a sound framework of corporate governance. This point can't be emphasized too much, because most of the problems that companies experience can usually be identified by failings in the way in which they are governed. When covering subjects in later chapters, the underlying assumption is that corporate executives are acting in the interests of shareholders, and that the firm is well governed.

When a company does not have strong corporate governance, it may make decisions that do not maximize share value. For example, a firm may choose to invest in projects that maximize managers' own wealth and not that of shareholders. They may also make financing decisions that minimize the risk of the firm for the management but not necessarily for shareholders. This would lead them to make investment and financing decisions different from those that would be recommended in later chapters.

Country	Code
Australia	Revised Corporate Governance Principles and Recommendations (2007)
Austria	Austrian Code of Corporate Governance (2009)
Belgium	The 2009 Belgian Code on Corporate Governance (2009)
China	The Code of Corporate Governance for Listed Companies in China (2001)
Denmark	Revised Recommendations for Corporate Governance in Denmark (2008)
EU	Euroshareholders Corporate Governance Guidelines 2000 (2002)
Finland	Finnish Corporate Governance Code (2008)
France	Recommendations on Corporate Governance (2010)
Germany	German Corporate Governance Code (2002, Amended 2009)
Greece	Principles of Corporate Governance (2001)
India	Corporate Governance Voluntary Guidelines (2009)
Ireland	Corporate Governance, Share Option and Other Incentive Schemes (1999)
Italy	Codice di Autodisciplina (2006)
Netherlands	Dutch Corporate Governance Code (2008)
Norway	The Norwegian Code of Practice for Corporate Governance (2009)
OECD	OECD Principles of Corporate Governance (2004)
Pakistan	Code of Corporate Governance (2002)
Poland	Code of Best Practice for WSE Companies (2007)
Portugal	CMVM Corporate Governance Code (2010)
South Africa	King Code of Corporate Governance for South Africa (2009)
Spain	Unified Good Governance Code (2006)
Sweden	Swedish Code of Corporate Governance (2009)
Switzerland	Swiss Code of Best Practice for Corporate Governance (2008)
Thailand	The Principles of Good Corporate Governance for Listed Companies (2006)
UK	The Stewardship Code for Institutional Investors (2010) The Audit Firm Governance Code (2009) Review of the Combined Code: Final Report (2009) A Review of Corporate Governance in UK Banks and Other Financial Industry Entities (The Walker Review) (2009) The Combined Code of Corporate Governance (2008)
US	Key Agreed Principles to Strengthen Corporate Governance for US Publicly Traded Corporations (2008) Final NYSE Corporate Governance Rules (2003) The Sarbanes-Oxley Act (2002)

Table 2.5 Country codes of corporate governance

Transparency and timely information disclosure are major aspects of good governance. Without these, investors would find it extremely difficult to value a firm or assess the risk of its operations. Part Three of the textbook assumes that share prices efficiently incorporate information about a company. However, if the management of a firm do not see transparency and disclosure as important parts of their responsibilities, then share prices will be uninformative, and risk assessment would be meaningless.

Most countries have their own code of corporate governance that guides companies on how they should be governed. Largely, they are very similar, with only slight country-level differences. Table 2.5 lists the main corporate governance codes and their date of publication for different countries.

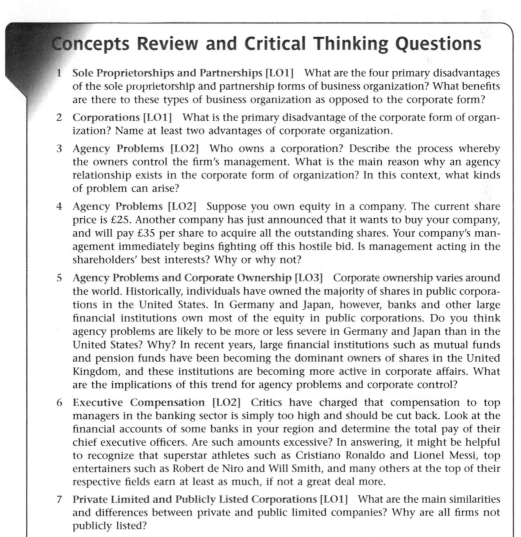

Summary and Conclusions

All the material in this textbook makes the assumption that firms are run properly, efficiently, and ethically. Unfortunately, in practice this may not be the case. Corporate governance is concerned with the way in which a firm is managed. There are a number of basic principles that should be followed to minimize the danger of firms getting into difficulty because of the way they are managed. The budding financial manager must be aware of, and familiar with, the basic principles underlying the way in which his or her company should be run. Without this knowledge, he or she will not be in a position to make the best financial decisions for the company's shareholders.

Concepts Review and Critical Thinking Questions

1   **Sole Proprietorships and Partnerships [LO1]**   What are the four primary disadvantages of the sole proprietorship and partnership forms of business organization? What benefits are there to these types of business organization as opposed to the corporate form?

2   **Corporations [LO1]**   What is the primary disadvantage of the corporate form of organization? Name at least two advantages of corporate organization.

3   **Agency Problems [LO2]**   Who owns a corporation? Describe the process whereby the owners control the firm's management. What is the main reason why an agency relationship exists in the corporate form of organization? In this context, what kinds of problem can arise?

4   **Agency Problems [LO2]**   Suppose you own equity in a company. The current share price is £25. Another company has just announced that it wants to buy your company, and will pay £35 per share to acquire all the outstanding shares. Your company's management immediately begins fighting off this hostile bid. Is management acting in the shareholders' best interests? Why or why not?

5   **Agency Problems and Corporate Ownership [LO3]**   Corporate ownership varies around the world. Historically, individuals have owned the majority of shares in public corporations in the United States. In Germany and Japan, however, banks and other large financial institutions own most of the equity in public corporations. Do you think agency problems are likely to be more or less severe in Germany and Japan than in the United States? Why? In recent years, large financial institutions such as mutual funds and pension funds have been becoming the dominant owners of shares in the United Kingdom, and these institutions are becoming more active in corporate affairs. What are the implications of this trend for agency problems and corporate control?

6   **Executive Compensation [LO2]**   Critics have charged that compensation to top managers in the banking sector is simply too high and should be cut back. Look at the financial accounts of some banks in your region and determine the total pay of their chief executive officers. Are such amounts excessive? In answering, it might be helpful to recognize that superstar athletes such as Cristiano Ronaldo and Lionel Messi, top entertainers such as Robert de Niro and Will Smith, and many others at the top of their respective fields earn at least as much, if not a great deal more.

7   **Private Limited and Publicly Listed Corporations [LO1]**   What are the main similarities and differences between private and public limited companies? Why are all firms not publicly listed?

8   **Macro Governance [LO3]**   Why do you think corporate behaviour in bank-based financial systems would be different from that in market-based financial systems? How do you think other differences in the macro environment can affect corporate objectives?

9   **Corporate Governance [LO3]** Why is corporate governance important to the shareholders of a firm? Should the same corporate governance rules be applied to all companies? Why or why not?

10 **Corporate Governance [LO1]** Explain why the corporate governance of a sole proprietorship should be different from that of a partnership, which in turn should be different from that of a limited corporation.

11 **Corporate Governance across the World [LO3]** Why is there no single code of corporate governance applied to all the countries of the world? Would emerging-market firms have different issues to consider?

12 **Sole Proprietorship [LO1]** Sole proprietorship is the most common type of corporation throughout the world. Why do you think this is the case? What are the benefits of sole proprietorships over other corporate forms?

13 **Partnerships [LO1]** What are the differences between a general partnership and a limited partnership? Why do firms choose to be partnerships instead of limited liability corporations?

14 **Organizations [LO1]** Review the differences between various corporate forms. Why would an owner move from being a sole owner to a partner to a controlling shareholder in a limited corporation?

15 **Government Ownership [LO3]** In recent years, governments have taken control of banks through buying their shares. What impact does this have on the lending culture of these banks? Is this consistent with shareholder maximization? Use an example to illustrate your answer.

16 **Stakeholders [LO2]** Discuss what is meant by a stakeholder. In what ways are stakeholders represented in two-tier board structures? How does this differ from companies with a unitary board structure? Use real examples to illustrate your answer.

17 **Institutional Shareholders [LO2]** Regulators have developed a number of new policies with respect to institutional shareholder involvement in the running of firms. Review the reasons why regulators would prefer more or less involvement of institutions in the running of corporations. In addition, discuss the proposals that have been put forward by regulators in your own country, and whether these are likely to be effective.

18 **Managerial Objectives [LO2]** Why would we expect managers of a corporation to pursue the objectives of shareholders? What about bondholders?

MINI CASE | Tadcaster Wines Limited

In early 2007 Kevin and Michelle Tadcaster formed Tadcaster Wines Limited. The company produced a full line of English wines, and its specialities included tonic wine, crazy dog wine, Temeke Wine and Tyson Wine. The two formed the company as an outside interest, and both continued to work at their existing jobs. Kevin did all the wine growing, and Michelle handled the marketing and distribution. With good product quality and a sound marketing plan, the company grew rapidly. In early 2010 the company was featured in a widely distributed entrepreneurial magazine. Later that year the company was featured in *Gourmet Wines*, a leading speciality wine magazine. After the article appeared in *Gourmet Wines* sales exploded, and the company began receiving orders from all over the world.

Because of the increased sales, Kevin left his other job, followed shortly by Michelle. The company hired additional workers to meet demand. Unfortunately, the fast growth experienced by the company led to cash flow and capacity problems. The company is currently producing as many wines as possible with the assets it owns, but demand for its wines is still growing. Further, the company has been approached by a national supermarket chain with a proposal to put four of its wines in all of the chain's stores, and a national restaurant chain has contacted the company about selling Tadcaster Wines in its restaurants. The restaurant would sell the wines without a brand name.

Kevin and Michelle have operated the company as a sole proprietorship. They have approached you to help manage and direct the company's growth. Specifically, they have asked you to answer the following questions.

QUESTIONS

1 What are the advantages and disadvantages of changing the company organization from a sole proprietorship to a partnership?

2 What are the advantages and disadvantages of changing the company organization from a sole proprietorship to a corporation?

3 Ultimately, what action would you recommend the company undertake? Why?

Online **LearningCentre**

To help you grasp the key concepts of this chapter check out the extra resources posted on the Online Learning Centre at **www.mcgraw-hill.co.uk/textbooks/hillier**

Among other helpful resources there are mini-cases tailored to each chapter.

CHAPTER 3

Financial Analysis and Planning

KEY NOTATIONS

b	retention ratio
NWC	net working capital
P/E ratio	price–earnings ratio
PPE	property, plant and equipment
ROA	return on assets
ROE	return on equity

LEARNING OBJECTIVES

After studying this chapter, you should understand:

LO1 The three main financial statements that are produced by corporations: the statement of financial position, the income statement, and the statement of cash flows.

LO2 How to compute and, more importantly, interpret some common ratios.

LO3 How to undertake long-term financial planning using financial statements.

A WRITE-OFF BY A COMPANY frequently means that the value of the company's assets has declined. In 2008 and 2009 almost all banks wrote off billions of euros of loans they did not expect to receive in the future. Royal Bank of Scotland, for example, took a write-off of £16.2 billion in 2008, meaning that it was reducing income for the year by that amount.

So did Royal Bank of Scotland shareholders actually lose £16.2 billion? The answer is no. Understanding why ultimately leads us to the main subject of this chapter: that all-important substance known as *cash flow*.

In this chapter we examine financial statements, taxes and cash flow. Our emphasis is not on preparing financial statements. Instead, we recognize that financial statements are frequently a key source of information for financial decisions, so our goal is to briefly examine such statements and point out some of their more relevant features. We also pay special attention to some of the practical details of cash flow.

As you read, pay particular attention to two important differences: (1) the difference between accounting value and market value; and (2) the difference between accounting income and cash flow. These distinctions will be important throughout the book.

3.1   The Annual Report

Every year, a company will release its annual report. In addition to information relating to the performance and activities of the firm over the previous year, the annual report presents three financial statements:

Chapter 3 Financial Analysis and Planning

1   The statement of financial position, or balance sheet

2   The income statement

3   The statement of cash flows

We shall now discuss each statement in turn.

statement of financial position (balance sheet) Financial statement showing a firm's accounting value on a particular date.

The Statement of Financial Position

The **statement of financial position** or **balance sheet** is a snapshot of the firm. It is a convenient means of organizing and summarizing what a firm owns (its assets), what the firm owes (its liabilities), and the difference between the two (the firm's equity) at a given point in time. Figure 3.1 illustrates how the statement of financial position is constructed. As shown, the left side lists the assets of the firm, and the right side lists the liabilities and equity.

Assets: The Left Side   Assets are classified as either *current* or *non-current*. A non-current asset is one that has a relatively long life (greater than 12 months). Non-current assets can be either *tangible*, such as a truck or a computer, or *intangible*, such as a trademark or patent. A current asset has a life of less than one year. This means that the asset will convert to cash within 12 months. For example, inventory would normally be purchased and sold within a year, and is thus classified as a current asset. Obviously, cash itself is a current asset. Trade receivables (money owed to the firm by its customers) are also current assets.

Liabilities and Owners' Equity: The Right Side   The firm's liabilities are the first thing listed on the right side of the statement of financial position. These are classified as either *current* or *non-current*. Current liabilities, like current assets, have a life of less than one year (meaning they must be paid within the year), and are usually listed before non-current liabilities. Trade payables (money the firm owes to its suppliers) are one example of a current liability.

A debt that is not due in the coming year is classified as a non-current liability. A loan that the firm will pay off in five years is one such non-current liability. Firms borrow in the long term from a variety of sources. We shall tend to use the terms *bond* and *bondholders* generically to refer to long-term debt and long-term creditors, respectively.

FIGURE 3.1

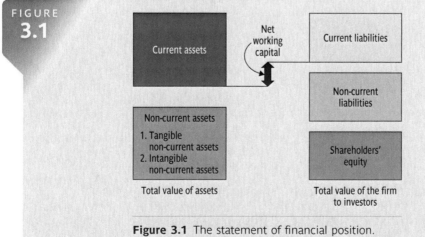

Total value of assets   Total value of the firm to investors

Figure 3.1 The statement of financial position. Left side: total value of assets. Right side: total value of liabilities and shareholders' equity.

Finally, by definition, the difference between the total value of the assets (current and non-current) and the total value of the liabilities (current and non-current) is the *shareholders' equity*, also called *ordinary equity* or *owners' equity*. This feature of the statement of financial position is intended to reflect the fact that, if the firm were to sell all its assets and use the money to pay off its debts, then whatever residual value remained would belong to the shareholders. So the statement of financial position or balance sheet 'balances' because the value of the left side always equals the value of the right side. That is, the value of the firm's assets is equal to the sum of its liabilities and shareholders' equity:

$$\text{Assets} = \text{Liabilities} + \text{Shareholders' equity} \qquad (3.1)$$

This is the *balance sheet identity*, or equation, and it always holds, because shareholders' equity is defined as the difference between assets and liabilities.

Net Working Capital As shown in Fig. 3.1, the difference between a firm's current assets and its current liabilities is called **net working capital**. Net working capital is positive when current assets exceed current liabilities. Based on the definitions of current assets and current liabilities, this means the cash that will become available over the next 12 months exceeds the cash that must be paid over the same period. For this reason, net working capital is usually positive in a healthy firm.

> **net working capital**
> Current assets less current liabilities.

Building the Statement of Financial Position

EXAMPLE 3.1

From British Airways' 2009 annual report, it had current assets of £2.346 billion, non-current assets of £8.142 billion, current liabilities of £4.142 billion, and non-current liabilities of £4.5 billion. What does British Airways' statement of financial position or balance sheet look like? What is shareholders' equity? What is net working capital?

In this case, total assets are £2.346 + £8.142 = £10.488 billion and total liabilities are £4.142 + £4.5 = £8.642 billion, so shareholders' equity is the difference: £10.488 − £8.642 = £1.846 billion. The statement of financial position for British Airways would look like this:

Assets (£ billions)		Liabilities and shareholders' equity (£ billions)	
Current assets	2.346	Current liabilities	4.142
Non-current assets	8.142	Non-current liabilities	4.5
		Shareholders' equity	1.846
Total assets	10.488	Total liabilities and shareholders' equity	10.488

Net working capital is the difference between current assets and current liabilities, or £2.346 − £4.142 = −£1.796 billion. Given that British Airways' net working capital is negative, its managers would have had to consider ways in which to raise cash to meet the company's commitments in 2009/2010. History tells us that they merged with the Spanish airline Iberia to capture economies of scale and compete on a level playing field with other European operators, such as Air France-KLM.

Table 3.1 shows a real-life statement of financial position for the global plumbing and heating firm Wolseley plc. The assets on the statement of financial position can be listed in order of the length of time it takes for them to convert to cash in the normal course of business. Similarly, the liabilities are listed in the order in which they would normally be paid. There are other ways in which the statements can be presented. For example, in the UK, non-current assets are sometimes called *fixed assets*, non-current liabilities are known as *long-term debt*, and the statement of financial position is presented as fixed assets + current assets − current liabilities = long-term debt + shareholders' equity.

Market Value versus Book Value The values shown in the statement of financial position for the firm's assets are *book values*, and generally are not normally what the assets are

Chapter 3 Financial Analysis and Planning

TABLE 3.1	Group balance sheet As at 31 July 2009			
		Notes	2009 £m	2008 £m
Assets				
Non-current assets				
Intangible assets: goodwill		12	1,514	1,995
Intangible assets: other		12	709	841
Property, plant and equipment		12	1,593	1,842
Investment in associate			53	–
Financial assets: available-for-sale investments			3	4
Deferred tax assets			244	52
Trade and other receivables			116	96
Derivative financial assets			34	–
			4,266	4,830
Current assets				
Inventories			1,624	2,025
Trade and other receivables			1,983	2,804
Current tax receivable			124	18
Financial assets: trading investments			155	5
Derivative financial assets			23	16
Financial receivables: construction loans (secured)			163	237
Cash and cash equivalents			635	231
			4,707	5,426
Assets held for sale			88	43
Total assets			9,061	10,299
Liabilities				
Current liabilities				
Trade and other payables			2,586	2,956
Current tax payable			173	219
Borrowings: construction loans (unsecured)			163	237
Bank loans and overdrafts			42	276
Obligations under finance leases			12	19
Derivative financial liabilities			25	8
Provisions		13	122	60
Retirement benefit obligations		14	33	22
			3,156	3,797
Non-current liabilities				
Trade and other payables			59	68
Bank loans			1,657	2,440
Obligations under finance leases			59	68

Table 3.1 Statements of financial position

TABLE 3.1			
Derivative financial liabilities		11	–
Deferred tax liabilities		176	235
Provisions	13	244	118
Retirement benefit obligations	14	308	214
		2,514	3,143
Liabilities of disposal groups held for sale		15	–
Total liabilities		5,685	6,940
Net assets		3,376	3,359
Shareholders' equity			
Called up share capital		241	165
Share premium account		1,152	949
Foreign currency translation reserve		228	(52)
Retained earnings		1,755	2,290
Equity shareholders' funds	15	3,376	3,359

Source: Wolseley plc 2009 annual report, www.wolseley.com

Table 3.1 *Continued*

actually worth. Under **International Accounting Standards (IAS)** financial statements in Europe and many other countries can show assets in two ways. The most common presentation uses the *historical cost model*, in which assets are valued at what the firm paid for them, no matter how long ago they were purchased or how much they are worth today. Another approach uses the *revaluation model*, which present an asset's value as what it is worth in the market today. This is known as the *fair value amount*.

For current assets market value and book value might be somewhat similar, because current assets are bought and converted into cash over a relatively short span of time. In other circumstances the two values might differ quite a bit. Moreover, for non-current assets under the cost model it would be purely a coincidence if the actual market value of an asset (what the asset could be sold for) were equal to its book value. For example, a railroad might own enormous tracts of land purchased a century or more ago. What the railroad paid for that land could be hundreds or thousands of times less than what the land is worth today. The statement of financial position would nonetheless show the historical cost if the cost model were used.

The difference between market value and book value is important for understanding the impact of reported gains and losses. For example, to open the chapter we discussed the huge charges against earnings taken by the Royal Bank of Scotland. What actually happened is that these charges came from recognizing a reduction in the book value of certain types of asset. However, this recognition had no effect on the amount the assets in question could actually sell for in the market. Instead, the market value of an asset depends on things such as its riskiness and cash flows, neither of which has anything to do with accounting.

The statement of financial position is potentially useful to many different parties. A supplier might look at the size of trade payables to see how promptly the firm pays its bills. A potential creditor would examine the liquidity and degree of financial leverage. Managers within the firm can track things such as the amount of cash and the amount of inventory the firm keeps on hand. Uses such as these are discussed in more detail later in the chapter.

International Accounting Standards (IAS) The common set of standards and procedures by which audited financial statements are prepared in Europe and many other countries.

Chapter 3 Financial Analysis and Planning

Managers and investors will frequently be interested in knowing the value of the firm. This information is not in the statement of financial position. The fact that assets may be listed at cost means that there is no necessary connection between the total assets shown and the value of the firm. Indeed, many of the most valuable assets a firm might have – good management, a good reputation, talented employees – don't appear in the statement of financial position at all.

Similarly, the shareholders' equity figure in the statement of financial position and the true value of the equity need not be related. For example, in early 2010 the book value of BP's equity was about £55 billion, whereas the market value was £110 billion. Similarly, Wolseley's book value of equity was approximately £3.4 billion, and its market value was £3.9 billion.

For financial managers, then, the accounting value of the equity is not an especially important concern; it is the market value that matters. Henceforth, whenever we speak of the value of an asset or the value of the firm, we shall normally mean its *market value*. So, for example, when we say the goal of the financial manager is to increase the value of the equity, we mean the market value of the equity.

EXAMPLE 3.2

Market Value versus Book Value

Siouxsie plc has non-current assets with a book value of £700 and an appraised market value of about £1,000. Net working capital is £400 on the books, but approximately £600 would be realized if all the current accounts were liquidated. Siouxsie has £500 in long-term debt, both book value and market value. What is the book value of the equity? What is the market value?

We can construct two simplified statements of financial position, one in accounting (book value) terms and one in economic (market value) terms:

SIOUXSIE PLC Statements of financial position Market value versus book value					
Assets			**Liabilities and shareholders' equity**		
	Book **£**	**Market** **£**		**Book** **£**	**Market** **£**
Net working capital	400	600	Non-current liabilities	500	500
Non-current assets	700	1,000	Shareholders' equity	600	1,100
	1,100	1,600		1,100	1,600

In this example shareholders' equity is actually worth almost twice as much as what is shown on the books. The distinction between book and market values is important precisely because book values can be so different from true economic value.

The Income Statement

income statement Financial statement summarizing a firm's performance over a period of time.

The **income statement** measures performance over some period of time, usually a quarter, six months or a year. The income statement equation is

$$\text{Revenues} - \text{Expenses} = \text{Income} \qquad (3.2)$$

If you think of the statement of financial position as a snapshot, then you can think of the income statement as a video recording covering the period between before and after pictures. Table 3.2 shows a real-life income statement for Wolseley plc.

TABLE 3.2	Group income statement Year ended 31 July 2009			
	Notes	2009 Before exceptional items £m	2009 Exceptional items £m	2009 Total £m
Continuing operations				
Revenue	2	14,441	–	14,441
Cost of sales		(10,436)	(28)	(10,464)
Gross profit		4,005	(28)	3,977
Distribution costs		(2,831)	(266)	(3,097)
Administrative expenses:				
amortization of acquired intangibles		(105)	–	(105)
impairment of acquired intangibles		(490)	–	(490)
other		(743)	(164)	(907)
Administrative expenses: total		(1,338)	(164)	(1,502)
Other income		16	–	16
Operating (loss)/profit	2	(148)	(458)	(606)
Finance revenue	4	72	–	72
Finance costs	5	(217)	–	(217)
Share of after-tax loss of associate	6	(9)	(6)	(15)
(Loss)/profit before tax		(302)	(464)	(766)
Tax income/(expense)	7	(72)	106	34
(Loss)/profit from continuing operations		(374)	(358)	(732)
Loss from discontinued operations	8	(265)	(176)	(441)
(Loss)/profit for the year attributable to equity shareholders		(639)	(534)	(1,173)
(Loss)/earnings per share	10			
Continuing operations and discontinued operations				
Basic (loss)/earnings per share				(558.0)p
Diluted (loss)/earnings per share				(558.0)p
Continuing operations only				
Basic (loss)/earnings per share				(348.2)p
Diluted (loss)/earnings per share				(348.2)p

Source: Wolseley plc 2009 annual report, www.wolseley.com

Table 3.2 Income statement

TABLE
3.3

15. Reconciliation of movements in shareholders' funds	2009 £m	2008 £m
(Loss)/profit for the year attributable to equity shareholders	(1,173)	74
Other recognized income and expense	187	40
Dividends paid	–	(215)
Credit to equity for share-based payments	9	5
New share capital subscribed	999	4
Purchase of own shares by employee benefit trusts	(5)	–
Net addition to/(reduction in) shareholders' funds	17	(92)
Opening shareholders' funds	3,359	3,451
Closing shareholders' funds	3,376	3,359

Source: Wolseley plc 2009 annual report, www.wolseley.com

Table 3.3 Note 15 to Wolseley 2009 annual report

The first thing reported in an income statement would usually be revenue and expenses from the firm's principal operations. Subsequent parts include, among other things, financing expenses such as interest paid. Taxes paid are reported separately. The last item is *(loss)/ profit from continuing operations*, also known as *net income* (the so-called bottom line). Net income is often expressed on a per-share basis and called *earnings per share (EPS)*.

Wolseley did not pay any dividends to its shareholders in 2009, probably because it had made such a large loss. You may also be wondering why shareholders' equity increased from £3.359 billion in 2008 to £3.376 billion in 2009 (see Table 3.1), when the firm lost £1.173 billion. This information can be found in the notes to the accounts, and is presented in Table 3.3. The main factor was that Wolseley raised £999 million in cash from shareholders, and this was used to shore up the company's finances during an exceptionally tough year.

 EXAMPLE
3.3

Calculating Earnings and Dividends per Share

Wolseley plc had 210 million shares after its 2009 share issue. Based on the income statement in Table 3.2, what was EPS? What were dividends per share?

From the income statement we see that Wolseley had a net loss of £732 million for the year from continuing operations. No dividends were paid. We can calculate earnings per share, or EPS, and dividends per share as follows:

Earnings per share = profit/loss from continuing operations/Total shares outstanding
= −£732/210 = −£3.48 per share

Dividends per share = Total dividends/Total shares outstanding
= £0/210 = £0 per share

This is confirmed from looking at the bottom of Table 3.2. We could, of course, have used the profit/loss from continuing and discounted operations (£1,173 million) and arrived at an earnings per share of −£5.58 per share. Clearly, the two values are very different, and so it is exceptionally important to know what EPS is actually measuring.

A Digression: Taxes

Taxes can be one of the largest cash outflows a firm experiences. For example, for the fiscal year 2008 the global energy firm Total SA's earnings before taxes were about €180 billion. Its tax bill, including all taxes paid worldwide, was a whopping €14 billion. Also for fiscal year 2008, Telefonica had a taxable income of €10.9 billion, and the company paid €3 billion in taxes, an average tax rate of 27.5 per cent.

The size of a company's tax bill is determined by the tax code, an often amended set of rules. In this section we examine corporate tax rates and how taxes are calculated. If the various rules of taxation seem a little bizarre or convoluted to you, keep in mind that the tax code is the result of political, not economic, forces. As a result, there is no reason why it has to make economic sense.

Corporate Tax Rates   An overview of corporate tax rates for a sample of countries that were in effect for 2010 is shown in Table 3.4. Corporate taxes are not normally a simple arithmetic deduction from profit before taxes. Almost all countries in the world allow firms to carry forward losses they've made in previous years to offset their tax bill in the future. In addition, there are a number of adjustments and modifications to the tax figure that affect what is actually paid. This is what happened in 2009 to British Airways, which made a loss of £401 million before taxes. Although the corporate tax rate in the UK was 28 per cent, British Airways received a tax credit (to offset the loss) of only £43 million. This is only 10.7 per cent of £401 million.

The tax rates presented in Table 3.4 are average tax rates for the largest companies. Many countries apply differential taxation, depending on how much a company earns in any given year. In the UK, for example, there are two corporation tax bands. Firms that earn between £0 and £300,000 per annum have a tax rate of 22 per cent. Firms that earn above £1,500,000 must pay 28 per cent (as presented in Table 3.4). Firms that report annual turnover between

TABLE 3.4	Country	Corporation tax (%)	Country	Corporation tax (%)
	Australia	30	New Zealand	30
	Austria	25	Nigeria	30
	Belgium	33.99	Norway	28
	Brazil	34	Pakistan	35
	Canada	19.5	Poland	19
	China	25	Portugal	25
	Denmark	25	Russia	20
	Finland	26	South Africa	28
	France	33.33	Spain	32.50
	Germany	29.8	Sweden	28
	Greece	25	Switzerland	21.30
	India	30	Taiwan	25
	Ireland	12.50	Tanzania	30
	Italy	31.4	Thailand	30
	Japan	30	Turkey	20
	Malaysia	26	United Kingdom	28
	Netherlands	20/25.5	United States	40

Source: Federation of International Trade Associations, KPMG.

Table 3.4 Corporate tax rates for large firms around the world

Chapter 3 Financial Analysis and Planning

£300,000 and £1,500,000 receive a rebate called marginal tax relief that allows them to transition their tax rates gradually between the small companies tax rate and the standard rate.

Average versus Marginal Tax Rates In making financial decisions, it is frequently important to distinguish between average and marginal tax rates. Your average tax rate is your tax bill divided by your taxable income – in other words, the percentage of your income that goes to pay taxes. Your marginal tax rate is the tax you would pay (in per cent) if you earned one more unit of currency. The percentage tax rates shown in Table 3.4 for the Netherlands are marginal rates. On the first €200,000 of earnings, Dutch firms must pay 20 per cent tax. Any extra earnings are charged 25.5 per cent tax. Put another way, marginal tax rates apply to the part of income in the indicated range only, not all income.

The difference between average and marginal tax rates can best be illustrated with a simple example. Suppose our Dutch corporation has a taxable income of €400,000. What is the tax bill? Using Table 3.4, we can figure our tax bill like this:

$$
\begin{aligned}
0.20 \times €200,000 &= €40,000 \\
0.255 \times (€400,000 - 200,000) &= \underline{€51,000} \\
&= \underline{\underline{€91,000}}
\end{aligned}
$$

Our total tax is thus €91,000.

In our example, what is the average tax rate? We had a taxable income of €400,000 and a tax bill of €91,000, so the average tax rate is €91,000/400,000 = 22.75%. What is the marginal tax rate? If we made one more euro, the tax on that euro would be 25.5 cents, so our marginal rate is 25.5 per cent.

With a flat-rate tax there is only one tax rate, so the rate is the same for all income levels. With such a tax the marginal tax rate is always the same as the average tax rate. As it stands now, corporate taxation in the United Kingdom is based on a modified flat-rate tax, which becomes a true flat rate for the highest incomes.

Normally, the marginal tax rate will be relevant for financial decision-making. The reason is that any new cash flows will be taxed at that marginal rate. Because financial decisions usually involve new cash flows or changes in existing ones, this rate will tell us the marginal effect of a decision on our tax bill.

Statement of Cash Flows

At this point we are ready to discuss perhaps one of the most important pieces of financial information that can be gleaned from financial statements: cash flow. By *cash flow* we simply mean the difference between the cash that came in and the cash that went out. For example, if you were the owner of a business, you might be very interested in how much cash you actually took out of your business in a given year. How to determine this amount is one of the things we discuss next.

No standard financial statement always presents this information in the way that we wish. We shall therefore discuss how to calculate cash flow for Wolseley plc, and point out how the result may differ from that of standard financial statement calculations. It is also important to note that the accounting standards used in Europe are different from those in the US, and this leads to differences in the way the cash flow statement is presented. Our focus is on International Accounting Standards, because these are followed by large European firms.

From the balance sheet identity, we know that the value of a firm's assets is equal to the value of its liabilities plus the value of its equity. Similarly, the cash flow from the firm's assets must equal the sum of the cash flow to creditors and the cash flow to shareholders (or owners):

> **total cash flow**
> The total of cash flow from operating activities, investing activities and financing activities.

Cash flow from assets = Cash flow to creditors + Cash flow to shareholders   (3.3)

This is the *cash flow identity*. It says that the cash flow from the firm's assets is equal to the cash flow paid to suppliers of capital to the firm. What it reflects is

A common variation on EBITDA is earnings before interest, taxes, and depreciation (EBITD – say 'ebbit-dee'). In this variation, only depreciation is considered.

Asset Management, or Turnover, Measures

We next turn our attention to the efficiency with which a company uses its assets. The measures in this section are sometimes called *asset utilization ratios*. The specific ratios we discuss can all be interpreted as measures of turnover. What they are intended to describe is how efficiently or intensively a firm uses its assets to generate sales. We first look at two important current assets: inventory and receivables.

Inventory Turnover and Days' Sales in Inventory   *Inventory turnover* can be calculated as follows:

$$\text{Inventory turnover} = \frac{\text{Cost of goods sold}}{\text{Inventory}} \qquad (3.12)$$

As long as we are not running out of stock and thereby forgoing sales, the higher this ratio is, the more efficiently we are managing inventory.

If we know the inventory turnover, we can immediately figure out how long it took us to turn it over on average. The result is the average *days' sales in inventory*:

$$\text{Days' sales in inventory} = \frac{365 \text{ days}}{\text{Inventory turnover}} \qquad (3.13)$$

In many of the ratios we discuss in this chapter, average figures could just as well be used. Again, it depends on whether we are worried about the past, in which case averages are appropriate, or the future, in which case ending figures might be better. Also, using ending figures is common in reporting industry averages; so, for comparison purposes, ending figures should be used in such cases.

Receivables Turnover and Days' Sales in Receivables   Our inventory measures give some indication of how fast we can sell our product. We now look at how fast we collect on those sales. The *receivables turnover* is defined much like inventory turnover:

$$\text{Receivable turnover} = \frac{\text{Sales}}{\text{Trade receivables}} \qquad (3.14)$$

This ratio makes more sense if we convert it to days, so here is the *days' sales in receivables*:

$$\text{Days' sales in receivables} = \frac{365 \text{ days}}{\text{Receivables turnover}} \qquad (3.15)$$

For obvious reasons, this ratio is frequently called the *average collection period (ACP)*.

Asset Turnover Ratios   Moving away from specific accounts such as inventory or receivables, we can consider several 'big picture' ratios. For example, *NWC turnover* is

$$\text{NWC turnover} = \frac{\text{Sales}}{\text{NWC}} \qquad (3.16)$$

This ratio measures how much 'work' we get out of our working capital. Once again, assuming we aren't missing out on sales, a high value is preferred. (Why?)

Similarly, *PPE turnover* is

$$\text{PPE turnover} = \frac{\text{Sales}}{\text{Property, plant and equipment}} \qquad (3.17)$$

Our final asset management ratio, the *total asset turnover*, comes up quite a bit. We shall see it later in this chapter. As the name suggests, the total asset turnover is

$$\text{Total asset turnover} = \frac{\text{Sales}}{\text{Total assets}} \qquad (3.18)$$

Profitability Measures

The three measures we discuss in this section are probably the best known and most widely used of all financial ratios. In one form or another, they are intended to measure how efficiently a firm uses its assets and manages its operations. The focus in this group is on the bottom line, net income.

Profit Margin   Companies pay a great deal of attention to their *profit margins*:

$$\text{Profit margin} = \frac{\text{Net income}}{\text{Sales}} \qquad (3.19)$$

All other things being equal, a relatively high profit margin is obviously desirable. This situation corresponds to low expense ratios relative to sales. However, we hasten to add that other things are often not equal.

For example, lowering our sales price will usually increase unit volume, but will normally cause profit margins to shrink. Total profit (or, more important, operating cash flow) may go up or down; so the fact that margins are smaller isn't necessarily bad.

Return on Assets   *Return on assets (ROA)* is a measure of profit per unit cash of assets. It can be defined in several ways, but the most common is this:

$$\text{Return on assets} = \frac{\text{Net income}}{\text{Total assets}} \qquad (3.20)$$

Return on Equity   *Return on equity (ROE)* is a measure of how the shareholders fared during the year. Because benefiting shareholders is our goal, ROE is, in an accounting sense, the true bottom-line measure of performance. ROE is usually measured as follows:

$$\text{Return on equity} = \frac{\text{Net income}}{\text{Total equity}} \qquad (3.21)$$

Because ROA and ROE are such commonly cited numbers, we stress that it is important to remember they are accounting rates of return. For this reason, these measures should properly be called *return on book assets* and *return on book equity*. In fact, ROE is sometimes called *return on net worth*. Whatever it's called, it would be inappropriate to compare the result with, for example, an interest rate observed in the financial markets. We shall have more to say about accounting rates of return in later chapters.

Market Value Measures

Our final group of measures is based, in part, on information not necessarily contained in financial statements – the market price per share of equity. Obviously, these measures can be calculated directly only for publicly traded companies.

Price–Earnings Ratio   The first of our market value measures, the *price–earnings (P/E) ratio* (or multiple), is defined here:

$$\text{P/E ratio} = \frac{\text{Price per share}}{\text{Earnings per share}} \qquad (3.22)$$

Earnings per share is simply net income divided by the number of shares.

Because the P/E ratio measures how much investors are willing to pay per unit of current earnings, higher P/Es are often taken to mean the firm has significant prospects for future growth. Of course, if a firm had no or almost no earnings, its P/E would probably be quite large: so, as always, care is needed in interpreting this ratio.

Sometimes analysts divide P/E ratios by expected future earnings growth rates (after multiplying the growth rate by 100). The result is the PEG ratio. The idea behind the PEG ratio is that whether a P/E ratio is high or low depends on expected future growth. High PEG ratios suggest that the P/E is too high relative to growth, and vice versa.

Price–Sales Ratio   In some cases, companies will have negative earnings for extended periods, so their P/E ratios are not very meaningful. A good example is a recent start-up. Such companies usually do have some revenues, so analysts will often look at the *price–sales ratio*:

$$\text{Price–sales ratio} = \frac{\text{Price per share}}{\text{Sales per share}} \tag{3.23}$$

As with P/E ratios, whether a particular price–sales ratio is high or low depends on the industry involved.

Market-to-Book Ratio   A second commonly quoted market value measure is the *market-to-book ratio*:

$$\text{Market-to-book ratio} = \frac{\text{Market value per share}}{\text{Book value per share}} \tag{3.24}$$

Notice that book value per share is total equity (not just ordinary shares) divided by the number of shares outstanding.

Because book value per share is an accounting number, it reflects historical costs. In a loose sense, the market-to-book ratio therefore compares the market value of the firm's investments with their cost. A value less than 1 could mean that the firm has not been successful overall in creating value for its shareholders.

Another ratio, called *Tobin's Q ratio*, is much like the market-to-book ratio. Tobin's Q is the market value of the firm's assets divided by their replacement cost:

$$\begin{aligned} \text{Tobin's Q} &= \frac{\text{Market value of firm's assets}}{\text{Replacement cost of firm's assets}} \\ &= \frac{\text{Market value of firm's debt and equity}}{\text{Replacement cost of firm's assets}} \end{aligned} \tag{3.25}$$

Notice that we used two equivalent numerators here: the market value of the firm's assets, and the market value of its debt and equity.

Conceptually, the Q ratio is superior to the market-to-book ratio, because it focuses on what the firm is worth today relative to what it would cost to replace it today. Firms with high Q ratios tend to be those with attractive investment opportunities or significant competitive advantages (or both). In contrast, the market-to-book ratio focuses on historical costs, which are less relevant.

As a practical matter, however, Q ratios are difficult to calculate with accuracy, because estimating the replacement cost of a firm's assets is not an easy task. Also, market values for a firm's debt are often unobservable. Book values can be used instead in such cases, but accuracy may suffer.

Conclusion

This completes our definitions of some common ratios. We could tell you about more of them, but these are enough for now. We'll go on to discuss some ways of using these ratios instead of just how to calculate them. Table 3.9 summarizes the ratios we've discussed.

TABLE
3.9

Short-term solvency, or liquidity, ratios

$$\text{Current ratio} = \frac{\text{Current assets}}{\text{Current liabilities}}$$

$$\text{Quick ratio} = \frac{\text{Current assets} - \text{Inventory}}{\text{Current liabilities}}$$

$$\text{Cash ratio} = \frac{\text{Cash}}{\text{Current liabilities}}$$

$$\frac{\text{Net working capital}}{\text{to total assets}} = \frac{\text{Net working capital}}{\text{Total assets}}$$

$$\frac{\text{Interval}}{\text{measure}} = \frac{\text{Current assets}}{\text{Average daily operating costs}}$$

Asset management, or turnover, ratios

$$\text{Inventory turnover} = \frac{\text{Cost of goods sold}}{\text{Inventory}}$$

$$\frac{\text{Days' sales}}{\text{in inventory}} = \frac{365 \text{ days}}{\text{Inventory turnover}}$$

$$\frac{\text{Receivables}}{\text{turnover}} = \frac{\text{Sales}}{\text{Accounts receivable}}$$

$$\frac{\text{Days' sales in}}{\text{receivables}} = \frac{365 \text{ days}}{\text{Receivables turnover}}$$

$$\text{NWC turnover} = \frac{\text{Sales}}{\text{NWC}}$$

$$\frac{\text{PPE}}{\text{turnover}} = \frac{\text{Sales}}{\text{Property, plant and equipment}}$$

$$\text{Total asset turnover} = \frac{\text{Sales}}{\text{Total assets}}$$

Long-term solvency, or financial leverage, ratios

$$\text{Total debt ratio} = \frac{\text{Total assets} - \text{Total equity}}{\text{Total assets}}$$

$$\text{Debt-equity ratio} = \frac{\text{Total debt}}{\text{Total equity}}$$

$$\text{Equity multiplier} = \frac{\text{Total assets}}{\text{Total equity}}$$

$$\frac{\text{Long-term}}{\text{debt ratio}} = \frac{\text{Long-term debt}}{\text{Long-term debt} + \text{Total equity}}$$

$$\frac{\text{Times interest}}{\text{earned ratio}} = \frac{\text{Operating profit}}{\text{Interest}}$$

$$\frac{\text{Cash}}{\text{coverage}} = \frac{\text{Operating profit} + \text{Non-cash adjustments}}{\text{Interest}}$$

Profitability ratios

$$\text{Profit margin} = \frac{\text{Net income}}{\text{Sales}}$$

$$\text{Return on assets (ROA)} = \frac{\text{Net income}}{\text{Total assets}}$$

$$\text{Return on equity (ROE)} = \frac{\text{Net income}}{\text{Total equity}}$$

$$\text{ROE} = \frac{\text{Net income}}{\text{Sales}} \times \frac{\text{Sales}}{\text{Assets}} \times \frac{\text{Assets}}{\text{Equity}}$$

Market value ratios

$$\text{Price-earnings ratio} = \frac{\text{Price per share}}{\text{Earnings per share}}$$

$$\text{PEG ratio} = \frac{\text{Price-earnings ratio}}{\text{Earnings growth rate (\%)}}$$

$$\text{Price-sales ratio} = \frac{\text{Price per share}}{\text{Sales per share}}$$

$$\frac{\text{Market-to-}}{\text{book ratio}} = \frac{\text{Market value per share}}{\text{Book value per share}}$$

$$\text{Tobin's } Q \text{ ratio} = \frac{\text{Market value of assets}}{\text{Replacement cost of assets}}$$

Table 3.9 Common financial ratios

CONCEPT QUESTIONS	3.2a What are the five groups of ratios? Give two or three examples of each kind.
	3.2b Given the total debt ratio, what other two ratios can be computed? Explain how.
	3.2c Turnover ratios all have one of two figures as the numerator. What are these two figures? What do these ratios measure? How do you interpret the results?
	3.2d Profitability ratios all have the same figure in the numerator. What is it? What do these ratios measure? How do you interpret the results?

3.3 The Du Pont Identity

As we mentioned in discussing ROA and ROE, the difference between these two profitability measures is a reflection of the use of debt financing, or financial leverage. We illustrate the relationship between these measures in this section by investigating a famous way of decomposing ROE into its component parts.

A Closer Look at ROE

To begin, let's recall the definition of ROE:

$$\text{Return on equity} = \frac{\text{Net income}}{\text{Total equity}}$$

If we were so inclined, we could multiply this ratio by Assets/Assets without changing anything:

$$\text{Return on equity} = \frac{\text{Net income}}{\text{Total equity}} = \frac{\text{Net income}}{\text{Total equity}} \times \frac{\text{Assets}}{\text{Assets}}$$

$$= \frac{\text{Net income}}{\text{Assets}} \times \frac{\text{Assets}}{\text{Total equity}}$$

Notice that we have expressed the ROE as the product of two other ratios – ROA and the equity multiplier:

$$\text{ROE} = \text{ROA} \times \text{Equity multiplier}$$
$$= \text{ROA} \times (1 + \text{Debt–equity ratio})$$

The difference between ROE and ROA can be substantial, particularly for certain businesses that have borrowed a lot of money. We can further decompose ROE by multiplying the top and bottom by total sales:

$$\text{ROE} = \frac{\text{Sales}}{\text{Sales}} \times \frac{\text{Net income}}{\text{Assets}} \times \frac{\text{Assets}}{\text{Total equity}}$$

If we rearrange things a bit, ROE looks like this:

$$\text{ROE} = \underbrace{\frac{\text{Net income}}{\text{Sales}} \times \frac{\text{Sales}}{\text{Assets}}}_{\text{Return on assets}} \times \frac{\text{Assets}}{\text{Total equity}} \tag{3.26}$$

$$= \text{Profit margin} \times \text{Total asset turnover} \times \text{Equity multiplier}$$

What we have now done is to partition ROA into its two component parts: profit margin and total asset turnover. The last expression of the preceding equation is called the **Du Pont identity**, after the Du Pont Corporation, which popularized its use.

The Du Pont identity tells us that ROE is affected by three things:

1 Operating efficiency (as measured by profit margin)

2 Asset use efficiency (as measured by total asset turnover)

3 Financial leverage (as measured by the equity multiplier)

Weakness in either operating or asset use efficiency (or both) will show up in a diminished return on assets, which will translate into a lower ROE.

Considering the Du Pont identity, it appears that the ROE could be leveraged up by increasing the amount of debt in the firm. However, notice that increasing debt also increases interest expense, which reduces profit margins, which acts to reduce

> **Du Pont identity** Popular expression breaking ROE into three parts: operating efficiency, asset use efficiency, and financial leverage.

ROE. So ROE could go up or down. More important, the use of debt financing has a number of other effects, and as we discuss at some length in Part Six, the amount of leverage a firm uses is governed by its capital structure policy.

The decomposition of ROE we've discussed in this section is a convenient way of systematically approaching financial statement analysis. If ROE is unsatisfactory by some measure, then the Du Pont identity tells you where to start looking for the reasons.

CONCEPT QUESTIONS	**3.3a** Return on assets, or ROA, can be expressed as the product of two ratios. Which two?
	3.3b Return on equity, or ROE, can be expressed as the product of three ratios. Which three?

3.4   Using Financial Statement Information

We now discuss in more detail some practical aspects of financial statement analysis. In particular, we shall look at reasons for analysing financial statements, how to get benchmark information, and some problems that come up in the process.

Why Evaluate Financial Statements?

As we have discussed, the primary reason for looking at accounting information is that we don't have, and can't reasonably expect to get, market value information. We stress that whenever we have market information, we shall use it instead of accounting data. Also, if there is a conflict between accounting and market data, market data should be given precedence.

Financial statement analysis is essentially an application of 'management by exception'. In many cases such analysis will boil down to comparing ratios for one business with average or representative ratios. Those ratios that seem to differ the most from the averages are tagged for further study.

Internal Uses   Financial statement information has a variety of uses within a firm. Among the most important of these is performance evaluation. For example, managers are frequently evaluated and compensated on the basis of accounting measures of performance such as profit margin and return on equity. Also, firms with multiple divisions frequently use financial statement information to compare the performance of those divisions.

Another important internal use we shall explore is planning for the future. As we shall see, historical financial statement information is useful for generating projections about the future, and for checking the realism of assumptions made in those projections.

External Uses   Financial statements are useful to parties outside the firm, including short-term and long-term creditors and potential investors. For example, we would find such information quite useful in deciding whether to grant credit to a new customer.

We would also use this information to evaluate suppliers, and suppliers would review our statements before deciding to extend credit to us. Large customers use this information to decide whether we are likely to be around in the future. Credit-rating agencies rely on financial statements in assessing a firm's overall creditworthiness. The common theme here is that financial statements are a prime source of information about a firm's financial health.

We would also find such information useful in evaluating our main competitors. We might be thinking of launching a new product. A prime concern would be whether the competition would jump in shortly thereafter. In this case we would be interested in learning about our competitors' financial strength to see whether they could afford the necessary development.

Finally, we might be thinking of acquiring another firm. Financial statement information would be essential in identifying potential targets and deciding what to offer.

no magic mirrors, of course, so the best we can hope for is a logical and organized procedure for exploring the unknown. Financial planning establishes guidelines for change and growth in a firm. It normally focuses on the big picture. This means it is concerned with the major elements of a firm's financial and investment policies, without examining the individual components of those policies in detail.

Financial planning formulates the way in which financial goals are to be achieved. A financial plan is thus a statement of what is to be done in the future. Many decisions have long lead times, which means they take a long time to implement. In an uncertain world, this requires that decisions be made far in advance of their implementation. If a firm wants to build a factory in 2014, for example, it might have to begin lining up contractors and financing in 2012 or even earlier.

Growth as a Financial Management Goal

Because the subject of growth will be discussed in various places in this chapter, we need to start out with an important warning: growth, by itself, is not an appropriate goal for the financial manager. As we discussed in Chapter 1, the appropriate goal is increasing the market value of the owners' equity. Of course, if a firm is successful in doing this, then growth will usually result. Growth may thus be a desirable consequence of good decision-making, but it is not an end unto itself. We discuss growth simply because growth rates are so commonly used in the planning process. As we shall see, growth is a convenient means of summarizing various aspects of a firm's financial and investment policies. Also, if we think of growth as growth in the market value of the equity in the firm, then goals of growth and increasing the market value of the equity in the firm are not all that different.

What Can Planning Accomplish?

Because a company is likely to spend a lot of time examining the different scenarios that will become the basis for its financial plan, it seems reasonable to ask what the planning process will accomplish.

Examining Interactions   As we discuss in greater detail in the following pages, the financial plan must make explicit the linkages between investment proposals for the different operating activities of the firm and its available financing choices. In other words, if the firm is planning on expanding and undertaking new investments and projects, where will the financing be obtained to pay for this activity?

Exploring Options   The financial plan allows the firm to develop, analyse, and compare many different scenarios in a consistent way. Various investment and financing options can be explored, and their impact on the firm's shareholders can be evaluated. Questions concerning the firm's future lines of business and optimal financing arrangements are addressed. Options such as marketing new products or closing plants might be evaluated.

Avoiding Surprises   Financial planning should identify what may happen to the firm if different events take place. In particular, it should address what actions the firm will take if things go seriously wrong or, more generally, if assumptions made today about the future are seriously in error. As physicist Niels Bohr once observed, 'Prediction is very difficult, particularly when it concerns the future.' Thus one purpose of financial planning is to avoid surprises and develop contingency plans.

Ensuring Feasibility and Internal Consistency   Beyond a general goal of creating value, a firm will normally have many specific goals. Such goals might be couched in terms of market share, return on equity, financial leverage, and so on. At times, the linkages

Chapter 3 Financial Analysis and Planning

between different goals and different aspects of a firm's business are difficult to see. Not only does a financial plan make these linkages explicit, it also imposes a unified structure for reconciling goals and objectives. In other words, financial planning is a way of verifying that the goals and plans made for specific areas of a firm's operations are feasible and internally consistent. Conflicting goals will often exist. To generate a coherent plan, goals and objectives will therefore have to be modified, and priorities will have to be established.

For example, one goal a firm might have would be 12 per cent growth in unit sales per year. Another goal might be to reduce the firm's total debt ratio from 40 to 20 per cent. Are these two goals compatible? Can they be accomplished simultaneously? Maybe yes, maybe no. As we shall discuss, financial planning is a way of finding out just what is possible – and, by implication, what is not possible.

Conclusion Probably the most important result of the planning process is that it forces managers to think about goals and establish priorities. In fact, conventional business wisdom holds that financial plans don't work, but financial planning does. The future is inherently unknown. What we can do is establish the direction in which we want to travel, and make some educated guesses about what we shall find along the way. If we do a good job, we won't be caught off guard when the future rolls around.

CONCEPT QUESTIONS

3.5a What are the two dimensions of the financial planning process?
3.5b Why should firms draw up financial plans?

3.6 Financial Planning Models: A First Look

Just as companies differ in size and products, the financial planning process will differ from firm to firm. In this section we discuss some common elements in financial plans, and develop a basic model to illustrate these elements. What follows is just a quick overview; later sections will take up the various topics in more detail.

We can begin our discussion of long-term planning models with a relatively simple example. Chute SA's financial statements from the most recent year are as follows:

Chute SA Financial statements				
Income statement		**Statement of financial position**		
	€		€	€
Sales	1,000	Assets	500	Debt	250
Costs	800			Equity	250
Net profit	200	Total	500	Total	500

Unless otherwise stated, the financial planners at Chute assume that all variables are tied directly to sales, and current relationships are optimal. This means that all items will grow at exactly the same rate as sales. This is obviously oversimplified; we use this assumption only to make a point.

Suppose sales increase by 20 per cent, rising from €1,000 to €1,200. Planners would then also forecast a 20 per cent increase in costs, from £800 to £800 × 1.2 = £960. The pro forma income statement would thus be:

Pro forma income statement	
	€
Sales	1,200
Costs	960
Net profit	240

The assumption that all variables will grow by 20 per cent lets us easily construct the pro forma statement of financial position as well:

Pro forma balance sheet			
	€		€
Assets	600 (+100)	Debt	300 (+50)
		Equity	300 (+50)
Total	600 (+100)	Total	600 (+100)

Notice that we have simply increased every item by 20 per cent. The numbers in parentheses are the euro changes for the different items.

Now we have to reconcile these two pro formas. How, for example, can net profit be equal to €240 and equity increase by only €50? The answer is that Chute must have paid out the difference of €240 − 50 = €190, possibly as a cash dividend. In this case, dividends are the plug variable.

Suppose Chute does not pay out the €190. In this case, the addition to retained earnings is the full €240. Chute's equity will thus grow to €250 (the starting amount) plus €240 (net income), or €490, and debt must be retired to keep total assets equal to €600.

With €600 in total assets and €490 in equity, debt will have to be €600 − 490 = €110. Because we started with €250 in debt, Chute will have to retire €250 − 110 = €140 in debt. The resulting pro forma statement of financial position would look like this:

Pro forma statement of financial position			
Assets	€600 (+100)	Debt	€110 (−140)
		Equity	490 (+240)
Total	€600 (+100)	Total	€600 (+100)

In this case, debt is the plug variable used to balance projected total assets and liabilities.

This example shows the interaction between sales growth and financial policy. As sales increase, so do total assets. This occurs because the firm must invest in net working capital and non-current assets (such as property, plant and equipment) to support higher sales levels. Because assets are growing, total liabilities and equity (the right side of the balance sheet) will grow as well.

The thing to notice from our simple example is that the way the liabilities and owners' equity change depends on the firm's financing policy and its dividend policy. The growth in assets requires that the firm decides on how to finance that growth. This is strictly a managerial decision. Note that, in our example, the firm needed no outside funds.

In the Chute SA example we described a simple planning model in which every item increased at the same rate as sales. This may be a reasonable assumption for some elements. For others, such as long-term borrowing, it probably is not: the amount of long-term borrowing is something set by management, and it does not necessarily relate directly to the level of sales.

We now describe an extended version of our simple model. The basic idea is to separate the income statement and balance sheet accounts into two groups – those that vary directly with sales, and those that do not. Given a sales forecast, we shall then be able to calculate how much financing the firm will need to support the predicted sales level.

Chapter 3 Financial Analysis and Planning

percentage of sales approach A financial planning method in which accounts are varied depending on a firm's predicted sales level.

The financial planning model we describe next is based on the **percentage of sales approach**. Our goal here is to develop a quick and practical way of generating pro forma statements. We defer discussion of some 'bells and whistles' to a later section.

The Income Statement

We start out with the most recent income statement for Bogle plc, as shown in Table 3.10. Notice that we have still simplified things by including costs, depreciation, and interest in a single cost figure.

Bogle has projected a 25 per cent increase in sales for the coming year, so we are anticipating sales of £1,000 × 1.25 = £1,250. To generate a pro forma income statement, we assume that total costs will continue to run at £800/1,000 = 80 per cent of sales. With this assumption, Bogle's pro forma income statement is shown in Table 3.11. The effect here of assuming that costs are a constant percentage of sales is to assume that the profit margin is constant. To check this, notice that the profit margin was £144/1,000 = 14.4 per cent. In our pro forma the profit margin is £180/1,250 = 14.4 per cent: so it is unchanged.

TABLE 3.10

Bogle plc Income statement		
	£	£
Sales		1,000
Costs		800
Profit before taxes		200
Taxes (28%)		56
Profit attributable to shareholders		144
Dividends	48	
Addition to retained earnings	96	

Table 3.10 Bogle plc: income statement

TABLE 3.11

Bogle plc Income statement		
	£	£
Sales		1,250
Costs		1,000
Profit before taxes		250
Taxes (28%)		70
Profit attributable to shareholders		180
Dividends	60	
Addition to retained earnings	120	

Table 3.11 Bogle plc: income statement

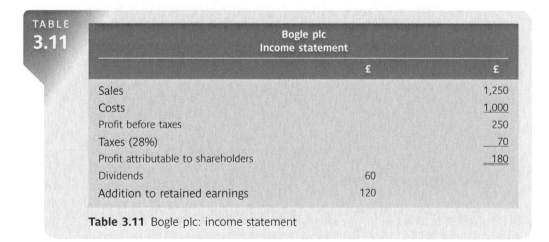

Next, we need to project the dividend payment. This amount is up to Bogle's management. We shall assume Bogle has a policy of paying out a constant fraction of net income in the form of a cash dividend. For the most recent year, the **dividend payout ratio** was this:

$$\text{Dividend payout ratio} = \text{Cash dividends/Net income}$$
$$= £48/144 = 1/3 \qquad (3.27)$$

> **dividend payout ratio** The amount of cash paid out to shareholders divided by net income.

We can also calculate the ratio of the addition to retained earnings to net income:

$$\text{Addition to retained earnings/Net income} = £96/144 = 2/3$$

This ratio is called the **retention ratio** or **ploughback ratio**, and it is equal to 1 minus the dividend payout ratio, because everything not paid out is retained. Assuming that the payout ratio is constant, here are the projected dividends and addition to retained earnings:

> **retention ratio** The addition to retained earnings divided by net income. Also called the **ploughback ratio**.

$$\text{Projected dividends paid to shareholders} = £188 \times 1/3 = \quad £60$$
$$\text{Projected addition to retained earnings} = £188 \times 2/3 = \underline{£120}$$
$$\underline{£180}$$

The Statement of Financial Position

To generate a pro forma statement of financial position, we start with the most recent statement, as shown in Table 3.12.

On our statement of financial position, we assume that some items vary directly with sales and others do not. For items that vary with sales, we express each as a percentage of

TABLE 3.12

Bogle plc — Statement of financial position					
Assets			**Liabilities and owners' equity**		
	£	Percentage of sales		£	Percentage of sales
Current assets			**Current liabilities**		
Cash	160	16	Trade payables	300	30
Trade receivables	440	44	Notes payable	100	n/a
Inventory	600	60			
Total	1,200	120	Total	400	n/a
Non-current assets			**Long-term debt**	800	n/a
Property, plant and equipment	1,800	180	**Owners' equity**		
			Ordinary shares and paid-in surplus	800	n/a
			Retained earnings	1,000	n/a
			Total	1,800	n/a
Total assets	3,000	300	**Total liabilities and owners' equity**	3,000	n/a

Table 3.12 Bogle plc: statement of financial position

Chapter 3 Financial Analysis and Planning

sales for the year just completed. When an item does not vary directly with sales, we write 'n/a' for 'not applicable'.

For example, on the asset side, inventory is equal to 60 per cent of sales (= £600/1,000) for the year just ended. We assume this percentage applies to the coming year, so for each £1 increase in sales, inventory will rise by £0.60. More generally, the ratio of total assets to sales for the year just ended is £3,000/1,000 = 3, or 300 per cent.

This ratio of total assets to sales is sometimes called the **capital intensity ratio**. It tells us the amount of assets needed to generate £1 in sales; so the higher the ratio, the more capital-intensive the firm. Notice also that this ratio is just the reciprocal of the total asset turnover ratio we defined in the last chapter.

For Bogle, assuming that this ratio is constant, it takes £3 in total assets to generate £1 in sales (apparently Bogle is in a relatively capital-intensive business). Therefore, if sales are to increase by £100, Bogle will have to increase total assets by three times this amount, or £300.

> **capital intensity ratio**
> A firm's total assets divided by its sales, or the amount of assets needed to generate £1 in sales.

On the liability side of the statement of financial position, we show trade payables varying with sales. The reason is that we expect to place more orders with our suppliers as sales volume increases, so payables will change 'spontaneously' with sales. Notes payable, on the other hand, represent short-term debt such as bank borrowing. This item will not vary unless we take specific actions to change the amount, so we mark it as 'n/a'.

Similarly, we use 'n/a' for long-term debt because it won't automatically change with sales. The same is true for ordinary shares and paid-in surplus. The last item on the right side, retained earnings, will vary with sales, but it won't be a simple percentage of sales. Instead, we shall explicitly calculate the change in retained earnings based on our projected net income and dividends.

We can now construct a partial pro forma statement of financial position for Bogle. We do this by using the percentages we have just calculated wherever possible to calculate the projected amounts. For example, property, plant and equipment are 180 per cent of sales: so, with a new sales level of £1,250, the property, plant and equipment amount will be $1.80 \times £1,250 = £2,250$, representing an increase of £2,250 − 1,800 = £450. It is important to note that for items that don't vary directly with sales, we initially assume no change and simply write in the original amounts. The result is shown in Table 3.13. Notice that the change in retained earnings is equal to the £110 addition to retained earnings we calculated earlier.

Inspecting our pro forma statement of financial position, we notice that assets are projected to increase by £750. However, without additional financing, liabilities and equity will increase by only £195, leaving a shortfall of £750 − 185 = £555. We label this amount *external financing needed (EFN)*.

A Particular Scenario

Our financial planning model now reminds us of one of those good news–bad news jokes. The good news is we're projecting a 25 per cent increase in sales. The bad news is that this isn't going to happen unless Bogle can somehow raise £555 in new financing.

This is a good example of how the planning process can point out problems and potential conflicts. If, for example, Bogle has a goal of not borrowing any additional funds and not selling any new equity, then a 25 per cent increase in sales is probably not feasible.

If we take the need for £555 in new financing as given, we know that Bogle has three possible sources: short-term borrowing, long-term borrowing, and new equity. The choice of some combination among these three is up to management; we shall illustrate only one of the many possibilities.

Suppose Bogle decides to borrow the needed funds. In this case, the firm might choose to borrow some over the short term and some over the long term. For example, current assets increased by £300 whereas current liabilities rose by only £75. Bogle could borrow £300 − 75 = £225 in short-term notes payable and leave total net working capital unchanged. With £555 needed, the remaining £555 − 225 = £330 would have to come from long-term debt. Table 3.14 shows the completed pro forma statement of financial position for Bogle.

3.7 External Financing and Growth

External financing needed (EFN) and growth are obviously related. All other things staying the same, the higher the rate of growth in sales or assets, the greater will be the need for external financing. In the previous section we took a growth rate as given, and then we determined the amount of external financing needed to support that growth. In this section we turn things around a bit. We shall take the firm's financial policy as given, and then examine the relationship between that financial policy and the firm's ability to finance new investments and thereby grow.

Once again, we emphasize that we are focusing on growth not because growth is an appropriate goal; instead, for our purposes, growth is simply a convenient means of examining the interactions between investment and financing decisions.

EFN and Growth

The first thing we need to do is establish the relationship between EFN and growth. To do this, we introduce the simplified income statement and balance sheet (statement of financial position) for Hoffman AG in Table 3.15. Notice that we have simplified the statement of financial position by combining short-term and long-term debt into a single total debt figure. Effectively, we are assuming that none of the current liabilities varies spontaneously with sales. This assumption isn't as restrictive as it sounds. If any current liabilities (such as trade payables) vary with sales, we can assume that any such accounts have been netted out in current assets. Also, we continue to combine depreciation, interest, and costs on the income statement.

TABLE 3.15

Hoffman AG Income statement		
	€	€
Sales		500
Costs		400
Profit before taxes		100
Taxes (34%)		34
Profit attributable to shareholders		66
Dividends	22	
Addition to retained earnings	44	

Statement of financial position					
Assets			**Liabilities and owners' equity**		
	€	Percentage of sales		€	Percentage of sales
Current assets	200	40	Total liabilities	250	n/a
Non-current assets	300	60	Owners' equity	250	n/a
Total assets	500	100	Total liabilities and owners' equity	500	n/a

Table 3.15 Hoffman AG: income statement and statement of financial position

TABLE
3.16

Hoffman AG Income statement		
	€	€
Sales (projected)		600.0
Costs (80% of sales)		480.0
Profit before taxes		120.0
Taxes (34%)		40.8
Profit attributable to shareholders		79.2
Dividends	26.4	
Addition to retained earnings	52.8	

Statement of financial position					
Assets			**Liabilities and owners' equity**		
	€	Percentage of sales		€	Percentage of sales
Current assets	240.0	40	Total Liabilities	50.0	n/a
Non-current assets	360.0	60	Owners' equity	302.8	n/a
Total assets	600.0	100	Total liabilities and owners' equity	552.8	n/a
			External financing needed	47.2	n/a

Table 3.16 Hoffman AG: income statement and statement of financial position

Suppose Hoffman is forecasting next year's sales level at €600, a €100 increase. Notice that the percentage increase in sales is €100/500 = 20%. Using the percentage of sales approach and the figures in Table 3.15, we can prepare a pro forma income statement and balance sheet as in Table 3.16. As Table 3.16 illustrates, at a 20 per cent growth rate Hoffman needs €100 in new assets (assuming full capacity). The projected addition to retained earnings is €52.8, so the external financing needed is €100 – 52.8 = €47.2.

Notice that the debt–equity ratio for Hoffman was originally (from Table 3.15) equal to €250/250 = 1.0. We shall assume Hoffman does not wish to sell new equity. In this case, the €47.2 in EFN will have to be borrowed. What will the new debt–equity ratio be? From Table 3.16, we know that total owners' equity is projected at €302.8. The new total debt will be the original €250 plus €47.2 in new borrowing, or €297.2 total. The debt–equity ratio thus falls slightly from 1.0 to €297.2/302.8 = 0.98.

Work the Web

Calculating company growth rates can involve detailed research, and a major part of an equity analyst's job is to estimate them. Places to find earnings and sales growth rates on the Web are Yahoo! Finance and Reuters. We visited Reuters, pulled up a quote for British Airways plc, and followed the 'Estimates' link. Here is an abbreviated look at the results:

Here ROA is the return on assets, and b is the ploughback, or retention, ratio defined earlier in this chapter.

For Hoffman AG, net income was €66 and total assets were €500. ROA is thus €66/500 = 13.2 per cent. Of the €66 net income, €44 was retained, so the ploughback ratio, b, is €44/66 = 2/3. With these numbers, we can calculate the internal growth rate:

$$\text{Internal growth rate} = \frac{\text{ROA} \times b}{1 - \text{ROA} \times b}$$

$$= \frac{0.132 \times (2/3)}{1 - 0.132 \times (2/3)}$$

$$= 9.65\%$$

Thus Hoffman AG can expand at a maximum rate of 9.65 per cent per year without external financing.

The Sustainable Growth Rate We have seen that if Hoffman AG wishes to grow more rapidly than at a rate of 9.65 per cent per year, external financing must be arranged. The second growth rate of interest is the maximum growth rate a firm can achieve with no external *equity* financing while it maintains a constant debt–equity ratio. This rate is commonly called the **sustainable growth rate**, because it is the maximum rate of growth a firm can maintain without increasing its financial leverage.

There are various reasons why a firm might wish to avoid equity sales. For example, as we discuss in Chapter 14, new equity sales can be expensive. Alternatively, the current owners may not wish to bring in new owners or contribute additional equity. Why a firm might view a particular debt–equity ratio as optimal is discussed in Chapters 13 and 15; for now, we shall take it as given.

> **sustainable growth rate** The maximum growth rate a firm can achieve without external equity financing while maintaining a constant debt–equity ratio.

Based on Table 3.17, the sustainable growth rate for Hoffman is approximately 20 per cent, because the debt–equity ratio is near 1.0 at that growth rate. The precise value can be calculated:

$$\text{Sustainable growth rate} = \frac{\text{ROE} \times b}{1 - \text{ROE} \times b} \qquad (3.29)$$

This is identical to the internal growth rate except that ROE, return on equity, is used instead of ROA.

For Hoffman AG, net income was €66 and total equity was €250; ROE is thus €66/250 = 26.4 per cent. The ploughback ratio, b, is still 2/3, so we can calculate the sustainable growth rate as follows:

$$\text{Sustainable growth rate} = \frac{\text{ROE} \times b}{1 - \text{ROE} \times b}$$

$$= \frac{0.264 \times (2/3)}{1 - 0.264 \times (2/3)}$$

$$= 21.36\%$$

Thus Hoffman AG can expand at a maximum rate of 21.36 per cent per year without external equity financing.

Determinants of Growth We have seen that the return on equity, ROE, could be decomposed into its various components using the Du Pont identity. Because ROE appears so prominently in the determination of the sustainable growth rate, it is obvious that the factors important in determining ROE are also important determinants of growth. We know that ROE can be written as the product of three factors:

$$\text{ROE} = \text{Profit margin} \times \text{Total asset turnover} \times \text{Equity multiplier}$$

If we examine our expression for the sustainable growth rate, we see that anything that increases ROE will increase the sustainable growth rate by making the top bigger and the bottom smaller. Increasing the ploughback ratio will have the same effect.

Putting it all together, what we have is that a firm's ability to sustain growth depends explicitly on the following four factors:

1 *Profit margin*: An increase in profit margin will increase the firm's ability to generate funds internally and thereby increase its sustainable growth.

2 *Dividend policy*: A decrease in the percentage of profit attributable to shareholders (net income) paid out as dividends will increase the retention ratio. This increases internally generated equity and thus increases sustainable growth.

3 *Financial policy*: An increase in the debt–equity ratio increases the firm's financial leverage. Because this makes additional debt financing available, it increases the sustainable growth rate.

4 *Total asset turnover*: An increase in the firm's total asset turnover increases the sales generated for each pound or euro in assets. This decreases the firm's need for new assets as sales grow and thereby increases the sustainable growth rate. Notice that increasing total asset turnover is the same thing as decreasing capital intensity.

The sustainable growth rate is a very useful planning number. What it illustrates is the explicit relationship between the firm's four major areas of concern: its operating efficiency as measured by profit margin, its asset use efficiency as measured by total asset turnover, its dividend policy as measured by the retention ratio, and its financial policy as measured by the debt–equity ratio.

Given values for all four of these, there is only one growth rate that can be achieved. This is an important point, so it bears restating:

If a firm does not wish to sell new equity and its profit margin, dividend policy, financial policy and total asset turnover (or capital intensity) are all fixed, then there is only one possible growth rate.

As we described early in this chapter, one of the primary benefits of financial planning is that it ensures internal consistency among the firm's various goals. The concept of the sustainable growth rate captures this element nicely. Also, we now see how a financial planning model can be used to test the feasibility of a planned growth rate. If sales are to grow at a rate higher than the sustainable growth rate, the firm must increase profit margins, increase total asset turnover, increase financial leverage, increase earnings retention, or sell new shares.

CONCEPT QUESTIONS	3.7a	How is a firm's sustainable growth related to its accounting return on equity (ROE)?
	3.7b	What are the determinants of growth?

3.8 Some Caveats Regarding Financial Planning Models

Financial planning models do not always ask the right questions. A primary reason is that they tend to rely on accounting relationships and not financial relationships. In particular, the three basic elements of firm value tend to get left out – namely cash flow size, risk, and timing.

Because of this, financial planning models sometimes do not produce meaningful clues about what strategies will lead to increases in value. Instead, they divert the user's attention to questions concerning the association of, say, the debt–equity ratio and firm growth.

3.2 **ROE and the Du Pont Identity** Calculate the 2008 ROE for Thomas Cook Group, and then break down your answer into its component parts using the Du Pont identity.

3.3 **Calculating EFN** Based on the following information for the pharmaceutical firm AstraZeneca plc, what is EFN if sales are predicted to grow by 15 per cent? Use the percentage of sales approach, and assume the company is operating at full capacity. The payout ratio is constant.

AstraZeneca plc					
Financial statements for Y/E 2008					
Income statement		**Statement of financial position**			
	$m	**Assets**	**$m**	**Liabilities and owners' equity**	**$m**
Sales	31,601	Current assets	16,152	Current liabilities	13,320
Costs	22,920	Non-current assets	30,632	Non-current liabilities	17,552
Profit before taxes	8,861			Owners' equity	15,912
Taxes (29.39%)	2,551				
				Total liabilities and owners'	
Net income	6,130	Total assets	46,784	equity	46,784
Dividends	2,971				
Addition to retained earnings	3,159				

3.4 **EFN and Capacity Use** Based on the information in Problem 3.3, what is EFN, assuming 60 per cent capacity usage for non-current assets? What is it, assuming 95 per cent capacity?

3.5 **Sustainable Growth** Based on the information in Problem 3.3, what growth rate can AstraZeneca maintain if no external financing is used? What is the sustainable growth rate?

Answers to Chapter Review and Self-Test Problems

3.1 We've calculated the following ratios based on the ending figures.

Current ratio	£2,079.70/£3,748.40	= 0.55 times
Quick ratio	£2,055.50/£3,748.40	= 0.55 times
Cash ratio	£761.30/£3,748.40	= 0.20 times
Inventory turnover	£6,282.50/£24.2	= 259.61 times
Receivables turnover	£8,167.10/£347.1	= 23.52 times
Days' sales in inventory	365/259.61	= 1.41 days
Days' sales in receivables	365/23.52	= 15.51 days
Total debt ratio	£5,021.90/£7,018.40	= 71.55%
Long-term debt ratio	£711.30/£2,707.80	= 26.27%
Times interest earned ratio	£109/£114	= 0.96 times
Cash coverage ratio	£236.60/£114	= 2.08 times

Chapter 3 Financial Analysis and Planning

3.2 The return on equity is the ratio of net income to total equity. For Thomas Cook Group, this is £44.7/£1,996.6 = 2.2 per cent, which is not outstanding.

Given the Du Pont identity, ROE can be written as follows:

$$\text{ROE} = \text{Profit margin} \times \text{Total asset turnover} \times \text{Equity multiplier}$$
$$= £44.7/£8,167.1 \times £8,167.1/£7,018.4 \times £7,018.4/£1,996.5$$
$$= 0.55\% \times 1.16 \times 3.52$$
$$= 2.2\%$$

Notice that return on assets, ROA, is £44.7/£7,018.4 = 0.64 per cent.

3.3 We can calculate EFN by preparing the pro forma statements using the percentage of sales approach. Note that sales are forecast to be $31,601 × 1.10 = $34,761.

AstraZeneca plc Pro forma financial statements			
Income statement ($m)			
Sales	36,341	Forecast	
Costs	26,358	72.53% of sales	
Profit before taxes	9,983		
Taxes (29.39%)	2,934		
Net income	7,050		
Dividends	3,417	48.47% of net income	
Addition to retained earnings	3,633		

Statement of financial position					
Assets			**Liabilities and owners' equity**		
	$m	**%**		**$m**	**%**
Current assets	18,575	51.11	Current liabilities	15,318	42.15
Non-current assets	35,227	96.93	Non-current liabilities	17,552	n/a
			Owners' equity	19,545	n/a
Total assets	53,802	148.05	Total liabilities and owners' equity	52,415	n/a
			EFN	1,387	n/a

3.4 Full-capacity sales are equal to current sales divided by the capacity utilization. At 60 per cent of capacity:

$$\$31,601 = 0.60 \times \text{Full-capacity sales}$$
$$\$52,668 = \text{Full-capacity sales}$$

With a sales level of $36,341, no new non-current assets will be needed, so our earlier estimate is too high. We estimated an increase in non-current assets of $35,227 − 30,632 = $4,595. The new EFN will thus be $1,387 − 4,595 = −$3,208, a surplus. No external financing is needed in this case.

At 95 per cent capacity, full-capacity sales are $33,264. The ratio of non-current assets to full-capacity sales is thus $30,632/33,264 = 92.08 per cent. At a sales level of $36,341, we shall thus need $36,341 × 0.9208 = $33,465 in non-current assets, an increase of $2,833. This is $4,595 − 2,833 = $1,762 less than we originally predicted, so the EFN is now $1,387 − 1,762 = −$375, a surplus. No additional financing is needed.

3.5 AstraZeneca retains $b = 1 − 0.4847 = 51.53$ per cent of net income. Return on assets is $6,130/46,784 = 13.10 per cent. The internal growth rate is thus

$$\frac{\text{ROA} \times b}{1 - (\text{ROA} \times b)} = \frac{0.1310 \times 0.5153}{1 - (0.1310 \times 0.5153)}$$
$$= 7.24\%$$

Return on equity for AstraZeneca is $6,130/15,912 = 38.52\%$, so we can calculate the sustainable growth rate as follows:

$$\frac{\text{ROE} \times b}{1 - (\text{ROE} \times b)} = \frac{0.3852 \times 0.5153}{1 - (0.3852 \times 0.5153)}$$
$$= 24.77\%$$

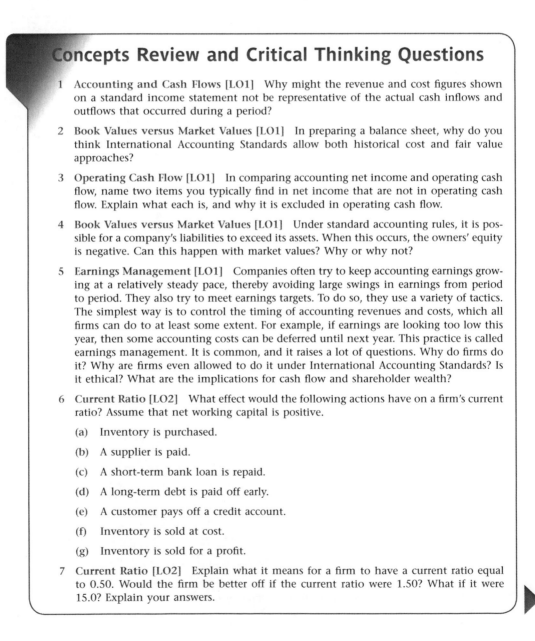

Concepts Review and Critical Thinking Questions

1 **Accounting and Cash Flows [LO1]** Why might the revenue and cost figures shown on a standard income statement not be representative of the actual cash inflows and outflows that occurred during a period?

2 **Book Values versus Market Values [LO1]** In preparing a balance sheet, why do you think International Accounting Standards allow both historical cost and fair value approaches?

3 **Operating Cash Flow [LO1]** In comparing accounting net income and operating cash flow, name two items you typically find in net income that are not in operating cash flow. Explain what each is, and why it is excluded in operating cash flow.

4 **Book Values versus Market Values [LO1]** Under standard accounting rules, it is possible for a company's liabilities to exceed its assets. When this occurs, the owners' equity is negative. Can this happen with market values? Why or why not?

5 **Earnings Management [LO1]** Companies often try to keep accounting earnings growing at a relatively steady pace, thereby avoiding large swings in earnings from period to period. They also try to meet earnings targets. To do so, they use a variety of tactics. The simplest way is to control the timing of accounting revenues and costs, which all firms can do to at least some extent. For example, if earnings are looking too low this year, then some accounting costs can be deferred until next year. This practice is called earnings management. It is common, and it raises a lot of questions. Why do firms do it? Why are firms even allowed to do it under International Accounting Standards? Is it ethical? What are the implications for cash flow and shareholder wealth?

6 **Current Ratio [LO2]** What effect would the following actions have on a firm's current ratio? Assume that net working capital is positive.

   (a) Inventory is purchased.

   (b) A supplier is paid.

   (c) A short-term bank loan is repaid.

   (d) A long-term debt is paid off early.

   (e) A customer pays off a credit account.

   (f) Inventory is sold at cost.

   (g) Inventory is sold for a profit.

7 **Current Ratio [LO2]** Explain what it means for a firm to have a current ratio equal to 0.50. Would the firm be better off if the current ratio were 1.50? What if it were 15.0? Explain your answers.

8 **Financial Ratios [LO2]** Fully explain the kind of information the following financial ratios provide about a firm:

(a) Quick ratio.

(b) Cash ratio.

(c) Total asset turnover.

(d) Equity multiplier.

(e) Long-term debt ratio.

(f) Times interest earned ratio.

(g) Profit margin.

(h) Return on assets.

(i) Return on equity.

(j) Price–earnings ratio.

9 **Du Pont Identity [LO2]** Why is the Du Pont identity a valuable tool for analysing the performance of a firm? Discuss the types of information it reveals, compared with ROE considered by itself.

10 **Industry-Specific Ratios [LO2]** Specialized ratios are sometimes used in specific industries. For example, the so-called book-to-bill ratio is closely watched for semiconductor manufacturers. A ratio of 0.93 indicates that for every €100 worth of chips shipped over some period, only €93 worth of new orders were received. In October 2009 the semiconductor equipment industry's book-to-bill ratio was 1.10, compared with 1.17 during the month of September 2009. The book-to-bill ratio reached a recent low of 0.47 during January 2009. The three-month average of worldwide bookings in October 2009 was $756.2 million, a decrease of $2.7 million from September 2009, while the three-month average of billings was $689.8 million, an increase of $41.1 million from September 2009. What is this ratio intended to measure? Why do you think it is so closely followed?

11 **Sustainable Growth [LO3]** In the chapter we used Bogle plc to demonstrate how to calculate EFN. The ROE for Bogle is about 8 per cent, and the ploughback ratio is about 67 per cent. If you calculate the sustainable growth rate for Bogle, you will find it is only 5.63 per cent. In our calculation for EFN we used a growth rate of 25 per cent. Is this possible? (*Hint*: Yes. How?)

12 **External Financing Needed [LO3]** GNR NV uses no external financing and maintains a positive retention ratio. When sales grow by 15 per cent, the firm has a negative projected EFN. What does this tell you about the firm's internal growth rate? How about the sustainable growth rate? At this same level of sales growth, what will happen to the projected EFN if the retention ratio is increased? What if the retention ratio is decreased? What happens to the projected EFN if the firm pays out all of its earnings in the form of dividends?

Use the following information to answer the next six questions. A small business called The Grandmother Calendar Company began selling personalized photo calendar kits. The kits were a hit, and sales soon sharply exceeded forecasts. The rush of orders created a huge backlog, so the company leased more space and expanded capacity, but it still could not keep up with demand. Equipment failed from overuse, and quality suffered. Working capital was drained to expand production, and at the same time payments from customers were often delayed until the product was shipped. Unable to deliver on orders, the company became so strapped for cash that employee pay cheques began to bounce. Finally, out of cash, the company ceased operations entirely, three years later.

13 **Product Sales [LO3]** Do you think the company would have suffered the same fate if its product had been less popular? Why or why not?

14   **Cash Flow [LO3]**   The Grandmother Calendar Company clearly had a cash flow problem. What was the impact of customers not paying until orders were shipped?

15   **Product Pricing [LO3]**   The firm actually priced its product to be about 20 per cent less than that of competitors, even though the Grandmother calendar was more detailed. In retrospect, was this a wise choice?

16   **Corporate Borrowing [LO3]**   If the firm was so successful at selling, why wouldn't a bank or some other lender step in and provide it with the cash it needed to continue?

17   **Cash Flow [LO3]**   Which was the biggest culprit here: too many orders, too little cash, or too little production capacity?

18   **Cash Flow [LO3]**   What are some of the actions that a small company like The Grandmother Calendar Company can take if it finds itself in a situation in which growth in sales outstrips production capacity and available financial resources? What other options (besides expansion of capacity) are available to a company when orders exceed capacity?

connect Questions and Problems

BASIC
1–15

1   **Building a Statement of Financial Position [LO1]**   On 31 March 2009 Cable & Wireless plc had current assets of £1.541 billion, non-current assets of £3.650 billion, current liabilities of £1.856 billion, and non-current liabilities of £1.291 billion. What is the value of the shareholders' equity account for this firm? How much is net working capital?

2   **Building an Income Statement [LO1]**   For the year ending 31 March 2009, Johnson Matthey plc had revenues of £7.848 billion, costs of £7.324 billion, depreciation expense of £108.9 million, interest expense of £42.7 million, and a tax rate of 28 per cent. What is the net income for this firm?

3   **Cost and Revaluation Methods of Accounting [LO1]**   Klingon Widgets plc purchased new cloaking machinery three years ago for £7 million. The machinery can be sold to the Romulans today for £4.9 million. Klingon's current statement of financial position shows non-current assets of £3.7 million, current liabilities of £1.1 million, and net working capital of £380,000. If all the current assets were liquidated today, the company would receive £1.6 million cash. What is the book value of Klingon's assets today if the historical cost method of accounting is used? What is the value of its assets if the revaluation method is used?

4   **Calculating Liquidity Ratios [LO2]**   For the year ending December 2008, Xstrata plc had current assets of $6,987, current liabilities of $5,060, and inventory of $3,573. What is the current ratio? What is the quick ratio?

5   **Calculating Profitability Ratios [LO2]**   For the year ending December 2008, Volkswagen AG had sales of €113,808 million, total assets of €167,919 million, and total debt of €69,380 million. If the profit margin is 4.173 per cent, what was net income? What was ROA? What was ROE?

6   **Calculating Leverage Ratios [LO2]**   GNR plc has a total debt ratio of 0.63. What is its debt–equity ratio? What is its equity multiplier?

7   **Calculating Market Value Ratios [LO2]**   Axel plc had additions to retained earnings for the year just ended of £430,000. The firm paid out £175,000 in cash dividends, and it has ending total equity of £5.3 million. If the company currently has 210,000 shares of equity outstanding, what are earnings per share? Dividends per share? Book value per share? If the equity currently sells for £63 per share, what is the market-to-book ratio? The price–earnings ratio? If the company had sales of £4.5 million, what is the price–sales ratio?

Chapter 3 Financial Analysis and Planning

8 **Du Pont Identity [LO2]**   If Roten Rooters NV has an equity multiplier of 2.80, total asset turnover of 1.15, and a profit margin of 5.5 per cent, what is its ROE?

9 **Pro Forma Statements [LO3]**   Consider the following simplified 2008 financial statements for Nokia Oyj (ignoring taxes):

Income statement		Statement of financial position			
	€m		**€m**		**€m**
Sales	50,710	Assets	39,582	Debt	23,072
Costs	45,740			Equity	16,510
Net profit	4,970	Total	39,582	Total	39,582

Nokia has predicted a sales increase of 15 per cent. It has predicted that every item on the statement of financial position will increase by 15 per cent as well. Create the pro forma statements, and reconcile them. What is the plug variable here?

10 **Pro Forma Statements and EFN [LO3]**   In the previous question, assume Nokia pays out half of net profit in the form of a cash dividend. Costs and assets vary with sales, but debt and equity do not. Prepare the pro forma statements and determine the external financing needed.

11 **EFN [LO3]**   The 2008 financial statements for WPP plc are shown here:

Income statement		Statement of financial position			
	£m		**£m**		**£m**
Sales	7,477	Current assets	11,108	Current liabilities	12,136
Costs	6,730	Non-current assets	13,355	Non-current liabilities	6,565
Profit before taxes	747			Total liabilities	18,701
Tax	233 31.19%			Equity	5,762
Net profit	514	Total assets	24,463	Total	24,463

Assets, costs, and current liabilities are proportional to sales. Non-current liabilities and equity are not. The company maintains a constant 40 per cent dividend payout ratio. As with every other firm in its industry, next year's sales are projected to increase by exactly 15 per cent. What is the external financing needed?

12 **Calculating Internal Growth [LO3]**   The 2009 financial statements for Siemens AG are shown here:

Income statement		Statement of financial position			
	€m		**€m**		**€m**
Sales	76,651	Current assets	44,129	Current liabilities	37,005
Costs	72,760	Non-current assets	50,797	Non-current liabilities	31,275
Profit before taxes	3,891			Total liabilities	68,280
Tax	1,434 36.85%			Equity	26,646
Net profit	2,457	Total assets	94,926	Total	94,926

Assets and costs are proportional to sales. Debt and equity are not. The company maintains a constant 30 per cent dividend payout ratio. No external equity financing is possible. What is the internal growth rate?

Statements of financial position LVMH Moet Hennessy Louis Vuitton					
	Dec 08	Dec 07		Dec 08	Dec 07
	€m	€m		€m	€m
Current assets			**Current liabilities**		
Cash and short-term investments	1,013	1,559	Trade payables	2,292	2,095
Trade receivables	1,650	1,595	Accrued expenses	1,866	1,552
Receivables – other	229	151	Notes payable/ short-term debt	1,571	2,212
Total inventory	5,767	4,812	Current port. of LT debt/capital leases	276	926
Other current assets	1,695	2,001	Other current liabilities	610	628
Total current assets	**10,354**	**10,118**	**Total current liabilities**	**6,615**	**7,413**
Non-current assets			**Non-current liabilities**		
Property/plant/ equipment	6,081	5,419	Total long-term debt	3,738	2,477
Goodwill, net	4,423	4,818	Deferred income tax	3,113	2,843
Intangibles, net	8,523	7,999	Minority interest	989	938
Long-term investments	591	952	Other liabilities	4,224	5,123
Other long-term assets	1,511	1,078	**Total non-current liabilities**	**12,064**	**11,381**
Total non-current assets	**21,129**	**20,266**	**Total liabilities**	**18,679**	**18,794**
			Shareholders' equity		
			Ordinary shares	147	147
			Additional paid-in capital	1,737	1,736
			Retained earnings (accumulated deficit)	12,274	11,192
			Treasury stock – common	–983	–877
			Other equity, total	–371	–608
			Total equity	**12,804**	**11,590**
Total assets	**31,483**	**30,384**	**Total liabilities and shareholders' equity**	**31,483**	**30,384**

23 Calculating Financial Ratios [LO2]   Find the following financial ratios for LVMH Moet Hennessy Louis Vuitton SA (use year-end figures rather than average values where appropriate):

Short-term solvency ratios:

(a)   Current ratio   _____

(b)   Quick ratio   _____

(c)   Cash ratio   _____

Asset utilization ratios:

(d)   Total asset turnover   _____

(e)   Inventory turnover   _____

(f)   Receivables turnover   _____

Chapter 3 Financial Analysis and Planning

Long-term solvency ratios:

(g)   Total debt ratio   _____

(h)   Debt–equity ratio   _____

(i)   Equity multiplier   _____

(j)   Times interest earned ratio   _____

Profitability ratios:

(k)   Profit margin   _____

(l)   Return on assets   _____

(m) Return on equity   _____

24   **Du Pont Identity [LO2]**   Construct the Du Pont identity for LVMH Moet Hennessy Louis Vuitton SA.

25   **Market Value Ratios [LO2]**   LVMH Moet Hennessy Louis Vuitton SA has 473.06 million ordinary shares outstanding, and the market price for a share of equity at the end of 2008 was €46.79. What is the price–earnings ratio? What is the market-to-book ratio at the end of 2008? If the company's growth rate is 9 per cent, what is the PEG ratio?

26   **Tobin's Q [LO2]**   What is Tobin's Q for LVMH Moet Hennessy Louis Vuitton SA? What assumptions are you making about the book value of debt and the market value of debt? What about the book value of assets and the market value of assets? Are these assumptions realistic? Why or why not?

27   **Full-Capacity Sales [LO3]**   Seaweed Manufacturing is currently operating at only 95 per cent of non-current asset capacity. Current sales are £600,000. How fast can sales grow before any new non-current assets are needed?

28   **Non-Current Assets and Capacity Usage [LO3]**   For the company in the previous problem, suppose non-current assets are £440,000 and sales are projected to grow to £830,000. How much in new non-current assets is required to support this growth in sales? Assume the company maintains its current operating capacity.

29   **Growth and Assets [LO3]**   A firm wishes to maintain an internal growth rate of 8 per cent and a dividend payout ratio of 25 per cent. The current profit margin is 5 per cent, and the firm uses no external financing sources. What must total asset turnover be?

30   **Sustainable Growth Rate [LO3]**   Coheed plc had equity of £135,000 at the beginning of the year. At the end of the year the company had total assets of £250,000. During the year the company sold no new equity. Net income for the year was £19,000, and dividends were £3,500. What is the sustainable growth rate for the company? What is the sustainable growth rate if you use the formula ROE $\times b$ and beginning of period equity? What is the sustainable growth rate if you use end of period equity in this formula? Is this number too high or too low? Why?

31   **Internal Growth Rates [LO3]**   Calculate the internal growth rate for the company in the previous problem. Now calculate the internal growth rate using ROA $\times b$ for both beginning of period and end of period total assets. What do you observe?

CHALLENGE

32 – 36

32   **Non-Current Assets and Depreciation [LO1]**   On the simplified statement of financial position, the non-current assets (NCA) account is equal to the gross property, plant and equipment (PPE) account (which records the acquisition cost of property, plant and equipment) minus the accumulated depreciation (AD) account (which records the total depreciation taken by the firm against its property, plant and equipment). Using the fact that NCA = PPE − AD, show that the expression for net capital spending, $NCA_{end} - NCA_{beg} + D$ (where D is the depreciation expense during the year), is equivalent to $PPE_{end} - PPE_{beg}$.

1   Calculate all the ratios listed in the industry table for West Coast Yachts.

2   Compare the performance of West Coast Yachts with that of the industry as a whole. For each ratio, comment on why it might be viewed as positive or negative relative to the industry. Suppose you create an inventory ratio calculated as inventory divided by current liabilities. How do you interpret this ratio? How does West Coast Yachts compare with the industry average?

3   Calculate the sustainable growth rate of West Coast Yachts. Calculate external funds needed (EFN), and prepare a pro forma income statement and statement of financial position, assuming growth at precisely this rate. Recalculate the ratios in the previous question. What do you observe?

4   As a practical matter, West Coast Yachts is unlikely to be willing to raise external equity capital, in part because the owners don't want to dilute their existing owner-ship and control positions. However, West Coast Yachts is planning for a growth rate of 20 per cent next year. What are your conclusions and recommendations about the feasibility of West Coast's expansion plans?

5   Most assets can be increased as a percentage of sales. For instance, cash can be increased by any amount. However, non-current assets often must be increased in specific amounts, because it is impossible, as a practical matter, to buy part of a new plant or machine. In this case a company has a 'staircase' or 'lumpy' fixed cost structure. Assume that West Coast Yachts is currently producing at 100 per cent of capacity. As a result, to expand production, the company must set up an entirely new line at a cost of £25,000,000. Calculate the new EFN with this assumption. What does this imply about capacity utilization for West Coast Yachts next year?

Online
LearningCentre

To help you grasp the key concepts of this chapter check out the extra resources posted on the Online Learning Centre at **www.mcgraw-hill.co.uk/textbooks/hillier**

Among other helpful resources there are mini-cases tailored to individual chapters.

CHAPTER 4

Introduction to Valuation: The Time Value of Money

LEARNING OBJECTIVES

After studying this chapter, you should understand:

LO1 How to determine the future value of an investment made today.

LO2 How to determine the present value of cash to be received at a future date.

LO3 How to find the return on an investment.

LO4 How long it takes for an investment to reach a desired value.

INTERCONTINENTAL HOTELS offered some securities for sale to the public on 9 December 2009. Under the terms of the deal InterContinental promised to repay the owner of one of these securities £50,000 on 9 December 2016, and £3,000 every year in between. Investors paid InterContinental £49,732.50 for each of these securities; so they gave up £49,732.50 on 9 December 2009 for the promise of £71,000 (£21,000 in interest and £50,000 original amount) over the subsequent seven years. Is giving up £49,732.50 in exchange for £71,000 over seven years a good deal? On the plus side, you get back about £1.42 for every £1 you put up. That probably sounds good; but on the down side, you have to wait seven years to get it. What you need to know is how to analyse this trade-off; this chapter gives you the tools you need.

One of the basic problems faced by the financial manager is how to determine the value today of cash flows expected in the future. For example, the InterContinental security paid £71,000 in total. Does this mean that time security was worth £71,000? The answer is no, because the security was actually going to pay out over a seven-year period at a rate of £3,000 per year, with a final payment of £50,000 after seven years. How much was the security worth then? The answer depends on the time value of money, the subject of this chapter.

In the most general sense, the phrase *time value of money* refers to the fact that a euro (or pound) in the hand today is worth more than a euro promised at some time in the future. On a practical level, one reason for this is that you could earn interest while you waited; so a euro today would grow to more than a euro later. The trade-off between money now and money later thus depends on, among other things, the rate you can earn by investing. Our goal in this chapter is to evaluate explicitly this trade-off between euros (or any other currency) today and at some future time.

A thorough understanding of the material in this chapter is critical to understanding material in subsequent chapters, so you should study it with particular care. We shall present a number of examples in this chapter. In many problems your answer may differ from ours slightly. This can happen because of rounding, and is not a cause for concern.

4.1 Future Value and Compounding

The first thing we shall study is future value. **Future value (FV)** refers to the amount of money an investment will grow to over some period of time at some given interest rate. Put another way, future value is the cash value of an investment at some time in the future. We start out by considering the simplest case: a single-period investment.

> **future value (FV)**
> The amount an investment is worth after one or more periods.

Investing for a Single Period

Suppose you invest £100 in a savings account that pays 10 per cent interest per year. How much will you have in one year? You will have £110. This £110 is equal to your original *principal* of £100 plus £10 in interest that you earn. We say that £110 is the future value of £100 invested for one year at 10 per cent, and we simply mean that £100 today is worth £110 in one year, given that 10 per cent is the interest rate.

In general, if you invest for one period at an interest rate of r, your investment will grow to $(1 + r)$ per pound invested. In our example, r is 10 per cent, so your investment grows to $1 + 0.10 = 1.1$ pounds per pound invested. You invested £100 in this case, so you ended up with $£100 \times 1.10 = £110$.

> **compounding**
> The process of accumulating interest on an investment over time to earn more interest.
>
> **interest on interest**
> Interest earned on the reinvestment of previous interest payments.

Investing for More than One Period

Going back to our £100 investment, what will you have after two years, assuming the interest rate doesn't change? If you leave the entire £110 in the bank, you will earn $£110 \times 0.10 = £11$ in interest during the second year, so you will have a total of $£110 + 11 = £121$. This £121 is the future value of £100 in two years at 10 per cent. Another way of looking at it is that one year from now you are effectively investing £110 at 10 per cent for a year. This is a single-period problem, so you'll end up with £1.10 for every pound invested, or $£110 \times 1.1 = £121$ total.

This £121 has four parts. The first part is the £100 original principal. The second part is the £10 in interest you earned in the first year, and the third part is another £10 you earn in the second year, for a total of £120. The last £1 you end up with (the fourth part) is interest you earn in the second year on the interest paid in the first year: $£10 \times 0.10 = £1$.

This process of leaving your money and any accumulated interest in an investment for more than one period, and thereby *reinvesting* the interest, is called **compounding**. Compounding the interest means earning **interest on interest**, so we call the result **compound interest**. With **simple interest** the interest is not reinvested, so interest is earned each period only on the original principal.

> **compound interest**
> Interest earned on both the initial principal and the interest reinvested from prior periods.
>
> **simple interest**
> Interest earned only on the original principal amount invested.

Chapter 4 Introduction to Valuation: The Time Value of Money

EXAMPLE
4.1
Interest on Interest

Suppose you locate a two-year investment that pays 14 per cent per year. If you invest €325, how much will you have at the end of the two years? How much of this is simple interest? How much is compound interest?

At the end of the first year you will have €325 × (1 + 0.14) = €370.50. If you reinvest this entire amount and thereby compound the interest, you will have €370.50 × 1.14 = €422.37 at the end of the second year. The total interest you earn is thus €422.37 − 325 = €97.37. Your €325 original principal earns €325 × 0.14 = €45.50 in interest each year, for a two-year total of €91 in simple interest. The remaining €97.37 − 91 = €6.37 results from compounding. You can check this by noting that the interest earned in the first year is €45.50. The interest on interest earned in the second year thus amounts to €45.50 × 0.14 = €6.37, as we calculated.

We now take a closer look at how we calculated the £121 future value. We multiplied £110 by 1.1 to get £121. The £110, however, was £100 also multiplied by 1.1. In other words:

$$
\begin{aligned}
£121 &= £110 \times 1.1 \\
&= (£100 \times 1.1) \times 1.1 \\
&= £100 \times (1.1 \times 1.1) \\
&= £100 \times 1.1^2 \\
&= £100 \times 1.21
\end{aligned}
$$

At the risk of belabouring the obvious, let's ask: how much would our £100 grow to after three years? Once again, in two years we'll be investing £121 for one period at 10 per cent. We'll end up with £1.10 for every pound we invest, or £121 × 1.1 = £133.10 total. This £133.10 is thus

$$
\begin{aligned}
£133.10 &= £121 \times 1.1 \\
&= (£110 \times 1.1) \times 1.1 \\
&= (£100 \times 1.1) \times 1.1 \times 1.1 \\
&= £100 \times (1.1 \times 1.1 \times 1.1) \\
&= £100 \times 1.1^3 \\
&= £100 \times 1.331
\end{aligned}
$$

You're probably noticing a pattern to these calculations, so we can now go ahead and state the general result. As our examples suggest, the future value of £1 invested for t periods at a rate of r per period is this:

$$\text{Future value} = £1 \times (1 + r)^t \tag{4.1}$$

The expression $(1 + r)^t$ is sometimes called the *future value interest factor* (or just *future value factor*) for £1 invested at r per cent for t periods, and can be abbreviated as FVIF(r, t).

In our example, what would your £100 be worth after five years? We can first compute the relevant future value factor as follows:

$$(1 + r)^t = (1 + 0.10)^5 = 1.1^5 = 1.6105$$

Your £100 will thus grow to

$$£100 \times 1.6105 = £161.05$$

The growth of your £100 each year is illustrated in Table 4.1. As shown, the interest earned in each year is equal to the beginning amount multiplied by the interest rate of 10 per cent.

In Table 4.1, notice that the total interest you earn is £61.05. Over the five-year span of this investment the simple interest is £100 × 0.10 = £10 per year, so you accumulate £50 this way. The other £11.05 is from compounding.

TABLE 4.1	Year	Beginning amount (£)	Simple interest (£)	Compound interest (£)	Total interest earned (£)	Ending amount (£)
	1	100.00	10	0.00	10.00	110.00
	2	110.00	10	1.00	11.00	121.00
	3	121.00	10	2.10	12.10	133.10
	4	133.10	10	3.31	13.31	146.41
	5	146.41	10	4.64	14.64	161.05
			Total £50 simple interest	Total £11.05 compound interest	Total £61.05 interest	

Table 4.1 Future value of £100 at 10 per cent

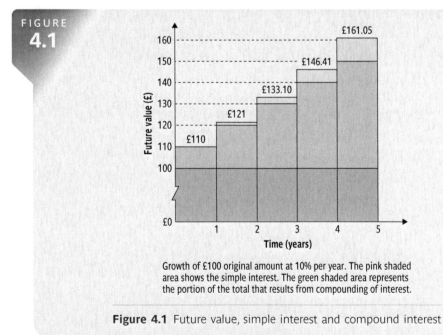

Growth of £100 original amount at 10% per year. The pink shaded area shows the simple interest. The green shaded area represents the portion of the total that results from compounding of interest.

Figure 4.1 Future value, simple interest and compound interest

Figure 4.1 illustrates the growth of the compound interest in Table 4.1. Notice how the simple interest is constant each year, but the amount of compound interest you earn gets bigger every year. The amount of the compound interest keeps increasing because more and more interest builds up and there is thus more to compound.

Future values depend critically on the assumed interest rate, particularly for long-lived investments. Figure 4.2 illustrates this relationship by plotting the growth of £1 for different rates and lengths of time. Notice that the future value of £1 after 10 years is about £6.20 at a 20 per cent rate, but it is only about £2.60 at 10 per cent. In this case, doubling the interest rate more than doubles the future value.

To solve future value problems, we need to come up with the relevant future value factors. There are several different ways of doing this. In our example, we could have multiplied 1.1 by itself five times. This would work just fine, but it would get to be very tedious for, say, a 30-year investment.

FIGURE
4.2

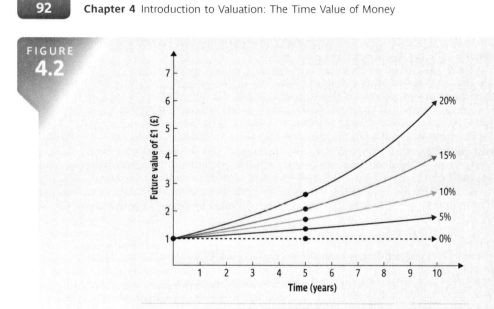

Figure 4.2 Future value of £1 for different periods and rates

TABLE
4.2

Number of periods	Interest rate (%)			
	5	10	15	20
1	1.0500	1.1000	1.1500	1.2000
2	1.1025	1.2100	1.3225	1.4400
3	1.1576	1.3310	1.5209	1.7280
4	1.2155	1.4641	1.7490	2.0736
5	1.2763	1.6105	2.0114	2.4883

Table 4.2 Future value interest factors

Fortunately, there are several easier ways to get future value factors. Most calculators have a key labelled 'y^x.' You can usually just enter 1.1, press this key, enter 5, and press the '=' key to get the answer. This is an easy way to calculate future value factors, because it's quick and accurate.

Alternatively, you can use a table that contains future value factors for some common interest rates and time periods. Table 4.2 contains some of these factors. Table A.1 in the appendix at the end of the book contains a much larger set. To use the table, find the column that corresponds to 10 per cent. Then look down the rows until you come to five periods. You should find the factor that we calculated, 1.6105.

Tables such these are not as common as they once were, because they pre-date inexpensive calculators or spreadsheets, and are available only for a relatively small number of rates. Interest rates are often quoted to three or four decimal places, so the tables needed to deal with these accurately would be quite large. As a result, the real world has moved away from using them. We shall emphasize the use of a calculator or spreadsheet in this chapter.

These tables still serve a useful purpose, though. To make sure you are doing the calculations correctly, pick a factor from the table and then calculate it yourself to see that you get the same answer. There are plenty of numbers to choose from.

The Single-Period Case

We've seen that the future value of £1 invested for one year at 10 per cent is £1.10. We now ask a slightly different question: how much do we have to invest today at 10 per cent to get £1 in one year? In other words, we know the future value here is £1, but what is the **present value (PV)**? The answer isn't too hard to figure out. Whatever we invest today will be 1.1 times bigger at the end of the year. Because we need £1 at the end of the year:

> **present value (PV)**
> The current value of future cash flows discounted at the appropriate discount rate.

Present value × 1.1 = £1

Or solving for the present value:

Present value = £1/1.1 = £0.909

In this case the present value is the answer to the following question: what amount, invested today, will grow to £1 in one year if the interest rate is 10 per cent? Present value is thus just the reverse of future value. Instead of compounding the money forward into the future, we **discount** it back to the present.

> **discount**
> Calculate the present value of some future amount.

EXAMPLE 4.5   Single-Period PV

Suppose you need €400 to buy textbooks next year. You can earn 7 per cent on your money. How much do you have to put up today?

We need to know the PV of €400 in one year at 7 per cent. Proceeding as in the previous example:

Present value × 1.07 = €400

We can now solve for the present value:

Present value = €400 × (1/1.07) = €373.83

Thus €373.83 is the present value. Again, this just means that investing this amount for one year at 7 per cent will give you a future value of €400.

From our examples, the present value of £1 to be received in one period is generally given as follows:

$$PV = £1 \times \left(\frac{1}{1+r} \right)$$
$$= \frac{£1}{1+r}$$

We next examine how to get the present value of an amount to be paid in two or more periods into the future.

Present Values for Multiple Periods

Suppose you need to have €1,000 in two years. If you can earn 7 per cent, how much do you have to invest to make sure you have the €1,000 when you need it? In other words, what is the present value of €1,000 in two years if the relevant rate is 7 per cent?

Based on your knowledge of future values, you know the amount invested must grow to €1,000 over the two years. In other words, it must be the case that:

$$€1,000 = PV \times 1.07 \times 1.07$$
$$= PV \times 1.07^2$$
$$= PV \times 1.1449$$

Given this, we can solve for the present value:

$$\text{Present value} = €1,000/1.1449 = €873.44$$

Therefore €873.44 is the amount you must invest to achieve your goal.

Saving Up

EXAMPLE 4.6

You would like to buy a new car. You have £50,000 or so, but the car costs £68,500. If you can earn 9 per cent, how much do you have to invest today to buy the car in two years? Do you have enough? Assume the price will stay the same.

What we need to know is the present value of £68,500 to be paid in two years, assuming a 9 per cent rate. Based on our discussion, this is

$$PV = £68,500/1.09^2 = £68,500/1.1881 = £57,655.08$$

You're still about £7,655 short, even if you're willing to wait two years.

As you have probably recognized by now, calculating present values is quite similar to calculating future values, and the general result looks much the same. The present value of £1 to be received t periods into the future at a discount rate of r is

$$PV = £1 \times \left[\frac{1}{(1+r)^t}\right]$$
$$= \frac{£1}{(1+r)^t}$$

(4.2)

discount rate
The rate used to calculate the present value of future cash flows.

discounted cash flow (DCF) valuation
Calculating the present value of a future cash flow to determine its value today.

The quantity in brackets, $1/(1 + r)^t$, goes by several different names. Because it's used to discount a future cash flow, it is often called a *discount factor*. With this name, it is not surprising that the rate used in the calculation is often called the **discount rate**. We shall tend to call it this in talking about present values. The quantity in brackets is also called the *present value interest factor* (or just *present value factor*) for £1 at r per cent for t periods, and is sometimes abbreviated as PVIF(r, t). Finally, calculating the present value of a future cash flow to determine its worth today is commonly called **discounted cash flow (DCF) valuation**.

To illustrate, suppose you need €1,000 in three years. You can earn 15 per cent on your money. How much do you have to invest today? To find out, we have to determine the present value of €1,000 in three years at 15 per cent. We do this by discounting €1,000 back three periods at 15 per cent. With these numbers, the discount factor is

$$1/(1 + 0.15)^3 = 1/1.5209 = 0.6575$$

The amount you must invest is thus

$$€1,000 \times 0.6575 = €657.50$$

EXAMPLE 4.8

Evaluating Investments

To give you an idea of how we shall be using present and future values, consider the following simple investment. Your company proposes to buy an asset for £335. This investment is very safe. You would sell off the asset in three years for £400. You know you could invest the £335 elsewhere at 10 per cent with very little risk. What do you think of the proposed investment?

This is not a good investment. Why not? Because you can invest the £335 elsewhere at 10 per cent. If you do, after three years it will grow to

$$£335 \times (1 + r)^t = £335 \times 1.1^3$$
$$= £335 \times 1.331$$
$$= £445.89$$

Because the proposed investment pays out only £400, it is not as good as other alternatives we have. Another way of seeing the same thing is to notice that the present value of £400 in three years at 10 per cent is

$$£400 \times \left[\frac{1}{(1 + r)^t} \right] = £400/1.1^3$$
$$= £400/1.331$$
$$= £300.53$$

This tells us that we have to invest only about £300 to get £400 in three years, not £335. We shall return to this type of analysis later on.

Determining the Discount Rate

We frequently need to determine what discount rate is implicit in an investment. We can do this by looking at the basic present value equation:

$$PV = \frac{FV_t}{(1 + r)^t}$$

There are only four parts to this equation: the present value (PV), the future value (FV$_t$), the discount rate (r), and the life of the investment (t). Given any three of these, we can always find the fourth.

EXAMPLE 4.9

Finding *r* for a Single-Period Investment

You are considering a one-year investment. If you put up €1,250, you will get back €1,350. What rate is this investment paying?

First, in this single-period case, the answer is fairly obvious. You are getting a total of €100 in addition to your €1,250. The implicit rate on this investment is thus €100/1,250 = 8 per cent.

More formally, from the basic present value equation, the present value (the amount you must put up today) is €1,250. The future value (what the present value grows to) is €1,350. The time involved is one period, so we have

$$€1,250 = €1,350/(1 + r)^1$$
$$1 + r = €1,350/1,250 = 1.08$$
$$r = 8\%$$

In this simple case, of course, there was no need to go through this calculation. But as we describe next, it gets a little harder with more than one period.

Chapter 4 Introduction to Valuation: The Time Value of Money

To illustrate what happens with multiple periods, let's say we are offered an investment that costs us £100 and will double our money in eight years. To compare this with other investments, we should like to know what discount rate is implicit in these numbers. This discount rate is called the *rate of return*, or sometimes just the *return*, on the investment. In this case we have a present value of £100, a future value of £200 (double our money), and an eight-year life. To calculate the return, we can write the basic present value equation as

$$PV = \frac{FV_t}{(1+r)^t}$$

$$£100 = \frac{£200}{(1+r)^8}$$

It could also be written as

$$(1+r)^8 = £200/100 = 2$$

We now need to solve for r. There are three ways we could do it:

1   Use a financial calculator or a spreadsheet.

2   Solve the equation for $1 + r$ by taking the eighth root of both sides. Because this is the same thing as raising both sides to the power of 1/8 or 0.125, this is actually easy to do with the 'y^x' key on a calculator. Just enter 2, then press 'y^x', enter 0.125, and press the '=' key. The eighth root should be about 1.09, which implies that r is 9 per cent.

3   Use a future value table. The future value factor after eight years is equal to 2. If you look across the row corresponding to eight periods in Table A.1, you will see that a future value factor of 2 corresponds to the 9 per cent column, again implying that the return here is 9 per cent.

Actually, in this particular example there is a useful 'back of the envelope' means of solving for r: the Rule of 72. For reasonable rates of return, the time it takes to double your money is given approximately by $72/r\%$. In our example this means that $72/r\% = 8$ years, implying that r is 9 per cent, as we calculated. This rule is fairly accurate for discount rates in the range 5 to 20 per cent.

EXAMPLE
4.10

Comic Collectibles as Investments

In January 2010 *Amazing Fantasy* No. 15, the first Marvel comic in which Spiderman appeared, was valued at $50,000 in mint condition. 'Experts' on such collectibles often argue that a mint condition *Amazing Fantasy* No. 15 would double in value to $100,000 by the end of 2019.

So would the comic have been a good investment? By the Rule of 72, you already know the experts were predicting that the comic would double in value in 10 years; so the return predicted would be about $72/10 = 7.2$ per cent per year, which is only so-so.

At one time at least, a rule of thumb in the rarefied world of fine art collecting was 'Your money back in 5 years, double your money in 10 years.' Given this, let's see how an investment stacked up. In 1998 the Alberto Giacometti bronze statue *Homme Qui Marche III* sold for €2,016,000. Five years later the statue was sold again, walking out of the door at a price of €2,740,000. How did the seller do?

The rule of thumb has us doubling our money in 10 years; so, from the Rule of 72, we have that 7.2 per cent per year was the norm. The statue was resold in almost exactly five years. The present value is €2,016,000, and the future value is €2,740,000. We need to solve for the unknown rate, r, as follows:

$$€2,016,000 = \frac{€2,740,000}{(1+r)^5}$$
$$(1+r)^5 = 1.3591$$

Solving for r, we find that the seller earned about 6.33 per cent per year – less than the 7.2 per cent rule of thumb. At least the seller made his money back.

 EXAMPLE 4.11

Saving for University

You estimate that you will need about £80,000 to send your child to university in eight years. You have about £35,000 now. If you can earn 20 per cent per year, will you make it? At what rate will you just reach your goal?

If you can earn 20 per cent, the future value of your £35,000 in eight years will be

$$FV = £35,000 \times 1.20^8 = £35,000 \times 4.2998 = £150,493.59$$

So you will make it easily. The minimum rate is the unknown r in the following:

$$FV = £35,000 \times (1+r)^8 = £80,000$$
$$(1+r)^8 = £80,000/35,000 = 2.2857$$

Therefore the future value factor is 2.2857. Looking at the row in Table A.1 that corresponds to eight periods, we see that our future value factor is roughly halfway between the ones shown for 10 per cent (2.1436) and 12 per cent (2.4760), so you will just reach your goal if you earn approximately 11 per cent. To get the exact answer, we would solve for r:

$$(1+r)^8 = £80,000/35,000 = 2.2857$$
$$1+r = 2.2857^{(1/8)} = 2.2857^{0.125} = 1.1089$$
$$r = 10.89\%$$

 EXAMPLE 4.12

Only 18,262.5 Days to Retirement

You would like to retire in 50 years as a millionaire. If you have €10,000 today, what rate of return do you need to earn to achieve your goal?

The future value is €1,000,000. The present value is €10,000, and there are 50 years until payment. We need to calculate the unknown discount rate in the following:

$$€10,000 = €1,000,000/(1+r)^{50}$$
$$(1+r)^{50} = 100$$

The future value factor is thus 100. You can verify that the implicit rate is about 9.65 per cent.

Finding the Number of Periods

Suppose we are interested in purchasing an asset that costs £50,000. We currently have £25,000. If we can earn 12 per cent on this £25,000, how long until we have the £50,000? Finding the answer involves solving for the last variable in the basic present value

Chapter 4 Introduction to Valuation: The Time Value of Money

equation, the number of periods. You already know how to get an approximate answer to this particular problem. Notice that we need to double our money. From the Rule of 72, this will take about $72/12 = 6$ years at 12 per cent.

To come up with the exact answer, we can again manipulate the basic present value equation. The present value is £25,000, and the future value is £50,000. With a 12 per cent discount rate, the basic equation takes one of the following forms:

$$£25,000 = £50,000/1.12^t$$
$$£50,000/25,000 = 1.12^t = 2$$

We thus have a future value factor of 2 for a 12 per cent rate. We now need to solve for t. If you look down the column in Table A.1 that corresponds to 12 per cent, you will see that a future value factor of 1.9738 occurs at six periods. It will thus take about six years, as we calculated. To get the exact answer, we have to explicitly solve for t. If you do this, you will see that the answer is 6.1163 years, so our approximation was quite close in this case.

EXAMPLE
4.13

Waiting for Godot

You've been saving up to buy Godot Ltd. The total cost will be £10 million. You currently have about £2.3 million. If you can earn 5 per cent on your money, how long will you have to wait? At 16 per cent, how long must you wait?

At 5 per cent, you'll have to wait a long time. From the basic present value equation:

$$£2.3 \text{ million} = £10 \text{ million}/1.05^t$$
$$1.05^t = 4.35$$
$$t = 30 \text{ years}$$

At 16 per cent, things are a little better. Verify for yourself that it will take about 10 years.

Spreadsheet Strategies

Using a Spreadsheet for Time Value of Money Calculations

More and more, businesspeople from many different areas (not just finance and accounting) rely on spreadsheets to do all the different types of calculation that come up in the real world. As a result, in this section we shall show you how to use a spreadsheet to handle the various time value of money problems we presented in this chapter. We shall use Microsoft Excel™, but the commands are similar for other types of software. We assume you are already familiar with basic spreadsheet operations.

As we have seen, you can solve for any one of the following four potential unknowns: future value, present value, the discount rate, or the number of periods. With a spreadsheet, there is a separate formula for each. In Excel, these are as follows:

To find	Enter this formula
Future value	= FV (rate,nper,pmt,pv)
Present value	= PV (rate,nper,pmt,fv)
Discount rate	= RATE (nper,pmt,pv,fv)
Number of periods	= NPER (rate,pmt,pv,fv)

In these formulae, pv and fv are present and future value, nper is the number of periods, and rate is the discount, or interest, rate.

Two things are a little tricky here. First, the spreadsheet requires that the rate be entered as a decimal. Second, you have to put a negative sign on either the present value or the future value to solve for the rate or the number of periods. For the same reason, if you solve for a present value, the answer will have a negative sign unless you input a negative future value. The same is true when you compute a future value.

To illustrate how you might use these formulae, we shall go back to an example in the chapter. If you invest £25,000 at 12 per cent per year, how long until you have £50,000? You might set up a spreadsheet like this:

	A	B	C	D	E	F	G	H
1	Present Value (pv)	£25,000		Periods	6.116255			
2	Future Value (fv)	£50,000						
3	Rate (rate)	12%		Formula in cell E1 is =NPER (B3,0,-B1,B2)				
4								
5								

This example finishes our introduction to basic time value concepts. Table 4.4 summarizes present and future value calculations for future reference.

TABLE 4.4

Symbols

PV = Present value; what future cash flows are worth today

FV_t = Future value; what cash flows are worth in the future

R = Interest rate, rate of return, or discount rate per period – typically, but not always, one year

T = Number of periods – typically, but not always, the number of years

C = Cash amount

Future value of C invested at r per cent for t periods

$FV_t = C \times (1 + r)^t$

The term $(1 + r)^t$ is called the *future value factor*.

Present value of C to be received in t periods at r per cent per period

$PV = C/(1 + r)^t$

The term $1/(1 + r)^t$ is called the *present value factor*.

The basic present value equation giving the relationship between present and future value

$PV = FV_t/(1 + r)^t$

Table 4.4 Summary of time value calculations

CONCEPT QUESTIONS

4.3a   What is the basic present value equation?

4.3b   What is the Rule of 72?

Summary and Conclusions

This chapter has introduced you to the basic principles of present value and discounted cash flow valuation. In it, we explained a number of things about the time value of money, including these:

1   For a given rate of return, we can determine the value at some point in the future of an investment made today by calculating the future value of that investment.

2   We can determine the current worth of a future cash flow or series of cash flows for a given rate of return by calculating the present value of the cash flow(s) involved.

3   The relationship between present value (PV) and future value (FV) for a given rate r and time t is given by the basic present value equation:

$$PV = \frac{FV_t}{(1 + r)^t}$$

As we have shown, it is possible to find any one of the four components (PV, FV_t, r or t) given the other three.

The principles developed in this chapter will figure prominently in the chapters to come. The reason for this is that most investments, whether they involve real assets or financial assets, can be analysed using the discounted cash flow (DCF) approach. As a result, the DCF approach is broadly applicable and widely used in practice. Before going on, therefore, you might want to do some of the problems that follow.

Chapter Review and Self-Test Problems

4.1   **Calculating Future Values**   Assume you deposit 10,000 Swedish kroner today in an account that pays 6 per cent interest. How much will you have in five years?

4.2   **Calculating Present Values**   Suppose you have just celebrated your 19th birthday. A rich uncle has set up a trust fund for you that will pay you £150,000 when you turn 30. If the relevant discount rate is 9 per cent, how much is this fund worth today?

4.3   **Calculating Rates of Return**   You've been offered an investment that will double your money in 10 years. What rate of return are you being offered? Check your answer using the Rule of 72.

4.4   **Calculating the Number of Periods**   You've been offered an investment that will pay you 9 per cent per year. If you invest £15,000, how long until you have £30,000? How long until you have £45,000?

Answers to Chapter Review and Self-Test Problems

4.1   We need to calculate the future value of SKr10,000 at 6 per cent for five years. The future value factor is

$$1.06^5 = 1.3382$$

The future value is thus SKr10,000 × 1.3382 = SKr13,382.26.

5 **Calculating the Number of Periods [LO4]** Solve for the unknown number of years in each of the following:

Present value (NKr)	Years	Interest rate (%)	Future value (NKr)
560		10	1,284
810		7	4,341
18,400		15	364,518
21,500		12	173,439

6 **Calculating Interest Rates [LO3]** Assume the total cost of a university education will be €290,000 when your child enters college in 18 years. You currently have €40,000 to invest. What annual rate of interest must you earn on your investment to cover the cost of your child's university education?

7 **Calculating the Number of Periods [LO4]** At 6 per cent interest, how long does it take to double your money? To quadruple it?

8 **Calculating Interest Rates [LO3]** In 2010 the average price per metre for owner-occupied flats in Copenhagen was about 23,000 Danish kroner. In 1995 the average price was around 6,000 Danish kroner. What was the annual increase in selling price?

9 **Calculating the Number of Periods [LO4]** You're trying to save to buy a new €170,000 Ferrari. You have €40,000 today that can be invested at your bank. The bank pays 5 per cent annual interest on its accounts. How long will it be before you have enough to buy the car?

10 **Calculating Present Values [LO2]** Imprudential plc has an unfunded pension liability of £800 million that must be paid in 20 years. To assess the value of the firm's equity, financial analysts want to discount this liability back to the present. If the relevant discount rate is 7 per cent, what is the present value of this liability?

11 **Calculating Present Values [LO2]** You have just received notification that you have won the €1 million first prize in the Euro Lottery. However, the prize will be awarded on your 100th birthday (assuming you're around to collect), 80 years from now. What is the present value of your windfall if the appropriate discount rate is 12 per cent?

12 **Calculating Future Values [LO1]** Your coin collection contains fifty 1952 silver dollars. If your grandparents purchased them for their face value when they were new, how much will your collection be worth when you retire in 2057, assuming they appreciate at a 4.5 per cent annual rate?

13 **Calculating Interest Rates and Future Values [LO1, LO3]** In 1968 prize money for the Wimbledon Tennis Championships was first awarded. The winner of the men's singles was £2,000 and for the ladies' singles it was £750. In 2009 both winners received £850,000. What was the percentage increase per year in the winner's cheque for men and women over this period? If the winner's prize increases at the same rate, what will the men's and ladies' singles tournament winners receive in 2040? Do you think this will actually happen? Explain.

14 **Calculating Interest Rates [LO3]** In 2008 a gold Morgan dollar minted in 1895 sold for $43,125. For this to have been true, what rate of return did this coin return for the lucky numismatist?

15 **Calculating Rates of Return [LO3]** On 8 February 2009 John Madejski, chairman of Reading Football Club, sold the Edgar Degas bronze sculpture *Petite Danseuse de Quatorze Ans* at auction for a world record price of £13.3 million. He bought the statue in 2004 for £5 million. What was his annual rate of return on this sculpture?

Chapter 4 Introduction to Valuation: The Time Value of Money

INTERMEDIATE

16–20

16 **Calculating Rates of Return [LO3]**   Consider again the security issue by Spanish Word Ltd that in return for receiving £24,099 today from investors, they will pay back £100,000 in 30 years.

(a) Based on the £24,099 price, what rate was Spanish Word paying to borrow money?

(b) Suppose that in 2020 this security's price is £38,260. If an investor had purchased it for £24,099 in 2010 and sold it in 2020, what annual rate of return would she have earned?

(c) If an investor had purchased the security at market in 2020, and held it until it matured, what annual rate of return would she have earned?

17 **Calculating Present Values [LO2]**   Suppose you are still committed to owning a €170,000 Ferrari (see Problem 9). If you believe your mutual fund can achieve a 12 per cent annual rate of return and you want to buy the car in 9 years on the day you turn 30, how much must you invest today?

18 **Calculating Future Values [LO1]**   You have just made your first £4,000 contribution to your retirement account. Assuming you earn a 10 per cent rate of return and make no additional contributions, what will your account be worth when you retire in 45 years? What if you wait 10 years before contributing? (Does this suggest an investment strategy?)

19 **Calculating Future Values [LO1]**   You are scheduled to receive £30,000 in two years. When you receive it, you will invest it for six more years at 8.4 per cent per year. How much will you have in eight years?

20 **Calculating the Number of Periods [LO4]**   You expect to receive €10,000 at graduation in two years. You plan on investing it at 10 per cent until you have €75,000. How long will you have to wait from now?

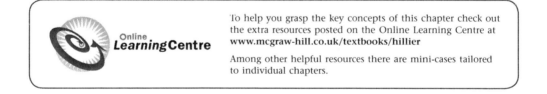

To help you grasp the key concepts of this chapter check out the extra resources posted on the Online Learning Centre at **www.mcgraw-hill.co.uk/textbooks/hillier**

Among other helpful resources there are mini-cases tailored to individual chapters.

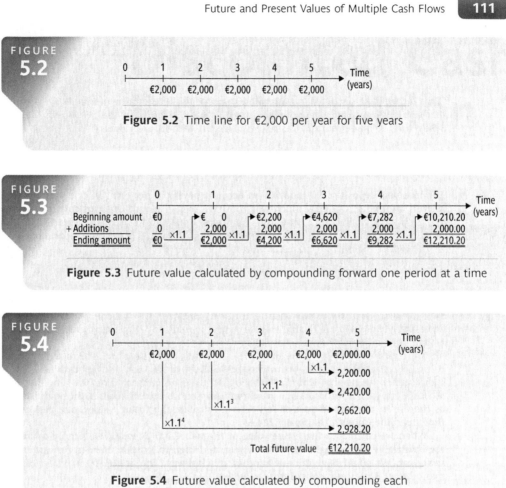

FIGURE **5.2**

Figure 5.2 Time line for €2,000 per year for five years

FIGURE **5.3**

Figure 5.3 Future value calculated by compounding forward one period at a time

FIGURE **5.4**

Figure 5.4 Future value calculated by compounding each cash flow separately

The total future value, as we previously calculated, is equal to the sum of these two future values:

$$€116.64 + 108 = €224.64$$

Based on this example, there are two ways to calculate future values for multiple cash flows: (1) compound the accumulated balance forward one year at a time; or (2) calculate the future value of each cash flow first and then add them up. Both give the same answer, so you can do it either way.

To illustrate the two different ways of calculating future values, consider the future value of €2,000 invested at the end of each of the next five years. The current balance is zero, and the rate is 10 per cent. We first draw a time line, as shown in Fig. 5.2.

On the time line, notice that nothing happens until the end of the first year, when we make the first €2,000 investment. This first €2,000 earns interest for the next four (not five) years. Also notice that the last €2,000 is invested at the end of the fifth year, so it earns no interest at all.

Figure 5.3 illustrates the calculations involved if we compound the investment one period at a time. As illustrated, the future value is €12,210.20.

Figure 5.4 goes through the same calculations, but the second technique is used. Naturally, the answer is the same.

EXAMPLE 5.1

Saving Up Once Again

If you deposit 100 Swedish kroner (SKr) in one year, SKr200 in two years, and SKr300 in three years, how much will you have in three years? How much of this is interest? How much will you have in five years if you don't add additional amounts? Assume a 7 per cent interest rate throughout.

We shall calculate the future value of each amount in three years. Notice that the SKr100 earns interest for two years, and the SKr200 earns interest for one year. The final SKr300 earns no interest. The future values are thus

$$
\begin{aligned}
\text{SKr100} \times 1.07^2 &= \text{SKr114.49} \\
\text{SKr200} \times 1.07 &= 214.00 \\
+\ \text{SKr300} &= \underline{300.00} \\
\text{Total future value} &= \underline{\text{SKr628.49}}
\end{aligned}
$$

The total future value is thus SKr628.49. The total interest is

$$
\text{SKr628.49} - (100 + 200 + 300) = \text{SKr28.49}
$$

How much will you have in five years? We know that you will have SKr628.49 in three years. If you leave that in for two more years, it will grow to

$$
\text{SKr628.49} \times 1.07^2 = \text{SKr628.49} \times 1.1449 = \text{SKr719.56}
$$

Notice that we could have calculated the future value of each amount separately. Once again, be careful about the lengths of time. As we previously calculated, the first SKr100 earns interest for only four years, the second deposit earns three years' interest, and the last earns two years' interest:

$$
\begin{aligned}
\text{SKr100} \times 1.07^4 &= \text{SKr100} \times 1.3108 = \text{SKr131.08} \\
\text{SKr200} \times 1.07^3 &= \text{SKr200} \times 1.2250 = 245.01 \\
+\text{SKr300} \times 1.07^2 &= \text{SKr300} \times 1.1449 = \underline{343.47} \\
\text{Total future value} &= \underline{\text{SKr719.56}}
\end{aligned}
$$

Present Value with Multiple Cash Flows

We often need to determine the present value of a series of future cash flows. As with future values, there are two ways we can do it. We can either discount back one period at a time, or we can just calculate the present values individually and add them up.

Suppose you need €1,000 in one year and €2,000 more in two years. If you can earn 9 per cent on your money, how much do you have to put up today to exactly cover these amounts in the future? In other words, what is the present value of the two cash flows at 9 per cent?

The present value of €2,000 in two years at 9 per cent is

$$
€2,000/1.09^2 = €1,683.36
$$

The present value of €1,000 in one year is

$$
€1,000/1.09 = €917.43
$$

Therefore the total present value is

$$
€1,683.36 + 917.43 = €2,600.79
$$

114

FIGURE
5.5

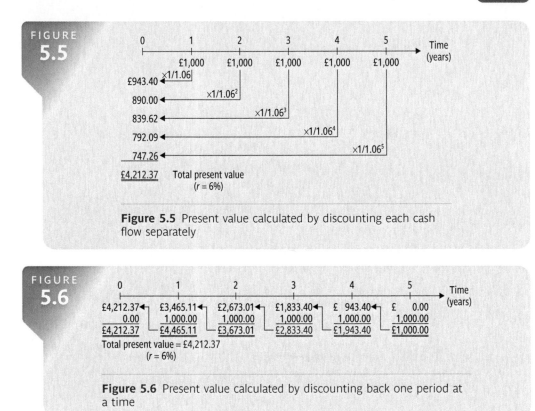

Figure 5.5 Present value calculated by discounting each cash flow separately

FIGURE
5.6

Figure 5.6 Present value calculated by discounting back one period at a time

An alternative way of calculating present values for multiple future cash flows is to discount back to the present, one period at a time. To illustrate, suppose we had an investment that was going to pay £1,000 at the end of every year for the next five years. To find the present value, we could discount each £1,000 back to the present separately and then add them up. Figure 5.5 illustrates this approach for a 6 per cent discount rate; as shown, the answer is £4,212.37 (ignoring a small rounding error).

Alternatively, we could discount the last cash flow back one period and add it to the next-to-last cash flow:

$$(\pounds1,000/1.06) + 1,000 = \pounds943.40 + 1,000 = \pounds1,943.40$$

We could then discount this amount back one period and add it to the year 3 cash flow:

$$(\pounds1,943.40/1.06) + 1,000 = \pounds1,833.40 + 1,000 = \pounds2,833.40$$

This process could be repeated as necessary. Figure 5.6 illustrates this approach, and the remaining calculations.

EXAMPLE
5.2

How Much Is It Worth?

You are offered an investment that will pay you £200 in one year, £400 the next year, £600 the next year, and £800 at the end of the fourth year. You can earn 12 per cent on similar investments. What is the most you should pay for this one?
   We need to calculate the present value of these cash flows at 12 per cent. Taking them one at a time gives

$$£200 \times 1/1.12^1 = £200/1.1200 = £178.57$$
$$£400 \times 1/1.12^2 = £400/1.2544 = 318.88$$
$$£600 \times 1/1.12^3 = £600/1.4049 = 427.07$$
$$+£800 \times 1/1.12^4 = £800/1.5735 = \underline{508.41}$$
$$\text{Total present value} = \underline{£1,432.93}$$

If you can earn 12 per cent on your money, then you can duplicate this investment's cash flows for £1,432.93, so this is the most you should be willing to pay.

How Much Is It Worth? Part 2

EXAMPLE 5.3

You are offered an investment that will make three €5,000 payments. The first payment will occur four years from today. The second will occur in five years, and the third will follow in six years. If you can earn 11 per cent, what is the most this investment is worth today? What is the future value of the cash flows?

We shall answer the questions in reverse order to illustrate a point. The future value of the cash flows in six years is

$$(€5,000 \times 1.11^2) + (5,000 \times 1.11) + 5,000 = €6,160.50 + 5,550 + 5,000$$
$$= €16,710.50$$

The present value must be

$$€16,710.50/1.11^6 = €8,934.12$$

Let's check this. Taking them one at a time, the PVs of the cash flows are

$$€5,000 \times 1/1.11^6 = €5,000/1.8704 = €2,673.20$$
$$€5,000 \times 1/1.11^5 = €5,000/1.6851 = 2,967.26$$
$$+€5,000 \times 1/1.11^4 = €5,000/1.5181 = \underline{3,293.65}$$
$$\text{Total present value} = \underline{€8,934.12}$$

This is as we previously calculated. The point we want to make is that we can calculate present and future values in any order, and convert between them using whatever way seems most convenient. The answers will always be the same as long as we stick with the same discount rate, and are careful to keep track of the right number of periods.

Spreadsheet Strategies

How to Calculate Present Values with Multiple Future Cash Flows Using a Spreadsheet

Just as we did in our previous chapter, we can set up a basic spreadsheet to calculate the present values of the individual cash flows as follows. Notice that we have simply calculated the present values one at a time and added them up:

	A	B	C	D	E	
1	Rate	0.12				
2	Year	1	2	3	4	
3	Cash Flow	£200.00	£400.00	£600.00	£800.00	
4	Present Value	£178.57	£318.88	£427.07	£508.41	
5	Formula Used	=PV($B$1,B2,0,-B3)	=PV($B$1,C2,0,-C3)	=PV($B$1,D2,0,-D3)	=PV($B$1,E2,0,-E3)	
6						
7	Total PV	£1,432.93				
8	Formula Used	=SUM(B5:E5)				
9						

A Note about Cash Flow Timing

In present and future value problems, cash flow timing is critically important. In almost all such calculations, it is implicitly assumed that the cash flows occur at the *end* of each period. In fact, all the formulae we have discussed, all the numbers in a standard present value or future value table, and (very important) all the preset (or default) settings in a spreadsheet assume that cash flows occur at the end of each period. Unless you are explicitly told otherwise, you should always assume that this is what is meant.

As a quick illustration of this point, suppose you are told that a three-year investment has a first-year cash flow of £100, a second-year cash flow of £200, and a third-year cash flow of £300. You are asked to draw a time line. Without further information, you should always assume that the time line looks like this:

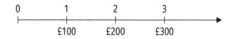

On our time line, notice how the first cash flow occurs at the end of the first period, the second at the end of the second period, and the third at the end of the third period.

We shall close this section by answering the question we posed at the beginning of the chapter concerning footballer Cristiano Ronaldo's contract. Recall that the contract called for £9.5 million in the first year, increasing by 25 per cent over the next five years. If 12 per cent is the appropriate interest rate, what kind of deal did the Real Madrid player have?

To answer, we can calculate the present value by discounting each year's salary back to the present as follows (notice we assume that all the payments are made at year-end):

$$
\begin{aligned}
&\text{Year 0 (2009): } £9,500,000 && = £9,500,000.00 \\
&\text{Year 1 (2010): } £9,500,000 \times 1.25 \times 1/1.12^1 &&= £10,602,678.57 \\
&\text{Year 2 (2011): } £9,500,000 \times 1.25^2 \times 1/1.12^2 &&= £11,833,346.62 \\
&\text{Year 3 (2012): } £9,500,000 \times 1.25^3 \times 1/1.12^3 &&= £13,206,860.07 \\
&\text{Year 4 (2013): } £9,500,000 \times 1.25^4 \times 1/1.12^4 &&= £14,739,799.18 \\
&\text{Year 5 (2014): } £9,500,000 \times 1.25^5 \times 1/1.12^5 &&= £16,450,668.73
\end{aligned}
$$

Adding the individual cash flows together, you will see that Ronaldo's contract had a present value of about £76 million, or about 71 per cent of the stated £107 million value.

CONCEPT QUESTIONS		
	5.1a	Describe how to calculate the future value of a series of cash flows.
	5.1b	Describe how to calculate the present value of a series of cash flows.
	5.1c	Unless we are explicitly told otherwise, what do we always assume about the timing of cash flows in present and future value problems?

5.2 Valuing Level Cash Flows: Annuities and Perpetuities

We shall frequently encounter situations in which we have multiple cash flows that are all the same amount. For example, a common type of loan repayment plan calls for the borrower to repay the loan by making a series of equal payments over some length of time. Almost all consumer loans (such as car loans) and home mortgages feature equal payments, usually made each month.

Chapter 5 Discounted Cash Flow Valuation

> **annuity**
> A level stream of cash flows for a fixed period of time.

More generally, a series of constant or level cash flows that occur at the end of each period for some fixed number of periods is called an ordinary **annuity**; more correctly, the cash flows are said to be in *ordinary annuity form*. Annuities appear frequently in financial arrangements, and there are some useful shortcuts for determining their values. We consider these next.

Present Value for Annuity Cash Flows

Suppose we are examining an asset that promises to pay £500 at the end of each of the next three years. The cash flows from this asset are in the form of a three-year, £500 annuity. If we wanted to earn 10 per cent on our money, how much would we offer for this annuity?

From the previous section, we know that we can discount each of these £500 payments back to the present at 10 per cent to determine the total present value:

$$\text{Present value} = (£500/1.1^1) + (500/1.1^2) + (500/1.1^3)$$
$$= (£500/1.1) + (500/1.21) + (500/1.331)$$
$$= £454.55 + 413.22 + 375.66$$
$$= £1{,}243.43$$

This approach works just fine. However, we shall often encounter situations in which the number of cash flows is quite large. For example, a typical home mortgage calls for monthly payments over 25 years, for a total of 300 payments. If we were trying to determine the present value of those payments, it would be useful to have a shortcut.

Because the cash flows of an annuity are all the same, we can come up with a handy variation on the basic present value equation. The present value of an annuity of £C (or any other currency) per period for t periods when the rate of return or interest rate is r is given by

$$\text{Annuity present value} = C \bigg/ \left[\frac{1 - \text{Present value factor}}{r}\right]$$
$$= C \times \left\{\frac{1 - [1/(1 + r)^t]}{r}\right\} \qquad (5.1)$$
$$= C \times \left\{\frac{1}{r} - \frac{1}{r(1 + r)^t}\right\}$$

The term in parentheses on the first line is sometimes called the *present value interest factor for annuities* and abbreviated PVIFA(r, t).

The expression for the annuity present value may look a little complicated, but it isn't difficult to use. Notice that the term in square brackets on the second line, $1/(1 + r)^t$, is the same present value factor we've been calculating. In our example from the beginning of this section the interest rate is 10 per cent, and there are three years involved. The usual present value factor is thus

$$\text{Present value factor} = 1/1.1^3 = 1/1.331 = 0.751315$$

To calculate the annuity present value factor, we just plug this in:

$$\text{Annuity present value factor} = (1 - \text{Present value factor})/r$$
$$= (1 - 0.751315)/0.10$$
$$= 0.248685/0.10 = 2.48685$$

Just as we calculated before, the present value of our £500 annuity is then

$$\text{Annuity present value} = £500 \times 2.48685 = £1{,}243.43$$

What we have here is an annuity of €20 per month at 1.5 per cent per month for some unknown length of time. The present value is €1,000 (the amount you owe today). We need to do a little algebra (or use a calculator):

$$€1,000 = €20 \times [(1 - \text{Present value factor})/0.015]$$
$$(€1,000/20) \times 0.015 = 1 - \text{Present value factor}$$
$$\text{Present value factor} = 0.25 = 1/(1 + r)^t$$
$$1.015^t = 1/0.25 = 4$$

At this point the problem boils down to asking: how long does it take for your money to quadruple at 1.5 per cent per month? Based on our previous chapter, the answer is about 93 months:

$$1.015^{93} = 3.99 \approx 4$$

It will take you about 93/12 = 7.75 years to pay off the €1,000 at this rate.

Finding the Rate   The last question we might want to ask concerns the interest rate implicit in an annuity. For example, an insurance company offers to pay you £1,000 per year for 10 years if you will pay £6,710 up front. What rate is implicit in this 10-year annuity?

In this case we know the present value (£6,710), we know the cash flows (£1,000 per year), and we know the life of the investment (10 years). What we don't know is the discount rate:

$$£6,710 = £1,000 \times [(1 - \text{Present value factor})/r]$$
$$£6,710/1,000 = 6.71$$
$$= \{1 - [1/(1 + r)^{10}]\}/r$$

So the annuity factor for 10 periods is equal to 6.71, and we need to solve this equation for the unknown value of r. Unfortunately, this is mathematically impossible to do directly. The only way to do it is to use a table, or trial and error, to find a value for r.

If you look across the row corresponding to 10 periods in Table A.3 you will see a factor of 6.7101 for 8 per cent, so we see right away that the insurance company is offering just about 8 per cent. Alternatively, we could just start trying different values until we got very close to the answer. Using this trial-and-error approach can be a little tedious, but fortunately computers are good at that sort of thing.

To illustrate a situation in which finding the unknown rate can be useful, let us consider that a lottery offers you a choice of how to take your winnings. In a recent drawing participants were offered the option of receiving a lump sum payment of €250,000 or an annuity of €500,000 to be received in equal instalments over a 25-year period. Which option was better?

To answer, suppose you were to compare €250,000 today with an annuity of €500,000/ 25 = €20,000 per year for 25 years. At what rate do these have the same value? This is the same type of problem we've been looking at; we need to find the unknown rate r for a present value of €250,000, a €20,000 payment, and a 25-year period. If you grind through the calculations (or get a little computer assistance), you should find that the unknown rate is about 6.24 per cent. You should take the annuity option if that rate is attractive relative to other investments available to you. Notice that we have ignored taxes in this example, and taxes can significantly affect our conclusion. Be sure to consult your tax adviser any time you win the lottery.

Future Value for Annuities

Sometimes it's also handy to know a shortcut for calculating the future value of an annuity. As you might guess, there are future value factors for annuities as well as present value factors. In general, here is the future value factor for an annuity:

$$\text{Annuity FV factor} = \frac{\text{Future value factor} - 1}{r}$$

$$= \frac{(1 + r)^t - 1}{r}$$

(5.2)

$$= \frac{(1 + r)^t}{r} - \frac{1}{r}$$

To see how we use annuity future value factors, suppose you plan to contribute £2,000 every year to a retirement account paying 8 per cent. If you retire in 30 years, how much will you have?

The number of years here, t, is 30, and the interest rate, r, is 8 per cent; so we can calculate the annuity future value factor as:

$$\text{Annuity FV factor} = (\text{Future value factor} - 1)/r$$
$$= (1.08^{30} - 1)/0.08$$
$$= (10.0627 - 1)/0.08$$
$$= 113.2832$$

The future value of this 30-year, £2,000 annuity is thus

$$\text{Annuity future value} = £2,000 \times 113.28$$
$$= £226,566$$

A Note about Annuities Due

So far we have only discussed ordinary annuities. These are the most important, but there is a fairly common variation. Remember that with an ordinary annuity the cash flows occur at the end of each period. When you take out a loan with monthly payments, for example, the first loan payment normally occurs one month after you get the loan. However, when you lease an apartment, the first lease payment is usually due immediately. The second payment is due at the beginning of the second month, and so on. A lease is an example of an **annuity due**. An annuity due is an annuity for which the cash flows occur at the beginning of each period. Almost any type of arrangement in which we have to prepay the same amount each period is an annuity due.

> **annuity due**
> An annuity for which the cash flows occur at the beginning of the period.

Suppose an annuity due has five payments of £400 each, and the relevant discount rate is 10 per cent. The time line looks like this:

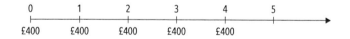

Notice how the cash flows here are the same as those for a *four*-year ordinary annuity, except that there is an extra £400 at time 0. For practice, check to see that the value of a four-year ordinary annuity at 10 per cent is £1,267.95. If we add on the extra £400, we get £1,667.95, which is the present value of this annuity due.

> **perpetuity**
> An annuity in which the cash flows continue for ever.
>
> **consol**
> A type of perpetuity.

Perpetuities

We've seen that a series of level cash flows can be valued by treating those cash flows as an annuity. An important special case of an annuity arises when the level stream of cash flows continues for ever. Such an asset is called a **perpetuity**, because the cash flows are perpetual. Perpetuities are also called **consols**, particularly in the United Kingdom. See Example 5.6 for an important example of a perpetuity.

Before we go on, there is one important note about our formulae for growing annuities and perpetuities. In both cases, the cash flow in the formula, C, is the cash flow that is going to occur exactly one period from today.

CONCEPT QUESTIONS

5.2a In general, what is the present value of an annuity of C per period at a discount rate of r per period? The future value?

5.2b In general, what is the present value of a perpetuity?

5.3 Comparing Rates: The Effect of Compounding

The next issue we need to discuss has to do with the way interest rates are quoted. This subject causes a fair amount of confusion, because rates are quoted in many different ways. Sometimes the way a rate is quoted is the result of tradition, and sometimes it's the result of legislation. Unfortunately, at times, rates are quoted in deliberately deceptive ways to mislead borrowers and investors. We shall discuss these topics in this section.

Effective Annual Percentage Rates and Compounding

If a rate is quoted as 10 per cent compounded semi-annually, this means the investment actually pays 5 per cent every six months. A natural question then arises: is 5 per cent every six months the same thing as 10 per cent per year? It's easy to see that it is not. If you invest €1 at 10 per cent per year, you will have €1.10 at the end of the year. If you invest at 5 per cent every six months, then you'll have the future value of €1 at 5 per cent for two periods:

$$€1 \times 1.05^2 = €1.1025$$

> **nominal interest rate** The interest rate expressed in terms of the interest payment made each period. Also known as the *stated or quoted interest rate.*

This is €0.0025 more. The reason is simple: your account was credited with €1 × 0.05 = 5 cents in interest after six months. In the following six months, you earned 5 per cent on that five cents, for an extra 5 × 0.05 = 0.25 cents.

As our example illustrates, 10 per cent compounded semi-annually is actually equivalent to 10.25 per cent per year. Put another way, we would be indifferent between 10 per cent compounded semi-annually and 10.25 per cent compounded annually. Any time we have compounding during the year, we need to be concerned about what the rate really is.

In our example, the 10 per cent is called a **nominal**, **stated** or **quoted interest rate**. Other names are used as well. The 10.25 per cent, which is actually the rate you will earn, is called the **effective annual percentage rate (EAR)**. To compare different investments or interest rates, we shall always need to convert to effective rates. Some general procedures for doing this are discussed next.

> **effective annual percentage rate (EAR)** The interest rate expressed as if it were compounded once per year.

Calculating and Comparing Effective Annual Rates

To see why it is important to work only with effective rates, suppose you've shopped around and come up with the following three rates:

Bank A: 15 per cent compounded daily

Bank B: 15.5 per cent compounded quarterly

Bank C: 16 per cent compounded annually

Which of these is the best if you are thinking of opening a savings account? Which of these is best if they represent loan rates?

Chapter 5 Discounted Cash Flow Valuation

To begin, Bank C is offering 16 per cent per year. Because there is no compounding during the year, this is the effective rate. Bank B is actually paying $0.155/4 = 0.03875$ or 3.875 per cent per quarter. At this rate, an investment of £1 for four quarters would grow to

$$£1 \times 1.03875^4 = £1.1642$$

The effective annual rate (EAR), therefore, is 16.42 per cent. For a saver, this is much better than the 16 per cent rate Bank C is offering; for a borrower, it's worse.

Bank A is compounding every day. This may seem a little extreme, but it is common to calculate interest daily. In this case, the daily interest rate is actually

$$0.15/365 = 0.000411$$

This is 0.0411 per cent per day. At this rate, an investment of £1 for 365 periods would grow to

$$£1 \times 1.000411^{365} = £1.1618$$

The EAR is 16.18 per cent. This is not as good as Bank B's 16.42 per cent for a saver, and not as good as Bank C's 16 per cent for a borrower.

This example illustrates two things. First, the highest quoted rate is not necessarily the best. Second, compounding during the year can lead to a significant difference between the quoted rate and the effective rate. Remember that the effective rate is what you actually get or what you pay.

If you look at our examples, you see that we computed the EARs in three steps. We first divided the quoted rate by the number of times that the interest is compounded. We then added 1 to the result and raised it to the power of the number of times the interest is compounded. Finally, we subtracted the 1. If we let m be the number of times the interest is compounded during the year, these steps can be summarized simply as

$$\text{EAR} = [1 + (\text{Quoted rate}/m)]^m - 1 \qquad (5.6)$$

For example, suppose you are offered 12 per cent compounded monthly. In this case, the interest is compounded 12 times a year; so m is 12. You can calculate the effective rate as

$$
\begin{aligned}
\text{EAR} &= [1 + (\text{Quoted rate}/m)]^m - 1 \\
&= [1 + (0.12/12)]^{12} - 1 \\
&= 1.01^{12} - 1 \\
&= 1.126825 - 1 \\
&= 12.6825\%
\end{aligned}
$$

What's the EAR?

EXAMPLE 5.7

A bank is offering 12 per cent compounded quarterly. If you put £100 in an account, how much will you have at the end of one year? What's the EAR? How much will you have at the end of two years?

The bank is effectively offering $12\%/4 = 3\%$ every quarter. If you invest £100 for four periods at 3 per cent per period, the future value is

$$
\begin{aligned}
\text{Future value} &= £100 \times 1.03^4 \\
&= £100 \times 1.1255 \\
&= £112.55
\end{aligned}
$$

The EAR is 12.55 per cent: $£100 \times (1 + 0.1255) = £112.55$.

TABLE 5.3	Compounding period	Number of times compounded	Effective annual rate (%)
	Year	1	10.00000
	Quarter	4	10.38129
	Month	12	10.47131
	Week	52	10.50648
	Day	365	10.51558
	Hour	8,760	10.51703
	Minute	525,600	10.51709

Table 5.3 Compounding frequency and effective annual rates

As the numbers in Table 5.3 seem to suggest, there is an upper limit to the EAR. If we let q stand for the quoted rate, then, as the number of times the interest is compounded gets extremely large, the EAR approaches

$$\text{EAR} = e^q - 1 \tag{5.8}$$

where e is the number 2.71828 (look for a key labelled 'e^x' on your calculator). For example, with our 10 per cent rate, the highest possible EAR is

$$
\begin{aligned}
\text{EAR} &= e^q - 1 \\
&= 2.71828^{10} - 1 \\
&= 1.1051709 - 1 \\
&= 10.51709\%
\end{aligned}
$$

In this case we say that the money is continuously, or instantaneously, compounded. Interest is being credited the instant it is earned, so the amount of interest grows continuously.

5.4   Loan Types and Loan Amortization

Whenever a lender extends a loan, some provision will be made for repayment of the principal (the original loan amount). A loan might be repaid in equal instalments, for example, or it might be repaid in a single lump sum. Because the way that the principal and interest are paid is up to the parties involved, there are actually an unlimited number of possibilities.

In this section we describe a few forms of repayment that come up quite often, and more complicated forms can usually be built up from these. The three basic types of loan are pure discount loans, interest-only loans, and amortized loans. Working with these loans is a very straightforward application of the present value principles that we have already developed.

Pure Discount Loans

The *pure discount loan* is the simplest form of loan. With such a loan the borrower receives money today, and repays a single lump sum at some time in the future. A one-year, 10 per cent pure discount loan, for example, would require the borrower to repay £1.10 in one year for every pound borrowed today.

Because a pure discount loan is so simple, we already know how to value one. Suppose a borrower was able to repay £25,000 in five years. If we, acting as the lender, wanted a 12 per cent interest rate on the loan, how much would we be willing to lend? Put another way, what value would we assign today to that £25,000 to be repaid in five years? Based on our work in Chapter 4, we know the answer is just the present value of £25,000 at 12 per cent for five years:

$$\text{Present value} = £25,000/1.12^5$$
$$= £25,000/1.7623$$
$$= £14,186$$

Pure discount loans are common when the loan term is short – say a year or less. In recent years they have become increasingly common for much longer periods.

EXAMPLE 5.10

Treasury Bills

When a government borrows money on a short-term basis (a year or less), it does so by selling what are called *Treasury bills*, or *T-bills* for short. A T-bill is a promise by the government to repay a fixed amount at some time in the future – for example, 3 months or 12 months.

Treasury bills are pure discount loans. If a T-bill promises to repay £10,000 in 12 months, and the market interest rate is 7 per cent, how much will the bill sell for in the market?

Because the going rate is 7 per cent, the T-bill will sell for the present value of £10,000 to be repaid in one year at 7 per cent:

$$\text{Present value} = £10,000/1.07 = £9,345.79$$

Interest-Only Loans

A second type of loan repayment plan calls for the borrower to pay interest each period, and to repay the entire principal (the original loan amount) at some point in the future. Loans with such a repayment plan are called *interest-only loans*. Notice that if there is just one period, a pure discount loan and an interest-only loan are the same thing.

For example, with a three-year, 10 per cent, interest-only loan of €1,000, the borrower would pay €1,000 × 0.10 = €100 in interest at the end of the first and second years. At the end of the third year the borrower would return the €1,000 along with another €100 in interest for that year. Similarly, a 50-year interest-only loan would call for the borrower to pay interest every year for the next 50 years, and then repay the principal. In the extreme, the borrower pays the interest every period for ever and never repays any principal. As we discussed earlier in the chapter, the result is a perpetuity.

Most corporate bonds have the general form of an interest-only loan. Because we shall be considering bonds in some detail in the next chapter, we shall defer further discussion of them for now.

Amortized Loans

With a pure discount or interest-only loan the principal is repaid all at once. An alternative is an *amortized loan*, with which the lender may require the borrower to repay parts of the loan amount over time. The process of providing for a loan to be paid off by making regular principal reductions is called *amortizing* the loan.

A simple way of amortizing a loan is to have the borrower pay the interest each period, plus some fixed amount. This approach is common with medium-term business loans. For example, suppose a business takes out a £5,000, five-year loan at 9 per cent. The loan agreement calls for the borrower to pay the interest on the loan balance each year, and to reduce the loan balance each year by £1,000. Because the loan amount declines by £1,000 each year, it is fully paid in five years.

In the case we are considering, notice that the total payment will decline each year. The reason is that the loan balance goes down, resulting in a lower interest charge each year, whereas the £1,000 principal reduction is constant. For example, the interest in the first year will be £5,000 × 0.09 = £450. The total payment will be £1,000 + 450 = £1,450. In the second year the loan balance is £4,000, so the interest is £4,000 × 0.09 = £360, and the total payment is £1,360. We can calculate the total payment in each of the remaining years by preparing a simple *amortization schedule* as follows:

Year	Beginning balance (£)	Total payment (£)	Interest paid (£)	Principal paid (£)	Ending balance (£)
1	5,000	1,450	450	1,000	4,000
2	4,000	1,360	360	1,000	3,000
3	3,000	1,270	270	1,000	2,000
4	2,000	1,180	180	1,000	1,000
5	1,000	1,090	90	1,000	0
Totals		6,350	1,350	5,000	

Notice that in each year the interest paid is given by the beginning balance multiplied by the interest rate. Also notice that the beginning balance is given by the ending balance from the previous year.

Probably the most common way of amortizing a loan is to have the borrower make a single, fixed payment every period. Almost all consumer loans (such as car loans) and mortgages work this way. For example, suppose our five-year, 9 per cent, £5,000 loan was amortized this way. How would the amortization schedule look?

We first need to determine the payment. From our discussion earlier in the chapter we know that this loan's cash flows are in the form of an ordinary annuity. In this case, we can solve for the payment as follows:

$$£5,000 = C \times \{[1 - (1/1.09^5)]/0.09\}$$
$$= C \times [(1 - 0.6499)/0.09]$$

This gives us

$$C = £5,000/3.8897$$
$$= £1285.46$$

The borrower will therefore make five equal payments of £1,285.46. Will this pay off the loan? We shall check by filling in an amortization schedule.

In our previous example we knew the principal reduction each year. We then calculated the interest owed to get the total payment. In this example we know the total payment. We shall thus calculate the interest, and then subtract it from the total payment to calculate the principal portion in each payment.

In the first year the interest is £450, as we calculated before. Because the total payment is £1,285.46, the principal paid in the first year must be

$$\text{Principal paid} = £1,285.46 - 450 = £835.46$$

The ending loan balance is thus

$$\text{Ending balance} = £5,000 - 835.46 = £4,164.54$$

Chapter 5 Discounted Cash Flow Valuation

The interest in the second year is £4,164.54 × 0.09 = £374.81, and the loan balance declines by £1,285.46 − 374.81 = £910.65. We can summarize all of the relevant calculations in the following schedule:

Year	Beginning balance (£)	Total payment (£)	Interest paid (£)	Principal paid (£)	Ending balance (£)
1	5,000.00	1,285.46	450.00	835.46	4,164.54
2	4,164.54	1,285.46	374.81	910.65	3,253.88
3	3,253.88	1,285.46	292.85	992.61	2,261.27
4	2,261.27	1,285.46	203.51	1,081.95	1,179.32
5	1,179.32	1,285.46	106.14	1,179.32	0.00
Totals		6,427.30	1,427.31	5,000.00	

Because the loan balance declines to zero, the five equal payments do pay off the loan. Notice that the interest paid declines each period. This isn't surprising, because the loan balance is going down. Given that the total payment is fixed, the principal paid must be rising each period.

If you compare the two loan amortizations in this section, you will see that the total interest is greater for the equal total payment case: £1,427.31 versus £1,350. The reason for this is that the loan is repaid more slowly early on, so the interest is somewhat higher. This doesn't mean that one loan is better than the other; it simply means that one is effectively paid off faster than the other. For example, the principal reduction in the first year is £835.46 in the equal total payment case as compared to £1,000 in the first case.

EXAMPLE 5.11

Partial Amortization, or 'Bite the Bullet'

A common arrangement in property lending might call for a 5-year loan with, say, a 15-year amortization. What this means is that the borrower makes a payment every month of a fixed amount based on a 15-year amortization. However, after 60 months the borrower makes a single, much larger payment called a 'balloon' or 'bullet' to pay off the loan. Because the monthly payments don't fully pay off the loan, the loan is said to be partially amortized.

Suppose we have a €100,000 commercial mortgage with a 1 per cent monthly effective interest rate and a 20-year (240-month) amortization. Further suppose the mortgage has a five-year balloon. What will the monthly payment be? How big will the balloon payment be?

The monthly payment can be calculated based on an ordinary annuity with a present value of €100,000. There are 240 payments, and the interest rate is 1 per cent per month. The payment is

$$€100,000 = C \times \{[1 - (1/1.01^{240})]/0.01\}$$
$$= C \times 90.8194$$
$$C = €1,101.09$$

Now there is an easy way and a hard way to determine the balloon payment. The hard way is to actually amortize the loan for 60 months to see what the balance is at that time. The easy way is to recognize that, after 60 months, we have a 240 − 60 = 180-month loan. The payment is still €1,101.09 per month, and the interest rate is still 1 per cent per month. The loan balance is thus the present value of the remaining payments:

$$\text{Loan balance} = €1,101.09 \times \{[1 - (1/1.01^{180})]/0.01\}$$
$$= €1,101.09 \times 83.3217$$
$$= €91,744.69$$

The balloon payment is a substantial €91,744. Why is it so large? To get an idea, consider the first payment on the mortgage. The interest in the first month is €100,000 × 0.01 = €1,000. Your payment is €1,101.09, so the loan balance declines by only €101.09. Because the loan balance declines so slowly, the cumulative 'pay down' over five years is not great.

Spreadsheet Strategies

Loan Amortization Using a Spreadsheet

Loan amortization is a common spreadsheet application. To illustrate, we shall set up the problem that we examined earlier: a five-year, £5,000, 9 per cent loan with constant payments. Our spreadsheet looks like this:

	A	B	C
1	Loan Amount	£5,000	
2	Interest rate	9%	
3	Loan Term	5	
4	Loan Payment	£1,285.46	
5			
6			

Loan payment formula: = PMT(B2,B3,-B1)

	A	B	C	D	E	F	G
6	Year	Beginning Balance	Total Payment	Interest Paid	Principal Paid	Ending Balance	
7	1	£5,000	£1,285.46	450	£835.46	£4,165	
8	2	£4,165	£1,285.46	374.809	£910.65	£3,254	
9	3	£3,254	£1,285.46	292.85	£992.61	£2,261	
10	4	£2,261	£1,285.46	203.515	£1,081.94	£1,179	
11	5	£1,179	£1,285.46	106.14	£1,179.32	£0	
12	Totals		£6,427.30	1427.31	£4,999.99		
13							
14							

Notice the slight rounding error in cell E12, which sometimes happens when one uses spreadsheets.

Year	Beginning balance	Total payment	Interest paid	Principal paid	Ending balance
1	=B1	=$B$4	=B7*$B$2	=C7-D7	=B7-E7
2	=F7	=$B$4	=B8*$B$2	=C8-D8	=B8-E8
3	=F8	=$B$4	=B9*$B$2	=C9-D9	=B9-E9
4	=F9	=$B$4	=B10*$B$2	=C10-D10	=B10-E10
5	=F10	=$B$4	=B11*$B$2	=C11-D11	=B11-E11
Totals		=SUM(C7:C11)	=SUM(D7:D11)	=SUM(E7:E11)	

CONCEPT QUESTIONS	5.4a What is a pure discount loan? An interest-only loan?
	5.4b What does it mean to amortize a loan?
	5.4c What is a balloon payment? How do you determine its value?

Summary and Conclusions

This chapter rounded out your understanding of fundamental concepts related to the time value of money and discounted cash flow valuation. Several important topics were covered:

1 There are two ways of calculating present and future values when there are multiple cash flows. Both approaches are straightforward extensions of our earlier analysis of single cash flows.

2 A series of constant cash flows that arrive or are paid at the end of each period is called an ordinary annuity, and we described some useful shortcuts for determining the present and future values of annuities.

3 Interest rates can be quoted in a variety of ways. For financial decisions, it is important that any rates being compared be first converted to effective rates. The relationship between a quoted rate, and an effective annual rate (EAR) is given by

$$EAR = [1 + (\text{Quoted rate}/m)]^m - 1$$

where m is the number of times during the year the money is compounded or, equivalently, the number of payments during the year.

4 Many loans are annuities. The process of providing for a loan to be paid off gradually is called amortizing the loan, and we discussed how amortization schedules are prepared and interpreted.

5 The annual percentage rate (APR) is used by countries in the European Union to provide a consistent way of presenting interest rates that have been applied to loans. The APR should include all fees and charges related to setting up a loan. The expression is

$$PV = C_0 + \frac{C_1}{1 + APR} + \frac{C_2}{(1 + APR)^2} + \dots + \frac{C_T}{(1 + APR)^T}$$

$$= C_0 + \sum_{i=1}^{T} \frac{C_i}{(1 + APR)^i}$$

The principles developed in this chapter will figure prominently in the chapters to come. The reason for this is that most investments, whether they involve real assets or financial assets, can be analysed using the discounted cash flow (DCF) approach. As a result, the DCF approach is broadly applicable and widely used in practice. For example, the next two chapters show how to value bonds and shares using an extension of the techniques presented in this chapter. Before going on, therefore, you might want to do some of the problems that follow.

Chapter Review and Self-Test Problems

5.1 **Present Values with Multiple Cash Flows** A top footballer has been signed to a three-year, £10 million contract. The details provide for an immediate cash bonus of £2 million. The player is to receive £2 million in salary at the end of the first year, £3 million the next, and £3 million at the end of the last year. Assuming a 15 per cent discount rate, is this package worth £10 million? If not, how much is it worth?

5.2 **Future Value with Multiple Cash Flows** You plan to make a series of deposits in an individual retirement account. You will deposit £1,000 today, £2,000 in two years, and £2,000 in five years. If you withdraw £1,500 in three years and £1,000 in seven years, assuming no withdrawal penalties, how much will you have after eight years if the interest rate is 7 per cent? What is the present value of these cash flows?

year, compounded monthly for the first six months, increasing thereafter to 18 per cent compounded monthly. Assuming you transfer the €5,000 balance from your existing credit card and make no subsequent payments, how much interest will you owe at the end of the first year?

32 **Calculating Future Values [LO1]** You have an investment that will pay you 1.17 per cent per month. How much will you have per euro invested in one year? In two years?

33 **Calculating Annuity Payments [LO1]** You want to be a millionaire when you retire in 40 years. How much do you have to save each month if you can earn a 10 per cent annual return? How much do you have to save if you wait 10 years before you begin your deposits? 20 years?

34 **Calculating Rates of Return [LO2]** Suppose an investment offers to triple your money in 12 months (don't believe it). What rate of return per quarter are you being offered?

35 **Comparing Cash Flow Streams [LO1]** You've just joined the investment banking firm of Dewey, Cheatum and Howe. They've offered you two different salary arrangements. You can have €120,000 per year for the next two years, or you can have €80,000 per year for the next two years, along with a €45,000 signing bonus today. The bonus is paid immediately, and the salary is paid at the end of each year. If the quoted interest rate is 12 per cent compounded monthly, which do you prefer?

36 **Growing Annuity [LO1]** You have just won the lottery and will receive €1,000,000 in one year. You will receive payments for 30 years, which will increase 5 per cent per year. If the appropriate discount rate is 8 per cent, what is the present value of your winnings?

37 **Growing Annuity [LO1]** Your job pays you only once a year for all the work you did over the previous 12 months. Today, 31 December, you have just received your salary of £50,000, and you plan to spend all of it. However, you want to start saving for retirement beginning next year. You have decided that one year from today you will begin depositing 5 per cent of your annual salary in an account that will earn 11 per cent per year. Your salary will increase at 4 per cent per year throughout your career. How much money will you have on the date of your retirement 40 years from today?

38 **Present Value and Interest Rates [LO1]** What is the relationship between the value of an annuity and the level of interest rates? Suppose you just bought a 20-year annuity of £19,000 per year at the current interest rate of 8 per cent per year. What happens to the value of your investment if interest rates suddenly drop to 3 per cent? What if interest rates suddenly rise to 13 per cent?

39 **Calculating the Number of Payments [LO2]** You're prepared to make monthly payments of €640, beginning at the end of this month, into an account that pays 9 per cent interest compounded monthly. How many payments will you have made when your account balance reaches €20,000?

40 **Calculating Annuity Present Values [LO2]** You want to borrow £100,000 from your local bank to buy a new yacht. You can afford to make monthly payments of £2,000, but no more. Assuming monthly compounding, what is the highest rate you can afford on a 60-month loan?

41 **Calculating Loan Payments [LO2]** You need a 25-year, fixed-rate mortgage to buy a new home for £450,000. Your mortgage bank will lend you the money at a 5.65 per cent APR for this 300-month loan. However, you can afford monthly payments of only £1,500, so you offer to pay off any remaining loan balance at the end of the loan in the form of a single balloon payment. How large will this balloon payment have to be for you to keep your monthly payments at £1,500?

Chapter 5 Discounted Cash Flow Valuation

42 **Present and Future Values [LO1]** The present value of the following cash flow stream is €9,000 when discounted at 8 per cent annually. What is the value of the missing cash flow?

Year	Cash flow (€)
1	1,700
2	?
3	2,100
4	2,800

43 **Calculating Present Values [LO1]** You have just won the Lottery. You will receive £10 million today plus another 10 annual payments that increase by £1 million per year. Thus, in one year, you receive £11 million. In two years you get £12 million, and so on. If the appropriate interest rate is 9 per cent, what is the present value of your winnings?

44 **EAR versus Quoted Rate [LO4]** You have just purchased a new warehouse. To finance the purchase, you've arranged for a 30-year mortgage loan for 80 per cent of the £2,900,000 purchase price. The monthly payment on this loan will be £15,000. What is the APR on this loan? The quoted rate?

45 **Present Value and Break-Even Interest [LO1]** Consider a firm with a contract to sell an asset for £200,000 four years from now. The asset costs £95,000 to produce today. Given a relevant discount rate on this asset of 16 per cent per year, will the firm make a profit on this asset? At what rate does the firm just break even?

46 **Present Value and Multiple Cash Flows [LO1]** What is the present value of SKr4,000 per year, at a discount rate of 10 per cent, if the first payment is received 8 years from now and the last payment is received 25 years from now?

47 **Variable Interest Rates [LO1]** A 15-year annuity pays £1,500 per month, and payments are made at the end of each month. If the interest rate is 11 per cent compounded monthly for the first seven years, and 7 per cent compounded monthly thereafter, what is the present value of the annuity?

48 **Comparing Cash Flow Streams [LO1]** You have your choice of two investment accounts. Investment A is a 20-year annuity that features end-of-month NKr12,000 payments and has an interest rate of 6 per cent compounded monthly. Investment B is an 8 per cent continuously compounded lump sum investment, also good for 15 years. How much money would you need to invest in B today for it to be worth as much as investment A 20 years from now?

49 **Calculating Present Value of a Perpetuity [LO1]** Given an interest rate of 6.2 per cent per year, what is the value at date $t = 7$ of a perpetual stream of 3,500 payments that begins at date $t = 15$?

50 **Calculating APR [LO4]** A local finance company quotes a 16 per cent interest rate on one-year loans. So, if you borrow €25,000, the interest for the year will be €4,000. Because you must repay a total of €29,000 in one year, the finance company requires you to pay €29,000/12, or €2,416.67, per month over the next 12 months. Is this a 16 per cent loan? What rate would legally have to be quoted?

51 **Calculating Present Values [LO1]** A 10-year annuity of twenty £10,000 semi-annual payments will begin 8 years from now, with the first payment coming 8.5 years from now. If the discount rate is 10 per cent compounded monthly, what is the value of this annuity five years from now? What is the value three years from now? What is the current value of the annuity?

52 **Calculating Annuities Due [LO1]** Suppose you are going to receive £15,000 per year for four years. The appropriate interest rate is 10 per cent.

interest per year. She wants to make equal annual payments on each birthday into the account established at the credit union for her retirement fund.

(a) If she starts making these deposits on her 36th birthday and continues to make deposits until she is 65 (the last deposit will be on her 65th birthday), what amount must she deposit annually to be able to make the desired withdrawals at retirement?

(b) Suppose your friend has just inherited a large sum of money. Rather than make equal annual payments, she has decided to make one lump sum payment on her 35th birthday to cover her retirement needs. What amount does she have to deposit?

(c) Suppose your friend's employer will contribute £1,500 to the account every year as part of the company's profit-sharing plan. In addition, your friend expects a £150,000 distribution from a family trust fund on her 55th birthday, which she will also put into the retirement account. What amount must she deposit annually now to be able to make the desired withdrawals at retirement?

66 **Calculating the Number of Periods [LO2]** Your Christmas skiing holiday was great, but it unfortunately ran a bit over budget. All is not lost: you just received an offer in the mail to transfer your €15,000 balance from your current credit card, which charges an annual rate of 21.4 per cent, to a new credit card charging a rate of 5 per cent. How much faster could you pay the loan off by making your planned monthly payments of €300 with the new card? What if there was a 2 per cent fee charged on any balances transferred?

67 **Future Value and Multiple Cash Flows [LO1]** An insurance company is offering a new policy to its customers. Typically, the policy is bought by a parent or grandparent for a child at the child's birth. The details of the policy are as follows. The purchaser (say, the parent) makes the following six payments to the insurance company:

First birthday:	£900
Second birthday:	£900
Third birthday:	£1,000
Fourth birthday:	£1,000
Fifth birthday:	£1,100
Sixth birthday:	£1,100

After the child's sixth birthday, no more payments are made. When the child reaches age 65, he or she receives £500,000. If the relevant interest rate is 12 per cent for the first six years and 8 per cent for all subsequent years, is the policy worth buying?

68 **Calculating a Balloon Payment [LO2]** You have just arranged for a €750,000 mortgage to finance the purchase of a large tract of land. The mortgage has an 8.1 per cent APR, and it calls for monthly payments over the next 30 years. However, the loan has an eight-year balloon payment, meaning that the loan must be paid off then. How big will the balloon payment be?

69 **Calculating Interest Rates [LO4]** A financial planning service offers a university savings programme. The plan calls for you to make six annual payments of £9,000 each, with the first payment occurring today, your child's 12th birthday. Beginning on your child's 18th birthday, the plan will provide £20,000 per year for four years. What return is this investment offering?

70 **Break-Even Investment Returns [LO4]** Your financial planner offers you two different investment plans. Plan X is a 100,000 dinari annual perpetuity. Plan Y is a 20-year, 150,000 dinari annual annuity. Both plans will make their first payment

one year from today. At what discount rate would you be indifferent between these two plans?

71 **Perpetual Cash Flows [LO1]**   What is the value of an investment that pays £15,000 every *other* year for ever, if the first payment occurs one year from today and the discount rate is 10 per cent compounded daily? What is the value today if the first payment occurs four years from today?

72 **Ordinary Annuities and Annuities Due [LO1]**   As discussed in the text, an annuity due is identical to an ordinary annuity except that the periodic payments occur at the beginning of each period and not at the end of the period. Show that the relationship between the value of an ordinary annuity and the value of an otherwise equivalent annuity due is

$$\text{Annuity due value} = \text{Ordinary annuity value} \times (1 + r)$$

Show this for both present and future values.

73 **Calculating Growing Annuities [LO1]**   You have 40 years left until retirement and want to retire with £2 million. Your salary is paid annually, and you will receive £40,000 at the end of the current year. Your salary will increase at 3 per cent per year, and you can earn an 11 per cent return on the money you invest. If you save a constant percentage of your salary, what percentage of your salary must you save each year?

74 **Calculating EAR [LO4]**   A pawnbroker's shop is in the business of making personal loans to walk-in customers. The shop makes only one-week loans at 7 per cent interest per week.

(a)   What APR must the shop report to its customers?

(b)   Now suppose the shop makes one-week loans at 7 per cent discount interest per week (see Problem 59). What's the APR now?

(c)   The pawnbroker also makes one-month add-on interest loans at 7 per cent discount interest per week. Thus if you borrow €100 for one month (four weeks), the interest will be (€100 × 1.07⁴) − 100 = €31.08. Because this is discount interest, your net loan proceeds today will be €68.92. You must then repay the shop €100 at the end of the month. To help you out, though, the shop lets you pay off this €100 in instalments of €25 per week. What is the APR of this loan?

75 **Present Value of a Growing Perpetuity [LO1]**   What is the equation for the present value of a growing perpetuity with a payment of C one period from today if the payments grow by C each period?

76 **Rule of 72 [LO4]**   Earlier, we discussed the Rule of 72, a useful approximation for many interest rates and periods for the time it takes a lump sum to double in value. For a 10 per cent interest rate, show that the 'Rule of 73' is slightly better. For what rate is the Rule of 72 exact? (*Hint:* Use the Solver function in Microsoft Excel.)

77 **Rule of 69.3 [LO4]**   A corollary to the Rule of 72 is the Rule of 69.3. The Rule of 69.3 is exactly correct except for rounding when interest rates are compounded continuously. Prove the Rule of 69.3 for continuously compounded interest.

MINI CASE

The MBA Decision

Ben Bates graduated from university six years ago with a finance undergraduate degree. Although he is satisfied with his current job, his goal is to become an investment banker. He feels that an MBA degree would allow him to achieve this goal. After examining schools, he has narrowed his choice to either Wilton University or Mount Perry University. Although internships are encouraged by both schools, to get class credit for the internship no salary can be paid. Other than internships, neither school will allow its students to work while enrolled in its MBA programme.

Ben currently works at the money management firm of Dewey and Louis. His annual salary at the firm is £75,000 per year, and his salary is expected to increase at 3 per cent per year until retirement. He is currently 28 years old and expects to work for 38 more years. His current job includes a fully paid health insurance plan, and his current average tax rate is 35 per cent. Ben has a savings account with enough money to cover the entire cost of his MBA programme.

The Ritter College of Business at Wilton University is one of the top MBA programmes in the country. The MBA degree requires two years of full-time enrolment at the university. The annual tuition fee is £30,000, payable at the beginning of each school year. Books and other supplies are estimated to cost £2,500 per year. Ben expects that after graduation from Wilton he will receive a job offer for about £98,000 per year, with a £15,000 signing bonus. The salary at this job will increase at 4 per cent per year. Because of the higher salary, his average income tax rate will increase to 40 per cent.

The Bradley School of Business at Mount Perry University began its MBA programme 16 years ago. The Bradley School is smaller and less well known than the Ritter College. Bradley offers an accelerated one-year programme, with a tuition cost of £20,000 to be paid upon matriculation. Books and other supplies for the programme are expected to cost £3,500. Ben thinks that he will receive an offer of £90,000 per year upon graduation, with a £10,000 signing bonus. The salary at this job will increase at 3.5 per cent per year. His average tax rate at this level of income will be 35 per cent.

Both schools offer a health insurance plan that will cost £3,000 per year, payable at the beginning of the year. Ben also estimates that room and board expenses will cost £20,000 per year at both schools. The appropriate discount rate is 6.5 per cent.

QUESTIONS

1 How does Ben's age affect his decision to get an MBA?

2 What other, perhaps non-quantifiable, factors affect Ben's decision to get an MBA?

3 Assuming all salaries are paid at the end of each year, what is the best option for Ben from a strictly financial standpoint?

4 Ben believes that the appropriate analysis is to calculate the future value of each option. How would you evaluate this statement?

5 What initial salary would Ben need to receive to make him indifferent between attending Wilton University and staying in his current position?

6 Suppose, instead of being able to pay cash for his MBA, Ben must borrow the money. The current borrowing rate is 5.4 per cent. How would this affect his decision?

CHAPTER 6

Bond Valuation

KEY NOTATIONS

C	Coupon
FV	Face value of bond
h	Inflation rate
PV	Present value
r	Interest rate or discount rate
t	Number of periods
YTM	Yield to maturity

LEARNING OBJECTIVES

After studying this chapter, you should understand:

LO1   Important bond features and types of bond.
LO2   Bond values and yields, and why they fluctuate.
LO3   Bond ratings, and what they mean.
LO4   The impact of inflation on interest rates.
LO5   The term structure of interest rates, and the determinants of bond yields.

IN ITS MOST BASIC FORM, a bond is a fairly simple thing. You lend a company some money, say €1,000. The company pays you interest regularly, and it repays the original loan amount of €1,000 at some point in the future. Bonds can also have complex features, and in 2008 a type of bond known as *a mortgage-backed security*, or *MBS*, caused havoc in the global financial system.

An MBS, as the name suggests, is a bond that is backed by a pool of home mortgages. The bondholders receive payments derived from payments on the underlying mortgages, and these payments can be divided up in various ways to create different classes of bond. Defaults on the underlying mortgages lead to losses for MBS bondholders. Since most mortgage-backed securities were held and issued by banks, the collapse in the housing market (particularly in the US) led to a global credit crunch in 2008 that nearly halted the global business economy. Because some of the world's largest banks had to be rescued through state bail-outs, many governments had to implement stringent public sector spending cuts and tax increases to bring budgets back into balance. This was still affecting European countries in 2011, and the repercussions are likely to be felt for a number of years yet.

Our goal in this chapter is to introduce you to bonds. We begin by showing how the techniques we developed in Chapters 4 and 5 can be applied to bond valuation. From there, we go on to discuss bond features, and how bonds are bought and sold. One important thing we learn is that bond values depend, in large part, on interest rates. We therefore close the chapter with an examination of interest rates and their behaviour.

6.1   Bonds and Bond Valuation

When a corporation or government wishes to borrow money from the public on a long-term basis, it usually does so by issuing or selling debt securities that are generically called *bonds*. In this section we describe the various features of corporate bonds, and some of the terminology associated with bonds. We then discuss the cash flows associated with a bond, and how bonds can be valued using our discounted cash flow procedure.

Bond Features and Prices

As we mentioned in our previous chapter, a bond is normally an interest-only loan, meaning that the borrower will pay the interest every period, but none of the principal will be repaid until the end of the loan. For example, suppose Pixie plc wants to borrow £1,000 for 30 years. The interest rate on similar debt issued by similar corporations is 12 per cent. Pixie will thus pay 0.12 × £1,000 = £120 in interest every year for 30 years. At the end of 30 years Pixie will repay the £1,000. As this example suggests, a bond is a fairly simple financing arrangement. There is, however, a rich jargon associated with bonds, so we shall use this example to define some of the more important terms.

In our example, the £120 regular interest payments that Pixie promises to make are called the bond's **coupons**. Because the coupon is constant and paid every year, the type of bond we are describing is sometimes called a *level coupon bond*. The amount that will be repaid at the end of the loan is called the bond's **face value**, or **par value**. As in our example, this par value is usually £1,000 for corporate bonds, and a bond that sells for its par value is called a *par value bond*. Government bonds frequently have much larger face, or par, values. Finally, the annual coupon divided by the face value is called the **coupon rate** on the bond: in this case, because £120/1,000 = 12%, the bond has a 12 per cent coupon rate.

The number of years until the face value is paid is called the bond's time to **maturity**. A corporate bond will frequently have a maturity of 30 years when it is originally issued, but this varies. Once the bond has been issued, the number of years to maturity declines as time goes by.

> **coupon**
> The stated interest payment made on a bond.
>
> **face value**
> The principal amount of a bond that is repaid at the end of the term. Also called *par value*.
>
> **coupon rate**
> The annual coupon divided by the face value of a bond.
>
> **maturity**
> The specified date on which the principal amount of a bond is paid.

Bond Values and Yields

As time passes, interest rates change in the marketplace. The cash flows from a bond, however, stay the same. As a result, the value of the bond will fluctuate. When interest rates rise, the present value of the bond's remaining cash flows declines, and the bond is worth less. When interest rates fall, the bond is worth more.

To determine the value of a bond at a particular point in time, we need to know the number of periods remaining until maturity, the face value, the coupon, and the market interest rate for bonds with similar features. The interest rate required in the market on a bond is called the bond's **yield to maturity (YTM)**. This rate is sometimes called the bond's *yield* for short. Given all this information, we can calculate the present value of the cash flows as an estimate of the bond's current market value.

> **yield to maturity (YTM)**
> The rate required in the market on a bond.

For example, suppose Pixie plc were to issue a bond with 10 years to maturity. The Pixie bond has an annual coupon of £80. Similar bonds have a yield to maturity of 8 per cent. Based on our preceding discussion, the Pixie bond will pay £80 per year for the next 10 years in coupon interest. In 10 years, Pixie will pay £1,000 to the owner of the bond. The cash flows from the bond are shown in Fig. 6.1. What would this bond sell for?

As illustrated in Fig. 6.1, the Pixie bond's cash flows have an annuity component (the coupons) and a lump sum (the face value paid at maturity). We thus estimate the market value of the bond by calculating the present value of these two components separately and adding the results together. First, at the going rate of 8 per cent, the present value of the £1,000 paid in 10 years is

$$\text{Present value} = £1{,}000/1.08^{10} = £1{,}000/2.1589 = £463.19$$

Chapter 6 Bond Valuation

FIGURE **6.1**

Cash flows

Year	0	1	2	3	4	5	6	7	8	9	10
Coupon		£80	£80	£80	£80	£80	£80	£80	£80	£80	£80
Face value											1,000
		£80	£80	£80	£80	£80	£80	£80	£80	£80	£1,080

As shown, the Pixie bond has an annual coupon of £80 and a face, or per, value of £1,000 paid at maturity in 10 years.

Figure 6.1 Cash flows for Pixie plc bond

Second, the bond offers £80 per year for 10 years; the present value of this annuity stream is

$$\text{Annuity present value} = £80 \times (1 - 1/1.08^{10})/0.08$$
$$= £80 \times (1 - 1/2.1589)/0.08$$
$$= £80 \times 6.7101$$
$$= £536.81$$

We can now add the values for the two parts together to get the bond's value:

$$\text{Total bond value} = £463.19 + 536.81 = £1,000$$

This bond sells for exactly its face value. This is not a coincidence. The going interest rate in the market is 8 per cent. Considered as an interest-only loan, what interest rate does this bond have? With an £80 coupon, this bond pays exactly 8 per cent interest only when it sells for £1,000.

To illustrate what happens as interest rates change, suppose a year has gone by. The Pixie bond now has nine years to maturity. If the interest rate in the market has risen to 10 per cent, what will the bond be worth? To find out, we repeat the present value calculations with 9 years instead of 10, and a 10 per cent yield instead of an 8 per cent yield. First, the present value of the £1,000 paid in nine years at 10 per cent is

$$\text{Present value} = £1,000/1.10^9 = £1,000/2.3579 = £424.10$$

Second, the bond now offers £80 per year for nine years; the present value of this annuity stream at 10 per cent is

$$\text{Annuity present value} = £80 \times (1 - 1/1.10^9)/0.10$$
$$= £80 \times (1 - 1/2.3579)/0.10$$
$$= £80 \times 5.7590$$
$$= £460.72$$

We can now add the values for the two parts together to get the bond's value:

$$\text{Total bond value} = £424.10 + 460.72 = £884.82$$

Therefore the bond should sell for about £885. In the vernacular, we say that this bond, with its 8 per cent coupon, is priced to yield 10 per cent at £885.

The Pixie plc bond now sells for less than its £1,000 face value. Why? The market interest rate is 10 per cent. Considered as an interest-only loan of £1,000, this bond pays only 8 per cent, its coupon rate. Because this bond pays less than the going rate, investors are

TABLE 6.1

Finding the value of a bond

Bond value = $C \times [1 - 1/(1 + r)^t]/r + F/(1 + r)^t$

where

C = coupon paid each period

r = rate per period

t = number of periods

F = bond's face value

Finding the yield on a bond

Given a bond value, coupon, time to maturity and face value, it is possible to find the implicit discount rate, or yield to maturity, by trial and error only. To do this, try different discount rates until the calculated bond value equals the given value (or let a financial calculator do it for you). Remember that increasing the rate decreases the bond value.

Table 6.1 Summary of bond valuation

Current Events

EXAMPLE 6.2

A bond has a quoted price of £108,042. It has a face value of £100,000, a semi-annual coupon of £3,000, and a maturity of five years. What is its current yield? What is its yield to maturity? Which is bigger? Why?

Notice that this bond makes semi-annual payments of £3,000, so the annual payment is £6,000. The current yield is thus £6,000/108,042 = 5.55 per cent. To calculate the yield to maturity, refer back to Example 6.1. In this case the bond pays £3,000 every six months, and has 10 six-month periods until maturity. So we need to find r as follows:

$$£108,042 = £3,000 \times [1 - 1/(1 + r)^{10}]/r + 100,000/(1 + r)^{10}$$

After some trial and error we find that r is equal to 2.1 per cent. But the tricky part is that this 2.1 per cent is the yield *per six months*. We have to double it to get the yield to maturity, so the yield to maturity is 4.2 per cent, which is less than the current yield. The reason is that the current yield ignores the built-in loss of the premium between now and maturity.

Bond Yields

EXAMPLE 6.3

You're looking at two bonds identical in every way except for their coupons and, of course, their prices. Both have 12 years to maturity. The first bond has a 10 per cent annual coupon rate and sells for £93,508. The second has a 12 per cent annual coupon rate. What do you think it would sell for?

Because the two bonds are similar, they will be priced to yield about the same rate. We first need to calculate the yield on the 10 per cent coupon bond. Proceeding as before, we know that the yield must be greater than 10 per cent, because the bond is selling at a discount. The bond has a fairly long maturity of 12 years. We've seen that long-term bond prices are relatively sensitive to interest rate changes, so the yield is probably close to 10 per cent. A little trial and error reveals that the yield is actually 11 per cent:

$$
\begin{aligned}
\text{Bond value} &= £10,000 \times (1 - 1/1.11^{12})/0.11 + 100,000/1.11^{12} \\
&= £10,000 \times 6.4924 + 100,000/3.4985 \\
&= £64,924 + 28,584 \\
&= £93,508
\end{aligned}
$$

With an 11 per cent yield, the second bond will sell at a premium because of its £12,000 coupon. Its value is

$$\text{Bond value} = £12,000 \times (1 - 1/1.11^{12})/0.11 + 100,000/1.11^{12}$$
$$= £12,000 \times 6.4924 + 100,000/3.4985$$
$$= £77,908 + 28,584$$
$$= £106,492$$

Spreadsheet Strategies

How to Calculate Bond Prices and Yields Using a Spreadsheet

Most spreadsheets have fairly elaborate routines available for calculating bond values and yields; many of these routines involve details we have not discussed. However, setting up a simple spreadsheet to calculate prices or yields is straightforward, as our next two spreadsheets show.

Suppose we have a bond with 22 years to maturity, a coupon rate of 8 per cent, and a yield to maturity of 9 per cent. If the bond makes semi-annual payments, what is its price today?

	B8	f_x =PRICE(B1,B2,B3,B4,B5,B6)		
	A	B	C	D
1	Settlement Date	01/01/2010		
2	Maturity Date	01/01/2032		
3	Annual Coupon Rate	8%		
4	Yield to Maturity	9%		
5	Face Value (% of par)	100		
6	Coupons per Year	2		
7				
8	Bond Price (% of par)	90.49		

The formula for the bond price is given in the formula bar, and is '=PRICE(B1,B2,B3,B4,B5,B6)'. In our spreadsheet, notice that we had to enter two dates: a settlement date and a maturity date. The settlement date is just the date when you actually pay for the bond, and the maturity date is the day the bond actually matures. In most of our problems we don't explicitly have these dates, so we have to make them up. For example, because our bond has 22 years to maturity, we just picked 1/1/2010 (1 January 2010) as the settlement date and 1/1/2032 (1 January 2032) as the maturity date. Any two dates would do as long as they are exactly 22 years apart, but these are particularly easy to work with. Finally, notice that we had to enter the coupon rate and yield to maturity in annual terms and then explicitly provide the number of coupon payments per year.

Now suppose we have a bond with 22 years to maturity, a coupon rate of 8 per cent, and a price of €960.17. If the bond makes semi-annual payments, what is its yield to maturity?

	A	B
1	Settlement Date	01/01/2010
2	Maturity Date	01/01/2032
3	Annual Coupon Rate	8%
4	Bond Price (% of par)	96.017
5	Face Value (% of par)	100
6	Coupons per Year	2
7		
8	Yield to Maturity	8.40%

The formula for yield to maturity is '=YIELD(B1,B2,B3,B4,B5,B6)'.

> **CONCEPT QUESTIONS**
>
> 6.1a What are the cash flows associated with a bond?
> 6.1b What is the general expression for the value of a bond?
> 6.1c Is it true that the only risk associated with owning a bond is that the issuer will not make all the payments? Explain.

6.2 More about Bond Features

In this section we continue our discussion of corporate debt by describing in some detail the basic terms and features that make up a typical long-term corporate bond. We discuss additional issues associated with long-term debt in subsequent sections.

Securities issued by corporations may be classified roughly as *equity securities* or *debt securities*. At the crudest level, a debt represents something that must be repaid; it is the result of borrowing money. When corporations borrow, they generally promise to make regularly scheduled interest payments, and to repay the original amount borrowed (that is, the principal). The person or firm making the loan is called the *creditor* or *lender*. The corporation borrowing the money is called the *debtor* or *borrower*.

From a financial point of view, the main differences between debt and equity are the following.

1 Debt is not an ownership interest in the firm. Creditors generally do not have voting power.

2 The corporation's payment of interest on debt is considered a cost of doing business, and is fully tax deductible. Dividends paid to shareholders are *not* tax deductible.

3 Unpaid debt is a liability of the firm. If it is not paid, the creditors can legally claim the assets of the firm. This action can result in liquidation or reorganization, two of the possible consequences of bankruptcy. Thus one of the costs of issuing debt is the possibility of financial failure. This possibility does not arise when equity is issued.

Is It Debt or Equity?

Sometimes it is not clear whether a particular security is debt or equity. For example, suppose a corporation issues a perpetual bond with interest payable solely from corporate income if and only if earned. Whether this is really a debt is hard to say, and is primarily a legal and semantic issue. Courts and tax authorities would have the final say.

Corporations are adept at creating exotic, hybrid securities that have many features of equity but are treated as debt. Obviously, the distinction between debt and equity is important for tax purposes. So one reason why corporations try to create a debt security that is really equity is to obtain the tax benefits of debt and the bankruptcy benefits of equity.

As a general rule, equity represents an ownership interest, and it is a residual claim. This means that equity holders are paid after debt holders. As a result, the risks and benefits associated with owning debt and equity are different. To give just one example, note that the maximum reward for owning a debt security is ultimately fixed by the amount of the loan, whereas there is no upper limit to the potential reward from owning an equity interest.

Long-Term Debt: The Basics

Ultimately, all long-term debt securities are promises made by the issuing firm to pay principal when due, and to make timely interest payments on the unpaid balance. Beyond this, a number of features distinguish these securities from one another. We discuss some of these features next.

TABLE 6.2

Term		Explanation
Amount of issue	€1 billion	The company issued €1 billion worth of bonds.
Date of issue	3/02/2010	The bonds were sold on 3 February 2010.
Maturity	03/02/2015	The bonds mature on 3 February 2015.
Face value	€1,000	The denomination of the bonds is €1,000.
Annual coupon	3.25	Each bondholder will receive €32.50 per bond per year (3.25% of face value).
Offer price	99.864	The offer price was 99.864% of the €1,000 face value, or €998.64, per bond.
Coupon payment dates	1 August, 1 February	Coupons of €32.50/2 = €16.25 will be paid on these dates.
Security	None	The bonds are guaranteed by the Kingdom of Spain.
Sinking fund	None	The bonds have no sinking fund.
Call provision	None	The bonds do not have a call provision.
Rating	Moody's Aaa; S&P AA+; Fitch AAA	The bonds have a very high credit rating.

Table 6.2 Features of an ICO bond

The maturity of a long-term debt instrument is the length of time the debt remains outstanding with some unpaid balance. Debt securities can be *short-term* (with maturities of one year or less) or *long-term* (with maturities of more than one year).[1] Short-term debt is sometimes referred to as *unfunded debt*.[2]

Debt securities are typically called *notes*, *debentures* or *bonds*. Strictly speaking, a bond is a secured debt. However, in common usage the word 'bond' refers to all kinds of secured and unsecured debt. We shall therefore continue to use the term generically to refer to long-term debt. Also, usually the only difference between a note and a bond is the original maturity. Issues with an original maturity of 10 years or less are often called notes. Longer-term issues are called bonds.

The two major forms of long-term debt are public issue and privately placed. We concentrate on public-issue bonds. Most of what we say about them holds true for private-issue, long-term debt as well. The main difference between public-issue and privately placed debt is that the latter is placed directly with a lender and not offered to the public. Because this is a private transaction, the specific terms are up to the parties involved.

There are many other aspects of long-term debt, including such things as security, call features, sinking funds, ratings and protective covenants. Table 6.2 illustrates these features for a bond issued by the Instituto de Crédito Oficial (ICO), the Spanish state financing organization. If some of these terms are unfamiliar, have no fear. We shall discuss them all presently.

Many of these features will be detailed in the bond indenture, so we discuss this first.

The Indenture

> **indenture**
> The written agreement between the corporation and the lender detailing the terms of the debt issue.

The **indenture** is the written agreement between the corporation (the borrower) and its creditors. It is sometimes referred to as the *deed of trust*.[3] Usually, a trustee (a bank, perhaps) is appointed by the corporation to represent the bondholders. The trust company must: (1) make sure the terms of the indenture are obeyed; (2) manage the sinking fund (described in the following pages); and (3) represent the bondholders in default – that is, if the company defaults on its payments to them.

Protective Covenants A **protective covenant** is that part of the indenture or loan agreement that limits certain actions a company might otherwise wish to take during the term of the loan. Protective covenants can be classified into two types: negative covenants and positive (or affirmative) covenants.

A *negative covenant* is a 'thou shalt not' type of covenant. It limits or prohibits actions the company might take. Here are some typical examples:

- The firm must limit the amount of dividends it pays according to some formula.

- The firm cannot pledge any assets to other lenders.

- The firm cannot merge with another firm.

- The firm cannot sell or lease any major assets without approval by the lender.

- The firm cannot issue additional long-term debt.

A *positive covenant* is a 'thou shalt' type of covenant. It specifies an action the company agrees to take, or a condition the company must abide by. Here are some examples:

- The company must maintain its working capital at or above some specified minimum level.

- The company must periodically furnish audited financial statements to the lender.

- The firm must maintain any collateral or security in good condition.

This is only a partial list of covenants; a particular indenture may feature many different ones.

CONCEPT QUESTIONS	6.2a	What are the distinguishing features of debt compared with equity?
	6.2b	What is the indenture? What are protective covenants? Give some examples.
	6.2c	What is a sinking fund?

6.3 Bond Ratings

Firms frequently pay to have their debt rated. The three leading bond-rating firms are Moody's, Standard & Poor's (S&P) and Fitch. The debt ratings are an assessment of the creditworthiness of the corporate issuer. The definitions of creditworthiness used by Moody's, S&P and Fitch are based on how likely the firm is to default, and on the protection that creditors have in the event of a default.

It is important to recognize that bond ratings are concerned *only* with the possibility of default. Earlier we discussed interest rate risk, which we defined as the risk of a change in the value of a bond resulting from a change in interest rates. Bond ratings do not address this issue. As a result, the price of a highly rated bond can still be quite volatile.

Bond ratings are constructed from information supplied by the corporation. The rating classes, and some information concerning them, are shown in Table 6.3.

The highest rating a firm's debt can have is AAA or Aaa, and such debt is judged to be the best quality and to have the lowest degree of risk. A large part of corporate borrowing takes the form of low-grade, or 'junk', bonds. If these low-grade corporate bonds are rated at all, they are rated below investment grade by the major rating agencies. Investment-grade bonds are bonds rated at least BBB by S&P and Fitch, or Baa by Moody's.

Rating agencies don't always agree. To illustrate, some bonds are known as 'crossover' or '5B' bonds. For example, in April 2008 CenterPoint Energy sold an issue of 10-year notes rated BBB by S&P and Ba1 by Moody's.

A bond's credit rating can change as the issuer's financial strength improves or deteriorates. For example, in January 2010 S&P downgraded Japan Airlines' long-term debt to junk bond status. Bonds that drop into junk territory like this are called *fallen angels*. After

TABLE 6.3

Moody's		Investment-quality bond ratings				Low-quality, speculative and/or 'junk' bond ratings					
		High grade		**Medium grade**		**Low grade**		**Very low grade**			
Moody's		Aaa	Aa	A	Baa	Ba	B	Caa	Ca	C	
Standard & Poor's		AAA	AA	A	BBB	BB	B	CCC	CC	C	D
Fitch		AAA	AA+	A	BBB	BB	B	CCC			D

Moody's	S&P	Fitch	
Aaa	AAA	AAA	Debt rated Aaa and AAA has the highest rating. Capacity to pay interest and principal is extremely strong.
Aa	AA	AA+	Debt rated Aa, AA and AA+ has a very strong capacity to pay interest and repay principal. Together with the highest rating, this group constitutes the high-grade bond class.
A	A	A	Debt rated A has a strong capacity to pay interest and repay principal, although it is somewhat more susceptible to the adverse effects of changes in circumstances and economic conditions than debt in high-rated categories.
Baa	BBB	BBB	Debt rated Baa and BBB is regarded as having an adequate capacity to pay interest and repay principal. Whereas it normally exhibits adequate protection parameters, adverse economic conditions or changing circumstances are more likely to lead to a weakened capacity to pay interest and repay principal for debt in this category than in higher-rated categories. These bonds are medium-grade obligations.
Ba; B Caa Ca C	BB; B CCC CC C	BB; B CCC	Debt rated in these categories is regarded, on balance, as predominantly speculative with respect to capacity to pay interest and repay principal in accordance with the terms of the obligation. BB and Ba indicate the lowest degree of speculation, and Ca, CC, and C the highest degree of speculation. Although such debt is likely to have some quality and protective characteristics, these are outweighed by large uncertainties or major risk exposures to adverse conditions. Issues rated C by Moody's are typically in default.
	D	D	Debt rated D is in default, and payment of interest and/or repayment of principal is in arrears.

Note: At times, Moody's, S&P and Fitch use adjustments (called notches) to these ratings. S&P uses plus and minus signs: A+ is the strongest A rating and A− the weakest. Moody's uses a 1, 2, or 3 designation, with 1 being the highest.

Table 6.3 Bond ratings

2 The coupon rate has a floor and a ceiling, meaning that the coupon is subject to a minimum and a maximum. In this case the coupon rate is said to be 'capped', and the upper and lower rates are sometimes called the *collar*.

A particularly interesting type of floating-rate bond is an *inflation-linked* bond. Such bonds have coupons that are adjusted according to the rate of inflation (the principal amount may be adjusted as well). The UK and French governments are the biggest European issuers of inflation-linked bonds, and they are called inflation-linked gilts (ILGs) in the UK and OATi and OAT€i in France. Other countries, including the US, Germany, Greece, Italy and Iceland, have issued similar securities.

Other Types of Bond

Many bonds have unusual or exotic features. So-called *catastrophe*, or *cat*, *bonds* provide an interesting example. In December 2009 Swiss Reinsurance Company Ltd issued $150 million in cat bonds (reinsurance companies sell insurance to insurance companies). These cat bonds, which matured in late 2010, were issued at a large discount to par value. Investors in the cat bond would have received a high return if no trigger events (such as hurricanes, flooding or earthquakes) occurred. However, in the event of a major natural disaster, investors would lose their full investment.

The largest single cat bond issue to date is a series of six bonds sold by Merna Reinsurance in 2007. The six bond issues were to cover various catastrophes the company faced owing to its reinsurance of State Farm. The six bonds totalled about $1.2 billion in par value, a large portion of the record $7 billion in cat bonds issued during 2007.

At this point, cat bonds probably seem pretty risky. It might therefore be surprising to learn that, since cat bonds were first issued in 1997, only one has not been paid in full. Because of Hurricane Katrina, bondholders in that one issue lost $190 million.

Another possible bond feature is a *warrant*. A warrant gives the buyer of a bond the right to purchase shares of equity in the company at a fixed price. Such a right would be very valuable if the share price climbed substantially (a later chapter discusses this subject in greater depth). Because of the value of this feature, bonds with warrants are often issued at a very low coupon rate.

As these examples illustrate, bond features are really limited only by the imaginations of the parties involved. Unfortunately, there are far too many variations for us to cover in detail here. We therefore close this discussion by mentioning a few of the more common types.

Income bonds are similar to conventional bonds, except that coupon payments depend on company income. Specifically, coupons are paid to bondholders only if the firm's income is sufficient. This would appear to be an attractive feature, but income bonds are not very common.

A *convertible bond* can be swapped for a fixed number of shares of equity any time before maturity at the holder's option. Convertibles are relatively common, but the number has been decreasing in recent years.

A *put bond* allows the *holder* to force the issuer to buy back the bond at a stated price. For example, 3i Group plc, the private equity firm, has bonds outstanding that allow the holder to force 3i Group to buy the bonds back at 100 per cent of face value if certain relevant 'risk' events happen. One such event is a change in credit rating by Moody's or S&P from investment grade to lower than investment grade. The put feature is therefore just the reverse of the call provision.

A given bond may have many unusual features. Two of the most recent exotic bonds are *CoCo bonds*, which have a coupon payment, and *NoNo bonds*, which are zero coupon bonds. CoCo and NoNo bonds are contingent convertible, puttable, callable, subordinated bonds. The contingent convertible clause is similar to the normal conversion feature, except that the contingent feature must be met. For example, a contingent feature may require that the company equity trade at 110 per cent of the conversion price for 20 out of the most recent 30 days. Because they are so complex, valuation of NoNo and CoCo bonds is exceptionally difficult.

6.4a   Why might an income bond be attractive to a corporation with volatile cash flows? Can you think of a reason why income bonds are not more popular?

6.4b   What do you think would be the effect of a put feature on a bond's coupon? How about a convertibility feature? Why?

6.5   Bond Markets

Bonds are bought and sold in enormous quantities every day. You may be surprised to learn that the trading volume in bonds on a typical day is many, many times larger than the trading volume in equities (by *trading volume* we simply mean the amount of money that changes hands). Here is a finance trivia question: where does most trading of financial securities take place? Most people would guess the stock exchanges. In fact, the largest securities market in the world in terms of trading volume is the government treasury market.

How Bonds Are Bought and Sold

Most trading in bonds takes place over the counter, or OTC, which means there is no particular place where buying and selling occur. Instead, dealers around the world stand ready to buy and sell. The various dealers are connected electronically. In 2010 the London Stock Exchange introduced a new electronic trading system for bonds that allowed private investors to buy bonds in denominations of £1,000. This retail market for individuals was a new innovation for UK bonds, since most British bonds have a face value of at least £50,000. In the Eurozone the main bond markets are Deutsche Böerse and Euronext, where many corporate bonds are traded through an electronic trading system.

One reason why the bond markets are so big is that the number of bond issues far exceeds the number of equity issues. There are two reasons for this. First, a corporation would typically have only one ordinary equity issue outstanding (there are exceptions to this, which we discuss in our next chapter). However, a single large corporation could easily have a dozen or more note and bond issues outstanding. Beyond this, government and local borrowing is simply enormous. For example, many large cities will have a wide variety of notes and bonds outstanding, representing money borrowed to pay for things such as roads, sewers and schools. When you think about how many large cities there are in the world, you begin to get the picture!

Although the total volume of trading in bonds far exceeds that in equities, only a small fraction of the total bond issues that exist actually trade on a given day. This fact, combined with the lack of transparency in the bond market, means that it can be difficult or impossible to get up-to-date prices on individual bonds, particularly for smaller corporate or municipal issues. Instead, a variety of sources of estimated prices exist and are commonly used.

Bond Price Reporting

In recent years, transparency in the corporate bond market has improved dramatically. The advent of high-speed Internet connections has allowed real-time updates on bond prices and trading volumes directly from the stock exchange. Our nearby *Work the Web* box shows you how to get this information.

FIGURE 6.4

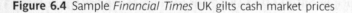

UK GILTS - cash market
www.ft.com/gilts

Jan 8	Price £	Day's chng	W'ks chng	Int yield	Red yield	Red yield Day's chng	W'ks chng	Mth's chng	Year chng	52 Week High	Low	Amnt £m	Last xd date	Interest due
Shorts (Lives up to Five Years)														
Tr 4.75pc '10	101.75	-0.04	-0.12	4.67	0.41	+0.01	+0.02	+0.01	-0.62	105.39	101.60	21,285	28/11	7 Jun/Dec
Tr 6.25pc '10	104.96	-0.04	-0.10	5.95	0.53	-0.01	-0.02	-0.05	-0.47	109.97	104.74	6,719	16/11	25 May/Nov
Tr 3.25pc '11	103.74	-0.01	+0.12	3.13	1.26	0.00	-0.04	+0.12	-0.88	115.22	102.24	15,747	28/11	7 Jun/Dec
Tr 4.25pc '11	104.02	-0.01	+0.02	4.09	0.74	-0.02	-0.05	+0.09	-0.93	106.45	103.78	23,651	29/08	7 Mar/Sep
Cn 9pc Ln '11	111.98	-0.05	-0.08	8.03	0.95	-0.01	-0.04	+0.08	-0.77	118.61	99.40	7,312	01/07	12 Jan/Jul
Tr 5pc '12	107.30	-0.01	+0.04	4.66	1.54	-0.01	-0.01	+0.20	-0.68	109.96	106.56	26,867	29/08	7 Mar/Sep
Tr 5.25pc '12	108.08	-0.02	+0.02	4.86	1.80	0.00	+0.01	+0.24	-0.51	111.11	107.21	21,583	28/11	7 Jun/Dec
Tr 9pc '12	117.81	-0.03	-0.07	7.64	1.87	-0.01	+0.01	+0.22	-0.56	124.11	116.18	204	28/07	6 Feb/Aug
Tr 8pc '13	119.98	-0.04	-0.15	6.67	2.34	0.00	+0.05	+0.26	-0.23	125.99	119.27	8,377	16/09	27 Mar/Sep
Tr 4.5pc '13	106.80	-0.01	-0.01	4.21	2.25	0.00	+0.04	+0.24	-0.23	109.94	105.08	29,287	29/08	7 Mar/Sep
Tr 2.25pc '14	98.15	-0.03	-0.09	2.29	2.72	+0.01	+0.08	+0.30	-	120.73	95.03	29,123	29/08	7 Mar/Sep
Tr 5pc '14	109.28	-0.04	-0.13	4.57	2.86	+0.01	+0.07	+0.28	+0.14	115.60	108.74	28,057	29/08	7 Mar/Sep
Five to Ten Years														
Tr 7.75pc '12-15	112.26	-0.03	-0.03	6.90	1.62	-0.01	-0.01	+0.18	-0.69	116.94	112.09	407	15/07	26 Jan/Jul
Tr 2.75pc '15	98.40	-0.02	+0.11	2.79	3.10	+0.01	+0.03	+0.30	-	100.12	98.00	15,060	13/07	22 Jan/Jul
Tr 4.75pc '15	108.16	-0.05	-0.07	4.39	3.16	+0.01	+0.06	+0.31	+0.17	115.18	107.64	24,968	29/08	7 Mar/Sep
Tr 8pc '15	125.48	-0.08	-0.15	6.37	3.23	+0.01	+0.06	+0.32	-0.01	135.52	125.11	9,997	28/11	7 Jun/Dec

Source: REUTERS Ltd, via www.ft.com/gilts

Figure 6.4 Sample *Financial Times* UK gilts cash market prices

If you go to the website and click on a particular bond, you will get a lot of information about the bond, including the credit rating, the call schedule, original issue information, and trade information.

As we mentioned before, the government Treasury market is the largest securities market in the world. As with bond markets in general, it is an OTC market, so there is limited transparency. However, unlike the situation with bond markets in general, trading in Treasury issues, particularly recently issued ones, is very heavy. Each day, representative prices for outstanding Treasury issues are reported.

Figure 6.4 shows a portion of the daily Treasury note and bond listings from the *Financial Times* website, ft.com. The entry that begins 'Tr 8pc '15' is highlighted. This information tells us that the bond will mature in 2015 and has an 8 per cent coupon. The next column is the price, which is £125.48. 'Day's chng' tells you that the price has fallen by £0.08 since the day before, and by £0.15 over the previous week. 'Int yield' is the interest yield or current yield (%), and you can calculate this by dividing the coupon (£8) by the bond price (£125.48). The redemption yield, 'Red yield', is the internal rate of return or yield to maturity of the bond, assuming that the bond is held to maturity and all the coupon payments are paid on time. For the 'Tr 8pc '15' bond this is 3.23 per cent. UK Treasury bonds (gilts) all make semi-annual payments and have a face value of £100, so this bond will pay £40 per six months until it matures.

The next four columns deal with changes in the bond's redemption yield (yield to maturity). Finally, the amount of bonds traded is presented (Amnt £m), the final date at which an individual is eligible to receive the bond's coupon (Last xd date), and the dates on which coupon payments are due.

If you examine the yields on the various issues in Fig. 6.4, you will clearly see that they vary by maturity. Why this occurs, and what it might mean, are things that we discuss in our next section.

A Note about Bond Price Quotes

If you buy a bond between coupon payment dates, the price you pay is usually more than the price you are quoted. The reason is that standard convention in the bond market is to quote prices net of 'accrued interest', meaning that accrued interest is deducted to arrive at the quoted price. This quoted price is called the **clean price**. The price you actually pay, however, includes the accrued interest. This price is the **dirty price**,

clean price
The price of a bond net of accrued interest; this is the price that is typically quoted.

dirty price
The price of a bond including accrued interest, also known as the *full* or *invoice* price. This is the price the buyer actually pays.

also known as the 'full' or 'invoice' price. If you look back to Fig. 6.3, you will see the accrued interest presented for a number of corporate bonds.

An example is the easiest way to understand these issues. Suppose you buy a bond with a 12 per cent annual coupon, payable semi-annually. You actually pay €1,080 for this bond, so €1,080 is the dirty, or invoice, price. Further, on the day you buy it, the next coupon is due in four months, so you are between coupon dates. Notice that the next coupon will be €60.

The accrued interest on a bond is calculated by taking the fraction of the coupon period that has passed, in this case two months out of six, and multiplying this fraction by the next coupon, €60. So, the accrued interest in this example is $2/6 \times €60 = €20$. The bond's quoted price (that is, its clean price) would be €1,080 − €20 = €1,060.

CONCEPT QUESTIONS

6.5a   What is meant by a bond's redemption yield and interest yield?
6.5b   What is the difference between a bond's clean price and dirty price?

6.6   Inflation and Interest Rates

So far, we haven't considered the role of inflation in our various discussions of interest rates, yields and returns. Because this is an important consideration, we consider the impact of inflation next.

Real versus Nominal Rates

real rates
Interest rates or rates of return that have been adjusted for inflation.

nominal rates
Interest rates or rates of return that have not been adjusted for inflation.

In examining interest rates, or any other financial market rates such as discount rates, bond yields, rates of return or required returns, it is often necessary to distinguish between **real rates** and **nominal rates**. Nominal rates are called 'nominal' because they have not been adjusted for inflation. Real rates are rates that have been adjusted for inflation.

To see the effect of inflation, suppose prices are currently rising by 5 per cent per year. In other words, the rate of inflation is 5 per cent. An investment is available that will be worth £115.50 in one year. It costs £100 today. Notice that with a present value of £100 and a future value in one year of £115.50, the investment has a 15.5 per cent rate of return. In calculating this 15.5 per cent return, we did not consider the effect of inflation, however, so this is the nominal return.

What is the impact of inflation here? To answer, suppose pizzas cost £5 apiece at the beginning of the year. With £100, we can buy 20 pizzas. Because the inflation rate is 5 per cent, pizzas will cost 5 per cent more, or £5.25, at the end of the year. If we take the investment, how many pizzas can we buy at the end of the year? Measured in pizzas, what is the rate of return on this investment?

Our £115.50 from the investment will buy us £115.50/5.25 = 22 pizzas. This is up from 20 pizzas, so our pizza rate of return is 10 per cent. What this illustrates is that even though the nominal return on our investment is 15.5 per cent, our buying power goes up by only 10 per cent, because of inflation. Put another way, we are really only 10 per cent richer. In this case we say that the real return is 10 per cent.

Alternatively, we can say that with 5 per cent inflation each of the £115.50 nominal pounds we get is worth 5 per cent less in real terms, so the real cash value of our investment in a year is

$$£115.50/1.05 = £110$$

What we have done is to *deflate* the £115.50 by 5 per cent. Because we give up £100 in current buying power to get the equivalent of £110, our real return is again 10 per cent.

Because we have removed the effect of future inflation here, this £110 is said to be measured in current pounds.

The difference between nominal and real rates is important, and bears repeating:

The nominal rate on an investment is the percentage change in the amount of cash you have.

The real rate on an investment is the percentage change in how much you can buy with your cash – in other words, the percentage change in your buying power.

The Fisher Effect

Our discussion of real and nominal returns illustrates a relationship often called the **Fisher effect** (after the great economist Irving Fisher). Because investors are ultimately concerned with what they can buy with their money, they require compensation for inflation. Let R stand for the nominal rate and r stand for the real rate. The Fisher effect tells us that the relationship between nominal rates, real rates and inflation can be written as

> **Fisher effect**
> The relationship between nominal returns, real returns and inflation.

$$1 + R = (1 + r) \times (1 + h) \tag{6.2}$$

where h is the inflation rate.

In the preceding example, the nominal rate was 15.50 per cent and the inflation rate was 5 per cent. What was the real rate? We can determine it by plugging in these numbers:

$$1 + 0.1550 = (1 + r) \times (1 + 0.05)$$
$$1 + r = 1.1550/1.05 = 1.10$$
$$r = 10\%$$

This real rate is the same as we found before. If we take another look at the Fisher effect, we can rearrange things a little as follows:

$$1 + R = (1 + r) \times (1 + h)$$
$$R = r + h + r \times h \tag{6.3}$$

What this tells us is that the nominal rate has three components. First, there is the real rate on the investment, r. Next, there is the compensation for the decrease in the value of the money originally invested because of inflation, h. The third component represents compensation for the fact that the money earned on the investment is also worth less because of the inflation.

This third component is usually small, so it is often dropped. The nominal rate is then approximately equal to the real rate plus the inflation rate:

$$R \approx r + h \tag{6.4}$$

 EXAMPLE 6.4

The Fisher Effect

If investors require a 10 per cent real rate of return, and the inflation rate is 8 per cent, what must be the approximate nominal rate? The exact nominal rate?

The nominal rate is approximately equal to the sum of the real rate and the inflation rate: 10% + 8% = 18%. From the Fisher effect, we have

$$1 + R = (1 + r) \times (1 + h)$$
$$= 1.10 \times 1.08$$
$$= 1.1880$$

Therefore the nominal rate will actually be closer to 19 per cent.

Chapter 6 Bond Valuation

It is important to note that financial rates, such as interest rates, discount rates and rates of return, are almost always quoted in nominal terms. To remind you of this, we shall henceforth use the symbol R instead of r in most of our discussions about such rates.

Inflation and Present Values

One question that often comes up is the effect of inflation on present value calculations. The basic principle is simple: either discount nominal cash flows at a nominal rate, or discount real cash flows at a real rate. As long as you are consistent, you will get the same answer.

To illustrate, suppose you want to withdraw money each year for the next three years, and you want each withdrawal to have £25,000 worth of purchasing power as measured in current pounds. If the inflation rate is 4 per cent per year, then the withdrawals will simply have to increase by 4 per cent each year to compensate. The withdrawals each year will thus be

$$C_1 = £25,000(1.04) = £26,000$$
$$C_2 = £25,000(1.04)^2 = £27,040$$
$$C_3 = £25,000(1.04)^3 = £28,121.60$$

What is the present value of these cash flows if the appropriate nominal discount rate is 10 per cent? This is a standard calculation, and the answer is

$$PV = \frac{£26,000}{1.10} + \frac{£27,040}{1.10^2} + \frac{£28,121.60}{1.10^3}$$
$$= £67,111.65$$

Notice that we discounted the nominal cash flows at a nominal rate.

To calculate the present value using real cash flows, we need the real discount rate. Using the Fisher equation, the real discount rate is obtained from

$$1 + R = (1 + r)(1 + h)$$
$$1 + 0.10 = (1 + r)(1 + 0.04)$$
$$r = 0.0577$$

By design, the real cash flows are an annuity of £25,000 per year. So the present value in real terms is

$$PV = £25,000[1 - (1/1.0577^3)]/0.0577 = £67,111.65$$

Thus we get exactly the same answer (after allowing for a small rounding error in the real rate). Of course, you could also use the growing annuity equation we discussed in the previous chapter. The withdrawals are increasing at 4 per cent per year: so, using the growing annuity formula, the present value is

$$PV = £26,000 \left[\frac{1 - \left(\frac{1 + 0.04}{1 + 0.10}\right)^3}{0.10 - 0.04} \right]$$
$$= £26,000(2.58122)$$
$$= £67,111.65$$

This is exactly the same present value we calculated before.

6.7 Determinants of Bond Yields

We are now in a position to discuss the determinants of a bond's yield. As we shall see, the yield on any particular bond reflects a variety of factors, some common to all bonds and some specific to the issue under consideration.

The Term Structure of Interest Rates

At any one time, short-term and long-term interest rates will generally be different. Sometimes short-term rates are higher, sometimes lower. Figure 6.5 gives us a long-range perspective on this by showing over two centuries of short- and long-term interest rates for the US (this is the only country that has such a long time period of data). As shown, through time, the difference between short- and long-term rates has ranged from essentially zero to up to several percentage points, both positive and negative.

The relationship between short- and long-term interest rates is known as the **term structure of interest rates**. To be a little more precise, the term structure of interest rates tells us what *nominal* interest rates are on *default-free, pure discount* bonds of all maturities. These rates are, in essence, 'pure' interest rates, because they involve no risk of default and a single, lump sum future payment. In other words, the term structure tells us the pure time value of money for different lengths of time.

When long-term rates are higher than short-term rates, we say that the term structure is upward sloping; when short-term rates are higher, we say it is downward sloping. The

> **term structure of interest rates** The relationship between nominal interest rates on default-free, pure discount securities and time to maturity: that is, the pure time value of money.

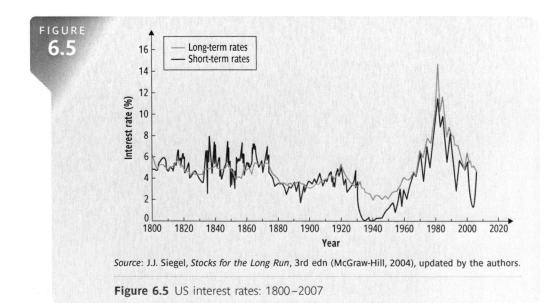

FIGURE **6.5**

Source: J.J. Siegel, *Stocks for the Long Run*, 3rd edn (McGraw-Hill, 2004), updated by the authors.

Figure 6.5 US interest rates: 1800–2007

Chapter 6 Bond Valuation

term structure can also be 'humped'. When this occurs, it is usually because rates increase at first, but then begin to decline as we look at longer- and longer-term rates. The most common shape of the term structure, particularly in modern times, is upward sloping, but the degree of steepness has varied quite a bit.

What determines the shape of the term structure? There are three basic components. The first two are the ones we discussed in our previous section: the real rate of interest and the rate of inflation. The real rate of interest is the compensation that investors demand for forgoing the use of their money. You can think of it as the pure time value of money after adjusting for the effects of inflation.

The real rate of interest is the basic component underlying every interest rate, regardless of the time to maturity. When the real rate is high, all interest rates will tend to be higher, and vice versa. Thus the real rate doesn't really determine the shape of the term structure; instead, it mostly influences the overall level of interest rates.

In contrast, the prospect of future inflation strongly influences the shape of the term structure. Investors thinking about lending money for various lengths of time recognize that future inflation erodes the value of the cash that will be returned. As a result, investors demand compensation for this loss in the form of higher nominal rates. This extra compensation is called the **inflation premium**.

inflation premium The portion of a nominal interest rate that represents compensation for expected future inflation.	If investors believe the rate of inflation will be higher in the future, then long-term nominal interest rates will tend to be higher than short-term rates. Thus an upward-sloping term structure may reflect anticipated increases in inflation. Similarly, a downward-sloping term structure probably reflects the belief that inflation will be falling in the future.
interest rate risk premium The compensation investors demand for bearing interest rate risk.	The third, and last, component of the term structure has to do with interest rate risk. As we discussed earlier in the chapter, longer-term bonds have much greater risk of loss resulting from changes in interest rates than do shorter-term bonds. Investors recognize this risk, and they demand extra compensation in the form of higher rates for bearing it. This extra compensation is called the **interest rate risk premium**. The longer is the term to maturity, the greater is the interest rate risk, so the interest rate risk premium increases with maturity. However, as we discussed earlier, interest rate risk increases at a decreasing rate, so the interest rate risk premium does as well.[6]

Putting the pieces together, we see that the term structure reflects the combined effect of the real rate of interest, the inflation premium, and the interest rate risk premium. Figure 6.6 shows how these can interact to produce an upward-sloping term structure (in the top part of the figure) or a downward-sloping term structure (in the bottom part).

In the top part of Fig. 6.6, notice how the rate of inflation is expected to rise gradually. At the same time, the interest rate risk premium increases at a decreasing rate, so the combined effect is to produce a pronounced upward-sloping term structure. In the bottom part of Fig. 6.6, the rate of inflation is expected to fall in the future, and the expected decline is enough to offset the interest rate risk premium and produce a downward-sloping term structure. Notice that if the rate of inflation was expected to decline by only a small amount, we could still get an upward-sloping term structure because of the interest rate risk premium.

We assumed in drawing Fig. 6.6 that the real rate would remain the same. Actually, expected future real rates could be larger or smaller than the current real rate. Also, for simplicity, we used straight lines to show expected future inflation rates as rising or declining, but they do not necessarily have to look like this. They could, for example, rise and then fall, leading to a humped yield curve.

Bond Yields and the Yield Curve: Putting It All Together

Going back to Fig. 6.4, recall that we saw that the yields on Treasury notes and bonds of different maturities are not the same. Each day, in addition to the Treasury prices and yields shown in Fig. 6.4, the *Financial Times* provides a plot of Treasury yields relative to maturity.

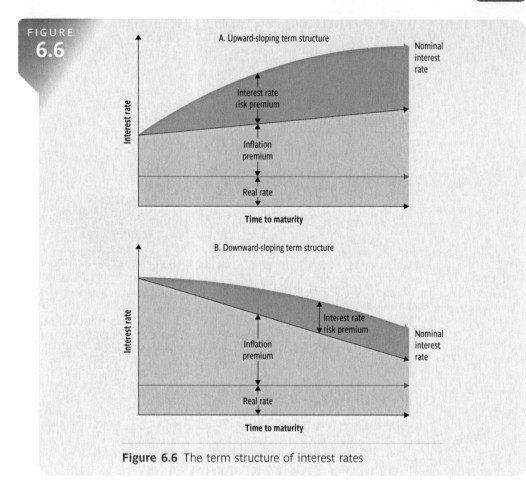

Figure 6.6 The term structure of interest rates

This plot is called the **Treasury yield curve** (or just the *yield curve*). Figure 6.7 shows the yield curve for the UK and Eurozone in early 2010. As can be seen both are upward sloping.

As you probably now suspect, the shape of the yield curve reflects the term structure of interest rates. In fact, the Treasury yield curve and the term structure of interest rates are almost the same thing. The only difference is that the term structure is based on pure discount bonds, whereas the yield curve is based on coupon bond yields. As a result, Treasury yields depend on the three components that underlie the term structure – the real rate, expected future inflation, and the interest rate risk premium.

Treasury notes and bonds have three important features that we need to remind you of: they are default-free (except for Eurozone countries), they are taxable, and they are highly liquid. This is not true of bonds in general, so we need to examine what additional factors come into play when we look at bonds issued by corporations or municipalities.

The first thing to consider is credit risk – that is, the possibility of default. Investors recognize that in most countries (except the Eurozone) issuers other than the Treasury may or may not make all the promised payments on a bond, so they demand a higher yield as compensation for this risk. This extra compensation is called the **default risk premium**. Earlier in the chapter we saw how bonds were rated based on their credit risk. What you will find if you start looking at bonds of different ratings is that lower-rated bonds have higher yields.

Treasury yield curve
A plot of the yields on Treasury notes and bonds relative to maturity.

default risk premium
The portion of a nominal interest rate or bond yield that represents compensation for the possibility of default.

FIGURE
6.7

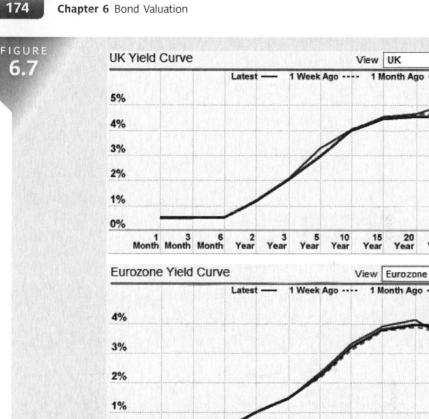

Source: ft.com, 12 February 2010. © The Financial Times Ltd 2010.

Figure 6.7 Yield curve: UK and Eurozone

taxability premium
The portion of a nominal interest rate or bond yield that represents compensation for unfavourable tax status.

liquidity premium
The portion of a nominal interest rate or bond yield that represents compensation for lack of liquidity.

An important thing to recognize about a bond's yield is that it is calculated assuming that all the promised payments will be made. As a result, it is really a promised yield, and it may or may not be what you will earn. In particular, if the issuer defaults, your actual yield will be lower – probably much lower. This fact is particularly important when it comes to junk bonds. Thanks to a clever bit of marketing, such bonds are now commonly called high-yield bonds, which has a much nicer ring to it; but now you recognize that these are really high *promised* yield bonds.

Next, recall that we discussed earlier how government bonds are free from most taxes and, as a result, have much lower yields than taxable bonds. Investors demand the extra yield on a taxable bond as compensation for the unfavourable tax treatment. This extra compensation is the **taxability premium**.

Finally, bonds have varying degrees of liquidity. As we discussed earlier, there are an enormous number of bond issues, most of which do not trade regularly. As a result, if you wanted to sell quickly, you would probably not get as good a price as you could otherwise. Investors prefer liquid assets to illiquid ones, so they demand a **liquidity premium** on top of all the other premiums we have discussed. As a result, all else being the same, less liquid bonds will have higher yields than more liquid bonds.

Conclusion

If we combine all of the things we have discussed regarding bond yields, we find that bond yields represent the combined effect of no fewer than six things. The first is the real rate of interest. On top of the real rate are five premiums representing compensation for:

1   Expected future inflation

2   Interest rate risk

3   Default risk

4   Taxability

5   Lack of liquidity

As a result, determining the appropriate yield on a bond requires careful analysis of each of these effects.

CONCEPT QUESTIONS

6.7a   What is the term structure of interest rates? What determines its shape?

6.7b   What is the Treasury yield curve?

6.7c   What six components make up a bond's yield?

Summary and Conclusions

This chapter has explored bonds, bond yields, and interest rates:

1   Determining bond prices and yields is an application of basic discounted cash flow principles.

2   Bond values move in the direction opposite to that of interest rates, leading to potential gains or losses for bond investors.

3   Bonds have a variety of features, spelled out in a document called the indenture.

4   Bonds are rated based on their default risk. Some bonds, such as Treasury bonds, have no risk of default, whereas so-called junk bonds have substantial default risk.

5   A wide variety of bonds exist, many of which contain exotic or unusual features.

6   Much bond trading is OTC, with little or no market transparency in many cases. As a result, bond price and volume information can be difficult to find for some types of bond.

7   Bond yields and interest rates reflect the effect of six different things: the real interest rate, and five premiums that investors demand as compensation for inflation, interest rate risk, default risk, taxability and lack of liquidity.

In closing, we note that bonds are a vital source of financing for governments and corporations of all types. Bond prices and yields are a rich subject, and our one chapter necessarily touches on only the most important concepts and ideas. There is a great deal more we could say, but instead we shall move on to equities in our next chapter.

Chapter Review and Self-Test Problems

6.1 **Bond Values** A Svenska AB bond has a 10 per cent coupon rate and a SKr1,000 face value. Interest is paid semi-annually, and the bond has 20 years to maturity. If investors require a 12 per cent yield, what is the bond's value? What is the effective annual yield on the bond?

6.2 **Bond Yields** An Ekornes ASA bond carries an 8 per cent coupon, paid semi-annually. The par value is NKr1,000, and the bond matures in six years. If the bond currently sells for NKr911.37, what is its yield to maturity? What is the effective annual yield?

Answers to Chapter Review and Self-Test Problems

6.1 Because the bond has a 10 per cent coupon yield and investors require a 12 per cent return, we know that the bond must sell at a discount. Notice that, because the bond pays interest semi-annually, the coupons amount to SKr100/2 = SKr50 every six months. The required yield is 12%/2 = 6% every six months. Finally, the bond matures in 20 years, so there are a total of 40 six-month periods.

The bond's value is thus equal to the present value of SKr50 every six months for the next 40 six-month periods plus the present value of the SKr1,000 face amount:

$$\text{Bond value} = \text{SKr50} \times \left[\frac{1 - 1/1.06^{40}}{0.06}\right] + \frac{1,000}{1.06^{40}}$$
$$= \text{SKr50} \times 15.04630 + 1,000/10.2857$$
$$= \text{SKr849.54}$$

Notice that we discounted the SKr1,000 back 40 periods at 6 per cent per period, rather than 20 years at 12 per cent. The reason is that the effective annual yield on the bond is $1.06^2 - 1 = 12.36\%$, not 12 per cent. We thus could have used 12.36 per cent per year for 20 years when we calculated the present value of the SKr1,000 face amount, and the answer would have been the same.

6.2 The present value of the bond's cash flows is its current price, NKr911.37. The coupon is NKr40 every six months for 12 periods. The face value is NKr1,000. So the bond's yield is the unknown discount rate in the following:

$$\text{NKr911.37} = \text{NKr40} \times \left[\frac{1 - 1/(1+r)^{12}}{r}\right] + \frac{1,000}{(1+r)^{12}}$$

The bond sells at a discount. Because the coupon rate is 8 per cent, the yield must be something in excess of that.

If we were to solve this by trial and error, we might try 12 per cent (or 6 per cent per six months):

$$\text{Bond value} = \text{NKr40} \times \left[\frac{1 - 1/1.06^{12}}{0.06}\right] + \frac{1,000}{1.06^{12}}$$
$$= \text{NKr832.32}$$

This is less than the actual value, so our discount rate is too high. We now know that the yield is somewhere between 8 and 12 per cent. With further trial and error (or a little computer assistance), the yield works out to be 10 per cent, or 5 per cent every six months.

By convention, the bond's yield to maturity would be quoted as $2 \times 5\% = 10\%$. The effective yield is thus $1.05^2 - 1 = 10.25\%$.

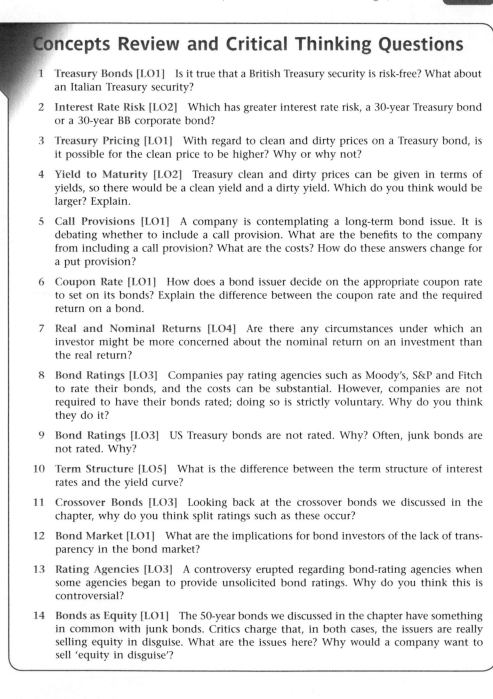

Concepts Review and Critical Thinking Questions

1 **Treasury Bonds [LO1]** Is it true that a British Treasury security is risk-free? What about an Italian Treasury security?

2 **Interest Rate Risk [LO2]** Which has greater interest rate risk, a 30-year Treasury bond or a 30-year BB corporate bond?

3 **Treasury Pricing [LO1]** With regard to clean and dirty prices on a Treasury bond, is it possible for the clean price to be higher? Why or why not?

4 **Yield to Maturity [LO2]** Treasury clean and dirty prices can be given in terms of yields, so there would be a clean yield and a dirty yield. Which do you think would be larger? Explain.

5 **Call Provisions [LO1]** A company is contemplating a long-term bond issue. It is debating whether to include a call provision. What are the benefits to the company from including a call provision? What are the costs? How do these answers change for a put provision?

6 **Coupon Rate [LO1]** How does a bond issuer decide on the appropriate coupon rate to set on its bonds? Explain the difference between the coupon rate and the required return on a bond.

7 **Real and Nominal Returns [LO4]** Are there any circumstances under which an investor might be more concerned about the nominal return on an investment than the real return?

8 **Bond Ratings [LO3]** Companies pay rating agencies such as Moody's, S&P and Fitch to rate their bonds, and the costs can be substantial. However, companies are not required to have their bonds rated; doing so is strictly voluntary. Why do you think they do it?

9 **Bond Ratings [LO3]** US Treasury bonds are not rated. Why? Often, junk bonds are not rated. Why?

10 **Term Structure [LO5]** What is the difference between the term structure of interest rates and the yield curve?

11 **Crossover Bonds [LO3]** Looking back at the crossover bonds we discussed in the chapter, why do you think split ratings such as these occur?

12 **Bond Market [LO1]** What are the implications for bond investors of the lack of transparency in the bond market?

13 **Rating Agencies [LO3]** A controversy erupted regarding bond-rating agencies when some agencies began to provide unsolicited bond ratings. Why do you think this is controversial?

14 **Bonds as Equity [LO1]** The 50-year bonds we discussed in the chapter have something in common with junk bonds. Critics charge that, in both cases, the issuers are really selling equity in disguise. What are the issues here? Why would a company want to sell 'equity in disguise'?

connect Questions and Problems

BASIC
1–14

1   **Interpreting Bond Yields [LO1]**   Is the yield to maturity on a bond the same thing as the required return? Is YTM the same thing as the coupon rate? Suppose today a 10 per cent coupon bond sells at par. Two years from now, the required return on the same bond is 8 per cent. What is the coupon rate on the bond then? The YTM?

2   **Interpreting Bond Yields [LO2]**   Suppose you buy a 7 per cent coupon, 20-year bond today when it's first issued. If interest rates suddenly rise to 15 per cent, what happens to the value of your bond? Why?

3   **Bond Prices [LO2]**   Staind plc has 8.5 per cent coupon bonds on the market that have 10 years left to maturity. The bonds make annual payments. If the YTM on these bonds is 9.75 per cent, what is the current bond price?

4   **Bond Yields [LO2]**   Ackerman plc has 10 per cent coupon bonds on the market, with nine years left to maturity. The bonds make annual payments. If the bond currently sells for £9,340 and the face value of the bonds is £10,000, what is its YTM?

5   **Coupon Rates [LO2]**   Steen Familie NV has bonds on the market making annual payments, with 13 years to maturity, and selling for €1,045. At this price, the bonds yield 7.5 per cent. What must the coupon rate be on the bonds?

6   **Bond Yields [LO2]**   In March 2009 the auto firm Daimler AG issued a 15-month bond with a face value of €1,000, and an annual coupon rate of 6.875 per cent, paid every quarter. The issue price was €9,997. What was its YTM?

7   **Bond Yields [LO2]**   Ngata SA issued 10-year bonds two years ago at a coupon rate of 7.5 per cent. The bonds make semi-annual payments. If these bonds currently sell for 105 per cent of par value, what is the YTM?

8   **Coupon Rates [LO2]**   Stand AG has bonds on the market with 17.5 years to maturity, a YTM of 8 per cent, and a current price of €924. The bonds make semi-annual payments. What must the coupon rate be on these bonds?

9   **Calculating Real Rates of Return [LO4]**   If Treasury bills are currently paying 7 per cent and the inflation rate is 3.8 per cent, what is the approximate real rate of interest? The exact real rate?

10   **Inflation and Nominal Returns [LO4]**   Suppose the real rate is 4 per cent and the inflation rate is 4.7 per cent. What rate would you expect to see on a Treasury bill?

11   **Nominal and Real Returns [LO4]**   An investment offers a 15 per cent total return over the coming year. You think the total real return on this investment will be only 9 per cent. What do you believe the inflation rate will be over the next year?

12   **Nominal versus Real Returns [LO4]**   A six-year government bond makes annual coupon payments of 5 per cent and offers a yield of 3 per cent annually compounded. Suppose that one year later the bond still yields 3 per cent. What return has the bondholder earned over the 12-month period? Now suppose that the bond yields 2 per cent at the end of the year. What return would the bondholder earn in this case?

13   **Using Treasury Quotes [LO2]**   Locate the 5 per cent coupon Treasury issue in Fig. 6.4 maturing in 2012. Is this a note or a bond? What is its interest yield? What is its redemption yield? What was the *previous* day's price?

14   **Using Treasury Quotes [LO2]**   Locate the 2.75 per cent coupon Treasury bond in Fig. 6.4 maturing in 2015. Is this a premium or a discount bond? What is its current yield? What is its yield to maturity?

INTERMEDIATE
15-28

15 **Bond Price Movements [LO2]** Bond X is a premium bond making annual payments. The bond pays an 8 per cent coupon, has a YTM of 6 per cent, and has 13 years to maturity. Bond Y is a discount bond making annual payments. This bond pays a 6 per cent coupon, has a YTM of 8 per cent, and also has 13 years to maturity. If interest rates remain unchanged, what do you expect the price of these bonds to be one year from now? In three years? In eight years? In 12 years? In 13 years? What's going on here? Illustrate your answers by plotting bond prices against time to maturity.

16 **Interest Rate Risk [LO2]** Both Bond Tony and Bond Peter have 10 per cent coupons, make semi-annual payments, and are priced at par value. Bond Tony has 3 years to maturity, whereas Bond Peter has 20 years to maturity. If interest rates suddenly rise by 2 per cent, what is the percentage change in the price of Bond Tony? Of Bond Peter? If rates were to suddenly fall by 2 per cent instead, what would the percentage change in the price of Bond Tony be then? Of Bond Peter? Illustrate your answers by plotting bond prices against YTM. What does this problem tell you about the interest rate risk of longer-term bonds?

17 **Interest Rate Risk [LO2]** Bond J is a 4 per cent coupon bond. Bond K is a 12 per cent coupon bond. Both bonds have nine years to maturity, make semi-annual payments, and have a YTM of 8 per cent. If interest rates suddenly rise by 2 per cent, what is the percentage price change of these bonds? What if rates suddenly fall by 2 per cent instead? What does this problem tell you about the interest rate risk of lower-coupon bonds?

18 **Bond Yields [LO2]** One More Time Software has 10.2 per cent coupon bonds on the market with nine years to maturity. The bonds make semi-annual payments and currently sell for 105.8 per cent of par. What is the current yield on the bonds? The YTM? The effective annual yield?

19 **Bond Yields [LO2]** Seether plc wants to issue new 20-year bonds for some much-needed expansion projects. The company currently has 8 per cent coupon bonds on the market that sell for £93,000 with a par value of £100,000, make semi-annual payments, and mature in 20 years. What coupon rate should the company set on its new bonds if it wants them to sell at par?

20 **Accrued Interest [LO2]** You purchase a bond with an invoice price of £9,680. The bond has a coupon rate of 7.4 per cent, and there are four months to the next semi-annual coupon date. What is the clean price of the bond?

21 **Accrued Interest [LO2]** You purchase a bond with a coupon rate of 6.8 per cent and a clean price of £10,730. If the next semi-annual coupon payment is due in two months, what is the invoice price?

22 **Finding the Bond Maturity [LO2]** Fluss AB has 8 per cent coupon bonds making annual payments with a YTM of 7.2 per cent. The current yield on these bonds is 7.55 per cent. How many years do these bonds have left until they mature?

23 **Using Bond Quotes [LO2]** Suppose the following bond quotes for Giorni di Estate SpA appear in the financial page of today's newspaper. Assume the bond has a face value of €1,000 and the current date is 15 February 2010. What is the yield to maturity of the bond? What is the current yield?

Company (ticker)	Coupon	Maturity	Last price	Last yield	Est vol (000s)
Giorni di Estate	9.2	15 Feb 2023	108.96	??	1,827

24 **Bond Prices versus Yields [LO2]**

   (a) What is the relationship between the price of a bond and its YTM?

   (b) Explain why some bonds sell at a premium over par value while other bonds sell at a discount. What do you know about the relationship between the coupon rate and the YTM for premium bonds? What about for discount bonds? For bonds selling at par value?

(c)   What is the relationship between the current yield and YTM for premium bonds? For discount bonds? For bonds selling at par value?

25   **Interest on Zeros [LO2]**   Tesla plc needs to raise funds to finance a plant expansion, and it has decided to issue 20-year zero coupon bonds to raise the money. The required return on the bonds will be 12 per cent. What will these bonds sell for at issuance?

26   **Zero Coupon Bonds [LO2]**   Suppose your company needs to raise €30 million and you want to issue 30-year bonds for this purpose. Assume the required return on your bond issue will be 8 per cent, and you're evaluating two issue alternatives: an 8 per cent semi-annual coupon bond and a zero coupon bond. Your company's tax rate is 35 per cent.

(a)   How many of the coupon bonds would you need to issue to raise the €30 million? How many of the zeros would you need to issue?

(b)   In 30 years, what will your company's repayment be if you issue the coupon bonds? What if you issue the zeros?

(c)   Based on your answers in (a) and (b), why would you ever want to issue the zeros? To answer, calculate the firm's after-tax cash outflows for the first year under the two different scenarios.

27   **Finding the Maturity [LO2]**   You've just found a 12 per cent coupon bond on the market that sells for par value. What is the maturity on this bond?

28   **Real Cash Flows [LO4]**   You want to have €1.5 million in real euros in an account when you retire in 40 years. The nominal return on your investment is 11 per cent and the inflation rate is 3.8 per cent. What real amount must you deposit each year to achieve your goal?

29   **Components of Bond Returns [LO2]**   Bond P is a premium bond with a 12 per cent coupon. Bond D is a 6 per cent coupon bond currently selling at a discount. Both bonds make annual payments, have a YTM of 9 per cent, and have five years to maturity. What is the current yield for bond P? For bond D? If interest rates remain unchanged, what is the expected capital gains yield over the next year for bond P? For bond D? Explain your answers and the interrelationships among the various types of yield.

30   **Holding Period Yield [LO2]**   The YTM on a bond is the interest rate you earn on your investment if interest rates don't change. If you actually sell the bond before it matures, your realized return is known as the *holding period yield* (HPY).

(a)   Suppose that today you buy a 7 per cent annual coupon bond for £106, when its face value is £100. The bond has 10 years to maturity. What rate of return do you expect to earn on your investment?

(b)   Two years from now, the YTM on your bond has declined by 1 per cent, and you decide to sell. What price will your bond sell for? What is the HPY on your investment? Compare this yield with the YTM when you first bought the bond. Why are they different?

31   **Valuing Bonds [LO2]**   Keegan plc has two different bonds currently outstanding. Bond M has a face value of £20,000 and matures in 20 years. The bond makes no payments for the first six years, then pays £1,100 every six months over the subsequent eight years, and finally pays £1,400 every six months over the last six years. Bond N also has a face value of £20,000 and a maturity of 20 years; it makes no coupon payments over the life of the bond. If the required return on both these bonds is 7 per cent compounded semi-annually, what is the current price of bond M? Of bond N?

CHAPTER

7

Equity Valuation

WHEN THE STOCK MARKET CLOSED on 19 February 2010, the equity of Daimler AG, manufacturer of automobiles, was selling for €32.36 per share. On that same day, shares in SAP AG, the software firm, closed at €32.90, while shares in Saint Gobain, the glass manufacturer, closed at €33.92. Because the share prices of these three companies were so similar, you might expect that they would be offering similar dividends to their shareholders, but you would be wrong. In fact, Daimler's annual dividend was €0.60 per share, Saint Gobain's was €1.98 per share, and SAP was paying no dividends at all!

As we shall see in this chapter, the dividends currently being paid are one of the primary factors we look at when attempting to value equities. However, it is obvious from looking at SAP that current dividends are not the end of the story. This chapter explores dividends, share prices, and the connection between the two.

In our previous chapter we introduced you to bonds and bond valuation. In this chapter, we turn to the other major source of financing for corporations: ordinary and preference shares. We first describe the cash flows associated with a share of equity, and then go on to develop a famous result, the dividend growth model. From there we move on to examine various important features of ordinary and preference shares, focusing on shareholder rights. We close the chapter with a discussion of how shares of equity are traded, and how share prices and other important information are reported in the financial press.

7.1 Share Valuation

Share prices are more difficult to value in practice than a bond, for at least three reasons. First, with equity, not even the promised cash flows are known in advance. Second, the life of the investment is essentially for ever, because equity has no maturity. Third, there is no way to easily observe the rate of return that the market requires. Nonetheless, as we shall see, there are cases in which we can come up with the present value of the future cash flows for a share of equity, and thus determine its value.

Chapter 7 Equity Valuation

Cash Flows

Imagine that you are considering buying a share of equity today. You plan to sell the equity in one year. You somehow know that it will be worth £70 at that time. You predict that the equity will also pay a £10 per share dividend at the end of the year. If you require a 25 per cent return on your investment, what is the most you would pay for the equity? In other words, what is the present value of the £10 dividend along with the £70 ending value at 25 per cent?

If you buy the equity today and sell it at the end of the year, you will have a total of £80 in cash. At 25 per cent:

$$\text{Present value} = \frac{£10 + 70}{1.25} = £64$$

Therefore £64 is the value you would assign to the equity today.

More generally, let P_0 be the current share price, and assign P_1 to be the price in one period. If D_1 is the cash dividend paid at the end of the period, then

$$P_0 = \frac{D_1 + P_1}{1 + R} \tag{7.1}$$

where R is the required return in the market on this investment.

Notice that we really haven't said much so far. If we wanted to determine the share price today (P_0), we would first have to come up with the value in one year (P_1). This is even harder to do, so we've only made the problem more complicated.

What is the price in one period, P_1? We don't know in general. Instead, suppose we somehow knew the price in two periods, P_2. Given a predicted dividend in two periods, D_2, the share price in one period would be

$$P_1 = \frac{D_2 + P_2}{1 + R}$$

If we were to substitute this expression for P_1 into our expression for P_0, we would have

$$P_0 = \frac{D_1 + P_1}{1 + R} = \frac{D_1 + (D_2 + P_2)/(1 + R)}{1 + R}$$

$$= \frac{D_1}{(1 + R)^1} + \frac{D_2}{(1 + R)^2} + \frac{P_2}{(1 + R)^2}$$

Now we need to get a price in two periods. We don't know this either, so we can procrastinate again and write

$$P_2 = \frac{D_3 + P_3}{1 + R}$$

If we substitute this back in for P_2, we have

$$P_0 = \frac{D_1}{(1 + R)^1} + \frac{D_2}{(1 + R)^2} + \frac{P_2}{(1 + R)^2}$$

$$= \frac{D_1}{(1 + R)^1} + \frac{D_2}{(1 + R)^2} + \frac{(D_3 + P_3)/(1 + R)}{(1 + R)^2}$$

$$= \frac{D_1}{(1 + R)^1} + \frac{D_2}{(1 + R)^2} + \frac{D_3}{(1 + R)^3} + \frac{P_3}{(1 + R)^3}$$

You should start to notice that we can push the problem of coming up with the share price off into the future for ever. Note that no matter what the share price is, the present value is essentially zero if we push the sale of the equity far enough away.[1] What we are eventually left with is the result that the current price of the equity can be written as the present value of the dividends beginning in one period and extending out for ever:

$$P_0 = \frac{D_1}{(1 + R)^1} + \frac{D_2}{(1 + R)^2} + \frac{D_3}{(1 + R)^3} + \frac{D_4}{(1 + R)^4} + \frac{D_5}{(1 + R)^5} + \dots$$

We have illustrated here that the share price today is equal to the present value of all of the future dividends. How many future dividends are there? In principle, there can be an infinite number. This means that we still can't compute a value for the equity, because we would have to forecast an infinite number of dividends and then discount them all. In the next section we consider some special cases in which we can get around this problem.

> **EXAMPLE 7.1**
>
> ## Growth Stocks
>
> You might be wondering about shares of equity in companies such as SAP AG that currently pay no dividends. In addition, small, growing companies frequently plough back everything and thus pay no dividends. Are such shares worth nothing? It depends. When we say that the value of the equity is equal to the present value of the future dividends, we don't rule out the possibility that some of those dividends are zero. They just can't *all* be zero.
>
> Imagine a company that has a provision in its articles and memorandum of association that prohibits the paying of dividends now or ever. The corporation never borrows any money, never pays out any money to shareholders in any form whatsoever, and never sells any assets. Such a corporation couldn't really exist, because the tax authorities wouldn't like it, and the shareholders could always vote to amend the articles and memorandum if they wanted to. If it did exist, however, what would the equity be worth?
>
> The shares are worth absolutely nothing. Such a company is a financial 'black hole'. Money goes in, but nothing valuable ever comes out. Because nobody would ever get any return on this investment, the investment has no value. This example is a little absurd, but it illustrates that when we speak of companies that don't pay dividends, what we really mean is that they are not *currently* paying dividends.

Some Special Cases

In a few useful special circumstances we can come up with a value for the equity. What we have to do is make some simplifying assumptions about the pattern of future dividends. The three cases we consider are the following:

1   The dividend has a zero growth rate.

2   The dividend grows at a constant rate.

3   The dividend grows at a constant rate after some length of time.

We consider each of these separately.

Zero Growth   The case of zero growth is one we've already seen. A share of equity in a company with a constant dividend is much like a preference share. For a zero-growth share of equity, this implies that

$$D_1 = D_2 = D_3 = D = \text{constant}$$

So the value of the equity is

$$P_0 = \frac{D}{(1 + R)^1} + \frac{D}{(1 + R)^2} + \frac{D}{(1 + R)^3} + \frac{D}{(1 + R)^4} + \frac{D}{(1 + R)^5} + \dots$$

Chapter 7 Equity Valuation

Because the dividend is always the same, the share price can be viewed as an ordinary perpetuity with a cash flow equal to D every period. The per-share value is thus given by

$$P_0 = D/R \qquad (7.2)$$

where R is the required return.

For example, suppose Paradise Prototyping has a policy of paying a €10 per share dividend every year. If this policy is to be continued indefinitely, what is the value of a share of equity if the required return is 20 per cent? The equity in this case amounts to an ordinary perpetuity, so it is worth €10/0.20 = €50 per share.

Constant Growth   Suppose we know that the dividend for some company always grows at a steady rate. Call this growth rate g. If we let D_0 be the dividend just paid, then the next dividend, D_1, is

$$D_1 = D_0 \times (1 + g)$$

The dividend in two periods is

$$\begin{aligned} D_2 &= D_1 \times (1 + g) \\ &= [D_0 \times (1 + g)] \times (1 + g) \\ &= D_0 \times (1 + g)^2 \end{aligned}$$

We could repeat this process to come up with the dividend at any point in the future. In general, from our discussion of compound growth in Chapter 4, we know that the dividend t periods into the future, D_t, is given by

$$D_t = D_0 \times (1 + g)^t$$

As we have previously seen, an asset with cash flows that grow at a constant rate for ever is called a *growing perpetuity*.

The assumption of steady dividend growth might strike you as peculiar. Why would the dividend grow at a constant rate? The reason is that, for many companies, steady growth in dividends is an explicit goal. For example, in 2009, Procter & Gamble, the US-based maker of personal care and household products, increased its dividend by 13.1 per cent to $1.64 per share: this increase was notable because it was the 53rd in a row. The subject of dividend growth falls under the general heading of dividend policy, so we shall defer further discussion of it to a later chapter.

EXAMPLE 7.2

Dividend Growth

Oasis plc has just paid a dividend of £3 per share. The dividend of this company grows at a steady rate of 8 per cent per year. Based on this information, what will the dividend be in five years?

Here we have a £3 current amount that grows at 8 per cent per year for five years. The future amount is thus

$$£3 \times 1.08^5 = £3 \times 1.4693 = £4.41$$

The dividend will therefore increase by £1.41 over the coming five years.

If the dividend grows at a steady rate, then we have replaced the problem of forecasting an infinite number of future dividends with the problem of coming up with a single growth rate – a considerable simplification. In this case, if we take D_0 to be the dividend just paid, and g to be the constant growth rate, the value of a share of equity can be written as

$$P_0 = \frac{D_1}{(1+R)^1} + \frac{D_2}{(1+R)^2} + \frac{D_3}{(1+R)^3} + \cdots$$

$$= \frac{D_0 \times (1+g)^1}{(1+R)^1} + \frac{D_0 \times (1+g)^2}{(1+R)^2} + \frac{D_0 \times (1+g)^3}{(1+R)^3} + \cdots$$

As long as the growth rate, g, is less than the discount rate, r, the present value of this series of cash flows can be written simply as

$$P_0 = \frac{D_0 \times (1+g)}{R-g}$$

$$= \frac{D_1}{R-g}$$

(7.3)

This elegant result goes by a lot of different names. We shall call it the **dividend growth model**. By any name, it is easy to use. To illustrate, suppose D_0 is £2.30, R is 13 per cent, and g is 5 per cent. The share price in this case is

$$
\begin{aligned}
P_0 &= D_0 \times (1+g)/(R-g) \\
&= £2.30 \times 1.05/(0.13 - 0.05) \\
&= £2.415/0.08 \\
&= £30.19
\end{aligned}
$$

> **dividend growth model**
> A model that determines the current share price as its dividend next period divided by the discount rate less the dividend growth rate.

We can actually use the dividend growth model to get the share price at any point in time, not just today. In general, the share price as of time t is

$$P_t = \frac{D_t \times (1+g)}{R-g} = \frac{D_{t+1}}{R-g}$$

(7.4)

In our example, suppose we are interested in the share price in five years, P_5. We first need the dividend at time 5, D_5. Because the dividend just paid is £2.30 and the growth rate is 5 per cent per year, D_5 is

$$D_5 = £2.30 \times 1.05^5 = £2.30 \times 1.2763 = £2.935$$

From the dividend growth model, we get the share price in five years:

$$
\begin{aligned}
P_5 &= \frac{D_5 \times (1+g)}{R-g} \\
&= \frac{£2.935 \times 1.05}{0.13 - 0.05} \\
&= \frac{£3.0822}{0.08} \\
&= £38.53
\end{aligned}
$$

> **EXAMPLE 7.3**
>
> ## Gordon Growth Limited
>
> The next dividend for Gordon Growth Limited will be £4 per share. Investors require a 16 per cent return on companies such as Gordon. Gordon's dividend increases by 6 per cent every year. Based on the dividend growth model, what is the value of Gordon's equity today? What is the value in four years?
>
> The only tricky thing here is that the next dividend, D_1, is given as £4, so we won't multiply this by $(1+g)$. With this in mind, the share price is given by

$$P_0 = D_1/(R - g)$$
$$= £4/(0.16 - 0.06)$$
$$= £4/0.10$$
$$= £40$$

Because we already have the dividend in one year, we know that the dividend in four years is equal to $D_1 \times (1 + g)^3 = £4 \times 1.06^3 = £4.764$. The price in four years is therefore

$$P_4 = D_4 \times (1 + g)/(R - g)$$
$$= £4.764 \times 1.06/(0.16 - 0.06)$$
$$= £5.05/0.10$$
$$= £50.50$$

Notice in this example that P_4 is equal to $P_0 \times (1 + g)^4$:

$$P_4 = £50.50$$
$$= £40 \times 1.06^4$$
$$= P_0 \times (1 + g)^4$$

To see why this is so, notice first that

$$P_4 = D_5/(R - g)$$

However, D_5 is just equal to $D_1 \times (1 + g)^4$, so we can write P_4 as

$$P_4 = D_1 \times (1 + g)^4/(R - g)$$
$$= [D_1/(R - g)] \times (1 + g)^4$$
$$= P_0 \times (1 + g)^4$$

This last example illustrates that the dividend growth model makes the implicit assumption that the share price will grow at the same constant rate as the dividend. This really isn't too surprising. What it tells us is that if the cash flows on an investment grow at a constant rate through time, so does the value of that investment.

You might wonder what would happen with the dividend growth model if the growth rate, g, were greater than the discount rate, R. It looks like we would get a negative share price, because $R - g$ would be less than zero. This is not what would happen.

Instead, if the constant growth rate exceeds the discount rate, then the share price is infinitely large. Why? If the growth rate is bigger than the discount rate, the present value of the dividends keeps getting bigger. Essentially the same is true if the growth rate and the discount rate are equal. In both cases, the simplification that allows us to replace the infinite stream of dividends with the dividend growth model is 'illegal', so the answers we get from the dividend growth model are nonsense unless the growth rate is less than the discount rate.

Finally, the expression we came up with for the constant growth case will work for any growing perpetuity, not just dividends on ordinary equity. As we saw in Chapter 4, if C is the next cash flow on a growing perpetuity, then the present value of the cash flows is given by

$$\text{Present value} = \frac{C_1}{(R - g)}$$
$$= \frac{C_0(1 + g)}{R - g}$$

Notice that this expression looks like the result for an ordinary perpetuity, except that we have $R - g$ on the bottom instead of just R.

$$P_0 = \frac{D_1}{(1+R)^1} + \frac{D_2}{(1+R)^2} + \frac{D_3}{(1+R)^3} + \frac{P_3}{(1+R)^3}$$

$$= \frac{€6.50}{1.20} + \frac{8.45}{1.20^2} + \frac{10.985}{1.20^3} + \frac{120.835}{1.20^3}$$

$$= €5.42 + 5.87 + 6.36 + 69.93$$

$$= €87.58$$

The total value of the equity today is thus €87.58 million. If there were, for example, 20 million shares, then the equity would be worth €87.58/20 = €4.38 per share.

Two-Stage Growth The last case we consider is a special case of non-constant growth: two-stage growth. Here, the idea is that the dividend will grow at a rate of g_1 for t years and then grow at a rate of g_2 thereafter for ever. In this case the value of the equity can be written as

$$P_0 = \frac{D_1}{R - g_1} \times \left[1 - \left(\frac{1 + g_1}{1 + R} \right)^t \right] + \frac{P_t}{(1 + R)^t} \qquad (7.5)$$

Notice that the first term in our expression is the present value of a growing annuity, which we discussed in Chapter 4. In this first stage, g_1 can be greater than R. The second part is the present value of the share price once the second stage begins at time t.

We can calculate P_t as follows:

$$P_t = \frac{D_{t+1}}{R - g_2} = \frac{D_0 \times (1 + g_1)^t \times (1 + g_2)}{R - g_2} \qquad (7.6)$$

In this calculation we need the dividend at time $t + 1$, D_{t+1}, to get the share price at time t, P_t. Notice that, to get it, we grew the current dividend, D_0, at rate g_1 for t periods and then grew it one period at rate g_2. Also, in this second stage, g_2 must be less than R.

EXAMPLE 7.5

Two-Stage Growth

Alto Campo's dividend is expected to grow at 20 per cent for the next five years. After that, the growth is expected to be 4 per cent for ever. If the required return is 10 per cent, what's the value of the equity? The dividend just paid was €2.

There is a fair amount of computation here, but it is mostly just 'plug and chug' with a calculator. We can start by calculating the share price five years from now, P_5:

$$P_5 = \frac{D_6}{R - g_2} = \frac{D_0 \times (1 + g_1)^5 \times (1 + g_2)}{R - g_2}$$

$$= \frac{€2 \times (1 + 0.20)^5 \times (1 + 0.04)}{0.10 - 0.04}$$

$$= \frac{€5.18}{0.06}$$

$$= €86.26$$

We then plug into our two-stage growth formula to get the price today:

$$P_0 = \frac{D_1}{R - g_1} \times \left[1 - \left(\frac{1 + g_1}{1 + R} \right)^t \right] + \frac{P_t}{(1 + R)^t}$$

$$= \frac{€2 \times (1 + 0.20)}{0.10 - 0.20} \times \left[1 - \left(\frac{1 + 0.20}{1 + 0.10} \right)^5 \right] + \frac{€86.26}{(1 + 0.10)^5}$$

$$= €66.64$$

Notice that we were given $D_0 = €2$ here, so we had to grow it by 20 per cent for one period to get D_1. Notice also that g_1 is bigger than R in this problem, but that fact does not cause a problem.

There are many reasons why dividend growth rates may change in the future. By far the most common reason is competition from other companies. Consider Apple, which has been incredibly successful over the past few years with its iPod, iPhone and iPad. Each product provided the company with exceptionally strong growth. However, within 12 months of launch, competitors released similar products. As competition grows, sales growth will naturally decrease, having a direct effect on dividend growth rates.

Dividend payout policy may also change, and this will also have an impact on growth rates. In Chapter 3 we discussed sustainable growth rates. If a company increases its total dividend as a proportion of its total earnings, growth will have to fall, because less money is retained to invest in value-maximizing projects. Holding everything else constant, if a company does increase its payout ratio, there will be a one-off increase in dividend (to reflect the bigger payout), followed by a lower growth rate in the future.

Components of the Required Return

Thus far we have taken the required return, or discount rate, R, as given. We shall have quite a bit to say about this subject in Chapters 11 and 13. For now, we want to examine the implications of the dividend growth model for this required return. Earlier, we calculated P_0 as

$$P_0 = D_1/(R - g)$$

If we rearrange this to solve for R, we get

$$R - g = D_1/P_0$$
$$R = D_1/P_0 + g \tag{7.7}$$

dividend yield
An equity's expected cash dividend divided by its current price.

capital gains yield
The dividend growth rate, or the rate at which the value of an investment grows.

This tells us that the total return, R, has two components. The first of these, D_1/P_0, is called the **dividend yield**. Because this is calculated as the expected cash dividend divided by the current price, it is conceptually similar to the current yield on a bond.

The second part of the total return is the growth rate, g. We know that the dividend growth rate is also the rate at which the share price grows (see Example 7.3). Thus this growth rate can be interpreted as the **capital gains yield** – that is, the rate at which the value of the investment grows.[2]

To illustrate the components of the required return, suppose we observe an equity selling for €20 per share. The next dividend will be €1 per share. You think that the dividend will grow by 10 per cent per year more or less indefinitely. What return does this equity offer if this is correct?

The dividend growth model calculates total return as

$$R = \text{Dividend yield} + \text{Capital gains yield}$$
$$= D_1/P_0 + g$$

In this case, total return works out to be

$$R = €1/20 + 10\%$$
$$= 5\% + 10\%$$
$$= 15\%$$

This equity therefore has an expected return of 15 per cent.

We can verify this answer by calculating the price in one year, P_1, using 15 per cent as the required return. Based on the dividend growth model, this price is

$$P_1 = D_1 \times (1 + g)/(R - g)$$
$$= €1 \times 1.10/(0.15 - 0.10)$$
$$= €1.10/0.05$$
$$= €22$$

Notice that this €22 is €20 × 1.1, so the share price has grown by 10 per cent as it should. If you pay €20 for the equity today, you will get a €1 dividend at the end of the year, and you will have a €22 − 20 = €2 gain. Your dividend yield is thus €1/20 = 5%. Your capital gains yield is €2/20 = 10%, so your total return would be 5% + 10% = 15%.

To get a feel for actual numbers in this context, consider that, according to Yahoo! Finance, Procter & Gamble's dividends were expected to grow by 8.5 per cent over the next five or so years, compared with a historical growth rate of 10.5 per cent over the preceding five years and 11 per cent over the preceding 10 years. In 2010 the projected dividend for the coming year was given as $1.77. The share price at that time was about $63 per share. What is the return investors require on P&G? Here, the dividend yield is 2.8 per cent and the capital gains yield is 8.5 per cent, giving a total required return of 11.3 per cent on P&G shares.

Our discussion of equity valuation is summarized in Table 7.1.

The Price – Earnings Ratio

In Chapter 3, via our discussion on financial ratios, we introduced the price–earnings ratio. Recall that the price–earnings ratio is the share price divided by earnings per share. P/E ratios are used by analysts to compare equity values across an industry, and they are used to complement other methods of equity valuation. The dividend growth model tells us that share value increases with growth rates, and so it implies that companies with high growth opportunities will have higher price–earnings ratios.

This explanation seems to hold fairly well in the real world. Electronic and other high-tech shares generally sell at very high P/E ratios (or multiples, as they are often called), because they are perceived to have high growth rates. In fact, some technology shares sell at high prices even though the companies have never earned a profit. Conversely, railroads, utilities and steel companies sell at lower multiples because of the prospects of lower growth. Figure 7.2 contains summary data for different UK industries in April 2010.

Notice the variation across industries, and how the P/E ratios are related to growth opportunities. TTM means 'trailing twelve months', and it says that the data (earnings and sales) are taken from the most recent financial report from the past year. Care should be taken with blindly using data such as P/E ratios, because sometimes strange figures appear. From looking at Fig. 7.2 you may be surprised to learn that the average P/E ratio for a UK company over the past 30 years has been between 12 and 18. The reason why the values are so large in Fig. 7.2 is that 2009 (the period for the earnings and sales figures) was a terrible year for companies, and average earnings were very low. With the recovery in the stock markets and share valuations in 2010, this resulted in very high P/E and P/Sale ratios.

Chapter 7 Equity Valuation

TABLE
7.1

The general case

In general, the price today of a share of equity, P_0, is the present value of all of its future dividends, $D_1, D_2, D_3, \ldots$:

$$P_0 = \frac{D_1}{(1+R)^1} + \frac{D_2}{(1+R)^2} + \frac{D_3}{(1+R)^3} + \cdots$$

where R is the required return.

Constant growth case

If the dividend grows at a steady rate, g, then the price can be written as

$$P_0 = \frac{D_1}{R-g}$$

This result is called the *dividend growth model.*

Non-constant growth

If the dividend grows steadily after t periods, then the price can be written as

$$P_0 = \frac{D_1}{(1+R)^1} + \frac{D_2}{(1+R)^2} + \cdots + \frac{D_t}{(1+R)^t} + \frac{P_t}{(1+R)^t}$$

where

$$P_t = \frac{D_t \times (1+g)}{(R-g)}$$

Two-stage growth

If the dividend grows at rate g_1 for t periods and then grows at rate g_2 thereafter, then the price can be written as

$$P_0 = \frac{D_1}{R-g_1} \times \left[1 - \left(\frac{1+g_1}{1+R} \right)^t \right] + \frac{P_t}{(1+R)^t}$$

where

$$P_t = \frac{D_{t+1}}{R-g_2} = \frac{D_0 \times (1+g_1)^t \times (1+g_2)}{R-g_2}$$

The required return

The required return, R, can be written as the sum of two things:

$$R = D_1/P_0 + g$$

where D_1/P_0 is the *dividend yield* and g is the *capital gains yield* (which is the same thing as the growth rate in dividends for the steady growth case).

Table 7.1 Summary of equity valuation

FIGURE 7.2

Sectors

Performance | Summary

Sectors	Average Market Cap	P/E TTM	Div Yield	Price-To-Sales Ratio TTM	EPS Growth (5 years)
Basic Materials	4.83t	61.9	1.40%	39.4	+8.33%
Consumer Goods	5.17t	48.5	2.00%	3.4	+6.87%
Consumer Services	4.24t	69.6	1.82%	7.1	+7.40%
Financials	11.41t	52.9	2.28%	67.7	+7.10%
Health Care	3.03t	22.9	2.08%	111.0	+14.29%
Industrials	79.98t	4.1	0.14%	177,553.2	+0.64%
Oil & Gas	4.74t	25.0	2.54%	28.5	+7.19%
Technology	3.87t	35.8	1.06%	6.6	+17.11%
Telecommunications	2.35t	76.3	4.25%	10.1	+7.01%
Utilities	2.18t	20.0	3.71%	2.6	+11.99%

As of Apr 15 2010 09:48 BST. Quotes are delayed by a least 20 minutes.

Source: *Financial Times.* © The Financial Times Ltd 2010.

Figure 7.2 Summary equity data for selected UK industries, 15 April 2010

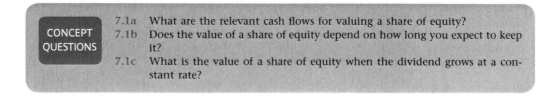

CONCEPT QUESTIONS

7.1a   What are the relevant cash flows for valuing a share of equity?

7.1b   Does the value of a share of equity depend on how long you expect to keep it?

7.1c   What is the value of a share of equity when the dividend grows at a constant rate?

7.2   Some Features of Ordinary and Preference Shares

In discussing ordinary equity features we focus on shareholder rights and dividend payments. For preference shares we explain what *preference* means, and we also debate whether preference shares are really debt or equity.

Ordinary Equity Features

The term **ordinary equity** means different things to different people, but it is usually applied to equity that has no special preference either in receiving dividends or in bankruptcy.

Preference Share Features

Preference shares differ from ordinary equity because they have preference over ordinary equity in the payment of dividends, and in the distribution of corporation

ordinary equity
Equity without priority for dividends or in bankruptcy.

preference shares
Equity with dividend priority over ordinary shares, normally with a fixed dividend rate, sometimes without voting rights.

assets in the event of liquidation. *Preference* means only that the holders of the preference shares must receive a dividend (in the case of an ongoing firm) before holders of ordinary shares are entitled to anything.

A preference share is a form of equity, from a legal and tax standpoint. It is important to note, however, that holders of preference shares sometimes have no voting privileges.

Stated Value   Preference shares have a stated liquidating value, such as £100 or €100 per share. The cash dividend is described as a percentage of stated value. For example, Unilever plc '4% preference shares' easily translates into a dividend yield of 4 per cent of stated value, or £4 per share.

Cumulative and Non-cumulative Dividends   A preference share dividend is *not* like interest on a bond. The board of directors may decide not to pay the dividends on preference shares, and their decision may have nothing to do with the current net income of the corporation.

Dividends payable on preference shares are either *cumulative* or *non-cumulative*; most are cumulative. If preferred dividends are cumulative and are not paid in a particular year, they will be carried forward as an *arrearage*. Usually, both the accumulated (past) preferred dividends and the current preferred dividends must be paid before the ordinary shareholders can receive anything.

Unpaid preferred dividends are *not* debts of the firm. Directors elected by the ordinary shareholders can defer preferred dividends indefinitely. However, in such cases ordinary shareholders must also forgo dividends. In addition, holders of preference shares are often granted voting and other rights if preferred dividends have not been paid for some time. Because preference shareholders receive no interest on the accumulated dividends, some have argued that firms have an incentive to delay paying preferred dividends, but, as we have seen, this may mean sharing control with preference shareholders.

Are Preference Shares Really Debt?   A good case can be made that preference shares are really debt in disguise, a kind of equity bond. Preference shareholders receive a stated dividend only; and if the corporation is liquidated, preference shareholders get a stated value. Often, preference shares carry credit ratings much like those of bonds. Furthermore, preference shares are sometimes convertible into ordinary shares, and preference shares are often callable.

In addition, many preference share issues have obligatory sinking funds. The existence of such a sinking fund effectively creates a final maturity, because it means that the entire issue will ultimately be retired. For these reasons, preference shares seem to be a lot like debt. However, for tax purposes, preferred dividends are treated like ordinary share dividends.

International Accounting Standards (IAS 32: *Financial Instruments: Presentation*) recommend that the equity-like features of preference shares should be treated as equity in the company's financial accounts. Similarly, the bond-like features of a preference share should be treated as debt. So, if a preference share has a fixed dividend that has a mandatory redemption property at some future date, then it should be treated as a liability. If there is no redemption date, and the dividends are not mandatory, it should be treated as equity.

CONCEPT QUESTIONS

7.2a   Why is a preference share called *preference*?

7.2b   How can a preference share sometimes be treated as debt and at other times be treated as equity?

7.2c   What is the difference between cumulative and non-cumulative dividends?

Answers to Chapter Review and Self-Test Problems

7.1 The last dividend, D_0, was £2. The dividend is expected to grow steadily at 8 per cent. The required return is 16 per cent. Based on the dividend growth model, we can say that the current price is

$$P_0 = D_1/(R - g) = D_0 \times (1 + g)/(R - g)$$
$$= £2 \times 1.08/(0.16 - 0.08)$$
$$= £2.16/0.08$$
$$= £27$$

We could calculate the price in five years by calculating the dividend in five years and then using the growth model again. Alternatively, we could recognize that the share price will increase by 8 per cent per year and calculate the future price directly. We'll do both. First, the dividend in five years will be

$$D_5 = D_0 \times (1 + g)^5$$
$$= £2 \times 1.08^5$$
$$= £2.9387$$

The price in five years would therefore be

$$P_5 = D_5 \times (1 + g)/(R - g)$$
$$= £2.9387 \times 1.08/0.08$$
$$= £3.1738/0.08$$
$$= £39.67$$

Once we understand the dividend model, however, it's easier to notice that

$$P_5 = P_0 \times (1 + g)^5$$
$$= £27 \times 1.08^5$$
$$= £27 \times 1.4693$$
$$= £39.67$$

Notice that both approaches yield the same price in five years.

7.2 In this scenario we have supernormal growth for the next three years. We'll need to calculate the dividends during the rapid growth period, and the share price in three years. The dividends are

$$D_1 = £2.00 \times 1.20 = £2.400$$
$$D_2 = £2.40 \times 1.20 = £2.880$$
$$D_3 = £2.88 \times 1.20 = £3.456$$

After three years the growth rate falls to 8 per cent indefinitely. The price at that time, P_3, is thus

$$P_3 = D_3 \times (1 + g)/(R - g)$$
$$= £3.456 \times 1.08/(0.16 - 0.08)$$
$$= £3.7325/0.08$$
$$= £46.656$$

To complete the calculation of the share's present value, we have to determine the present value of the three dividends and the future price:

$$P_0 = \frac{D_1}{(1 + R)^1} + \frac{D_2}{(1 + R)^2} + \frac{D_3}{(1 + R)^3} + \frac{P_3}{(1 + R)^3}$$
$$= \frac{£2.40}{1.16} + \frac{2.88}{1.16^2} + \frac{3.456}{1.16^3} + \frac{46.656}{1.16^3}$$
$$= £2.07 + 2.14 + 2.21 + 29.89$$
$$= £36.31$$

Concepts Review and Critical Thinking Questions

1   **Share Valuation [LO1]**   Why does the value of a share of equity depend on dividends?

2   **Share Valuation [LO1]**   A substantial percentage of the companies listed on European stock exchanges don't pay dividends, but investors are nonetheless willing to buy shares in them. How is this possible, given your answer to the previous question?

3   **Dividend Policy [LO1]**   Referring to the previous questions, under what circumstances might a company choose not to pay dividends?

4   **Dividend Growth Model [LO1]**   Under what two assumptions can we use the dividend growth model presented in the chapter to determine the share price? Comment on the reasonableness of these assumptions.

5   **Ordinary versus Preference Shares [LO1]**   Suppose a company has a preference share issue and an ordinary share issue. Both have just paid a £2 dividend. Which do you think will have a higher price, the preference share or the ordinary share?

6   **Dividend Growth Model [LO1]**   Based on the dividend growth model, what are the two components of the total return on a share of equity? Which do you think is typically larger?

7   **Growth Rate [LO1]**   In the context of the dividend growth model, is it true that the growth rate in dividends and the growth rate in the share price are identical?

8   **Share Valuation [LO1]**   Evaluate the following statement: managers should not focus on the current share price, because doing so will lead to an overemphasis on short-term profits at the expense of long-term profits.

9   **Two-Stage Dividend Growth Model [LO1]**   One of the assumptions of the two-stage growth model is that the dividends drop immediately from the high growth rate to the perpetual growth rate. What do you think about this assumption? What happens if this assumption is violated?

connect Questions and Problems

BASIC
1–9

1   **Share Values [LO1]**   In 2010, Daimler AG announced that it would not pay a dividend because of the atrocious trading conditions in the previous year. However, analysts expect the company to pay a dividend of €0.60 in 2011. If dividends are expected to grow at a constant rate of 8 per cent per year indefinitely, and investors require a 10 per cent return on the company, what is the current price? What will the price be in three years? In 15 years?

2   **Share Values [LO1]**   The next dividend payment by Modern Times Group AB will be SKr5 per share. The dividends are anticipated to maintain a 5 per cent growth rate for ever. If the equity currently sells for SKr397.3 per share, what is the required return?

3   **Share Values [LO1]**   For the company in the previous problem, what is the dividend yield? What is the expected capital gains yield?

4   **Share Values [LO1]**   British American Tobacco plc will pay an £8.82 per share dividend next year. The company pledges to increase its dividend by 3.8 per cent per year indefinitely. If you require a 30 per cent return on your investment, how much will you pay for the company's equity today? Look up Yahoo! Finance and find the current price of British American Tobacco plc. How does the existing share price compare with the theoretical share price?

5   **Share Valuation [LO1]** Credit Agricole SA is expected to maintain a constant 5.2 per cent growth rate in its dividends indefinitely. If the company has a dividend yield of 4.27 per cent, what is the required return on the company's shares?

6   **Share Valuation [LO1]** Suppose you know that a company's equity currently sells for £47 per share, and the required return on the equity is 11 per cent. You also know that the total return on the equity is evenly divided between a capital gains yield and a dividend yield. If it's the company's policy to always maintain a constant growth rate in its dividends, what is the current dividend per share?

7   **Share Valuation [LO1]** Vivendi SA pays a constant €1.40 dividend on its equity. The company will maintain this dividend for the next 11 years, and will then cease paying dividends for ever. If the required return on this equity is 10 per cent, what is the current share price?

8   **Valuing Preference Shares [LO1]** Resnor plc has an issue of preference shares outstanding that pays a £3.40 dividend every year in perpetuity. If this issue currently sells for £69 per share, what is the required return?

9   **Share Valuation and Required Return [LO1]** Red plc, Yellow plc and Blue plc each will pay a dividend of £2.35 next year. The growth rate in dividends for all three companies is 5 per cent. The required return for each company's shares is 8 per cent, 11 per cent and 14 per cent, respectively. What is the share price for each company? What do you conclude about the relationship between the required return and the share price?

10   **Share Valuation [LO1]** Unilever NV just paid a dividend of €0.51 on its equity. The growth rate in dividends is expected to be a constant 5 per cent per year indefinitely. Investors require a 14 per cent return on the equity for the first three years, a 12 per cent return for the next three years, and a 10 per cent return thereafter. What is the current share price?

11   **Non-Constant Growth [LO1]** Metallica Bearings plc is a young start-up company. No dividends will be paid on the equity over the next nine years, because the firm needs to plough back its earnings to fuel growth. The company will pay a £1 per share dividend in 10 years, and will increase the dividend by 5 per cent per year thereafter. If the required return on this equity is 16 per cent, what is the current share price?

12   **Non-Constant Dividends [LO1]** Bread plc has an odd dividend policy. The company has just paid a dividend of £5 per share, and has announced that it will increase the dividend by £2 per share for each of the next five years, and then never pay another dividend. If you require an 18 per cent return on the company's equity, how much will you pay for a share today?

13   **Non-Constant Dividends [LO1]** Far Side SpA is expected to pay the following dividends over the next four years: €12, €10, €6 and €3. Subsequently, the company pledges to maintain a constant 5 per cent growth rate in dividends for ever. If the required return on the equity is 12 per cent, what is the current share price?

14   **Supernormal Growth [LO1]** Marcel AG is growing quickly. Dividends are expected to grow at a 30 per cent rate for the next three years, with the growth rate falling off to a constant 6 per cent thereafter. If the required return is 13 per cent and the company just paid a €1.80 dividend, what is the current share price?

15   **Supernormal Growth [LO1]** Eva AB is experiencing rapid growth. Dividends are expected to grow at 20 per cent per year during the next three years, 15 per cent over the following year, and then 10 per cent per year indefinitely. The required return on this equity is 13 per cent, and it currently sells for €56 per share. What is the projected dividend for the coming year?

16 **Negative Growth [LO1]** Antiques R Us is a mature manufacturing firm. The company just paid a €12 dividend, but management expects to reduce the payout by 4 per cent per year indefinitely. If you require an 11 per cent return on this equity, what will you pay for a share today?

17 **Finding the Dividend [LO1]** Teder plc shares currently sell for £64 per share. The market requires a 10 per cent return on the firm's equity. If the company maintains a constant 4.5 per cent growth rate in dividends, what was the most recent dividend per share paid on the equity?

18 **Valuing Preference Shares [LO1]** E-Eyes.com Bank just issued some new preference shares. The issue will pay a £20 annual dividend in perpetuity, beginning 20 years from now. If the market requires a 6.4 per cent return on this investment, how much does a preference share cost today?

19 **Using Share Price Quotes [LO3]** You have found the following share price quote for HBooks plc, in the financial pages of today's newspaper. What was the closing price for this equity that appeared in *yesterday's* paper? If the company currently has 25 million shares of equity outstanding, what was net income for the most recent year?

52-WEEK						NET	
HI	LO	EQUITY (DIV)	YLD %	P/E	VOL 100s	CLOSE	CHG
72.18	53.17	HBOOKS 1.48	2.1	19	17652	??	−.23

20 **Two-Stage Dividend Growth Model [LO1]** Thirsty Cactus SA just paid a dividend of €2.50 per share. The dividends are expected to grow at 25 per cent for the next eight years, and then level off to an 8 per cent growth rate indefinitely. If the required return is 13 per cent, what is the share price today?

21 **Two-Stage Dividend Growth Model [LO1]** Chartreuse County Choppers plc is experiencing rapid growth. The company expects dividends to grow at 20 per cent per year for the next 11 years before levelling off at 5 per cent into perpetuity. The required return on the company's equity is 14 per cent. If the dividend per share just paid was $1.74, what is the share price?

CHALLENGE
22–28

22 **Capital Gains versus Income [LO1]** Consider four different equities, all of which have a required return of 16 per cent and a most recent dividend of £2.50 per share. Equities W, X and Y are expected to maintain constant growth rates in dividends for the foreseeable future of 10 per cent, 0 per cent and –5 per cent per year, respectively. Equity Z is a growth stock that will increase its dividend by 20 per cent for the next two years, and then maintain a constant 12 per cent growth rate thereafter. What is the dividend yield for each of these four equities? What is the expected capital gains yield? Discuss the relationship among the various returns that you find for each of these equities.

23 **Share Valuation [LO1]** Most corporations pay semi-annual dividends on their ordinary equity rather than annual dividends. Barring any unusual circumstances during the year, the board raises, lowers or maintains the current dividend once a year and then pays this dividend out in equal six-monthly instalments to its shareholders.

(a) Suppose a company currently pays a £3.20 annual dividend on its ordinary equity in a single annual instalment, and management plans to raise this dividend by 6 per cent per year indefinitely. If the required return on this equity is 14 per cent, what is the current share price?

(b) Now suppose the company in (a) actually pays its annual dividend in equal six-monthly instalments: thus the company has just paid a £1.60 dividend per share, as it has for the previous six-month period. What is your value for the current share price now? (*Hint:* Find the equivalent annual end-of-year dividend for each year.) Comment on whether you think this model of share valuation is appropriate.

24 **Non-constant Growth [LO1]** Storico plc has just paid a dividend of £2.45 per share. The company will increase its dividend by 20 per cent next year, and will then reduce its dividend growth rate by 5 percentage points per year until it reaches the industry average of 5 per cent dividend growth, after which the company will keep a constant growth rate for ever. If the required return on Storico shares is 11 per cent, what will a share of equity sell for today?

25 **Non-Constant Growth [LO1]** This one's a little harder. Suppose the current share price for the firm in the previous problem is £63.82, and all the dividend information remains the same. What required return must investors be demanding on Storico equity? (*Hint:* Set up the valuation formula with all the relevant cash flows, and use trial and error to find the unknown rate of return.)

26 **Constant Dividend Growth Model [LO1]** Assume an equity has dividends that grow at a constant rate for ever. If you value the shares using the constant dividend growth model, how many years worth of dividends constitute one-half of the share's current price?

27 **Two-Stage Dividend Growth [LO1]** Regarding the two-stage dividend growth model in the chapter, show that the price of a share of equity today can be written as follows:

$$P_0 = \frac{D_0 \times (1 + g_1)}{R - g_1} \times \left[1 - \left(\frac{1 + g_1}{1 + R}\right)^t\right] + \left(\frac{1 + g_1}{1 + R}\right)^t \times \frac{D_0 \times (1 + g_2)}{R - g_2}$$

Can you provide an intuitive interpretation of this expression?

28 **Two-Stage Dividend Growth [LO1]** The chapter shows that in the two-stage dividend growth model, the growth rate in the first stage, g_1, can be greater than or less than the discount rate, R. Can they be exactly equal? (*Hint:* Yes, but what does the expression for the share value look like?)

MINI CASE   Share Valuation at Ragan plc.

Ragan plc was founded nine years ago by brother and sister Carrington and Genevieve Ragan. The company manufactures and installs commercial heating, ventilation and cooling (HVAC) units. Ragan plc has experienced rapid growth because of a proprietary technology that increases the energy efficiency of its units. The company is equally owned by Carrington and Genevieve. The original partnership agreement between the siblings gave each 50,000 shares of equity. In the event either wished to sell stock, the shares first had to be offered to the other at a discounted price.

Although neither sibling wants to sell, they have decided they should value their holdings in the company. To get started, they have gathered the following information about their main competitors:

	EPS (£)	DPS (£)	Share price (£)	ROE (%)	R (%)
			Ragan plc competitors		
Arctic Cooling plc	0.79	0.20	14.18	10.00	10.00
National Heating & Cooling	1.38	0.62	11.87	13.00	13.00
Expert HVAC plc	−0.48	0.38	13.21	14.00	12.00
Industry Average	0.56	0.40	13.09	12.33	11.67

Expert HVAC plc's negative earnings per share were the result of an accounting write-off last year. Without the write-off, earnings per share for the company would have been £1.06.

Last year, Ragan plc had an EPS of £4.54 and paid a dividend to Carrington and Genevieve of £63,000 each. The company also had a return on equity of 25 per cent. The siblings believe that 20 per cent is an appropriate required return for the company.

QUESTIONS

1 Assuming the company continues its current growth rate, what is the share price of the company's equity?

2 To verify their calculations, Carrington and Genevieve have hired Josh Schlessman as a consultant. Josh was previously an equity analyst, and covered the HVAC industry. Josh has examined the company's financial statements, as well as examining its competitors. Although Ragan plc currently has a technological advantage, his research indicates that other companies are investigating methods to improve efficiency. Given this, Josh believes that the company's technological advantage will last only for the next five years. After that period, the company's growth is likely to slow to the industry growth average. Additionally, Josh believes that the required return used by the company is too high. He believes the industry average required return is more appropriate. Under this growth rate assumption, what is your estimate of the share price?

3 What is the industry average price–earnings ratio? What is the price–earnings ratio for Ragan plc? Is this the relationship you would expect between the two ratios? Why?

4 Carrington and Genevieve are unsure how to interpret the price–earnings ratio. After some head scratching, they've come up with the following expression for the price–earnings ratio:

$$\frac{P_0}{E_1} = \frac{1-b}{R - (\text{ROE} \times b)}$$

Beginning with the constant dividend growth model, verify this result. What does this expression imply about the relationship between the dividend payout ratio, the required return on the equity, and the company's ROE?

5 Assume the company's growth rate slows to the industry average in five years. What future return on equity does this imply, assuming a constant payout ratio?

6 After discussing the share value with Josh, Carrington and Genevieve agree that they would like to increase the value of the company equity. Like many small business owners, they want to retain control of the company, but they do not want to sell equity to outside investors. They also feel that the company's debt is at a manageable level, and do not want to borrow more money. How can they increase the share price? Are there any conditions under which this strategy would not increase the share price?

Endnotes

1 The only assumption we make about the share price is that it is a finite number, no matter how far away we push it. It can be extremely large, just not infinitely so. Because no one has ever observed an infinite share price, this assumption is plausible.

2 Here and elsewhere, we use the term *capital gains* a little loosely. For the record, a capital gain (or loss) is, strictly speaking, something defined by a country's tax authority. For our purposes, it would be more accurate (but less common) to use the term *price appreciation* instead of *capital gain*.

it costs us to acquire. How can something be worth more than it costs? It's a case of the whole being worth more than the cost of the parts.

For example, suppose you buy a run-down house for £25,000 and spend another £25,000 on painters, plumbers and so on to get it renovated. Your total investment is £50,000. When the work is completed, you place the house back on the market and find that it's worth £60,000. The market value (£60,000) exceeds the cost (£50,000) by £10,000. What you have done here is act as a manager and bring together some non-current assets (a house), some labour (plumbers, carpenters, and others) and some materials (carpeting, paint, and so on). The net result is that you have created £10,000 in value. Put another way, this £10,000 is the *value added* by management.

With our house example, it turned out *after the fact* that £10,000 in value had been created. Things thus worked out nicely. The real challenge, of course, would have been somehow to identify *ahead of time* whether investing the necessary £50,000 was a good idea in the first place. This is what capital budgeting is all about – namely, trying to determine whether a proposed investment or project will be worth more, once it is in place, than it costs.

For reasons that will be obvious in a moment, the difference between an investment's market value and its cost is called the **net present value** of the investment, abbreviated to NPV. In other words, net present value is a measure of how much value is created or added today by undertaking an investment. Given our goal of creating value for the shareholders, the capital budgeting process can be viewed as a search for investments with positive net present values.

net present value (NPV) The difference between an investment's market value and its cost.

With our run-down house, you can probably imagine how we would go about making the capital budgeting decision. We would first look at what comparable, renovated properties were selling for in the market. We would then get estimates of the cost of buying a particular property and bringing it to market. At this point, we would have an estimated total cost and an estimated market value. If the difference was positive, then this investment would be worth undertaking, because it would have a positive estimated net present value. There is risk, of course, because there is no guarantee that our estimates will turn out to be correct.

As our example illustrates, investment decisions are greatly simplified when there is a market for assets similar to the investment we are considering. Capital budgeting becomes much more difficult when we cannot observe the market price for at least roughly comparable investments. The reason is that we then face the problem of estimating the value of an investment using only indirect market information. Unfortunately, this is precisely the situation the financial manager usually encounters. We examine this issue next.

Estimating Net Present Value

Imagine we are thinking of starting a business to produce and sell a new product – organic fertilizer, say. We can estimate the start-up costs with reasonable accuracy, because we know what we shall need to buy to begin production. Would this be a good investment? Based on our discussion, you know that the answer depends on whether the value of the new business exceeds the cost of starting it. In other words, does this investment have a positive NPV?

This problem is much more difficult than our renovated house example, because entire fertilizer companies are not routinely bought and sold in the marketplace, so it is essentially impossible to observe the market value of a similar investment. As a result, we must somehow estimate this value by other means.

discounted cash flow (DCF) valuation The process of valuing an investment by discounting its future cash flows.

Based on our work in Chapters 4 and 5, you may be able to guess how we shall go about estimating the value of our fertilizer business. We shall first try to estimate the future cash flows we expect the new business to produce. We shall then apply our basic discounted cash flow procedure to estimate the present value of those cash flows. Once we have this estimate, we shall then estimate NPV as the difference between the present value of the future cash flows and the cost of the investment. As we mentioned in Chapter 5, this procedure is often called **discounted cash flow (DCF) valuation**.

Chapter 8 Net Present Value and Other Investment Criteria

Time (years)	0	1	2	3	4	5	6	7	8
Initial cost	−£30								
Inflows		£20	£20	£20	£20	£20	£20	£20	£20
Outflows		−14	−14	−14	−14	−14	−14	−14	−14
Net inflow		£ 6	£ 6	£ 6	£ 6	£ 6	£ 6	£ 6	£ 6
Salvage									2
Net cash flow	−£30	£ 6	£ 6	£ 6	£ 6	£ 6	£ 6	£ 6	£ 8

Figure 8.1 Project cash flows (£000)

To see how we might go about estimating NPV, suppose we believe the cash revenues from our fertilizer business will be £20,000 per year, assuming everything goes as expected. Cash costs (including taxes) will be £14,000 per year. We shall wind down the business in eight years. Plant, property and equipment will be worth £2,000 as salvage at that time. The project costs £30,000 to launch. We use a 15 per cent discount rate on new projects such as this one. Is this a good investment? If there are 1,000 shares of equity outstanding, what will be the effect on the share price of taking this investment?

From a purely mechanical perspective, we need to calculate the present value of the future cash flows at 15 per cent. The net cash inflow will be £20,000 cash income less £14,000 in costs per year for eight years. These cash flows are illustrated in Fig. 8.1. As Fig. 8.1 suggests, we effectively have an eight-year annuity of £20,000 − 14,000 = £6,000 per year, along with a single lump-sum inflow of £2,000 in eight years. Calculating the present value of the future cash flows thus comes down to the same type of problem we considered in Chapter 5. The total present value is

$$\text{Present value} = £6,000 \times [1 - (1/1.15^8)]/0.15 + (2,000/1.15^8)$$
$$= (£6,000 \times 4.4873) + (2,000/3.0590)$$
$$= £26,924 + 654$$
$$= £27,578$$

When we compare this with the £30,000 estimated cost, we see that the NPV is

$$\text{NPV} = -£30,000 + 27,578 = -£2,422$$

Therefore this is *not* a good investment. Based on our estimates, taking it would *decrease* the total value of the equity by £2,422. With 1,000 shares outstanding, our best estimate of the impact of taking this project is a loss of value of £2,422/1,000 = £2.42 per share.

Our fertilizer example illustrates how NPV estimates can be used to determine whether an investment is desirable. From our example, notice that if the NPV is negative, the effect on share value will be unfavourable. If the NPV were positive, the effect would be favourable. As a consequence, all we need to know about a particular proposal for the purpose of making an accept–reject decision is whether the NPV is positive or negative.

Given that the goal of financial management is to increase share value, our discussion in this section leads us to the *net present value rule*:

An investment should be accepted if the net present value is positive, and rejected if it is negative.

In the unlikely event that the net present value turned out to be exactly zero, we would be indifferent between taking the investment and not taking it.

Two comments about our example are in order. First, and foremost, it is not the rather mechanical process of discounting the cash flows that is important. Once we have the cash flows and the appropriate discount rate, the required calculations are fairly straightforward. The task of coming up with the cash flows and the discount rate is much more challenging. We shall have much more to say about this in the next few chapters. For the remainder of this chapter we take it as a given that we have estimates of the cash revenues and costs and, where needed, an appropriate discount rate.

The second thing to keep in mind about our example is that the −£2,422 NPV is an estimate. Like any estimate, it can be high or low. The only way to find out the true NPV would be to place the investment up for sale and see what we could get for it. We generally won't be doing this, so it is important that our estimates are reliable. Once again, we shall say more about this later. For the rest of this chapter we shall assume that the estimates are accurate.

EXAMPLE 8.1

Using the NPV Rule

Suppose we are asked to decide whether a new consumer product should be launched. Based on projected sales and costs, we expect that the cash flows over the five-year life of the project will be £2,000 in the first two years, £4,000 in the next two, and £5,000 in the last year. It will cost about £10,000 to begin production. We use a 10 per cent discount rate to evaluate new products. What should we do here?

Given the cash flows and discount rate, we can calculate the total value of the product by discounting the cash flows back to the present:

$$\text{Present value} = (£2,000/1.1) + (2,000/1.1^2) + (4,000/1.1^3)$$
$$+ (4,000/1.1^4) + (5,000/1.1^5)$$
$$= £1,818 + 1,653 + 3,005 + 2,732 + 3,105$$
$$= £12,313$$

The present value of the expected cash flows is £12,313, but the cost of getting those cash flows is only £10,000, so the NPV is £12,313 − 10,000 = £2,313. This is positive; so, based on the net present value rule, we should take on the project.

As we have seen in this section, estimating NPV is one way of assessing the value of a proposed investment. It is certainly not the only way value is assessed, and we now turn to some alternatives. As we shall see, when compared with NPV, each of the alternative ways we shall examine is flawed in some key way; so NPV is the preferred approach in principle, if not always in practice.

Spreadsheet Strategies

Calculating NPVs with a Spreadsheet
Spreadsheets are commonly used to calculate NPVs. Examining the use of spreadsheets in this context also allows us to issue an important warning. Let's redo Example 8.1:

	A	B	C	D	E	F	G	H
1	Year	0	1	2	3	4	5	
2	Cash Flow	-£10,000	£2,000	£2,000	£4,000	£4,000	£5,000	
3								
4	Discount Rate	10%						
5								
6	NPV =	£2,102.72	WRONG!!! Incorrect formula is =NPV(B4,B2:G2)					
7	NPV =	£2,312.99	CORRECT!!! Formula is =NPV(B4,C2:G2)+B2					
8								
9								

Chapter 8 Net Present Value and Other Investment Criteria

In our spreadsheet example, notice that we have provided two answers. By comparing the answers with that found in Example 8.1, we see that the first answer is wrong, even though we used the spreadsheet's NPV formula. What happened is that the 'NPV' function in our spreadsheet is actually a PV function; unfortunately, one of the original spreadsheet programs many years ago got the definition wrong, and subsequent spreadsheets have copied it! Our second answer shows how to use the formula properly.

The example here illustrates the danger of blindly using calculators or computers without understanding what is going on; we shudder to think of how many capital budgeting decisions in the real world are based on incorrect use of this particular function. We shall see another example of something that can go wrong with a spreadsheet later in the chapter.

CONCEPT QUESTIONS

8.1a   What is the net present value rule?
8.1b   If we say an investment has an NPV of €1,000, what exactly do we mean?

8.2   The Payback Rule

It is common in practice to talk of the payback on a proposed investment. Loosely, the *payback* is the length of time it takes to recover our initial investment. Because this idea is widely understood and used, we shall examine it in some detail.

Defining the Rule

payback period
The amount of time required for an investment to generate cash flows sufficient to recover its initial cost.

We can illustrate how to calculate a payback with an example. Figure 8.2 shows the cash flows from a proposed investment. How many years do we have to wait until the accumulated cash flows from this investment equal or exceed the cost of the investment? As Fig. 8.2 indicates, the initial investment is £50,000. After the first year, the firm has recovered £30,000, leaving £20,000. The cash flow in the second year is exactly £20,000, so this investment 'pays for itself' in exactly two years. Put another way, the **payback period** is two years. If we require a payback of, say, three years or less, then this investment is acceptable. This illustrates the *payback period rule*:

Based on the payback rule, an investment is acceptable if its calculated payback period is less than some pre-specified number of years.

In our example, the payback works out to be exactly two years. This won't usually happen, of course. When the numbers don't work out exactly, it is customary to work with fractional years. For example, suppose the initial investment is £60,000, and the cash flows are £20,000 in the first year and £90,000 in the second. The cash flows over the first two years are £110,000, so the project obviously pays back some time in the second year. After the first year, the project has paid back £20,000, leaving £40,000 to be recovered. To figure

FIGURE 8.2

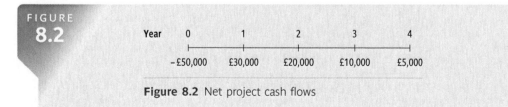

Year	0	1	2	3	4
	-£50,000	£30,000	£20,000	£10,000	£5,000

Figure 8.2 Net project cash flows

out the fractional year, note that this £40,000 is £40,000/90,000 = 4/9 of the second year's cash flow. Assuming that the £90,000 cash flow is received uniformly throughout the year, the payback would be $1^{4}/_{9}$ years.

EXAMPLE 8.2

Calculating Payback

Here are the projected cash flows from a proposed investment:

Year	Cash flow (€)
1	100
2	200
3	500

This project costs €500. What is the payback period for this investment?

The initial cost is €500. After the first two years, the cash flows total €300. After the third year, the total cash flow is €800, so the project pays back some time between the end of year 2 and the end of year 3. Because the accumulated cash flows for the first two years are €300, we need to recover €200 in the third year. The third-year cash flow is €500, so we shall have to wait €200/500 = 0.4 year to do this. The payback period is thus 2.4 years, or about two years and five months.

TABLE 8.1

Year	A (€)	B (€)	C (€)	D (€)	E (€)
0	−100	−200	−200	−200	−50
1	30	40	40	100	100
2	40	20	20	100	−50,000,000
3	50	10	10	−200	
4	60		130	200	

Table 8.1 Expected cash flows for projects A–E

Now that we know how to calculate the payback period on an investment, using the payback period rule for making decisions is straightforward. A particular cut-off time is selected – say, two years – and all investment projects that have payback periods of two years or less are accepted, whereas any that pay off in more than two years are rejected.

Table 8.1 illustrates cash flows for five different projects. The figures shown as the year 0 cash flows are the costs of the investments. We examine these to indicate some peculiarities that can, in principle, arise with payback periods.

The payback for the first project, A, is easily calculated. The sum of the cash flows for the first two years is €70, leaving us with €100 − 70 = €30 to go. Because the cash flow in the third year is €50, the payback occurs some time in that year. When we compare the €30 we need with the €50 that will be coming in, we get €30/50 = 0.6: so payback will occur 60 per cent of the way into the year. The payback period is thus 2.6 years.

Project B's payback is also easy to calculate: it *never* pays back, because the cash flows never total up to the original investment. Project C has a payback of exactly four years, because it supplies the €130 that B is missing in year 4. Project D is a little strange. Because of the negative cash flow in year 3, you can easily verify that it has two different payback periods, two years and four years. Which of these is correct? Both of them; the way the payback period is calculated doesn't guarantee a single answer. Finally, project E is obviously unrealistic, but it does pay back in six months, thereby illustrating the point that a rapid payback does not guarantee a good investment.

Chapter 8 Net Present Value and Other Investment Criteria

Year	Long (€)	Short (€)
0	–250	–250
1	100	100
2	100	200
3	100	0
4	100	0

TABLE 8.2

Table 8.2 Investment projected cash flows

Analysing the Rule

When compared with the NPV rule, the payback period rule has some rather severe short-comings. First, we calculate the payback period by simply adding up the future cash flows. There is no discounting involved, so the time value of money is completely ignored. The payback rule also fails to consider any risk differences. The payback would be calculated the same way for both very risky and very safe projects.

Perhaps the biggest problem with the payback period rule is coming up with the right cut-off period: we don't really have an objective basis for choosing a particular number. Put another way, there is no economic rationale for looking at payback in the first place, so we have no guide for how to pick the cut-off. As a result, we end up using a number that is arbitrarily chosen.

Suppose we have somehow decided on an appropriate payback period of two years or less. As we have seen, the payback period rule ignores the time value of money for the first two years. More seriously, cash flows after the second year are ignored entirely. To see this, consider the two investments, Long and Short, in Table 8.2. Both projects cost €250. Based on our discussion, the payback on Long is 2 + (€50/100) = 2.5 years, and the payback on Short is 1 + (€150/200) = 1.75 years. With a cut-off of two years, Short is acceptable and Long is not.

Is the payback period rule guiding us to the right decisions? Maybe not. Suppose we require a 15 per cent return on this type of investment. We can calculate the NPV for these two investments as

$$\text{NPV(Short)} = -€250 + (100/1.15) + (200/1.15^2) = -€11.81$$
$$\text{NPV(Long)} = -€250 + (100 \times \{[1 - (1/1.15^4)]/0.15\}) = €35.50$$

Now we have a problem. The NPV of the shorter-term investment is actually negative, meaning that taking it diminishes the value of the shareholders' equity. The opposite is true for the longer-term investment – it increases share value.

Our example illustrates two primary shortcomings of the payback period rule. First, by ignoring time value, we may be led to take investments (like Short) that are actually worth less than they cost. Second, by ignoring cash flows beyond the cut-off, we may be led to reject profitable long-term investments (like Long). More generally, using a payback period rule will tend to bias us towards shorter-term investments.

Redeeming Qualities of the Rule

Despite its shortcomings, the payback period rule is often used by large and sophisticated companies when they are making relatively minor decisions. There are several reasons for this. The primary reason is that many decisions simply do not warrant detailed analysis, because the cost of the analysis would exceed the possible loss from a mistake. As a practical matter, it can be said that an investment that pays back rapidly and has benefits extending beyond the cut-off period probably has a positive NPV.

Small investment decisions are made by the hundreds every day in large organizations. Moreover, they are made at all levels. As a result, it would not be uncommon for a corporation to require, for example, a two-year payback on all investments of a very small amount (say, less than £10,000). Larger investments would be subjected to greater scrutiny. The requirement of a two-year payback is not perfect, for reasons we have seen, but it does exercise some control over expenditures, and thus limits possible losses.

In addition to its simplicity, the payback rule has two other positive features. First, because it is biased towards short-term projects, it is biased towards liquidity. In other words, a payback rule tends to favour investments that free up cash for other uses quickly. This could be important for a small business; it would be less so for a large corporation. Second, the cash flows that are expected to occur later in a project's life are probably more uncertain. Arguably, a payback period rule adjusts for the extra riskiness of later cash flows, but it does so in a rather draconian fashion – by ignoring them altogether.

We should note here that some of the apparent simplicity of the payback rule is an illusion. The reason is that we must still come up with the cash flows first, and, as we discussed earlier, this is not at all easy to do. Thus it would probably be more accurate to say that the *concept* of a payback period is both intuitive and easy to understand.

Summary of the Rule

To summarize, the payback period is a kind of 'break-even' measure. Because time value is ignored, you can think of the payback period as the length of time it takes to break even in an accounting sense, but not in an economic sense. The biggest drawback to the payback period rule is that it doesn't ask the right question. The relevant issue is the impact an investment will have on the value of the equity, not how long it takes to recover the initial investment.

Nevertheless, because it is so simple, companies often use it as a screen for dealing with the myriad minor investment decisions they have to make. There is certainly nothing wrong with this practice. As with any simple rule of thumb, there will be some errors in using it; but it wouldn't have survived all this time if it weren't useful. Now that you understand the rule, you can be on the alert for circumstances under which it might lead to problems. To help you remember, Table 8.3 lists the pros and cons of the payback period rule.

TABLE 8.3	Advantages	Disadvantages
	1 Easy to understand.	1 Ignores the time value of money.
	2 Adjusts for uncertainty of later cash flows.	2 Requires an arbitrary cut-off point.
	3 Biased towards liquidity.	3 Ignores cash flows beyond the cut-off date.
		4 Biased against long-term projects, such as research and development, and new projects.

Table 8.3 Advantages and disadvantages of the payback period rule

CONCEPT QUESTIONS	
8.2a	In words, what is the payback period? The payback period rule?
8.2b	Why do we say that the payback period is, in a sense, an accounting break-even measure?

8.3 The Discounted Payback

discounted payback period
The length of time required for an investment's discounted cash flows to equal its initial cost.

We saw that one shortcoming of the payback period rule was that it ignored time value. A variation of the payback period, the discounted payback period, fixes this particular problem. The **discounted payback period** is the length of time until the sum of the discounted cash flows is equal to the initial investment. The *discounted payback rule* would be:

Based on the discounted payback rule, an investment is acceptable if its discounted payback is less than some pre-specified number of years.

To see how we might calculate the discounted payback period, suppose we require a 12.5 per cent return on new investments. We have an investment that costs €300 and has cash flows of €100 per year for five years. To get the discounted payback, we have to discount each cash flow at 12.5 per cent and then start adding them. We do this in Table 8.4. In Table 8.4 we have both the discounted and the undiscounted cash flows. Looking at the accumulated cash flows, we see that the regular payback is exactly three years. The discounted cash flows total €300 only after four years, however, so the discounted payback is four years, as shown.[1]

How do we interpret the discounted payback? Recall that the ordinary payback is the time it takes to break even in an accounting sense. Because it includes the time value of money, the discounted payback is the time it takes to break even in an economic or financial sense. Loosely speaking, in our example, we get our money back, along with the interest we could have earned elsewhere, in four years.

Figure 8.3 illustrates this idea by comparing the *future* value at 12.5 per cent of the €300 investment with the *future* value of the €100 annual cash flows at 12.5 per cent. Notice that the two lines cross at exactly four years. This tells us that the value of the project's cash flows catches up and then passes the original investment in four years.

Table 8.4 and Fig. 8.3 illustrate another interesting feature of the discounted payback period. If a project ever pays back on a discounted basis, then it must have a positive NPV.[2] This is true because, by definition, the NPV is zero when the sum of the discounted cash flows equals the initial investment. For example, the present value of all the cash flows in Table 8.4 is €355. The cost of the project was €300, so the NPV is obviously €55. This €55 is the value of the cash flow that occurs *after* the discounted payback (see the last line in Table 8.4). In general, if we use a discounted payback rule, we won't accidentally take any projects with a negative estimated NPV.

Based on our example, the discounted payback would seem to have much to recommend it. You may be surprised to find that it is rarely used in practice. Why? Probably because it really isn't any simpler to use than NPV. To calculate a discounted payback, you have to discount cash flows, add them up, and compare them with the cost, just as you do with NPV. So, unlike an ordinary payback, the discounted payback is not especially simple to calculate.

TABLE 8.4		Cash flow (€)		Accumulated cash flow (€)	
	Year	Undiscounted	Discounted	Undiscounted	Discounted
	1	100	89	100	89
	2	100	79	200	168
	3	100	70	300	238
	4	100	62	400	300
	5	100	55	500	355

Table 8.4 Ordinary and discounted payback

FIGURE
8.3

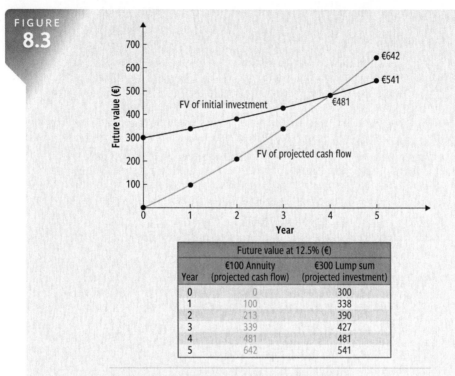

| | Future value at 12.5% (€) | |
Year	€100 Annuity (projected cash flow)	€300 Lump sum (projected investment)
0	0	300
1	100	338
2	213	390
3	339	427
4	481	481
5	642	541

Figure 8.3 Future value of project cash flows

A discounted payback period rule has a couple of other significant drawbacks. The biggest one is that the cut-off still has to be arbitrarily set, and cash flows beyond that point are ignored.[3] As a result, a project with a positive NPV may be found unacceptable because the cut-off is too short. Also, just because one project has a shorter discounted payback than another does not mean it has a larger NPV.

All things considered, the discounted payback is a compromise between a regular payback and NPV that lacks the simplicity of the first and the conceptual rigour of the second. Nonetheless, if we need to assess the time it will take to recover the investment required by a project, then the discounted payback is better than the ordinary payback, because it considers time value. In other words, the discounted payback recognizes that we could have invested the money elsewhere and earned a return on it. The ordinary payback does not take this into account. The advantages and disadvantages of the discounted payback rule are summarized in Table 8.5.

TABLE
8.5

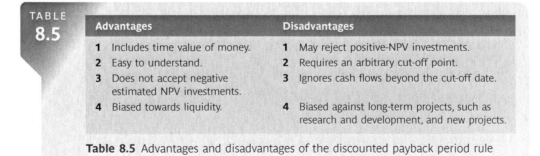

Advantages	Disadvantages
1 Includes time value of money.	1 May reject positive-NPV investments.
2 Easy to understand.	2 Requires an arbitrary cut-off point.
3 Does not accept negative estimated NPV investments.	3 Ignores cash flows beyond the cut-off date.
4 Biased towards liquidity.	4 Biased against long-term projects, such as research and development, and new projects.

Table 8.5 Advantages and disadvantages of the discounted payback period rule

EXAMPLE 8.3 — Calculating Discounted Payback

Consider an investment that costs £400 and pays £100 per year for ever. We use a 20 per cent discount rate on this type of investment. What is the ordinary payback? What is the discounted payback? What is the NPV?

The NPV and ordinary payback are easy to calculate in this case, because the investment is a perpetuity. The present value of the cash flows is £100/0.2 = £500, so the NPV is £500 − 400 = £100. The ordinary payback is obviously four years.

To get the discounted payback, we need to find the number of years such that a £100 annuity has a present value of £400 at 20 per cent. In other words, the present value annuity factor is £400/100 = 4, and the interest rate is 20 per cent per period; so what's the number of periods? If we solve for the number of periods, we find that the answer is a little less than nine years, so this is the discounted payback.

CONCEPT QUESTIONS

8.3a In words, what is the discounted payback period? Why do we say it is, in a sense, a financial or economic break-even measure?

8.3b What advantage(s) does the discounted payback have over the ordinary payback?

8.4 The Average Accounting Return

average accounting return (AAR)
An investment's average net income divided by its average book value.

Another attractive, but flawed, approach to making capital budgeting decisions involves the **average accounting return (AAR)**. There are many different definitions of the AAR. However, in one form or another, the AAR is always defined as

$$\frac{\text{Some measure of average accounting profit}}{\text{Some measure of average accounting value}}$$

The specific definition we shall use is

$$\frac{\text{Average net income}}{\text{Average book value}}$$

To see how we might calculate this number, suppose we are deciding whether to open a store in a new shopping centre. The required investment in improvements is £500,000. The store would have a five-year life, because everything reverts to the centre owners after that time. We shall assume that the required investment would be 100 per cent depreciated (straight-line) over five years,[4] so the depreciation would be £500,000/5 = £100,000 per year. The tax rate is 25 per cent. Table 8.6 contains the projected revenues and expenses. Net income in each year, based on these figures, is also shown.

To calculate the average book value for this investment, we note that we started out with a book value of £500,000 (the initial cost) and ended up at £0. The average book value during the life of the investment is thus (£500,000 + 0)/2 = £250,000. As long as we use straight-line depreciation, the average investment will always be one-half of the initial investment.[5]

Looking at Table 8.6, we see that net income is £100,000 in the first year, £150,000 in the second year, £50,000 in the third year, £0 in Year 4, and −£50,000 in Year 5. The average net income, then, is

[£100,000 + 150,000 + 50,000 + 0 + (−50,000)]/5 = £50,000

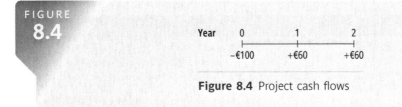

Figure 8.4 Project cash flows

This 10 per cent is what we have already called the return on this investment. What we have now illustrated is that the internal rate of return on an investment (or just 'return' for short) is the discount rate that makes the NPV equal to zero. This is an important observation, so it bears repeating:

The IRR on an investment is the required return that results in a zero NPV when it is used as the discount rate.

The fact that the IRR is simply the discount rate that makes the NPV equal to zero is important, because it tells us how to calculate the returns on more complicated investments. As we have seen, finding the IRR turns out to be relatively easy for a single-period investment. However, suppose you were now looking at an investment with the cash flows shown in Fig. 8.4. As illustrated, this investment costs €100 and has a cash flow of €60 per year for two years, so it's only slightly more complicated than our single-period example. However, if you were asked for the return on this investment, what would you say? There doesn't seem to be any obvious answer (at least not to us). However, based on what we now know, we can set the NPV equal to zero and solve for the discount rate:

$$NPV = 0 = -€100 + [60/(1 + IRR)] + [60/(1 + IRR)^2]$$

Unfortunately, the only way to find the IRR in general is by trial and error, either by hand or by calculator. This is precisely the same problem that came up in Chapter 4 when we found the unknown rate for an annuity and in Chapter 6 when we found the yield to maturity on a bond. In fact, we now see that in both of those cases we were finding an IRR.

In this particular case the cash flows form a two-period, €60 annuity. To find the unknown rate, we can try some different rates until we get the answer. If we were to start with a 0 per cent rate, the NPV would obviously be €120 − 100 = €20. At a 10 per cent discount rate, we would have

$$NPV = -€100 + (60/1.1) + (60/1.1^2) = €4.13$$

Now, we're getting close. We can summarize these and some other possibilities as shown in Table 8.8. From our calculations the NPV appears to be zero with a discount rate between 10 per cent and 15 per cent, so the IRR is somewhere in that range. With a little more effort we can find that the IRR is about 13.1 per cent.[7] So, if our required return were less than 13.1 per cent, we would take this investment. If our required return exceeded 13.1 per cent, we would reject it.

Discount rate (%)	NPV (€)
0	20.00
5	11.56
10	4.13
15	−2.46
20	−8.33

Table 8.8 NPV at different discount rates

FIGURE
8.5

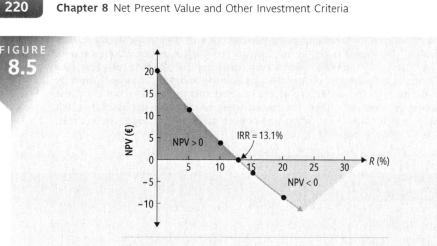

Figure 8.5 An NPV profile

By now you have probably noticed that the IRR rule and the NPV rule appear to be quite similar. In fact, the IRR is sometimes simply called the *discounted cash flow return*, or *DCF return*. The easiest way to illustrate the relationship between NPV and IRR is to plot the numbers we calculated for Table 8.8. We put the different NPVs on the vertical axis, or *y*-axis, and the discount rates on the horizontal axis, or *x*-axis. If we had a very large number of points the resulting picture would be a smooth curve called a **net present value profile**. Figure 8.5 illustrates the NPV profile for this project. Beginning with a 0 per cent discount rate, we have €20 plotted directly on the *y*-axis. As the discount rate increases, the NPV declines smoothly. Where will the curve cut through the *x*-axis? This will occur where the NPV is just equal to zero, so it will happen right at the IRR of 13.1 per cent.

In our example the NPV rule and the IRR rule lead to identical accept–reject decisions. We shall accept an investment using the IRR rule if the required return is less than 13.1 per cent. As Fig. 8.5 illustrates, however, the NPV is positive at any discount rate less than 13.1 per cent, so we would accept the investment using the NPV rule as well. The two rules give equivalent results in this case.

net present value profile
A graphical representation of the relationship between an investment's NPVs and various discount rates.

EXAMPLE
8.4

Calculating the IRR

A project has a total up-front cost of €435.44. The cash flows are €100 in the first year, €200 in the second year, and €300 in the third year. What's the IRR? If we require an 18 per cent return, should we take this investment?

We'll describe the NPV profile and find the IRR by calculating some NPVs at different discount rates. You should check our answers for practice. Beginning with 0 per cent, we have:

Discount rate (%)	NPV (€)
0	164.56
5	100.36
10	46.15
15	0.00
20	−39.61

The NPV is zero at 15 per cent, so 15 per cent is the IRR. If we require an 18 per cent return, then we should not take the investment. The reason is that the NPV is negative at 18 per cent (verify that it is −€24.47). The IRR rule tells us the same thing in this case. We shouldn't take this investment, because its 15 per cent return is below our required 18 per cent return.

Non-conventional cash flows can occur in a variety of ways. For example, ore mining firms open and close operations depending on the price of the ore that is being extracted. This results in negative cash flows during the periods in which the mine is closed, and positive cash flows when it is open. Sometimes the cost of maintaining a disused mine is significantly better than running a loss-making mining operation.

The moral of the story is that when the cash flows aren't conventional, strange things can start to happen to the IRR. This is not anything to get upset about, however, because the NPV rule, as always, works just fine. This illustrates the fact that, oddly enough, the obvious question – What's the rate of return? – may not always have a good answer.

EXAMPLE 8.5

What's the IRR?

You are looking at an investment that requires you to invest €51 today. You'll get €100 in one year, but you must pay out €50 in two years. What is the IRR on this investment?

You're on the alert now for the non-conventional cash flow problem, so you probably wouldn't be surprised to see more than one IRR. However, if you start looking for an IRR by trial and error, it will take you a long time. The reason is that there is no IRR. The NPV is negative at every discount rate, so we shouldn't take this investment under any circumstances. What's the return on this investment? Your guess is as good as ours.

EXAMPLE 8.6

'I Think, Therefore I Know How Many IRRs There Can Be.'

We've seen that it's possible to get more than one IRR. If you wanted to make sure that you had found all the possible IRRs, how could you do it? The answer comes from the great mathematician, philosopher and financial analyst Descartes (of 'I think, therefore I am' fame). Descartes' Rule of Sign says that the maximum number of IRRs that there can be is equal to the number of times that the cash flows change sign from positive to negative and/or negative to positive.[8]

In our example with the 25 per cent and $33^1/_3$ per cent IRRs, could there be yet another IRR? The cash flows flip from negative to positive, then back to negative, for a total of two sign changes. Therefore, according to Descartes' rule, the maximum number of IRRs is two and we don't need to look for any more. Note that the actual number of IRRs can be less than the maximum (see Example 8.5).

Mutually Exclusive Investments   Even if there is a single IRR, another problem can arise concerning **mutually exclusive investment decisions**. If two investments, X and Y, are mutually exclusive, then taking one of them means that we cannot take the other. Two projects that are not mutually exclusive are said to be independent. For example, if we own one corner lot, then we can build a petrol station or an apartment building, but not both. These are mutually exclusive alternatives.

Thus far we have asked whether a given investment is worth undertaking. However, a related question comes up often: given two or more mutually exclusive investments, which one is the best? The answer is simple enough: the best one is the one with the largest NPV. Can we also say that the best one has the highest return? As we show, the answer is no.

To illustrate the problem with the IRR rule and mutually exclusive investments, consider the following cash flows from two mutually exclusive investments:

> **mutually exclusive investment decisions**
> A situation in which taking one investment prevents the taking of another.

Chapter 8 Net Present Value and Other Investment Criteria

Year	Investment A (€)	Investment B (€)
0	−100	−100
1	50	20
2	40	40
3	40	50
4	30	60

The IRR for A is 24 per cent, and the IRR for B is 21 per cent. Because these investments are mutually exclusive, we can take only one of them. Simple intuition suggests that investment A is better because of its higher return. Unfortunately, simple intuition is not always correct.

To see why investment A is not necessarily the better of the two investments, we've calculated the NPV of these investments for different required returns:

Discount rate (%)	NPV(A) (€)	NPV(B) (€)
0	60.00	70.00
5	43.13	47.88
10	29.06	29.79
15	17.18	14.82
20	7.06	2.31
25	−1.63	−8.22

The IRR for A (24 per cent) is larger than the IRR for B (21 per cent). However, if you compare the NPVs, you'll see that which investment has the higher NPV depends on our required return. B has greater total cash flow, but it pays back more slowly than A. As a result, it has a higher NPV at lower discount rates.

In our example, the NPV and IRR rankings conflict for some discount rates. If our required return is 10 per cent, for instance, then B has the higher NPV and is thus the better of the two, even though A has the higher return. If our required return is 15 per cent, then there is no ranking conflict: A is better.

The conflict between the IRR and NPV for mutually exclusive investments can be illustrated by plotting the investments' NPV profiles as we have done in Fig. 8.8. In Fig. 8.8

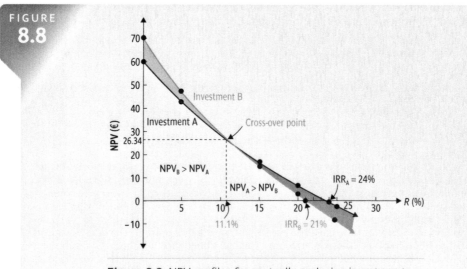

Figure 8.8 NPV profiles for mutually exclusive investments

	Advantages	Disadvantages
1	Closely related to NPV, often leading to identical decisions.	**1** May result in multiple answers, or not deal with non-conventional cash flows.
2	Easy to understand and communicate.	**2** May lead to incorrect decisions in comparisons of mutually exclusive investments.

Table 8.9 Advantages and disadvantages of the internal rate of return

Finally, under certain circumstances, the IRR may have a practical advantage over the NPV. We can't estimate the NPV unless we know the appropriate discount rate, but we can still estimate the IRR. Suppose we didn't know the required return on an investment, but we found, for example, that it had a 40 per cent return. We would probably be inclined to take it, because it would be unlikely that the required return would be that high. The advantages and disadvantages of the IRR are summarized in Table 8.9.

The Modified Internal Rate of Return (MIRR)

To address some of the problems that can crop up with the standard IRR, it is often proposed that a modified version be used. As we shall see, there are several different ways of calculating a modified IRR, or MIRR, but the basic idea is to modify the cash flows first and then calculate an IRR using the modified cash flows.

To illustrate, let's go back to the cash flows in Fig. 8.6: −€60, +€155 and −€100. As we saw, there are two IRRs, 25 per cent and $33^1/_3$ per cent. We next illustrate three different MIRRs, all of which have the property that only one answer will result, thereby eliminating the multiple IRR problem.

Method 1: The Discounting Approach   With the discounting approach, the idea is to discount all negative cash flows back to the present at the required return and add them to the initial cost, and then calculate the IRR. Because only the first modified cash flow is negative, there will be only one IRR. The discount rate used might be the required return, or it might be some other externally supplied rate. We shall use the project's required return.

If the required return on the project is 20 per cent, then the modified cash flows look like this:

$$\text{Time 0: } -€60 + \frac{-€100}{1.20^2} = -€129.44$$
$$\text{Time 1: } +€155$$
$$\text{Time 2: } +€0$$

If you calculate the MIRR now, you should get 19.74 per cent.

Method 2: The Reinvestment Approach   With the reinvestment approach, we compound *all* cash flows (positive and negative) except the first out to the end of the project's life, and then calculate the IRR. In a sense, we are 'reinvesting' the cash flows, and not taking them out of the project until the very end. The rate we use could be the required return on the project, or it could be a separately specified 'reinvestment rate'. We shall use the project's required return. When we do, here are the modified cash flows:

$$\text{Time 0: } -€60$$
$$\text{Time 1: } +0$$
$$\text{Time 2: } -€100 + (€155 \times 1.2) = €86$$

Chapter 8 Net Present Value and Other Investment Criteria

The MIRR on this set of cash flows is 19.72 per cent, or a little lower than we got using the discounting approach.

Method 3: The Combination Approach   As the name suggests, the combination approach blends our first two methods. Negative cash flows are discounted back to the present, and positive cash flows are compounded to the end of the project. In practice, different discount or compounding rates might be used, but we shall again stick with the project's required return.

With the combination approach, the modified cash flows are as follows:

$$\text{Time 0: } -\text{€}60 + \frac{-\text{€}100}{1.20^2} = -\text{€}129.44$$

Time 1: +0
Time 2: €155 × 1.2 = €186

See if you don't agree that the MIRR is 19.87 per cent, the highest of the three.

MIRR or IRR: Which Is Better?   MIRRs are controversial. At one extreme are those who claim that MIRRs are always superior to IRRs. For example, by design, they clearly don't suffer from the multiple rate of return problem.

At the other end, detractors say that MIRR should stand for 'meaningless internal rate of return'. As our example makes clear, one problem with MIRRs is that there are different ways of calculating them, and there is no clear reason to say that one of our three methods is better than any other. The differences are small with our simple cash flows, but they could be much larger for a more complex project. Moreover, it's not clear how to interpret an MIRR. It may look like a rate of return, but it's a rate of return on a modified set of cash flows, not the project's actual cash flows.

We're not going to take sides. However, notice that calculating an MIRR requires discounting, compounding, or both, which leads to two obvious observations. First, if we have the relevant discount rate, why not calculate the NPV and be done with it? Second, because an MIRR depends on an externally supplied discount (or compounding) rate, the answer you get is not truly an 'internal' rate of return, which by definition depends only on the project's cash flows.

We shall take a stand on one issue that frequently comes up in this context. The value of a project does not depend on what the firm does with the cash flows generated by that project. A firm might use a project's cash flows to fund other projects, to pay dividends, or to buy an executive jet. It doesn't matter: how the cash flows are spent in the future does not affect their value today. As a result, there is generally no need to consider reinvestment of interim cash flows.

CONCEPT QUESTIONS

8.5a   Under what circumstances will the IRR and NPV rules lead to the same accept–reject decisions? When might they conflict?

8.5b   Is it generally true that an advantage of the IRR rule over the NPV rule is that we don't need to know the required return to use the IRR rule?

8.6 The Profitability Index

profitability index (PI)
The present value of an investment's future cash flows divided by its initial cost. Also called the *benefit–cost ratio.*

Another tool used to evaluate projects is called the **profitability index (PI)** or benefit–cost ratio. This index is defined as the present value of the future cash flows divided by the initial investment. So, if a project costs €200 and the present value of its future cash flows is €220, the profitability index value would be €220/200 = 1.1. Notice that the NPV for this investment is €20, so it is a desirable investment.

More generally, if a project has a positive NPV, then the present value of the future cash flows must be bigger than the initial investment. The profitability index

TABLE
8.10

Advantages	Disadvantages
1 Closely related to NPV, generally leading to identical decisions.	**1** May lead to incorrect decisions in comparisons of mutually exclusive investments.
2 Easy to understand and communicate.	
3 May be useful when available investment funds are limited.	

Table 8.10 Advantages and disadvantages of the profitability index

would thus be bigger than 1 for a positive-NPV investment and less than 1 for a negative-NPV investment.

How do we interpret the profitability index? In our example, the PI was 1.1. This tells us that, per euro invested, €1.10 in value or €0.10 in NPV results. The profitability index thus measures the value created per cash unit invested. For this reason, it is often proposed as a measure of performance for government or other not-for-profit investments. Also, when capital is scarce, it may make sense to allocate it to projects with the highest PIs. We shall return to this issue in a later chapter.

The PI is obviously similar to the NPV. However, consider an investment that costs €5 and has a €10 present value, and an investment that costs €100 with a €150 present value. The first of these investments has an NPV of €5 and a PI of 2. The second has an NPV of €50 and a PI of 1.5. If these are mutually exclusive investments, then the second one is preferred even though it has a lower PI. This ranking problem is similar to the IRR ranking problem we saw in the previous section. In all, there seems to be little reason to rely on the PI instead of the NPV. Our discussion of the PI is summarized in Table 8.10.

CONCEPT QUESTIONS	8.6a What does the profitability index measure?
	8.6b How would you state the profitability index rule?

8.7 The Practice of Capital Budgeting

Given that NPV seems to be telling us directly what we want to know, you might be wondering why there are so many other procedures, and why alternative procedures are commonly used. Recall that we are trying to make an investment decision, and that we are frequently operating under considerable uncertainty about the future. We can only *estimate* the NPV of an investment in this case. The resulting estimate can be very 'soft', meaning that the true NPV might be quite different.

Because the true NPV is unknown, the astute financial manager seeks clues to help in assessing whether the estimated NPV is reliable. For this reason, firms would typically use multiple criteria for evaluating a proposal. For example, suppose we have an investment with a positive estimated NPV. Based on our experience with other projects, this one appears to have a short payback and a very high AAR. In this case, the different indicators seem to agree that it's 'all systems go'. Put another way, the payback and the AAR are consistent with the conclusion that the NPV is positive.

On the other hand, suppose we had a positive estimated NPV, a long payback, and a low AAR. This could still be a good investment, but it looks as though we need to be much more careful in making the decision, because we are getting conflicting signals. If the estimated NPV is based on projections in which we have little confidence, then further analysis is probably in order. We shall consider how to evaluate NPV estimates in more detail in the next two chapters.

EXAMPLE
8.8

Bringing It All Together: Evaluating a Project Using Several Capital Budgeting Appraisal Techniques

Sandy Grey Ltd is in the process of deciding whether or not to revise its line of mobile phones that it manufactures and sells. Its sole market is large corporations, and it has not as yet focused on the retail sector. The company has estimated that the revision will cost £220,000. Cash flows from increased sales will be £80,000 in the first year. These cash flows will increase by 5% per year. The company estimates that the new line will be obsolete five years from now. Assume the initial cost is paid now, and all revenues are received at the end of each year. If the company requires a 10 per cent return for such an investment, should it undertake the revision? Use three investment evaluation techniques to arrive at your answer.

We shall look at NPV, IRR and the profitability index. However, it is easy to consider the payback period or discounted payback period.

If the cash flows increase by 5 per cent per year, they will be as follows:

Year	0	1	2	3	4	5
Cash flow (£)	−220,000	80,000	84,000	88,200	92,610	97,240.5

The NPV of the investment is

$$\text{NPV} = -£220,000 + \frac{£80,000}{(1+0.10)} + \frac{£84,000}{(1+0.10)^2} + \frac{£88,200}{(1+0.10)^3} + \frac{£92,610}{(1+0.10)^4} + \frac{£97,240.5}{(1+0.10)^5}$$

$$= £112,047$$

The IRR of the investment is

$$\text{NPV} = 0$$

$$= -£220,000 + \frac{£80,000}{(1+\text{IRR})} + \frac{£84,000}{(1+\text{IRR})^2} + \frac{£88,200}{(1+\text{IRR})^3} + \frac{£92,610}{(1+\text{IRR})^4} + \frac{£97,240.5}{(1+\text{IRR})^5}$$

Using trial and error, the IRR is

$$\text{IRR} = 27.69\%$$

The profitability index of the investment is

$$\text{PI} = \left[\frac{£80,000}{(1+\text{IRR})} + \frac{£84,000}{(1+\text{IRR})^2} + \frac{£88,200}{(1+\text{IRR})^3} + \frac{£92,610}{(1+\text{IRR})^4} + \frac{£97,240.5}{(1+\text{IRR})^5} \right] \Big/ £220,000$$

$$= 1.509$$

With all methods the project looks viable, and should be undertaken.

So far this chapter has asked 'Which capital budgeting methods should companies be using?' An equally important question is this: which methods *are* companies using? Table 8.11 helps to answer this question. As can be seen from the table, there is quite a strong variation in the frequency with which different techniques are utilized. Other more advanced techniques, such as real options, break-even and sensitivity analysis, are covered in later chapters.

Most companies use the IRR and NPV methods. This is not surprising, given the theoretical advantages of these approaches. The most interesting point is that for the UK, Germany and France, payback period is the most popular technique to appraise new projects, which is surprising, given the conceptual problems with this approach. However, as we have discussed, the flaws of payback period may be relatively easy to correct. For example,

TABLE 8.11	US	UK	The Netherlands	Germany	France
Net present value	74.93	46.97	70.00	47.58	35.09
Internal rate of return	75.61	53.13	56.00	42.15	44.07
Accounting rate of return	20.29	38.10	25.00	32.17	16.07
Profitability index	11.87	15.87	8.16	16.07	37.74
Payback period	56.74	69.23	64.71	50.00	50.88
Discounted payback	29.45	25.40	25.00	30.51	11.32
Hurdle rate	56.94	26.98	41.67	28.81	3.85
Sensitivity analysis	51.54	42.86	36.73	28.07	10.42
Real options	26.56	29.03	34.69	44.04	53.06

Source: Table 2 from D. Brounen, A. de Jong and K. Koedijk, 'Corporate finance in Europe: confronting theory and practice', *Journal of Banking and Finance* (2006), vol. 30, no. 5, pp. 1409–1442.

Table 8.11 Capital budgeting techniques in practice

although the payback method ignores all cash flows after the payback period, an alert manager can make ad hoc adjustments for a project with back-loaded cash flows.

For future reference, the various criteria we have discussed are summarized in Table 8.12.

TABLE 8.12

Discounted cash flow criteria

A *Net present value (NPV)*: The NPV of an investment is the difference between its market value and its cost. The NPV rule is to take a project if its NPV is positive. NPV is frequently estimated by calculating the present value of the future cash flows (to estimate market value) and then subtracting the cost. NPV has no serious flaws; it is the preferred decision criterion.

B *Internal rate of return (IRR)*: The IRR is the discount rate that makes the estimated NPV of an investment equal to zero; it is sometimes called the *discounted cash flow (DCF) return*. The IRR rule is to take a project when its IRR exceeds the required return. IRR is closely related to NPV, and it leads to exactly the same decisions as NPV for conventional, independent projects. When project cash flows are not conventional there may be no IRR, or there may be more than one. More seriously, the IRR cannot be used to rank mutually exclusive projects; the project with the highest IRR is not necessarily the preferred investment.

C *Modified internal rate of return (MIRR)*: The MIRR is a modification to the IRR. A project's cash flows are modified by: (1) discounting the negative cash flows back to the present; (2) compounding cash flows to the end of the project's life; or (3) combining (1) and (2). An IRR is then computed on the modified cash flows. MIRRs are guaranteed to avoid the multiple rate of return problem, but it is unclear how to interpret them; and they are not truly 'internal', because they depend on externally supplied discounting or compounding rates.

D *Profitability index (PI)*: The PI, also called the *benefit–cost ratio*, is the ratio of present value to cost. The PI rule is to take an investment if the index exceeds 1. The PI measures the present value of an investment per unit of currency invested. It is quite similar to NPV, but, like IRR, it cannot be used to rank mutually exclusive projects. However, it is sometimes used to rank projects when a firm has more positive NPV investments than it can currently finance.

Table 8.12 Summary of investment criteria

TABLE 8.12

Payback criteria
A *Payback period*: The payback period is the length of time until the sum of an investment's cash flows equals its cost. The payback period rule is to take a project if its payback is less than some cut-off. The payback period is a flawed criterion, primarily because it ignores risk, the time value of money, and cash flows beyond the cut-off point. **B** *Discounted payback period*: The discounted payback period is the length of time until the sum of an investment's discounted cash flows equals its cost. The discounted payback period rule is to take an investment if the discounted payback is less than some cut-off. The discounted payback rule is flawed, primarily because it ignores cash flows after the cut-off.

Accounting criterion
A *Average accounting return (AAR)*: The AAR is a measure of accounting profit relative to book value. It is *not* related to the IRR, but it is similar to the accounting return on assets (ROA) measure in Chapter 3. The AAR rule is to take an investment if its AAR exceeds a benchmark AAR. The AAR is seriously flawed for a variety of reasons, and it has little to recommend it.

Table 8.12 *Continued*

CONCEPT QUESTIONS

8.7a   What are the most commonly used capital budgeting procedures?

8.7b   If NPV is conceptually the best procedure for capital budgeting, why do you think multiple measures are used in practice?

Summary and Conclusions

This chapter has covered the different criteria used to evaluate proposed investments. The seven criteria, in the order we discussed them, are these:

1   Net present value (NPV)

2   Payback period

3   Discounted payback period

4   Average accounting return (AAR)

5   Internal rate of return (IRR)

6   Modified internal rate of return (MIRR)

7   Profitability index (PI)

We illustrated how to calculate each of these, and discussed the interpretation of the results. We also described the advantages and disadvantages of each of them. Ultimately a good capital budgeting criterion must tell us two things. First, is a particular project a good investment? Second, if we have more than one good project, but we can take only one of them, which one should we take? The main point of this chapter is that only the NPV criterion can always provide the correct answer to both questions.

Average book value is

$$\text{Average book value} = €12{,}000/2 = €6{,}000$$

So the average accounting return is

$$\text{AAR} = €4{,}000/6{,}000 = 66.67\%$$

This is an impressive return. Remember, however, that it isn't really a rate of return like an interest rate or an IRR, so the size doesn't tell us a lot. In particular, our money is probably not going to grow at a rate of 66.67 per cent per year, we're sorry to say.

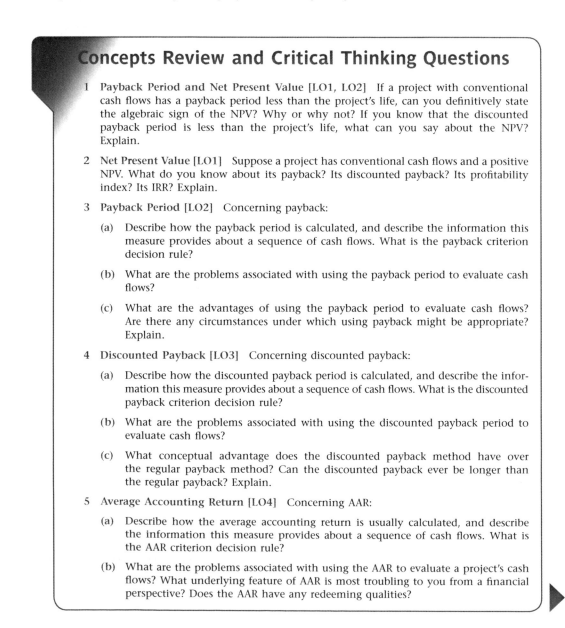

Concepts Review and Critical Thinking Questions

1 **Payback Period and Net Present Value [LO1, LO2]** If a project with conventional cash flows has a payback period less than the project's life, can you definitively state the algebraic sign of the NPV? Why or why not? If you know that the discounted payback period is less than the project's life, what can you say about the NPV? Explain.

2 **Net Present Value [LO1]** Suppose a project has conventional cash flows and a positive NPV. What do you know about its payback? Its discounted payback? Its profitability index? Its IRR? Explain.

3 **Payback Period [LO2]** Concerning payback:

(a) Describe how the payback period is calculated, and describe the information this measure provides about a sequence of cash flows. What is the payback criterion decision rule?

(b) What are the problems associated with using the payback period to evaluate cash flows?

(c) What are the advantages of using the payback period to evaluate cash flows? Are there any circumstances under which using payback might be appropriate? Explain.

4 **Discounted Payback [LO3]** Concerning discounted payback:

(a) Describe how the discounted payback period is calculated, and describe the information this measure provides about a sequence of cash flows. What is the discounted payback criterion decision rule?

(b) What are the problems associated with using the discounted payback period to evaluate cash flows?

(c) What conceptual advantage does the discounted payback method have over the regular payback method? Can the discounted payback ever be longer than the regular payback? Explain.

5 **Average Accounting Return [LO4]** Concerning AAR:

(a) Describe how the average accounting return is usually calculated, and describe the information this measure provides about a sequence of cash flows. What is the AAR criterion decision rule?

(b) What are the problems associated with using the AAR to evaluate a project's cash flows? What underlying feature of AAR is most troubling to you from a financial perspective? Does the AAR have any redeeming qualities?

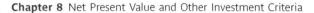

6   **Net Present Value [LO1]**   Concerning NPV:

(a)   Describe how NPV is calculated, and describe the information this measure provides about a sequence of cash flows. What is the NPV criterion decision rule?

(b)   Why is NPV considered a superior method of evaluating the cash flows from a project? Suppose the NPV for a project's cash flows is computed to be £2,500. What does this number represent with respect to the firm's shareholders?

7   **Internal Rate of Return [LO5]**   Concerning IRR:

(a)   Describe how the IRR is calculated, and describe the information this measure provides about a sequence of cash flows. What is the IRR criterion decision rule?

(b)   What is the relationship between IRR and NPV? Are there any situations in which you might prefer one method over the other? Explain.

(c)   Despite its shortcomings in some situations, why do most financial managers use IRR along with NPV when evaluating projects? Can you think of a situation in which IRR might be a more appropriate measure to use than NPV? Explain.

8   **Profitability Index [LO7]**   Concerning the profitability index:

(a)   Describe how the profitability index is calculated, and describe the information this measure provides about a sequence of cash flows. What is the profitability index decision rule?

(b)   What is the relationship between the profitability index and NPV? Are there any situations in which you might prefer one method over the other? Explain.

9   **Payback and Internal Rate of Return [LO2, LO5]**   A project has perpetual cash flows of C per period, a cost of I, and a required return of R. What is the relationship between the project's payback and its IRR? What implications does your answer have for long-lived projects with relatively constant cash flows?

10   **International Investment Projects [LO1]**   In January 2008 automobile manufacturer Volkswagen announced plans to build an automatic transmission and engine plant in the US. Volkswagen apparently felt that it would be better able to compete and create value in the US with US-based facilities rather than export its automobiles from Europe. Other companies, such as BMW, Fiat and Mercedes, have reached similar conclusions and taken similar actions. What are some of the reasons why manufacturers might arrive at the same conclusion to set up facilities abroad rather than simply export their products?

11   **Capital Budgeting Problems [LO1]**   What difficulties might come up in actual applications of the various criteria we have discussed in this chapter? Which one would be the easiest to implement in actual applications? The most difficult?

12   **Capital Budgeting in Not-for-Profit Entities [LO1]**   Are the capital budgeting criteria we have discussed applicable to not-for-profit corporations? How should such entities make capital budgeting decisions? What about governments? Should they evaluate spending proposals using these techniques?

13   **Modified Internal Rate of Return [LO6]**   One of the less flattering interpretations of the acronym MIRR is 'meaningless internal rate of return'. Why do you think this term is applied to MIRR?

14   **Net Present Value [LO1]**   It is sometimes stated that 'the net present value approach assumes reinvestment of the intermediate cash flows at the required return'. Is this claim correct? To answer, suppose you calculate the NPV of a project in the usual way. Next, suppose you do the following:

(a) Calculate the future value (as of the end of the project) of all the cash flows other than the initial outlay, assuming they are reinvested at the required return, and producing a single future value figure for the project.

(b) Calculate the NPV of the project using the single future value calculated in the previous step, and the initial outlay. It is easy to verify that you will get the same NPV as in your original calculation only if you use the required return as the reinvestment rate in the previous step.

15 **Internal Rate of Return [LO5]** It is sometimes stated that 'the internal rate of return approach assumes reinvestment of the intermediate cash flows at the internal rate of return'. Is this claim correct? To answer, suppose you calculate the IRR of a project in the usual way. Next, suppose you do the following:

(a) Calculate the future value (as of the end of the project) of all the cash flows other than the initial outlay, assuming they are reinvested at the IRR, and producing a single future value figure for the project.

(b) Calculate the IRR of the project using the single future value calculated in the previous step and the initial outlay. It is easy to verify that you will get the same IRR as in your original calculation only if you use the IRR as the reinvestment rate in the previous step.

connect Questions and Problems

BASIC

1–19

1 **Calculating Payback [LO2]** What is the payback period for the following set of cash flows?

Year	Cash flow (R)
0	−6,400
1	1,600
2	1,900
3	2,300
4	1,400

2 **Calculating Payback [LO2]** An investment project provides cash inflows of £765 per year for eight years. What is the project payback period if the initial cost is £2,400? What if the initial cost is £3,600? What if it is £6,500?

3 **Calculating Payback [LO2]** Koop Kust NV imposes a payback cut-off of three years for its international investment projects. If the company has the following two projects available, should it accept either of them?

Year	Cash flow (A) (€)	Cash flow (B) (€)
0	−50,000	−60,000
1	9,000	24,000
2	35,000	7,000
3	18,000	24,000
4	6,000	270,000

4 **Calculating Discounted Payback [LO3]** An investment project has annual cash inflows of €4,200, €5,300, €6,100 and €7,400, and a discount rate of 14 per cent. What is the discounted payback period for these cash flows if the initial cost is €7,000? What if the initial cost is €10,000? What if it is €13,000?

5 **Calculating Discounted Payback [LO3]** An investment project costs €30,000, and has annual cash flows of €8,300 for six years. What is the discounted payback period if the discount rate is zero per cent? What if the discount rate is 7 per cent? If it is 20 per cent?

6 **Calculating AAR [LO4]** You're trying to determine whether to expand your business by building a new manufacturing plant. The plant has an installation cost of £15 million, which will be depreciated straight-line to zero over its four-year life. If the plant has projected net income of £1,938,200, £2,201,600, £1,876,000 and £1,329,500 over these four years, what is the project's average accounting return (AAR)?

7 **Calculating IRR [LO5]** A firm evaluates all of its projects by applying the IRR rule. If the required return is 20 per cent, should the firm accept the following project?

Year	Cash flow (€)
0	−30,000
1	15,000
2	17,000
3	14,000

8 **Calculating NPV [LO1]** For the cash flows in the previous problem, suppose the firm uses the NPV decision rule. At a required return of 12 per cent, should the firm accept this project? What if the required return was 40 per cent?

9 **Calculating NPV and IRR [LO1, 5]** A project that provides annual cash flows of €28,500 for nine years costs €138,000 today. Is this a good project if the required return is 8 per cent? What if it's 20 per cent? At what discount rate would you be indifferent between accepting the project and rejecting it?

10 **Calculating IRR [LO5]** What is the IRR of the following set of cash flows?

Year	Cash flow (£)
1	9,800
2	10,300
3	8,600

11 **Calculating NPV [LO1]** For the cash flows in the previous problem, what is the NPV at a discount rate of zero per cent? What if the discount rate is 5 per cent? If it is 15 per cent? If it is 25 per cent?

12 **NPV versus IRR [LO1, LO5]** Mahjong SA has identified the following two mutually exclusive projects:

Year	Cash flow (A) (€)	Cash flow (B) (€)
0	−43,000	−43,000
1	23,000	7,000
2	17,900	13,800
3	12,400	24,000
4	9,400	26,000

(a) What is the IRR for each of these projects? Using the IRR decision rule, which project should the company accept? Is this decision necessarily correct?

(b) If the required return is 11 per cent, what is the NPV for each of these projects? Which project will the company choose if it applies the NPV decision rule?

(c)   Over what range of discount rates would the company choose project A? Project B? At what discount rate would the company be indifferent between these two projects? Explain.

13   **NPV versus IRR [LO1, LO5]**   Consider the following two mutually exclusive projects:

Year	Cash flow (X) (DKr)	Cash flow (Y) (DKr)
0	−15,000	−15,000
1	8,150	7,700
2	5,050	5,150
3	6,800	7,250

Sketch the NPV profiles for X and Y over a range of discount rates from zero to 25 per cent. What is the crossover rate for these two projects?

14   **Problems with IRR [LO5]**   Light Sweet Petroleum AG is trying to evaluate a generation project with the following cash flows:

Year	Cash flow (SKr)
0	−45,000,000
1	78,000,000
2	−14,000,000

(a)   If the company requires a 12 per cent return on its investments, should it accept this project? Why?

(b)   Compute the IRR for this project. How many IRRs are there? Using the IRR decision rule, should the company accept the project? What's going on here?

15   **Calculating Profitability Index [LO7]**   What is the profitability index for the following set of cash flows if the relevant discount rate is 10 per cent? What if the discount rate is 15 per cent? If it is 22 per cent?

Year	Cash flow (€)
0	−14,000
1	7,300
2	6,900
3	5,700

16   **Problems with Profitability Index [LO1, LO7]**   Weiland Computers GmbH is trying to choose between the following two mutually exclusive design projects:

Year	Cash flow (I) (€)	Cash flow (II) (€)
0	−53,000	−16,000
1	27,000	9,100
2	27,000	9,100
3	27,000	9,100

(a)   If the required return is 10 per cent and the company applies the profitability index decision rule, which project should the firm accept?

(b)   If the company applies the NPV decision rule, which project should it take?

(c)   Explain why your answers in (a) and (b) are different.

17   Comparing Investment Criteria [LO1, LO2, LO3, LO5, LO7]   Consider the following two mutually exclusive projects:

Year	Cash flow (A) (NKr)	Cash flow (B) (NKr)
0	–300,000	–40,000
1	20,000	19,000
2	50,000	12,000
3	50,000	18,000
4	390,000	10,500

Whichever project you choose, if any, you require a 15 per cent return on your investment.

(a)   If you apply the payback criterion, which investment will you choose? Why?

(b)   If you apply the discounted payback criterion, which investment will you choose? Why?

(c)   If you apply the NPV criterion, which investment will you choose? Why?

(d)   If you apply the IRR criterion, which investment will you choose? Why?

(e)   If you apply the profitability index criterion, which investment will you choose? Why?

(f)   Based on your answers in (a)–(e), which project will you finally choose? Why?

18   NPV and Discount Rates [LO1]   An investment has an installed cost of €700,000. The cash flows over the four-year life of the investment are projected to be €250,000, €300,000, €225,000 and €175,000. If the discount rate is zero, what is the NPV? If the discount rate is infinite, what is the NPV? At what discount rate is the NPV just equal to zero? Sketch the NPV profile for this investment, based on these three points.

19   MIRR [LO6]   Slow Ride plc is evaluating a project with the following cash flows:

Year	Cash flow (£)
0	–19,000
1	7,100
2	8,800
3	9,400
4	4,500
5	–7,100

The company uses a 12 per cent interest rate on all of its projects. Calculate the MIRR of the project using all three methods.

INTERMEDIATE

20–22

20   MIRR [LO6]   Suppose the company in the previous problem uses an 11 per cent discount rate and an 8 per cent reinvestment rate on all of its projects. Calculate the MIRR of the project using all three methods using these interest rates.

21   NPV and the Profitability Index [LO1, LO7]   If we define the NPV index as the ratio of NPV to cost, what is the relationship between this index and the profitability index?

22   Cash Flow Intuition [LO1, LO2]   A project has an initial cost of I, has a required return of R, and pays C annually for N years.

(a) Find C in terms of I and N such that the project has a payback period just equal to its life.

(b) Find C in terms of I, N and R such that this is a profitable project according to the NPV decision rule.

(c) Find C in terms of I, N and R such that the project has a benefit–cost ratio of 2.

CHALLENGE

23 – 28

23 **Payback and NPV [LO1, LO2]**   An investment under consideration has a payback of seven years and a cost of €724,000. If the required return is 12 per cent, what is the worst-case NPV? The best-case NPV? Explain. Assume the cash flows are conventional.

24 **Multiple IRRs [LO5]**   This problem is useful for testing the ability of financial calculators and computer software. Consider the following cash flows. How many different IRRs are there? (*Hint*: Search between 20 per cent and 70 per cent.) When should we take this project?

Year	Cash flow (£)
0	−1,512
1	8,586
2	−18,210
3	17,100
4	−6,000

25 **NPV Valuation [LO1]**   Yuvhadit Ltd wants to set up a private cemetery business. According to the CFO, Barry M. Deep, business is 'looking up'. As a result, the cemetery project will provide a net cash inflow of €80,000 for the firm during the first year, and the cash flows are projected to grow at a rate of 6 per cent per year for ever. The project requires an initial investment of €800,000.

(a) If Yuvhadit requires a 12 per cent return on such undertakings, should the cemetery business be started?

(b) The company is somewhat unsure about the assumption of a 6 per cent growth rate in its cash flows. At what constant growth rate would the company just break even if it still required a 12 per cent return on investment?

26 **Problems with IRR [LO5]**   A project has the following cash flows:

Year	Cash flow (£)
0	58,000
1	−34,000
2	−45,000

What is the IRR for this project? If the required return is 12 per cent, should the firm accept the project? What is the NPV of this project? What is the NPV of the project if the required return is 0 per cent? 24 per cent? What is going on here? Sketch the NPV profile to help you with your answer.

27 **Problems with IRR [LO5]**   McKeekin plc has a project with the following cash flows:

Year	Cash flow (£)
0	20,000
1	−26,000
2	13,000

What is the IRR of the project? What is happening here?

28 **NPV and IRR [LO1, LO5]** Gulliver International Limited is evaluating a project in Lilliput. The project will create the following cash flows:

Year	Cash flow (LP)
0	−750,000
1	205,000
2	265,000
3	346,000
4	220,000

All cash flows will occur in Lilliput and are expressed in Lilliputian pounds (LP). In an attempt to improve its economy, the Lilliputian government has declared that all cash flows created by a foreign company are 'blocked', and must be reinvested with the government for one year. The reinvestment rate for these funds is 4 per cent. If Gulliver uses an 11 per cent required return on this project, what are the NPV and IRR of the project? Is the IRR you calculated the MIRR of the project? Why or why not?

MINI CASE Davis Gold Mining

Dick Davies, the owner of Davies Gold Mining, is evaluating a new gold mine in Tanzania. Barry Koch, the company's geologist, has just finished his analysis of the mine site. He has estimated that the mine would be productive for eight years, after which the gold would be completely mined. Barry has taken an estimate of the gold deposits to Andy Marshall, the company's financial officer. Andy has been asked by Dick to perform an analysis of the new mine and present his recommendation on whether the company should open the new mine.

Andy has used the estimates provided by Barry to determine the revenues that could be expected from the mine. He has also projected the expense of opening the mine, and the annual operating expenses. If the company opens the mine, it will cost £500 million today, and it will have a cash outflow of £80 million nine years from today in costs associated with closing the mine and reclaiming the area surrounding it. The expected cash flows each year from the mine are shown in the following table. Davies Gold Mining has a 12 per cent required return on all of its gold mines.

Year	Cash flow (£)
0	−500,000,000
1	60,000,000
2	90,000,000
3	170,000,000
4	230,000,000
5	205,000,000
6	140,000,000
7	110,000,000
8	70,000,000
9	−80,000,000

1 Construct a spreadsheet to calculate the payback period, internal rate of return, modified internal rate of return, and net present value of the proposed mine.

2 Based on your analysis, should the company open the mine?

3 Bonus question: Most spreadsheets do not have a built-in formula to calculate the payback period. Write a VBA script that calculates the payback period for a project.

Endnotes

1   In this case the discounted payback is an even number of years. This won't ordinarily happen, of course. However, calculating a fractional year for the discounted payback period is more involved than it is for the ordinary payback, and it is not commonly done.

2   This argument assumes that the cash flows, other than the first, are all positive. If they are not, then these statements are not necessarily correct. Also, there may be more than one discounted payback.

3   If the cut-off were for ever, then the discounted payback rule would be the same as the NPV rule. It would also be the same as the profitability index rule considered in a later section.

4   Straight-line depreciation is not the normal way to depreciate assets in Europe, where the reducing-balance method is more common. To estimate reducing-balance depreciation you would subtract a certain percentage from the residual value of the asset. For example, assume that the asset is worth £500,000 and you are applying 20 per cent reducing-balance depreciation. The depreciation for this year would be 20% of £500,000, which is equal to £100,000. Next year, the residual value is £500,000 − £100,000 = £400,000, and depreciation next year would be 20% of this amount, £400,000, which is £80,000, and so on.

5   We could, of course, calculate the average of the six book values directly. In thousands, we would have (£500 + 400 + 300 + 200 + 100 + 0)/6 = £250.

6   The AAR is closely related to the return on assets (ROA) discussed in Chapter 3. In practice, the AAR is sometimes computed by first calculating the ROA for each year and then averaging the results. This produces a number that is similar, but not identical, to the one we computed.

7   With a lot more effort (or a personal computer), we can find that the IRR is approximately (to nine decimal places) 13.066238629 per cent – not that anybody would ever want this many decimal places!

8   To be more precise, the number of IRRs that are larger than −100 per cent is equal to the number of sign changes, or it differs from the number of sign changes by an even number. Thus, for example, if there are five sign changes, there are five IRRs, three IRRs, or one IRR. If there are two sign changes, there are either two IRRs or no IRRs.

Online
Learning Centre

To help you grasp the key concepts of this chapter check out the extra resources posted on the Online Learning Centre at **www.mcgraw-hill.co.uk/textbooks/hillier**

Among other helpful resources there are mini-cases tailored to individual chapters.

CHAPTER 9

Making Capital Investment Decisions

KEY NOTATIONS

AAR   Average accounting return
EAC   Equivalent annual cost
EBIT   Earnings before interest and taxes
NPV   Net present value
OCF   Operating cash flow

LEARNING OBJECTIVES

After studying this chapter, you should understand:

LO1   How to determine the relevant cash flows for a proposed project.
LO2   How to determine whether a project is acceptable.
LO3   How to set a bid price for a project.
LO4   How to evaluate the equivalent annual cost of a project.

MAKING CAPITAL INVESTMENT DECISIONS is not just about investing in one specific project. In an environment where cash is scarce, an investment decision in one area may lead to spending cuts in another area. This is what happened with Anglo American, the global mining firm, in 2010. With a number of potentially lucrative projects in the pipeline, the company had to reserve cash from its operations to fund the new investment. It refused to pay a dividend for 18 months, redesigned its global supply chain, and made 20,000 employees redundant in 2009, leading to cost savings of £1 billion (€1.14 billion). However, in return it invested £2.5 billion (€2.8 billion) in a large Brazilian iron ore project and invested new capital in its two affiliate companies, Anglo Platinum and De Beers. Management of Anglo American argued that the combined investment and cost savings would increase firm value by £1.3 billion (€1.5 billion).

As you no doubt recognize from your study of the previous chapter, Anglo American's decision to invest in new mining operations represents a capital budgeting decision. However, other decisions made by the firm are inextricably linked to the investments. In this chapter we further investigate such decisions, how they are made, and how to look at them objectively.

This chapter follows up on the previous one by delving more deeply into capital budgeting. We have two main goals. First, recall that in the last chapter we saw that cash flow estimates are the critical input into a net present value analysis, but we didn't say much about where these cash flows come from, so we shall now examine this question in some detail. Our second goal is to learn how to critically examine NPV estimates and, in particular, how to evaluate the sensitivity of NPV estimates to assumptions made about the uncertain future.

So far we've covered various parts of the capital budgeting decision. Our task in this chapter is to start bringing these pieces together. In particular, we'll show you how to 'spread the numbers' for a proposed investment or project and, based on those numbers, make an initial assessment about whether the project should be undertaken.

In the discussion that follows, we focus on the process of setting up a discounted cash flow analysis. From the previous chapter we know that the projected future cash flows are the key element in such an evaluation. Accordingly, we emphasize working with financial and accounting information to come up with these figures.

In evaluating a proposed investment we pay special attention to deciding what information is relevant to the decision at hand, and what information is not. As we shall see, it is easy to overlook important pieces of the capital budgeting puzzle.

We shall wait until the next chapter to describe in detail how to go about evaluating the results of our discounted cash flow analysis. Also, where needed, we shall assume that we know the relevant required return, or discount rate. We continue to defer in-depth discussion of this subject to Part Five.

9.1 Project Cash Flows: A First Look

The effect of taking a project is to change the firm's overall cash flows today, and in the future. To evaluate a proposed investment we must consider these changes in the firm's cash flows, and then decide whether they add value to the firm. The first (and most important) step, therefore, is to decide which cash flows are relevant.

Relevant Cash Flows

What is a relevant cash flow for a project? The general principle is simple enough: a relevant cash flow for a project is a change in the firm's overall future cash flow that comes about as a *direct* consequence of the decision to take that project. Because the relevant cash flows are defined in terms of changes in, or increments to, the firm's existing cash flow, they are called the **incremental cash flows** associated with the project.

> **incremental cash flows** The difference between a firm's future cash flows with a project and those without the project.

The concept of incremental cash flow is central to our analysis, so we shall state a general definition, and refer back to it as needed:

> *The incremental cash flows for project evaluation consist of* any and all *changes in the firm's future cash flows that are a direct consequence of taking the project.*

This definition of incremental cash flows has an obvious and important corollary: any cash flow that exists regardless of *whether or not* a project is undertaken is *not* relevant.

The Stand-Alone Principle

In practice, it would be cumbersome to actually calculate the future total cash flows to the firm with and without a project, especially for a large firm. Fortunately, it is not really necessary to do so. Once we have identified the effect of undertaking the proposed project on the firm's cash flows, we need focus only on the project's resulting incremental cash flows. This is called the **stand-alone principle**.

> **stand-alone principle** The assumption that evaluation of a project may be based on the project's incremental cash flows.

What the stand-alone principle says is that, once we have determined the incremental cash flows from undertaking a project, we can view that project as a kind of 'mini-firm' with its own future revenues and costs, its own assets and, of course, its own cash flows. We shall then be interested primarily in comparing the cash flows from this mini-firm with the cost of acquiring it. An important consequence of this approach is that we shall be evaluating the proposed project purely on its own merits, in isolation from any other activities or projects.

> **CONCEPT QUESTIONS**
>
> 9.1a   What are the relevant incremental cash flows for project evaluation?
> 9.1b   What is the stand-alone principle?

9.2 Incremental Cash Flows

We are concerned here only with cash flows that are incremental, and which result from a project. Looking back at our general definition, we might think it would be easy enough to decide whether a cash flow is incremental. Even so, in a few situations it is easy to make mistakes. In this section we describe some common pitfalls, and how to avoid them.

Sunk Costs

> **sunk cost**
> A cost that has already been incurred and cannot be removed, and which therefore should not be considered in an investment decision.

A **sunk cost**, by definition, is a cost we have already paid, or have already incurred the liability to pay. Such a cost cannot be changed by the decision today to accept or reject a project. Put another way, the firm will have to pay this cost no matter what. Based on our general definition of incremental cash flow, such a cost is clearly not relevant to the decision at hand. So we shall always be careful to exclude sunk costs from our analysis.

That a sunk cost is not relevant seems obvious given our discussion. Nonetheless, it's easy to fall prey to the fallacy that a sunk cost should be associated with a project. For example, suppose General Milk plc hires a financial consultant to help evaluate whether a line of chocolate milk should be launched. When the consultant turns in the report, General Milk objects to the analysis, because the consultant did not include the hefty consulting fee as a cost of the chocolate milk project.

Who is correct? By now, we know that the consulting fee is a sunk cost: it must be paid whether or not the chocolate milk line is actually launched (this is an attractive feature of the consulting business).

Opportunity Costs

> **opportunity cost**
> The most valuable alternative that is given up if a particular investment is undertaken.

When we think of costs, we normally think of out-of-pocket costs – namely those that require us to actually spend some amount of cash. An **opportunity cost** is slightly different; it requires us to give up a benefit. A common situation arises in which a firm already owns some of the assets a proposed project will be using. For example, we might be thinking of converting an old rustic cotton mill we bought years ago for €100,000 into up-market apartments.

If we undertake this project, there will be no direct cash outflow associated with buying the old mill, because we already own it. For purposes of evaluating the apartment project, should we then treat the mill as 'free'? The answer is no. The mill is a valuable resource used by the project. If we didn't use it here, we could do something else with it. Like what? The obvious answer is that, at a minimum, we could sell it. Using the mill for the apartment complex thus has an opportunity cost: we give up the valuable opportunity to do something else with the mill.

There is another issue here. Once we agree that the use of the mill has an opportunity cost, how much should we charge the apartment project for this use? Given that we paid €100,000, it might seem that we should charge this amount to the apartment project. Is this correct? The answer is no, and the reason is based on our discussion concerning sunk costs.

The fact that we paid €100,000 some years ago is irrelevant. That cost is sunk. At a minimum, the opportunity cost that we charge the project is what the mill would sell for today (net of any selling costs), because this is the amount we give up by using the mill instead of selling it.[1]

Side Effects

Remember that the incremental cash flows for a project include all the resulting changes in the *firm's* future cash flows. It would not be unusual for a project to have side, or spillover, effects, both good and bad. For example, in 2010 the time between the theatrical release of a feature film and the release of the DVD had shrunk to 98 days, compared with 200 days ten years earlier. This shortened release time was blamed for at least part of the decline in average movie theatre box office receipts. Of course, retailers cheered the move, because it was credited with increasing DVD sales. A negative impact on the cash flows of an existing product from the introduction of a new product is called **erosion**.[2] In this case the cash flows from the new line should be adjusted downwards to reflect lost profits on other lines.

> **erosion**
> The cash flows of a new project that come at the expense of a firm's existing projects.

In accounting for erosion, it is important to recognize that any sales lost as a result of launching a new product might be lost anyway because of future competition. Erosion is relevant only when the sales would not otherwise be lost.

Side effects show up in a lot of different ways. For example, one of Walt Disney Company's concerns when it built Euro Disney was that the new park would drain visitors from the Florida park, a popular vacation destination for Europeans.

There are beneficial spillover effects, of course. For example, you might think that Hewlett-Packard would have been concerned when the price of a printer that sold for £500–£600 in 1994 declined to below £100 by 2010, but such was not the case. HP realized that the big money is in the consumables that printer owners buy to keep their printers going, such as inkjet cartridges, laser toner cartridges and special paper. The profit margins for these products are substantial.

Net Working Capital

Normally a project will require that the firm invest in net working capital in addition to long-term assets. For example, a project will generally need some amount of cash on hand to pay any expenses that arise. In addition, a project will need an initial investment in inventories and trade receivables (to cover credit sales). Some of the financing for this will be in the form of amounts owed to suppliers (trade payables), but the firm will have to supply the balance. This balance represents the investment in net working capital.

It's easy to overlook an important feature of net working capital in capital budgeting. As a project winds down, inventories are sold, receivables are collected, bills are paid, and cash balances can be drawn down. These activities free up the net working capital originally invested. So the firm's investment in project net working capital closely resembles a loan. The firm supplies working capital at the beginning, and recovers it towards the end.

Financing Costs

In analysing a proposed investment, we shall *not* include interest paid or any other financing costs such as dividends or principal repaid, because we are interested in the cash flow generated by the assets of the project. As we mentioned in Chapter 3, interest paid, for example, is a component of cash flow to creditors, not cash flow from assets.

More generally, our goal in project evaluation is to compare the cash flow from a project with the cost of acquiring that project in order to estimate NPV. The particular mixture of debt and equity a firm actually chooses to use in financing a project is a managerial variable, and determines primarily how project cash flow is divided between owners and creditors. This is not to say that financing arrangements are unimportant; they are just something to be analysed separately. We shall cover this in later chapters.

Other Issues

There are some other things to watch out for. First, we are interested only in measuring cash flow. Moreover, we are interested in measuring it when it actually occurs, not when it accrues in an accounting sense. Second, we are always interested in *after-tax* cash flow, because taxes are definitely a cash outflow. In fact, whenever we write *incremental cash flows*, we mean after-tax incremental cash flows. Remember, however, that after-tax cash flow and accounting profit, or net income, are entirely different things.

CONCEPT QUESTIONS	
9.2a	What is a sunk cost? An opportunity cost?
9.2b	Explain what erosion is, and why it is relevant.
9.2c	Explain why interest paid is not a relevant cash flow for project evaluation.

9.3 Pro Forma Financial Statements and Project Cash Flows

The first thing we need when we begin evaluating a proposed investment is a set of pro forma, or projected, financial statements. Given these, we can develop the projected cash flows from the project. Once we have the cash flows, we can estimate the value of the project using the techniques we described in the previous chapter.

Getting Started: Pro Forma Financial Statements

pro forma financial statements
Financial statements projecting future years' operations.

Pro forma financial statements are a convenient and easily understood means of summarizing much of the relevant information for a project. To prepare these statements, we shall need estimates of quantities such as unit sales, the selling price per unit, the variable cost per unit, and total fixed costs. We shall also need to know the total investment required, including any investment in net working capital.

To illustrate, suppose we think we can sell 50,000 cans of shark attractant per year at a price of £4 per can. It costs us about £2.50 per can to make the attractant, and a new product such as this one typically has only a three-year life (perhaps because the customer base dwindles rapidly). We require a 20 per cent return on new products.

Fixed costs for the project, including such things as rent on the production facility, will run to £12,000 per year.[3] Further, we shall need to invest a total of £90,000 in manufacturing equipment. For simplicity, we shall assume that this £90,000 will be 100 per cent depreciated straight-line over the three-year life of the project.[4] Furthermore, the cost of removing the equipment will roughly equal its actual value in three years, so it will be essentially worthless on a market value basis as well. Finally, the project will require an initial £20,000 investment in net working capital, and the tax rate is 34 per cent.

In Table 9.1 we organize these initial projections by first preparing the pro forma income statement. Once again, notice that we have *not* deducted any interest expense. This will always be so. As we described earlier, interest paid is a financing expense, not a component of operating cash flow.

We can also prepare a series of abbreviated statements of financial position that show the capital requirements for the project, as we've done in Table 9.2. Here we have net working capital of £20,000 in each year. Non-current assets are £90,000 at the start of the project's life (year 0), and they decline by the £30,000 in depreciation each year, ending up at zero. Notice that the total investment given here for future years is the total book, or accounting, value, not market value.

At this point, we need to start converting this accounting information into cash flows. We consider how to do this next.

investment (the IRR) is about 26 per cent. The fact that the AAR is larger illustrates again why the AAR cannot be meaningfully interpreted as the return on a project.

CONCEPT QUESTIONS

9.3a What is the definition of project operating cash flow? How does this differ from net income?

9.3b For the shark attractant project, why did we add back the firm's net working capital investment in the final year?

9.4 More about Project Cash Flow

In this section we take a closer look at some aspects of project cash flow. In particular, we discuss project net working capital in more detail. We then examine current tax laws regarding depreciation. Finally, we work through a more involved example of the capital investment decision.

A Closer Look at Net Working Capital

In calculating operating cash flow, we did not explicitly consider the fact that some of our sales might be on credit. Also, we may not have actually paid some of the costs shown. In either case, the cash flow in question would not yet have occurred. We show here that these possibilities are not a problem as long as we don't forget to include changes in net working capital in our analysis. This discussion thus emphasizes the importance and the effect of doing so.

Suppose that during a particular year of a project we have the following simplified income statement:

Sales (€)	500
Costs (€)	310
Net income (€)	190

Depreciation and taxes are zero. No non-current assets are purchased during the year. Also, to illustrate a point, we assume that the only components of net working capital are trade receivables and payables. The beginning and ending amounts for these accounts are as follows:

	Beginning of year	End of year	Change
Trade receivables (€)	880	910	+30
Trade payables (€)	550	605	+55
Net working capital (€)	330	305	−25

Based on this information, what is total cash flow for the year? We can first just mechanically apply what we have been discussing to come up with the answer. Operating cash flow in this particular case is the same as net income, because there are no taxes or depreciation: thus it equals €190. Also, notice that net working capital actually *declined* by €25. This just means that €25 was freed up during the year. There was no capital spending, so the total cash flow for the year is

$$\text{Total cash flow} = \text{Operating cash flow} - \text{Change in NWC} - \text{Capital spending}$$
$$= €190 - (-25) - 0$$
$$= €215$$

Now, we know that this €215 total cash flow has to be 'euros in' less 'euros out' for the year. We could therefore ask a different question: what were cash revenues for the year? Also, what were cash costs?

To determine cash revenues, we need to look more closely at net working capital. During the year, we had sales of €500. However, trade receivables rose by €30 over the same time period. What does this mean? The €30 increase tells us that sales exceeded collections by €30. In other words, we haven't yet received the cash from €30 of the €500 in sales. As a result, our cash inflow is €500 − 30 = €470. In general, cash income is sales minus the increase in trade receivables.

Cash outflows can be similarly determined. We show costs of €310 on the income statement, but trade payables increased by €55 during the year. This means that we have not yet paid €55 of the €310, so cash costs for the period are just €310 − 55 = €255. In other words, in this case, cash costs equal costs less the increase in accounts payable.[8]

Putting this information together, we calculate that cash inflows less cash outflows are €470 − 255 = €215, just as we had before. Notice that

$$
\begin{aligned}
\text{Cash flow} &= \text{Cash inflow} - \text{Cash outflow} \\
&= (\text{€}500 - 30) - (310 - 55) \\
&= (\text{€}500 - 310) - (30 - 55) \\
&= \text{Operating cash flow} - \text{Change in NWC} \\
&= \text{€}190 - (-25) \\
&= \text{€}215
\end{aligned}
$$

More generally, this example illustrates that including net working capital changes in our calculations has the effect of adjusting for the discrepancy between accounting sales and costs and actual cash receipts and payments.

Cash Collections and Costs

For the year just completed, Combat Womble Telestat plc (CWT) reports sales of £998 and costs of £734. You have collected the following beginning and ending statement of financial position information:

	Beginning	Ending
Trade receivables (£)	100	110
Inventory (£)	100	80
Trade payables (£)	100	70
Net working capital (£)	100	120

Based on these figures, what are cash inflows? Cash outflows? What happened to each account? What is net cash flow?

Sales were £998, but receivables rose by £10. So cash collections were £10 less than sales, or £988. Costs were £734, but inventories fell by £20. This means that we didn't replace £20 worth of inventory, so costs are actually overstated by this amount. Also, payables fell by £30. This means that, on a net basis, we actually paid our suppliers £30 more than we received from them, resulting in a £30 understatement of costs. Adjusting for these events, we calculate that cash costs are £734 − 20 + 30 = £744. Net cash flow is £988 − 744 = £244.

Finally, notice that net working capital increased by £20 overall. We can check our answer by noting that the original accounting sales less costs (= £998 − 734) are £264. In addition, CWT spent £20 on net working capital, so the net result is a cash flow of £264 − 20 = £244, as we calculated.

Depreciation

As we note elsewhere, accounting depreciation is a non-cash deduction. As a result, depreciation has cash flow consequences only because it influences the tax bill. The way that depreciation is computed for tax purposes is thus the relevant method for capital investment decisions. Not surprisingly, the procedures are governed by tax law. We now discuss some specifics of the depreciation system that is enacted within the European Union. This system is known as the **reducing-balance method** (compared with the straight-line method presented in earlier examples).

> **reducing-balance method**
> A depreciation method allowing for the accelerated write-off of assets under various classifications.

Reducing-Balance Depreciation   The calculation of depreciation is normally mechanical, and assets are depreciated according to the tax rules that apply in each country. The UK system is very simple, with only two asset categories for depreciation: plant and machinery, and buildings. However, other countries may have more complex systems for estimating depreciation expenses, and these should be considered before carrying out a capital budgeting analysis.

Depreciation rates change regularly, and a financial manager must be up to date with the current applicable rates. For example, from 2010 the UK applied 20 per cent reducing-balance depreciation on plant and machinery. Buildings are depreciated using the straight-line method.

To understand how reducing-balance depreciation is calculated, it is useful to compare the methodology with the much simpler straight-line depreciation. Assume that you purchase an asset for €500,000, which has a five-year life, and at the end of its life the asset will be worthless.

With straight-line depreciation, since the asset's life is five years and its residual value is zero, the annual depreciation will be

$$\text{Annual depreciation} = \text{€}500,000/5 = \text{€}100,000$$

Reducing-balance Depreciation:

Assume that we apply 20 per cent reducing-balance method. This means that we shall depreciate the written-down (or residual) value of the asset by 20 per cent per annum.

	Year				
	1	**2**	**3**	**4**	**5**
Initial value (€)	500,000	400,000	320,000	256,000	204,800
Depreciation (20%) (€)	100,000	80,000	64,000	51,200	204,800
Written-down value (€)	400,000	320,000	256,000	204,800	0

Note how the depreciation amounts fall over time. This is because the amount that is being depreciated is less each year. In addition, given that the asset is worthless at the end of five years, the final-year depreciation is simply the starting year 5 value.

Currently, each country in the European Union has its own tax system, and this is seen as one of the major obstacles for full integration of the different European economies. However, a working group has been set up to develop a Common Consolidated Corporate Tax Base (CCCTB) for all countries. Although it will take several years for it to be enacted, the CCCTB is definitely a step in the right direction. The main recommendations of the working group are that all countries apply 20 per cent reducing-balance depreciation on plant and machinery, 2.5 per cent straight-line depreciation for buildings, and 4 per cent straight-line depreciation for long-term tangible assets (i.e. assets that will last for more than 25 years).

Book Value versus Market Value   In calculating depreciation under current tax law, the economic life and future market value of the asset are not an issue. As a result, the book value of an asset can differ substantially from its actual market value. Take, for example, a top of the range Chrysler Grand Voyager that is worth £35,000 new. With 20 per cent reducing-balance depreciation, the book value after the first year is £35,000 less the first year's depreciation of £7,000, or £28,000. The remaining book values are summarized in Table 9.5. After five years, the book value of the car is £11,469.

TABLE 9.5	Year				
	1	**2**	**3**	**4**	**5**
Initial value (£)	35,000	28,000	22,400	17,920	14,336
Depreciation (20%) (£)	7,000	5,600	4,480	3,584	2,867
Written-down value (£)	28,000	22,400	17,920	14,336	11,469

Table 9.5 Chrysler Grand Voyager book values

Suppose we wanted to sell the car after five years. Based on historical averages, it would be worth, say, 50 per cent of the purchase price, or $0.50 \times £35,000 = £17,500$. If we actually sold it for this, then we would have to pay taxes at the ordinary income tax rate on the difference between the sale price of £17,500 and the book value of £11,469. For a corporation in the 28 per cent bracket, the tax liability would be $0.28 \times £6,031 = £1,688.74$.

The reason why taxes must be paid in this case is that the difference between market value and book value is 'excess' depreciation, and it must be 'recaptured' when the asset is sold. What this means is that, as it turns out, we over-depreciated the asset by $£17,500 - £11,469 = £6,031$. Because we deducted £6,031 too much in depreciation, we paid £1,688.74 too little in taxes, and we simply have to make up the difference.

Notice that this is *not* a tax on a capital gain. As a general (albeit rough) rule, a capital gain occurs only if the market price exceeds the original cost. However, what is and what is not a capital gain is ultimately up to the taxation authorities, and the specific rules can be complex. We shall ignore capital gains taxes for the most part.

Finally, if the book value exceeds the market value, then the difference is treated as a loss for tax purposes. For example, if we sell the car after two years for £10,000, then the book value exceeds the market value by £1,469. In this case, a tax saving of $0.28 \times £1,469 = £411.32$ occurs.

Reducing-Balance Depreciation

EXAMPLE 9.2

Staple Supply Ltd has just purchased a new computerized information system with an installed cost of €160,000. What are the yearly depreciation allowances if 20 per cent reducing-balance depreciation is used? Based on historical experience, we think that the system will be worth only €10,000 when Staple gets rid of it in four years. What are the tax consequences of the sale if the tax rate is 34 per cent? What is the total after-tax cash flow from the sale?

The yearly depreciation allowances are presented below:

	Year			
	1	**2**	**3**	**4**
Initial value (€)	160,000	128,000	102,400	81,920
Depreciation (20%) (€)	32,000	25,600	20,480	16,384
Written-down value (€)	128,000	102,400	81,920	65,536

Notice that we have also computed the book value of the system as at the end of each year. The book value at the end of year 4 is €65,536. If Staple sells the system for €10,000 at that time, it will have a loss of €55,536 (the difference) for tax purposes. This loss, of course, is like depreciation because it isn't a cash expense.

What really happens? Two things. First, Staple gets €10,000 from the buyer. Second, it saves $0.34 \times €55,536 = €18,882$ in taxes. So the total after-tax cash flow from the sale is a €28,882 cash inflow.

An Example: Majestic Mulch and Compost Ltd (MMC)

At this point we want to go through a somewhat more involved capital budgeting analysis. Keep in mind as you read that the basic approach here is exactly the same as that in the shark attractant example used earlier. We have just added some real-world detail (and a lot more numbers).

MMC is investigating the feasibility of a new line of power mulching tools aimed at the growing number of home composters. Based on exploratory conversations with buyers for large garden shops, MMC projects unit sales as follows:

Year	Unit sales
1	3,000
2	5,000
3	6,000
4	6,500
5	6,000
6	5,000
7	4,000
8	3,000

The new power mulcher will sell for £120 per unit to start. When the competition catches up after three years, however, MMC anticipates that the price will drop to £110.

The power mulcher project will require £20,000 in net working capital at the start. Subsequently, total net working capital at the end of each year will be about 15 per cent of sales for that year. The variable cost per unit is £60, and total fixed costs are £25,000 per year.

It will cost about £800,000 to buy the equipment necessary to begin production. This investment is primarily in industrial equipment, which should be depreciated using the 20 per cent reducing-balance method. The equipment will actually be worth about 20 per cent of its cost in eight years, or $0.20 \times £800,000 = £160,000$. The relevant tax rate is 28 per cent, and the required return is 15 per cent. Based on this information, should MMC proceed?

Operating Cash Flows   There is a lot of information here that we need to organize. The first thing we can do is calculate projected sales. Sales in the first year are projected at 3,000 units at £120 apiece, or £360,000 total. The remaining figures are shown in Table 9.6.

TABLE 9.6	Year	Unit price (£)	Unit sales	Revenues (£)
	1	120	3,000	360,000
	2	120	5,000	600,000
	3	120	6,000	720,000
	4	110	6,500	715,000
	5	110	6,000	660,000
	6	110	5,000	550,000
	7	110	4,000	440,000
	8	110	3,000	330,000

Table 9.6 Projected revenues, power mulcher project

TABLE
9.7

Year	Initial value (£)	Depreciation (£)	Residual value (£)
1	800,000	160,000	640,000
2	640,000	128,000	512,000
3	512,000	102,400	409,600
4	409,600	81,920	327,680
5	327,680	65,536	262,144
6	262,144	52,429	209,715
7	209,715	41,943	167,772
8	167,772	7,772	160,000

Table 9.7 Annual depreciation, power mulcher project

TABLE
9.8

	Year							
	1	2	3	4	5	6	7	8
Unit price (£)	120	120	120	110	110	110	110	110
Unit sales	3,000	5,000	6,000	6,500	6,000	5,000	4,000	3,000
Revenues (£)	360,000	600,000	720,000	715,000	660,000	550,000	440,000	330,000
Variable cost (£)	180,000	300,000	360,000	390,000	360,000	300,000	240,000	180,000
Fixed costs (£)	25,000	25,000	25,000	25,000	25,000	25,000	25,000	25,000
Depreciation (£)	160,000	128,000	102,400	81,920	65,536	52,429	41,943	7,772
Profit before taxes (£)	−5,000	147,000	232,600	218,080	209,464	172,571	133,057	117,228
Taxes (28%) (£)	−1,400	41,160	65,128	61,062	58,650	48,320	37,256	32,824
Net income (£)	−3,600	105,840	167,472	157,018	150,814	124,251	95,801	84,404

Table 9.8 Projected income statements, power mulcher project

Next, we compute the depreciation on the £800,000 investment in Table 9.7. With this information, we can prepare the pro forma income statements, as shown in Table 9.8. From here, computing the operating cash flows is straightforward. The results are illustrated in the first part of Table 9.10.

Change in NWC   Now that we have the operating cash flows, we need to determine the changes in NWC. By assumption, net working capital requirements change as sales change. In each year, MMC will generally either add to or recover some of its project net working capital. Recalling that NWC starts out at £20,000 and then rises to 15 per cent of sales, we can calculate the amount of NWC for each year, as shown in Table 9.9.

As illustrated, during the first year net working capital grows from £20,000 to $0.15 \times £360,000 = £54,000$. The increase in net working capital for the year is thus £54,000 − 20,000 = £34,000. The remaining figures are calculated in the same way.

Remember that an increase in net working capital is a cash outflow, so we use a negative sign in this table to indicate an additional investment that the firm makes in net working capital. A positive sign represents net working capital returning to the firm. Thus, for example, £16,500 in NWC flows back to the firm in year 6. Over the project's life, net working capital builds to a peak of £108,000, and declines from there as sales begin to drop off.

Alternative Definitions of Operating Cash Flow   **259**

> **CONCEPT QUESTIONS**
>
> 9.4a   Why is it important to consider changes in net working capital in developing cash flows? What is the effect of doing so?
>
> 9.4b   How is depreciation calculated for non-current assets under current tax law? What effects do expected salvage value and estimated economic life have on the calculated depreciation deduction?

9.5 Alternative Definitions of Operating Cash Flow

The analysis we went through in the previous section is quite general, and can be adapted to just about any capital investment problem. In the next section we illustrate some particularly useful variations. Before we do so, we need to discuss the fact that there are different definitions of project operating cash flow that are commonly used, both in practice and in finance texts.

As we shall see, the different approaches to operating cash flow that exist all measure the same thing. If they are used correctly, they all produce the same answer, and one is not necessarily any better or more useful than another. Unfortunately, the fact that alternative definitions are used does sometimes lead to confusion. For this reason, we examine several of these variations next, to see how they are related.

In the discussion that follows, keep in mind that when we speak of cash flow, we literally mean cash in less cash out. This is all we are concerned with. Different definitions of operating cash flow simply amount to different ways of manipulating basic information about sales, costs, depreciation and taxes to get at cash flow.

For a particular project and year under consideration, suppose we have the following estimates:

Sales = €1,500
Costs = €700
Depreciation = €600

With these estimates, notice that earnings before interest and taxes (EBIT) is

$$\text{EBIT} = \text{Sales} - \text{Costs} - \text{Depreciation}$$
$$= €1,500 - 700 - 600$$
$$= €200$$

Once again, we assume that no interest is paid, so the tax bill is

$$\text{Taxes} = \text{EBIT} \times T$$
$$= €200 \times 0.34 = €68$$

where T, the corporate tax rate, is 34 per cent.

When we put all of this together, we see that project operating cash flow, OCF, is

$$\text{OCF} = \text{EBIT} + \text{Depreciation} - \text{Taxes}$$
$$= €200 + 600 - 68 = €732$$

There are some other ways to determine OCF that could be (and are) used. We consider these next.

The Bottom-Up Approach

Because we are ignoring any financing expenses, such as interest, in our calculations of project OCF, we can write project net income as

Chapter 9 Making Capital Investment Decisions

$$Project\ net\ income = EBIT - Taxes$$
$$= €200 - 68$$
$$= €132$$

If we simply add the depreciation to both sides, we arrive at a slightly different and very common expression for OCF:

$$OCF = Net\ income + Depreciation$$
$$= €132 + 600 \qquad\qquad (9.1)$$
$$= €732$$

This is the *bottom-up* approach. Here, we start with the accountant's bottom line (net income) and add back any non-cash deductions such as depreciation. It is crucial to remember that this definition of operating cash flow as net income plus depreciation is correct only if there is no interest expense subtracted in the calculation of net income.

For the shark attractant project, net income was £21,780 and depreciation was £30,000, so the bottom-up calculation is

$$OCF = £21,780 + 30,000 = £51,780$$

The Top-Down Approach

Perhaps the most obvious way to calculate OCF is

$$OCF = Sales - Costs - Taxes$$
$$= €1,500 - 700 - 68 = €732 \qquad (9.2)$$

This is the *top-down* approach, the second variation on the basic OCF definition. Here, we start at the top of the income statement with sales, and work our way down to net cash flow by subtracting costs, taxes and other expenses. Along the way, we simply leave out any strictly non-cash items such as depreciation.

For the shark attractant project the operating cash flow can be readily calculated using the top-down approach. With sales of £200,000, total costs (fixed plus variable) of £137,000, and a tax bill of £11,220, the OCF is

$$OCF = £200,000 - 137,000 - 11,220 = £51,780$$

This is just as we had before.

The Tax Shield Approach

The third variation on our basic definition of OCF is the *tax shield* approach. This approach will be useful for some problems we consider in the next section. The tax shield definition of OCF is

$$OCF = (Sales - Costs) \times (1 - T) + Depreciation \times T \qquad (9.3)$$

where T is again the corporate tax rate. Assuming that $T = 34\%$, the OCF works out to be

$$OCF = (€1,500 - 700) \times 0.66 + 600 \times 0.34$$
$$= €528 + 204$$
$$= €732$$

This is just as we had before.

To Buy or Not to Buy

EXAMPLE 9.3

We are considering the purchase of a €200,000 computer-based inventory management system. It will be depreciated 20 per cent reducing-balance over its four-year life. It will be worth €30,000 at the end of that time. The system will save us €60,000 before taxes in inventory-related costs. The relevant tax rate is 39 per cent. Because the new set-up is more efficient than our existing one, we shall be able to carry less total inventory and thus free up €45,000 in net working capital. What is the NPV at 16 per cent? What is the DCF return (the IRR) on this investment?

We can first calculate the operating cash flow. The depreciation schedule is given below:

Year	Initial value (€)	Depreciation (€)	Residual value (€)
1	200,000	40,000	160,000
2	160,000	32,000	128,000
3	128,000	25,600	102,400
4	102,400	72,400	30,000

Operating cash flow now follows:

	Year			
	1	2	3	4
Cash savings (€)	60,000	60,000	60,000	60,000
Depreciation (€)	40,000	32,000	25,600	72,400
Profit before taxes (€)	20,000	28,000	34,400	–12,400
Taxes (39%) (€)	7,800	10,920	13,416	–4,836
Net income (€)	12,200	17,080	20,984	–7,564
Plus depreciation (€)	40,000	32,000	25,600	72,400
Operating cash flow (€)	52,200	49,080	46,584	64,836

Finally, and this is the somewhat tricky part, the initial investment in net working capital is a €45,000 *inflow*, because the system frees up working capital. Furthermore, we shall have to put this back in at the end of the project's life. What this really means is simple: while the system is in operation, we have €45,000 to use elsewhere.

To finish our analysis, we can compute the total cash flows:

	Year				
	0	1	2	3	4
Operating cash flow (€)		52,200	49,080	46,584	64,836
Change in NWC (€)	45,000				–45,000
Capital spending (€)	–200,000				30,000
Net cash flow (€)	–155,000	52,200	49,080	46,584	49,836

At 16 per cent the NPV is –€16,157, so the investment is not attractive. After some trial and error, we find that the NPV is zero when the discount rate is 10.62 per cent, so the IRR on this investment is about 10.6 per cent.

Chapter 9 Making Capital Investment Decisions

Setting the Bid Price

Early on, we used discounted cash flow analysis to evaluate a proposed new product. A somewhat different (and common) scenario arises when we must submit a competitive bid to win a job. Under such circumstances, the winner is whoever submits the lowest bid.

There is an old joke concerning this process: the low bidder is whoever makes the biggest mistake. This is called the *winner's curse*. In other words, if you win, there is a good chance you underbid. In this section we look at how to go about setting the bid price to avoid the winner's curse. The procedure we describe is useful whenever we have to set a price on a product or service.

As with any other capital budgeting project, we must be careful to account for all relevant cash flows. For example, industry analysts estimated that the materials in Microsoft's Xbox 360 cost £313 before assembly. Other items such as the power supply, cables and controllers increased the materials cost by another £37. At a retail price of £160, Microsoft obviously loses a significant amount on each Xbox 360 it sells in the UK. Why would a manufacturer sell at a price well below break-even? A Microsoft spokesperson stated that the company believed that sales of its game software would make the Xbox 360 a profitable project.

To illustrate how to go about setting a bid price, imagine we are in the business of buying stripped-down truck platforms and then modifying them to customer specifications for resale. A local distributor has requested bids for five specially modified trucks each year for the next four years, for a total of 20 trucks in all.

We need to decide what price per truck to bid. The goal of our analysis is to determine the lowest price we can profitably charge. This maximizes our chances of being awarded the contract, while guarding against the winner's curse.

Suppose we can buy the truck platforms for €10,000 each. The facilities we need can be leased for €24,000 per year. The labour and material cost to do the modification works out to be about €4,000 per truck. Total cost per year will thus be €24,000 + 5 × (10,000 + 4,000) = €94,000.

We shall need to invest €60,000 in new equipment. For simplicity, this equipment will be depreciated straight-line to a zero salvage value over the four years. It will be worth about €5,000 at the end of that time. We shall also need to invest €40,000 in raw materials inventory and other working capital items. The relevant tax rate is 39 per cent. What price per truck should we bid if we require a 20 per cent return on our investment?

We start by looking at the capital spending and net working capital investment. We have to spend €60,000 today for new equipment. The after-tax salvage value is €5,000 × (1 − 0.39) = €3,050. Furthermore, we have to invest €40,000 today in working capital. We shall get this back in four years.

We can't determine the operating cash flow just yet, because we don't know the sales price. Thus, if we draw a time line, here is what we have so far:

	Year				
	0	**1**	**2**	**3**	**4**
Operating cash flow		+OCF	+OCF	+OCF	+OCF
Change in NWC (€)	−40,000				40,000
Capital spending (€)	−60,000				3,050
Total cash flow (€)	−100,000	+OCF	+OCF	+OCF	+OCF + 43,050

With this in mind, note that the key observation is the following: the lowest possible price we can profitably charge will result in a zero NPV at 20 per cent. At that price, we earn exactly 20 per cent on our investment.

Given this observation, we first need to determine what the operating cash flow must be for the NPV to equal zero. To do this, we calculate the present value of the €43,050 non-operating cash flow from the last year, and subtract it from the €100,000 initial investment:

267

EXAMPLE	**Equivalent Annual Costs**
9.4	This extended example illustrates what happens to the EAC when we consider taxes. You are evaluating two different pollution control options. A filtration system will cost €1.1 million to install and €60,000 annually, before taxes, to operate. It will

have to be completely replaced every five years. A precipitation system will cost €1.9 million to install but only €10,000 per year to operate. The precipitation equipment has an effective operating life of eight years. To simplify matters, straight-line depreciation is used throughout, and neither system has any salvage value. Which option should we select if we use a 12 per cent discount rate? The tax rate is 34 per cent.

We need to consider the EACs for the two systems, because they have different service lives and will be replaced as they wear out. The relevant information can be summarized as follows:

	Filtration system	**Precipitation system**
After-tax operating cost (€)	−39,600	−6,600
Depreciation tax shield (€)	74,800	80,750
Operating cash flow (€)	35,200	74,150
Economic life (years)	5	8
Annuity factor (12%) (€)	3.6048	4.9676
Present value of operating cash flow (€)	126,888	368,350
Capital spending (€)	−1,100,000	−1,900,000
Total PV of costs (€)	−973,112	−1,531,650

Notice that the operating cash flow is actually positive in both cases because of the large depreciation tax shields. This can occur whenever the operating cost is small relative to the purchase price.

To decide which system to purchase, we compute the EACs for both using the appropriate annuity factors:

$$\text{Filtration system:}$$
$$-€973{,}112 = \text{EAC} \times 3.6048$$
$$\text{EAC} = -€269{,}951$$

$$\text{Precipitation system:}$$
$$-€1{,}531{,}650 = \text{EAC} \times 4.9676$$
$$\text{EAC} = -€308{,}328$$

The filtration system is the cheaper of the two, so we select it. In this case the longer life and smaller operating cost of the precipitation system are not sufficient to offset its higher initial cost.

CONCEPT QUESTIONS	9.6a	In setting a bid price, we used a zero NPV as our benchmark. Explain why this is appropriate.
	9.6b	Under what circumstances do we have to worry about unequal economic lives? How do you interpret the EAC?

Summary and Conclusions

This chapter has described how to put together a discounted cash flow analysis. In it, we covered:

1   The identification of relevant project cash flows. We discussed project cash flows, and described how to handle some issues that often come up, including sunk costs, opportunity costs, financing costs, net working capital, and erosion.

2 Preparing and using pro forma, or projected, financial statements. We showed how information from such financial statements is useful in coming up with projected cash flows, and we also looked at some alternative definitions of operating cash flow.

3 The role of net working capital and depreciation in determining project cash flows. We saw that including the change in net working capital was important in cash flow analysis, because it adjusted for the discrepancy between accounting revenues and costs and cash revenues and costs. We also went over the calculation of depreciation expense under current tax law.

4 Some special cases encountered in using discounted cash flow analysis. Here we looked at three special issues: evaluating cost-cutting investments, how to go about setting a bid price, and the unequal lives problem.

The discounted cash flow analysis we've covered here is a standard tool in the business world. It is a very powerful tool, so care should be taken in its use. The most important thing is to identify the cash flows in a way that makes economic sense. This chapter gives you a good start in learning to do this.

Chapter Review and Self-Test Problems

9.1 Capital Budgeting for Project X Based on the following information for project X, should we undertake the venture? To answer, first prepare a pro forma income statement for each year. Next calculate operating cash flow. Finish the problem by determining total cash flow and then calculating NPV assuming a 28 per cent required return. Use a 34 per cent tax rate throughout. For help, look back at our shark attractant and power mulcher examples.

Project X involves a new type of graphite composite in-line skate wheel. We think we can sell 6,000 units per year at a price of €1,000 each. Variable costs will be about €400 per unit, and the product should have a four-year life.

Fixed costs for the project will be €450,000 per year. Further, we shall need to invest a total of €1,250,000 in manufacturing equipment. This equipment is depreciated using 20 per cent reducing-balance for tax purposes. In four years the equipment will be worth about half of what we paid for it. We shall have to invest €1,150,000 in net working capital at the start. After that, net working capital requirements will be 25 per cent of sales.

9.2 Calculating Operating Cash Flow Kilimanjaro Tents Ltd have projected a sales volume of R1,650 for the second year of a proposed expansion project. Costs normally run at 60 per cent of sales, or about R990 in this case. The depreciation expense will be R100, and the tax rate is 35 per cent. What is the operating cash flow? Calculate your answer using all the approaches (including the top-down, bottom-up and tax shield approaches) described in the chapter.

9.3 Spending Money to Save Money? For help on this one, refer back to the computerized inventory management system in Example 9.3. Here, we're contemplating a new automatic surveillance system to replace our current contract security system. It will cost SKr450,000 to get the new system. The cost will be depreciated straight-line to zero over the system's four-year expected life. The system is expected to be worth SKr250,000 at the end of four years after removal costs.

We think the new system will save us SKr125,000, before taxes, per year in contract security costs. The tax rate is 34 per cent. What are the NPV and IRR for buying the new system? The required return is 17 per cent.

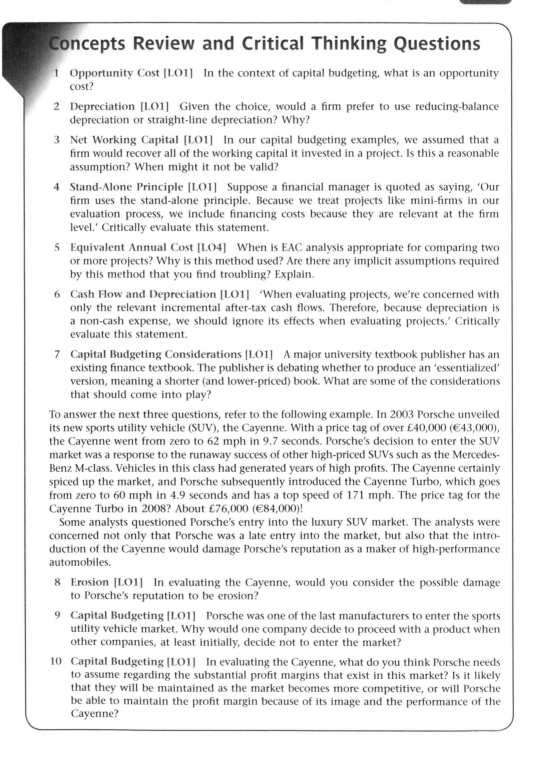

Concepts Review and Critical Thinking Questions

1 **Opportunity Cost [LO1]**   In the context of capital budgeting, what is an opportunity cost?

2 **Depreciation [LO1]**   Given the choice, would a firm prefer to use reducing-balance depreciation or straight-line depreciation? Why?

3 **Net Working Capital [LO1]**   In our capital budgeting examples, we assumed that a firm would recover all of the working capital it invested in a project. Is this a reasonable assumption? When might it not be valid?

4 **Stand-Alone Principle [LO1]**   Suppose a financial manager is quoted as saying, 'Our firm uses the stand-alone principle. Because we treat projects like mini-firms in our evaluation process, we include financing costs because they are relevant at the firm level.' Critically evaluate this statement.

5 **Equivalent Annual Cost [LO4]**   When is EAC analysis appropriate for comparing two or more projects? Why is this method used? Are there any implicit assumptions required by this method that you find troubling? Explain.

6 **Cash Flow and Depreciation [LO1]**   'When evaluating projects, we're concerned with only the relevant incremental after-tax cash flows. Therefore, because depreciation is a non-cash expense, we should ignore its effects when evaluating projects.' Critically evaluate this statement.

7 **Capital Budgeting Considerations [LO1]**   A major university textbook publisher has an existing finance textbook. The publisher is debating whether to produce an 'essentialized' version, meaning a shorter (and lower-priced) book. What are some of the considerations that should come into play?

To answer the next three questions, refer to the following example. In 2003 Porsche unveiled its new sports utility vehicle (SUV), the Cayenne. With a price tag of over £40,000 (€43,000), the Cayenne went from zero to 62 mph in 9.7 seconds. Porsche's decision to enter the SUV market was a response to the runaway success of other high-priced SUVs such as the Mercedes-Benz M-class. Vehicles in this class had generated years of high profits. The Cayenne certainly spiced up the market, and Porsche subsequently introduced the Cayenne Turbo, which goes from zero to 60 mph in 4.9 seconds and has a top speed of 171 mph. The price tag for the Cayenne Turbo in 2008? About £76,000 (€84,000)!

Some analysts questioned Porsche's entry into the luxury SUV market. The analysts were concerned not only that Porsche was a late entry into the market, but also that the introduction of the Cayenne would damage Porsche's reputation as a maker of high-performance automobiles.

8 **Erosion [LO1]**   In evaluating the Cayenne, would you consider the possible damage to Porsche's reputation to be erosion?

9 **Capital Budgeting [LO1]**   Porsche was one of the last manufacturers to enter the sports utility vehicle market. Why would one company decide to proceed with a product when other companies, at least initially, decide not to enter the market?

10 **Capital Budgeting [LO1]**   In evaluating the Cayenne, what do you think Porsche needs to assume regarding the substantial profit margins that exist in this market? Is it likely that they will be maintained as the market becomes more competitive, or will Porsche be able to maintain the profit margin because of its image and the performance of the Cayenne?

272   **Chapter 9** Making Capital Investment Decisions

connect Questions and Problems

BASIC
1 – 17

1   **Relevant Cash Flows [LO1]**   Parker & Stone NV is looking at setting up a new manufacturing plant in Rotterdam to produce garden tools. The company bought some land six years ago for €6 million in anticipation of using it as a warehouse and distribution site, but the company has since decided to rent these facilities from a competitor instead. If the land were sold today, the company would net €6.4 million. The company wants to build its new manufacturing plant on this land; the plant will cost €14.2 million to build, and the site requires €890,000 worth of grading before it is suitable for construction. What is the proper cash flow amount to use as the initial investment in non-current assets when evaluating this project? Why?

2   **Relevant Cash Flows [LO1]**   Winnebagel plc currently sells 30,000 mobile caravans per year at £53,000 each, and 12,000 luxury stationary caravans per year at £91,000 each. The company wants to introduce a new caravanette to fill out its product line; it hopes to sell 19,000 of these caravanettes per year at £13,000 each. An independent consultant has determined that if Winnebagel introduces the new caravanettes, it should boost the sales of its existing luxury stationary caravans by 4,500 units per year, and reduce the sales of its mobile caravans by 900 units per year. What is the amount to use as the annual sales figure when evaluating this project? Why?

3   **Calculating Projected Net Income [LO1]**   A proposed new investment has projected sales of £830,000. Variable costs are 60 per cent of sales, and fixed costs are £181,000; depreciation is £77,000. Prepare a pro forma income statement assuming a tax rate of 28 per cent. What is the projected net income?

4   **Calculating OCF [LO1]**   Consider the following income statement:

Sales (£)	1,824,500
Costs (£)	838,900
Depreciation (£)	226,500
Profit before taxes (£)	?
Taxes (28%) (£)	?
Net income (£)	?

Fill in the missing numbers and then calculate the OCF. What is the depreciation tax shield?

5   **OCF from Several Approaches [LO1]**   A proposed new project has projected sales of NKr108,000, costs of NKr51,000, and depreciation of NKr6,800. The tax rate is 35 per cent. Calculate operating cash flow using the four different approaches described in the chapter, and verify that the answer is the same in each case.

6   **Calculating Depreciation [LO1]**   A piece of newly purchased industrial equipment costs €1,080,000, and is depreciated using 20 per cent reducing-balance. Calculate the annual depreciation allowances and end-of-the-year book values for this equipment.

7   **Calculating Salvage Value [LO1]**   Consider an asset that costs €548,000 and is depreciated using 20 per cent reducing-balance. The asset is to be used in a five-year project; at the end of the project, the asset can be sold for €105,000. If the relevant tax rate is 35 per cent, what is the after-tax cash flow from the sale of this asset?

8   **Calculating Salvage Value [LO1]**   An asset used in a four-year project is to be depreciated using the 20 per cent reducing-balance method. The asset has an acquisition cost of DKr7,900,000 and will be sold for DKr1,400,000 at the end of the project. If the tax rate is 25 per cent, what is the after-tax salvage value of the asset?

25 **Break-Even Cost [LO2]** The previous problem suggests that using CFLs instead of incandescent bulbs is a no-brainer. However, electricity costs actually vary quite a bit, depending on location and user type (you can get information on your rates from your local power company). An industrial user in the Scottish Highlands might pay £0.04 per kilowatt-hour, whereas a residential user in Essex might pay £0.25. What's the break-even cost per kilowatt-hour in Problem 24?

26 **Break-Even Replacement [LO2]** The previous two problems suggest that using CFLs is a good idea from a purely financial perspective unless you live in an area where power is relatively inexpensive, but there is another wrinkle. Suppose you have a residence with a lot of incandescent bulbs that are used on average for 500 hours a year. The average bulb will be about halfway through its life, so it will have 500 hours remaining (and you can't tell which bulbs are older or newer). At what cost per kilowatt-hour does it make sense to replace your incandescent bulbs today?

27 **Issues in Capital Budgeting [LO1]** The debate regarding CFLs versus incandescent bulbs (see Problems 24–26) has even more wrinkles. In no particular order:

- Incandescent bulbs generate a lot more heat than CFLs.

- CFL prices will probably decline relative to incandescent bulbs.

- CFLs unavoidably contain small amounts of mercury, a significant environmental hazard, and special precautions must be taken in disposing of burned-out units (and also in cleaning up a broken lamp). Currently, there is no agreed-upon way to recycle a CFL. Incandescent bulbs pose no disposal/breakage hazards.

- Depending on a light's location (or the number of lights), there can be a non-trivial cost to change bulbs (i.e., labour cost in a business).

- Coal-fired power generation accounts for a substantial portion of the mercury emissions in Europe, though the emissions will drop sharply in the relatively near future.

- Power generation accounts for a substantial portion of CO_2 emissions in Europe.

- CFLs are more energy and material intensive to manufacture. On-site mercury contamination and worker safety are issues.

- If you install a CFL in a permanent lighting fixture in a building, you will probably move long before the CFL burns out.

- Another lighting technology based on light-emitting diodes (LEDs) exists, and is improving. LEDs are currently much more expensive than CFLs, but costs are coming down. LEDs last much longer than CFLs, and use even less power. Also, LEDs don't contain mercury.

Qualitatively, how do these issues affect your position in the CFL versus incandescent light bulb debate? Australia recently proposed banning the sale of incandescent bulbs altogether, as have several European countries. Does your analysis suggest such a move is wise? Are there other regulations, short of an outright ban, that make sense to you?

28 **Replacement Decisions [LO2]** Your small remodelling business has two hydrogen-battery/petrol hybrid eco-vehicles. One is a small passenger car used for job-site visits and for other general business purposes. The other is a heavy truck used to haul equipment. The car gets 50 miles per litre. The truck gets 20 miles per litre. You want to improve petrol mileage to save money, and you have enough money to upgrade one vehicle. The upgrade cost will be the same for both vehicles. An upgraded car will get 80 miles per litre; an upgraded truck will get 25 miles per litre. The cost of petrol is £1.09 per litre. Assuming an upgrade is a good idea in the first place, which one should you upgrade? Both vehicles are driven 12,000 miles per year.

29 **Replacement Decisions [LO2]** In the previous problem, suppose you drive the truck *x* miles per year. How many miles would you have to drive the car before upgrading the car would be the better choice? (*Hint:* Look at the relative petrol savings.)

CHALLENGE
30 – 34

30 **Calculating Project NPV [LO1]** You have been hired as a consultant for Pristine Urban-Tech Zither plc (PUTZ), manufacturers of fine zithers. The market for zithers is growing quickly. The company bought some land three years ago for £1.4 million in anticipation of using it as a toxic waste dump site, but has recently hired another company to handle all toxic materials. Based on a recent appraisal, the company believes it could sell the land for £1.5 million on an after-tax basis. In four years the land could be sold for £1.6 million after taxes. The company also hired a marketing firm to analyse the zither market, at a cost of £125,000. An excerpt of the marketing report is as follows:

> The zither industry will have a rapid expansion in the next four years. With the brand name recognition that PUTZ brings to bear, we feel that the company will be able to sell 3,200, 4,300, 3,900 and 2,800 units each year for the next four years, respectively. Again, capitalizing on the name recognition of PUTZ, we feel that a premium price of £780 can be charged for each zither. Because zithers appear to be a fad, we feel that, at the end of the four-year period, sales should be discontinued.

PUTZ believes that fixed costs for the project will be £425,000 per year, and variable costs are 15 per cent of sales. The equipment necessary for production will cost £4.2 million, and will be depreciated according to the 20 per cent reducing-balance method. At the end of the project the equipment can be scrapped for £400,000. Net working capital of £125,000 will be required immediately. PUTZ has a 28 per cent tax rate, and the required return on the project is 13 per cent. What is the NPV of the project? Assume the company has other profitable projects.

31 **Project Evaluation [LO1]** Aguilera Acoustics (AA) projects unit sales for a new seven-octave voice emulation implant as follows:

Year	Unit sales
1	85,000
2	98,000
3	106,000
4	114,000
5	93,000

Production of the implants will require €1,500,000 in net working capital to start, and additional net working capital investments each year equal to 15 per cent of the projected sales increase for the following year. Total fixed costs are €900,000 per year, variable production costs are €240 per unit, and the units are priced at €325 each. The equipment needed to begin production has an installed cost of €21,000,000. Because the implants are intended for professional singers, this equipment is considered industrial machinery, and is thus depreciated by the reducing-balance method at 20 per cent per annum. In five years this equipment can be sold for about 20 per cent of its acquisition cost. AA is in the 35 per cent marginal tax bracket, and has a required return on all its projects of 18 per cent. Based on these preliminary project estimates, what is the NPV of the project? What is the IRR?

32 **Calculating Required Savings [LO2]** A proposed cost-saving device has an installed cost of £480,000. The device will be used in a five-year project, and will be depreciated using the reducing-balance method at 20 per cent per annum. The required initial net working capital investment is £40,000, the marginal tax rate is 28 per cent, and the project discount rate is 12 per cent. The device has an estimated year 5 salvage value of £45,000. What level of pre-tax cost savings do we require for this project to be profitable?

33   **Calculating a Bid Price [LO3]**   Your company has been approached to bid on a contract to sell 10,000 voice recognition (VR) computer keyboards a year for four years. Because of technological improvements, beyond that time they will be outdated, and no sales will be possible. The equipment necessary for the production will cost £2.4 million and will be depreciated on a reducing-balance (20 per cent) method. Production will require an investment in net working capital of £75,000 to be returned at the end of the project, and the equipment can be sold for £200,000 at the end of production. Fixed costs are £500,000 per year, and variable costs are £165 per unit. In addition to the contract, you feel your company can sell 3,000, 6,000, 8,000 and 5,000 additional units to companies in other countries over the next four years, respectively, at a price of £275. This price is fixed. The tax rate is 28 per cent, and the required return is 13 per cent. Additionally, the managing director of the company will undertake the project only if it has an NPV of £100,000. What bid price should you set for the contract?

34   **Replacement Decisions [LO2]**   Suppose we are thinking about replacing an old computer with a new one. The old one cost us €650,000; the new one will cost €780,000. The new machine will be depreciated straight-line to zero over its five-year life. It will probably be worth about €150,000 after five years.

The old computer is being depreciated straight-line at a rate of €130,000 per year. It will be completely written off in three years. If we don't replace it now, we shall have to replace it in two years. We can sell it now for €210,000; in two years, it will probably be worth €60,000. The new machine will save us €145,000 per year in operating costs. The tax rate is 38 per cent, and the discount rate is 12 per cent.

(a)   Suppose we recognize that, if we don't replace the computer now, we shall be replacing it in two years. Should we replace now or should we wait? (*Hint*: What we effectively have here is a decision either to 'invest' in the old computer (by not selling it) or to invest in the new one. Notice that the two investments have unequal lives.)

(b)   Suppose we consider only whether we should replace the old computer now without worrying about what's going to happen in two years. What are the relevant cash flows? Should we replace it or not? (*Hint*: Consider the net change in the firm's after-tax cash flows if we do the replacement.)

MINI CASE   Conch Republic Electronics, Part 1

Conch Republic Electronics is a mid-sized electronics manufacturer located in Emilia-Romagna, Italy. The company president is Morena Moscardini, who inherited the company. When it was founded, over 70 years ago, the company originally repaired radios and other household appliances. Over the years the company expanded into manufacturing, and is now a reputable manufacturer of various electronic items. Jay McCanless, a recent MBA graduate, has been hired by the company's finance department.

One of the major revenue-producing items manufactured by Conch Republic is a personal digital assistant (PDA). Conch Republic currently has one PDA model on the market, and sales have been excellent. The PDA is a unique item in that it comes in a variety of tropical colours and is pre-programmed to play Billy Bragg music. However, as with any electronic item, technology changes rapidly, and the current PDA has limited features in comparison with newer models. Conch Republic spent €750,000 to develop a prototype for a new PDA that has all the features of the existing PDA but adds new features such as cell-phone capability. The company has spent a further €200,000 for a marketing study to determine the expected sales figures for the new PDA.

Conch Republic can manufacture the new PDA for €155 each in variable costs. Fixed costs for the operation are estimated to be €4.7 million per year. The estimated sales volumes are 74,000, 95,000, 125,000, 105,000 and 80,000 per year for the next five years,

Chapter 9 Making Capital Investment Decisions

respectively. The unit price of the new PDA will be €360. The necessary equipment can be purchased for €21.5 million, and will be depreciated using the 20 per cent reducing-balance method. It is believed the value of the equipment in five years will be €4.1 million.

As previously stated, Conch Republic currently manufactures a PDA. Production of the existing model is expected to be terminated in two years. If Conch Republic does not introduce the new PDA, sales will be 80,000 units and 60,000 units for the next two years, respectively. The price of the existing PDA is €290 per unit, with variable costs of €120 each and fixed costs of €1,800,000 per year. If Conch Republic does introduce the new PDA, sales of the existing PDA will fall by 15,000 units per year, and the price of the existing units will have to be lowered to €255 each. Net working capital for the PDAs will be 20 per cent of sales, and will occur with the timing of the cash flows for the year: for example, there is no initial outlay for NWC, but changes in NWC will first occur in year 1 with the first year's sales. Conch Republic has a 35 per cent corporate tax rate and a 12 per cent required return.

Morena has asked Jay to prepare a report that answers the following questions.

QUESTIONS

1   What is the payback period of the project?

2   What is the profitability index of the project?

3   What is the IRR of the project?

4   What is the NPV of the project?

Endnotes

1   If the asset in question is unique, then the opportunity cost might be higher, because there might be other valuable projects we could undertake that would use it. However, if the asset in question is of a type that is routinely bought and sold (a used car, perhaps), then the opportunity cost is always the going price in the market, because that is the cost of buying another similar asset.

2   More colourfully, erosion is sometimes called *piracy* or *cannibalism*.

3   By *fixed cost* we mean a cash outflow that will occur regardless of the level of sales. This should not be confused with some sort of accounting period charge.

4   We shall also assume that a full year's depreciation can be taken in the first year.

5   In reality, the firm would probably recover something less than 100 per cent of this amount because of bad debts, inventory loss, and so on. If we wanted to, we could just assume that, for example, only 90 per cent was recovered, and proceed from there.

6   We're guilty of a minor inconsistency here. When we calculated the NPV and the IRR, we assumed that all the cash flows occurred at end of year. When we calculated the payback, we assumed that the cash flows occurred uniformly throughout the year.

7   Notice that the average total book value is not the initial total of £110,000 divided by 2. The reason is that the £20,000 in working capital doesn't 'depreciate'.

8   If there were other accounts, we might have to make some further adjustments. For example, a net increase in inventory would be a cash outflow.

CHAPTER

10

Project Analysis and Evaluation

LEARNING OBJECTIVES

After studying this chapter, you should understand:

LO1 How to perform and interpret a sensitivity analysis for a proposed investment.

LO2 How to perform and interpret a scenario analysis for a proposed investment.

LO3 How to determine and interpret cash, accounting and financial break-even points.

LO4 How the degree of operating leverage can affect the cash flows of a project.

LO5 How capital rationing affects the ability of a company to accept projects.

IN THE SUMMER OF 2008 the movie *Speed Racer*, starring Emile Hirsch and Christina Ricci, spun its wheels at the box office. The *Speed Racer* slogan is 'Go Speed Racer, Go!', but critics said, 'Don't go (see) *Speed Racer*, don't go!' One critic said 'the races felt like a drag'. Others were even more harsh, saying the movie was 'like spending two hours caroming through a pinball machine' and a 'long, dreary, migraine-inducing slog'.

Looking at the numbers, Warner Brothers spent close to $150 million making the movie, plus millions more for marketing and distribution. Unfortunately for Warner Brothers, *Speed Racer* crashed and burned, pulling in only $90 million worldwide. In fact, about 4 of 10 movies lose money at the box office, though DVD sales often help the final tally. Of course, there are movies that do quite well. In 2009 the independent offering *Paranormal Activity* raked in over $100 million worldwide at a production cost of just $15,000!

Obviously, Warner Brothers didn't *plan* to lose $60 million on *Speed Racer*, but it happened. As the box office results for *Speed Racer* show, projects don't always go as companies think they will. This chapter explores how this can happen, and what companies can do to analyse and possibly avoid these situations.

In our previous chapter we discussed how to identify and organize the relevant cash flows for capital investment decisions. Our primary interest there was in coming up with a preliminary estimate of the net present value for a proposed project. In this chapter we focus on assessing the reliability of such an estimate, and on some additional considerations in project analysis.

We begin by discussing the need for an evaluation of cash flow and NPV estimates. We go on to develop some useful tools for such an evaluation. We also examine additional complications and concerns that can arise in project evaluation.

10.1   Evaluating NPV Estimates

As we discussed in Chapter 9, an investment has a positive net present value if its market value exceeds its cost. Such an investment is desirable, because it creates value for its owner. The primary problem in identifying such opportunities is that usually we can't actually observe the relevant market value; instead, we estimate it. Having done so, it is only natural to wonder whether our estimates are at least close to the true values. We consider this question next.

The Basic Problem

Suppose we are working on a preliminary discounted cash flow analysis along the lines we described in the previous chapter. We carefully identify the relevant cash flows, avoiding such things as sunk costs, and we remember to consider working capital requirements. We add back any depreciation; we account for possible erosion; and we pay attention to opportunity costs. Finally, we double-check our calculations; when all is said and done, the bottom line is that the estimated NPV is positive.

Now what? Do we stop here and move on to the next proposal? Probably not. The fact that the estimated NPV is positive is definitely a good sign; but, more than anything, this tells us that we need to take a closer look.

If you think about it, there are two circumstances under which a DCF analysis could lead us to conclude that a project has a positive NPV. The first possibility is that the project really does have a positive NPV. That's the good news. The bad news is the second possibility: a project may appear to have a positive NPV because our estimate is inaccurate.

Notice that we could also err in the opposite way. If we conclude that a project has a negative NPV when the true NPV is positive, we lose a valuable opportunity.

Projected versus Actual Cash Flows

There is a somewhat subtle point we need to make here. When we say something like 'The projected cash flow in year 4 is €700', what exactly do we mean? Does this mean that we think the cash flow will actually be €700? Not really. It could happen, of course, but we would be surprised to see it turn out exactly that way. The reason is that the €700 projection is based only on what we know today. Almost anything could happen between now and then to change that cash flow.

Loosely speaking, we really mean that if we took all the possible cash flows that could occur in four years and averaged them, the result would be €700. So we don't really expect a projected cash flow to be exactly right in any one case. What we *do* expect is that, if we evaluate a large number of projects, our projections will be right – on average.

Forecasting Risk

The key inputs into a DCF analysis are projected future cash flows. If the projections are seriously in error, then we have a classic GIGO (garbage in, garbage out) system. In such a case, no matter how carefully we arrange the numbers and manipulate them, the resulting answer can still be grossly misleading. This is the danger in using a relatively sophisticated technique like DCF. It is sometimes easy to get caught up in number crunching and forget the underlying nuts-and-bolts economic reality.

forecasting risk
The possibility that errors in projected cash flows will lead to incorrect decisions. Also, *estimation risk*.

The possibility that we shall make a bad decision because of errors in the projected cash flows is called **forecasting risk** (or *estimation risk*). Because of forecasting risk, there is the danger that we shall think a project has a positive NPV when really it does not. How is this possible? It happens if we are overly optimistic about the future, and, as a result, our projected cash flows don't realistically reflect the possible future cash flows.

Forecasting risk can take many forms. For example, Microsoft spent several billion dollars developing and bringing the Xbox game console to market. Technologically more sophisticated than existing products on the market, the Xbox was the best way to play against competitors over the Internet. Unfortunately, Microsoft sold only 9 million Xboxes in the first 14 months of sales, at the low end of Microsoft's expected range. The Xbox was arguably the best available game console at the time, so why didn't it sell better? The reason given by analysts was that there were far fewer games made for the Xbox. For example, the PlayStation enjoyed a two-to-one advantage in the number of games made for it.

So far, we have not explicitly considered what to do about the possibility of errors in our forecasts, so one of our goals in this chapter is to develop some tools that are useful in identifying areas where potential errors exist, and where they might be especially damaging. In one form or another, we shall be trying to assess the economic 'reasonableness' of our estimates. We shall also be wondering how much damage will be done by errors in those estimates.

Sources of Value

The first line of defence against forecasting risk is simply to ask, 'What is it about this investment that leads to a positive NPV?' We should be able to point to something specific as the source of value. For example, if the proposal under consideration involved a new product, then we might ask questions such as the following. Are we certain that our new product is significantly better than that of the competition? Can we truly manufacture at lower cost, or distribute more effectively, or identify undeveloped market niches, or gain control of a market?

These are just a few of the potential sources of value. There are many others. For example, in 2004 Google announced a new, free email service: Gmail. Why? Free email services were already widely available from big hitters like Microsoft and Yahoo! The answer is that Google's mail service is integrated with its acclaimed search engine, thereby giving it an edge. Also, offering email lets Google expand its lucrative keyword-based advertising delivery. So Google's source of value is leveraging its proprietary web search and advertisement delivery technologies.

A key factor to keep in mind is the degree of competition in the market. A basic principle of economics is that positive-NPV investments will be rare in a highly competitive environment. Therefore proposals that appear to show significant value in the face of stiff competition are particularly troublesome, and the likely reaction of the competition to any innovations must be closely examined.

To give an example, in 2010 demand for touch screen smartphones was high, prices were high, and profit margins were fat for retailers. But also in 2010 manufacturers of smartphones, such as Apple, Nokia and HTC, were projected to pour several billion euros into new production facilities as the market matured. Thus anyone thinking of entering this highly profitable market would do well to reflect on what the supply (and profit margin) situation will look like in just a few years.

It is also necessary to think about *potential* competition. For example, suppose home improvement retailer B&Q identifies an area that is underserved, and is thinking about opening a store. If the store is successful, what will happen? The answer is that Focus or Homebase (other competitors) would probably also build a store, thereby driving down volume and profits. So we always need to keep in mind that success attracts imitators and competitors.

The point to remember is that positive-NPV investments are probably not all that common, and the number of positive-NPV projects is almost certainly limited for any given firm. If we can't articulate some sound economic basis for thinking – ahead of time – that we have found something special, then the conclusion that our project has a positive NPV should be viewed with some suspicion.

CONCEPT QUESTIONS

> 10.1a   What is forecasting risk? Why is it a concern for the financial manager?
> 10.1b   What are some potential sources of value in a new project?

10.2   Scenario and Other What-If Analyses

Our basic approach to evaluating cash flow and NPV estimates involves asking what-if questions. Accordingly, we discuss some organized ways of going about a what-if analysis. Our goal in performing such an analysis is to assess the degree of forecasting risk, and to identify the most critical components of the success or failure of an investment.

Getting Started

We are investigating a new project. Naturally, the first thing we do is estimate NPV, based on our projected cash flows. We shall call this initial set of projections the *base case*. Now, however, we recognize the possibility of error in these cash flow projections. After completing the base case, we thus wish to investigate the impact on our estimates of different assumptions about the future.

One way to organize this investigation is to put upper and lower bounds on the various components of the project. For example, suppose we forecast sales at 100 units per year. We know this estimate may be high or low, but we are relatively certain it is not off by more than 10 units in either direction. We thus pick a lower bound of 90 and an upper bound of 110. We go on to assign such bounds to any other cash flow components we are unsure about.

When we pick these upper and lower bounds, we are not ruling out the possibility that the actual values could be outside this range. What we are saying, again loosely speaking, is that it is unlikely that the true average (as opposed to our estimated average) of the possible values is outside this range.

An example is useful to illustrate the idea here. The project under consideration costs €200,000, has a five-year life, and has no salvage value. For simplicity, depreciation is straight-line to zero. The required return is 12 per cent, and the tax rate is 34 per cent. In addition, we have compiled the following information:

	Base case	Lower bound	Upper bound
Unit sales	6,000	5,500	6,500
Price per unit (€)	80	75	85
Variable costs per unit (€)	60	58	62
Fixed costs per year (€)	50,000	45,000	55,000

With this information we can calculate the base-case NPV by first calculating net income:

Sales (€)	480,000
Variable costs (€)	360,000
Fixed costs (€)	50,000
Depreciation (€)	40,000
Profit before taxes (€)	30,000
Taxes (34%) (€)	10,200
Net income	19,800

Operating cash flow is thus €19,800 + 40,000 = €59,800 per year. At 12 per cent, the five-year annuity factor is 3.6048, so the base-case NPV is

$$\text{Base-case NPV} = -€200{,}000 + 59{,}800 \times 3.6048$$
$$= €15{,}567$$

Thus the project looks good so far.

Scenario Analysis

The basic form of what-if analysis is called **scenario analysis**. What we do is investigate the changes in our NPV estimates that result from asking questions such as: what if unit sales realistically should be projected at 5,500 units instead of 6,000?

> **scenario analysis** The determination of what happens to NPV estimates when we ask what-if questions.

Once we start looking at alternative scenarios, we might find that most of the plausible ones result in positive NPVs. In this case we have some confidence in proceeding with the project. If a substantial percentage of the scenarios look bad, the degree of forecasting risk is high, and further investigation is in order.

We can consider a number of possible scenarios. A good place to start is with the worst-case scenario. This will tell us the minimum NPV of the project. If this turns out to be positive, we shall be in good shape. While we are at it, we shall go ahead and determine the other extreme, the best case. This puts an upper bound on our NPV.

To get the worst case, we assign the least favourable value to each item. This means *low* values for items such as units sold and price per unit, and *high* values for costs. We do the reverse for the best case. For our project, these values would be the following:

	Worst case	Best case
Unit sales	5,500	6,500
Price per unit (€)	75	85
Variable costs per unit (€)	62	58
Fixed costs per year (€)	55,000	45,000

With this information we can calculate the net income and cash flows under each scenario (check these for yourself):

Scenario	Net income (€)	Cash flow (€)	Net present value (€)	IRR (%)
Base case	19,800	59,800	15,567	15.1
Worst case*	−15,510	24,490	−111,719	−14.4
Best case	59,730	99,730	159,504	40.9

*We assume a tax credit is created in our worst-case scenario.

What we learn is that, under the worst scenario, the cash flow is still positive at €24,490. That's good news. The bad news is that the return is −14.4 per cent in this case, and the NPV is −€111,719. Because the project costs €200,000, we stand to lose a little more than half of the original investment under the worst possible scenario. The best case offers an attractive 41 per cent return.

The terms *best case* and *worst case* are commonly used, and we shall stick with them; but they are somewhat misleading. The absolutely best thing that could happen would be something absurdly unlikely, such as launching a new diet soft drink and subsequently learning that our (patented) formulation also just happens to cure the common cold. Similarly, the true worst case would involve some incredibly remote possibility of total disaster. We're not claiming that these things don't happen; once in a while they do. Some products, such as iPhones, succeed beyond the wildest expectations; and some, such as asbestos, turn out to be absolute catastrophes. Our point is that, in assessing the reasonableness of an NPV estimate, we need to stick to cases that are reasonably likely to occur.

Instead of *best* and *worst*, then, it is probably more accurate to use the words *optimistic* and *pessimistic*. In broad terms, if we were thinking about a reasonable range for, say, unit sales, then what we call the best case would correspond to something near the upper end of that range. The worst case would simply correspond to the lower end.

Depending on the project, the best- and worst-case estimates can vary greatly. For example, in 2008 Roche Carolina, a subsidiary of the Roche Group, a Swiss global health care company, announced plans for converting its site to a solar heating and cooling system. The initial cost was estimated at €350,000, including a government grant. The range used for this initial cost was ±15 per cent. The annual savings were estimated at €29,000, with a range of ±30 per cent. In the end, the NPV was estimated at €125,000, with a range of €42,000 to €208,000, and the IRR was 18 per cent, with a range of 11 per cent to 25 per cent.

As we have mentioned, there are an unlimited number of different scenarios that we could examine. At a minimum, we might want to investigate two intermediate cases by going halfway between the base amounts and the extreme amounts. This would give us five scenarios in all, including the base case.

Beyond this point, it is hard to know when to stop. As we generate more and more possibilities, we run the risk of experiencing 'paralysis of analysis'. The difficulty is that, no matter how many scenarios we run, all we can learn are possibilities – some good and some bad. Beyond that, we don't get any guidance as to what to do. Scenario analysis is thus useful in telling us what could happen, and in helping us gauge the potential for disaster, but it does not tell us whether to take a project.

Unfortunately, in practice, even the worst-case scenarios may not be low enough. Two recent examples show what we mean. The Eurotunnel, or Chunnel, may be one of the new wonders of the world. The tunnel under the English Channel connects Britain to France and covers 38 km. It took 8,000 workers eight years to remove 7.5 million cubic metres of rock. When the tunnel was finally built, it cost £11.9 billion (€13.1 billion), or slightly more than twice the original estimate of £5.9 billion (€6.5 billion). And things got worse. Forecasts called for 16.8 million passengers in the first year, but only 4 million actually used it. Revenue estimates for 2003 were £1.92 billion (€2.12 billion), but actual revenue was only about one-third of that. The major problems faced by the Eurotunnel were increased competition from ferry services, which dropped their prices, and the rise of low-cost airlines. In 2006 things got so bad that the company operating the Eurotunnel was forced into negotiations with creditors to chop its £7.4 billion (€8.2 billion) debt in half to avoid bankruptcy. The debt reduction appeared to help. In 2007 the Eurotunnel reported its first profit, of £0.9 million (€1 million). Of course, this profit paled in comparison with the £185 million (€204 million) in losses accumulated since the Chunnel first opened in 1994.

Another example is Toyota, which had long been regarded as a very reliable carmaker. In 2010 complaints started to trickle out that the accelerator pedal in some of its cars would stick, leading to uncontrolled increases in speed. By April 2010 Toyota had recalled over 8 million cars, which resulted in a catastrophic decline in its reputation, and a collapse in Toyota car sales throughout the world.

Moving forward to 2010, analysts would have had even more difficulty in forecasting the eruption of the Icelandic volcano, Eyjafjallajökull, which grounded European flights for weeks and forced many people into using other sources of transport, such as the Eurotunnel. The last time that Eyjafjallajökull erupted (in the nineteenth century), its eruptions lasted for nearly two years. Furthermore, the volcano's larger neighbour, Katla, could also erupt, and if this happens, European flights will be the least of our worries . . .

sensitivity analysis
Investigation of what happens to NPV when only one variable is changed.

Sensitivity Analysis

Sensitivity analysis is a variation on scenario analysis that is useful in pinpointing the areas where forecasting risk is especially severe. The basic idea with a sensitivity

Given that Libertad produces gas and Galoc produces oil, we can concentrate on three main uncertainties: the future gas price, the future oil price, and the future extraction capabilities of the hydrocarbon fields owned by Forum Energy.

The wholesale gas price in April 2010 was around £2.63 per barrel and the oil price was around £54.61 per barrel. Assume that one barrel of gas is equal to 6 cubic feet. The expected extraction rates and other information for each hydrocarbon field are as follows:

Field	Interest	Expected reserves	Reserves × Interest	Barrels equivalent	Annual output
Libertad Gas	66.7%	1.14 billion cubic feet	760 million cubic feet	127 million barrels	423,333 barrels/year (assuming 300 years' life)
Galoc Oil	2.27%	2.3 million barrels/year	52,210 barrels/year	52,210 barrels/year	52,210 barrels/year

This is all the information we have to work with, and so we have to make a number of assumptions. Assume that the relevant discount rate for the oil field is 12 per cent, and the discount rate for the gas field is 15 per cent. Assume also that the oil field lasts for 10 years, and the gas field has enough gas to last for 300 years. Also assume that energy prices may be 20 per cent higher or lower than anticipated, and extraction capabilities may be 10 per cent higher or lower than expected. The assumptions are provided in tabular form below:

Input	Worst case	Expected	Best case
Oil price (£)	43.68	54.61	65.53
Gas price (£)	2.11	2.63	3.16
Oil extraction capacity (barrels)	46,989	52,210	57,431
Gas extraction capacity (barrels)	381,000	423,333	465,667

Now that we have our different assumptions, we are in a position to value Forum Energy plc. Taking the expected scenario first, we value the oil and gas fields separately:

- **Galoc oil field** The oil in the Galoc field will last for 10 years. If the oil price is £54.61 per barrel, and 52,210 barrels are extracted annually, then the annual revenues from Galoc will be £54.61 × 52,210 = £2,850,941. The present value of a 10-year annuity of £2,850,941 discounted at a rate of 12 per cent is approximately equal to £16,108,451.

- **Libertad gas field** The gas in the Libertad field will last for 300 years. The gas price is £2.63 per barrel, and 423,333 barrels are extracted annually, giving annual cash flows of £2.63 × 423,333 = £1,114,034. The present value of a 300-year annuity of £1,114,034 discounted at a rate of 15 per cent is approximately equal to £7,426,895.

The total market value of Forum Energy's assets (ignoring the Sampaguita gas field) is equal to the sum of the two main operations, which is £16,108,451 + £7,426,895 = £23,535,346. With 33,092,533 shares, the expected share price should be £0.711, which is almost exactly the same as the actual share price of £0.715. This gives us confidence that our analysis is in roughly the same area as that of the market. If our valuation was significantly different from the existing share price, it would be important to reassess the various inputs into the analysis.

For information, the spreadsheet that was used in the analysis is presented overleaf. Clearly any layout could be used.

Chapter 10 Project Analysis and Evaluation

◢	A	B	C	D	E
1	Forum Energy plc				
2					
3	Share Price	£0.715			
4	Number of Shares	33092533			
5	Market Cap	£23,661,161			
6					
7	$/£	1.52			
8	Oil Price ($83)	£54.61			
9	Gas Price ($4)	£2.63			
10					
11	Oil Barrels	52,210		Gas Barrels	423,333
12	Annual Oil Revenu	£2,850,940.79		Annual Gas Revenues	£1,114,034.21
13	years	10		years	300
14	r	12%		r	15%
15					
16	PV Oil	£16,108,451.30		PV Gas	£7,426,894.74
17					
18	Total Value	£23,535,346.04			
19	Share Price	£0.711			
20					

The next stage in our valuation should be the sensitivity analysis. In the table below we present the expected share prices in each situation by varying only one input at a time. From the table it can be seen that the Forum Energy share price is most sensitive to changes in the oil price. Thus analysts should focus more heavily on predicting changes in future oil prices when considering Forum Energy's value.

Worst case Oil = £43.68	Best case Oil = £65.53	Worst case Gas = £2.11	Best case Gas = £3.16
Share price = £0.614	Share price = £0.809	Share price = £0.667	Share price = £0.756
Worst case Oil = 46,989 barrels	Best case Oil = 57,431 barrels	Worst case Gas = 381,000 barrels	Best case Gas = 465,667 barrels
Share price = £0.662	Share price = £0.760	Share price = £0.689	Share price = £0.734

We can also carry out a scenario analysis for Forum Energy by looking at the best- and worst-case scenarios. These are the times when the worst (or best) case estimates for all the inputs occur simultaneously. When the worst-case scenario occurs, the gas price will be £2.11, the oil price will be £43.68, the oil production will be 46,989 barrels, and the gas production will be 381,000 barrels. The share price of Forum Energy plc when this happens will only be £0.512, significantly less than the current share price. Similarly, under the best-case scenario, Forum Energy's share price will be £0.939.

So what should the share price be? It all depends on the likelihood of each scenario or outcome in the future. Further analysis is definitely required at this point. For example, we have not considered the valuation effects of the Sampaguita gas field and the possible

> **EXAMPLE 10.1**
>
> # Variable Costs
>
> Blume plc is a manufacturer of pencils. It has received an order for 5,000 pencils, and the company has to decide whether to accept the order. From recent experience, the company knows that each pencil requires £0.05 in raw materials and £0.50 in direct labour costs. These variable costs are expected to continue to apply in the future. What will Blume's total variable costs be if it accepts the order?
>
> In this case the cost per unit is £0.50 in labour plus £0.05 in materials, for a total of £0.55 per unit. At 5,000 units of output, we have
>
> $$\begin{aligned} VC &= Q \times v \\ &= 5{,}000 \times £0.55 \\ &= £2{,}750 \end{aligned}$$
>
> Therefore total variable costs will be £2,750.

Fixed Costs   Fixed costs, by definition, do not change during a specified time period. So, unlike variable costs, they do not depend on the amount of goods or services produced during a period (at least within some range of production). For example, the lease payment on a production facility and the company chairman's salary are fixed costs, at least over some period.

> **fixed costs**
> Costs that do not change when the quantity of output changes during a particular time period.

Naturally, fixed costs are not fixed for ever. They are fixed only during some particular time, say a quarter or a year. Beyond that time, leases can be terminated and executives 'retired'. More to the point, any fixed cost can be modified or eliminated given enough time; so, in the long run, all costs are variable.

Notice that when a cost is fixed, that cost is effectively a sunk cost, because we are going to have to pay it no matter what.

Total Costs   Total costs (TC) for a given level of output are the sum of variable costs (VC) and fixed costs (FC):

$$\begin{aligned} TC &= VC + FC \\ &= v \times Q + FC \end{aligned}$$

So, for example, if we have variable costs of €3 per unit and fixed costs of €8,000 per year, our total cost is

$$TC = €3 \times Q + €8{,}000$$

If we produce 6,000 units, our total production cost will be €3 × 6,000 + €8,000 = €26,000. At other production levels, we have the following:

Quantity produced	Total variable costs (€)	Fixed costs (€)	Total costs (€)
0	0	8,000	8,000
1,000	3,000	8,000	11,000
5,000	15,000	8,000	23,000
10,000	30,000	8,000	38,000

> **marginal, or incremental, cost**
> The change in costs that occurs when there is a small change in output.

By plotting these points in Fig. 10.3 we see that the relationship between quantity produced and total costs is given by a straight line. In Fig. 10.3, notice that total costs equal fixed costs when sales are zero. Beyond that point, every one-unit increase in production leads to a €3 increase in total costs, so the slope of the line is 3. In other words, the **marginal**, or **incremental**, **cost** of producing one more unit is €3.

FIGURE
10.3

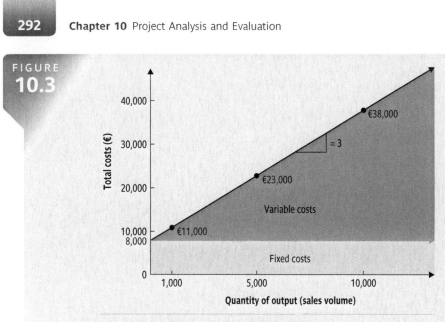

Figure 10.3 Output level and total costs

EXAMPLE
10.2

Average Cost versus Marginal Cost

Suppose Blume plc has a variable cost per pencil of £0.55. The lease payment on the production facility is £5,000 per month. If Blume produces 100,000 pencils per year, what are the total costs of production? What is the average cost per pencil?

The fixed costs are £5,000 per month, or £60,000 per year. The variable cost is £0.55 per pencil. So the total cost for the year, assuming that Blume produces 100,000 pencils, is

$$\text{Total cost} = v \times Q + FC$$
$$= £0.55 \times 100,000 + £60,000$$
$$= £115,000$$

The average cost per pencil is £115,000/100,000 = £1.15.

Now suppose that Blume has received a special, one-off order for 5,000 pencils. Blume has sufficient capacity to manufacture the 5,000 pencils on top of the 100,000 already produced, so no additional fixed costs will be incurred. Also, there will be no effect on existing orders. If Blume can get £0.75 per pencil for this order, should the order be accepted?

> **marginal, or incremental, revenue**
> The change in revenue that occurs when there is a small change in output.

What this boils down to is a simple proposition. It costs £0.55 to make another pencil. Anything Blume can get for this pencil in excess of the £0.55 incremental cost contributes in a positive way towards covering fixed costs. The £0.75 **marginal**, or **incremental**, **revenue** exceeds the £0.55 marginal cost, so Blume should take the order.

The fixed cost of £60,000 is not relevant to this decision, because it is effectively sunk, at least for the current period. In the same way, the fact that the average cost is £1.15 is irrelevant, because this average reflects the fixed cost. As long as producing the extra 5,000 pencils truly does not cost anything beyond the £0.55 per pencil, then Blume should accept anything over £0.55.

Accounting Break-Even

The most widely used measure of break-even is **accounting break-even**. The accounting break-even point is simply the sales level that results in a zero project net income.

To determine a project's accounting break-even, we start off with some common sense. Suppose we retail USB flash drives for £5 apiece. We can buy drives from a wholesale supplier for £3 apiece. We have accounting expenses of £600 in fixed costs and £300 in depreciation. How many drives do we have to sell to break even – that is, for net income to be zero?

For every drive we sell, we pick up £5 – 3 = £2 towards covering our other expenses (this £2 difference between the selling price and the variable cost is often called the *contribution margin per unit*). We have to cover a total of £600 + 300 = £900 in accounting expenses, so we obviously need to sell £900/2 = 450 drives. We can check this by noting that at a sales level of 450 units our revenues are £5 × 450 = £2,250 and our variable costs are £3 × 450 = £1,350. Thus here is the income statement:

Sales (£)	2,250
Variable costs (£)	1,350
Fixed costs (£)	600
Depreciation (£)	300
Profit before taxes (£)	0
Taxes (28%) (£)	0
Net income (£)	0

Remember, because we are discussing a proposed new project, we do not consider any interest expense in calculating net income or cash flow from the project. Also, notice that we include depreciation in calculating expenses here, even though depreciation is not a cash outflow. That is why we call it an *accounting* break-even. Finally, notice that when net income is zero, so are pre-tax income and, of course, taxes. In accounting terms, our revenues are equal to our costs, so there is no profit to tax.

Figure 10.4 presents another way to see what is happening. This figure looks a lot like Fig. 10.3 except that we add a line for revenues. As indicated, total revenues are zero when output is zero. Beyond that, each unit sold brings in another £5, so the slope of the revenue line is 5.

From our preceding discussion we know that we break even when revenues are equal to total costs. The line for revenues and the line for total costs cross exactly where output is at 450 units. As illustrated, at any level of output below 450 our accounting profit is negative, and at any level above 450 we have a positive net income.

Accounting Break-Even: A Closer Look

In our numerical example, notice that the break-even level is equal to the sum of fixed costs and depreciation, divided by price per unit less variable costs per unit. This is always true. To see why, we recall all of the following variables:

P = Selling price per unit

v = Variable cost per unit

Q = Total units sold

S = Total sales = $P \times Q$

VC = Total variable costs = $v \times Q$

FC = Fixed costs

D = Depreciation

T = Tax rate

FIGURE
10.4

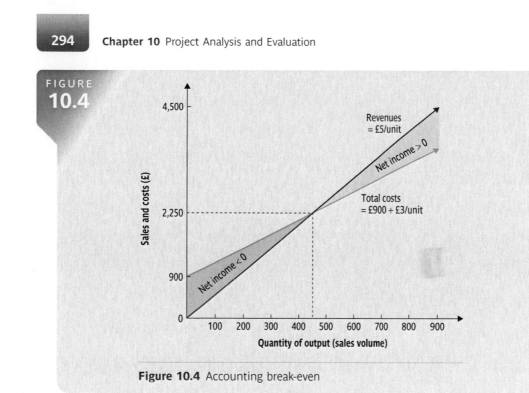

Figure 10.4 Accounting break-even

Project net income is given by

Net income = (Sales − Variable costs − Fixed costs − Depreciation) × (1 − T)
= (S − VC − FC − D) × (1 − T)

From here, it is not difficult to calculate the break-even point. If we set this net income equal to zero, we get

Net income $\stackrel{\text{SET}}{=}$ 0 − (S − VC − FC − D) × (1 − T)

Divide both sides by (1 − T) to get

$$S - \text{VC} - \text{FC} - D = 0$$

As we have seen, this says that when net income is zero, so is pre-tax income. If we recall that $S = P \times Q$ and VC = $v \times Q$, then we can rearrange the equation to solve for the break-even level:

$$S - \text{VC} = \text{FC} + D$$
$$P \times Q - v \times Q = \text{FC} + D$$
$$(P - v) \times Q = \text{FC} + D \qquad (10.1)$$
$$Q = (\text{FC} + D)/(P - v)$$

This is the same result we described earlier.

Uses for the Accounting Break-Even

Why would anyone be interested in knowing the accounting break-even point? To illustrate how it can be useful, suppose we are a small ice cream manufacturer with a strictly local distribution. We are thinking about expanding into new markets. Based on the estimated cash flows, we find that the expansion has a positive NPV.

Going back to our discussion of forecasting risk, we know that it is likely that what will make or break our expansion is sales volume. The reason is that, in this case at least, we probably have a fairly good idea of what we can charge for the ice cream. Further, we know relevant production and distribution costs reasonably well, because we are already in the business. What we do not know with any real precision is how much ice cream we can sell.

Given the costs and selling price, however, we can immediately calculate the break-even point. Once we have done so, we might find that we need to get 30 per cent of the market just to break even. If we think that this is unlikely to occur, because, for example, we have only 10 per cent of our current market, then we know our forecast is questionable, and there is a real possibility that the true NPV is negative. On the other hand, we might find that we already have firm commitments from buyers for about the break-even amount, so we are almost certain we can sell more. In this case the forecasting risk is much lower, and we have greater confidence in our estimates.

There are several other reasons why knowing the accounting break-even can be useful. First, as we shall discuss in more detail later, accounting break-even and payback period are similar measures. Like payback period, accounting break-even is relatively easy to calculate and explain.

Second, managers are often concerned with the contribution a project will make to the firm's total accounting earnings. A project that does not break even in an accounting sense actually reduces total earnings.

Third, a project that just breaks even on an accounting basis loses money in a financial or opportunity cost sense. This is true because we could have earned more by investing elsewhere. Such a project does not lose money in an out-of-pocket sense. As described in the following pages, we get back exactly what we put in. For non-economic reasons, opportunity losses may be easier to live with than out-of-pocket losses.

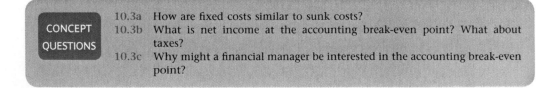

CONCEPT QUESTIONS		
	10.3a	How are fixed costs similar to sunk costs?
	10.3b	What is net income at the accounting break-even point? What about taxes?
	10.3c	Why might a financial manager be interested in the accounting break-even point?

10.4   Operating Cash Flow, Sales Volume and Break-Even

Accounting break-even is one tool that is useful for project analysis. Ultimately, however, we are more interested in cash flow than in accounting income. So, for example, if sales volume is the critical variable, then we need to know more about the relationship between sales volume and cash flow than just the accounting break-even.

Our goal in this section is to illustrate the relationship between operating cash flow and sales volume. We also discuss some other break-even measures. To simplify matters somewhat, we shall ignore the effect of taxes. We start off by looking at the relationship between accounting break-even and cash flow.

Accounting Break-Even and Cash Flow

Now that we know how to find the accounting break-even, it is natural to wonder what happens with cash flow. To illustrate, suppose Wettway Yachts Ltd is considering whether to launch its new Margo-class yacht. The selling price will be £40,000 per boat. The variable costs will be about half that, or £20,000 per boat, and fixed costs will be £500,000 per year.

The Base Case The total investment needed to undertake the project is £3,500,000. For simplicity, this amount will be depreciated straight-line to zero over the five-year life of the equipment.[1] The salvage value is zero, and there are no working capital consequences. Wettway has a 20 per cent required return on new projects.

Based on market surveys and historical experience, Wettway projects total sales for the five years at 425 boats, or about 85 boats per year. Ignoring taxes, should this project be launched?

To begin, ignoring taxes, the operating cash flow at 85 boats per year is

$$\begin{aligned}
\text{Operating cash flow} &= \text{EBIT} + \text{Depreciation} - \text{Taxes} \\
&= (S - VC - FC - D) + D - 0 \\
&= 85 \times (£40{,}000 - 20{,}000) - 500{,}000 \\
&= £1{,}200{,}000 \text{ per year}
\end{aligned}$$

At 20 per cent, the five-year annuity factor is 2.9906, so the NPV is

$$\begin{aligned}
\text{NPV} &= -£3{,}500{,}000 + 1{,}200{,}000 \times 2.9906 \\
&= -£3{,}500{,}000 + 3{,}588{,}720 \\
&= £88{,}720
\end{aligned}$$

In the absence of additional information, the project should be launched.

Calculating the Break-Even Level To begin looking a little closer at this project, you might ask a series of questions. For example, how many new boats does Wettway need to sell for the project to break even on an accounting basis? If Wettway does break even, what will be the annual cash flow from the project? What will be the return on the investment in this case?

Before fixed costs and depreciation are considered, Wettway generates £40,000 – 20,000 = £20,000 per boat (this is revenue less variable cost). Depreciation is £3,500,000/5 = £700,000 per year. Fixed costs and depreciation together total £1.2 million, so Wettway needs to sell $(FC + D)/(P - v)$ = £1.2 million/20,000 = 60 boats per year to break even on an accounting basis. This is 25 boats fewer than projected sales: so, assuming that Wettway is confident its projection is accurate to within, say, 15 boats, it appears unlikely that the new investment will fail to at least break even on an accounting basis.

To calculate Wettway's cash flow in this case, we note that if 60 boats are sold, net income will be exactly zero. Recalling from the previous chapter that operating cash flow for a project can be written as net income plus depreciation (the bottom-up definition), we can see that the operating cash flow is equal to the depreciation, or £700,000 in this case. The internal rate of return is exactly zero (why?).

Payback and Break-Even As our example illustrates, whenever a project breaks even on an accounting basis, the cash flow for that period will equal the depreciation. This result makes perfect accounting sense. For example, suppose we invest £100,000 in a five-year project. The depreciation is straight-line to a zero salvage, or £20,000 per year. If the project exactly breaks even in every period, then the cash flow will be £20,000 per period.

The sum of the cash flows for the life of this project is 5 × £20,000 = £100,000, the original investment. What this shows is that a project's payback period is exactly equal to its life if the project breaks even in every period. Similarly, a project that does better than break even has a payback that is shorter than the life of the project, and has a positive rate of return.

The bad news is that a project that just breaks even on an accounting basis has a negative NPV and a zero return. For our yacht project, the fact that Wettway will almost surely break even on an accounting basis is partially comforting, because it means that the firm's 'downside' risk (its potential loss) is limited, but we still don't know whether the project is truly profitable. More work is needed.

$$£3,500 = OCF \times 2.9906$$
$$OCF = £3,500/2.9906$$
$$= £1,170$$

Wettway thus needs an operating cash flow of £1,170 each year to break even. We can now plug this OCF into the equation for sales volume:

$$Q = (£500 + 1,170)/20$$
$$= 83.5$$

So, Wettway needs to sell about 84 boats per year. This is not good news.

As indicated in Fig. 10.5, the financial break-even is substantially higher than the accounting break-even. This will often be the case. Moreover, what we have discovered is that the yacht project has a substantial degree of forecasting risk. We project sales of 85 boats per year, but it takes 84 just to earn the required return.

Conclusion   Overall, it seems unlikely that the Wettway yacht project would fail to break even on an accounting basis. However, there appears to be a very good chance that the true NPV is negative. This illustrates the danger in looking at just the accounting break-even.

What should Wettway do? Is the new project all wet? The decision at this point is essentially a managerial issue – a judgement call. The crucial questions are these:

1   How much confidence do we have in our projections?

2   How important is the project to the future of the company?

3   How badly will the company be hurt if sales turn out to be low? What options are available to the company in this case?

We shall consider questions such as these in a later section. For future reference, our discussion of the different break-even measures is summarized in Table 10.1.

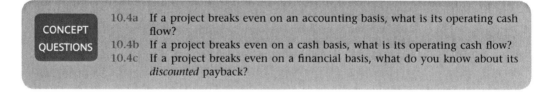

CONCEPT QUESTIONS

10.4a   If a project breaks even on an accounting basis, what is its operating cash flow?

10.4b   If a project breaks even on a cash basis, what is its operating cash flow?

10.4c   If a project breaks even on a financial basis, what do you know about its *discounted* payback?

10.5 Operating Leverage

We have discussed how to calculate and interpret various measures of break-even for a proposed project. What we have not explicitly discussed is what determines these points, and how they might be changed. We now turn to this subject.

The Basic Idea

Operating leverage is the degree to which a project or firm is committed to fixed production costs. A firm with low operating leverage will have low fixed costs compared with a firm with high operating leverage. Generally speaking, projects with a relatively heavy investment in plant and equipment will have a relatively high degree of operating leverage. Such projects are said to be *capital intensive*.

Whenever we are thinking about a new venture, there will normally be alternative ways of producing and delivering the product. For example, Wettway can purchase the necessary equipment and build all the components for its yachts in-house. Alternatively, some of the work could be farmed out to other firms. The

operating leverage
The degree to which a firm or project relies on fixed costs.

Chapter 10 Project Analysis and Evaluation

TABLE 10.1

The general break-even expression

Ignoring taxes, the relation between operating cash flow (OCF) and quantity of output or sales volume (Q) is

$$Q = \frac{FC + OCF}{P - v}$$

where
  FC = Total fixed costs
  P = Price per unit
  v = Variable cost per unit
As shown next, this relation can be used to determine the accounting, cash, and financial break-even points.

The accounting break-even point

Accounting break-even occurs when net income is zero. Operating cash flow is equal to depreciation when net income is zero, so the accounting break-even point is

$$Q = \frac{FC + D}{P - v}$$

A project that always just breaks even on an accounting basis has a payback exactly equal to its life, a negative NPV, and an IRR of zero.

The cash break-even point

Cash break-even occurs when operating cash flow is zero. The cash break-even point is thus

$$Q = \frac{FC}{P - v}$$

A project that always just breaks even on a cash basis never pays back, has an NPV that is negative and equal to the initial outlay, and has an IRR of −100 per cent.

The financial break-even point

Financial break-even occurs when the NPV of the project is zero. The financial break-even point is thus

$$Q = \frac{FC + OCF^*}{P - v}$$

where OCF* is the level of OCF that results in a zero NPV. A project that breaks even on a financial basis has a discounted payback equal to its life, a zero NPV, and an IRR just equal to the required return.

Table 10.1 Summary of break-even measures

first option involves a greater investment in plant and equipment, greater fixed costs and depreciation, and, as a result, a higher degree of operating leverage.

Implications of Operating Leverage

Regardless of how it is measured, operating leverage has important implications for project evaluation. Fixed costs act like a lever in the sense that a small percentage change in operating revenue can be magnified into a large percentage change in operating cash flow and NPV. This explains why we call it operating 'leverage'.

The higher the degree of operating leverage, the greater is the potential danger from forecasting risk. The reason is that relatively small errors in forecasting sales volume can get magnified, or 'levered up', into large errors in cash flow projections.

From a managerial perspective, one way of coping with highly uncertain projects is to keep the degree of operating leverage as low as possible. This will generally have the effect of keeping the break-even point (however measured) at its minimum level. We shall illustrate this point shortly, but first we need to discuss how to measure operating leverage.

Measuring Operating Leverage

One way of measuring operating leverage is to ask: if quantity sold rises by 5 per cent, what will be the percentage change in operating cash flow? In other words, the **degree of operating leverage** (DOL) is defined such that

> **degree of operating leverage (DOL)** The percentage change in operating cash flow relative to the percentage change in quantity sold.

$$\text{Percentage change in OCF} = \text{DOL} \times \text{Percentage change in } Q$$

Based on the relationship between OCF and Q, DOL can be written as[2]

$$\text{DOL} = 1 + \text{FC}/\text{OCF} \qquad (10.4)$$

The ratio FC/OCF simply measures fixed costs as a percentage of total operating cash flow. Notice that zero fixed costs would result in a DOL of 1, implying that percentage changes in quantity sold would show up one for one in operating cash flow. In other words, no magnification, or leverage, effect would exist.

To illustrate this measure of operating leverage, we go back to the Wettway yacht project. Fixed costs were £500 and $(P - v)$ was £20, so OCF was

$$\text{OCF} = -£500 + 20 \times Q$$

Suppose Q is currently 50 boats. At this level of output, OCF is $-£500 + 1,000 = £500$.

If Q rises by 1 unit to 51, then the percentage change in Q is $(51 - 50)/50 = 0.02$, or 2 per cent. OCF rises to £520, a change of $P - v = £20$. The percentage change in OCF is $(£520 - 500)/500 = 0.04$, or 4 per cent. So a 2 per cent increase in the number of boats sold leads to a 4 per cent increase in operating cash flow. The degree of operating leverage must be exactly 2.00. We can check this by noting that

$$\begin{aligned} \text{DOL} &= 1 + \text{FC}/\text{OCF} \\ &= 1 + £500/500 \\ &= 2 \end{aligned}$$

This verifies our previous calculations.

Our formulation of DOL depends on the current output level, Q. However, it can handle changes from the current level of any size, not just one unit. For example, suppose Q rises from 50 to 75, a 50 per cent increase. With DOL equal to 2, operating cash flow should increase by 100 per cent, or exactly double. Does it? The answer is yes, because, at a Q of 75, OCF is

$$\text{OCF} = -£500 + 20 \times 75 = £1,000$$

Notice that operating leverage declines as output (Q) rises. For example, at an output level of 75, we have

$$\begin{aligned} \text{DOL} &= 1 + £500/1,000 \\ &= 1.50 \end{aligned}$$

The reason why DOL declines is that fixed costs, considered as a percentage of operating cash flow, get smaller and smaller, so the leverage effect diminishes.

EXAMPLE
10.3

Operating Leverage

Peigi Ltd currently sells gourmet dog food for £1.20 per can. The variable cost is £0.80 per can, and the packaging and marketing operations have fixed costs of £360,000 per year. Depreciation is £60,000 per year. What is the accounting break-even? Ignoring taxes, what will be the increase in operating cash flow if the quantity sold rises to 10 per cent above the break-even point?

The accounting break-even is £420,000/0.40 = 1,050,000 cans. As we know, the operating cash flow is equal to the £60,000 depreciation at this level of production, so the degree of operating leverage is

$$DOL = 1 + FC/OCF$$
$$= 1 + £360,000/60,000$$
$$= 7$$

Given this, a 10 per cent increase in the number of cans of dog food sold will increase operating cash flow by a substantial 70 per cent.

To check this answer, we note that if sales rise by 10 per cent, then the quantity sold will rise to 1,050,000 × 1.1 = 1,155,000. Ignoring taxes, the operating cash flow will be 1,155,000 × £0.40 – 360,000 = £102,000. Compared with the £60,000 cash flow we had, this is exactly 70 per cent more: £102,000/60,000 = 1.70.

Operating Leverage and Break-Even

We illustrate why operating leverage is an important consideration by examining the Wettway yacht project under an alternative scenario. At a Q of 85 boats, the degree of operating leverage for the yacht project under the original scenario is

$$DOL = 1 + FC/OCF$$
$$= 1 + £500/1,200$$
$$- 1.42$$

Also, recall that the NPV at a sales level of 85 boats was £88,720, and that the accounting break-even was 60 boats.

An option available to Wettway is to subcontract production of the boat hull assemblies. If the company does this, the necessary investment falls to £3,200,000 and the fixed operating costs fall to £180,000. However, variable costs will rise to £25,000 per boat, because subcontracting is more expensive than producing in-house. Ignoring taxes, evaluate this option.

For practice, see if you don't agree with the following:

NPV at 20% (85 units) = £74,720
Accounting break-even = 55 boats
Degree of operating leverage = 1.16

What has happened? This option results in a slightly lower estimated net present value, and the accounting break-even point falls to 55 boats from 60 boats.

Given that this alternative has the lower NPV, is there any reason to consider it further? Perhaps there is. The degree of operating leverage is substantially lower in the second case. If Wettway is worried about the possibility of an overly optimistic projection, then it might prefer to subcontract.

There is another reason why Wettway might consider the second arrangement. If sales turned out to be better than expected, the company would always have the option of starting to produce in-house at a later date. As a practical matter, it is much easier to increase operating leverage (by purchasing equipment) than to decrease it (by selling off equipment). As we discuss in a later chapter, one of the drawbacks of discounted cash flow analysis is that it is difficult to explicitly include options of this sort in the analysis, even though they may be quite important.

CONCEPT QUESTIONS	
10.5a	What is operating leverage?
10.5b	How is operating leverage measured?
10.5c	What are the implications of operating leverage for the financial manager?

10.6 Capital Rationing

Capital rationing is said to exist when we have profitable (positive NPV) investments available, but we can't get the funds needed to undertake them. For example, as division managers for a large corporation, we might identify €5 million in excellent projects, but find that, for whatever reason, we can spend only €2 million. Now what? Unfortunately, for reasons we shall discuss, there may be no truly satisfactory answer.

> **capital rationing** The situation that exists if a firm has positive-NPV projects but cannot find the necessary financing.

Soft Rationing

The situation we have just described is called **soft rationing**. This occurs when, for example, different units in a business are allocated some fixed amount of money each year for capital spending. Such an allocation is primarily a means of controlling and keeping track of overall spending. The important thing to note about soft rationing is that the corporation as a whole isn't short of capital; more can be raised on ordinary terms if management so desires.

> **soft rationing** The situation that occurs when units in a business are allocated a certain amount of financing for capital budgeting.

If we face soft rationing, the first thing to do is to try to get a larger allocation. Failing that, one common suggestion is to generate as large a net present value as possible within the existing budget. This amounts to choosing projects with the largest benefit–cost ratio (profitability index).

Strictly speaking, this is the correct thing to do only if the soft rationing is a one-time event – that is, if it won't exist next year. If the soft rationing is a chronic problem, then something is amiss. The reason goes all the way back to Chapter 1. Ongoing soft rationing means we are constantly bypassing positive-NPV investments. This contradicts our goal of the firm. If we are not trying to maximize value, then the question of which projects to take becomes ambiguous, because we no longer have an objective goal in the first place.

Hard Rationing

With **hard rationing**, a business cannot raise capital for a project under any circumstances. For large, healthy corporations this situation probably does not occur very often. This is fortunate, because with hard rationing our DCF analysis breaks down, and the best course of action is ambiguous.

> **hard rationing** The situation that occurs when a business cannot raise financing for a project under any circumstances.

The reason why DCF analysis breaks down has to do with the required return. Suppose we say our required return is 20 per cent. Implicitly, we are saying we shall take a project with a return that exceeds this. However, if we face hard rationing, then we are not going to take a new project, no matter what the return on that project is, so the whole concept of a required return is ambiguous. About the only interpretation we can give this situation is that the required return is so large that no project has a positive NPV in the first place.

Hard rationing can occur when a company experiences financial distress, meaning that bankruptcy is a possibility. Also, a firm may not be able to raise capital without violating a pre-existing contractual agreement. We discuss these situations in greater detail in a later chapter.

CONCEPT QUESTIONS

10.6a What is capital rationing? What types are there?

10.6b What problems does capital rationing create for discounted cash flow analysis?

Summary and Conclusions

In this chapter we looked at some ways of evaluating the results of a discounted cash flow analysis; we also touched on some of the problems that can come up in practice:

1 Net present value estimates depend on projected future cash flows. If there are errors in those projections, then our estimated NPVs can be misleading. We called this possibility *forecasting risk*.

2 Scenario and sensitivity analysis are useful tools for identifying which variables are critical to the success of a project, and where forecasting problems can do the most damage.

3 Break-even analysis in its various forms is a particularly common type of scenario analysis that is useful for identifying critical levels of sales.

4 Operating leverage is a key determinant of break-even levels. It reflects the degree to which a project or a firm is committed to fixed costs. The degree of operating leverage tells us the sensitivity of operating cash flow to changes in sales volume.

5 Projects usually have future managerial options associated with them. These options may be important, but standard discounted cash flow analysis tends to ignore them.

6 Capital rationing occurs when apparently profitable projects cannot be funded. Standard discounted cash flow analysis is troublesome in this case, because NPV is not necessarily the appropriate criterion.

The most important thing to carry away from reading this chapter is that estimated NPVs or returns should not be taken at face value. They depend critically on projected cash flows. If there is room for significant disagreement about those projected cash flows, the results from the analysis have to be taken with a pinch of salt.

Despite the problems we have discussed, discounted cash flow analysis is still *the* way of attacking problems, because it forces us to ask the right questions. What we have learned in this chapter is that knowing the questions to ask does not guarantee we shall get all the answers.

Chapter Review and Self-Test Problems

Use the following base-case information to work the self-test problems:

A project under consideration costs €750,000, has a five-year life, and has no salvage value. Depreciation is straight-line to zero. The required return is 17 per cent, and the tax rate is 34 per cent. Sales are projected at 500 units per year. Price per unit is €2,500, variable cost per unit is €1,500, and fixed costs are €200,000 per year.

10.1 **Scenario Analysis** Suppose you think that the unit sales, price, variable cost and fixed cost projections given here are accurate to within 5 per cent. What are the upper and lower bounds for these projections? What is the base-case NPV? What are the best- and worst-case scenario NPVs?

10.2 **Break-Even Analysis** Given the base-case projections in the previous problem, what are the cash, accounting and financial break-even sales levels for this project? Ignore taxes in answering.

Answers to Chapter Review and Self-Test Problems

10.1 We can summarize the relevant information as follows:

	Base case	Lower bound	Upper bound
Unit sales	500	475	525
Price per unit (€)	2,500	2,375	2,625
Variable cost per unit (€)	1,500	1,425	1,575
Fixed cost per year (€)	200,000	190,000	210,000

Depreciation is €150,000 per year; knowing this, we can calculate the cash flows under each scenario. Remember that we assign high costs and low prices and volume for the worst case, and just the opposite for the best case:

Scenario	Unit sales	Unit price (€)	Unit variable cost (€)	Fixed costs (€)	Cash flow (€)
Base case	500	2,500	1,500	200,000	249,000
Best case	525	2,625	1,425	190,000	341,400
Worst case	475	2,375	1,575	210,000	163,200

At 17 per cent the five-year annuity factor is 3.19935, so the NPVs are

$$\text{Base-case NPV} = -€750{,}000 + 3.19935 \times €249{,}000$$
$$= €46{,}638$$
$$\text{Best-case NPV} = -€750{,}000 + 3.19935 \times €341{,}400$$
$$= €342{,}258$$
$$\text{Worst-case NPV} = -€750{,}000 + 3.19935 \times €163{,}200$$
$$= -€227{,}866$$

10.2 In this case we have €200,000 in cash fixed costs to cover. Each unit contributes €2,500 − 1,500 = €1,000 towards covering fixed costs. The cash break-even is thus €200,000/€1,000 = 200 units. We have another €150,000 in depreciation, so the accounting break-even is (€200,000 + 150,000)/ €1,000 = 350 units.

To get the financial break-even, we need to find the OCF such that the project has a zero NPV. As we have seen, the five-year annuity factor is 3.19935 and the project costs €750,000, so the OCF must be such that

$$€750,000 = OCF \times 3.19935$$

So, for the project to break even on a financial basis, the project's cash flow must be €750,000/3.19935, or €234,423 per year. If we add this to the €200,000 in cash fixed costs, we get a total of €434,423 that we have to cover. At €1,000 per unit, we need to sell €434,423/€1,000 = 435 units.

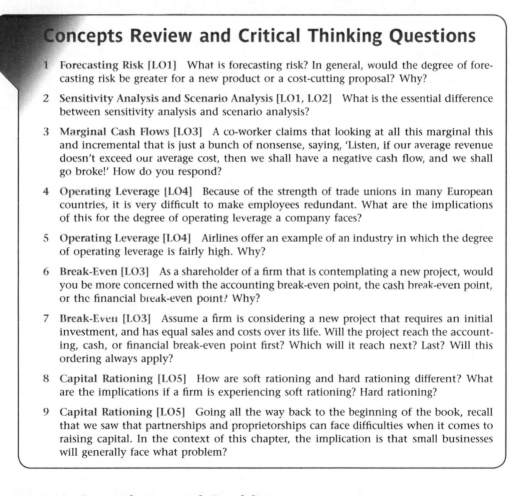

Concepts Review and Critical Thinking Questions

1   **Forecasting Risk [LO1]**   What is forecasting risk? In general, would the degree of forecasting risk be greater for a new product or a cost-cutting proposal? Why?

2   **Sensitivity Analysis and Scenario Analysis [LO1, LO2]**   What is the essential difference between sensitivity analysis and scenario analysis?

3   **Marginal Cash Flows [LO3]**   A co-worker claims that looking at all this marginal this and incremental that is just a bunch of nonsense, saying, 'Listen, if our average revenue doesn't exceed our average cost, then we shall have a negative cash flow, and we shall go broke!' How do you respond?

4   **Operating Leverage [LO4]**   Because of the strength of trade unions in many European countries, it is very difficult to make employees redundant. What are the implications of this for the degree of operating leverage a company faces?

5   **Operating Leverage [LO4]**   Airlines offer an example of an industry in which the degree of operating leverage is fairly high. Why?

6   **Break-Even [LO3]**   As a shareholder of a firm that is contemplating a new project, would you be more concerned with the accounting break-even point, the cash break-even point, or the financial break-even point? Why?

7   **Break-Even [LO3]**   Assume a firm is considering a new project that requires an initial investment, and has equal sales and costs over its life. Will the project reach the accounting, cash, or financial break-even point first? Which will it reach next? Last? Will this ordering always apply?

8   **Capital Rationing [LO5]**   How are soft rationing and hard rationing different? What are the implications if a firm is experiencing soft rationing? Hard rationing?

9   **Capital Rationing [LO5]**   Going all the way back to the beginning of the book, recall that we saw that partnerships and proprietorships can face difficulties when it comes to raising capital. In the context of this chapter, the implication is that small businesses will generally face what problem?

connect Questions and Problems

BASIC

1 – 15

1   **Calculating Costs and Break-Even [LO3]**   Night Shades NV (NS) manufactures biotech sunglasses. The variable materials cost is €5.43 per unit, and the variable labour cost is €3.13 per unit.

   (a)   What is the variable cost per unit?

   (b)   Suppose NS incurs fixed costs of €720,000 during a year in which total production is 280,000 units. What are the total costs for the year?

(c) If the selling price is €19.99 per unit, does NS break even on a cash basis? If depreciation is €220,000 per year, what is the accounting break-even point?

2 **Computing Average Cost [LO3]** Makaveli SpA can manufacture mountain climbing shoes for €24.86 per pair in variable raw material costs and €14.08 per pair in variable labour expense. The shoes sell for €135 per pair. Last year, production was 120,000 pairs. Fixed costs were €1,550,000. What were total production costs? What is the marginal cost per pair? What is the average cost? If the company is considering a one-time order for an extra 5,000 pairs, what is the minimum acceptable total revenue from the order? Explain.

3 **Scenario Analysis [LO2]** Olin Transmissions plc has the following estimates for its new gear assembly project: price = £1,900 per unit; variable costs = £240 per unit; fixed costs = £4.8 million; quantity = 95,000 units. Suppose the company believes all of its estimates are accurate only to within ±15 per cent. What values should the company use for the four variables given here when it performs its best-case scenario analysis? What about the worst-case scenario?

4 **Sensitivity Analysis [LO1]** For the company in the previous problem, suppose management is most concerned about the impact of its price estimate on the project's profitability. How could you address this concern? Describe how you would calculate your answer. What values would you use for the other forecast variables?

5 **Sensitivity Analysis and Break-Even [LO1, LO3]** We are evaluating a project that costs £724,000, has an eight-year life, and has no salvage value. Assume that depreciation is straight-line to zero over the life of the project. Sales are projected at 90,000 units per year. Price per unit is £43, variable cost per unit is £29, and fixed costs are £780,000 per year. The tax rate is 28 per cent, and we require a 15 per cent return on this project.

(a) Calculate the accounting break-even point. What is the degree of operating leverage at the accounting break-even point?

(b) Calculate the base-case cash flow and NPV. What is the sensitivity of NPV to changes in the sales figure? Explain what your answer tells you about a 500-unit decrease in projected sales.

(c) What is the sensitivity of OCF to changes in the variable cost figure? Explain what your answer tells you about a £1 decrease in estimated variable costs.

6 **Scenario Analysis [LO2]** In the previous problem, suppose the projections given for price, quantity, variable costs and fixed costs are all accurate to within ±10 per cent. Calculate the best-case and worst-case NPV figures.

7 **Calculating Break-Even [LO3]** In each of the following cases, calculate the accounting break-even and the cash break-even points. Ignore any tax effects in calculating the cash break-even.

Unit price (NKr)	Unit variable cost (NKr)	Fixed costs (NKr)	Depreciation (NKr)
3,020	2,275	14,000,000	6,500,000
2,938	27	73,000	150,000
2,811	4	1,200	840

8 Calculating Break-Even [LO3] In each of the following cases, find the unknown variable.

Accounting break-even	Unit price (£)	Unit variable cost (£)	Fixed costs (£)	Depreciation (£)
212,800	41	30	820,000	?
165,000	?	33	3,200,000	1,150,000
4,385	98	?	90,000	105,000

9 Calculating Break-Even [LO3] A project has the following estimated data: price = £60 per unit; variable costs = £32 per unit; fixed costs = £9,000; required return = 12 per cent; initial investment = £18,000; life = four years. Ignoring the effect of taxes, what is the accounting break-even quantity? The cash break-even quantity? The financial break-even quantity? What is the degree of operating leverage at the financial break-even level of output?

10 Using Break-Even Analysis [LO3] Consider a project with the following data: accounting break-even quantity = 17,500 units; cash break-even quantity = 13,200 units; life = five years; fixed costs = £140,000; variable costs = £24 per unit; required return = 16 per cent. Ignoring the effect of taxes, find the financial break-even quantity.

11 Calculating Operating Leverage [LO4] At an output level of 80,000 units, you calculate that the degree of operating leverage is 3.40. If output falls to 70,000 units, what will the percentage change in operating cash flow be? Will the new level of operating leverage be higher or lower? Explain.

12 Leverage [LO4] In the previous problem, suppose fixed costs are £130,000. What is the operating cash flow at 58,000 units? The degree of operating leverage?

13 Operating Cash Flow and Leverage [LO4] A proposed project has fixed costs of £83,000 per year. The operating cash flow at 8,000 units is £97,500. Ignoring the effect of taxes, what is the degree of operating leverage? If units sold rise from 8,000 to 8,500, what will be the increase in operating cash flow? What is the new degree of operating leverage?

14 Cash Flow and Leverage [LO4] At an output level of 10,000 units, you have calculated that the degree of operating leverage is 2.1. The operating cash flow is £43,000 in this case. Ignoring the effect of taxes, what are fixed costs? What will the operating cash flow be if output rises to 11,000 units? If output falls to 9,000 units?

15 Leverage [LO4] In the previous problem, what will be the new degree of operating leverage in each case?

INTERMEDIATE

16–24

16 Break-Even Intuition [LO3] Consider a project with a required return of R per cent that costs $€I$ and will last for N years. The project uses straight-line depreciation to zero over the N-year life; there is no salvage value or net working capital requirements.

(a) At the accounting break-even level of output, what is the IRR of this project? The payback period? The NPV?

(b) At the cash break-even level of output, what is the IRR of this project? The payback period? The NPV?

(c) At the financial break-even level of output, what is the IRR of this project? The payback period? The NPV?

17 Sensitivity Analysis [LO1] Consider a four-year project with the following information: initial fixed asset investment = €490,000; 20 per cent reducing-balance

(a) What is the estimated OCF for this project? The NPV? Should you pursue this project?

(b) Suppose you believe that the accounting department's initial cost and salvage value projections are accurate only to within ±15 per cent; the marketing department's price estimate is accurate only to within ±10 per cent; and the engineering department's net working capital estimate is accurate only to within ±5 per cent. What is your worst-case scenario for this project? Your best-case scenario? Do you still want to pursue the project?

28 **Sensitivity Analysis [LO1]**   In Problem 27, suppose you're confident about your own projections, but you're a little unsure about Detroit's actual machine screw requirement. What is the sensitivity of the project OCF to changes in the quantity supplied? What about the sensitivity of NPV to changes in quantity supplied? Given the sensitivity number you calculated, is there some minimum level of output below which you wouldn't want to operate? Why?

29 **Break-Even Analysis [LO3]**   Use the results of Problem 25 to find the accounting, cash, and financial break-even quantities for the company in Problem 27.

30 **Operating Leverage [LO4]**   Use the results of Problem 26 to find the degree of operating leverage for the company in Problem 27 at the base-case output level of 35,000 units. How does this number compare with the sensitivity figure you found in Problem 28? Verify that either approach will give you the same OCF figure at any new quantity level.

MINI CASE   Conch Republic Electronics, Part 2

Morena Moscardini, the owner of Conch Republic Electronics, had received the capital budgeting analysis from Jay McCanless for the new PDA the company is considering. Morena was pleased with the results, but she still had concerns about the new PDA. Conch Republic had used a small market research firm for the past 20 years, but recently the founder of that firm retired. Because of this, she was not convinced the sales projections presented by the market research firm were entirely accurate. Additionally, because of rapid changes in technology, she was concerned that a competitor could enter the market. This would probably force Conch Republic to lower the sales price of its new PDA. For these reasons, she has asked Jay to analyse how changes in the price of the new PDA and changes in the quantity sold will affect the NPV of the project.

Morena has asked Jay to prepare a memo answering the following questions.

QUESTIONS

1 How sensitive is the NPV to changes in the price of the new PDA?

2 How sensitive is the NPV to changes in the quantity sold of the new PDA?

Endnotes

1 We use straight-line depreciation to provide the intuition underlying break-even analysis. In practice, one would use the reducing-balance method. Given that the depreciation amount would be different each year, one would need to use a spreadsheet to find the break-even level. However, the intuition underlying the discussion remains the same.

2 To see this, note that if Q goes up by one unit, OCF will go up by $(P - v)$. In this case, the percentage change in Q is $1/Q$, and the percentage change in OCF is $(P - v)/\text{OCF}$. Given this, we have

Chapter 10 Project Analysis and Evaluation

$$\text{Percentage change in OCF} = \text{DOL} \times \text{Percentage change in } Q$$
$$(P - v)/\text{OCF} = \text{DOL} \times 1/Q$$
$$\text{DOL} = (P - v) \times Q/\text{OCF}$$

Also, based on our definitions of OCF:

$$\text{OCF} + \text{FC} = (P - v) \times Q$$

Thus DOL can be written as

$$\text{DOL} = (\text{OCF} + \text{FC})/\text{OCF}$$
$$= 1 + \text{FC}/\text{OCF}$$

Online
LearningCentre

To help you grasp the key concepts of this chapter check out the extra resources posted on the Online Learning Centre at **www.mcgraw-hill.co.uk/textbooks/hillier**

Among other helpful resources there are mini-cases tailored to individual chapters.

CHAPTER 11

Some Lessons from Recent Capital Market History

KEY NOTATIONS

D	Dividend
P	Share price
R	Return
$\bar{R}$	Average return
$SD(R)$ or σ	Standard deviation of returns
T	Number of historical returns
$Var(R)$ or σ^2	Variance of returns

LEARNING OBJECTIVES

After studying this chapter, you should understand:

LO1   How to calculate the return on an investment.

LO2   The historical returns on various important types of investment.

LO3   The historical risks on various important types of investment.

LO4   The implications of market efficiency.

RECENT YEARS have seen significant movements in financial markets, both up and down. Take the FTSE 100 as an example. Representing the fortunes of the 100 largest companies in the UK, it had an index value of 6,457 at the end of 2007. In the aftermath of the global credit crisis and the resulting collapse in equity valuations, it fell by 31 per cent to 4,434 – its worst calendar year performance since the index started in 1984. Although it slipped further in the early months of 2009 (its lowest point was in March, when it had a value of 3,512), it made an incredibly sharp recovery, and within one year (March 2010) it hit 5,600. As can be seen, between 2007 and 2010 there were tremendous potential profits to be made, but there was also the risk of losing money – lots of it. So what should you, as a stock market investor, expect when you invest your own money? In this chapter, we study market history to find out.

Thus far we haven't had much to say about what determines the required return on an investment. In one sense, the answer is simple: the required return depends on the risk of the investment. The greater the risk, the greater is the required return.

Having said this, we are left with a somewhat more difficult problem. How can we measure the amount of risk present in an investment? Put another way, what does it mean to say that one investment is riskier than another? Obviously, we need to define what we mean by *risk* if we are going to answer these questions. This is our task in the next two chapters.

From the last several chapters, we know that one of the responsibilities of the financial manager is to assess the value of proposed real asset investments. In doing this, it is important that we first look at what financial investments have to offer. At a minimum, the return we require from a proposed non-financial investment must be greater than what we can get by buying financial assets of similar risk.

Our goal in this chapter is to provide a perspective on what capital market history can tell us about risk and return. The most important thing to get out of this chapter is a feel for the numbers. What is a high return? What is a low one? More generally, what returns should we expect from financial assets, and what are the risks of such investments? This perspective is essential for understanding how to analyse and value risky investment projects.

We start our discussion of risk and return by describing the experience of investors in the world's financial markets. The introduction to this chapter showed the extent of volatility in the UK equity markets since 2007, which experienced the greatest year-on-year movements since the index started in 1984. The US has an even longer period to consider. In 1931, for example, the US stock market lost 43 per cent of its value, gaining 54 per cent just two years later. In more recent memory, the US market lost about 25 per cent of its value on one day alone (19 October 1987). What lessons, if any, can financial managers learn from such shifts in the stock market? We shall explore market history to find out.

Two central lessons emerge from our study of market history. First, there is a reward for bearing risk. Second, the greater the potential reward is, the greater is the risk. To illustrate these facts about market returns, we devote much of this chapter to reporting the statistics and numbers that make up the modern capital market history of Europe. In the next chapter these facts provide the foundation for our study of how financial markets put a price on risk.

11.1 Returns

We wish to discuss historical returns on different types of financial asset. The first thing we need to do, then, is to briefly discuss how to calculate the return from investing.

Cash Returns

If you buy an asset of any sort, your gain (or loss) from that investment is called the *return on your investment*. This return will usually have two components. First, you may receive some cash directly while you own the investment. This is called the *income component* of your return. Second, the value of the asset you purchase will often change. In this case, you have a capital gain or capital loss on your investment.[1]

To illustrate, suppose Video Concept has several thousand shares of equity outstanding. You purchased some of these shares at the beginning of the year. It is now year-end, and you want to determine how well you have done on your investment.

First, over the year, a company may pay cash dividends to its shareholders. As a shareholder in Video Concept, you are a part owner of the company. If the company is profitable, it may choose to distribute some of its profits to shareholders (we discuss the details of dividend policy in a later chapter). So, as the owner of some equity, you will receive some cash. This cash is the income component from owning the shares.

In addition to the dividend, the other part of your return is the capital gain or capital loss on the equity. This part arises from changes in the value of your investment. For example, consider the cash flows illustrated in Fig. 11.1. At the beginning of the year the equity was selling for £37 per share. If you had bought 100 shares, you would have had a total outlay of £3,700. Suppose that, over the year, the equity paid a dividend of £1.85 per share. By the end of the year, then, you would have received income of

$$\text{Dividend} = £1.85 \times 100 = £185$$

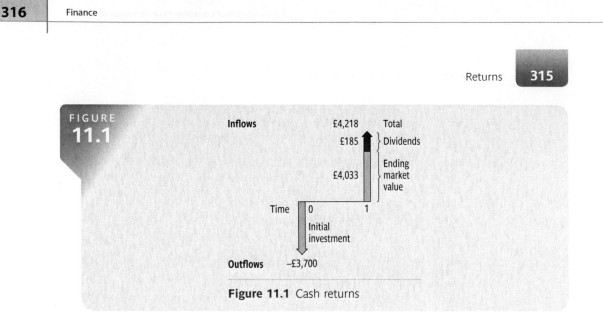

Figure 11.1 Cash returns

Also, the value of the equity has risen to £40.33 per share by the end of the year. Your 100 shares are now worth £4,033, so you have a capital gain of

$$\text{Capital gain} = (£40.33 - 37) \times 100 = £333$$

On the other hand, if the price had dropped to, say, £34.78, you would have a capital loss of

$$\text{Capital loss} = (£34.78 - 37) \times 100 = -£222$$

Notice that a capital loss is the same thing as a negative capital gain.

The total cash return on your investment is the sum of the dividend and the capital gain:

$$\text{Total cash return} = \text{Dividend income} + \text{Capital gain (or loss)} \qquad \text{(11.1)}$$

In our first example, the total cash return is thus given by

$$\text{Total cash return} = £185 + 333 = £518$$

Notice that if you sold the equity at the end of the year, the total amount of cash you would have would equal your initial investment plus the total return. In the preceding example, then:

$$\begin{aligned}\text{Total cash if equity is sold} &= \text{Initial investment} + \text{Total return} \qquad \text{(11.2)} \\ &= £3,700 + 518 \\ &= £4,218 \end{aligned}$$

As a check, notice that this is the same as the proceeds from the sale of the equity plus the dividends:

$$\begin{aligned}\text{Proceeds from equity sale} + \text{Dividends} &= £40.33 \times 100 + 185 \\ &= £4,033 + 185 \\ &= £4,218 \end{aligned}$$

Suppose you hold on to your Video Concept shares and don't sell them at the end of the year. Should you still consider the capital gain as part of your return? Isn't this only a 'paper' gain and not really a cash flow if you don't sell the equity?

The answer to the first question is a strong yes, and the answer to the second is an equally strong no. The capital gain is every bit as much a part of your return as the dividend, and you should certainly count it as part of your return. That you actually decided to keep the shares and not sell (you don't 'realize' the gain) is irrelevant, because you could have converted it to cash if you had wanted to. Whether you choose to do so or not is up to you.

After all, if you insisted on converting your gain to cash, you could always sell the shares at year-end and immediately reinvest by buying the shares back. There is no net difference between doing this and just not selling (assuming, of course, that there are no tax consequences from selling the shares). Again, the point is that whether you actually cash out and buy beer (or whatever) or reinvest by not selling doesn't affect the return you earn.

Percentage Returns

It is usually more convenient to summarize information about returns in percentage terms, rather than cash terms, because that way your return doesn't depend on how much you actually invest. The question we want to answer is this: how much do we get for each unit of cash we invest?

To answer this question, let P_t be the share price at the beginning of the year and let D_{t+1} be the dividend paid during the year. Consider the cash flows in Fig. 11.2. These are the same as those in Fig. 11.1, except that we have now expressed everything on a per-share basis.

In our example, the price at the beginning of the year was £37 per share and the dividend paid during the year on each share was £1.85. As we discussed in Chapter 7, expressing the dividend as a percentage of the beginning share price results in the dividend yield:

$$\text{Dividend yield} = D_{t+1}/P_t$$
$$= £1.85/37 = 0.05 = 5\%$$

This says that for each pound we invest, we get five pence in dividends.

The second component of our percentage return is the capital gains yield. Recall (from Chapter 7) that this is calculated as the change in the price during the year (the capital gain) divided by the beginning price:

$$\text{Capital gains yield} = (P_{t+1} - P_t)/P_t$$
$$= (£40.33 - 37)/37$$
$$= £3.33/37$$
$$= 9\%$$

So, per pound invested, we get nine pence in capital gains.

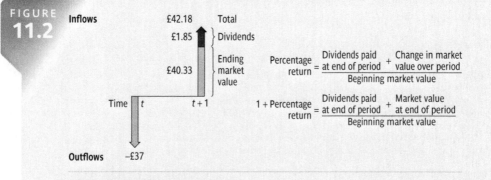

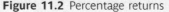

Figure 11.2 Percentage returns

Putting it together, per pound invested, we get 5 pence in dividends and 9 pence in capital gains; so we get a total of 14 pence. Our percentage return is 14 pence on the pound, or 14 per cent.

To check this, notice that we invested £3,700 and ended up with £4,218. By what percentage did our £3,700 increase? As we saw, we picked up £4,218 − 3,700 = £518. This is a £518/3,700 = 14% increase.

Calculating Returns

EXAMPLE 11.1

Suppose you bought some equity at the beginning of the year for €25 per share. At the end of the year, the share price is €35. During the year, you got a €2 dividend per share. This is the situation illustrated in Fig. 11.3. What is the dividend yield? The capital gains yield? The percentage return? If your total investment was €1,000, how much do you have at the end of the year?

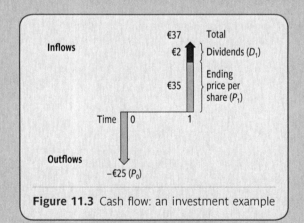

Figure 11.3 Cash flow: an investment example

Your €2 dividend per share works out to a dividend yield of

$$\text{Dividend yield} = D_{t+1}/P_t$$
$$= €2/25 = 0.08 = 8\%$$

The per-share capital gain is €10, so the capital gains yield is

$$\text{Capital gains yield} = (P_{t-1} - P_t)/P_t$$
$$= (€35 - 25)/25$$
$$= €10/25$$
$$= 40\%$$

The total percentage return is thus 48 per cent.

If you had invested €1,000, you would have €1,480 at the end of the year, representing a 48 per cent increase. To check this, note that your €1,000 would have bought you €1,000/25 = 40 shares. Your 40 shares would then have paid you a total of 40 × €2 = €80 in cash dividends. Your €10 per share gain would give you a total capital gain of €10 × 40 = €400. Add these together, and you get the €480 increase.

To give another example, equity in the mining firm Fresnillo began 2009 at £2.30 per share. Fresnillo paid dividends of £0.077 during 2009, and the share price at the end of the year was £7.819. What was the return on Fresnillo for the year? For practice, see if you agree that the answer is 243.3 per cent. Of course, negative returns occur as well. For example, again in 2009, Royal Bank of Scotland's share price at the beginning of the year was £0.494, and no dividends were paid. The equity ended the year at £0.292 per share. Verify that the loss was 40.8 per cent for the year.

CONCEPT QUESTIONS

11.1a What are the two parts of total return?

11.1b Why are unrealized capital gains or losses included in the calculation of returns?

11.1c What is the difference between a cash return and a percentage return? Why are percentage returns more convenient?

11.2 The Historical Record

In this section we shall discuss the historical rates of return on a number of different securities in different countries across Europe. The countries we look at are Belgium, Denmark, France, Germany, the Netherlands, Sweden and the UK. The large company share portfolios are based on indices representing the largest companies in each country. These are, respectively, the Bel-20 Index (Belgium), OMX Copenhagen 20 (Denmark), CAC 40 (France), DAX30 (Germany), Amsterdam SE All Shares (Netherlands), and the FTSE 100 (UK). We have also included the FTSE 250 Midcap Index, which represents smaller companies on the London Stock Exchange.

None of the returns are adjusted for taxes, transaction costs or inflation. Figure 11.4 shows the relative performance of different stock markets over the period 2001–2010. Clearly, a much longer period could have been considered, since European stock exchanges have been open for years and, in some cases, hundreds of years. The period (2001) starts with the collapse of the hi-tech bubble, when Internet stock valuations dropped precipitously. It took a number of years to recover, but this was a sustained growth period until 2007, when the subprime mortgage crisis erupted and caused the global credit crunch that markets faced in 2008. Fortunately, the world's stock markets showed exceptional performance in 2009, giving much needed returns to Europe's investors. Unfortunately, valuations in most European countries had still not reached the levels of 10 years earlier, and an investor who

FIGURE 11.4

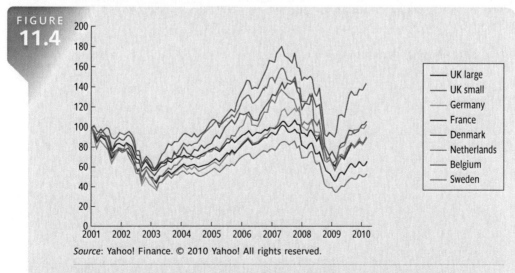

Figure 11.4 Stock market index levels for a number of European countries, 2001–2010

Date	UK large	UK small	Germany	France	Denmark	Netherlands	Belgium	Sweden
Jan 2000	6,268	6,181	6,835	5,659	250	612	2,806	N/A
Jan 2001	6,297	6,735	6,795	5,998	347	639	2,968	303
Jan 2002	5,164	5,849	5,107	4,461	263	500	2,764	225
Jan 2003	3,567	4,016	2,747	2,937	186	294	1,882	144
Jan 2004	4,390	6,023	4,058	3,638	261	353	2,383	205
Jan 2005	4,852	7,166	4,254	3,913	291	360	2,997	229
Jan 2006	5,760	9,172	5,674	4,947	389	450	3,744	307
Jan 2007	6,203	11,100	6,789	5,608	462	499	4,433	386
Jan 2008	5,879	9,881	6,851	4,869	407	441	3,722	309
Jan 2009	4,149	6,250	4,338	2,973	261	248	1,900	192
Jan 2010	5,188	9,237	5,608	3,739	354	327	2,505	301

TABLE 11.1

Source: Yahoo! Finance. © 2010 Yahoo! All rights reserved.

Table 11.1 Year-by-year stock market index levels for different countries, 2000–2010

bought shares in 2001 would have not recouped her investment in 2010 had she invested in large UK, French, German, Dutch or Belgian firms.

Table 11.1 presents the index values for each stock market for every year between 2001 and 2010. The numbers in Table 11.1 also show that an investor must be careful when reading information on company or stock market performance. For example, if one were to look at the return for the United Kingdom between 2000 and 2010, and compare this with the return for the same country in 2009, conflicting messages would be given. The average annual return (calculate the annual return for each year, and average over the full sample period) for the years 2000–2010 is 0.19 per cent, compared with the annual return for 2009 of 25.04 per cent! Which is the correct performance measure? Unfortunately, both are correct from different perspectives.

Figure 11.4 gives the growth of an investment in various stock markets between 2000 and 2010. In other words, it shows what the worth of the investment would have been if the money that was initially invested had been left in the stock market, and if each year the dividends from the previous year had been reinvested in more shares. If R_t is the return in year t (expressed in decimals), the value you would have at the end of year T is the product of 1 plus the return in each of the years:

$$(1 + R_1) \times (1 + R_2) \times \cdots \times (1 + R_t) \times \cdots \times (1 + R_T)$$

For example, in Table 11.2 the index values in Table 11.1 are presented as annual percentage returns.

The next thing to consider is the difference in performance between large and small companies (shown here for the UK). Notice how, in almost every year, small companies had larger returns (whether positive or negative) than large companies. We shall discuss why later in the chapter.

CONCEPT QUESTIONS

11.2a With 20/20 hindsight, what would you say was the best investment for the period from 2000 through 2010?

11.2b Why doesn't everyone just buy small equities as investments?

11.2c About how many times did large-company equities return more than 30 per cent? How many times did they return less than –20 per cent?

11.2d What was the longest 'winning streak' (years without a negative return) for large-company equities?

Chapter 11 Some Lessons from Recent Capital Market History

TABLE
11.2

Year	UK large	UK small	Germany	France	Denmark	Netherlands	Belgium	Sweden
2000	0.46	8.96	-0.59	5.99	38.80	4.41	5.77	–
2001	-17.99	-13.16	-24.84	-25.63	-24.21	-21.75	-6.87	-25.74
2002	-30.93	-31.34	-46.21	-34.16	-29.28	-41.20	-31.91	-36.00
2003	23.07	49.98	47.72	23.87	40.32	20.07	26.62	42.36
2004	10.52	18.98	4.83	7.56	11.49	1.98	25.77	11.71
2005	18.71	27.99	33.38	26.42	33.68	25.00	24.92	34.06
2006	7.69	21.02	19.65	13.36	18.77	10.89	18.40	25.73
2007	-5.22	-10.98	0.91	-13.18	-11.90	-11.62	-16.04	-19.95
2008	-29.43	-36.75	-36.68	-38.94	-35.87	-43.76	-48.95	-37.86
2009	25.04	47.79	29.28	25.77	35.63	31.85	31.84	56.77

Table 11.2 Year-by-year stock market returns (percentages) for different countries, 2000–2009

11.3 Average Returns: The First Lesson

As you've probably begun to notice, the history of capital market returns is too complicated to be of much use in its undigested form. We need to begin summarizing all these numbers. Accordingly, we discuss how to go about condensing the detailed data. We start out by calculating average returns.

Calculating Average Returns

The obvious way to calculate the average returns on the different indices in Table 11.2 is simply to add up the yearly returns and divide by 10. The result is the historical average of the individual values.

For example, if you add up the returns for the UK large company equities for the 10 years, you will get about 1.94. The average annual return is thus 1.94/10 = 0.194%. You interpret this 0.194 per cent, just like any other average. If you were to pick a year at random from the 10-year history, and you had to guess what the return in that year was, the best guess would be 0.194 per cent.

Average Returns: The Historical Record

Table 11.3 shows the average returns for the indices we have discussed. As shown, in a typical year, UK small company equities increased in value by 8.25 per cent. Notice also how much larger the small company returns are than the large company returns.

Clearly, the 10-year period between 2001 and 2010 has been exceptional in the history of stock markets. A much longer period to assess average returns would be better, because then short-term volatility would be likely to even out. Fortunately, the US has data starting in 1927, and the average returns for a variety of instruments are presented in Table 11.4.

These averages are of course nominal, because we haven't worried about inflation. Notice that the average inflation rate in the US was 3.1 per cent per year over this 82-year span. The nominal return on US Treasury bills was 3.8 per cent per year. The average real return on US Treasury bills was thus approximately 0.7 per cent per year: so the real return on US T-bills has been quite low historically.

11.4   The Variability of Returns: The Second Lesson

We have already seen that the year-to-year returns on equities tend to be more volatile than the returns on, say, long-term government bonds. We now discuss measuring this variability of equity returns so that we can begin examining the subject of risk.

Return Variability

What we need to do is to measure the spread in returns. We know, for example, that the return on UK small company equities in a typical year was 8.25 per cent. We now want to know how much the actual return deviates from this average in a typical year. In other words, we need a measure of how volatile the return is. The **variance** and its square root, the **standard deviation**, are the most commonly used measures of volatility. We describe how to calculate them next.

> **variance**
> The average squared difference between the actual return and the average return.
>
> **standard deviation**
> The positive square root of the variance.

The Historical Variance and Standard Deviation

The variance essentially measures the average squared difference between the actual returns and the average return. The bigger this number is, the more the actual returns tend to differ from the average return. Also, the larger the variance or standard deviation is, the more spread out the returns will be.

The way we calculate the variance and standard deviation will depend on the specific situation. In this chapter we are looking at historical returns, so the procedure we describe here is the correct one for calculating the *historical* variance and standard deviation. If we were examining projected future returns, then the procedure would be different. We describe this procedure in the next chapter.

To illustrate how we calculate the historical variance, suppose a particular investment has had returns of 10 per cent, 12 per cent, 3 per cent and –9 per cent over the last four years. The average return is $(0.10 + 0.12 + 0.03 - 0.09)/4 = 4\%$. Notice that the return is never actually equal to 4 per cent. Instead, the first return deviates from the average by $0.10 - 0.04 = 0.06$, the second return deviates from the average by $0.12 - 0.04 = 0.08$, and so on. To compute the variance, we square each of these deviations, add them up, and divide the result by the number of returns less 1, or 3 in this case. Most of this information is summarized in the following table:

	(1) Actual return	(2) Average return	(3) Deviation (1)–(2)	(4) Squared deviation
	0.10	0.04	0.06	0.0036
	0.12	0.04	0.08	0.0064
	0.03	0.04	−0.01	0.0001
	−0.09	0.04	−0.13	0.0169
Totals	0.16		0.00	0.0270

In the first column we write the four actual returns. In the third column we calculate the difference between the actual returns and the average by subtracting 4 per cent. Finally, in the fourth column we square the numbers in the third column to get the squared deviations from the average.

The variance can now be calculated by dividing 0.0270, the sum of the squared deviations, by the number of returns less 1. Let Var(R), or σ^2 (read this as 'sigma squared'), stand for the variance of the return:

$$\text{Var}(R) = \sigma^2 = 0.027/(4 - 1) = 0.009$$

The standard deviation is the square root of the variance. So if SD(R), or σ, stands for the standard deviation of return:

$$\text{SD}(R) = \sigma = \sqrt{0.009} = 0.09487$$

The square root of the variance is used because the variance is measured in 'squared' percentages and thus is hard to interpret. The standard deviation is an ordinary percentage, so the answer here could be written as 9.487 per cent.

In the preceding table, notice that the sum of the deviations is equal to zero. This will always be the case, and it provides a good way to check your work. In general, if we have T historical returns, where T is some number, we can write the historical variance as

$$\text{Var}(R) = \frac{1}{T-1}[(R_1 - \bar{R})^2 + \cdots + (R_T - \bar{R})^2]$$ (11.3)

This formula tells us to do what we just did: take each of the T individual returns (R_1, R_2, . . .) and subtract the average return, $\bar{R}$; square the results, and add them all up; and finally, divide this total by the number of returns less 1, $(T - 1)$. The standard deviation is always the square root of Var(R). Standard deviations are a widely used measure of volatility. Our nearby Work the Web box gives a real-world example.

EXAMPLE 11.2

Calculating the Variance and Standard Deviation

Suppose Supertech and Hyperdrive have experienced the following returns in the last four years:

Year	Supertech return	Hyperdrive return
2007	−0.20	0.05
2008	0.50	0.09
2009	0.30	−0.12
2010	0.10	0.20

What are the average returns? The variances? The standard deviations? Which investment was more volatile?

To calculate the average returns, we add up the returns and divide by 4. The results are:

Supertech average return $\bar{R} = 0.70/4 = 0.175$
Hyperdrive average return $\bar{R} = 0.22/4 = 0.055$

To calculate the variance for Supertech, we can summarize the relevant calculations as follows:

Year	(1) Actual return	(2) Average return	(3) Deviation (1)−(2)	(4) Squared deviation
2007	−0.20	0.175	−0.375	0.140625
2008	0.50	0.175	0.325	0.105625
2009	0.30	0.175	0.125	0.015625
2010	0.10	0.175	−0.075	0.005625
Totals	0.70		0.000	0.267500

Because there are four years of returns, we calculate the variance by dividing 0.2675 by (4 − 1) = 3:

	Supertech	Hyperdrive
Variance (σ^2)	0.2675/3 = 0.0892	0.0529/3 = 0.0176
Standard deviation (σ)	$\sqrt{0.0892} = 0.2987$	$\sqrt{0.0176} = 0.1327$

For practice, verify that you get the same answer as we do for Hyperdrive. Notice that the standard deviation for Supertech, 29.87 per cent, is a little more than twice Hyperdrive's 13.27 per cent: Supertech is thus the more volatile investment.

FIGURE 11.5

Series	Average return (%)	Standard deviation (%)	Distribution
US large-company equities	12.3	20.0	
US small-company equities	17.1	32.6	
Long-term corporate bonds	6.2	8.4	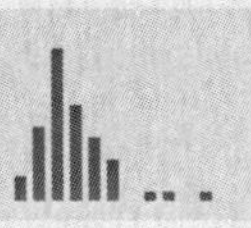
Long-term government bonds	5.8	9.2	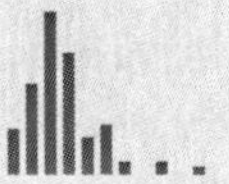
Intermediate-term government bonds	5.5	5.7	
US Treasury bills	3.8	3.1	
Inflation	3.1	4.2	

The 1933 small company equity total return was 142.9 per cent.

Source: Modified from *Ibbotson® Stocks, Bonds, Bills and Inflation 2008 Yearbook*; annually updates work by Roger G. Ibbotson and Rex A. Sinquefield (Chicago: Morningstar). All rights reserved.

Figure 11.5 US historical returns, standard deviations, and frequency distributions: 1926–2007

The Historical Record

Figure 11.5 summarizes US capital market history in more detail. It displays average returns, standard deviations and frequency distributions of annual returns on a common scale. In Fig. 11.5, for example, notice that the standard deviation for the small company portfolio (32.6 per cent per year) is more than 10 times larger than the T-bill portfolio's standard deviation (3.1 per cent per year). We shall return to these figures shortly.

Normal Distribution

For many different random events in nature, a particular frequency distribution, the **normal distribution** (or *bell curve*), is useful for describing the probability of ending up in a given range.

> **normal distribution**
> A symmetric, bell-shaped frequency distribution that is completely defined by its mean and standard deviation.

Work the Web

Standard deviations are widely reported for mutual funds. For example, consider the Henderson All Stocks Credit A Investment Trust. How volatile is it? To find out, we went to www.morningstar. co.uk, searched on the fund's name, and hit the 'Risk/Measures' link. Here is what we found:

Henderson All Stocks Credit A Inc

Morningstar Rating™(Relative to Category)   28/02/2010

	Morningstar Return		Morningstar Risk	Morningstar Rating™
3-Year	Average		Below Average	★★★★
5-Year	Average		Below Average	★★★★
10-Year	-		-	Not Rated
Overall	Average		Below Average	★★★★

Category : Sterling Corporate Bond   Click here to see our Methodology

Volatility Measurements				28/02/2010
3-Yr Std Dev	6.19 %		3-Yr Sharpe Ratio	-0.13
3-Yr Mean Return	3.00 %			

Modern Portfolio Statistics			28/02/2010
		Standard Index	Best Fit Index
		IBOXX GBP Corp TR	IBOXX GBP Corp TR
3-Yr R-Squared		85.11	85.11
3-Yr Beta		0.64	0.64
3-Yr Alpha		0.21	0.21

Over the last three years the standard deviation of the return on the fund was 6.19 per cent. When you consider that the average share price has a standard deviation of about 50 per cent, this seems like a low number. But the All Stocks Credit A fund is a relatively well-diversified portfolio of low-risk corporate bonds, so this is an illustration of the power of diversification and asset risk, a subject we shall discuss in detail later. The mean is the average return: so over the last three years investors in the Henderson fund experienced fairly poor performance, with a return of 3 per cent per year. Also under the Volatility Measurements section you will see the Sharpe ratio. The Sharpe ratio is defined as the risk premium of the asset divided by the standard deviation. It is a measure of return to the level of risk taken (as measured by standard deviation). The 'beta' for the All Stocks Credit A Fund is 0.64. We shall have more to say about this number – lots more – in the next chapter.

QUESTIONS

1 Go to the Morningstar website at www.morningstar.com. Get a quote for the Aberdeen Asian Income fund. How does this compare with the Henderson All Stocks Investment Trust?

2 What style is this fund? What are the five sectors that have the highest percentage investment for this fund? What are the five equities with the highest percentage investment?

Figure 11.6 illustrates a normal distribution, and its distinctive bell shape. As you can see, this distribution has a much cleaner appearance than the actual return distributions illustrated in Fig. 11.5. Even so, like the normal distribution, the actual distributions do appear to be at least roughly mound-shaped and symmetric. When this is true, the normal distribution is often a very good approximation.

Also, keep in mind that the distributions in Fig. 11.5 are based on only 82 yearly observations, whereas Fig. 11.6 is, in principle, based on an infinite number. So if we had been able to observe returns for, say, 1,000 years, we might have filled in a lot of the irregularities and ended up with a much smoother picture in Fig. 11.5. For our purposes it is enough to observe that the returns are at least roughly normally distributed.

The usefulness of the normal distribution stems from the fact that it is completely described by the average and the standard deviation. If you have these two numbers, then there is nothing else to know. For example, with a normal distribution, the probability that we shall end up within one standard deviation of the average is about 2/3. The probability that we shall end up within two standard deviations is about 95 per cent. Finally, the probability of being more than three standard deviations away from the average is less than 1 per cent. These ranges, and the probabilities, are illustrated in Fig. 11.6.

To see why this is useful, recall from Fig. 11.5 that the standard deviation of returns on the US large company equities is 20 per cent. The average return is 12.3 per cent. So,

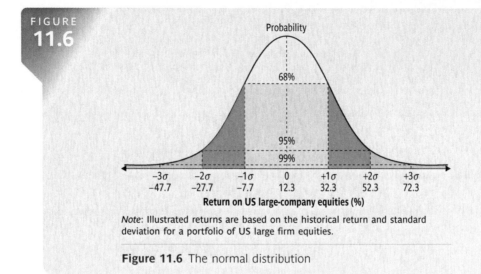

Note: Illustrated returns are based on the historical return and standard deviation for a portfolio of US large firm equities.

Figure 11.6 The normal distribution

assuming that the frequency distribution is at least approximately normal, the probability that the return in a given year is in the range –7.7 to 32.3 per cent (12.3 per cent plus or minus one standard deviation, 20 per cent) is about 2/3. This range is illustrated in Fig. 11.6. In other words, there is about one chance in three that the return will be *outside* this range. This literally tells you that, if you buy equities in large US companies, you should expect to be outside this range in one year out of every three. This reinforces our earlier observations about stock market volatility. However, there is only a 5 per cent chance (approximately) that we would end up outside the range –27.7 to 52.3 per cent (12.3 per cent plus or minus 2 × 20%). These points are also illustrated in Fig. 11.6.

The Second Lesson

Our observations concerning the year-to-year variability in returns are the basis for our second lesson from capital market history. On average, bearing risk is handsomely rewarded; but in a given year there is a significant chance of a dramatic change in value. Thus our second lesson is this: the greater the potential reward, the greater is the risk.

Using Capital Market History

Based on the discussion in this section, you should begin to have an idea of the risks and rewards from investing. For example, in early 2010 one-year UK Treasury bills were paying about 0.75 per cent. Suppose we had an investment that we thought had about the same risk as a portfolio of small UK company equities. At a minimum, what return would this investment have to offer for us to be interested?

From Table 11.3 we see that the average return earned by small UK company equities was 8.25 per cent per annum, and so a reasonable estimate of the risk premium was 7.5 per cent (= 8.25 – 0.75) over the 10-year period 2001 to 2010. This may strike you as being high, but if we were thinking of starting a new business, then the risks of doing so might resemble those of investing in small-company equities.

Clearly, there are major problems with this analysis when such a short period is used to estimate risk premiums. Take, for example, large UK company equities, which had an average annual return of 0.19 per cent over the period 2001–2010. In this case the estimated risk premium is negative, which is nonsense.

It makes sense to look at data over a much longer period, and a glance at the 82-year US sample in Table 11.5 shows a much more sensible pattern across securities. Small-company equities have a higher risk premium than large-company equities, which in turn is greater than the risk premium for corporate and government bonds.

We shall discuss the relationship between risk and required return in more detail in the next chapter. For now, you should notice that a projected internal rate of return, or IRR, on a risky investment in the 10 to 20 per cent range isn't particularly outstanding. It depends on how much risk there is. This, too, is an important lesson from capital market history.

EXAMPLE 11.3

Investing in Growth Stocks

The term *growth stock* is frequently used as a euphemism for small-company equities. Are such investments suitable for 'widows and orphans'? Before answering, you should consider the historical volatility. For example, from the historical US record, what is the approximate probability that you will actually lose more than 16 per cent of your money in a single year if you buy a portfolio of shares of such companies?

Looking back at Fig. 11.5, we see that the average return on small US company equities is 17.1 per cent, and the standard deviation is 32.6 per cent. Assuming the returns are approximately normal, there is about a 1/3 probability that you will experience a return outside the range −15.5 to 49.7 per cent (17.1% ± 32.6%).

Because the normal distribution is symmetric, the odds of being above or below this range are equal. There is thus a 1/6 chance (half of 1/3) that you will lose more than 15.5 per cent. So you should expect this to happen once in every six years, on average. Such investments can thus be *very* volatile, and they are not well suited for those who cannot afford the risk.

More on the Stock Market Risk Premium

As we have discussed, the historical stock market risk premium has been substantial. In fact, based on standard economic models, it has been argued that the historical risk premium is *too* big, and is thus an overestimate of what is likely to happen in the future.

Of course, whenever we use the past to predict the future, there is the danger that the past period we observe isn't representative of what the future will hold. For example, in this chapter we have studied the period 2001–2010. Investors were obviously highly unlucky over this period, and earned abysmally low returns. With that in mind, the average annual return (March to February) on the FTSE 100 since it started in 1984 is 7.9 per cent, significantly greater than 0.19 per cent (2001–2010), but still low compared with other major countries, such as the US.

Data from earlier years are available, but are not of such high quality. Figure 11.7 shows the historical average stock market risk premium for 17 countries over the 106-year period 1900–2005. Looking at the numbers, we can see that Italy had the highest risk premium, at 10.5 per cent, and Denmark was lowest, at 4.5 per cent. The overall average risk premium is 7.1 per cent. These numbers make it clear most investors did well, but not exceptionally well.

So, are market risk premiums estimated too high? The evidence seems to suggest that the answer is 'maybe a little' for some countries and 'definitely not' for others.

CONCEPT QUESTIONS

11.4a In words, how do we calculate a variance? A standard deviation?

11.4b With a normal distribution, what is the probability of ending up more than one standard deviation below the average?

11.4c Assuming that long-term corporate bonds have an approximately normal distribution, what is the approximate probability of earning 14.6 per cent or more in a given year? With T-bills, roughly what is this probability?

11.4d What is the second lesson from capital market history?

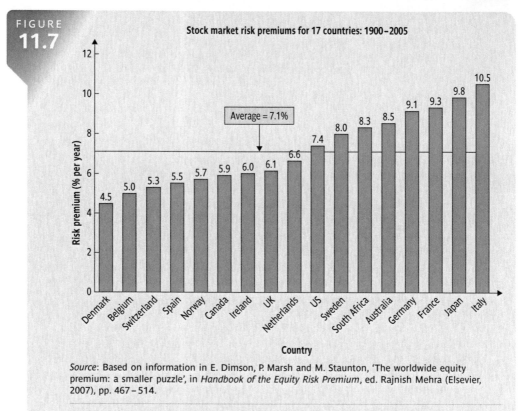

Figure 11.7 Stock market risk premiums for 17 countries: 1900–2005

Source: Based on information in E. Dimson, P. Marsh and M. Staunton, 'The worldwide equity premium: a smaller puzzle', in *Handbook of the Equity Risk Premium*, ed. Rajnish Mehra (Elsevier, 2007), pp. 467–514.

11.5 More about Average Returns

Thus far in this chapter we have looked closely at simple average returns. But there is another way of computing an average return. The fact that average returns are calculated in two different ways leads to some confusion, so our goal in this section is to explain the two approaches, and also the circumstances under which each is appropriate.

Arithmetic versus Geometric Averages

Let's start with a simple example. Suppose you buy a particular equity for £100. Unfortunately, the first year you own it, it falls to £50. The second year you own it, it rises back to £100, leaving you where you started (no dividends were paid).

What was your average return on this investment? Common sense seems to say that your average return must be exactly zero, because you started with £100 and ended with £100. But if we calculate the returns year by year, we see that you lost 50 per cent the first year (you lost half of your money). The second year, you made 100 per cent (you doubled your money). Your average return over the two years was thus (−50% + 100%)/2 = 25%!

So which is correct, 0 per cent or 25 per cent? Both are correct: they just answer different questions. The 0 per cent is called the **geometric average return**. The 25 per cent is called the **arithmetic average return**. The geometric average return

geometric average return The average compound return earned per year over a multi-year period.

arithmetic average return The return earned in an average year over a multi-year period.

Chapter 11 Some Lessons from Recent Capital Market History

answers the question 'What was your average compound return per year over a particular period?' The arithmetic average return answers the question 'What was your return in an average year over a particular period?'

Notice that in previous sections the average returns we calculated were all arithmetic averages, so we already know how to calculate them. What we need to do now is: (1) learn how to calculate geometric averages; and (2) learn the circumstances under which one average is more meaningful than the other.

Calculating Geometric Average Returns

First, to illustrate how we calculate a geometric average return, suppose a particular investment had annual returns of 10 per cent, 12 per cent, 3 per cent, and –9 per cent over the last four years. The geometric average return over this four-year period is calculated as $(1.10 \times 1.12 \times 1.03 \times 0.91)^{1/4} - 1 = 3.66\%$. In contrast, the average arithmetic return we have been calculating is $(0.10 + 0.12 + 0.03 - 0.09)/4 = 4.0\%$.

In general, if we have T years of returns, the geometric average return over these T years is calculated using this formula:

$$\text{Geometric average return} = [(1 + R_1) \times (1 + R_2) \times \cdots \times (1 + R_T)]^{1/T} - 1 \qquad (11.4)$$

This formula tells us that four steps are required:

1 Take each of the T annual returns $R_1, R_2, \ldots, R_T$ and add 1 to each (after converting them to decimals!).

2 Multiply all the numbers from step 1 together.

3 Take the result from step 2 and raise it to the power $1/T$.

4 Finally, subtract 1 from the result of step 3. The result is the geometric average return.

 EXAMPLE 11.4

Calculating the Geometric Average Return

Calculate the geometric average return for Danish equities for the first five years in Table 11.1, 2001–2005.

First, convert percentages to decimal returns, add 1, and then calculate their product:

Danish returns (%)	Product
38.80	1.3880
–24.21	× 0.7579
–29.28	× 0.7072
40.32	× 1.4032
11.49	× 1.1149
	1.1640

Notice that the number 1.1640 is what our investment is worth after five years if we started with a 1 kroner investment. The geometric average return is then calculated as follows:

$$\text{Geometric average return} = 1.1640^{1/5} - 1 = 0.0308, \text{ or } 3.08\%$$

Thus the geometric average return is about 3.08 per cent in this example. Here is a tip: if you are using a financial calculator, you can put '1' in as the present value, '1.5291' as the future value, and '5' as the number of periods. Then solve for the unknown rate. You should get the same answer that we did.

| | Average return (%) | | Standard deviation (%) |
Series	Geometric	Arithmetic	
Large US company equities	10.4	12.3	20.0
Small US company equities	12.5	17.1	32.6
Long-term US corporate bonds	5.9	6.2	8.4
Long-term US government bonds	5.5	5.8	9.2
Intermediate-term US government bonds	5.3	5.5	5.7
US Treasury bills	3.7	3.8	3.1
Inflation	3.0	3.1	4.2

Table 11.6 Geometric versus arithmetic average US returns: 1926–2007

One thing you may have noticed in our examples thus far is that the geometric average returns seem to be smaller. This will always be true (as long as the returns are not all identical, in which case the two 'averages' would be the same). To illustrate, Table 11.6 shows the arithmetic averages and standard deviations from Fig. 11.5, along with the geometric average returns.

As shown in Table 11.6, the geometric averages are all smaller, but the magnitude of the difference varies quite a bit. The reason is that the difference is greater for more volatile investments. In fact, there is a useful approximation. Assuming all the numbers are expressed in decimals (as opposed to percentages), the geometric average return is approximately equal to the arithmetic average return minus half the variance. For example, looking at the large company equities, the arithmetic average is 0.123 and the standard deviation is 0.20, implying that the variance is 0.04. The approximate geometric average is thus 0.123 – 0.04/2 = 0.103, which is quite close to the actual value.

More Geometric Averages

EXAMPLE 11.5

Take a look back at Table 11.1. There we showed that the small UK company index grew from 6,181 to 9,237 over 10 years. The 10-year return is given below:

$$\text{Ten-year return} = (9{,}237/6{,}181) - 1 = 49.44\%$$

The geometric average annual return is thus

$$\text{Geometric average return} = 1.4944^{1/10} - 1 = 0.0409, \text{ or } 4.09\%$$

For practice, check some of the other countries in Table 11.1 the same way.

Arithmetic Average Return or Geometric Average Return?

When we look at historical returns, the difference between the geometric and arithmetic average returns isn't too hard to understand. To put it slightly differently, the geometric average tells you what you actually earned per year on average, compounded annually. The arithmetic average tells you what you earned in a typical year. You should use whichever one answers the question you want answered.

A somewhat trickier question concerns which average return to use when forecasting future wealth levels, and there's a lot of confusion on this point among analysts and financial planners. First, let's get one thing straight: if you *know* the true arithmetic average return, then this is what you should use in your forecast. For example, if you know the arithmetic return is 10 per cent, then your best guess of the value of a €1,000 investment in 10 years is the future value of €1,000 at 10 per cent for 10 years, or €2,593.74.

The problem we face, however, is that we usually have only *estimates* of the arithmetic and geometric returns, and estimates have errors. In this case the arithmetic average return is probably too high for longer periods, and the geometric average is probably too low for shorter periods. So you should regard long-run projected wealth levels calculated using arithmetic averages as optimistic. Short-run projected wealth levels calculated using geometric averages are probably pessimistic.

The good news is that there is a simple way of combining the two averages, which we shall call *Blume's formula*.[2] Suppose we have calculated geometric and arithmetic return averages from N years of data, and we wish to use these averages to form a T-year average return forecast, $R(T)$, where T is less than N. Here's how we do it:

$$R(T) = \frac{T-1}{N-1} \times \text{Geometric average} + \frac{N-T}{N-1} \times \text{Arithmetic average} \qquad (11.5)$$

For example, suppose that from 25 years of annual returns data we calculate an arithmetic average return of 12 per cent and a geometric average return of 9 per cent. From these averages we wish to make one-year, five-year and ten-year average return forecasts. These three average return forecasts are calculated as follows:

$$R(1) = \frac{1-1}{24} \times 9\% + \frac{25-1}{24} \times 12\% = 12\%$$

$$R(5) = \frac{5-1}{24} \times 9\% + \frac{25-5}{24} \times 12\% = 11.5\%$$

$$R(10) = \frac{10-1}{24} \times 9\% + \frac{25-10}{24} \times 12\% = 10.875\%$$

Thus we see that one-year, five-year and ten-year forecasts are 12 per cent, 11.5 per cent and 10.875 per cent, respectively.

As a practical matter, Blume's formula says that if you are using averages calculated over a long period to forecast up to a decade or so into the future, then you should use the arithmetic average. If you are forecasting a few decades into the future (as you might do for retirement planning), then you should just split the difference between the arithmetic and geometric average returns. Finally, if for some reason you are doing very long forecasts covering many decades, use the geometric average.

This concludes our discussion of geometric versus arithmetic averages. One last note: in the future, when we say 'average return', we mean arithmetic unless we explicitly say otherwise.

CONCEPT QUESTIONS

11.5a If you want to forecast what the stock market is going to do over the next year, should you use an arithmetic or geometric average?

11.5b If you want to forecast what the stock market is going to do over the next century, should you use an arithmetic or geometric average?

11.6 Capital Market Efficiency

Capital market history suggests that the market values of equities and bonds can fluctuate widely from year to year. Why does this occur? At least part of the answer is that prices change because new information arrives, and investors reassess asset values based on that information.

The behaviour of market prices has been extensively studied. A question that has received particular attention is whether prices adjust quickly and correctly when new information arrives. A market is said to be 'efficient' if this is the case. To be more precise, in an **efficient capital market** current market prices fully reflect available information. By this we simply mean that, based on available information, there is no reason to believe that the current price is too low or too high.

> **efficient capital market**
> A market in which security prices reflect available information.

The concept of market efficiency is a rich one, and much has been written about it. A full discussion of the subject goes beyond the scope of our study of corporate finance. However, because the concept figures so prominently in studies of market history, we briefly describe the key points here.

Price Behaviour in an Efficient Market

To illustrate how prices behave in an efficient market, suppose F-Stop Camera Corporation (FCC) has, through years of secret research and development, developed a camera with an autofocusing system whose speed will double that of the autofocusing systems now available. FCC's capital budgeting analysis suggests that launching the new camera will be a highly profitable move; in other words, the NPV appears to be positive and substantial. The key assumption thus far is that FCC has not released any information about the new system, so the fact of its existence is 'inside' information only.

Now consider a share of equity in FCC. In an efficient market, its price reflects what is known about FCC's current operations and profitability, and it reflects market opinion about FCC's potential for future growth and profits. The value of the new autofocusing system is not reflected, however, because the market is unaware of the system's existence.

If the market agrees with FCC's assessment of the value of the new project, FCC's share price will rise when the decision to launch is made public. For example, assume the announcement is made in a press release on Wednesday morning. In an efficient market, the price of shares in FCC will adjust quickly to this new information. Investors should not be able to buy the equity on Wednesday afternoon and make a profit on Thursday. This would imply that it took the stock market a full day to realize the implication of the FCC press release. If the market is efficient, the FCC share price on Wednesday afternoon will already reflect the information contained in the Wednesday morning press release.

Figure 11.8 presents three possible share price adjustments for FCC. In Fig. 11.8 day 0 represents the announcement day. As illustrated, before the announcement FCC sells for £140 per share. The NPV per share of the new system is, say, £40, so the new price will be £180 once the value of the new project is fully reflected.

The solid line in Fig. 11.8 represents the path taken by the share price in an efficient market. In this case the price adjusts immediately to the new information, and no further changes in the share price take place. The broken line in Fig. 11.8 depicts a delayed reaction. Here it takes the market eight days or so to fully absorb the information. Finally, the dotted line illustrates an overreaction and subsequent adjustment to the correct price.

The broken line and the dotted line in Fig. 11.8 illustrate paths that the share price might take in an inefficient market. If, for example, share prices don't adjust immediately to new information (the broken line), then buying shares immediately following the release of new information and then selling it several days later would be a positive-NPV activity because the price is too low for several days after the announcement.

The Efficient Markets Hypothesis

The **efficient markets hypothesis (EMH)** asserts that well-organized capital markets, such as the London Stock Exchange or Euronext, are efficient markets, at least as a practical matter. In other words, an advocate of the EMH might argue that although inefficiencies may exist, they are relatively small and not common.

> **efficient markets hypothesis (EMH)**
> The hypothesis that actual capital markets are efficient.

If a market is efficient, then there is a very important implication for market participants: all investments in that market are zero-NPV investments. The reason is not complicated. If prices are neither too low nor too high, then the difference between the market value of an investment and its cost is zero: hence the NPV is zero. As a

FIGURE
11.8

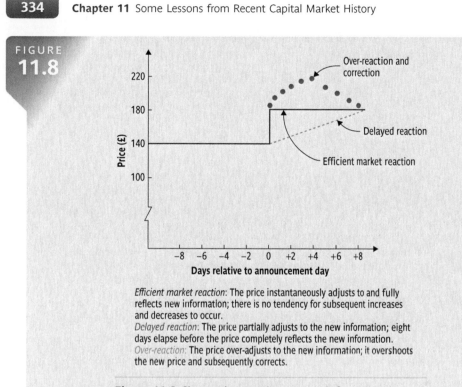

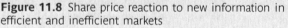

Efficient market reaction: The price instantaneously adjusts to and fully reflects new information; there is no tendency for subsequent increases and decreases to occur.
Delayed reaction: The price partially adjusts to the new information; eight days elapse before the price completely reflects the new information.
Over-reaction: The price over-adjusts to the new information; it overshoots the new price and subsequently corrects.

Figure 11.8 Share price reaction to new information in efficient and inefficient markets

result, in an efficient market investors get exactly what they pay for when they buy securities, and firms receive exactly what their equities and bonds are worth when they sell them.

What makes a market efficient is competition among investors. Many individuals spend their entire lives trying to find mispriced equities. For any given equity, they study what has happened in the past to the share price and the equity's dividends. They learn, to the extent possible, what a company's earnings have been, how much the company owes to creditors, what taxes it pays, what businesses it is in, what new investments are planned, how sensitive it is to changes in the economy, and so on.

Not only is there a great deal to know about any particular company, but there is also a powerful incentive for knowing it – namely, the profit motive. If you know more about some company than other investors in the marketplace, you can profit from that knowledge by investing in the company's shares if you have good news and by selling them if you have bad news.

The logical consequence of all this information-gathering and analysis is that mispriced equities will become fewer and fewer. In other words, because of competition among investors, the market will become increasingly efficient. A kind of equilibrium comes into being, with which there is just enough mispricing around for those who are best at identifying it to make a living at it. For most other investors the activity of information-gathering and analysis will not pay.[3]

Some Common Misconceptions about the EMH

No other idea in finance has attracted as much attention as that of efficient markets, and not all of the attention has been flattering. Rather than rehash the arguments here, we shall be content to observe that some markets are more efficient than others. For example, financial markets on the whole are probably much more efficient than real asset markets.

Having said this, however, we can also say that much of the criticism of the EMH is misguided, because it is based on a misunderstanding of what the hypothesis says and what it doesn't say. For example, when the notion of market efficiency was first publicized and debated in the popular financial press, it was often characterized by words to the effect that 'throwing darts at the financial page will produce a portfolio that can be expected to do as well as any managed by professional security analysts'.[4]

Confusion over statements of this sort has often led to a failure to understand the implications of market efficiency. For example, sometimes it is wrongly argued that market efficiency means that it doesn't matter how you invest your money, because the efficiency of the market will protect you from making a mistake. However, a random dart thrower might wind up with all of the darts sticking into one or two high-risk equities that deal in genetic engineering. Would you really want all of your money in two such companies?

A contest run by the *Wall Street Journal* provides a good example of the controversy surrounding market efficiency. Each month the *Journal* asked four professional money managers to pick one equity each. At the same time it threw four darts at the equities page to select a comparison group. In the 147 five- and one-half month contests from July 1990 to September 2002 the pros won 90 times.

The fact that the pros are ahead of the darts by 90 to 57 suggests that markets are not efficient. Or does it? One problem is that the darts naturally tend to select equities of average risk. The pros, however, are playing to win, and naturally select riskier equities, or so it is argued. If this is true, then on average we *expect* the pros to win. Furthermore, the pros' picks are announced to the public at the start. This publicity may boost the prices of the shares involved somewhat, leading to a partially self-fulfilling prophecy. Unfortunately, the *Journal* discontinued the contest in 2002, so this test of market efficiency is no longer continuing.

More than anything else, what efficiency implies is that the price a firm will obtain when it sells a share of its equity is a 'fair' price in the sense that it reflects the value of that equity, given the information available about the firm. Shareholders do not have to worry that they are paying too much for an equity with a low dividend or some other sort of characteristic, because the market has already incorporated that characteristic into the price. We sometimes say that the information has been 'priced out'.

The concept of efficient markets can be explained further by replying to a frequent objection. It is sometimes argued that the market cannot be efficient, because share prices fluctuate from day to day. If the prices are right, the argument goes, then why do they change so much and so often? From our discussion of the market we can see that these price movements are in no way inconsistent with efficiency. Investors are bombarded with information every day. The fact that prices fluctuate is, at least in part, a reflection of that information flow. In fact, the absence of price movements in a world that changes as rapidly as ours would suggest inefficiency.

The Forms of Market Efficiency

It is common to distinguish between three forms of market efficiency. Depending on the degree of efficiency, we say that markets are either *weak-form efficient*, *semi-strong-form efficient*, or *strong-form efficient*. The difference between these forms relates to what information is reflected in prices.

We start with the extreme case. If the market is strong-form efficient, then *all* information of *every* kind is reflected in share prices. In such a market there is no such thing as inside information. Therefore, in our FCC example, we apparently were assuming that the market was not strong-form efficient.

Casual observation, particularly in recent years, suggests that inside information does exist, and it can be valuable to possess. Whether it is lawful or ethical to use that information is another issue. In any event, we conclude that private information about a particular equity may exist that is not currently reflected in the share price. For example, prior knowledge of a takeover attempt could be very valuable.

The second form of efficiency, semi-strong-form efficiency, is the most controversial. If a market is semi-strong-form efficient, then all *public* information is reflected in the share price. The reason why this form is controversial is that it implies that a security analyst who tries to identify mispriced equities using, for example, financial statement information is wasting time, because that information is already reflected in the current price.

The third form of efficiency, weak-form efficiency, suggests that, at a minimum, the current share price reflects the equity's own past prices. In other words, studying past prices in an attempt to identify mispriced securities is futile if the market is weak-form efficient. Although this form of efficiency might seem rather mild, it implies that searching for patterns in historical prices that will be useful in identifying mispriced equities will not work (this practice is quite common).

What does capital market history say about market efficiency? Here again there is great controversy. At the risk of going out on a limb, we can say that the evidence seems to tell us three things. First, prices appear to respond rapidly to new information, and the response is at least not grossly different from what we would expect in an efficient market. Second, the future of market prices, particularly in the short run, is difficult to predict based on publicly available information. Third, if mispriced equities exist, then there is no obvious means of identifying them. Put another way, simple-minded schemes based on public information will probably not be successful.

Many people do not believe that markets are efficient at all. The recent stock market bubbles at the beginning of the century and, more recently, in the mid-2000s have led to a new interest in what is known as *behavioural finance*. This is covered in more detail in Chapter 19.

CONCEPT QUESTIONS

11.6a   What is an efficient market?

11.6b   What are the forms of market efficiency?

Summary and Conclusions

This chapter has explored the subject of capital market history. Such history is useful, because it tells us what to expect in the way of returns from risky assets. We summed up our study of market history with two key lessons:

1   Risky assets, on average, earn a risk premium. There is a reward for bearing risk.

2   The greater the potential reward from a risky investment, the greater is the risk.

These lessons have significant implications for the financial manager. We shall consider these implications in the chapters ahead.

We also discussed the concept of market efficiency. In an efficient market, prices adjust quickly and correctly to new information. Consequently, asset prices in efficient markets are rarely too high or too low. How efficient capital markets (such as the London Stock Exchange or Euronext) are is a matter of debate; but, at a minimum, they are probably much more efficient than most real asset markets.

8 **Stocks versus Gambling [LO4]** Critically evaluate the following statement: 'Playing the stock market is like gambling. Such speculative investing has no social value other than the pleasure people get from this form of gambling.'

9 **Efficient Markets Hypothesis [LO4]** Several celebrated investors and stock pickers frequently mentioned in the financial press have recorded huge returns on their investments over the past two decades. Is the success of these particular investors an invalidation of the EMH? Explain.

10 **Efficient Markets Hypothesis [LO4]** For each of the following scenarios, discuss whether profit opportunities exist from trading in the equity of the firm under the conditions that: (1) the market is not weak-form efficient; (2) the market is weak-form but not semi-strong-form efficient; (3) the market is semi-strong-form but not strong-form efficient; and (4) the market is strong-form efficient.

(a) The share price has risen steadily each day for the past 30 days.

(b) The financial statements for a company were released three days ago, and you believe you've uncovered some anomalies in the company's inventory and cost control reporting techniques that are causing the firm's true liquidity strength to be understated.

(c) You observe that the senior managers of a company have been buying a lot of the company's equities on the open market over the past week.

connect Questions and Problems

BASIC
1 – 11

1 **Calculating Returns [LO1]** At the beginning of 2009 the price of Anheuser-Busch was €19.67, it paid a dividend of €0.28 per share during the year, and had an ending share price of €36.40. Compute the percentage total return.

2 **Calculating Yields [LO1]** In Problem 1, what was the dividend yield? The capital gains yield?

3 **Return Calculations [LO1]** Rework Problems 1 and 2 assuming the ending share price is €30.

4 **Calculating Returns [LO1]** Suppose you bought a 7 per cent coupon bond one year ago for £104. The bond sells for £107 today.

(a) Assuming a £100 face value, what was your total cash return on this investment over the past year?

(b) What was your total nominal rate of return on this investment over the past year?

(c) If the inflation rate last year was 4 per cent, what was your total real rate of return on this investment?

5 **Nominal versus Real Returns [LO2]** What was the average annual return on UK large company shares from 2001 through to 2010:

(a) In nominal terms?

(b) In real terms if the average rate of inflation was 1 per cent?

6 **Bond Returns [LO2]** What is the historical real return on long-term US government bonds? On long-term US corporate bonds?

340 **Chapter 11** Some Lessons from Recent Capital Market History

7   Calculating Returns and Variability [LO1]   Using the following returns, calculate the arithmetic average returns, the variances, and the standard deviations for X and Y.

Year	Returns (%)	
	X	**Y**
1	8	16
2	21	38
3	17	14
4	−16	−21
5	9	26

8   Risk Premiums [LO2, LO3]   Refer to Table 11.1 in the text and look at the period from 2003 through to 2007.

  (a)   Calculate the arithmetic average returns for all the indices in the table over this period.

  (b)   Calculate the standard deviation of the returns for all the indices over this period.

9   Calculating Returns and Variability [LO1]   You've observed the following returns on Crash-n-Burn Computers' equity over the past five years: 7 per cent, −12 per cent, 11 per cent, 38 per cent and 14 per cent.

  (a)   What was the arithmetic average return on Crash-n-Burn's shares over this five-year period?

  (b)   What was the variance of Crash-n-Burn's returns over this period? The standard deviation?

10   Calculating Real Returns and Risk Premiums [LO1]   For Problem 9, suppose the average inflation rate over this period was 3.5 per cent and the average T-bill rate over the period was 4.2 per cent.

  (a)   What was the average real return on Crash-n-Burn's shares?

  (b)   What was the average nominal risk premium on Crash-n-Burn's shares?

11   Calculating Real Rates [LO1]   Given the information in Problem 10, what was the average real risk-free rate over this time period? What was the average real risk premium?

12   Calculating Investment Returns [LO1]   You bought one of Blueboy plc's 8 per cent coupon bonds one year ago for £103,000. These bonds make annual payments, and mature six years from now. Suppose you decide to sell your bonds today, when the required return on the bonds is 8 per cent. If the inflation rate was 3.2 per cent over the past year, what was your total real return on investment?

13   Calculating Returns and Variability [LO1]   You find a certain equity that had returns of 7 per cent, −12 per cent, 18 per cent and 19 per cent for four of the last five years. If the average return of the equity over this period was 10.5 per cent, what was the equity's return for the missing year? What is the standard deviation of the equity's return?

14   Arithmetic and Geometric Returns [LO1]   An equity has had returns of 6 per cent, 14 per cent, 21 per cent, −15 per cent, 29 per cent and −13 per cent over the last six years. What are the arithmetic and geometric returns for the equity?

15   **Arithmetic and Geometric Returns [LO1]**   An equity has had the following year-end prices and dividends:

Year	Price (£)	Dividend (£)
1	60.18	–
2	73.66	0.60
3	94.18	0.64
4	89.35	0.72
5	78.49	0.80
6	95.05	1.20

What are the arithmetic and geometric returns for the equity?

16   **Using Return Distributions [LO3]**   Suppose the returns on long-term corporate bonds are normally distributed. Based on the historical record, what is the approximate probability that your return on these bonds will be less than –2.2 per cent in a given year? What range of returns would you expect to see 95 per cent of the time? What range would you expect to see 99 per cent of the time?

17   **Using Return Distributions [LO3]**   Assuming that the returns from holding Dutch equities are normally distributed, what is the approximate probability that your money will double in value in a single year? What about triple in value?

18   **Distributions [LO3]**   In Problem 17, what is the probability that the return is less than –100 per cent (think)? What are the implications for the distribution of returns?

19   **Blume's Formula [LO1]**   Over a 40-year period an asset had an arithmetic return of 15.3 per cent and a geometric return of 11.9 per cent. Using Blume's formula, what is your best estimate of the future annual returns over 5 years? 10 years? 20 years?

20   **Blume's Formula [LO1, LO2]**   Assume that the historical return on German equities is a predictor of the future returns. What return would you estimate for German equities over the next year? The next 5 years?

21   **Using Probability Distributions [LO3]**   Suppose the returns on large company UK equities are normally distributed. Based on the historical record, use the cumulative normal probability table (rounded to the nearest table value) in the appendix of the text to determine the probability that in any given year you will lose money by investing in small company UK equities.

22   **Using Probability Distributions [LO3]**   Suppose the returns on German and Danish equities are normally distributed. Based on the historical record, use the cumulative normal probability table (rounded to the nearest table value) in the appendix of the text to answer the following questions:

(a)   What is the probability that, in any given year, the return on German equities will be greater than 10 per cent? Less than 0 per cent?

(b)   What is the probability that in any given year, the return on Danish equities will be greater than 10 per cent? Less than 0 per cent?

(c)   In 2008 the return on German equities was –36.68 per cent. How likely is it that such a low return will recur at some point in the future? In 2009 German equities had a return of 29.28 per cent. How likely is it that such a high return on German equities will recur at some point in the future?

MINI
CASE

A Job at West Coast Yachts

You recently graduated from university, and your job search led you to West Coast Yachts at Kip Marina. Because you felt the company's business was seaworthy, you accepted a job offer. The first day on the job, while you are finishing your employment paperwork, Dan Ervin, who works in Finance, stops by to inform you about the company's retirement plan.

Retirement plans are offered by many companies, and are tax-deferred savings vehicles, meaning that any deposits you make into the plan are deducted from your current pre-tax income, so no current taxes are paid on the money. For example, assume your salary will be £50,000 per year. If you contribute £3,000 to the plan, you will pay taxes on only £47,000 in income. There are also no taxes paid on any capital gains or income while you are invested in the plan, but you do pay taxes when you withdraw money at retirement. As is fairly common, the company also has a 5 per cent matched funding. This means that the company will match your contribution up to 5 per cent of your salary, but you must contribute to get the match.

The retirement plan has several options for investments, most of which are mutual funds. A mutual fund is a portfolio of assets. When you purchase shares in a mutual fund, you are actually purchasing partial ownership of the fund's assets. The return of the fund is the weighted average of the return of the assets owned by the fund, minus any expenses. The largest expense is typically the management fee paid to the fund manager. The management fee is compensation for the manager, who makes all the investment decisions for the fund.

West Coast Yachts uses Skandla Life Assurance Company Ltd as its retirement plan administrator. Here are the investment options offered for employees:

- **Company Shares** One option in the retirement plan is equity ownership of West Coast Yachts. The company is currently privately held. However, when you were interviewed by the owner, Larissa Warren, she informed you that the company shares were expected to go public in the next three to four years. Until then, a company share price is simply set each year by the board of directors.

- **Skandla Market Index Fund** This mutual fund tracks the FTSE 100 index. Equities in the fund are weighted exactly the same as the FTSE 100. This means that the fund return is approximately the return on the FTSE 100, minus expenses. Because an index fund purchases assets based on the compensation of the index it is following, the fund manager is not required to research stocks or make investment decisions. The result is that the fund expenses are usually low. The Skandla Index Fund charges expenses of 0.15 per cent of assets per year.

- **Skandla Small-Cap Fund** This fund invests primarily in small-capitalization companies. The returns of the fund are therefore more volatile. The fund can also invest 10 per cent of its assets in companies based outside the United Kingdom. This fund charges 1.70 per cent in expenses.

- **Skandla Large-Company Equity Fund** This fund invests primarily in large-capitalization companies based in the United Kingdom. The fund is managed by Evan Skandla, and has outperformed the market in six of the last eight years. The fund charges 1.50 per cent in expenses.

- **Skandla Bond Fund** This fund invests in long-term corporate bonds issued by UK-domiciled companies. The fund is restricted to investments in bonds with an investment-grade credit rating. This fund charges 1.40 per cent in expenses.

- **Skandla Money Market Fund** This fund invests in short-term, high–credit quality debt instruments, which include Treasury bills. The return on the money market fund is therefore only slightly higher than the return on Treasury bills. Because of the credit quality and short-term nature of the investments, there is only a very slight risk of negative return. The fund charges 0.60 per cent in expenses.

QUESTIONS

1 What advantages do the mutual funds offer compared with the company equity?

2 Assume that you invest 5 per cent of your salary and receive the full 5 per cent match from West Coast Yachts. What APR do you earn from the match? What conclusions do you draw about matching plans?

3 Assume you decide you should invest at least part of your money in large-capitalization companies based in the United Kingdom. What are the advantages and disadvantages of choosing the Skandla Large-Company Equity Fund compared with the Skandla Market Index Fund?

4 The returns on the Skandla Small-Cap Fund are the most volatile of all the mutual funds offered in the retirement plan. Why would you ever want to invest in this fund? When you examine the expenses of the mutual funds, you will notice that this fund also has the highest expenses. Does this affect your decision to invest in this fund?

5 A measure of risk-adjusted performance that is often used is the Sharpe ratio. The Sharpe ratio is calculated as the risk premium of an asset divided by its standard deviation. The standard deviation and return of the funds over the past 10 years are listed here. Calculate the Sharpe ratio for each of these funds. Assume that the expected return and standard deviation of the company equity will be 18 per cent and 70 per cent, respectively. Calculate the Sharpe ratio for the company shares. How appropriate is the Sharpe ratio for these assets? When would you use the Sharpe ratio?

	10-Year annual return (%)	Standard deviation (%)
Skandla Market Index Fund	11.48	15.82
Skandla Small-Cap Fund	16.68	19.64
Skandla Large-Company Equity Fund	11.85	15.41
Skandla Bond Fund	9.67	10.83

6 What portfolio allocation would you choose? Why? Explain your thinking carefully.

Endnotes

1 As we mentioned in an earlier chapter, strictly speaking, what is and what is not a capital gain (or loss) is determined by a country's tax authority. We thus use the terms loosely.

2 This elegant result is due to Marshal Blume ('Unbiased estimates of long-run expected rates of return', *Journal of the American Statistical Association*, September 1974, pp. 634–638).

3 The idea behind the EMH can be illustrated by the following short story. A student was walking down the hall with her finance professor when they both saw a €500 note on the ground. As the student bent down to pick it up, the professor shook his head slowly and, with a look of disappointment on his face, said patiently to the student, 'Don't bother. If it were really there, someone else would have picked it up already.' The moral of the story reflects the logic of the efficient markets hypothesis: if you think you have found a pattern in share prices or a simple device for picking winners, you probably have not.

4 B.G. Malkiel, *A Random Walk Down Wall Street* (revised and updated ed.) (New York: Norton, 2003).

PART SIX: TOPICS IN CORPORATE FINANCE

CHAPTER 18

International Corporate Finance

KEY NOTATIONS

F	Forward exchange rate
FC	Foreign country
h	Inflation rate
HC	Home country
IFE	International Fisher effect
IRP	Interest rate parity
NPV	Net present value
P	Price
PPP	Purchasing power parity
R	Risk-free rate
S	Exchange rate
UFR	Unbiased forward rate
UIP	Uncovered interest parity

LEARNING OBJECTIVES

After studying this chapter, you should understand:

LO1 How exchange rates are quoted, what they mean, and the difference between spot and forward exchange rates.

LO2 Purchasing power parity, interest rate parity, unbiased forward rates, uncovered interest rate parity and the international Fisher effect, and their implications for exchange rate changes.

LO3 The different types of exchange rate risk, and ways in which firms manage exchange rate risk.

LO4 The impact of political risk on international business investing.

RELATIVELY FEW LARGE COMPANIES operate in a single country. As a financial manager in a corporation, even if your sales are not overseas, it is highly likely that you have competitors or suppliers with operations overseas. In most industries, raw materials and components are sourced and imported from abroad, and many services and products are sold to other countries.

For example, an analysis of 2009 import and export revenue for the United Kingdom shows that most of Britain's export revenue comes from the US (13.8%), Germany (11.5%), the Netherlands (7.8%) France (7.6%), Ireland (7.5%), Belgium (5.3%) and Spain (4.1%). Similarly, the United Kingdom's main import partners are Germany (13%), the US (8.7%), China (7.5%), the Netherlands (7.4%), France (6.8%), Belgium (4.7%) and Italy (4.1%).

Currency fluctuations will clearly have an impact on firms. For example, if the euro strengthens against the British pound, British exports become more competitive in Europe. Similarly, raw materials sourced from Europe will become more expensive, and British corporations will look elsewhere for cheaper inputs. One of the reasons why European Monetary Union was adopted in 2000 was precisely that many countries in the Eurozone traded heavily with each other. With a single currency, the risk of fluctuations is eradicated. For companies outside the Eurozone who have Eurozone customers or suppliers, currency fluctuations (and hence currency risk) may even become worse. For example, when Greek sovereign debt was reduced to junk status in 2010, the euro was exceptionally volatile. In this chapter we explore the roles played by currencies and exchange rates, along with a number of other key topics in international corporate finance.

Corporations with significant foreign operations are often called *international corporations* or *multinationals*. Such corporations must consider many financial factors that do not directly affect purely domestic firms. These include foreign exchange rates, differing interest rates from country to country, complex accounting methods for foreign operations, foreign tax rates, and foreign government intervention.

The basic principles of corporate finance still apply to international corporations: like domestic companies, these firms seek to invest in projects that create more value for the shareholders than they cost, and to arrange financing that raises cash at the lowest possible cost. In other words, the net present value principle holds for both foreign and domestic operations, although it is usually more complicated to apply the NPV rule to foreign investments.

One of the most significant complications of international finance is foreign exchange. The foreign exchange markets provide important information and opportunities for an international corporation when it undertakes capital budgeting and financing decisions. As we shall discuss, international exchange rates, interest rates and inflation rates are closely related. We shall spend much of this chapter exploring the connection between these financial variables.

We shan't have much to say here about the role of cultural and social differences in international business. Nor shall we be discussing the implications of differing political and economic systems. These factors are of great importance to international businesses, but it would take another book to do them justice. Consequently, we shall focus only on some purely financial considerations in international finance, and on some key aspects of foreign exchange markets.

18.1 Terminology

A common buzzword for the student of business finance is *globalization*. The first step in learning about the globalization of financial markets is to conquer the new vocabulary. As with any speciality, international finance is rich in jargon. Accordingly, we get started on the subject with a highly eclectic vocabulary exercise.

The terms that follow are presented alphabetically, and they are not all of equal importance. We choose these particular ones either because they appear frequently in the financial press, or because they illustrate the colourful nature of the language of international finance.

American depositary receipt (ADR)
A security issued in the United States representing shares of a foreign equity, and allowing that equity to be traded in the United States.

cross-rate
The implicit exchange rate between two currencies quoted in some third currency.

Eurobonds
International bonds issued in multiple countries but denominated in a single currency (usually the issuer's currency).

1 An **American depositary receipt (ADR)** is a security issued in the United States that represents shares of a foreign equity, allowing that equity to be traded in the United States. Foreign companies use ADRs, which are issued in US dollars, to expand the pool of potential US investors. ADRs are available in two forms for a large and growing number of foreign companies: company-sponsored, which are listed on an exchange; and unsponsored, which usually are held by the bank that makes a market in the ADR. Both forms are available to individual investors, but only company-sponsored issues are quoted daily in newspapers. A *global depositary receipt* (GDR) is an equivalent security denominated in sterling or euros, and issued and traded in financial centres such as London or Frankfurt.

2 The **cross-rate** is the implicit exchange rate between two currencies when both are quoted in some third currency.

3 A **Eurobond** is a bond issued in multiple countries, but denominated in a single currency, usually the issuer's home currency. Such bonds have become an important way to raise capital for many international companies and governments. Eurobonds are issued outside the restrictions that apply to domestic offerings, and are syndicated and traded mostly from London. Trading takes place anywhere there is a buyer and a seller.

4 **Eurocurrency** is money deposited in a financial centre outside the country whose currency is involved. For instance, Eurodollars – the most widely used Eurocurrency – are US dollars deposited in banks outside the US. Eurosterling and euroyen are British and Japanese equivalents.

> **Eurocurrency** Money deposited in a financial centre outside the country whose currency is involved.

5 **Foreign bonds**, unlike Eurobonds, are issued in a single country and are usually denominated in that country's currency. Often, the country in which these bonds are issued will draw distinctions between them and bonds issued by domestic issuers, including different tax laws, restrictions on the amount issued, and tougher disclosure rules.

> **foreign bonds** International bonds issued in a single country, usually denominated in that country's currency.

Foreign bonds often are nicknamed for the country where they are issued: Yankee bonds (United States), Samurai bonds (Japan), Rembrandt bonds (the Netherlands), and Bulldog bonds (Britain). Partly because of tougher regulations and disclosure requirements, the foreign bond market hasn't grown in past years with the vigour of the Eurobond market.

6 **Gilts**, technically, are British and Irish government securities, although the term also includes issues of local British authorities and some overseas public sector offerings.

> **gilts** British and Irish government securities.

7 The **London Interbank Offered Rate (LIBOR)** is the rate that most international banks charge one another for loans overnight in the London market. LIBOR is a cornerstone in the pricing of money market issues and other short-term debt issues by both government and corporate borrowers. Interest rates are frequently quoted as some spread over LIBOR, and they then float with the LIBOR rate. EURIBOR is the Eurozone equivalent.

> **London Interbank Offered Rate (LIBOR)** The rate most international banks charge one another for overnight loans.

8 There are two basic kinds of **swap**: interest rate swaps and currency swaps. An interest rate swap occurs when two parties exchange a floating-rate payment for a fixed-rate payment or vice versa. Currency swaps are agreements to deliver one currency in exchange for another. Often, both types of swap are used in the same transaction when debt denominated in different currencies is swapped.

> **swaps** Agreements to exchange two securities or currencies.

CONCEPT QUESTIONS

18.1a What are the differences between a Eurobond and a foreign bond?
18.1b What are Eurodollars?

18.2 Foreign Exchange Markets and Exchange Rates

The **foreign exchange market** is undoubtedly the world's largest financial market. It is the market where one country's currency is traded for another's. Most of the trading takes place in a few currencies: the US dollar ($), the British pound sterling (£), the Japanese yen (¥) and the euro (€). Table 18.1 lists some of the more common currencies and their symbols.

> **foreign exchange market** The market in which one country's currency is traded for another's.

The foreign exchange market is an over-the-counter market, so there is no single location where traders get together. Instead, market participants are located in the major banks around the world. They communicate using computer terminals, telephones, and other telecommunications devices. For example, one communications network for foreign transactions is maintained by the Society for Worldwide Interbank Financial Telecommunication (SWIFT), a Belgian not-for-profit co-operative. Using data transmission lines, a bank in New York can send messages to a bank in London via SWIFT regional processing centres.

556   **Chapter 18** International Corporate Finance

Country	Currency	Symbol
Australia	Dollar	A$
Canada	Dollar	C$
China	Yuan (renminbi)	¥
Denmark	Krone	DKr
EMU (Eurozone)	Euro	€
India	Rupee	Rs
Iran	Rial	IR
Japan	Yen	¥
Kuwait	Dinar	KD
Mexico	Peso	Ps
Norway	Krone	NKr
Saudi Arabia	Riyal	SR
Singapore	Dollar	S$
South Africa	Rand	R
Sweden	Krona	SKr
Switzerland	Franc	SFr
United Kingdom	Pound	£
United States	Dollar	$

TABLE 18.1

Table 18.1 International currency symbols

Work the Web

You have just returned from your dream backpacking trip to Vietnam, and you feel rich because you have 10,000 Vietnamese dong left over. You now need to convert this to euros. How much will you have? You can look up the current exchange rate and do the conversion yourself, or simply work the Web. We went to www.xe.com and used the currency converter on the site to find out. This is what we found:

Universal Currency Converter™ Results   Mid-market rates refreshed minutely. More currencies...

Currency Rates   Quick Links

Live rates at 2010.08.18 15:25:00 UTC

10,000.00 VND = 0.400331 EUR

Vietnam Dong   Euro
1 VND = 0.0000400331 EUR   1 EUR = 24,979.31 VND   View Chart

Trade Currencies. Click here!!

○ **Free Forex News**
○ XE Currency Rates
○ Monitor This Rate
○ Tell a friend
○ Free rates by email
○ Free converter for your site

Tip: Bookmark this conversion

It looks as though you left Vietnam just before you ran out of money!

QUESTIONS

1 Using this currency converter, what is the current EUR/VND exchange rate?

2 The website www.xe.com also lists cross-rates. What is the current ¥/€ cross-rate?

The many different types of participant in the foreign exchange market include the following:

1   Importers who pay for goods using foreign currencies

2   Exporters who receive foreign currency and may want to convert to the domestic currency

3   Portfolio managers who buy or sell foreign equities and bonds

4   Foreign exchange brokers who match buy and sell orders

5   Traders who 'make a market' in foreign currencies

6   Speculators who try to profit from changes in exchange rates

Exchange Rates

An **exchange rate** is simply the price of one country's currency expressed in terms of another country's currency. In practice, almost all trading of currencies takes place in terms of the US dollar, the yen and the euro. For example, both the Swiss franc and the Japanese yen are traded with their prices quoted in US dollars. Exchange rates are constantly changing. Our nearby Work the Web box shows you how to get up-to-the-minute rates.

> **exchange rate**
> The price of one country's currency expressed in terms of another country's currency.

Exchange Rate Quotations   Figure 18.1 reproduces exchange rate quotations as they appeared in the *Financial Times* in 2010. The three main columns give the number of units of foreign currency it takes to buy one dollar, euro or pound, respectively. Because this is the price in foreign currency with respect to dollars, euros or pounds, it is called an indirect quote. For example, the Thai baht is quoted at 49.2861 against the pound, which means that you can buy one British pound with 49.2861 Thai baht.

Cross-Rates and Triangle Arbitrage   The *Financial Times* quotes exchange rates in terms of the US dollar, euro and British pound. Using any of these currencies as the common denominator in quoting exchange rates greatly reduces the number of possible cross-currency quotes. For example, with five major currencies there would potentially be ten exchange rates instead of just four.[1] Also, the fact that one currency (the dollar, euro or pound) is used throughout decreases inconsistencies in the exchange rate quotations.

> **EXAMPLE**
> **18.1**
>
> # A Yen for Euros
>
> Suppose you have £1,000. Based on the rates in Fig. 18.1, how many South African rand can you get? Alternatively, if a Porsche costs €100,000, how many pounds will you need to buy it?
> The exchange rate in terms of rand per pound is 11.1965. Your £1,000 will thus get you
>
> $$£1,000 \times 11.1965 \text{ rand per } £1 = 11,197 \text{ rand}$$
>
> Because the exchange rate in terms of pounds per euro is 0.9056, you will need
>
> $$€100,000 \times £0.9056 \text{ per } € = £90,560$$

Earlier, we defined the cross-rate as the exchange rate for a foreign currency expressed in terms of another foreign currency. For example, suppose we observe the following for the Russian rouble and the Bahraini dinar:

Russian rouble per €1 = 45.8022
Bahraini dinar per €1 = 0.4831

FIGURE 18.1

Mar 16	Currency	DOLLAR Closing Mid	DOLLAR Day's Change	EURO Closing Mid	EURO Day's Change	POUND Closing Mid	POUND Day's Change
Argentina	(Peso)	3.8613	-0.0018	5.3124	0.0388	5.8664	0.0557
Australia	(A$)	1.0933	-0.0037	1.5042	0.0066	1.6611	0.0109
Bahrain	(Dinar)	0.3770	0.0000	0.5187	0.0040	0.5728	0.0057
Bolivia	(Boliviano)	7.0200	-	9.6581	0.0747	10.6655	0.1060
Brazil	(R$)	1.7622	-0.0048	2.4244	0.0122	2.6773	0.0193
Canada	(C$)	1.0149	-0.0068	1.3963	0.0015	1.5419	0.0050
Chile	(Peso)	523.950	7.7000	720.850	16.0917	796.037	19.4940
China	(Yuan)	6.8259	-0.0001	9.3911	0.0725	10.3706	0.1030
Colombia	(Peso)	1896.45	-6.0500	2609.14	11.9381	2881.28	19.5361
Costa Rica	(Colon)	527.820	-13.7850	726.176	-13.1971	801.918	-12.7654
Czech Rep.	(Koruna)	18.5347	-0.1446	25.5000	0.0624	28.1598	0.0624
Denmark	(DKr)	5.4081	-0.0426	7.4405	-0.0006	8.2166	0.0176
Egypt	(Egypt £)	5.4815	-0.0005	7.5415	0.0577	8.3281	0.0820
Estonia	(Kroon)	11.3727	-0.0887	15.6465		17.2785	0.0383
Hong Kong	(HK$)	7.7608	0.0017	10.6772	0.0850	11.7909	0.1199
Hungary	(Forint)	191.838	-2.1705	263.930	-0.9200	291.459	-0.3681
India	(Rs)	45.5350	-0.0500	62.6471	0.4167	69.1813	0.6123
Indonesia	(Rupiah)	9165.00	-	12609.2	97.6075	13924.4	138.391
Iran	(Rial)	9887.50	-	13603.2	105.302	15022.1	149.301
Israel	(Shk)	3.7263	-0.0023	5.1266	0.0366	5.6613	0.0529
Japan	(Y)	90.4300	-0.0350	124.414	0.9153	137.390	1.3129
One Month		90.4102	0.0001	124.390	0.0018	137.335	0.0024
Three Month		90.3755	0.0010	124.344	0.0021	137.235	0.0022
One Year		89.9980	0.0015	123.746	0.0012	136.495	-0.0109
Kenya	(Shilling)	76.9000	0.0500	105.799	0.8872	116.834	1.2364
Kuwait	(Dinar)	0.2879	-0.0003	0.3961	0.0026	0.4374	0.0039
Malaysia	(M$)	3.3200	-0.0010	4.5677	0.0339	5.0441	0.0486
Mexico	(New Peso)	12.5208	-0.0448	17.2261	0.0722	19.0228	0.1218
New Zealand	(NZ$)	1.4139	-0.0150	1.9453	-0.0053	2.1482	-0.0012
Nigeria	(Naira)	150.000	-0.4300	206.370	1.0105	227.895	1.6182
Norway	(NKr)	5.8260	-0.0494	8.0154	-0.0053	8.8515	0.0138
Pakistan	(Rupee)	84.4000	-0.1000	116.118	0.7624	128.229	1.1241
Peru	(New Sol)	2.8368	-0.0027	3.9029	0.0265	4.3100	0.0387
Philippines	(Peso)	45.7200	0.0075	62.9016	0.4972	69.4624	0.7017

	Currency	DOLLAR Closing Mid	DOLLAR Day's Change	EURO Closing Mid	EURO Day's Change	POUND Closing Mid	POUND Day's Change
Poland	(Zloty)	2.8203	-0.0334	3.8802	-0.0156	4.2849	-0.0078
Romania	(New Leu)	2.9738	-0.0219	4.0913	0.0018	4.5180	0.0120
Russia	(Rouble)	29.3013	-0.1480	40.3127	0.1099	44.5174	0.2198
Saudi Arabia	(SR)	3.7503	0.0001	5.1596	0.0401	5.6978	0.0567
Singapore	(S$)	1.3950	-0.0031	1.9192	0.0107	2.1194	0.0165
South Africa	(R)	7.3695	-0.0505	10.1390	0.0095	11.1965	0.0353
South Korea	(Won)	1132.65	-2.0500	1558.30	9.2642	1720.84	14.0194
Sweden	(SKr)	7.0648	-0.0691	9.7198	-0.0190	10.7336	0.0029
Switzerland	(SFr)	1.0557	-0.0077	1.4524	0.0006	1.6039	0.0042
Taiwan	(T$)	31.8155	0.0005	43.7718	0.3395	48.3373	0.4812
Thailand	(Bt)	32.4400	-0.1300	44.6310	0.1680	49.2861	0.2943
Tunisia	(Dinar)	1.3769	-0.0097	1.8944	0.0015	2.0920	0.0062
Turkey	(Lira)	1.5227	-0.0076	2.0949	0.0058	2.3134	0.0116
UAE	(Dirham)	3.6730	-	5.0533	0.0391	5.5804	0.0555
UK (0.6582)*	(£)	1.5193	0.0151	0.9056	-0.0020		
One Month		1.5190	0.0000	0.9058	0.0000		
Three Month		1.5185	0.0000	0.9061	0.0000		
One Year		1.5167	-0.0001	0.9066	0.0001		
Ukraine	(Hryvnia)	7.9875	0.0140	10.9892	0.0001	12.1355	0.1417
Uruguay	(Peso)	19.5500	0.0500	26.8969		29.7024	0.3704
USA	($)			1.3758	0.0106	1.5193	0.0151
One Month				1.3759	0.0000	1.5190	0.0000
Three Month				1.3759	0.0000	1.5185	0.0000
One Year				1.3750	0.0001	1.5167	-0.0001
Venezuela †(Bolivar Fuerte)		4.2947		5.9086	0.0458	6.5249	-0.0649
Vietnam	(Dong)	19090.0		26264.0	203.309	29003.4	288.259
Euro (0.7268)*	(Euro)	1.3758	0.0106			1.1043	0.0025
One Month		1.3759	0.0000			1.1041	
Three Month		1.3759	0.0000			1.1037	
One Year		1.3750	0.0001			1.1030	-0.0001
SDR	-	0.6508	-0.0024	0.8953	0.0036	0.9887	0.0062

Source: ft.com, 17 March 2010. © The Financial Times Ltd 2010.

Figure 18.1 Exchange rate quotations

Suppose the cross-rate is quoted as

$$\text{Dinar per rouble} = 0.01$$

What do you think?

The cross-rate here is inconsistent with the exchange rates. To see this, suppose you have €100. If you convert this to Russian roubles, you will receive

$$\text{€100} \times 45.8022 \text{ roubles per €1} = 4{,}580.22 \text{ roubles}$$

If you convert this to dinar at the cross-rate, you will have

$$4{,}580.22 \text{ roubles} \times 0.01 \text{ per rouble} = 45.8022 \text{ dinar}$$

However, if you just convert your euros to dinar without going through Russian roubles, you will have

$$\text{€100} \times 0.4831 \text{ dinar per €1} = 48.31 \text{ dinar}$$

What we see is that the dinar has two prices, 0.4831 dinar per €1 and 0.4580 dinar per €1, with the price we pay depending on how we get the dinar.

To make money, we want to buy low and sell high. The important thing to note is that dinar are cheaper if you buy them with euros, because you get 0.4831 dinar instead of just 0.4580 dinar. You should proceed as follows:

1   Buy 48.31 dinar for €100.

2   Use the 48.31 dinar to buy Russian roubles at the cross-rate. Because it takes 0.01 dinar to buy a Russian rouble, you will receive 48.31 dinar/0.01 roubles = 4,831 roubles.

3   Use the 4,831 roubles to buy euros. Because the exchange rate is 45.8022 roubles per euro, you receive 4,831 roubles/45.8022 = €105.48, for a round-trip profit of €5.48.

4   Repeat steps 1–3.

This particular activity is called *triangle arbitrage*, because the arbitrage involves moving through three different exchange rates:

0.4831 Dinar/€1

45.8022 Rouble/€1
= €0.02183/Rouble

Dinar/1 Rouble
= 100 Rouble/1 Dinar

To prevent such opportunities, it is not difficult to see that because a euro will buy you either 45.8022 Russian roubles or 0.4831 Bahraini dinar, the cross-rate must be

$$(0.4831 \text{ dinar/€1})/(45.8022 \text{ rouble/€1}) = 0.010548 \text{ dinar/rouble}$$

That is, the cross-rate must be 0.010548 Bahraini dinar per 1 Russian rouble. If it were anything else, there would be a triangle arbitrage opportunity.

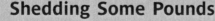

EXAMPLE
18.2

Shedding Some Pounds

According to Fig. 18.1, the exchange rates for the British pound against the euro and dollar are

$$\text{€/£} = 1.1043$$
$$\text{\$/£} = 1.5193$$

> The US dollar/euro exchange rate is quoted as \$1.3758/€. Show that the exchange rates are consistent.
>
> Taking the two British pound exchange rates, we find that the cross-rate is
>
> $$\$/€ = (\$/£)/(€/£) = 1.5193/1.1043 = 1.3758$$
>
> The exchange rates are consistent.

Types of Transaction There are two basic types of trade in the foreign exchange market: spot trades and forward trades. A **spot trade** is an agreement to exchange currency 'on the spot', which actually means that the transaction will be completed or settled within two business days. The exchange rate on a spot trade is called the **spot exchange rate**. Implicitly, all the exchange rates and transactions we have discussed so far have referred to the spot market.

A **forward trade** is an agreement to exchange currency at some time in the future. The exchange rate that will be used is agreed upon today and is called the **forward exchange rate**. A forward trade will normally be settled some time in the next 12 months.

If you look back at Fig. 18.1 you will see forward exchange rates quoted for the dollar, the euro and the pound. For example, the spot €/£ exchange rate is €1.1043/£. The one-year forward exchange rate is €1.1030/£. This means that you can buy a pound today for €1.1043, or you can agree to take delivery of a pound in one year and pay €1.1030 at that time.

Notice that the British pound is less expensive in the forward market (€1.1030 versus €1.1043). Because the British pound is less expensive in the future than it is today, it is said to be selling at a *discount* relative to the euro. For the same reason, the euro is said to be selling at a *premium* relative to the British pound.

Why does the forward market exist? One answer is that it allows businesses and individuals to lock in a future exchange rate today, thereby eliminating any risk from unfavourable shifts in the exchange rate.

spot trade
An agreement to trade currencies based on the exchange rate today for settlement within two business days.

spot exchange rate
The exchange rate on a spot trade.

forward trade
An agreement to exchange currency at some time in the future.

forward exchange rate
The agreed-upon exchange rate to be used in a forward trade.

EXAMPLE
18.3

Looking Forward

Suppose you are a British business and are expecting to receive one million euros in three months, and you agree to a forward trade to exchange your euros for pounds. Based on Fig. 18.1, how many pounds will you get in three months? Is the euro selling at a discount or a premium relative to the pound?

In Fig. 18.1 the spot exchange rate and the three-month forward rate in terms of pounds per euros are £0.9056 = €1 and £0.9061 = €1, respectively. If you expect €1 million in three months, then you will get €1 million × 0.9061 per pound = £906,100. Because it is less expensive to buy a pound in the forward market than in the spot market (£0.9061 versus £0.9056), the pound is said to be selling at a discount relative to the euro.

As we mentioned earlier, it is standard practice around the world (with a few exceptions) to quote exchange rates in terms of the dollar, euro or pound. This means that rates are quoted as the amount of currency per dollar, euro or pound. For the remainder of this chapter we shall stick with this form. Things can get extremely confusing if you forget this. Thus when we say things like 'the exchange rate is expected to rise', it is important to remember that we are talking about the exchange rate quoted as units of foreign currency per dollar, euro or pound.

18.3 Purchasing Power Parity

Now that we have discussed what exchange rate quotations mean, we can address an obvious question: what determines the level of the spot exchange rate? In addition, because we know that exchange rates change through time, we can ask the related question: what determines the rate of change in exchange rates? At least part of the answer in both cases goes by the name of **purchasing power parity** (PPP): the idea that the exchange rate adjusts to keep purchasing power constant among currencies. As we discuss next, there are two forms of PPP, *absolute* and *relative*.

> **purchasing power parity (PPP)** The idea that the exchange rate adjusts to keep purchasing power constant among currencies.

Absolute Purchasing Power Parity

The basic idea behind **absolute purchasing power parity** is that a commodity costs the same, regardless of what currency is used to purchase it or where it is selling. This is a straightforward concept. If a beer costs 50 kroner in Oslo, and the exchange rate is NKr10 per pound, then a beer costs NKr50/10 = £5 in London. In other words, absolute PPP says that £1 or €1 will buy you the same number of, say, beers anywhere in the world.

More formally, let S_0 be the spot exchange rate between the euro and the dollar today (time 0), and we are quoting exchange rates as the amount of foreign currency per euro. Let P_{US} and P_{euro} be the current US and euro prices, respectively, on a particular commodity, say, apples. Absolute PPP simply says that

$$P_{US} = S_0 \times P_{euro}$$

This tells us that the US price for something is equal to the euro price for that same something multiplied by the exchange rate.

The rationale behind PPP is similar to that behind triangle arbitrage. If PPP did not hold, arbitrage would be possible (in principle) if apples were moved from one country to another. For example, suppose apples are selling in Milan for €2 per bushel, whereas in New York the price is $3 per bushel. Absolute PPP implies that

$$P_{US} = S_0 \times P_{euro}$$
$$\$3 = S_0 \times €2$$
$$S_0 = \$3/€2 = \$1.50/€$$

That is, the implied spot exchange rate is $1.50 per euro. Equivalently, a dollar is worth €1/$1.5 = €0.667/$.

Suppose instead that the actual exchange rate is $1.2815/€. Starting with €2, a trader could buy a bushel of apples in Madrid, ship it to New York, and sell it there for $3. Our trader could then convert the $3 into euros at the prevailing exchange rate, $S_0 = \$1.2815/€$, yielding a total of $3/€1.2815 = €2.34. The round-trip gain would be 34 cents.

Because of this profit potential, forces are set in motion to change the exchange rate and/or the price of apples. In our example, apples would begin moving from Madrid to New York. The reduced supply of apples in Madrid would raise the price of apples there, and the increased supply in the US would lower the price of apples in New York.

In addition to moving apples around, apple traders would be busily converting dollars back into euros to buy more apples. This activity would increase the supply of dollars, and

In general, relative PPP says that the expected exchange rate at some time in the future, $E(S_t)$, is

$$E(S_t) = S_0 \times [1 + (h_{FC} - h_{HC})]^t$$

As we shall see, this is a very useful relationship.

Because we don't really expect absolute PPP to hold for most goods, we shall focus on relative PPP in our following discussion. Henceforth, when we refer to PPP without further qualification, we mean relative PPP.

It's All Relative

EXAMPLE 18.4

From Fig. 18.1, the Turkish lira-euro exchange rate is 2.0949 lira per euro. The inflation rate in Turkey over the next three years will be, say, 10 per cent per year, whereas the Eurozone inflation rate will be 2 per cent. Based on relative PPP, what will the exchange rate be in three years?

Because the Eurozone inflation rate is lower, we expect that a euro will become more valuable. The exchange rate change will be 10 per cent – 2 per cent = 8 per cent per year. Over three years the exchange rate will rise to

$$
\begin{aligned}
E(S_3) &= S_0 \times [1 + (h_{FC} - h_{HC})]^3 \\
&= 2.0949 \times [1 + (0.08)]^3 \\
&= 2.6390
\end{aligned}
$$

Currency Appreciation and Depreciation We frequently hear things like 'the euro strengthened (or weakened) in financial markets today' or 'the euro is expected to appreciate (or depreciate) relative to the pound.' When we say that the euro strengthens or appreciates, we mean that the value of a euro rises, so it takes more foreign currency to buy a euro.

What happens to the exchange rates as currencies fluctuate in value depends on how exchange rates are quoted. Because we are quoting them as units of foreign currency per home currency, the exchange rate moves in the same direction as the value of the home currency: it rises as the home currency strengthens, and it falls as the home currency weakens.

Relative PPP tells us that the exchange rate will rise if the home currency inflation rate is lower than the foreign country's. This happens because the foreign currency depreciates in value and therefore weakens relative to the home currency.

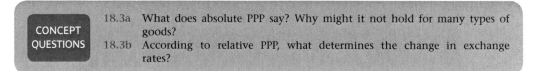

CONCEPT QUESTIONS	18.3a	What does absolute PPP say? Why might it not hold for many types of goods?
	18.3b	According to relative PPP, what determines the change in exchange rates?

18.4 Interest Rate Parity, Unbiased Forward Rates and the International Fisher Effect

The next issue we need to address is the relationship between spot exchange rates, forward exchange rates, and interest rates. To get started, we need some additional notation:

$$
\begin{aligned}
F_t &= \text{Forward exchange rate for settlement at time } t \\
R_{HC} &= \text{Home country nominal risk-free interest rate} \\
R_{FC} &= \text{Foreign country nominal risk-free interest rate}
\end{aligned}
$$

As before, we shall use S_0 to stand for the spot exchange rate. You can take the home country's nominal risk-free rate, R_{HC}, to be the home country's T-bill rate.

Covered Interest Arbitrage

We observe the following information about the British pound and the US dollar:

$$
\begin{aligned}
S_0 &= \$1.5193 \\
F_1 &= \$1.5167 \\
R_{HC} &= 2.13\% \\
R_{FC} &= 0.27\%
\end{aligned}
$$

where R_{FC} is the nominal risk-free rate in the United States. The period is one year, so F_1 is the 360-day forward rate.

Do you see an arbitrage opportunity here? Suppose you have £10,000 to invest, and you want a riskless investment. One option you have is to invest the £10,000 in a riskless UK investment such as a 360-day T-bill. If you do this, then in one period your £1 will be worth

$$
\begin{aligned}
\text{£ value in 1 period} &= £1 \times (1 + R_{HC}) \\
&= £10,213
\end{aligned}
$$

Alternatively, you can invest in the US risk-free investment. To do this, you need to convert your £10,000 to US dollars and simultaneously execute a forward trade to convert dollars back to pounds in one year. The necessary steps would be as follows:

1 Convert your £10,000 to £10,000 $\times S_0 = \$15,193$.

2 At the same time, enter into a forward agreement to convert US dollars back to pounds in one year. Because the forward rate is $1.5167, you will get £1 for every $1.5167 that you have in one year.

3 Invest your $15,193 in the United States at R_{FC}. In one year, you will have

$$
\begin{aligned}
\text{\$ value in 1 year} &= \$15,193 \times (1 + R_{FC}) \\
&= \$15,193 \times 1.0027 \\
&= \$15,234
\end{aligned}
$$

4 Convert your $15,234 back to pounds at the agreed-upon rate of $1.5167 = £1. You end up with

$$
\begin{aligned}
\text{£ value in 1 year} &= \$15,234/1.5167 \\
&= £10,044
\end{aligned}
$$

Notice that the value in one year resulting from this strategy can be written as

$$
\begin{aligned}
\text{£ value in 1 year} &= £10,000 \times S_0 \times (1 + R_{FC})/F_1 \\
&= £10,000 \times 1.5193 \times 1.0027/1.5167 \\
&= £10,044
\end{aligned}
$$

The return on this investment is apparently 0.44 per cent. This is lower than the 2.13 per cent we get from investing in the United Kingdom. Because both investments are risk-free, there is an arbitrage opportunity.

To exploit the difference in interest rates, you need to borrow, say, $10 million at the lower US rate and invest it at the higher British rate. What is the round-trip profit from doing this? To find out, we can work through the steps outlined previously:

1 Convert the $10 million at $1.5193/£ to get £6,581,979.

2 Agree to exchange dollars for pounds in one year at $1.5167 to the pound.

3 Invest the £6,581,979 for one year at $R_{UK} = 2.13$ per cent. You end up with £6,722,175.

4 Convert the £6,722,175 back to dollars to fulfil the forward contract. You receive £6,722,175 $\times$ $1.5167/£ = $10,195,522.

5 Repay the loan with interest. You owe $10 million plus 0.27 per cent interest, for a total of $10,027,000. You have $10,195,522, so your round-trip profit is a risk-free $168,522.

The activity that we have illustrated here goes by the name of *covered interest arbitrage*. The term *covered* refers to the fact that we are covered in the event of a change in the exchange rate because we lock in the forward exchange rate today.

Interest Rate Parity

If we assume that significant covered interest arbitrage opportunities do not exist, then there must be some relationship between spot exchange rates, forward exchange rates, and relative interest rates. To see what this relationship is, note that, in general, Strategy 1, from the preceding discussion, investing in a riskless home country investment, gives us $1 + R_{HC}$ for every unit of cash in home currency we invest. Strategy 2, investing in a foreign risk-free investment, gives us $S_0 \times (1 + R_{FC})/F_1$ for every unit of cash in home currency we invest. Because these have to be equal to prevent arbitrage, it must be the case that

> **interest rate parity (IRP)**
> The condition stating that the interest rate differential between two countries is equal to the percentage difference between the forward exchange rate and the spot exchange rate.

$$1 + R_{HC} = S_0 \times \frac{1 + R_{FC}}{F_1}$$

Rearranging this a bit gets us the famous **interest rate parity (IRP)** condition:

$$\frac{F_1}{S_0} = \frac{1 + R_{FC}}{1 + R_{HC}} \tag{18.3}$$

There is a very useful approximation for IRP that illustrates very clearly what is going on, and is not difficult to remember. If we define the percentage forward premium or discount as $(F_1 - S_0)/S_0$, then IRP says that this percentage premium or discount is *approximately* equal to the difference in interest rates:

$$(F_1 - S_0)/S_0 = R_{FC} - R_{HC} \tag{18.4}$$

Very loosely, what IRP says is that any difference in interest rates between two countries for some period is just offset by the change in the relative value of the currencies, thereby eliminating any arbitrage possibilities. Notice that we could also write

$$F_1 = S_0 \times [1 + (R_{FC} - R_{HC})] \tag{18.5}$$

In general, if we have t periods instead of just one, the IRP approximation is written as

$$F_t = S_0 \times [1 + (R_{FC} - R_{HC})]^t \tag{18.6}$$

EXAMPLE
18.5

Parity Check

Suppose the exchange rate for the South African rand, S_0, is currently R13.0745 = €1. If the interest rate in the Eurozone is R_{Euro} = 2.12 per cent and the interest rate in South Africa is R_{SA} = 10.95 per cent, then what must the forward rate be to prevent covered interest arbitrage?

From IRP, we have

$$\begin{aligned} F_1 &= S_0 \times [1 + (R_{SA} - R_{Euro})] \\ &= R13.0745 \times [1 + (0.1095 - 0.0212)] \\ &= R13.0745 \times 1.0883 \\ &= R14.2290 \end{aligned}$$

Notice that the rand will sell at a discount relative to the euro. (Why?)

Forward Rates and Future Spot Rates

In addition to PPP and IRP, we need to discuss one more basic relationship. What is the connection between the forward rate and the expected future spot rate? The **unbiased forward rates (UFR)** condition says that the forward rate, F_1, is equal to the *expected* future spot rate, $E(S_1)$:

$$F_1 = E(S_1)$$

With t periods, UFR would be written as

$$F_t = E(S_t)$$

> **unbiased forward rates (UFR)**
> The condition stating that the current forward rate is an unbiased predictor of the future spot exchange rate.

Loosely, the UFR condition says that, on average, the forward exchange rate is equal to the future spot exchange rate.

If we ignore risk, then the UFR condition should hold. Suppose the forward rate for the South African rand is consistently lower than the future spot rate by, say, 10 rand. This means that anyone who wanted to convert euros to rand in the future would consistently get more rand by not agreeing to a forward exchange. The forward rate would have to rise to get anyone interested in a forward exchange.

Similarly, if the forward rate were consistently higher than the future spot rate, then anyone who wanted to convert rand to euros would get more euros per rand by not agreeing to a forward trade. The forward exchange rate would have to fall to attract such traders.

For these reasons, the forward and actual future spot rates should be equal to each other on average. What the future spot rate will actually be is uncertain, of course. The UFR condition may not hold if traders are willing to pay a premium to avoid this uncertainty. If the condition does hold, then the 180-day forward rate that we see today should be an unbiased predictor of what the exchange rate will actually be in 180 days.

Putting It All Together

We have developed three relationships, PPP, IRP and UFR, that describe the interaction between key financial variables such as interest rates, exchange rates and inflation rates. We now explore the implications of these relationships as a group.

Uncovered Interest Parity   To start, it is useful to collect our international financial market relationships in one place:

$$\text{PPP: } E(S_1) = S_0 \times [1 + (h_{FC} - h_{HC})]$$
$$\text{IRP: } F_1 = S_0 \times [1 + (R_{FC} - R_{HC})]$$
$$\text{UFR: } F_1 = E(S_1)$$

We begin by combining UFR and IRP. Because we know that $F_1 = E(S_1)$ from the UFR condition, we can substitute $E(S_1)$ for F_1 in IRP. The result is

$$\text{UIP: } E(S_1) = S_0 \times [1 + (R_{FC} - R_{HC})] \qquad \textbf{(18.7)}$$

> **uncovered interest parity (UIP)**
> The condition stating that the expected percentage change in the exchange rate is equal to the difference in interest rates.

This important relationship is called **uncovered interest parity (UIP)**, and it will play a key role in our international capital budgeting discussion that follows. With t periods, UIP becomes

$$E(S_t) = S_0 \times [1 + (R_{FC} - R_{HC})]^t \qquad \textbf{(18.8)}$$

The International Fisher Effect   Next, we compare PPP and UIP. Both of them have $E(S_1)$ on the left-hand side, so their right-hand sides must be equal. We thus have that

> **international Fisher effect (IFE)**
> The theory that real interest rates are equal across countries.

$$S_0 \times [1 + (h_{FC} - h_{HC})] = S_0 \times [1 + (R_{FC} - R_{HC})]$$
$$h_{FC} - h_{HC} = R_{FC} - R_{HC}$$

This tells us that the difference in returns between the home country and a foreign country is just equal to the difference in inflation rates. Rearranging this slightly gives us the **international Fisher effect (IFE)**:

$$\text{IFE: } R_{HC} - h_{HC} = R_{FC} - h_{FC} \qquad (18.9)$$

The IFE says that *real* rates are equal across countries.[2]

The conclusion that real returns are equal across countries is really basic economics. If real returns were higher in, say, Britain than in the Eurozone, money would flow out of Eurozone financial markets and into British markets. Asset prices in Britain would rise and their returns would fall. At the same time, asset prices in Europe would fall and their returns would rise. This process acts to equalize real returns.

Having said all this, we need to note a couple of things. First of all, we really haven't explicitly dealt with risk in our discussion. We might reach a different conclusion about real returns once we do, particularly if people in different countries have different tastes and attitudes towards risk. Second, there are many barriers to the movement of money and capital around the world. Real returns might be different in two different countries for long periods of time if money can't move freely between them.

Despite these problems, we expect that capital markets will become increasingly internationalized. As this occurs, any differences in real rates that do exist will probably diminish. The laws of economics have very little respect for national boundaries.

CONCEPT QUESTIONS

18.4a What is covered interest arbitrage?
18.4b What is the international Fisher effect?

18.5 International Capital Budgeting

Kihlstrom Equipment, a US-based international company, is evaluating an overseas investment. Kihlstrom's exports of drill bits have increased to such a degree that it is considering building a distribution centre in France. The project will cost €2 million to launch. The cash flows are expected to be €0.9 million a year for the next three years.

The current spot exchange rate for euros is €0.5. Recall that this is euros per dollar, so a euro is worth $1/0.5 = $2. The risk-free rate in the United States is 5 per cent, and the risk-free rate in the Eurozone is 7 per cent. Note that the exchange rate and the two interest rates are observed in financial markets, not estimated.[3] Kihlstrom's required return on dollar investments of this sort is 10 per cent.

Should Kihlstrom take this investment? As always, the answer depends on the NPV; but how do we calculate the net present value of this project in US dollars? There are two basic methods:

1 *The home currency approach*: Convert all the euro cash flows into dollars, and then discount at 10 per cent to find the NPV in dollars. Notice that for this approach we have to come up with the future exchange rates to convert the future projected euro cash flows into dollars.

2 *The foreign currency approach*: Determine the required return on euro investments, and then discount the euro cash flows to find the NPV in euros. Then convert this euro NPV to a dollar NPV. This approach requires us to somehow convert the 10 per cent dollar required return to the equivalent euro required return.

The difference between these two approaches is primarily a matter of when we convert from euros to dollars. In the first case we convert before estimating the NPV. In the second case we convert after estimating the NPV.

It might appear that the second approach is superior, because we have to come up with only one number, the euro discount rate. Furthermore, because the first approach requires us to forecast future exchange rates, it probably seems that there is greater room for error with this approach. As we illustrate next, however, based on our previous results, the two approaches are really the same.

Method 1: The Home Currency Approach

To convert the projected future cash flows into dollars, we shall invoke the uncovered interest parity, or UIP, relation to come up with the projected exchange rates. Based on our earlier discussion, the expected exchange rate at time t, $E(S_t)$, is

$$E(S_t) = S_0 \times [1 + (R_\epsilon - R_{US})]^t$$

where R_ϵ stands for the nominal risk-free rate in the Eurozone. Because R_ϵ is 7 per cent, R_{US} is 5 per cent, and the current exchange rate (S_0) is €0.5:

$$E(S_t) = 0.5 \times [1 + (0.07 - 0.05)]^t$$
$$= 0.5 \times 1.02^t$$

The projected exchange rates for the drill bit project are thus

Year	Expected exchange rate
1	€0.5 × 1.02^1 = €0.5100
2	€0.5 × 1.02^2 = €0.5202
3	€0.5 × 1.02^3 = €0.5306

Using these exchange rates, along with the current exchange rate, we can convert all of the euro cash flows to dollars (note that all of the cash flows in this example are in millions):

Year	(1) Cash flow in € millions	(2) Expected exchange rate (€/$)	(3) Cash flow in $ millions (1)/(2)
0	−2.0	0.5000	−4.00
1	0.9	0.5100	1.76
2	0.9	0.5202	1.73
3	0.9	0.5306	1.70

To finish off, we calculate the NPV in the ordinary way:

$$NPV_\$ = -\$4 + \$1.76/1.10 + \$1.73/1.10^2 + \$1.70/1.10^3$$
$$= \$0.3 \text{ million}$$

So the project appears to be profitable.

Method 2: The Foreign Currency Approach

Kihlstrom requires a nominal return of 10 per cent on the dollar-denominated cash flows. We need to convert this to a rate suitable for euro-denominated cash flows. Based on the international Fisher effect, we know that the difference in the nominal rates is

$$R_{€} - R_{US} = h_{€} - h_{US}$$
$$= 7\% - 5\%$$
$$= 2\%$$

The appropriate discount rate for estimating the euro cash flows from the drill bit project is approximately equal to 10 per cent plus an extra 2 per cent to compensate for the greater euro inflation rate.

If we calculate the NPV of the euro cash flows at this rate, we get

$$NPV_{€} = -€2 + €0.9/1.12 + €0.9/1.12^2 + €0.9/1.12^3$$
$$= €0.16 \text{ million}$$

The NPV of this project is €0.16 million. Taking this project makes us €0.16 million richer today. What is this in dollars? Because the exchange rate today is €0.5, the dollar NPV of the project is

$$NPV_{\$} = NPV_{€}/S_0$$
$$= €0.16/0.5$$
$$= \$0.3 \text{ million}$$

This is the same dollar NPV that we previously calculated.

The important thing to recognize from our example is that the two capital budgeting procedures are actually the same, and will always give the same answer.[4] In this second approach, the fact that we are implicitly forecasting exchange rates is simply hidden. Even so, the foreign currency approach is computationally a little easier.

Unremitted Cash Flows

The previous example assumed that all after-tax cash flows from the foreign investment could be remitted to (paid out to) the parent firm. Actually, substantial differences can exist between the cash flows generated by a foreign project and the amount that can actually be remitted, or 'repatriated', to the parent firm.

A foreign subsidiary can remit funds to a parent in many forms, including the following:

- Dividends

- Management fees for central services

- Royalties on the use of trade names and patents

However cash flows are repatriated, international firms must pay special attention to remittances, because there may be current and future controls on remittances. Many governments are sensitive to the charge of being exploited by foreign national firms. In such cases, governments are tempted to limit the ability of international firms to remit cash flows. Funds that cannot currently be remitted are sometimes said to be *blocked*.

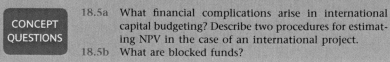

CONCEPT QUESTIONS

18.5a What financial complications arise in international capital budgeting? Describe two procedures for estimating NPV in the case of an international project.

18.5b What are blocked funds?

exchange rate risk
The risk related to having international operations in a world where relative currency values vary.

18.6 Exchange Rate Risk

Exchange rate risk is the natural consequence of international operations in a world where relative currency values move up and down. Managing exchange rate risk is an important part of international finance. As we discuss next, there are three different types of exchange rate risk, or exposure: short-run exposure, long-run exposure, and translation exposure.

Short-Run Exposure

The day-to-day fluctuations in exchange rates create short-run risks for international firms. Most such firms have contractual agreements to buy and sell goods in the near future at set prices. When different currencies are involved, such transactions have an extra element of risk.

For example, imagine that you are importing imitation pasta from Italy and reselling it in the United Kingdom under the Impasta brand name. Your largest customer has ordered 10,000 cases of Impasta. You place the order with your supplier today, but you won't pay until the goods arrive in 60 days. Your selling price is £6 per case. Your cost is €8.4 per case, and the exchange rate is currently €1.50, so it takes €1.50 to buy £1.

At the current exchange rate, your cost in pounds of filling the order is €8.4/0.5 = £5.60 per case, so your pre-tax profit on the order is 10,000 × (£6 − 5.60) = £4,000. However, the exchange rate in 60 days will probably be different, so your profit will depend on what the future exchange rate turns out to be.

For example, if the rate goes to €1.6, your cost is €8.4/1.6 = £5.25 per case. Your profit goes to £7,500. If the exchange rate goes to, say, €1.4, then your cost is €8.4/1.4 = £6, and your profit is zero.

The short-run exposure in our example can be reduced or eliminated in several ways. The most obvious way is by entering into a forward exchange agreement to lock in an exchange rate. For example, suppose the 60-day forward rate is €1.58. What will be your profit if you hedge? What profit should you expect if you don't?

If you hedge, you lock in an exchange rate of €1.58. Your cost in pounds will thus be €8.4/1.58 = £5.32 per case, so your profit will be 10,000 × (£6 − 5.32) = £6,800. If you don't hedge, then, assuming that the forward rate is an unbiased predictor (in other words, assuming the UFR condition holds), you should expect that the exchange rate will actually be €1.58 in 60 days. You should expect to make £6,800.

Alternatively, if this strategy is not feasible, you could simply borrow the pounds today, convert them into euros, and invest the euros for 60 days to earn some interest. Based on IRP, this amounts to entering into a forward contract.

Long-Run Exposure

In the long run, the value of a foreign operation can fluctuate because of unanticipated changes in relative economic conditions. For example, imagine that we own a labour-intensive assembly operation located in another country to take advantage of lower wages. Through time, unexpected changes in economic conditions can raise the foreign wage levels to the point where the cost advantage is eliminated, or even becomes negative.

The impact of changes in exchange rate levels can be substantial. For example, during early 2010 the euro varied between €1.15/£ and €1.10/£, with it strengthening over the period and then weakening because of the Greek debt crisis. This meant that Eurozone manufacturers took home less for each pound's worth of sales they made, depending on when they traded. Currency gains and losses can be enormous. For example, during 2009 Barclays lost £853 million as a result of exchange rate changes. This compares with a gain of £2,233 million in 2008.

Hedging long-run exposure is more difficult than hedging short-term risks. For one thing, organized forward markets don't exist for such long-term needs. Instead, the primary option that firms have is to try to match up foreign currency inflows and outflows. The same thing goes for matching foreign-currency-denominated assets and liabilities. For example, a firm that sells in a foreign country might try to concentrate its raw material purchases and labour expense in that country. In that way, the home currency values of its revenues and costs will move up and down together. Probably the best examples of this type of hedging are the so-called *transplant auto manufacturers* such as BMW, Honda, Mercedes and Toyota, which now build in the United States a substantial portion of the cars they sell there, thereby obtaining some degree of immunization against exchange rate movements.

For example, BMW produces 160,000 cars in the US and exports about 100,000 of them. The costs of manufacturing the cars are paid mostly in dollars; when BMW exports the cars to Europe, it receives euros. When the dollar weakens, these vehicles become more profitable for BMW. At the same time, BMW exports about 217,000 cars to the United States each year. The costs of manufacturing these imported cars are mostly in euros, so they become less profitable when the dollar weakens. Taken together, these gains and losses tend to offset each other and provide BMW with a natural hedge.

Similarly, a firm can reduce its long-run exchange rate risk by borrowing in the foreign country. Fluctuations in the value of the foreign subsidiary's assets will then be at least partially offset by changes in the value of the liabilities.

Translation Exposure

When a British company calculates its accounting net income and EPS for some period, it must 'translate' everything into pounds. This can create some problems for the accountants when there are significant foreign operations. In particular, two issues arise:

1 What is the appropriate exchange rate to use for translating each balance sheet account?

2 How should balance sheet accounting gains and losses from foreign currency translation be handled?

To illustrate the accounting problem, suppose we started a small foreign subsidiary in Lilliputia a year ago. The local currency is the gulliver, abbreviated GL. At the beginning of the year, the exchange rate was GL2 = €1, and the balance sheet in gullivers looked like this:

	GL		GL
Assets	1,000	Liabilities	500
		Equity	500

At two gullivers to the euro, the beginning balance sheet in euros was as follows:

	€		€
Assets	500	Liabilities	250
		Equity	250

Lilliputia is a quiet place, and nothing at all actually happened during the year. As a result, net income was zero (before consideration of exchange rate changes). However, the exchange rate did change to 4 gullivers = €1, purely because the Lilliputian inflation rate is much higher than the Eurozone inflation rate.

Because nothing happened, the accounting ending balance sheet in gullivers is the same as the beginning one. However, if we convert it to euros at the new exchange rate, we get

	€		€
Assets	250	Liabilities	125
		Equity	125

Notice that the value of the equity has gone down by €125, even though net income was exactly zero. Despite the fact that absolutely nothing really happened, there is a €125 accounting loss. How to handle this €125 loss has been a controversial accounting question.

One obvious and consistent way to handle this loss is simply to report the loss on the parent's income statement. During periods of volatile exchange rates this kind of treatment can dramatically impact on an international company's reported EPS. This is a purely accounting phenomenon; but, even so, such fluctuations are disliked by some financial managers.

The current approach to handling translation gains and losses is based on rules set out in the International Accounting Standards Board (IASB) International Accounting Standard No. 21 (IAS 21). For the most part, IAS 21 requires that all assets and liabilities be translated from the subsidiary's currency into the parent's currency using the exchange rate that currently prevails. Income and expenses are treated differently, and these are translated at the exchange rate that prevails at the time of the transaction, or at the average rate for the period when this is a reasonable approximation. In contrast to US accounting rules, the impact of translation gains and losses is explicitly recognized in net income. In the US, the translation gain or loss is not recognized until the underlying assets and liabilities are sold or otherwise liquidated.

Managing Exchange Rate Risk

For a large multinational firm the management of exchange rate risk is complicated by the fact that there can be many different currencies involved in many different subsidiaries. A change in some exchange rate will probably benefit some subsidiaries and hurt others. The net effect on the overall firm depends on its net exposure.

For example, suppose a firm has two divisions. Division A buys goods in Italy for euros and sells them in Britain for pounds. Division B buys goods in Britain for pounds and sells them in Italy for euros. If these two divisions are of roughly equal size in terms of their inflows and outflows, then the overall firm obviously has little exchange rate risk.

In our example the firm's net position in pounds (the amount coming in less the amount going out) is small, so the exchange rate risk is small. However, if one division, acting on its own, were to start hedging its exchange rate risk, then the overall firm's exchange rate risk would go up. The moral of the story is that multinational firms have to be conscious of their overall positions in a foreign currency. For this reason, management of exchange rate risk is probably best handled on a centralized basis.

CONCEPT QUESTIONS	18.6a	What are the different types of exchange rate risk?
	18.6b	How can a firm hedge short-run exchange rate risk? Long-run exchange rate risk?

18.7 Political Risk

One final element of risk in international investing is **political risk**. Political risk refers to changes in value that arise as a consequence of political actions. This is not a problem faced exclusively by international firms. For example, changes in British tax laws and regulations may benefit some British firms and hurt others, so political risk exists nationally as well as internationally.

> **political risk**
> Risk related to changes in value that arise because of political actions.

Some countries do have more political risk than others, however. When firms operate in these riskier countries, the extra political risk may lead the firms to require higher returns on overseas investments to compensate for the possibility that funds may be blocked, critical operations interrupted, or contracts abrogated. In the most extreme case the possibility of outright confiscation may be a concern in countries with relatively unstable political environments.

Political risk also depends on the nature of the business: some businesses are less likely to be confiscated, because they are not particularly valuable in the hands of a different owner. An assembly operation supplying subcomponents that only the parent company uses would not be an attractive 'takeover' target, for example. Similarly, a manufacturing operation that requires the use of specialized components from the parent is of little value without the parent company's co-operation.

Natural resource developments, such as copper mining or oil drilling, are just the opposite. Once the operation is in place, much of the value is in the commodity. The political risk for such investments is much higher for this reason. Also, the issue of exploitation is more pronounced with such investments, again increasing the political risk.

Corruption is a very big issue in many countries, and the payment of kickbacks or 'business facilitation fees' is the norm in many areas. Government officials, petty bureaucrats and cumbersome administrative regulations can significantly restrict the efficiency of international operations.

Many organizations present rankings of political risk in countries, and it is important that these are considered before any foreign direct investment takes place. Transparency International's 'perceptions of corruption' ranking is an example of such an assessment, and is presented in Table 18.2.

Political risk can be hedged in several ways, particularly when confiscation or nationalization is a concern. The use of local financing, perhaps from the government of the foreign country in question, reduces the possible loss, because the company can refuse to pay the debt in the event of unfavourable political activities. Based on our discussion in this section, structuring the operation in such a way that it requires significant parent company involvement to function is another way to reduce political risk.

TABLE 18.2

Country/territory	CPI 2009 score	Country/territory	CPI 2009 score
New Zealand	9.4	United States	7.5
Denmark	9.3	Belgium	7.1
Sweden	9.2	France	6.9
Switzerland	9.0	Cyprus	6.6
Finland	8.9	Spain	6.1
Netherlands	8.9	Portugal	5.8
Australia	8.7	South Africa	4.7
Iceland	8.7	Italy	4.3
Norway	8.6	Greece	3.8
Germany	8.0	China	3.6
Ireland	8.0	India	3.4
Austria	7.9	Thailand	3.4
Japan	7.7	Tanzania	2.6
United Kingdom	7.7	Somalia	1.1

Countries with lower numbers are more corrupt. *Source*: Transparency International.

Table 18.2 Perceptions of Corruption Index 2009

CONCEPT QUESTIONS

18.7a What is political risk?

18.7b What are some ways of hedging political risk?

Summary and Conclusions

The international firm has a more complicated life than the purely domestic firm. Management must understand the connection between interest rates, foreign currency exchange rates and inflation, and it must become aware of many different financial market regulations and tax systems. This chapter is intended to be a concise introduction to some of the financial issues that come up in international investing.

Our coverage has been necessarily brief. The main topics we discussed are the following:

1   *Some basic vocabulary*: We briefly defined some exotic terms such as LIBOR and Eurocurrency.

2   *The basic mechanics of exchange rate quotations*: We discussed the spot and forward markets, and how exchange rates are interpreted.

3   *The fundamental relationships between international financial variables*:

    (a)   Absolute and relative purchasing power parity, PPP.

    (b)   Interest rate parity, IRP.

    (c)   Unbiased forward rates, UFR.

    Absolute purchasing power parity states that £1 or €1 should have the same purchasing power in each country. This means that an orange costs the same whether you buy it in London or in Madrid.

    Relative purchasing power parity means that the expected percentage change in exchange rates between the currencies of two countries is equal to the difference in their inflation rates.

    Interest rate parity implies that the percentage difference between the forward exchange rate and the spot exchange rate is equal to the interest rate differential. We showed how covered interest arbitrage forces this relationship to hold.

    The unbiased forward rates condition indicates that the current forward rate is a good predictor of the future spot exchange rate.

4   *International capital budgeting*: We showed that the basic foreign exchange relationships imply two other conditions:

    (a)   Uncovered interest parity.

    (b)   The international Fisher effect.

    By invoking these two conditions, we learned how to estimate NPVs in foreign currencies and how to convert foreign currencies into home currencies to estimate NPV in the usual way.

5   *Exchange rate and political risk*: We described the various types of exchange rate risk, and discussed some commonly used approaches to managing the effect of fluctuating exchange rates on the cash flows and value of the international firm. We also discussed political risk, and some ways of managing exposure to it.

Chapter Review and Self-Test Problems

18.1   **Relative Purchasing Power Parity**   The inflation rate in the United Kingdom is projected at 3 per cent per year for the next several years. The Swiss inflation rate is projected to be 5 per cent during that time. The exchange rate is currently SFr 1.66. Based on relative PPP, what is the expected exchange rate in two years?

18.2   **Covered Interest Arbitrage**   The spot and 360-day forward rates on the Turkish lira to the euro are L2.1/€ and L1.9/€, respectively. Assume that the risk-free interest rate in Europe is 6 per cent, and the risk-free rate in Turkey is 4 per cent. Is there an arbitrage opportunity here? How would you exploit it?

Answers to Chapter Review and Self-Test Problems

18.1   Based on relative PPP, the expected exchange rate in two years, $E(S_2)$, is

$$E(S_2) = S_0 \times [1 + (h_{FC} - h_{HC})]^2$$

where h_{FC} is the Swiss inflation rate. The current exchange rate is SFr 1.66, so the expected exchange rate is

$$\begin{aligned} E(S_2) &= SFr1.66 \times [1 + (0.05 - 0.03)]^2 \\ &= SFr1.66 \times 1.02^2 \\ &= SFr1.73 \end{aligned}$$

18.2   Based on interest rate parity, the forward rate should be (approximately)

$$\begin{aligned} F_1 &= S_0 \times [1 + (R_{FC} - R_{HC})] \\ &= 2.1 \times [1 + (0.04 - 0.06)] \\ &= 2.06 \end{aligned}$$

Because the forward rate is actually L1.9/€, there is an arbitrage opportunity.

To exploit the arbitrage opportunity, you first note that euros are selling for L1.9 each in the forward market. Based on IRP, this is too cheap, because they should be selling for L2.06. So you want to arrange to buy euros with Turkish lira in the forward market. To do this, you can:

1   *Today*: Borrow, say, €1 million for 360 days. Convert it to L2.1 million in the spot market, and buy a forward contract at L1.9 to convert it back to euros in 360 days. Invest the L2.1 million at 4 per cent.

2   *In one year*: Your investment has grown to L2.1 million × 1.04 = L2.184 million. Convert this to euros at the rate of L1.9/€. You will have L2.184 million/1.9 = €1,149,474. Pay off your loan with 6 per cent interest at a cost of €1 million × 1.06 = €1,060,000 and pocket the difference of €89,474.

Concepts Review and Critical Thinking Questions

1   **Spot and Forward Rates [LO1]**   Suppose the exchange rate for the Norwegian krone is quoted as NKr9.96/£ in the spot market and NKr10/£ in the 90-day forward market.

  (a)   Is the British pound selling at a premium or a discount relative to the krone?

  (b)   Does the financial market expect the krone to weaken relative to the pound? Explain.

  (c)   What do you suspect is true about relative economic conditions in the United Kingdom and Norway?

2   **Exchange Rates [LO1]**   Suppose the rate of inflation in the Eurozone will be about 3 per cent higher than the UK inflation rate over the next several years. All other things being the same, what will happen to the euro versus pound exchange rate? What relationship are you relying on in answering?

3   **Bulldog Bonds [LO3]**   Which of the following most accurately describes a Bulldog bond?

  (a)   A bond issued by Vodafone in Frankfurt with the interest payable in British pounds.

  (b)   A bond issued by Vodafone in Frankfurt with the interest payable in euros.

  (c)   A bond issued by BMW in Germany with the interest payable in British pounds.

(d) A bond issued by BMW in London with the interest payable in British pounds.

(e) A bond issued by BMW worldwide with the interest payable in British pounds.

4 **Exchange Rates [LO1]** Are exchange rate changes necessarily good or bad for a particular company?

5 **International Risks [LO4]** At one point, Duracell International confirmed that it was planning to open battery-manufacturing plants in China and India. Manufacturing in these countries allows Duracell to avoid import duties of between 30 and 35 per cent that have made alkaline batteries prohibitively expensive for some consumers. What additional advantages might Duracell see in this proposal? What are some of the risks to Duracell?

6 **Multinational Corporations [LO3]** Given that many multinationals based in many countries have much greater sales outside their domestic markets than within them, what is the particular relevance of their domestic currency?

7 **Exchange Rate Movements [LO3]** Are the following statements true or false? Explain why.

(a) If the general price index in Great Britain rises faster than that in the United States, we would expect the pound to appreciate relative to the dollar.

(b) Suppose you are a German machine tool exporter, and you invoice all of your sales in foreign currency. Further suppose that the European Central Bank begins to undertake an expansionary monetary policy. If it is certain that the easy money policy will result in higher inflation rates in Germany relative to those in other countries, then you should use the forward markets to protect yourself against future losses resulting from the deterioration in the value of the euro.

(c) If you could accurately estimate differences in the relative inflation rates of two countries over a long period while other market participants were unable to do so, you could successfully speculate in spot currency markets.

8 **Exchange Rate Movements [LO3]** Some countries encourage movements in their exchange rate relative to those of some other country as a short-term means of addressing foreign trade imbalances. For each of the following scenarios, evaluate the impact the announcement would have on a Danish importer and a Danish exporter doing business with the foreign country:

(a) Officials in the Danish government announce that they are comfortable with a rising krone relative to the euro.

(b) The Bank of England announces that it feels the krone has been driven too low by currency speculators relative to the British pound.

(c) The European Central Bank announces that it will print billions of new euros and inject them into the economy in an effort to reduce the country's unemployment rate.

9 **International Capital Market Relationships [LO2]** We discussed five international capital market relationships: relative PPP, IRP, UFR, UIP and the international Fisher effect. Which of these would you expect to hold most closely? Which do you think would be most likely to be violated?

578   **Chapter 18** International Corporate Finance

connect Questions and Problems

1   Using Exchange Rates [LO1]   Take a look back at Fig. 18.1 to answer the following questions:

   (a)   If you have €100, how many British pounds can you get?

   (b)   How much is one pound worth?

   (c)   If you have 5 million pounds, how many euros do you have?

   (d)   Which is worth more, a New Zealand dollar or a Singapore dollar?

   (e)   Which is worth more, a Mexican peso or a Chilean peso?

   (f)   How many Mexican pesos can you get for an Israeli sheqel? What do you call this rate?

   (g)   Per unit, what is the most valuable currency of those listed? The least valuable?

2   Using the Cross-Rate [LO1]   Use the information in Fig. 18.1 to answer the following questions:

   (a)   Which would you rather have, €100 or £100? Why?

   (b)   Which would you rather have, 100 Swiss francs (SFr) or 100 Norwegian kroner (NKr)? Why?

   (c)   What is the cross-rate for Swiss francs in terms of Norwegian kroner? For Norwegian kroner in terms of Swiss francs?

3   Forward Exchange Rates [LO1]   Use the information in Fig. 18.1 to answer the following questions:

   (a)   What is the three-month forward rate for the US dollar per euro? Is the dollar selling at a premium or a discount? Explain.

   (b)   What is the three-month forward rate for British pounds in euros per pound? Is the euro selling at a premium or a discount? Explain.

   (c)   What do you think will happen to the value of the euro relative to the dollar and the pound, based on the information in the figure? Explain.

4   Using Spot and Forward Exchange Rates [LO1]   Suppose the spot exchange rate for the South African rand is R15/£ and the six-month forward rate is R16/£.

   (a)   Which is worth more, the British pound or the South African rand?

   (b)   Assuming absolute PPP holds, what is the cost in the United Kingdom of a Castle beer if the price in South Africa is R20? Why might the beer actually sell at a different price in the United Kingdom?

   (c)   Is the British pound selling at a premium or a discount relative to the South African rand?

   (d)   Which currency is expected to appreciate in value?

   (e)   Which country do you think has higher interest rates – the United Kingdom or South Africa? Explain.

5   Cross-Rates and Arbitrage [LO1]   Use Fig. 18.1 to answer the following questions

   (a)   What is the cross-rate in terms of Iranian rial per Thai baht?

   (b)   Suppose the cross-rate is 279 rial = 1 Thai baht. Is there an arbitrage opportunity here? If there is, explain how to take advantage of the mispricing.

6   Interest Rate Parity [LO2]   Use Fig. 18.1 to answer the following questions: Suppose interest rate parity holds, and the current one-year risk-free rate in the Eurozone is

3.8 per cent. What must the one-year risk-free rate be in Great Britain? In Japan? In the US?

7   **Interest Rates and Arbitrage [LO2]**   The treasurer of a major British firm has £30 million to invest for three months. The annual interest rate in the United Kingdom is 0.45 per cent per month. The interest rate in the Eurozone is 0.6 per cent per month. The spot exchange rate is €1.12/£, and the three-month forward rate is €1.15/€. Ignoring transaction costs, in which country would the treasurer want to invest the company's funds? Why?

8   **Inflation and Exchange Rates [LO2]**   Suppose the current exchange rate for the Polish zloty is Z5/£. The expected exchange rate in three years is Z5.2/£. What is the difference in the annual inflation rates for the United Kingdom and Poland over this period? Assume that the anticipated rate is constant for both countries. What relationship are you relying on in answering?

9   **Exchange Rate Risk [LO3]**   Suppose your company, which is based in Nantes, imports computer motherboards from Singapore. The exchange rate is S$1.9361/€1. You have just placed an order for 30,000 motherboards at a cost to you of 168.5 Singapore dollars each. You will pay for the shipment when it arrives in 90 days. You can sell the motherboards for €100 each. Calculate your profit if the exchange rate goes up or down by 10 per cent over the next 90 days. What is the break-even exchange rate? What percentage rise or fall does this represent in terms of the Singapore dollar versus the euro?

10   **Exchange Rates and Arbitrage [LO2]**   Suppose the spot and six-month forward rates on the Swedish krona are SKr11.95/£ and SKr12.00/£, respectively. The annual risk-free rate in the United Kingdom is 2.5 per cent, and the annual risk-free rate in Sweden is 1.13 per cent.

(a)   Is there an arbitrage opportunity here? If so, how would you exploit it?

(b)   What must the six-month forward rate be to prevent arbitrage?

11   **The International Fisher Effect [LO2]**   You observe that the inflation rate in the United Kingdom is 3.5 per cent per year, and that T-bills currently yield 3.9 per cent annually. What do you estimate the inflation rate to be in

(a)   Australia if short-term Australian government securities yield 5 per cent per year?

(b)   Canada if short-term Canadian government securities yield 7 per cent per year?

(c)   Taiwan if short-term Taiwanese government securities yield 10 per cent per year?

12   **Spot versus Forward Rates [LO1]**   Suppose the spot and three-month forward rates for the Indian rupee are R62.5/€ and R61.8/€, respectively.

(a)   Is the rupee expected to get stronger or weaker?

(b)   What would you estimate is the difference between the inflation rates of the Eurozone and India?

13.   **Expected Spot Rates [LO2]**   Suppose the spot exchange rate for the Tanzanian shilling is TSh2000/£. The inflation rate in the United Kingdom is 3.5 per cent and it is 8.6 per cent in Tanzania. What do you predict the exchange rate will be in one year? In two years? In five years? What relationship are you using?

14   **Capital Budgeting [LO2]**   The Dutch firm ABS Equipment has an investment opportunity in the United Kingdom. The project costs £12 million, and is expected to produce cash flows of £2.7 million in year 1, £3.5 million in year 2, and £3.3 million in year 3. The current spot exchange rate is €1.12/£ and the current

risk-free rate in the Eurozone is 2.12 per cent, compared with that in the United Kingdom of 2.13 per cent. The appropriate discount rate for the project is estimated to be 13 per cent, the Eurozone cost of capital for the company. In addition, the subsidiary can be sold at the end of three years for an estimated £7.4 million. What is the NPV of the project?

INTERMEDIATE
15–17

15 **Capital Budgeting [LO2]** As a German company, you are evaluating a proposed expansion of an existing subsidiary located in Switzerland. The cost of the expansion would be SFr27.0 million. The cash flows from the project would be SFr7.5 million per year for the next five years. The euro required return is 13 per cent per year, and the current exchange rate is SFr1.48/€. The going rate on EURIBOR is 8 per cent per year. It is 7 per cent per year on Swiss francs.

(a) What do you project will happen to exchange rates over the next four years?

(b) Based on your answer in (a), convert the projected franc flows into euro cash flows and calculate the NPV.

(c) What is the required return on franc cash flows? Based on your answer, calculate the NPV in francs and then convert to euros.

16 **Translation Exposure [LO3]** Atreides International has operations in Arrakis. The balance sheet for this division in Arrakeen solaris shows assets of 23,000 solaris, debt in the amount of 9,000 solaris, and equity of 14,000 solaris.

(a) If the current exchange ratio is 1.20 solaris per euro, what does the balance sheet look like in euros?

(b) Assume that one year from now the balance sheet in solaris is exactly the same as at the beginning of the year. If the exchange rate is 1.40 solaris per euro, what does the balance sheet look like in euros now?

(c) Rework part (b) assuming the exchange rate is 1.12 solaris per euro.

17 **Translation Exposure [LO3]** In the previous problem, assume the equity increases by 1,250 solaris as a result of retained earnings. If the exchange rate at the end of the year is 1.24 solaris per euro, what does the balance sheet look like?

CHALLENGE
18

18 **Using the Exact International Fisher Effect [LO2]** From our discussion of the Fisher effect in Chapter 6, we know that the actual relationship between a nominal rate R, a real rate r and an inflation rate h can be written as

$$1 + r = (1 + R)/(1 + h)$$

This is the *domestic* Fisher effect.

(a) What is the non-approximate form of the international Fisher effect?

(b) Based on your answer in (a), what is the exact form for UIP? (*Hint*: Recall the exact form of IRP, and use UFR.)

(c) What is the exact form for relative PPP? (*Hint*: Combine your previous two answers.)

(d) Recalculate the NPV for the Kihlstrom drill bit project (discussed in Sec. 18.5) using the exact forms for UIP and the international Fisher effect. Verify that you get precisely the same answer either way.

MINI CASE West Coast Yachts Goes International

Larissa Warren, the owner of West Coast Yachts, has been in discussions with a yacht dealer in Monaco about selling the company's yachts in Europe. Jarek Jachowicz, the dealer, wants to add West Coast Yachts to his current retail line. Jarek has told Larissa that he feels the retail sales will be approximately €5 million per month. All sales will be made in euros, and Jarek will retain 5 per cent of the retail sales as commission, which will be paid in euros. Because the yachts will be customized to order, the first sales will take place in one month. Jarek will pay West Coast Yachts for the order 90 days after it is filled. This payment schedule will continue for the length of the contract between the two companies.

Larissa is confident the company can handle the extra volume with its existing facilities, but she is unsure about any potential financial risks of selling yachts in Europe. In her discussion with Jarek she found that the current exchange rate is €1.12/£. At this exchange rate the company would spend 70 per cent of the sales income on production costs. This number does not reflect the sales commission to be paid to Jarek.

Larissa has decided to ask Dan Ervin, the company's financial analyst, to prepare an analysis of the proposed international sales. Specifically she asks Dan to answer the following questions:

1 What are the pros and cons of the international sales plan? What additional risks will the company face?

2 What will happen to the company's profits if the British pound strengthens? What if the British pound weakens?

3 Ignoring taxes, what are West Coast Yacht's projected gains or losses from this proposed arrangement at the current exchange rate of €1.12/£? What will happen to profits if the exchange rate changes to €1.20/£? At what exchange rate will the company break even?

4 How can the company hedge its exchange rate risk? What are the implications for this approach?

5 Taking all factors into account, should the company pursue international sales further? Why or why not?

Endnotes

1 There are four exchange rates instead of five because one exchange rate would involve the exchange of a currency for itself. More generally, it might seem that there should be 25 exchange rates with five currencies. There are 25 different combinations, but, of these, five involve the exchange of a currency for itself. Of the remaining 20, half are redundant because they are just the reciprocals of another exchange rate. Of the remaining 10, six can be eliminated by using a common denominator.

2 Notice that our result here is in terms of the approximate real rate, $R - h$ (see Chapter 6), because we used approximations for PPP and IRP. For the exact result see Problem 18 at the end of the chapter.

3 For example, the interest rates might be the short-term Eurodollar and euro deposit rates offered by large money centre banks.

4 Actually, there will be a slight difference because we are using the approximate relationships. If we calculate the required return as $1.10 \times (1 + 0.02) - 1 = 12.2\%$, then we get exactly the same NPV. See Problem 18 for more detail.

CHAPTER

19

Behavioural Finance

LEARNING OBJECTIVES

After studying this chapter, you should understand:

LO1   How behaviours such as overconfidence, over-optimism and confirmation bias can affect decision-making.

LO2   How framing effects can result in inconsistent and/or incorrect decisions.

LO3   How the use of heuristics can lead to suboptimal financial decisions.

LO4   The shortcomings of and limitations to market efficiency from the behavioural finance view.

EUROPEAN STOCK MARKETS WERE RAGING in the mid-2000s, and most stock indices nearly doubled in value between 2003 and 2007. Of course, that spectacular run came to a jarring halt when the global credit crunch imploded market valuations in October 2007. Take, for example, the UK, where the FTSE 100 Index fell by 50 per cent between its highest point in October 2007 and its lowest point in March 2009. The FTSE 350 Construction and Materials Index, an index of construction-related UK companies, rose from 1,561 in March 2003 to 6,386 in October 2007, a gain of about 300 per cent. It then fell like a rock to 2,472 by October 2008. The performance of the FTSE 100 over this period, and particularly the rise and fall of construction companies, has been described by many as a major bubble. The argument is that prices were inflated to economically ridiculous levels by market participants (banks in particular) before investors came to their senses, which then caused the bubble to pop and prices to plunge. Debate over whether the stock market movements of recent years have been bubbles has generated much controversy. In this chapter we introduce the subject of behavioural finance, which deals with questions such as how bubbles can come to exist. Some of the issues we discuss are quite controversial and unsettled. We shall describe competing ideas, present some evidence on both sides, and examine the implications for financial managers.

Be honest: do you think of yourself as a better than average driver? If you do, you are not alone. About 80 per cent of the people who are asked this question will say yes. Evidently, we tend to overestimate our abilities behind the wheel. Is the same true when it comes to making financial management decisions?

It will probably not surprise you when we say that human beings sometimes make errors in judgement. How these errors, and other aspects of human behaviour, affect financial managers falls under the general heading of *behavioural finance*. In this chapter our goal is to acquaint you with some common types of mistake, and their financial implications. As you will see, researchers have identified a wide variety of potentially damaging behaviours. By learning to recognize situations in which mistakes are common, you will become a better decision-maker, both in the context of financial management and elsewhere.

19.1 Introduction to Behavioural Finance

Sooner or later, you are going to make a financial decision that winds up costing you (and possibly your employer and/or shareholders) a lot of money. Why is this going to happen? You already know the answer. Sometimes you make sound decisions, but you get unlucky in the sense that something happens that you could not have reasonably anticipated. At other times (however painful it is to admit) you just make a bad decision, one that could (and should) have been avoided. The beginning of business wisdom is to recognize the circumstances that lead to poor decisions, and thereby cut down on the damage done by financial blunders.

> **behavioural finance**
> The area of finance dealing with the implications of reasoning errors on financial decisions.

As we have previously noted, the area of research known as **behavioural finance** attempts to understand and explain how reasoning errors influence financial decisions. Much of the research done in the behavioural finance area stems from work in cognitive psychology, which is the study of how people, including financial managers, think, reason, and make decisions. Errors in reasoning are often called *cognitive errors*. In the next several subsections we shall review three main categories of such errors: (1) biases; (2) framing effects; and (3) heuristics.

19.2 Biases

If your decisions exhibit systematic biases, then you will make systematic errors in judgement. The type of error depends on the type of bias. In this section, we discuss three particularly relevant biases: (1) overconfidence; (2) over-optimism; and (3) confirmation bias.

Overconfidence

Serious errors in judgement occur in the business world as a result of **overconfidence**. We are all overconfident about our abilities in at least some areas (recall our question about driving ability at the beginning of the chapter). Here is another example that we see a lot: ask yourself what grade you will receive in this course (in spite of the arbitrary and capricious nature of the professor). In our experience, almost everyone will either say 'A' or, at worst 'B'. Sadly, when this happens, we are always confident (but not overconfident) that at least some of our students are going to be disappointed.

> **overconfidence**
> The belief that your abilities are better than they really are.

In general, you are overconfident when you overestimate your ability to make the correct choice or decision. For example, most business decisions require judgements about the unknown future. The belief that you can forecast the future with precision is a common form of overconfidence.

Another good example of overconfidence comes from studies of equity investors. Researchers have examined large numbers of actual brokerage accounts to see how investors fare when they choose equities. Overconfidence by investors would cause them to overestimate their ability to pick the best equities, leading to excessive trading. The evidence supports this view. First, investors hurt themselves by trading. The accounts that have the most trading significantly underperform the accounts with the least trading, primarily because of the costs associated with trades.

A second finding is equally interesting. Accounts registered to men underperform those registered to women. The reason is that men trade more on average. This extra trading is consistent with evidence from psychology that men have greater degrees of overconfidence than women.

584 **Chapter 19** Behavioural Finance

Over-Optimism

> **over-optimism**
> Taking an overly optimistic view of potential outcomes.
>
> **confirmation bias**
> Searching for (and giving more weight to) information and opinion that confirms what you believe, rather than information and opinion to the contrary.

Over-optimism leads to overestimating the likelihood of a good outcome and underestimating the likelihood of a bad outcome. Over-optimism and overconfidence are related, but they are not the same thing. An overconfident individual could (over-confidently) forecast a bad outcome, for example.

Optimism is usually thought of as a good thing. Optimistic people have 'upbeat personalities' and 'sunny dispositions'. However, excessive optimism leads to bad decisions. In a capital budgeting context, overly optimistic analysts will consistently overestimate cash flows and underestimate the probability of failure. Doing so leads to upward-biased estimates of project NPVs, a common occurrence in the business world.

Confirmation Bias

When you are evaluating a decision, you collect information and opinions. A common bias in this regard is to focus more on information that agrees with your opinion, and to downplay or ignore information that doesn't agree with or support your position. This phenomenon is known as **confirmation bias**, and people who suffer from it tend to spend too much time trying to prove themselves right rather than searching for information that might prove them wrong.

Here is a classic example from psychology. Below are four cards. Notice that the cards are labelled *a*, *b*, 2 and 3. You are asked to evaluate the following statement: 'Any card with a vowel on one side has an even number on the other.' You are asked which of the four cards has to be turned over to decide whether the statement is true or false. It costs €100 to turn over a card, so you want to be economical as possible. What do you do?

You would probably begin by turning over the card with an *a* on it, which is correct. If we find an odd number, then we are done, because the statement is not correct.

Suppose we find an even number. What next? Most people will turn over the card with a 2. Is that the right choice? If we find a vowel, then we confirm the statement, but if we find a consonant, we don't learn anything. In other words, this card can't prove that the statement is wrong; it can only confirm it, so selecting this card is an example of confirmation bias.

Continuing, there is no point in turning over the card labelled '*b*', because the statement doesn't say anything about consonants, which leaves us with the last card. Do we have to turn it over? The answer is yes, because it might have a vowel on the other side, which would disprove the statement, but most people will choose the 2 card over the 3 card.

Confirmation bias can lead managers to ignore negative information about potential investments and focus only on that information which proves they are correct in their opinions. This can lead to a number of poor decisions that reduce firm value. For example, in 2007 most investors believed that the banking system was stable, and that the incredibly high levels of lending were sustainable in the long term. Even though the signs were there to see that people and companies were becoming over-indebted, most individuals didn't see the signals until it was too late.

CONCEPT QUESTIONS

19.2a What is overconfidence? How is it likely to be costly?
19.2b What is over-optimism? How is it likely to be costly?
19.2c What is confirmation bias? How is it likely to be costly?

19.3 Framing Effects

You are susceptible to framing effects if your decisions depend on how a problem or question is framed. Consider the following example. A disaster has occurred, 600 people are at risk, and you are in charge. You must choose between the two following rescue operations:

Scenario 1

Option A: Exactly 200 people will be saved.

Option B: There is a 1/3 chance that all 600 people will be saved and a 2/3 chance that no people will be saved.

Which would you choose? There is no necessarily right answer, but most people will choose Option A. Now suppose your choices are as follows:

Scenario 2

Option C: Exactly 400 people will die.

Option D: There is a 1/3 chance that nobody will die and a 2/3 chance that all 600 will die.

> **frame dependence** The tendency of individuals to make different (and potentially inconsistent) decisions, depending on how a question or problem is framed.

Now which do you pick? Again, there is no right answer, but most people will choose option D. Although most people will choose options A and D in our hypothetical scenarios, you probably see that doing so is inconsistent, because options A and C are identical, as are options B and D. Why do people make inconsistent choices? It's because the options are framed differently. The first scenario is positive, because it emphasizes the number that will be saved. The second is negative, because it focuses on losses, and people react differently to positive and negative framing, which is a form of **frame dependence.**

Loss Aversion

Here is another example that illustrates a particular type of frame dependence:

Scenario 1

Suppose we give you £1,000. You have the following choices:

Option A: You can receive another £500 for sure.

Option B: You can flip a fair coin. If the coin flip comes up heads, you get another £1,000, but if it comes up tails, you get nothing.

Scenario 2

Suppose we give you £2,000. You have the following choices:

Option C: You can lose £500 for sure.

Option D: You can flip a fair coin. If the coin flip comes up heads, you lose £1,000, but if it comes up tails, you lose nothing.

What were your answers? Did you choose option A in the first scenario and option D in the second? If that's what you did, you are guilty of focusing just on gains and losses, and not paying attention to what really matters, namely the impact on your wealth. However, you are not alone. About 85 per cent of the people who are presented with the first scenario choose option A, and about 70 per cent of the people who are presented with the second scenario choose option D.

If you look closely at the two scenarios, you will see that they are actually identical. You end up with £1,500 for sure if you pick option A or C, or else you end up with a

50–50 chance of either £1,000 or £2,000 if you pick option B or D. So you should pick the same option in both scenarios. Which option you prefer is up to you, but the point is that you should never pick option A in our first scenario and option D in our second one.

This example illustrates an important aspect of financial decision-making. Focusing on gains and losses instead of overall wealth is an example of narrow framing, and it leads to a phenomenon known as *loss aversion*. In fact, the reason why most people avoid option C in scenario 2 in our example is that it is expressed as a sure loss of £500. In general, researchers have found that individuals are reluctant to realize losses and will, for example, gamble at unfavourable odds to avoid doing so.

Loss aversion is also known as the *break-even effect*, because it frequently shows up as individuals and companies hang on to bad investments and projects (and perhaps even invest more), hoping that something will happen that will allow them to break even and thereby escape without a loss. For example, we discussed the irrelevance of sunk costs in the context of capital budgeting, and the idea of a sunk cost seems clear. Nonetheless, we constantly see companies (and individuals) throw good money after bad rather than just recognize a loss in the face of sunk costs.

How destructive is the break-even effect? Perhaps the most famous case occurred in 1995, when 28-year-old Nicholas Leeson caused the collapse of his employer, the 233-year-old Barings Bank. At the end of 1992 Mr Leeson had lost about £2 million, which he hid in a secret account. By the end of 1993 his losses were about £23 million, and they mushroomed to £208 million at the end of 1994.

Instead of admitting to these losses, Mr Leeson gambled more of the bank's money in an attempt to 'double up and catch up'. On 23 February 1995 Mr Leeson's losses were about £827 million, and his trading irregularities were uncovered. Although he attempted to flee from prosecution, he was caught, arrested, tried, convicted and imprisoned. Also, his wife divorced him.

Do you suffer from the break-even effect? Perhaps so. Consider the following scenario. You have just lost €78 somehow. You can just live with the loss, or you can make a bet. If you make the bet, there is an 80 per cent chance that your loss will grow to €100 (from €78) and a 20 per cent chance that your loss will be nothing. Do you take the loss or take the bet? We bet you choose the bet. If you do, you suffer from the break-even effect, because the bet is a bad one. Instead of a sure loss of €78, your expected loss from the bet is $0.80 \times €100 + 0.20 \times €0 = €80$.

In corporate finance, loss aversion can be quite damaging. We have already mentioned the pursuit of sunk costs. We also might see managers bypassing positive-NPV projects because they have the possibility of large losses (perhaps with low probability). Another phenomenon that we see is *debt avoidance*. As we discuss in our coverage of capital structure, debt financing generates valuable tax shields for profitable companies. Even so, there are hundreds of profitable companies listed on major stock exchanges that completely (or almost completely) avoid debt financing. Because debt financing increases the likelihood of losses, and even bankruptcy, this potentially costly behaviour could be due to loss aversion.

House Money

Casinos know all about a concept called *playing with house money*. They have found that gamblers are far more likely to take big risks with money that they have won from the casino (i.e., house money). Also, casinos have found that gamblers are not as upset about losing house money as they are about losing the money they brought with them to gamble.

It may seem natural for you to feel that some money is precious, because you earned it through hard work, sweat and sacrifice, whereas other money is less precious, because it came to you as a windfall. But these feelings are plainly irrational, because any cash you have buys the same amount of goods and services, no matter how you obtained that cash.

Let's consider another common situation to illustrate several of the ideas we have explored thus far. Consider the following two investments:

Investment 1: You bought 100 shares in Jayz plc for £35 per share. The shares immediately fell to £20 each.

Investment 2: At the same time you bought 100 shares in Streets plc for £5 per share. The shares immediately jumped to £20 each.

How would you feel about your investments? You would probably feel pretty good about your Streets investment and be unhappy with your Jayz investment. Here are some other things that might occur:

1   You might tell yourself that your Streets investment was a great idea on your part; you're a stock-picking genius. The drop in value on the Jayz shares wasn't your fault – it was just bad luck. This is a form of confirmation bias, and it also illustrates self-attribution bias, which is taking credit for good outcomes that occur for reasons beyond your control, while attributing bad outcomes to bad luck or misfortune.

2   You might be unhappy that your big winner was essentially nullified by your loser, but notice in our example that your overall wealth did not change. Suppose instead that shares in both companies didn't change in price at all, so that your overall wealth was unchanged. Would you feel the same way?

3   You might be inclined to sell your Streets shares to 'realize' the gain, but hold on to your Jayz shares in hopes of avoiding the loss (which is, of course, loss aversion). The tendency to sell winners and hold losers is known as the *disposition effect*. Plainly, the rational thing to do is to decide whether the equities are attractive investments at their new prices, and react accordingly.

Suppose you decide to keep both equities a little longer. Once you do, both decline to £15. You might now feel very differently about the decline, depending on which equity you looked at. With Jayz, the decline makes a bad situation even worse. Now you are down £20 per share on your investment. On the other hand, with Streets you only 'give back' some of your 'paper profit'. You are still way ahead. This kind of thinking is playing with house money; whether you lose from your original investment or from your investment gains is irrelevant.

Our Jayz and Streets example illustrates what can happen when you become emotionally invested in decisions such as equity purchases. When you add a new equity to your portfolio, it is human nature for you to associate the equity with its purchase price. As the share price changes through time, you will have unrealized gains or losses when you compare the current price with the purchase price. Through time, you will mentally account for these gains and losses, and how you feel about the investment depends on whether you are ahead or behind. This behaviour is known as *mental accounting*.

When you engage in mental accounting, you unknowingly have a personal relationship with each of your investments. As a result, it becomes harder to sell one of them. It is as if you have to 'break up' with this investment, or 'fire' it from your portfolio. As with personal relationships, these investment relationships can be complicated and, believe it or not, make selling shares or dropping projects difficult at times. What can you do about mental accounting? Legendary investor Warren Buffet offers the following advice: 'The investment doesn't know you own it. You have feelings about it, but it has no feelings about you. The investment doesn't know what you paid. People shouldn't get emotionally involved with their investments.'

Loss aversion, mental accounting and the house money effect are important examples of how narrow framing leads to poor decisions. Other, related types of judgement error have been documented. Here are a few examples:

1   *Myopic loss aversion*: This behaviour is the tendency to focus on avoiding short-term losses, even at the expense of long-term gains. For example, you might fail to invest in equities for long-term retirement purposes because you have a fear of loss in the near term. Another example is that managers may avoid investing in long-term projects with little positive cash flow for a number of years because they fear the impact the investment has on the firm's short-term earnings. Projects with shorter payback periods may be preferred in this case.

2 *Regret aversion*: This aversion is the tendency to avoid making a decision because you fear that, in hindsight, the decision would have been less than optimal. Regret aversion relates to myopic loss aversion.

3 *Endowment effect*: This effect is the tendency to consider something that you own to be worth more than it would be if you did not own it. Because of the endowment effect, people sometimes demand more money to give up something than they would be willing to pay to acquire it. The endowment effect can sometimes explain why acquiring firms find it so difficult to persuade shareholders of a target firm that the value of the target is less than the shareholders believe.

4 *Money illusion*: If you suffer from a money illusion, you are confused between real buying power and nominal buying power (i.e., you do not account for the effects of inflation).

CONCEPT QUESTIONS	19.3a	What is frame dependence? How is it likely to be costly?
	19.3b	What is loss aversion? How is it likely to be costly?
	19.3c	What is the house money effect? Why is it irrational?

19.4 Heuristics

Financial managers (and managers in general) often rely on rules of thumb, or **heuristics**, in making decisions. For example, a manager might decide that any project with a payback period of less than two years is acceptable, and therefore not bother with additional analysis. As a practical matter, this mental shortcut might be fine for most circumstances, but we know that sooner or later it will lead to the acceptance of a negative-NPV project.

heuristics
Shortcuts or rules of thumb used to make decisions.

affect heuristic
The reliance on instinct instead of analysis in making decisions.

The Affect Heuristic

We frequently hear business and political leaders talk about following their gut instinct. In essence, such people are making decisions based on whether the chosen outcome or path feels 'right' emotionally. Psychologists use the term *affect* (as in *affection*) to refer to emotional feelings, and the reliance on gut instinct is called the **affect heuristic**.

Reliance on instinct is closely related to reliance on intuition and/or experience. Both intuition and experience are important, and, used properly, help decision-makers to identify potential risks and rewards. However, instinct, intuition and experience should be viewed as complements to formal analysis, not substitutes. Overreliance on emotions in making decisions will almost surely lead (at least on occasion) to costly outcomes that could have been avoided with careful, structured thinking. An obvious example would be making capital budgeting decisions based on instinct rather than on market research and discounted cash flow analysis.

The Representativeness Heuristic

People often assume that a particular person, object or outcome is broadly representative of a larger class. For example, suppose an employer hired a graduate of your high-quality educational institution and, in fact, is quite pleased with that person. The employer might be inclined to look to your institution again for future employees, because the students are so good. Of course, in doing so, the employer is assuming that the recent hire is representative of all the students, which is an example of the **representativeness heuristic**. A little more generally, the representativeness heuristic is the reliance on stereotypes, analogies or limited samples to form opinions about an entire class.

representativeness heuristic
The reliance on instinct instead of analysis in making decisions.

Representativeness and Randomness

Another implication of the representativeness heuristic has to do with perceiving patterns or causes where none exist. For example, soccer fans generally believe that success breeds success. Suppose we look at the recent performance of two football players named Wayne and Cristiano. Both of these players have a 50 per cent goal to shoot ratio. But Wayne has just scored two goals in a row, whereas Cristiano has just missed two in a row. Researchers have found that if they ask 100 football fans which player has the better chance of scoring the next goal, 91 of them will say Wayne. Further, 84 of these fans believe that it is important for teammates to pass the ball to Wayne after he has scored two or three goals in a row.

But, and the sports fans among you will have a hard time with this, researchers have found that this (known as the *hot hands effect* from basketball) is an illusion. That is, players really do not deviate much from their long-run scoring averages – although fans, players, commentators and coaches think they do. Cognitive psychologists actually studied the shooting percentage of one professional basketball team for a season. Here is what they found:

Shooting percentages and the history of previous attempts	
Shooting percentage on next shot (%)	History of previous attempts
46	Has made 3 in a row
50	Has made 2 in a row
51	Has made 1 in a row
52	First shot of the game
54	Has missed 1 in a row
53	Has missed 2 in a row
56	Has missed 3 in a row

Detailed analysis of scoring data failed to show that players score or miss shots more or less frequently than what would be expected by chance. That is, statistically speaking, all the scoring percentages listed here are the same.

It is true that footballers score in streaks. But these streaks are within the bounds of long-run goal scoring percentages. So it is an illusion that players are either 'hot' or 'cold'. If you are a believer in the hot hand (or hot foot), however, you are likely to reject these facts, because you 'know better' from watching your favourite teams over the years. If you do, you are being fooled by randomness.

The *clustering illusion* is our human belief that random events that occur in clusters are not really random. For example, it strikes most people as very unusual if heads comes up four times in a row during a series of coin flips. However, if a fair coin is flipped 20 times, there is about a 50 per cent chance of getting four heads in a row. Ask yourself, if you flip four heads in a row, do you think you have a 'hot hand' at coin flipping?

The Gambler's Fallacy

People commit the *gambler's fallacy* when they assume that a departure from what occurs on average, or in the long run, will be corrected in the short run. Interestingly, some people suffer from both the hot-hand illusion (which predicts continuation in the short run) and the gambler's fallacy (which predicts reversal in the short run)! The idea is that because an event has not happened recently, it has become overdue and is more likely to occur. People sometimes refer (wrongly) to the law of averages in such cases.

Roulette is a random gambling game where gamblers can make various bets on the spin of the wheel. There are 37 numbers on a roulette table: 1 green one, 18 red ones, and 18 black ones. One possible bet is whether the spin will result in a red number or in a black number. Suppose a red number has appeared five times in a row. Gamblers will often

The 3Com/Palm Mispricing   On 2 March 2000 3Com, a profitable provider of computer networking products and services, sold 5 per cent of its Palm subsidiary to the public via an initial public offering (IPO). 3Com planned to distribute the remaining Palm shares to 3Com shareholders at a later date. Under the plan, if you owned one share of 3Com, you would receive 1.5 shares of Palm. So, after 3Com sold part of Palm via the IPO, investors could buy Palm shares directly, or they could buy them indirectly by purchasing shares of 3Com.

What makes this case interesting is what happened in the days that followed the Palm IPO. If you owned one 3Com share, you would be entitled, eventually, to 1.5 shares of Palm. Therefore each 3Com share should be worth *at least* 1.5 times the value of each Palm share. We say *at least*, because the other parts of 3Com were profitable. As a result, each 3Com share should have been worth much more than 1.5 times the value of one Palm share. But, as you might guess, things did not work out this way.

The day before the Palm IPO, shares in 3Com sold for $104.13. After the first day of trading, Palm closed at $95.06 per share. Multiplying $95.06 by 1.5 results in $142.59, which is the minimum value one would expect to pay for 3Com. But the day Palm closed at $95.06, 3Com shares closed at $81.81, more than $60 lower than the price implied by Palm. It gets stranger.

A 3Com price of $81.81 when Palm is selling for $95.06 implies that the market values the rest of 3Com's businesses (per share) at: $81.81 − 142.59 = −$60.78. Given the number of 3Com shares outstanding at the time, this means the market placed a *negative value* of about −$22 billion on the rest of 3Com's businesses. Of course, a share price cannot be negative. This means, then, that the price of Palm relative to 3Com was much too high, and investors should have bought and sold such that the negative value was instantly eliminated.

What happened? As you can see in Fig. 19.1, the market valued 3Com and Palm shares in such a way that the non-Palm part of 3Com had a negative value for about two months, from 2 March 2000 until 8 May 2000. Even then, it took approval by the US tax authorities for 3Com to proceed with the planned distribution of Palm shares before the non-Palm part of 3Com once again had a positive value.

FIGURE
19.1

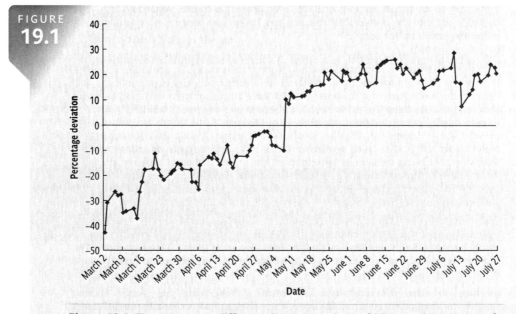

Figure 19.1 The percentage difference between 1 share of 3Com and 1.5 shares of Palm, 2 March 2000 to 27 July 2000

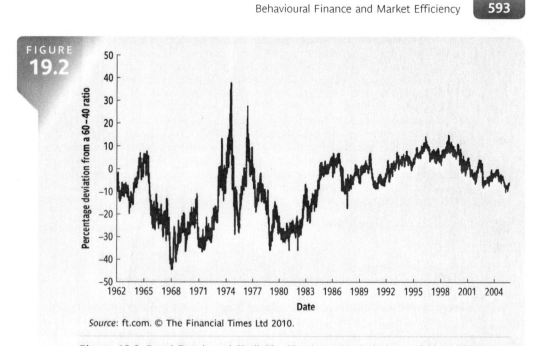

FIGURE
19.2

Source: ft.com. © The Financial Times Ltd 2010.

Figure 19.2 Royal Dutch and Shell 60–40 price ratio deviations, 1962 to 2005

The Royal Dutch/Shell Price Ratio   Another fairly well-known example of an apparent mispricing involves two large oil companies. In 1907 Royal Dutch of the Netherlands and Shell of the UK agreed to merge their business enterprises and split operating profits on a 60–40 basis. So, whenever the share prices of Royal Dutch and Shell are not in a 60–40 ratio, there is a potential opportunity to make an arbitrage profit.

Figure 19.2 contains a plot of the daily deviations from the 60–40 ratio of the Royal Dutch price to the Shell price. If the prices of Royal Dutch and Shell are in a 60–40 ratio, there is a zero percentage deviation. If the price of Royal Dutch is too high compared with the Shell price, there is a positive deviation. If the price of Royal Dutch is too low compared with the price of Shell, there is a negative deviation. As you can see in Fig. 19.2, there have been large and persistent deviations from the 60–40 ratio. In fact, the ratio is seldom at 60–40 for most of the time from 1962 until mid-2005 (when the companies merged).

Bubbles and Crashes

A **bubble** occurs when market prices soar far in excess of what normal and rational analysis would suggest. Investment bubbles eventually pop, because they are not based on fundamental values. When a bubble does pop, investors find themselves holding assets with plummeting values.

A **crash** is a significant and sudden drop in market-wide values. Crashes are generally associated with a bubble. Typically, a bubble lasts much longer than a crash. A bubble can form over weeks, months, or even years. Crashes, on the other hand, are sudden, generally lasting less than a week. However, the disastrous financial aftermath of a crash can last for years.

The High-Technology Bubble and Crash   How many websites do you think existed at the end of 1994? Would you believe only about 10,000? By the end of 1999 the number of active websites stood at about 9,500,000, and at the beginning of 2010 there were about 108,000,000 active websites.

bubble
A situation where observed prices soar far higher than fundamentals and rational analysis would suggest.

crash
A situation where market prices collapse significantly and suddenly.

By the mid-1990s the rise in Internet use and its international growth potential had fuelled widespread excitement over the 'new economy'. Investors did not seem to care about solid business plans – only big ideas. Investor euphoria led to a surge in Internet and high-technology IPOs. Of course, the lack of solid business models doomed many of the newly formed companies. Many of them suffered huge losses, and some folded relatively shortly after their IPOs.

An example of the craziness in valuations that occurred during the time is Think Tools AG, a Swiss IT company. Coming into its IPO at the peak of the hi-tech bubble in March 2000, the firm reported sales of 10.6 million Swiss francs (SFr) for the previous year. The IPO issue price was SFr270, but by the end of the day's trading the share price stood at an amazing SFr1,050, nearly four times its issue price, and representing a market valuation of SFr2.52 billion. Unfortunately, along with other high-tech firms of the dot-com era, its fortunes quickly reversed, and within 18 months the price of Think Tools was less than SFr30.

To give you some idea of the bubble that was forming in Europe between 1994 and 2000, the FTSE 100 Index in the UK more than doubled in value from 3,000 at the beginning of 1994 to nearly 7,000 at the beginning of 2000. Over the next three years the index lost 50 per cent of its value.

The Global Credit Crunch   More recently, the world is just recovering from what many believe was the worst financial crisis in modern history. Analysts will be dissecting the events of 2007 and 2008 for many decades, but almost all agree that the cause of the crisis was a combination of investor irrationality and an almost blind view of the riskiness of bank strategies in the years before the crash.

Although the crisis originated in the US through the mass provision of risky subprime mortgages to people ill placed to afford them over the longer term, Europe gleefully took full advantage of the cheap credit that was available at the time. Faced with increasing competition from other countries, many banks maximized the size of their loan portfolios through significantly increased levels of lending to risky borrowers. What made this strategy particularly risky was that the long-term loans were funded by short-term borrowing in the money markets. Since 2001, short-term borrowing had been exceptionally cheap, and bankers believed this was going to continue for the foreseeable future. To further cement their view, the increase in loan portfolios led to very high earnings growth, which was supported by shareholders, who were delighted with the returns they were receiving. Governments, too, were happy to allow the risky funding strategy to continue, because they were receiving significant tax revenues on the back of the banks' performance.

It is clear that several behavioural biases were at work here. First, everyone was overly optimistic about the cheap credit continuing. Even with inflation growing fast, and bad debt levels increasing, market participants ignored the warning signs. Confirmation bias was also exhibited by bankers and shareholders, who argued that the bank funding and lending strategy was obviously a good one, because it had provided such strong performance in the recent past.

As markets descended into chaos in 2008, share price valuations exhibited massive degrees of volatility, as can be seen for the VDAX index of German market volatility in Fig. 19.3. Moreover, the heightened levels of market volatility did not return to pre-crisis levels until late 2009.

The global financial crisis of 2008 is the most recent and dramatic example of a bubble and crash. However, there are many more examples of bubbles, and some of these are presented in Table 19.1.

As a result of the events of recent years, many people now believe that markets are not efficient, but instead are driven by behavioural biases of the type discussed in this chapter. However, many others believe that the markets are efficient in general, but that there are times when a fundamental shock leads to a period of transition.

Behavioural finance supporters may have the final say in this debate by stating that the global credit crunch and the resulting financial crisis were actually caused by traders who blindly believed in efficient markets. Because they think that share prices will always

Period	Name	Description
1633–1637	Tulpenmanie	The price of one tulip bulb in The Netherlands rose to 10 times the annual income of a skilled worker, and cost the equivalent of 12 acres (5 hectares) of land. When the bubble burst, the bulb price fell to 0.001 per cent of its previous high.
1720	The South Sea Bubble	Share valuations in European companies that traded in South America grew 1,000 per cent and collapsed to pre-bubble levels within one year. A very famous example of the silliness was the successful public equity issue of a company whose business model was to 'carry out an undertaking of great advantage'. We still don't know today what that undertaking was.
1920–1929	The Roaring Twenties	Very similar to the bubbles of this century in that new technologies and economic prosperity drove stock market valuations to extreme highs. The crash led to the great depression of the 1930s.
1997	The South East Asian Bubble	Significant foreign capital inflows in search of lucrative gains led to the South East Asian economies becoming overheated. When the bubble burst, the economies went with it.
1995–2007	The Celtic Tiger	The Irish economy grew sharply over this period until the global credit crisis in 2007. The economy subsequently contracted by more than 10 per cent in a year, and made the country one of the riskiest in the Eurozone.
2006–present	The Property Bubble	Property prices are at historically extreme levels, with the majority of individuals being unable to comfortably afford mortgages. It is argued that property bubbles currently exist in China, France, Greece, India, Ireland, Italy, the Netherlands, Norway, Spain, the UK and the US. The bubble hasn't burst yet . . .

Table 19.1 Bubbles in history

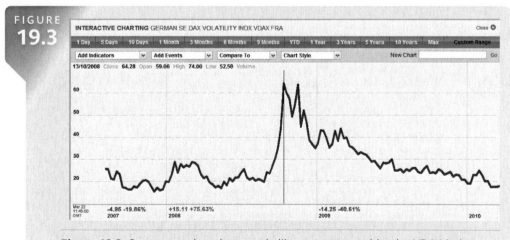

Figure 19.3 German stock exchange volatility as represented by the VDAX index

596 **Chapter 19** Behavioural Finance

reflect the true value of underlying equities, proponents of efficient markets will not see asset bubbles forming, and will therefore extend their duration and exacerbate the negative impact when the bubble inevitably bursts.

In Their Own Words . . .

Hersh Shefrin on Behavioural Finance

Most of the chief financial officers (CFOs) I know admit that there is a gap between what they learned about corporate finance in business schools and what they put into practice as executives. A major reason for this gap is the material you are studying in this chapter. It really is true that financial managers do not practise textbook corporate finance. In the 1990s I became convinced that this was the case after I joined the organization Financial Executives International (FEI), which gave me an opportunity to meet many CFOs on a regular basis and discuss with them how they practise corporate finance. In doing so, I gained a great deal of information that led me to conclude that behavioural finance was highly applicable to corporate life.

Behavioural corporate finance is important for at least three reasons. First, being human, financial managers are susceptible to the behavioural phenomena you are reading about in this chapter. Textbook corporate finance offers many valuable concepts, tools, and techniques. My point is not that the material in traditional corporate finance textbooks lacks value, but that psychological obstacles often stand in the way of this material being implemented correctly. Second, the people with whom financial managers interact are also susceptible to mistakes. Expecting other people to be immune to mistakes is itself an error that can lead managers to make bad decisions. Third, investors' mistakes can sometimes lead prices to be inefficient. In this respect, managers can make one of two different mistakes. They might believe that prices are efficient when they are actually inefficient. Or they might believe that prices are inefficient when they are actually efficient. Managers need to know how to think about the vulnerability to both types of errors, and how to deal with each.

The material in this chapter is a wonderful start to learning about behavioural finance. However, for this material to really make a difference, you need to integrate the material with what you are learning about traditional topics such as capital budgeting, capital structure, valuation, payout policy, market efficiency, corporate governance, and mergers and acquisition. You need to study behavioural cases about real people making real decisions and see how psychology impacts those decisions. You need to learn from their mistakes in an effort to make better decisions yourself. This is how behavioural corporate finance will generate value for you.

Hersh Shefrin holds the Mario Belotti Chair in the Department of Finance at Santa Clara University's Leavey School of Business. Professor Shefrin is a pioneer of behavioural finance.

Summary and Conclusions

In this chapter we have examined some of the implications of research in cognitive psychology and behavioural finance. In the first part of the chapter we learned that a key to becoming a better financial decision-maker is to be aware of, and avoid, certain types of behaviour. By studying behavioural finance you can see the potential damage from errors due to biases, frame dependence, and heuristics. Biases can lead to bad decisions, because they lead to unnecessarily poor estimates of future outcomes. Over-optimism, for example, leads to overly favourable estimates and opinions. Frame dependence leads to narrow framing, which is focusing on the smaller picture instead of the bigger one. The use of heuristics as shortcuts ignores potentially valuable insights that more detailed analysis would reveal.

In the second part of the chapter we turned to a much more difficult question, and one where the evidence is not at all clear. Do errors in judgement by investors influence market prices and lead to market inefficiencies? This question is the subject of raging debate among researchers and practitioners, and we are not going to take sides. Instead, our goal is to introduce you to the ideas and issues. We saw that market inefficiencies can be difficult for arbitrageurs to exploit because of firm-specific risk, noise trader (or sentiment-based) risk, and implementation costs. We called these difficulties limits (or barriers) to arbitrage, and the implication is that some inefficiencies may only gradually disappear, and smaller inefficiencies can persist if they cannot be profitably exploited. Looking back at market history, we saw some examples of evident mispricing, such as Royal Dutch and Shell. We also saw that markets appear to be susceptible to bubbles and crashes, suggesting significant inefficiency.

Concepts Review and Critical Thinking Questions

1   **Limits to Arbitrage [LO4]**   In the chapter we discussed the 3Com/Palm and Royal Dutch/Shell mispricings. Which of the limits to arbitrage is least likely to have been the main reason for these mispricings? Explain.

2   **Overconfidence [LO1]**   How could overconfidence affect the financial manager of the firm, and the firm's shareholders?

3   **Frame Dependence [LO4]**   How can frame dependence lead to irrational investment decisions?

4   **Noise Trader Risk [LO4]**   What is noise trader risk? How can noise trader risk lead to market inefficiencies?

5   **Probabilities [LO3]**   Suppose you are flipping a fair coin in a coin-flipping contest and have flipped eight heads in a row. What is the probability of flipping a head on your next coin flip? Suppose you flipped a head on your ninth toss. What is the probability of flipping a head on your tenth toss?

6   **Efficient Market Hypothesis [LO4]**   The efficient market hypothesis implies that all mutual funds should obtain the same expected risk-adjusted returns. Therefore we can simply pick mutual funds at random. Is this statement true or false? Explain.

7   **Behavioural Finance and Efficient Markets [LO4]**   Proponents of behavioural finance use three concepts to argue that markets are not efficient. What are these arguments?

8   **Frame Dependence [LO2]**   In the chapter we presented an example where you had lost €78 and were given the opportunity to make a wager in which your loss would increase to €100 for 80 per cent of the time and decrease to €0 for 20 per cent of the time. Using the stand-alone principal from capital budgeting, explain how your decision to accept or reject the proposal could have been affected by frame dependence. In other words, reframe the question in a way in which most people are likely to analyse the proposal correctly.

Online LearningCentre

To help you grasp the key concepts of this chapter check out the extra resources posted on the Online Learning Centre at **www.mcgraw-hill.co.uk/textbooks/hillier**

Among other helpful resources there are mini-cases tailored to individual chapters.

Chapters from: Money, Banking and Financial Markets - Global Third Edition by Cecchetti

Chapter 1

An Introduction to Money and the Financial System

This morning, a typical American college student bought coffee at the local café, paying for it with an ATM card. Then she jumped into her insured car, and drove to the university, which she attends thanks to her student loan. She may have left her parents' home, which is mortgaged, a few minutes early to avoid construction work on a new dormitory, financed by bonds issued by the university. Or perhaps she needed to stop at the bookstore to purchase this book, using her credit card, before her first money and banking class began.

Beneath the surface, each financial transaction in this story—even the seemingly simple ones—is quite complicated. If the café owner and the student use different banks, paying for the coffee will require an interbank funds transfer. The company that insures the student's car has to invest the premiums she pays until they are needed to pay off claims. The student's parents almost surely obtained their home mortgage through a mortgage broker, whose job was to find the cheapest mortgage available. And the bonds the university issued to finance construction of the new dormitory were created with the aid of an investment bank.

This brief example hints at the complex web of interdependent institutions and markets that is the foundation for our daily financial transactions. The system is so large, so efficient, and generally speaking so well run that most of us rarely take note of it. But a financial system is like air to an economy: If it disappeared suddenly, everything would grind to a halt.

In the autumn of 2008, we came closer to such a financial meltdown than at any time since the 1930s. In the earlier episode, the collapse of the banking system led to the Great Depression. In the recent crisis, some of the world's largest financial institutions failed. Key markets stopped functioning. Credit dried up, even for healthy borrowers. As a result, vibrant companies that relied on short-term loans to pay their employees and buy materials faced potential ruin. Even some fundamental ways that we make payments for goods and services were threatened.

Gasping for air in this financial crisis, the global economy during 2008 and 2009 sank into the deepest, broadest, and longest downturn since World War II. Around the world, tens of millions of people lost their jobs. In the United States, millions lost their homes and their life's savings. Others became unable to borrow to buy a home or go to college. The chances are good that you know someone—in your neighborhood, your school, or your family—whose life was changed for the worse by the crisis.

So, what happens in the financial system—whether for good or for bad—matters greatly for all of us. To understand the system—both its strengths and its vulnerabilities—let's take a closer look.

The Six Parts of the Financial System

The financial system has six parts, each of which plays a fundamental role in our economy. Those parts are money, financial instruments, financial markets, financial institutions, government regulatory agencies, and central banks.

We use the first part of the system, money, to pay for our purchases and to store our wealth. We use the second part, financial instruments, to transfer resources from savers to investors and to transfer risk to those who are best equipped to bear it. Stocks, mortgages, and insurance policies are examples of financial instruments. The third part of our financial system, financial markets, allows us to buy and sell financial instruments quickly and cheaply. The New York Stock Exchange is an example of a financial market. Financial institutions, the fourth part of the financial system, provide a myriad of services, including access to the financial markets and collection of information about prospective borrowers to ensure they are creditworthy. Banks, securities firms, and insurance companies are examples of financial institutions. Government regulatory agencies form the fifth part of the financial system. They are responsible for making sure that the elements of the financial system—including its instruments, markets, and institutions—operate in a safe and reliable manner. Finally, central banks, the sixth part of the system, monitor and stabilize the economy. The Federal Reserve System is the central bank of the United States.

While the essential functions that define these six categories endure, their form is constantly evolving. *Money* once consisted of gold and silver coins, which were eventually replaced by paper currency, which today is being eclipsed by electronic funds transfers. Methods of accessing means of payment have changed dramatically as well. As recently as 1970, people customarily obtained currency from bank tellers when they cashed their paychecks or withdrew their savings from the local bank. Today, they can get cash from practically any ATM anywhere in the world. To pay their bills, people once wrote checks and put them in the mail, then waited for their monthly bank statements to make sure the transactions had been processed correctly. Today, payments can be made automatically, and account holders can check the transactions at any time on their bank's Web site.

Financial instruments (or securities, as they are often called) have evolved just as much as currency. In the last few centuries, investors could buy individual stocks through stockbrokers, but the transactions were costly. Furthermore, putting together a portfolio of even a small number of stocks and bonds was extremely time consuming; just collecting the information necessary to evaluate a potential investment was a daunting task. As a result, investing was an activity reserved for the wealthy. Today, financial institutions offer people with as little as $1,000 to invest the ability to purchase shares in *mutual funds*, which pool the savings of a large number of investors. Because of their size, mutual funds can construct portfolios of hundreds or even thousands of different stocks and/or bonds.

The markets where stocks and bonds are sold have undergone a similar transformation. Originally, *financial markets* were located in coffeehouses and taverns where individuals met to exchange financial instruments. The next step was to create organized markets, like the New York Stock Exchange—trading places specifically dedicated to the buying and selling of stocks and bonds. Today, much of the activity that once occurred at these big-city financial exchanges is handled by electronic networks. Buyers and sellers obtain price information and initiate transactions from their desktop computers or from handheld devices. Because electronic networks have reduced the cost of processing financial transactions, even small investors can afford to participate in them. Just as important, today's financial markets offer a much broader array of financial instruments than those available even 50 years ago.

Financial institutions have changed, as well. Banks began as vaults where people could store their valuables. Gradually, they developed into institutions that accepted deposits and made loans. For hundreds of years, in fact, that was what bankers did. Today, a bank is more like a financial supermarket. Walk in and you will discover

"This is Fluffy, my pet money."

SOURCE: © Danny Shanahan/The New Yorker
Collection/www.cartoonbank.com.

a huge assortment of financial products and services for sale, from access to the financial markets to insurance policies, mortgages, consumer credit, and even investment advice.

The activities of government regulatory agencies and the design of regulation have been evolving and have entered a period of more rapid change, too. In the aftermath of the financial crisis of 1929–1933, when the failure of thousands of banks led to the Great Depression, the U.S. government introduced regulatory agencies to provide wide-ranging financial regulation—rules for the operation of financial institutions and markets—and supervision—oversight through examination and enforcement. The U.S. agencies established in the 1930s to issue and enforce these financial rules still operate.

Yet, the evolution of financial instruments, institutions, and markets has led to many changes in the ways that regulatory agencies work. A bank examiner used to count the money in the cash drawers and call borrowers to see if the loans on a bank's books were real. They might even visit workplaces to see if the loans were used as designed to buy equipment or build a factory. Today, banks engage in millions of transactions, many of which are far more complex and difficult to understand than a loan or a mortgage. So, a government examiner also looks at the systems that a bank uses to manage its various risks. In doing so, regulators try to encourage best practices throughout the financial industry. However, the failure of regulators in the United States and elsewhere around the world to anticipate or prevent the financial crisis of 2007–2009 has led many governments to consider more far-reaching changes to financial regulation and the regulatory agencies. Such changes likely will affect the financial system for years to come.

Finally, *central banks* have changed a great deal. They began as large private banks founded by monarchs to finance wars. For instance, King William of Orange created the Bank of England in 1694 for the express purpose of raising taxes and borrowing to finance a war between Austria, England, and the Netherlands on one side and Louis XIV's France on the other. Eventually, these government treasuries grew into the modern central banks we know today. While only a few central banks existed in 1900, now nearly every country in the world has one, and they have become one of the most important institutions in government. Central banks control the availability of money and credit to ensure low inflation, high growth, and the stability of the financial system. Because their current mission is to serve the public at large rather than land-hungry monarchs, their operating methods have changed as well. Once the central bank's decisions were shrouded in mystery, but today's policymakers strive for transparency in their operations. Officials at the European Central Bank and the U.S. Federal Reserve—two of the most important central banks in the world—go out of their way to explain the rationale for their decisions.

Though the changing nature of our financial system is a fascinating topic, it poses challenges for both students and instructors. How can we teach and learn about money and banking in a way that will stand the test of time, so that the knowledge we gain won't become outmoded? The answer is that we must develop a way to understand

and adapt to the evolutionary structure of the financial system. That means discussing money and banking within a framework of core principles that do not change over time. The next section introduces the five core principles that will guide our studies throughout this book.

The Five Core Principles of Money and Banking

Five core principles will inform our analysis of the financial system and its interaction with the real economy. Once you have grasped these principles, you will have a better understanding not only of what is happening in the financial world today but of changes that will undoubtedly occur in the future. The five principles are based on **Time, Risk, Information, Markets,** and **Stability.**

Core Principle 1: Time Has Value

The first principle of money and banking is that *time has value*. At some very basic level, everyone knows this. If you take a job at the local supermarket, you will almost surely be paid by the hour. An hour's worth of work equals a certain number of dollars. Literally, your time has a price.

On a more sophisticated level, time affects the value of financial transactions. Most loan contracts allow the borrower to spread out the payments over time. If you take out an auto loan, for example, the lender will allow you to make a series of monthly payments over three, four, or even five years. If you add up the payments, you'll discover that the total exceeds the amount of the loan. At an interest rate of 6 percent, a four-year, $10,000 car loan will require 48 monthly payments of $235 each. That means you will repay a total of $11,280 (48 times $235). The reason your repayments total more than the loan amount is that you are paying interest to compensate the lender for the time during which you use the funds. That is, the resources you borrowed have an opportunity cost to the lender so you have to pay rent on them.

Interest payments are fundamental to a market economy. In Chapter 4, we will develop an understanding of interest rates and how to use them. Then, throughout the remainder of Part II, we will apply the principle that time has value in our discussion of the valuation of bonds, stocks, and other financial instruments involving future payments. How much should you be willing to pay for a particular stock or bond? Figuring out what alternative investments are worth, and comparing them, means valuing payments made on different future dates. The same principle applies to the question of how much you must invest today to achieve a particular financial objective in the future. How much of your salary, for example, do you need to save each month to meet your goal of buying a house? The length of time your savings will be earning interest is a key to answering this question.

Core Principle 2: Risk Requires Compensation

The world is filled with uncertainty. More events, both good and bad, *can* happen than *will* happen. Some of the possibilities, such as the likelihood of your home doubling in value after you buy it, are welcome. Other possibilities, such as the chance that you might lose your job and not be able to make your car payments, are distinctly unwelcome. Dealing effectively with risk requires that you consider the full range of possibilities in order to eliminate some risks, reduce others, pay someone to assume particularly onerous risks, and just live with what's left. Needless to say, no one will assume your risks for free, which brings us to the second core principle of money and banking: *Risk requires compensation*. In the financial world, compensation is made in the form of explicit payments. That is, investors must be paid to assume risk; the higher the risk, the bigger the required payment.

Car insurance is a common example of paying someone else to shoulder a risk you don't want to take. If your car is wrecked in an accident, you will want to be able to repair it. But beyond that, auto insurance shelters drivers from the possibility of losing all their wealth in the event that they cause an accident in which someone is seriously injured. Although the chances of causing such an accident are quite small, the results can be so serious that, even if the government didn't require it, most of us would voluntarily purchase auto insurance. Driving without it just isn't worth the risk. The insurance company pools the premiums that policyholders pay and invests them. Even though some of the premiums will be spent to settle claims when cars are stolen or damaged by collisions, the chance to make a profit is good. So both the insurance company and the drivers who buy policies are ultimately better off.

Bearing in mind that time has value and risk requires compensation, we can begin to see the rationale behind the valuation of a broad set of financial instruments. For example, a lender will charge a higher interest rate on a loan if there is a chance that the borrower will not repay. In Chapters 6 and 7, we will use this principle when we examine the interest rates on bonds. As we will see, a company that is on the verge of bankruptcy may still be able to issue bonds (called *junk bonds*), but it will have to pay an extremely high interest rate to do so. The reason is that the lender must be compensated for the substantial risk that the company will not repay the loan. Risk requires compensation.

Core Principle 3: Information Is the Basis for Decisions

Most of us collect information before making decisions. The more important the decision, the more information we gather. Think of the difference between buying a $5 sandwich and a $10,000 car. You will surely spend more time comparing cars than comparing sandwiches.

What's true for sandwiches and cars is true for finance as well. That is, *information is the basis for decisions*. In fact, the collection and processing of information is the foundation of the financial system. In Chapter 11, we will learn how financial institutions like banks funnel resources from savers to investors. Before a bank makes a loan, a loan officer will investigate the financial condition of the individual or firm seeking it. Banks want to provide loans only to the highest-quality borrowers. Thus, they spend a great deal of time gathering the information needed to evaluate the creditworthiness of loan applicants.

To understand the problem faced by the two parties to any financial transaction, think about a home mortgage. Before making the loan, the mortgage broker examines the applicant's finances and researches the home's value to make sure the applicant can afford the monthly payments and the property is more valuable than the loan.

And before the broker transfers the funds to the seller, the new homeowner must purchase fire insurance. All these requirements arise from the fact that the lender doesn't know much about the borrower and wants to make sure the loan will be repaid. When lenders fail to assess creditworthiness properly, they end up with more borrowers who are unable to repay their loans in the future. Large mistakes like these were a key factor in the wave of U.S. mortgage delinquencies and defaults that preceded the financial crisis of 2007–2009.

Information plays a key role in other parts of the financial system as well. In Chapters 2 and 3, we'll see that many types of transactions are arranged so that the buyer doesn't need to know anything about the seller. When merchants accept cash, they don't need to worry about the customer's identity. When stocks change hands, the buyer doesn't need to know anything about the seller, or vice versa. Stock exchanges are organized to eliminate the need for costly information gathering, facilitating the exchange of securities. In one way or another, information is the key to the financial system.

Core Principle 4: Markets Determine Prices and Allocate Resources

MARKETS

Markets are the core of the economic system. They are the place, physical or virtual, where buyers and sellers meet, where firms go to issue stocks and bonds, and where individuals go to purchase assets. Financial markets are essential to the economy, channeling its resources and minimizing the cost of gathering information and making transactions. In fact, well-developed financial markets are a necessary precondition for healthy economic growth. The better developed a country's financial markets, the faster the country will grow.

The reason for this connection between markets and growth is that *markets determine prices and allocate resources*. Financial markets gather information from a large number of individual participants and aggregate it into a set of prices that signals what is valuable and what is not. Thus, markets are sources of information. By attaching prices to different stocks or bonds, they provide a basis for the allocation of capital.

To see how prices in the financial markets allocate capital, think about a large firm wishing to finance the construction of a new factory costing several hundred million dollars. To raise the funds, the firm can go directly into the financial markets and issue stocks or bonds. The higher the price investors are willing to pay in the market, the more appealing the idea will be, and the more likely it is that the firm will issue securities to raise the capital for the investment.

We will refer to the financial markets throughout much of this book. While our primary focus in Part II will be the nature of financial instruments, we will also study the markets in which those instruments are traded. Chapters 6 through 10 describe the markets for bonds, stocks, derivatives, and foreign currencies.

Importantly, financial markets do not arise by themselves—at least, not the large, well-oiled ones we see operating today. Markets like the New York Stock Exchange, where billions of shares of stock change hands every day, require rules in order to work properly, as well as authorities to police them. Otherwise, they will not function. For people to be willing to participate in a market, they must perceive it as fair. As we will see, this creates an important role for the government. Regulators and supervisors of the financial system make and enforce the rules, punishing people who violate them. When the government protects investors, financial markets work well; otherwise they don't.

Finally, even well-developed markets can break down. When they do—as some did during the financial crisis of 2007–2009—the financial system as a whole can be at risk. So today, governments must also play a role in promoting the healthy operation of markets.

50 | Chapter 1   An Introduction to Money and the Financial System

Core Principle 5: Stability Improves Welfare

Most of us prefer stable to variable incomes. We like getting raises, but the prospect of a salary cut is not a pleasant one. This brings us to the fifth core principle of money and banking: *Stability improves welfare*. Stability is a desirable quality, not just in our personal lives but in the financial system as a whole. As we saw at the start of this chapter, financial instability in the autumn of 2008 brought us closer to a collapse of the system than at any time since the 1930s, triggering the worst global downturn since the Great Depression.

If you are wondering whether this principle is related to Core Principle 2 (risk requires compensation), you are right. Because volatility creates risk, reducing volatility reduces risk. But while individuals can eliminate many risks on their own (we'll see how when we study financial instruments in Part II), some risks can only be reduced by government policymakers. Business cycle fluctuations are an example of the sort of instability individuals can't eliminate on their own. And though "automatic stabilizers" like unemployment insurance and the income tax system reduce the burden of recessions on individuals, they cannot eliminate an economic slowdown. Monetary policymakers can moderate these downswings by carefully adjusting interest rates. In stabilizing the economy as a whole, they eliminate risks that individuals can't, improving everyone's welfare in the process.

As we will learn in Part IV of this book, stabilizing the economy is a primary function of central banks like the Federal Reserve and the European Central Bank. Officials of these institutions are charged with controlling inflation and reducing business cycle fluctuations. That is, they work to keep inflation low and stable and to keep growth high and stable. When they are successful, they reduce both the risk that individuals will lose their jobs and the uncertainty that firms face in making investment decisions. Not surprisingly, a stable economy grows faster than an unstable economy. Stability improves welfare.

Throughout the book you will notice icons like this in the margin at various points. These will guide you to the core principle that provides the foundation for what is being discussed at that point in the text.

Special Features of This Book

Every chapter of this book contains a series of important elements, beginning with an introduction. The introduction presents real-world examples that lead to the big questions the chapter is designed to answer: What is money? What do banks do? How does the bond market work? What does the Federal Reserve do to prevent or limit financial crises?

The text of each chapter presents the economic and financial theory you need to understand the topics covered. Each chapter also contains a series of inserts that apply the theory. There are five types of inserts: Your Financial World, Applying the Concept, Lessons from the Crisis, In the News, and Tools of the Trade. Here are some guidelines for using them.

Your Financial World

When most people decide to make a major purchase, they begin by collecting information. If they are considering buying a car, they will first try to decide which model

YOUR FINANCIAL WORLD
Guard Your Identity

There is a television commercial in which a middle-aged man is sitting in his living room drinking a beer. Out of the man's mouth comes the voice of a woman describing some very expensive clothing she just bought. She didn't care how much the clothes cost because she wasn't paying—she used a credit card that was in the man's name. The ad catches viewers' attention because it is funny. But its primary purpose is to serve as a warning about identity theft, in which one person takes on the identity of another to do things like make credit card purchases.

It is important to realize that someone who has a few pieces of key information about you can get a credit card in your name. To prevent this, you need to protect personal information. Do your best to never tell anyone your birth date and birthplace, your address, or your mother's maiden name. Most importantly, guard your Social Security number. Because it is unique, it is the key to identity theft. Give out your Social Security number only when absolutely necessary—on tax forms, for employment records,

and to open bank accounts. If your driver's license has your Social Security number on it, ask that it be removed. If a business requests it, ask if some alternative number can be used. Importantly, if you get a telephone call or an e-mail from someone you don't know asking for personal data, don't provide it.

Beyond protecting access to personal information, you need to monitor your financial statements closely, looking for things that shouldn't be there. Be on the lookout for unauthorized charges. This means maintaining careful records so that you know what should be on your bank and credit card statements.

Identity theft is a crime, and governments work hard to find and prosecute the offenders. Even so, millions of people are victims each year. Don't be one of them. For more information about identity theft and how to avoid being a victim, see the U.S. Department of Justice's Web site: www.justice.gov/criminal/fraud/websites/idtheft.html.

is best for them and then work hard to pay the lowest price possible. Even for smaller purchases, like clothes or groceries, people first gather information and then buy.

Financial transactions should be no different from consumer purchases. Become informed first, and then buy. If you're thinking, "That's easier said than done," you're right. The problem is that most people have very little knowledge of the financial system, so they don't know how to start or what kind of information to collect.

That's where Your Financial World comes in. These inserts provide basic guidelines for applying economic theory to the bread-and-butter financial decisions you make nearly every day. Your Financial World answers questions about:

- Banking and Payments
  - What's the difference between credit and debit cards?
  - How should you pick a bank?
- Investments
  - Should you own stocks or bonds or gold?
  - Should you invest in the company you work for?
- Credit, Loans, and Mortgages
  - What do you need to know when you shop for a mortgage?
  - What is your credit score and why is it important?
- Insurance
  - How much life insurance do you need?
  - How much car insurance do you need?
- Saving and Retirement
  - How big an emergency saving reserve should you have?
  - Is your retirement savings insured?

Applying the Concept

Each chapter in this book contains a series of applications called Applying the Concept, which show how to put theory into practice. These inserts provide real-world examples of the ideas introduced in the chapter, drawn primarily from history or from relevant public policy debates. Here are some of the questions examined in Applying the Concept:

- Why do interest rates rise when inflation goes up?
- Why does a country's exchange rate suddenly plummet?
- Why do large-scale frauds that damage investors occur repeatedly?
- Why is it important for central banks to be free of political influence?
- Can monetary policy be used to stabilize the economy?
- What determines inflation?
- What are the implications of China's exchange rate policy?

Lessons from the Crisis

These inserts cover episodes from the financial crisis of 2007–2009. One goal is to give you a framework for understanding the crisis and how it is transforming the world of finance. Another goal is to highlight the relevance and power of the ideas in the book more generally. Along the way, the various Lessons from the Crisis offer you insight into the sources and effects of financial instability. They also address the means that governments—including regulators and central bankers—use to counter financial instability. Most chapters contain one such insert.

The topics range from specific aspects of the crisis to key issues that have wide application. Here are some of the questions examined in Lessons from the Crisis:

- What factors led to the financial crisis of 2007–2009?
- What made financial institutions especially vulnerable in this period?
- Why do financial markets sometimes stop functioning?
- How do threats to the financial system differ from threats to specific financial institutions?
- When a crisis erupts, what can central banks do to prevent another Great Depression?

In the News

One of the primary purposes of this textbook is to help you understand the business and financial news. Critically evaluating what you read, hear, and see means developing a clear understanding of how the financial system works, as well as reading the news regularly. Like many other skills, critical reading of newspapers and magazines takes practice. You can't just pick up a newspaper and skim through it quickly and efficiently; you need to learn how. Your instructor will make suggestions about what you should read. See Table 1.1 for a list of reliable sources of information on the economy and the financial system.

Given your need to become a skilled consumer of financial information, each chapter in this book closes with an article drawn from the financial press. These stories from *The Wall Street Journal*, the *Financial Times*, *The Economist*, *BusinessWeek*, and

Table 1.1   Sources of Economic and Financial News and Data

Sources of Daily News

The Wall Street Journal and *www.wsj.com*

Available six days a week both in print and online, *The Wall Street Journal* provides general news along with comprehensive coverage of business and finance.

Financial Times and *www.ft.com*

The *Financial Times* offers reporting, analysis, and commentary on major business, political, financial, and economic events. The *FT* is written from a distinctly European perspective, and includes detailed coverage of non-U.S. business and financial news.

Bloomberg.com

Bloomberg offers a wide range of financial market services, including news. A wide variety of news and data can be found on the free portion of their Web site.

Sources of Weekly News

The Economist and *www.economist.com*

The Economist covers global politics, economics, business, finance, and science. It not only reports the facts, but gives analysis and policy conclusions. The Finance and Economics section is of particular interest.

BusinessWeek and *www.businessweek.com*

BusinessWeek is a U.S.-based publication that offers fair and balanced reporting and analysis of top economic, financial, business, and technological issues.

Economic and Financial Data

The Bureau of Labor Statistics supplies data on prices, employment and unemployment at www.bls.gov.

The Bureau of Economic Analysis provides information on gross domestic product, consumption, investment, and other macroeconomic data at www.bea.gov.

The Federal Reserve Board Web site www.federalreserve.gov provides a variety of banking, monetary, interest rate, and exchange rate data.

The Federal Reserve Bank of St. Louis maintains a comprehensive data base called ALFRED (Archive of Federal Reserve Economic Data) that you can access by going to www.stls.frb.org.

The European Central Bank maintains data on inflation, GDP, monetary aggregates, government finance, and a wide variety of other data for the euro area at www.ecb.int.

The Bank of England presents data on inflation targeting as well as a wide array of interest rates, exchange rates, and other financial data at www.bankofengland.co.uk.

Personal Finance Information

Among many Web sites offering personal finance resources and calculators are:

- www.choosetosave.org
- www.dinkytown.net
- www.wsj.com (go to "personal finance" then "family finances" and look for "tools")

other sources are reproduced under the heading In the News. Each provides an example of how the concepts introduced in the chapter are discussed in the real world, and each is followed by a brief summary.

Tools of the Trade

Many chapters in this book include an insert called Tools of the Trade that concentrates on practical knowledge relevant to the chapter. Some of these inserts cover basic skills, including how to read bond and stock tables, how to read charts, and how to do some simple algebraic calculations. Others provide brief reviews of material from principles of economics classes, such as the relationship between the current account and the capital account in the balance of payments. Still other Tools of the Trade inserts address questions such as:

- What is leverage, and how does it affect risk?
- What are hedge funds?
- What tools did the Fed use to address the financial crisis?
- How is a recession defined?

The Organization of This Book

This book is organized into five sections. Each one employs core principles to illuminate a particular part of the financial system and applies economic theory to the world around us. The next two chapters will continue our overview of the financial system. First, we'll study money—what it is and how it is used. We'll see that currency allows transactions to be made anonymously, which reduces the need to gather information. This advantage of currency is related to Core Principle 3: Information is the basis for decisions. In Chapter 3, we'll take a bird's-eye view of financial instruments, financial markets, and financial institutions. At various points in that chapter, we'll refer to the first four core principles.

Part II includes detailed descriptions of financial instruments. We'll study bonds, stocks, and derivatives, as well as exchange rates for foreign currency. The valuation of financial instruments requires a comparison of payments made on different dates as well as an estimate of the risk involved in each instrument. Thus, these chapters focus on Core Principles 1 and 2: Time has value and Risk requires compensation.

Throughout Part II and continuing in Part III, we'll discuss financial markets, whose purpose is to facilitate the buying and selling of financial instruments. No one would buy stocks or bonds if they could not be resold cheaply and easily. Financial markets also provide the information necessary to understand the value and risk that are associated with particular financial instruments. Core Principles 3 and 4 (Information is the basis for decisions and Markets determine prices and allocate resources) are both relevant to our discussion of markets.

Part III covers financial institutions, especially banks and their regulation. Earlier in this chapter (pages 48–49), we emphasized that financial institutions spend a great deal of time collecting and processing information. Without that information, many financial transactions could not take place. This dependence of banks on information is an example of Core Principle 3: Information is the basis for decisions. Financial regulation is driven by Core Principle 5: Stability improves welfare.

Part IV describes central banks, especially the Federal Reserve and the European Central Bank. These institutions exist to stabilize the real economy as well as the financial system. Thus, like financial regulators in Part III of the book, they embody Core Principle 5: Stability improves welfare. We'll see how central banks manipulate interest rates and other less conventional policy tools to stabilize the economy.

Finally, Part V brings together material covered in the first four sections to explain how the financial system influences the real economy. We'll use a macroeconomic model to analyze the mechanism through which central banks influence the economy, paying particular attention to the role of the financial system in determining inflation and growth.

Learning money and banking is going to be hard work. Reading and working through the remaining 22 chapters of this book will take lots of time and energy. But when you are done, you will be armed with the tools you need to understand how the financial system works and why it changes as it does. You will know how to be an informed reader of the financial and economic news and how to put the financial system to use for you. You will understand the various ways that you can pay for your morning coffee and how each one of them works. You will understand the usefulness of bonds and stocks as well as what financial institutions do and how central banks work. You will know how to make sound financial decisions for the rest of your life. You will understand how financial crises arise, how they threaten economic stability, and what can be done to prevent and contain them. Regardless of the career you choose to follow, a solid background in money, banking, and financial markets will help you make sound financial decisions from now on.

Terms

central bank, 45	markets, 49
European Central Bank, 46	money, 45
Federal Reserve System, 45	regulation, 46
financial institution, 45	regulatory agencies, 45
financial instrument, 45	risk, 48
financial market, 45	stability, 50
financial system, 44	supervision, 46
information, 48	time, 47

Chapter Lessons

1. A healthy and constantly evolving financial system is the foundation for economic efficiency and economic growth. It has six parts:
   a. Money is used to pay for purchases and to store wealth.
   b. Financial instruments are used to transfer resources and risk.
   c. Financial markets allow people to buy and sell financial instruments.
   d. Financial institutions provide access to the financial markets, collect information, and provide a variety of other services.

e. Government regulatory agencies aim to make the financial system operate safely and reliably.

f. Central banks stabilize the economy.

2. The core principles of money and banking are useful in understanding all six parts of the financial system.

a. Core Principle 1: Time has value.

b. Core Principle 2: Risk requires compensation.

c. Core Principle 3: Information is the basis for decisions.

d. Core Principle 4: Markets determine prices and allocate resources.

e. Core Principle 5: Stability improves welfare.

Conceptual Problems

1. Try to list the financial transactions you have engaged in over the past week. How might each one have been carried out 50 years ago?

2. Can you think of any examples of how you, or your family or friends, were affected by the failure of the financial system to function normally during the financial crisis of 2007–2009?

3. Describe the links among the six components of the financial system and the five core principles of money and banking.

4. Socialists argue that, to reduce the power exerted by the owners of capital, the state should control the allocation of resources. Thus, in a socialist system, the state allocates investment resources. In a market-based capitalist system, financial markets do that job. Which approach do you think works better, and why? Relate your answer to the core principle that markets determine prices and allocate resources.

5. Financial innovation has reduced individuals' need to carry cash. Explain how.

6.* Many people believe that, despite ongoing financial innovations, cash will always be with us to some degree as a form of money. What core principle could justify this view?

7. If you were a loan officer, what information would you request from a loan applicant in order to assess whether the applicant is creditworthy?

8. Merchants that accept Visa or MasterCard pay the issuer of the card a percentage of the transaction. For example, for each $100 charged on Visa cards, a merchant might receive only $98. Explain why Visa charges the fee and why the merchant pays it. (You should be able to use at least two core principles in your answer.)

9. Suppose central bankers have figured out a way to eliminate recessions. What financial and economic changes would you expect to see? Relate these changes to the core principle that stability improves welfare.

10.* Why do you think the global financial system has become more integrated over time? Can you think of any downside to this increased integration?

11. Suppose a central bank could regulate financial markets and institutions so completely as to eliminate risk. Would such a regulatory regime enhance or retard economic growth?

*Indicates more difficult problems

Analytical Problems

12. If offered the choice of receiving $1,000 today or $1,000 in one year's time, which option would you choose, and why?

13. If time has value, why are financial institutions often willing to extend you a 30-year mortgage at a lower annual interest rate than they would charge for a one-year loan?

14. Using Core Principle 2, under what circumstances would you expect a job applicant to accept an offer of a low base salary and an opportunity to earn commission over one with a higher base salary and no commission potential?

15. Suppose medical research confirms earlier speculation that red wine is good for you. Why would banks be willing to lend to vineyards that produce red wine at a lower interest rate than before?

16.* If the U.S. Securities and Exchange Commission eliminated its requirement for public companies to disclose information about their finances, what would you expect to happen to the stock prices for these companies?

17. If 2 percent growth is your break-even point for an investment project, under which outlook for the economy would you be more inclined to go ahead with the investment: (1) A forecast for economic growth that ranges from 0 to 4 percent, or (2) a forecast of 2 percent growth for sure, assuming the forecasts are equally reliable? What core principle does this illustrate?

18.* Why are large, publicly listed companies much more likely than small businesses to sell financial instruments such as bonds directly to the market, while small businesses get their financing from financial institutions such as banks?

19.* During the financial crisis of 2007–2009, some financial instruments that received high ratings in terms of their safety turned out to be much riskier than those ratings indicated. Explain why markets for other financial instruments might have been adversely affected by that development.

20. Suppose financial institutions didn't exist but you urgently needed a loan. Where would you most likely get this loan? Using core principles, identify an advantage and a disadvantage this arrangement might have over borrowing from a financial institution.

www.mhhe.com/cecchetti3e

Appendix to Chapter 1

Measuring Economic Activity, Prices, and the Inflation Rate

Measuring Economic Activity

Gross Domestic Product (GDP) is the most commonly used measure of economic activity. In order to see if the economy is improving, you can look at whether GDP is growing (or shrinking) and the rate of that growth. And to compare well-being in two countries, you can look at the GDP per person in each country—*per capita GDP*.

The definition of GDP is *the market value of final goods and services produced in a country during a year*. Let's look at the pieces of this definition:

- **Market value:** In order to add together production of cars, corn flakes, and computers, we take the market price of each and multiply it times the quantity of each that is produced, and sum the products together. That is, add up (market price of cars × quantity of cars produced) plus (market price of corn flakes × quantity of corn flakes produced), and so on.

- **Final goods and services:** We take only the price of the final product purchased by the person who uses it. For example, when a consumer buys a car, the car is considered a final good so it's included. But when the automobile manufacturer buys steel from a steel company in order to build the car, the steel is an intermediate product so it is not included.

- **In a country:** Only production within the country counts. This means that if a U.S. company owns a factory in China, the production of the factory is included in China's GDP.

- **During a year:** To measure production we need to specify a time period, and the time period is usually one year.

So, to compute U.S. GDP in 2010, for example, we sum the quantity of goods and services produced in the United States in 2010 times their 2010 prices. In an economy with only cars and corn flakes, the calculation would look like this:

GDP in 2010 = (2010 price of cars × quantity of cars produced in 2010)
        + (2010 price of corn flakes × quantity of corn flakes produced in 2010)

Note that we could always measure incomes rather than production. That is, instead of measuring total production, we can measure the total payments made to factors used to produce the output—the payments to labor, capital, and land. Because the revenue from selling all of the goods and services produced must always go to the people responsible for making them—the workers and the owners—total income equals GDP as well.

Real versus Nominal GDP

It is essential when measuring the level of economic activity to distinguish changes in prices from changes in quantities. As defined so far, GDP confuses the two changes. For example, U.S. GDP rose from $14.078 trillion in 2007 to $14.441 trillion in 2008. Computing the annual growth rate, the percentage change from one year to the next, means that the U.S. economy grew by 2.58 percent.

$$\text{GDP growth rate from 2007 to 2008} = \frac{\$14.441\,trillion - \$14.078\,trillion}{\$14.078\,trillion} \times 100$$

$$= 2.58\%$$

This number alone only tells us the sum of the growth in the quantity of output produced (something that is beneficial) and the change in prices (which is not so good). To see the point, look back at the computation for the car and corn flakes economy and note that GDP can rise either because quantities rise or because prices go up.

Separating changes in the quantities from changes in the prices requires computing *real* GDP. To do this, government statisticians fix the prices at a base-year level and then calculate the sum of the quantities times these base-year prices. Currently, real GDP in the United States is reported in year-2005 dollars. That is, statisticians sum up the value of all production in the United States during a year measured at the prices at which the goods and services were sold in the year 2005. This procedure isolates the part of change in GDP that is due to growth in the quantity produced from the part that came from changes in prices.

For the car and corn flakes economy, the formula looks like this:

Real GDP in 2010 = (2005 price of cars × quantity of cars produced in 2010)
        + (2005 price of corn flakes × quantity of corn flakes produced in 2010)

To see what this means for the United States as a whole, we can look at www.bea.gov and find that, in 2007, real GDP (in year-2005 dollars) was $13.254 trillion. In 2008, real GDP (again in year-2005 dollars) had increased to $13.312 trillion. That's an increase of 0.44 percent.

$$\text{Real GDP growth rate from 2007 to 2008} = \frac{\$13.312\,trillion - \$13.254\,trillion}{\$13.254\,trillion} \times 100$$

$$= 0.44\%$$

The GDP Deflator and the Inflation Rate

It should come as no surprise that from nominal and real GDP we get a measure of prices on average in the economy as a whole. We can start by thinking about nominal GDP as the product of real GDP times a measure of prices in the economy as a whole. That is:

$$Nominal\,GDP = Prices \times Real\,GDP$$

Looking at this expression, you can see that by taking the ratio of nominal GDP to real GDP we get a measure of prices. This is what's called the GDP *deflator*, and using the data from 2007, we get:

$$\text{GDP deflator in 2007} = \frac{\text{Nominal GDP in 2007}}{\text{Real GDP in 2007}} = \frac{\$14.078\,trillion}{\$13.254\,trillion} = 1.0621$$

The same computation for 2008 tells us that the GDP deflator in 2008 is 1.0848.

www.mhhe.com/cecchetti3e

No one spends much time worrying about the level of the GDP deflator. Instead, we are concerned with the rate at which the index is changing. The inflation rate is defined as the rate of growth in the price level. Using the GDP deflator from 2007 to 2008, we get an inflation rate of 2.14 percent.

$$\text{Inflation rate} = \frac{(1.0848 - 1.0621)}{1.0621} \times 100 = 2.14\%$$

This result makes sense. Since real GDP is designed to strip out the effect of price changes, the inflation rate should equal the growth rate of nominal GDP minus the growth rate of real GDP. And it does: $2.14 = 2.58 - 0.44$.

While it is the easiest to explain and compute, the GDP deflator is unfortunately not the most commonly used price index. The Consumer Price Index, or CPI, designed to measure the changes in the cost of living, lays claim to that title. We will learn more about the CPI throughout this book, starting with the Tools of the Trade in Chapter 2.

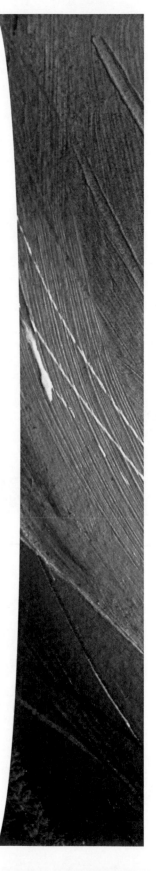

Chapter 2

Money and the Payments System

Parker Brothers' bestselling board game.

The makers of the board game Monopoly print about $50 billion of Monopoly money every year—coincidentally about the same as the amount of new U.S. currency issued in 2008. Every game has bills totaling 15,140 Monopoly dollars. At a cost of about 13 U.S. dollars per set, this "money" would be a good deal if you could buy things other than Boardwalk and Park Place with it. Unfortunately, attempts to pay for groceries, books, or rent with this particular form of money have been unsuccessful. And that's probably a good thing. Since the mid-1930s, Parker Brothers has sold more than 200 million Monopoly games, containing more than 3 trillion Monopoly dollars.[1]

When we pay for our purchases in the real world, we have lots of choices: crisp new $20 bills, credit cards, debit cards, checks, or more complicated electronic methods. Regardless of the choice we make, we are using *money* to buy our food and clothes and pay our bills. To make sure we can do it, thousands of people work through every night, for the payments system really never sleeps. And the volume of payments is astounding. The Federal Reserve reports that in 2006 there were 93 billion noncash payments made in the United States, 33 percent of which were paper checks. That means something like 120 million paper checks and 250 million electronic payments were processed on an average business day. And, regardless of how you choose to pay, the path that the payment follows is pretty complicated.

To understand why money is so important to the smooth functioning of the economy and how it improves everyone's well-being, we need to understand exactly what money is. Just why is a $20 bill issued by the U.S. government much more useful than $20 in Monopoly money? Furthermore, to quantify the impact of money on the economy, we need to be able to measure it. Those are the goals of this chapter: to understand what money is, how we use it, and how we measure it.

[1]For more fun facts about Monopoly, see www.monopoly.com.

Money and How We Use It

When people use the word *money* in conversation, they mean many different things. Someone who "makes lots of money" has a high income; a person who "has lots of money" is wealthy. We will use the word *money* in a narrower, specialized sense to mean anything that can readily be used to make economic transactions. Formally defined, money is *an asset that is generally accepted as payment for goods and services or repayment of debt.* Income, in contrast, is a flow of earnings over time. Wealth is the value of assets minus liabilities. Money is one of those assets, albeit a very minor one.

Money, in the sense we are talking about, has three characteristics. It is (1) a means of payment, (2) a unit of account, and (3) a store of value. The first of these characteristics is the most important. Anything that is used as a means of payment must be a store of value and thus is very likely to become a unit of account. Let's see why this is so.

Means of Payment

The primary use of money is as a **means of payment.** Most people insist on payment in money at the time a good or service is supplied because the alternatives just don't work very well. Barter, in which a good or service is exchanged directly for another good or service, requires that a plumber who needs food find a grocer who needs a plumbing repair. Relying on this "double coincidence of wants" surely causes the economy to run less smoothly. The plumber could pay for his breakfast cereal with a "promise" of plumbing services, which the grocer could then transfer to someone else. But while it would be possible to certify the plumber's trustworthiness, certainly taking payment in money is easier. Money finalizes payments so that buyers and sellers have no further claim on each other. That is money's special role. In fact, so long as a buyer has money, there is nothing more the seller needs to know.

As economies have become more complex and physically dispersed, reducing the likelihood that a seller will have good information about a buyer, the need for money has grown. The increase in both the number of transactions and the number of potential buyers and sellers (the vast majority of whom may never even have seen one another) argues for something that makes payment final and whose value is easily verified. That something is money.

Unit of Account

Just as we measure length using feet and inches, we measure value using dollars and cents. Money is the **unit of account** that we use to quote prices and record debts. We could also refer to it as a standard of value.

Having a unit of account is an incredible convenience. Remember from microeconomics that prices provide the information consumers and producers use to ensure that resources are allocated to their best uses. What matters are the *relative* prices of goods and services. When the price of one

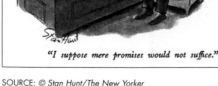

LOANS

"*I suppose mere promises would not suffice.*"

SOURCE: © Stan Hunt/The New Yorker Collection/www.cartoonbank.com.

YOUR FINANCIAL WORLD
Debit Cards versus Credit Cards

When you go shopping, should you pay with a credit card or a debit card? To decide, you need to understand the difference between the two. First make sure you know which one of your cards is which. Usually an ATM card (the one that you got from the bank when you opened your checking account) is a debit card. But check to make sure.

What's the real difference, from the shopper's point of view? A debit card works just like a check, only faster. When you write a paper check, it usually takes a day or two to go through the system. A debit card transaction goes through right away. The electronic message gets to your bank on the same day, and your account is debited immediately. So, if you want to use your debit card, your account balance has to be higher than the payment you want to make.

A credit card creates a deferred payment. The issuer agrees to make the payment for you, and you repay the debt later. That sounds good, but there's a catch. If you're late paying, there's a late fee. And if you don't pay the entire debt every month, you pay interest on the balance—at what is usually a very high interest rate. If you do pay the entire debt every month, however, there is no late fee and no interest charge. And because you don't pay right away, you get an interest-free loan from the time you make the purchase to the time you pay the balance. If you can pay off your credit cards in full and on time, it's to your advantage to use them.

Credit cards have another advantage over debit cards. They help you to build a credit history, which you'll need when the time comes to buy a car or a house. Because debit cards are just extensions of your bank account, they don't show potential lenders that you are creditworthy. In fact, some businesses, like car rental companies, require their customers to use credit cards for this reason.

product is higher than the price of another, that product is worth more to both producers and consumers. Using dollars makes these comparisons easy. Imagine what would happen if we needed to compute relative prices for each pair of goods. With two goods, we would need only one price. With three goods, we would need three prices. But with 100 goods, we would need 4,950 prices, and with 10,000 goods (substantially less than the 70,000 products in a typical supermarket), we would need nearly 50 million prices.[2] Using money as a yardstick and quoting all prices in dollars certainly is easier.

Store of Value

For money to function as a means of payment, it has to be a store of value, too. That is, if we are going to use money to pay for goods and services, then it must retain its worth from day to day. Sellers are much less likely to accept things that are perishable, like milk or lettuce. So the means of payment has to be durable and capable of transferring purchasing power from one day to the next. Paper currency does degrade with use ($1 bills have an average lifetime of 21 months in circulation), but regardless of its physical condition, it is usually accepted at face value in transactions.

Of course, money is not the only store of value. We hold our wealth in lots of other forms—stocks, bonds, houses, even cars. Many of these are actually preferable to money as stores of value. Some, like bonds, pay higher interest rates than money. Others, like stocks, offer the potential for appreciation in nominal value, which money does not. Still others, like houses, deliver other services over time. Yet we all hold

[2]The general formula is that for n goods we need $n(n-1)/2$ prices, so for 10,000 goods, the number would be $10,000\,(9,999)/2 = 49,995,000$.

money because money is liquid. Liquidity *is a measure of the ease with which an asset can be turned into a means of payment,* namely money. For example, a bond is much more liquid than a house because it is so much easier and cheaper to sell. The more costly it is to convert an asset into money, the less liquid it is. Because constantly transforming assets into money every time we wished to make a purchase would be extremely costly, we keep some money around.

Financial institutions often use a more specific term—market liquidity—for their ability to sell assets for money. A second, related concept—funding liquidity—refers to their ability to borrow money to buy securities or make loans. For financial institutions, liquidity in both those senses is critical to their daily operations: A shortfall of either type can lead to their outright failure (see Lessons from the Crisis: Market Liquidity, Funding Liquidity, and Making Markets on page 70).

The Functions of Money

1. Means of payment: Used in exchange for goods and services.
2. Unit of account: Used to quote prices.
3. Store of value: Used to move purchasing power into the future.

The Payments System

The payments system is the web of arrangements that allow for the exchange of goods and services, as well as assets, among different people. Because the efficient operation of our economy depends on the payments system, a critical public policy concern is that it functions well. As we will see in Part IV, that is why central banks are directly involved.

Money is at the heart of the payments system. Whether we realize it or not, virtually every transaction we engage in involves the use of money at some point. Let's go through all the possible methods of payment to see how the system works.

Commodity and Fiat Monies

The first means of payment were things with intrinsic value. These **commodity monies** included everything from silk in China to butter in Norway, whale teeth in Fiji, and salt in Venice. All these things had value even if they were not used as money. The worth of a block of salt, for instance, came from its value as a preservative. But successful commodity monies had other characteristics: They were usable in some form by most people; they could be made into standardized quantities; they were durable; they had high value relative to their weight and size so that they were easily transportable; and they were divisible into small units so that they were easy to trade. For most of human history, gold has been the most common commodity money. It is widely accepted as payment; can be purified and made into standard weight units like coins; and is extremely durable since it does not corrode or tarnish. Moreover, gold is rare (there is only enough in existence to fill about one-third of the Washington

A Revolutionary War "continental" issued
by the Continental Congress in 1775.
The new government of the United States
eventually printed $200 million worth, and
by 1781 they no longer had any value.

An assignat issued by the French
Revolutionary Government in 1793. Faced
with the need to finance wars and food
shortages, the government eventually
printed 40 billion of them and by the late
1790s they were worthless.

Monument with solid gold), so it has high value relative to weight. And it can be cut
into smaller pieces without losing its value.

In 1656, a Swede named Johan Palmstruck founded the Stockholm Banco. Five
years later he issued Europe's first paper money.[3] At the time, the Swedish currency
was copper ingots, which works poorly as money because of its low value per unit of
weight. (Today, copper is worth only about 18 cents per ounce, or roughly 1/100 the
value of silver and 1/6,000 the value of gold.) Thus, easy-to-handle paper was wel-
comed, at least at first.

After a few years of printing paper currency, Palmstruck and his sponsor, the King
of Sweden, became overly enamored of the new money. The king needed to finance
some wars he was fighting, so he convinced Palmstruck to print more and more notes.
Because the bills were redeemable on demand for metal, the system worked only as
long as people believed there was enough metal sitting in Palmstruck's vaults. As the
number of notes increased, Swedes lost confidence in them and started to redeem
them for the metal they supposedly stood for. But Palmstruck had issued too many
notes, and his bank failed.

Other people tried issuing paper money during the early 1700s. Eventually governments got into the act. In 1775, the newly formed Continental Congress of the United
States of America issued "continentals" to finance the Revolutionary War. Twenty
years later, revolutionary France issued the "assignat." Lacking any other source of
funding for their wars, both governments issued huge quantities of the currencies, and
both currencies eventually became worthless.

The reaction was predictable: People became suspicious of government-issued
paper money. But governments need funds and will use all available means to get

[3]The Chinese were the real monetary pioneers, issuing their first paper currency in the 7th century, 1,000 years
before the Europeans.

them. In the United States, the Civil War put pressure on government finances and the two warring parties had little choice but to issue paper money to pay for salaries and supplies. Beginning in 1862, both the Confederate and the Union governments printed and used paper money with no explicit backing. The North's "greenbacks" are still legal tender in the United States, but collectors are the only people who value the Confederate currency.

After the Civil War, the United States reverted to the use of gold as money. Both gold coins and notes backed by gold circulated well into the 20th century. Today, though, we use paper money—high-quality paper, nicely engraved, with lots of special security features. This type of currency is called fiat money, because its value comes from government decree, or *fiat*. Some countries print notes that are durable and attractive, bearing famous works of art in multiple colors. The Australians make their notes out of plastic. But in all cases the money has very little intrinsic worth, and the cost of production is only a small fraction of the face value. The U.S. Treasury's Bureau of Engraving and Printing pays less than 7 cents to print a note, regardless of whether it's a $1 or a $100 bill.

Why are we willing to accept these bills as payment for goods or in settlement of debts? There are two reasons. First, we take them because we believe we can use them in the future; someone else will take them from us. Second, the law says we must accept them. That is, the U.S. government stands behind its paper money. Since the first greenbacks were issued in 1862, all U.S. currency has borne the short and simple phrase "This note is legal tender for all debts, public and private." In practice, this means that private businesses must accept dollar bills as payment. More important, the U.S. government is committed to accepting the currency it has issued in settlement of debts. We will always be able to pay our taxes in dollars. As long as the government stands behind its paper money and doesn't issue too much of it, we will use it. In the end, money is about trust.

Checks

Checks are another way of paying for things. Unlike currency, the checks you use to pay your rent and electric bill are not legal tender. In fact, they aren't money at all. A check is just an instruction to the bank to take funds from your account and transfer them to the person or firm whose name you have written in the "Pay to the order of" line. Thus, when you give someone a check in exchange for a good or service, it is not a final payment—at least, not in the same sense as currency. Instead, your check sets in motion a series of transactions that eventually lead to the final payment.

Here are the steps. You hand the check over to a merchant, who then takes it to the bank. Depending on the arrangement, the bank will credit the amount of the check to the merchant's account either immediately or with a short lag. At the end of the day, the bank sends the check (or an electronic image) through the check-clearing system along with the other millions of checks to be processed that night by shipping them to a check-processing center run by the Federal Reserve or to a private check clearinghouse. (The first check clearinghouses were pubs where bank employees met to have a drink and exchange checks.) At the center, the check is transferred from the bank that sent it in to the bank on which it is written—your bank. The account of the bank presenting the check is credited, and the account of

Figure 2.1   The Path of a Paper Check

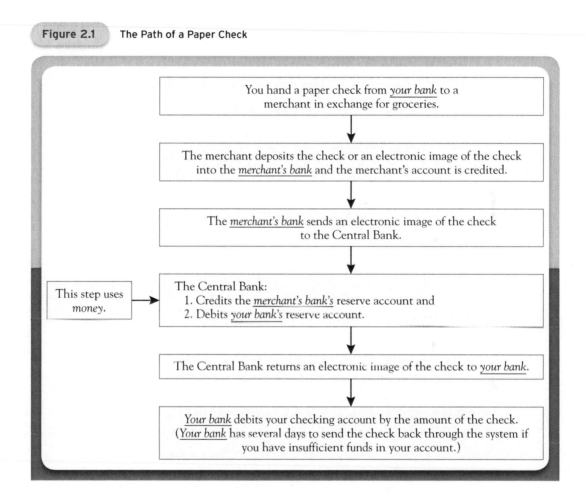

the bank on which the check is written is debited (see Figure 2.1). This is the step that uses *money*.

Finally, on receipt of the check, your bank debits your account. (If the balance in your account is insufficient to cover the check, your bank has a few days to return it to the sending bank, so the transaction isn't actually final until that period has passed.) In the past all paper checks were returned to the people who originally wrote them. Today, they are scanned and customers can view electronic images on their bank's Web sites. (See Your Financial World: Paper Checks Become Digital Images.)

Recently check volumes have fallen, but paper checks are still with us for several reasons. A canceled check is legal proof of payment and, in many states, laws require banks to return checks to customers. Then there is force of habit. Over time, people may get used to receiving bank statements without their checks, but so

YOUR FINANCIAL WORLD
Paper Checks Become Digital Images

For at least 30 years, there have been predictions that paper checks would disappear. Credit cards, ATM machines, debit cards, automatic bill payment, and Internet banking were all supposed to get rid of them. Instead, each month millions of people received thick envelopes from their banks that included canceled checks along with their monthly statements. Paper checks accounted for 60 percent of payments in 2000. But no more! On October 28, 2004, Check 21–the Check Clearing for the 21st Century Act–went into effect.

Banks are thrilled. Until the fall of 2004, the check verification and payment process required commercial banks to transport all paper checks to and from a Federal Reserve Bank, and eventually back to the people who wrote them. Paper checks were legal proof of payment, so customers wanted them back. But transporting tons and tons of checks around the country was an expensive headache for banks.

Check 21 gives banks the leeway to process checks electronically. Instead of shipping paper across the country, banks transmit digital images of each check that was written. These images create "substitute checks," and have the same legal standing as the original checks.

Payments in long-distance transactions are now much less complicated. Before Check 21, if someone living in Houston sent a check to make a payment to a business in Chicago, the piece of paper had to go from Texas to Illinois, and then back again. Now, the check can be scanned and shredded in Chicago and the image is saved and transmitted. If the person who wrote it in Houston wants a paper copy of the canceled check, their bank can print a substitute check. A check processing system that used to take a few days now takes a few hours.

Processing checks electronically is definitely cheaper. With the volume of paper checks dwindling and most checks now clearing electronically, the Federal Reserve has reduced the number of its processing centers to 1–down from 45 before Check 21. And, experts estimate that by scanning checks and transmitting the images, the banks will save $2 billion a year. These savings include $250 million spent on courier services to move checks around the country.

In fact, reducing the risks of physically transporting checks was one of the big reasons for the passage of Check 21. For several days following the September 11, 2001, terrorist attacks, only military planes were allowed to fly in U.S. airspace and that disrupted the check transportation system eventually grounding $47 billion worth of paper checks.

Speeding up paper check processing does have one downside: People can't write checks with the expectation that they will have a day or two to make a deposit to cover it. There is no more float. The new rules shrink the time between when a check is written and when the account is debited, especially for out-of-town checks.*

By speeding up the processing of paper checks, Check 21 provides a further incentive for individuals to use debit cards, credit cards, or other forms of electronic payments. Nevertheless, billions of checks are likely to be written for years to come.

For more details on Check 21, payments system development and policies, see the Federal Reserve Board's payment system Web site http://www.federalreserve.gov/paymentsys.htm.

*Just because banks are able to move checks through the clearing system more quickly doesn't mean that they are going to offer the depositor more timely access to the funds. In an attempt to reduce fraud, banks restrict access to funds from so-called high-risk checks, such as those for more than $5,000 that are deposited into newly opened accounts, for as long as 11 business days. If you have to shift large quantities of funds and use them quickly, it is important to find out the policies of the financial intermediaries involved before you do it.

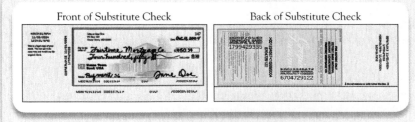

Front of Substitute Check   Back of Substitute Check

The front of the substitute check includes the following: "This is a legal copy of your check. You can use it the same way you would use the original check."

far not many people have chosen the option. Finally, new electronic mechanisms for clearing checks have lowered costs and kept checks as an attractive means of payment.

Electronic Payments

The third and final method of payment is electronic. We are all familiar with credit cards and debit cards. A less well-known form of payment is electronic funds transfers. While there are a large number of credit and debit card transactions, electronic funds transfers account for the bulk of the $35 trillion worth of noncash, noncheck payments made each year in the United States.

What is the difference between debit cards and credit cards? A debit card works the same way as a check in that it provides the bank with instructions to transfer funds from the cardholder's account directly to a merchant's account. There is usually a charge for this; the processor of the payment takes a fee based on the size of the transaction.

A credit card is a promise by a bank to lend the cardholder money with which to make purchases. When a shopper buys a pair of shoes with a credit card, the shoe store's bank account receives payment immediately, but the money that is used for payment does not belong to the buyer. Instead, the bank that issued the credit card makes the payment, creating a loan the cardholder must repay. For this reason, credit cards do not represent money; rather, they represent access to someone else's money.

Electronic funds transfers are movements of funds directly from one account to another. These transactions are used extensively by banks and are becoming increasingly popular for individuals as well. For individuals, the most common form is the automated clearinghouse transaction (ACH), which is generally used for recurring payments such as paychecks and utility bills. Some merchants use them for one-time transactions as well. ACH transactions are just like checks except that they are entirely electronic. Your bank account is debited or credited automatically, and you receive periodic notifications of the activity in your account.

Banks use electronic transfers to handle transactions among themselves. The most common method is to send money through a system maintained by the Federal Reserve, called Fedwire. The volume and value of payments made through this system are substantial. On a typical day in 2009, the system completed 495,000 transactions with a total value of about $2.5 trillion.

Retail businesses, together with their banks, are experimenting with a variety of new methods of electronic payment. One is the stored-value card, which looks like a credit or debit card except that it doesn't bear your name. To use one, you go to the bank or ATM machine and put the card into an electronic device that transfers funds from your checking account to your card. Then you take the card to a merchant who has a reader that is capable of deducting funds from the card and depositing them directly into the store's account. The stuff on the card is in fact money, and the system can be set up so that if you lose your card, its current value can be canceled.

So far, these cards have limited usefulness. The New York City Metropolitan Transit Authority and other city transit systems sell stored-value cards, but it's hard to buy anything with them other than subway and bus rides. The same is true of long-distance phone cards and gift cards sold by chain stores like Barnes & Noble.

70 | Chapter 2   Money and the Payments System

LESSONS FROM THE CRISIS
MARKET LIQUIDITY, FUNDING LIQUIDITY, AND MAKING MARKETS

A "market maker" in stocks, bonds, or other securities is usually a financial institution that buys and sells securities on behalf of clients. If buy orders at a market maker exceed sell orders for a particular security, the market maker must be able to act as the seller to clear the market. Therefore, market makers usually hold inventories of the specific financial instruments in which they trade, and they borrow to maintain inventories at adequate levels.

Market liquidity—the ability to sell assets—and *funding liquidity*—the ability to borrow money—are both needed to make financial markets function smoothly. If a loss of funding liquidity prevents market makers from holding adequate inventories, trading and market liquidity suffer. Conversely, if market liquidity for some financial instruments declines, the prices of those instruments will fall as they become less attractive to investors; resulting concerns about the safety of the market makers that hold the assets with falling prices may reduce their ability to borrow.

A sudden loss of liquidity was central to the 2007–2009 financial crisis. Before the crisis, many financial institutions relied on short-term borrowing to hold long-term financial instruments because their managers believed that funding liquidity would remain readily available. They also believed that markets would always be liquid—that is, they would always be able to sell the securities and loans that they held. They were wrong on both counts.

In the summer of 2007, investors began to doubt the value of a wide class of securities. As a result, market liquidity for those instruments disappeared, and financial institutions that held them faced large potential losses. In turn, funding liquidity for these institutions evaporated as the potential losses caused their lenders to worry about their safety.

This double "liquidity shock" led many financial institutions to increase cash holdings that they might otherwise have lent to others. Reduced loan supply intensified the vicious spiral of dwindling liquidity and falling securities prices. The financial system as a whole could not provide sufficient market liquidity or funding liquidity to satisfy heightened demands.

One lesson from the financial crisis is clear: Liquidity is a highly valuable resource that can disappear when it is most needed, so it should not be taken for granted. Even large and seemingly wealthy financial firms can fail if liquidity evaporates.

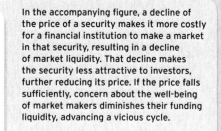

Liquidity Spiral

In the accompanying figure, a decline of the price of a security makes it more costly for a financial institution to make a market in that security, resulting in a decline of market liquidity. That decline makes the security less attractive to investors, further reducing its price. If the price falls sufficiently, concern about the well-being of market makers diminishes their funding liquidity, advancing a vicious cycle.

Attempts to implement the stored-value card more broadly haven't worked very well because most merchants lack the hardware to read the cards. And few of us know how to use them.

E-money is another new method of payment. It can be used to pay for purchases on the Internet. You open an account by transferring funds to the issuer of the e-money. Then, when you are shopping online, you instruct the issuer to send your e-money to the merchant.

E-money is really a form of private money. It is not issued or guaranteed by the government, so you can't use it to pay your taxes. It's hard to even define what the term *e-money* means. One definition that seems helpful is "monetary value, as represented by a claim on the issuer, which is (a) stored on an electronic device, (b) issued on receipt of funds, and (c) accepted as a means of payment by persons other than the issuer."[4]

But at this point, e-money is questionable at best. Will individuals develop enough trust in e-money to be willing to use it? Will merchants install the expensive equipment to handle it? Who will be allowed to issue e-money? Still, the day may come when you can park your car and pay the parking meter by simply punching a series of numbers into your cell phone that transfers e-money issued by your phone provider to the city government that owns the parking meter.

The Future of Money

Let's speculate about what might happen to money and each of its three functions in the future. As a *means of payment,* it has already undergone big changes. The time is rapidly approaching when safe and secure systems for payment will use virtually no money at all.

We will always need money as a *unit of account* in which to quote values and prices; the efficiency of quoting prices in commonly understood terms isn't going to change. But the question is, how many units of account will we need? Today, many countries have their own currencies, which give rise to their own units of account. In the future, though, there will be little reason to maintain different units of account across different countries. Price systems will be more like systems of weights and measures. Today, there are two commonly used systems of weights and measures: English ounces and yards and metric grams and meters. We will likely see a similar sort of standardization of money and a dramatic reduction in the number of units of account.

Finally, money as a *store of value* is clearly on the way out. With the advances in financial markets, many financial instruments have become highly liquid. They are easily bought and sold and can be converted into a means of payment quickly and cheaply. These instruments and the financial markets in which they trade are the subject of the next chapter. For now, though, we can conclude that in the future, there will almost surely be less and less money.

One caution is in order. As we look into the future and try to discern what will happen to money, we should remember that 150 years ago there was virtually no paper currency in circulation. The first credit card was issued in the early 1950s; the first ATM was installed around 1970. Not until the mid-1990s could we shop via the Internet. Forecasting most of these developments, as well as any other trend in technology, is nearly impossible. After all, who could have predicted even 10 years ago that today we would be able to check our bank balances, buy and sell stocks, and pay our utility bills 24 hours a day, seven days a week from the comfort of our homes? (See In the News: Dad, Can You Text Me $200?)

---

[4]This definition comes from Directive 2000/46 of the European Parliament and the Council of 18 September 2000, "On the Taking Up, Pursuit and Prudential Supervision of the Business of Electronic Money Institutions," *Official Journal of the European Communities,* 275/39, 27 October 2000.

IN THE NEWS
Dad, Can You Text Me $200?

THE WALL STREET JOURNAL.
WSJ.com

by Jonnelle Marte

June 23, 2009

Parents, used to receiving kids' requests for money via email and cellphone, are now able to send that money via text message, email or cell.

A new service by CashEdge Inc., which provides online banking services for financial institutions, would let users send money to friends and family through a text message or email—further cutting down on our need to stop at ATMs or write checks when we owe people money.

"Paper transactions are shrinking and electronic transactions are growing and this just seems to be the next step along that path," said Steve Kenneally of the American Bankers Association.

The new service, called POPmoney, will let consumers "Pay Other People" through their bank's online or mobile banking application by providing the recipient's email address, cell phone number or account number.

Once users enter their friends' information online, they would be able to send the person-to-person payments directly from their cell phones.

"You will be using your mobile phone to do small transfers over dinner" and to make other quick payments to friends or relatives, says CashEdge president Sanjeev Dheer.

OMG, plz txt me $!

Measuring Money

Changes in the amount of money in the economy are related to changes in interest rates, economic growth, and most important, inflation. Inflation is the rate at which prices in general are increasing over time—and the inflation rate is a measure of that process.[5] With inflation, you need more units of money to buy the same basket of goods you bought a month or a year ago. Put another way, inflation makes money less valuable. And the primary cause of inflation is the issuance of too much money. When the Continental Congress issued too much currency to finance the Revolutionary

[5] The terms "inflation" and "inflation rate" are often used interchangeably. We will refer to inflation as the process of prices rising, and inflation rate as the measurement of the process. The relationship between these terms is analogous to that between "heat" and "temperature." The second is the measure of the first.

Recipients at participating banks will be able to accept the cash deposits through their own online banking accounts. They can also automatically deposit payments from specific users. For example, college students could have payments from mom and dad automatically deposited into their checking accounts or vice versa.

The service will likely come with a fee, which Mr. Dheer says will be set by the financial institutions. A demo transaction showed a standard transfer, which could take a few days, costing $2 and an express one costing $10.

The concept isn't completely new. Mobile banking apps already let people check their balances and transfer money from one account to another by pushing a few buttons. PayPal, which most online shoppers know well, lets consumers send money electronically to friends using their email address. Zoompass, a service recently launched in Canada, lets users send, receive and request money from their mobile phones to an intermediary account—similar to PayPal—linked to their bank accounts.

But POPmoney's key feature is that it will allow users to send money directly from one bank account to another.

"This is a function that people should be able to do within their banks and not have to sign up for another service," says Mr. Dheer.

Those with banks that don't offer the service will be able to sign on to an online payment hub where they can provide their bank account information in order to receive the money.

Larger transactions will have added security measures, said Mr. Dheer. For instance, the person sending money will

have to give both an email and phone number for the recipient, who would be required to submit a code sent to them via text before they could accept the money.

At first, consumers will only have the option to send and accept cash, not to request it, but CashEdge is hoping to offer that feature in later releases, said Mr. Dheer. POPmoney will likely be up and running around September, after banks integrate the service into their online banking hubs, says Mr. Dheer.

SOURCE: *The Wall Street Journal Online*. "Dad, Can You Text Me $200?" by Jonnelle Marte, June 23, 2009. Copyright 2009 by Dow Jones & Company, Inc. Reproduced with permission of Dow Jones & Company, Inc. in the formats Textbook and Other Book via Copyright Clearance Center.

LESSONS OF THE ARTICLE

Technological advances are constantly creating new methods of payment. While their adoption depends on many things, one thing is for certain: Someone will always be searching for easier and cheaper ways for us to pay for things. And as the payments system evolves, so will the assets that we need to hold. As our cell phones transform into a part of the payments sytem, we will need to carry less and less cash.

War, the number of continentals people needed to purchase food and shelter rose dramatically. Continentals slowly became less valuable. So the value of the means of payment depends on how much of it is circulating.

To use the insight that money growth is somehow related to inflation, we must be able to measure how much money is circulating. This is no easy task. Let's start with money's primary function, as a means of payment. If that were the definition of money, we would measure the quantity of money as the quantity of currency in circulation—an unrealistically limited measure, since there are many ways to complete transactions (effect final payment) without using currency.

A reasonable alternative would be to consider the functionality of a broad category of financial assets and sort them by their degree of liquidity. That is, we could sort them by the ease with which they can be converted into a means of payment, arranging them along a spectrum from the most liquid (currency) to the least liquid (art,

Figure 2.2   The Liquidity Spectrum

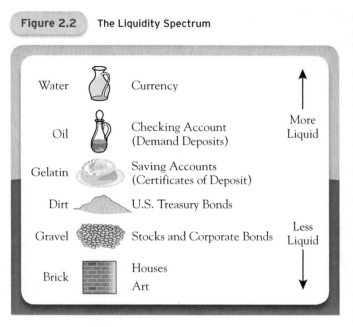

Liquidity is the ease with which you can turn an asset into a means of payment without loss of value.

antique cars, and the like). Figure 2.2 shows what our liquidity spectrum would look like.

Once we have our list, we could draw a line and include everything on one side of the line in our measure of money. Over the years, figuring out just where to draw the line has proven very difficult, especially since the introduction of new types of checking accounts. There really is no perfect solution. Instead, central bankers have drawn the line in several places and compute various measures of money, called **monetary aggregates**. In the U.S., they are called M1 and M2.[6] In the Euro zone they are M1 and M3.

Table 2.1 shows the components of M1 and M2 as defined by the Federal Reserve and M1 and M3 as defined by the European Central Bank, along with recent values. Each central bank has a narrow definition of money called M1, though the components differ a bit between the U.S. and the Euro zone. M1 in the U.S. includes currency and deposits upon which checks can be written. These are the most liquid assets in the financial system. Components of U.S. M1 include *currency in the hands of the public*, which is currency outside of bank vaults; *travelers' checks* issued by travel companies, banks, and credit card companies, which are guaranteed by the issuer and usually work just like cash; demand deposits at commercial banks, standard checking accounts paying no interest; and other checkable deposits, interest-bearing checking accounts. Euro area M1 is the sum of currency in circulation and overnight deposits, the most liquid assets in the European financial system.

U.S. M2 equals all of M1 plus assets that cannot be used directly as a means of payment and are difficult to turn into currency quickly. These assets in M2 include small denomination time deposits (less than $100,000) that cannot be withdrawn without advance notice; *savings deposits*, including *money-market deposit accounts*, which pay interest and offer limited check-writing privileges; and *retail money-market mutual fund shares*, shares in funds that collect relatively small sums from individuals, pool them together, and invest in short-term marketable debt issued by large corporations. Money-market mutual fund shares can be issued by nonbank financial intermediaries, such as brokerage firms. They do carry check-writing privileges. M2 is the most commonly quoted monetary aggregate, since its movements are most closely related to interest rates and economic growth. As with the U.S., the euro area's broader aggregate, M3, adds to its M1 slightly less liquid assets that can be converted into the means of payment.

To clarify what the monetary aggregates mean, let's compare their size to the size of the economy. For example, in winter 2010, nominal U.S. gross domestic product (GDP) was

[6]On March 23, 2006, the Federal Reserve Board ceased collection and publication of a third monetary aggregate, M3. In announcing their decision, officials wrote: "M3 does not appear to convey any additional information about economic activity that is not already embodied in M2 and has not played a role in the monetary policy process for many years."

Table 2.1	U.S. and Euro-Area Monetary Aggregates

A. Narrow Aggregates		**U.S. ($billions)**				**Euro Area (€ billions)**
M1	=	Currency in hands of public	861.1	M1	=	Currency in Circulation	785.0
	+	Traveler's Checks	5.1		+	Overnight Deposits	3875.2
	+	Demand Deposits	435.0			**Total M1**	**4660.2**
	+	Other Checkable Deposits	375.3				
		Total M1	**1676.5**				

B. Broad Aggregates

M2	=	M1		M3	=	M1	
	+	Small denomination time deposits	1139.8		+	Deposits with Maturity Up to 2 Years	1798.4
	+	Savings and Money Market Deposit Accounts	4856.5		+	Deposits Redeemable at Notice up to 3 Months	1841.0
	+	Retail Money Market Mutual Fund Shares	790.7		+	Repurchase Agreements	401.9
		Total M2	**8463.5**		+	Money Market Funds	604.1
					+	Debt Securities up to 2 Years	122.1
						Total M3	**9427.7**

Note: U.S. data for January 2010; Euro area data for June 2010.
SOURCE: *Board of Governors of the Federal Reserve System and European Central Bank.*

$14.5 trillion. Putting that number into the same units as those in Table 2.1, that's $14,500 billion. So U.S. GDP is nearly nine times as large as M1 and about 70 percent larger than M2.

Which one of the Ms should we use to understand inflation? That's a difficult question whose answer has changed over time for some countries. Until the early 1980s, economists and policymakers in the U.S. looked at M1. But with the introduction of substitutes for standard checking accounts, especially money-market mutual fund shares, M1 became less useful. These innovations enabled people to shift their balances out of the noninterest-bearing accounts in M1 and into accounts that paid interest. As Table 2.1 shows, U.S. demand deposits and other checkable deposits in M1 total about $810 billion, which represents less than 6 percent of GDP. By comparison, the savings deposits, money-market deposit accounts, and retail money-market mutual fund shares in M2 total over $6.7 trillion, representing nearly one-half of GDP. M1 is no longer a useful measure of money. In Europe, M3 is monitored for longer-run inflation implications.

Looking at Figure 2.3 on page 77, you can see that from 1960 to 1980 the growth rates of the two measures of money moved together. After 1980, however, M1 behaved very differently from M2. Here's what happened. In the late 1970s and early 1980s, inflation climbed to over 10 percent for a few years. Needless to say, people who had money in zero-interest checking accounts were upset. Their money was losing value at a rapid rate. They went looking for ways to get checking services along with interest. Soon financial firms began to offer "money market" accounts that compensated depositors at least in part for inflation. These accounts are part of M2. The movement of funds into the non-M1 portion of M2 meant that the two measures no longer moved together. At the same time, the new money market accounts made M2 accounts more liquid. Analysts stopped looking at M1 and began to look at M2.

TOOLS OF THE TRADE

Consumer Price Indexes in the U.S. and Europe

Understanding how to measure inflation is central to understanding economics and finance. Most of us gauge the purchasing power of our money by watching measures like the Consumer Price Index (CPI) in the U.S. or, in Europe, the Harmonized Index of Consumer Prices (HICP). And adjusting interest rates for inflation is critical for investment decisions. (See Chapter 4.)

These indices are designed to answer the following question: How much more would it cost for someone to purchase today the same basket of goods and services that they actually bought at some fixed time in the past?

To calculate these price indices, every few years government statisticians in various countries survey people to find out what they bought. This gives us the basket of goods and services bought by the typical consumer. Next, every month the statistical agencies collect information on the prices of thousands of goods and services—everything from breakfast cereal to gasoline to washing machines to the cost of cable television. Combining the expenditure and price surveys allows statisticians to compute the current cost of the basket. Finally, this current cost is compared to a benchmark to yield an index. And the percentage change in this index is a measure of inflation.

To see how this works, let's look at an example. Assume people spend 25 percent of their income on food, 50 percent on housing and 25 percent on transportation. That's the survey information. Examples of the prices are in Table 2.2. Importantly, these are the prices of exactly the same bundle of food, the same size and quality of housing, and the same transportation for each year.

Using the numbers in Table 2.2 we can compute the cost of the basket of goods in each year:

Cost of the basket in 2010

= 0.25 × Price of food + 0.5 × Price of housing

   + 0.25 × Price of transportation

= 0.25 × \$100 + 0.5 × \$200 + 0.25 × \$100

= \$150

And for 2011, we get \$165. Choosing 2010 as the base year, the index level in each year equals

$$CPI = \frac{\text{Cost of the basket in current year}}{\text{Cost of the basket in base year}} \times 100$$

The result of this computation is the fifth column of the table.

Finally, we can use the index number to compute the inflation rate from the previous year. From 2010 to 2011, this means that

$$\text{Inflation Rate 2011} = \frac{\text{CPI in 2011} - \text{CPI in 2010}}{\text{CPI in 2010}} \times 100$$

Using the numbers from Table 2.2 to compute the inflation rate in 2011, we get that

$$\frac{110 - 100}{100} \times 100 = 10\%$$

and for 2012 the result is

$$\frac{120 - 110}{110} \times 100 = 9.1\%$$

(These numbers are just for illustration. The U.S. inflation rate is closer to 2 percent.)

Inflation measured using the CPI or HICP tells us how much more money we need to give someone to restore purchasing power they had in the earlier period when the survey was done. But adjustments in wages based on fixed-expenditure-weight inflation indices are known to overcompensate people in an unintended way. This overstatement of inflation comes from what is known as *substitution bias*. Because inflation is not uniform, the prices of some products will increase by more than the prices of others. People can escape some of the inflation by *substituting* goods and services that have sustained less inflation for those that have sustained more. By assuming that any substitution makes people worse off, the index *overstates* the impact of price changes. To address this problem, and take into account changes in spending patterns, statistical agencies must now update the weights more frequently than earlier. As a result, the indices are much more accurate.

Table 2.2   Computing the Consumer Price Index

Year	Price of Food	Price of Housing	Price of Transportation	Cost of the Basket	Consumer Price Index
2010	\$100	\$200	\$100	\$150	100
2011	110	205	140	165	110
2012	120	210	180	180	120

APPLYING THE CONCEPT
WHERE ARE ALL THOSE $100 BILLS?

A quick look at the Federal Reserve's Web site, www.federalreserve.gov, tells us that during the winter of 2009, the public held about $880 billion in United States currency. That's a huge amount. To get some sense of the size of this number, you can divide it by the U.S. population, 310 million, to get roughly $2,800 per person. For a household of four, that's an average of more than $11,000 in cash. What's even more absurd is that nearly 80 percent of the $880 billion is held in the form of $100 bills, meaning that there must be twenty-two $100 bills for each United States resident. Clearly, we do not hold all this cash in our wallets or our homes, nor does it fill the cash registers of local businesses. Where are all those $100 bills?

Not in the United States. In many countries, people do not trust their governments to protect the value of the currency they print. They fear the authorities will print too much, creating inflation. And because money is all about trust, if you don't have confidence in your government, you don't want to hold your wealth in the government's money. In many cases, the lack of faith has been warranted. When the Soviet Union collapsed in the early 1990s, the currency issued by the old regime became nearly worthless. The same thing happened in Argentina in the 1980s.

When people stop trusting the local currency, they look for substitutes. The most sought-after is the U.S. dollar bill. With the stability of the constant addition of new security features, and the stability of the government, everyone seems to have faith in it.* The U.S. Treasury estimates that between two-thirds and three-quarters of U.S. currency is held outside the United States. That's around $600 billion—and most of it is in hundreds!

*For a guide to the security features in U.S. currency, go to www.moneyfactory.gov. This constant redesign has been successful in thwarting counterfeiting. Estimates are that the total quantity [of counterfeit bills] is less than 10,000 bills outstanding. This is definitely not something that anyone should worry about.

Figure 2.3   Growth Rates of Monetary Aggregates, 1960–2009

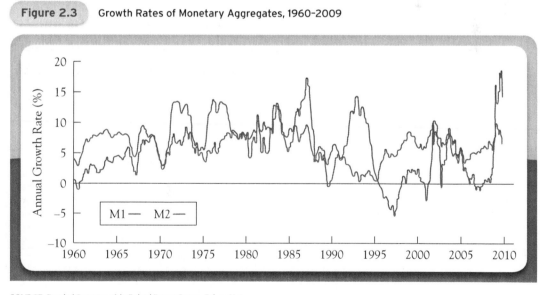

SOURCE: *Board of Governors of the Federal Reserve System, Release H.6.*

How useful is M2 in tracking inflation? We already know that when the quantity of money grows quickly, it produces very high inflation. A cross-country analysis of money growth supports this conclusion. In Turkey, Venezuela, and Ukraine, where in the last half of the 1990s the inflation rate ranged from 30 to 75 percent per year, the

Figure 2.4   Money Growth and Inflation, Monthly 1960-2009

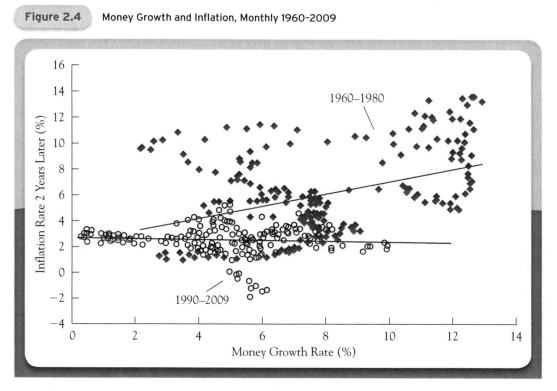

Money growth measured as the 12-month change in M2, and inflation measured as the 12-month change in the Consumer Price Index.

SOURCE: *Board of Governors of the Federal Reserve System and Bureau of Labor Statistics.*

money supply grew at comparable rates.[7] By contrast, in the United States, Canada, and Europe, the inflation rate averaged only about 2 percent, and the money growth rate stayed in the range of 6 to 7 percent. Because high money growth means high inflation, controlling inflation means controlling the money supply. Imagine how much inflation there would be if people could spend the $3 trillion in Monopoly dollars Parker Brothers has printed over the past seven decades!

How useful is money growth in helping us to control moderate inflation? We will address this question in detail in Chapter 20 of this book. For now, though, let's look at whether money growth helps to forecast inflation.

Figure 2.4 shows the inflation rate on the vertical axis and M2 growth *two years earlier* on the horizontal axis, both for the United States. The solid red diamonds represent data from 1960 to 1980. Note that, while the relationship is far from perfect

[7]From 1995 to 2000, inflation averaged 74 percent, 42 percent, and 30 percent, respectively, in Turkey, Venezuela, and Ukraine. At the same time, a measure of money that is close to U.S. M2 grew at 86, 33, and 36 percent per year. Data for these comparisons come from the International Monetary Fund's *International Financial Statistics.*

in those years, higher money growth was clearly associated with higher inflation two years later. In fact, the correlation was over 0.5.[8] But look at what has happened to the relationship more recently. The hollow blue dots represent data from 1990 to 2009, when there was virtually no relationship at all between the two measures. (The correlation was slightly negative.) Growth in M2 stopped being a useful tool for forecasting inflation.

According to the Organization for Economic Cooperation and Development, the ability of monetary aggregates to predict inflation in the euro area has also deteriorated. For core inflation, various aggregates "have virtually no predictive power over any horizon in the 2000–2005 period."[9]

There are two possible explanations for the fact that money may no longer predict inflation. One is that the relationship between the two applies only at high levels of inflation. In the United States, for instance, Figure 2.4 shows that during the period 1960–1980, the inflation rate often rose higher than 5 percent, but from 1990 to 2009, it rarely did. Maybe the relationship between money growth and inflation doesn't exist at low levels of inflation, or it shows up only over longer periods of time. All we really know is that at low levels of money growth, inflation is likely to stay low.

An alternative explanation is that we need a new measure of money that takes into account recent changes in the way we make payments and use money. Once economists have identified the right measure, we'll be able to predict inflation again.

---

[8]Correlation is a measure of how closely two quantities are related, or change together. The numerical value ranges from +1 to −1. A positive correlation signifies that the two variables move and down together, while a negative correlation means that they move in opposite directions.

[9]"Economic Survey of the Euro Area 2007: The Role of Monetary Aggregates in Monetary Policy," www.oecd .org/dataoecd/55/11/37861149.pdf

Terms

automated clearinghouse transaction (ACH), 69
check, 66
credit card, 69
currency, 63
debit card, 69
demand deposits, 74
electronic funds transfer, 69
e-money, 70
fiat money, 66
funding liquidity, 64
gross domestic product (GDP), 74
inflation, 72
inflation rate, 72

liquidity, 64
market liquidity, 64
M1, 74
M2, 74
M3, 74
means of payment, 62
monetary aggregates, 74
money, 62
payments system, 64
store of value, 63
stored-value card, 69
time deposits, 74
unit of account, 62
wealth, 62

www.mhhe.com/cecchetti3e

Chapter Lessons

1. Money is an asset that is generally accepted in payment for goods and services or repayment of debts.
   a. Money has three basic uses:
      i. Means of payment
      ii. Unit of account
      iii. Store of value
   b. Money is liquid. Liquidity is the ease with which an asset can be turned into a means of payment.
   c. For financial institutions, market liquidity is the ease with which they can sell a security or loan for money. Funding liquidity is the ease with which they can borrow to acquire a security or loan.

2. Money makes the payments system work. The payments system is the web of arrangements that allows people to exchange goods and services. There are three broad categories of payments, all of which use money at some stage.
   a. Cash
   b. Checks
   c. Electronic payments

3. In the future, money will be used less and less as a means of payment.

4. To understand the links among money, inflation, and economic growth, we need to measure the quantity of money in the economy. There are two basic measures of money.
   a. M1, the narrowest measure, includes only the most liquid assets.
   b. M2, a broader measure, includes assets not usable as means of payment.
   c. Countries with high money growth have high inflation.
   d. In countries with low inflation, money growth is a poor forecaster of inflation.

Conceptual Problems

1. The country of Brieonia has an economy that is based largely on farming and agricultural products. The inhabitants of Brieonia use cheese as their money.
   a. Not surprisingly, the Brieonians complain bitterly about the problems that their commodity money creates. What are they?
   b. Modern medical science arrives in Brieonia, and doctors begin giving the Brieonians cholesterol tests. The results lead to the recommendation that the Brieonians reduce the amount of cheese they eat. What is the impact of this recommendation on their economy?
   c. As the economy of Brieonia becomes industrialized, what changes in the monetary system would you expect to see, and why?

2. Describe at least three ways you could pay for your morning cup of coffee. What are the advantages and disadvantages of each?

3. Explain how money encourages specialization, and how specialization improves everyone's standard of living.

4.* Could the dollar still function as the unit of account in a totally cashless society?

5. Explain why a security for which there is a financial institution acting as a market maker would be more attractive to an investor.

6. As of March 2010, 16 of the 27 countries of the European Union have adopted the euro. The remaining 11 countries, including Great Britain, Denmark, and Sweden, have retained their own currencies. What are the advantages of a common currency for someone who is traveling through Europe?

7. Go to the website for the European Central Bank and find data on M3 along with information on population in the euro area. Compute the per capita quantity of money in the euro area. Does the value strike you as large or small? Explain.

8. Plot annual percentage changes in M1 and M3 from the euro area and compare with Figure 2.3 in the text. How do the patterns in the growth rates in the euro area compare with those in the United States?

9. During World War II, Germany used counterfeiting as a tool of war. Explain the reasoning behind this decision.

10.* You have decided to issue your own currency and use your computer to produce some impressive looking notes. What could you do to increase the chances of these notes being accepted as a means of payment?

11. Over a nine-year period in the 16th century, King Henry VIII reduced the silver content of the British pound to one-sixth its initial value. Why do you think he did so? What do you think happened to the use of pounds as a means of payment? If you held both the old and new pounds, which would you use first, and why?

Analytical Problems

12. Under what circumstances might you expect barter to reemerge in an economy that has fiat money as a means of payment? Can you think of an example of a country where this has happened recently?

13. You visit a tropical island that has only four goods in its economy—oranges, pineapples, coconuts, and bananas. There is no money in this economy.
   a. Draw a grid showing all the prices for this economy. (You should check your answer using the $n(n-1)/2$ formula where n is the number of goods.)
   b. An islander suggests designating oranges as the means of payment and unit of account for the economy. How many prices would there be if her suggestion was followed?
   c. Do you think the change suggested in part b is worth implementing? Why or why not?

14. Consider again the tropical island described in question 13. Under what circumstances would you recommend the issue of a paper currency by the government of the island? What advantages might this strategy have over the use of oranges as money?

*Indicates more difficult problems

15. What factors should you take into account when considering using the following assets as stores of value?
    a. Gold
    b. Real estate
    c. Stocks
    d. Government bonds

16.* Under what circumstances might money in the form of currency be the best option as a store of value?

17. Suppose a significant fall in the price of certain stocks caused the market makers in those stocks to worry about their funding liquidity. Under what circumstances might that development lead to liquidity problems in markets for other assets?

18.* Consider an economy that only produces and consumes two goods—food and apparel. Suppose the inflation rate based on the consumer price index is higher during the year than that based on the GDP deflator. Assuming underlying tastes and preferences in the economy stay the same, what can you say about food and apparel price movements during the year?

19. Suppose a regulator proposes placing an upper limit on the interest rate payable on checking and saving accounts. How would this help or hinder regulation of the banking system during a period of high interest rates?

20. If money growth is related to inflation, what would you expect to happen to the inflation rates of countries that join a monetary union and adopt a common currency such as the euro?

Chapter 3

Financial Instruments, Financial Markets, and Financial Institutions

Long before formal financial institutions and instruments became common, there were times when people lacked the resources to meet their immediate needs. In the terminology of introductory economics, people's incomes were exceeded by their necessary consumption. When a harvest was poor, they would dip into the reserves stored from previous years or exchange assets like land and livestock for food. But often those measures were insufficient, so communities developed informal financial arrangements that allowed people to borrow or lend among themselves. After a poor harvest, those people with relatively good yields would help those with relatively poor ones. When the tables were turned, help would flow the other way. In some societies, families spread out geographically to facilitate these arrangements. For example, in rural Indian communities, households deliberately married off their daughters to families in different regions to increase the chance that their in-laws would be able to respond in a time of crisis.[1] These informal insurance arrangements ensured that everyone had enough to eat.

While family members and friends still make loans among themselves, the informal arrangements that were the mainstay of the financial system centuries ago have given way to the formal financial instruments of the modern world. Today, the international financial system exists to facilitate the design, sale, and exchange of a broad set of contracts with a very specific set of characteristics. As shown in Figure 3.1 we obtain the financial resources we need through this system in two ways: directly from markets and indirectly through institutions.

In indirect finance, an institution like a bank stands between the lender and the borrower, borrowing from the lender and then providing the funds to the borrower. Most of us do our borrowing and lending indirectly. If we need a loan to buy a car, we get it from a bank or finance company—that's indirect finance. Once we get the loan, the car becomes one of our assets, and the loan becomes our liability. We all have assets and liabilities. Your assets probably include things of value like a bank account and a computer. If you have a student loan or credit card debt, those are your liabilities.

In direct finance, borrowers sell securities directly to lenders in the financial markets. Governments and corporations finance their activities in this way. These securities become assets for the lenders who buy them and liabilities to the government or corporation that initially sells them.

Financial development is inextricably linked to economic growth. A country's financial system has to grow as its level of economic activity rises, or the country will stagnate. The role of the financial system is to facilitate production, employment, and

---

[1] See M. R. Rosenzweig, "Risk, Implicit Contracts, and the Family in Rural Areas of Low-Income Countries," *Economic Journal* 98 (December 1988).

84 | Chapter 3   Financial Instruments, Financial Markets, and Financial Institutions

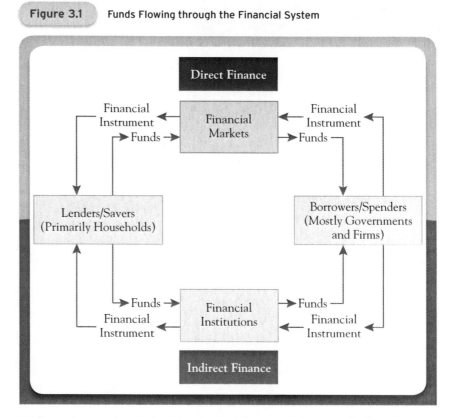

Figure 3.1   Funds Flowing through the Financial System

The financial system channels funds from lenders to borrowers in two ways: directly and indirectly. In **direct finance**, borrowers obtain resources by selling financial instruments like bonds and stocks in financial markets directly to lenders. In **indirect finance**, a financial institution like a bank takes the resources from the lender in the form of a deposit (or something like it) and then provides them to the borrower in the form of a loan (or the equivalent).

consumption. In a prosperous economy, people have the means to pay for things, and resources flow to their most efficient uses. Savings are funneled through the system so that they can finance investment and allow the economy to grow. The decisions made by the people who do the saving direct the investment.

In this chapter, we will survey the financial system in three steps. First, we'll study *financial instruments*, or *securities*, as they are often called. Stocks, bonds, and loans of all types are financial instruments, as are more exotic agreements like options and insurance. Exactly what are these financial instruments, and what is their role in our economy? Second, we'll look at *financial markets*, such as the New York Stock Exchange and the Nasdaq (National Association of Securities Dealers Automatic Quotations), where investors can buy and sell stocks, bonds, and various other instruments. And finally, we'll look at *financial institutions*—what they are and what they do.

Financial Instruments

A financial instrument is the *written legal obliga-*
tion of one party to transfer something of value, usu-
ally money, to another party at some future date,
under certain conditions. Let's dissect this definition
to understand it better. First, a financial instrument is a *written legal obligation* that is subject to
government enforcement. That is, a person can
be compelled to take the action specified in the
agreement. The enforceability of the obligation
is an important feature of a financial instrument.
Without enforcement of the specified terms, financial instruments would not exist.[2]

SOURCE: © Wayne Bressler/The New Yorker
Collection/www.cartoonbank.com.

Second, a financial instrument obligates *one*
party to transfer something of value, usually money,
to another party. By *party*, we mean a person, company, or government. Usually the financial instrument specifies that payments will be made. For
example, if you get a car loan, you are obligated
to make monthly payments of a particular amount
to the lender. And if you have an accident, your
insurance company is obligated to fix your car,
though the cost of the repair is left unspecified.

Third, a financial instrument specifies that
payment will be made *at some future date*. In
some cases, such as a car loan that requires payments, the dates may be very specific. In others,
such as car insurance, the payment is triggered when something specific happens,
like an accident.

Finally, a financial instrument *specifies certain conditions* under which a payment
will be made. Some agreements specify payments only when certain events happen.
That is clearly the case with car insurance and with stocks as well. The holder of a
stock owns a small part of a firm and so can expect to receive occasional cash payments, called *dividends,* when the company is profitable. There is no way to know in
advance, however, exactly when such payments will be made. In general, financial
instruments specify a number of possible contingencies under which one party is required to make a payment to another.

Uses of Financial Instruments

Stocks, loans, and insurance are all examples of financial instruments. Taking them
as a group, we can see that they have three functions (see Table 3.1). Financial instruments can act as a means of payment, and they can also be stores of value. Thus,
they offer two of the three uses of money. (Remember from Chapter 2 that money is a
means of payment, a unit of account, and a store of value.) But financial instruments
have a third function that can make them very different from money: They allow for
the transfer of risk.

---

[2]A myriad of financial arrangements that exist outside the legal system, like loan sharking, are also enforced,
but those sorts of obligations are not part of the formal financial system.

Table 3.1	Uses of Financial Instruments

Means of Payment: Purchase of goods or services.

Store of Value: Transfer of purchasing power into the future.

Transfer of Risk: Transfer of risk from one person or company to another.

Recall that a means of payment is something that is generally accepted as payment for goods and services or repayment of a debt. It is possible to pay for purchases with financial instruments, even if they don't look much like money. An example is the willingness of employees to accept a company's stock as payment for working. (This means of payment was very popular in the late 1990s, when the stock market was booming.) While we cannot yet pay for groceries with shares of stock, the time may come when we can. For now, although some financial instruments may function as means of payment, they aren't terribly good ones.

Having a store of value means that your consumption doesn't need to exactly match your income. For days, months, and years, if necessary, you can spend more than you make, repaying the difference later. Even though most of us are paid weekly or monthly, we eat every day. As stores of value, financial instruments like stocks and bonds are thought to be better than money. Over time, they generate increases in wealth that are bigger than those we can obtain from holding money in most of its forms. These higher payoffs are compensation for higher levels of risk, because the payoffs from holding most financial instruments are generally more uncertain than those that arise from holding money. Nevertheless, many financial instruments can be used to transfer purchasing power into the future.

RISK

The third use of a financial instrument lies in its ability to *transfer risk* between the buyer and the seller. Most financial instruments involve some sort of risk transfer. For example, think of wheat farmers. If only one farm has a huge harvest, that farmer does very well. But if everyone's harvest is huge, then prices can plummet and individual farms can lose money. The risk that the harvest will be too good, resulting in low grain prices, is a risk that most individual farmers do not want to take. A *wheat futures contract* allows the farmer to transfer that risk to someone else. A wheat futures contract is a financial instrument in which two parties agree to exchange a fixed quantity of wheat on a prearranged future date at a specified price. By fixing the price at which the crop will be sold well in advance of the harvest, the farmer can forget about what happens in the wheat market because the risk has been transferred to someone else.

Insurance contracts are another example of a financial instrument that transfers risk—in this case, from individuals to an insurance company. Because a car accident can be financially catastrophic, we buy car insurance and transfer the risk to an insurance company. Because insurance companies make similar guarantees to a large group of people, they have the capacity to shoulder the risk. While the timing of an individual automobile accident is impossible to forecast, a predictable percentage of a large group of drivers will experience accidents over a given period.

Characteristics of Financial Instruments: Standardization and Information

As is obvious from the definition of a financial instrument, these sorts of contracts can be very complex. If you don't believe it, take a look at the fine print in a car insurance policy, a student loan, or even a credit card agreement. Complexity is costly. The more complicated something is, the more it costs to create and the more difficult it is to

LESSONS FROM THE CRISIS
LEVERAGE

Households and firms often borrow to make investments. Obtaining a mortgage for a new home or selling a corporate bond to build a new plant are common examples. The use of borrowing to finance part of an investment is called *leverage*.* Leverage played a key role in the financial crisis of 2007-2009, so it is worth understanding how leverage relates to risk and how it can make the financial system vulnerable.

Modern economies rely heavily on borrowing to make investments. They are all leveraged. Yet, the more leverage, the greater the risk that an adverse surprise will lead to bankruptcy. If two households own houses of the same value, the one that has borrowed more—the one that is more highly leveraged and has less net worth—is the more likely to default during a temporary slump in income. This example could apply equally well to firms, financial institutions, or even countries.

Financial institutions are much more highly leveraged than households or firms, typically owning assets of about 10 times their net worth. During the crisis, some important financial firms leveraged more than 30 times their net worth.† Such high leverage meant that these firms would be vulnerable even to a minor decline in the value of their assets. For example, when a borrower is leveraged more

than 30 times, a drop as small as 3 percent in asset prices could eliminate the cushion created by the net worth and lead to bankruptcy.

When highly leveraged financial institutions experience a loss, they usually try to reduce their leverage—that is, to *deleverage*—by selling assets and issuing securities that raise their net worth (see accompanying figure). However, the financial system cannot deleverage all at once. When too many institutions try to sell assets simultaneously, their efforts will almost surely prove counterproductive: falling prices will mean more losses, diminishing their net worth further, raising leverage, and making the assets they hold seem riskier, thereby compelling further sales.

This "paradox of leverage" reinforces the destabilizing liquidity spiral discussed in Chapter 2 (see Lessons from the Crisis: Market Liquidity, Funding Liquidity, and Making Markets). Both spirals feed a vicious cycle of falling prices and widespread deleveraging that was a hallmark of the financial crisis of 2007-2009. The financial system steadied only after a plunge of many asset prices and massive government interventions.

*For a technical definition of leverage, see the Tools of the Trade box in Chapter 5.
†A bank's net worth—its assets minus liabilities—is commonly known as *bank capital*. We will discuss this in more detail in Chapter 12.

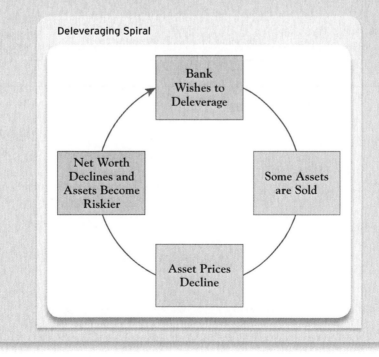

Deleveraging Spiral

- Bank Wishes to Deleverage
- Some Assets are Sold
- Asset Prices Decline
- Net Worth Declines and Assets Become Riskier

understand. As a rule, people do not want to bear these costs. Yes, the owner of an oil tanker may be willing to go to the expense of negotiating a specific insurance contract for each voyage a ship makes. The same owner may agree to make premium payments based on the load carried, the distance traveled, the route taken, and the weather expected. But for most of us, the cost of such custom contracts is simply too high.

In fact, people on both sides of financial contracts shy away from specialized agreements. Instead, they use standardized financial instruments to overcome the potential costs of complexity. Because of *standardization*, most of the financial instruments that we encounter on a day-to-day basis are very homogeneous. For example, most mortgages feature a standard application process and offer standardized terms. Automobile insurance contracts generally offer only certain standard options.

Standardization of terms makes sense. If all financial instruments differed in critical ways, most of us would not be able to understand them. Their usefulness would be severely limited. If the shares of Microsoft stock sold to one person differed in a crucial way from the shares sold to someone else, for instance, potential investors might not understand what they were buying. Even more important, the resale and trading of the shares would become virtually impossible, which would certainly discourage anyone from purchasing them in the first place. From this, we conclude that arrangements that obligate people to make payments to one another cannot all be one-of-a-kind arrangements.

Another characteristic of financial instruments is that they communicate *information*, summarizing certain essential details about the issuer. How much do you really want to learn about the original issuer of a financial instrument? Or if you are purchasing an existing instrument, how much do you want to have to know about the person who is selling it to you? Surely, the less you feel you need to know to feel secure about the transaction, the better. Regardless of whether the instrument is a stock, a bond, a futures contract, or an insurance contract, the holder does not want to have to watch the issuer too closely; continuous monitoring is costly and difficult. Thus, financial instruments are designed to eliminate the expensive and time-consuming process of collecting such information.

A number of mechanisms exist to reduce the cost of monitoring the behavior of the counterparties to a financial arrangement. A counterparty is the person or institution on the other side of a contract. If you obtain a car loan from your local bank, then you are the bank's counterparty and the bank is yours. In the case of a stock or bond, the issuing firm and the investors who hold the instrument are counterparties.

The solution to the high cost of obtaining information on the parties to a financial instrument is to standardize both the instrument and the information provided about the issuer. We can also hire a specialist whom we all trust to do the monitoring. The institutions that have arisen over the years to support the existence of financial instruments provide an environment in which everyone can feel secure about the behavior of the counterparties to an agreement.

In addition to simply summarizing information, financial instruments are designed to handle the problem of *asymmetric information*, which comes from the fact that borrowers have some information they don't disclose to lenders. Instead of buying new ovens, will a bread baker use a $50,000 loan to take an extended vacation in Tahiti? The lender wants to make sure the borrower is not misrepresenting what he or she will do with borrowed funds. Thus, the financial system is set up to gather information on borrowers before giving them resources and to monitor their use of the resources afterwards. These specialized mechanisms were developed to handle the problem of asymmetric information.

Underlying versus Derivative Instruments

There are two fundamental classes of financial instruments. The first, **underlying instruments** (sometimes called *primitive securities*), are used by savers/lenders to transfer resources directly to investors/borrowers. Through these instruments, the financial system improves the efficient allocation of resources in the real economy.

The primary examples of underlying securities or instruments are stocks and bonds that offer payments based solely on the issuer's status. Bonds, for example, make payments depending on the solvency of the firm that issued them. Stocks sometimes pay dividends when the issuing corporation's profits are sufficient.

The second class of financial instruments is known as **derivative instruments**. Their value and payoffs are "derived" from the behavior of the underlying instruments. The most common examples of derivatives are futures and options. In general, derivatives specify a payment to be made between the person who sells the instrument and the person who buys it. The amount of the payment depends on various factors associated with the price of the underlying asset. The primary use of derivatives is to shift risk among investors. We will see some examples in a moment; Chapter 9 discusses derivatives in detail.

A Primer for Valuing Financial Instruments

Why are some financial instruments more valuable than others? If you look at *The Wall Street Journal*, you'll see the prices of many bonds and stocks. They are quite different from each other. Not only that, but from day to day, the prices of an individual bond or stock can vary quite a bit. What characteristics affect the price someone will pay to buy or sell a financial instrument?

Four fundamental characteristics influence the value of a financial instrument (see Table 3.2): (1) the *size* of the payment that is promised, (2) *when* the promised payment is to be made, (3) the *likelihood* that the payment will be made, and (4) the *circumstances* under which the payment is to be made. Let's look at each one of these traits.

First, people will pay more for an instrument that obligates the issuer to pay the holder $1,000 than for one that offers a payment of $100. Regardless of any other conditions, this simply must be true: *The bigger the promised payment, the more valuable the financial instrument.*

Second, if you are promised a payment of $100 sometime in the future, you will want to know when you will receive it. Receiving $100 tomorrow is different from receiving $100 next year. This simple example illustrates a very general proposition: *The sooner the payment is made, the more valuable is the promise to make it.* Time has

TIME

Table 3.2	What Makes a Financial Instrument Valuable?

Size: Payments that are larger are more valuable.
Timing: Payments that are made sooner are more valuable.
Likelihood: Payments that are more likely to be made are more valuable.
Circumstances: Payments that are made when we need them most are more valuable.

value because of opportunity cost. If you receive a payment immediately, you have an opportunity to invest or consume it right away. If you don't receive the payment until later, you lose that opportunity.

The third factor that affects the value of a financial instrument is the odds that the issuer will meet the obligation to make the payment. Regardless of how conscientious and diligent the party who made the promise is, there remains some possibility that the payment will not be made. Because risk requires compensation, the impact of this uncertainty on the value of a financial instrument is clear: *The more likely it is that the payment will be made, the more valuable the financial instrument.*

Finally, the value of a financial instrument is affected by the conditions under which a promised payment is to be made. Insurance is the best example. We buy car insurance to receive a payment if we have an accident, so we can repair the car. No one buys insurance that pays off when good things happen. *Payments that are made when we need them most are more valuable than other payments.*[3]

Examples of Financial Instruments

We'll have quite a bit to say about financial instruments in Part II of the book. For now, let's take a look at some of the most common varieties. The best way to organize them is by whether they are used primarily as stores of value or for trading risk.

Financial Instruments Used Primarily as Stores of Value

1. **Bank loans.** A borrower obtains resources from a lender immediately in exchange for a promised set of payments in the future. The borrower, who can be either an individual or a firm, needs funds to make an investment or purchase, while the lender is looking for a way to store value into the future.

2. **Bonds.** Bonds are a form of loan. In exchange for obtaining funds today, a corporation or government promises to make payments in the future. While bond payments are often stated in fixed dollars, they need not be. Unlike most bank loans, most bonds can be bought and sold in financial markets. Like bank loans, bonds are used by the borrower to finance current operations and by the lender to store value.

3. **Home mortgages.** Most people who wish to purchase a home need to borrow some portion of the funds. A mortgage is a loan that is used to purchase real estate. In exchange for the funds, the borrower promises to make a series of payments. The house is collateral for the loan. Collateral is the term used to describe specific assets a borrower pledges to protect the lender's interests in the event of nonpayment. If the payments aren't made, the lender can take the house, a process called *foreclosure.*

4. **Stocks.** The holder of a share of a company's stock owns a small piece of the firm and is entitled to part of its profits. The owner of a firm sells stock as a way of raising funds to enlarge operations as well as a way of transferring the risk of ownership to someone else. Buyers of stocks use them primarily as stores of wealth.

---

[3]This conclusion is related to the principle of declining marginal utility, which you may recall from your study of microeconomics. The idea is that the satisfaction obtained from consumption declines as the level of consumption increases. Each succeeding candy bar brings less pleasure than the last one. Thus, a financial instrument that pays off when marginal utility is high is worth more than one that pays off when marginal utility is low. This means that payoffs that are made when income and wealth are low are more valuable than payoffs that are made when income and wealth are high.

YOUR FINANCIAL WORLD
Disability Income Insurance

People insure their houses so they can rebuild them if they burn down. They insure their cars so they can repair them if they have an accident. And they insure their lives so their families will be financially secure if they die prematurely. But few people insure their most important asset: their ability to produce an income. The biggest risk all of us face is that we will become disabled and lose our earning capacity. Insuring it should be one of our highest priorities.

If you think this advice is alarmist, just look at a few numbers. The odds of a man becoming disabled for 90 days or longer between the ages of 20 and 60 are one in five. For women they're somewhat lower, more like one in seven. In fact, the chance you'll become disabled during your working life is far higher than the chance of your house burning down—which over 40 years is about 1 in 30.*

Fortunately, you may already have some disability insurance. The government provides some through Social Security; your employer may insure you; and if you're injured on the job and can't work, there is always workers' compensation insurance. But is that enough? You should evaluate what your needs are likely to be. If the disability insurance you already have is not enough, you should buy more. While it isn't very pleasant to think about what would happen if you became disabled, you need to do it. Surely this is one risk you should transfer to someone else.

*The chance of any particular house burning down is 1 in 1,200 in a given year. So there is a 1,199 chance in 1,200 of a house *not* burning down in a particular year. This means that the probability of a house *not* burning down in 40 years is $(1,199/1,200)^{40} = 0.967$. So the probability of the house burning down is 0.033, which is 1 in 30.

5. **Asset-backed securities.** Asset-backed securities are shares in the returns or payments arising from specific assets, such as home mortgages, student loans, credit card debt, or even movie box-office receipts. Investors purchase shares in the revenue that comes from these underlying assets. The most prominent of these instruments are **mortgage-backed securities**, which bundle a large number of mortgages together into a pool in which shares are then sold. Securities backed by *subprime* mortgages—loans to borrowers who are less likely to repay than borrowers of conventional mortgages—played an important role in the financial crisis of 2007–2009 (see Chapter 7, Lessons from the Crisis: Subprime Mortgages). The owners of these securities receive a share of the payments made by the homeowners who borrowed the funds. Asset-backed securities are an innovation that allows funds in one part of the country to find productive uses elsewhere. Thus, the availability of some sorts of financing no longer depends on local credit conditions.[4]

Financial Instruments Used Primarily to Transfer Risk

1. **Insurance contracts.** The primary purpose of insurance policies is to assure that payments will be made under particular, and often rare, circumstances. These instruments exist expressly to transfer risk from one party to another.
2. **Futures contracts.** A futures contract is an agreement between two parties to exchange a fixed quantity of a commodity (such as wheat or corn) or an asset (such as a bond) at a fixed price on a set future date. A futures contract always specifies the *price* at which the transaction will take place. A futures contract is a

[4]For an introduction to how asset-backed securities work, see Andreas Jobst, "What is Securitization?" *Finance and Development*, International Monetary Fund, September 2008.

type of derivative instrument, since its value is based on the price of some other asset. It is used to transfer the risk of price fluctuations from one party to another.

3. **Options.** Like futures contracts, options are derivative instruments whose prices are based on the value of some underlying asset. Options give the holder the right, but not the obligation, to buy or sell a fixed quantity of the underlying asset at a predetermined price either on a specified date or at any time during a specified period.

These are just a few examples of the most prominent financial instruments. Together, they allow people to buy and sell almost any sort of payment on any date under any circumstances. Thus, they offer the opportunity to store value and trade risk in almost any way that one might want.[5] When you encounter a financial instrument for the first time, try to figure out whether it is used primarily for storing value or for transferring risk. Then try to identify which characteristics determine its value.

Financial Markets

Financial markets are the places where financial instruments are bought and sold. They are the economy's central nervous system, relaying and reacting to information quickly, allocating resources, and determining prices. In doing so, financial markets enable both firms and individuals to find financing for their activities. When they are working well, new firms can start up and existing firms can grow; individuals who don't have sufficient savings can borrow to purchase cars and houses. By ensuring that resources are available to those who can put them to the best use, and by keeping the costs of transactions as low as possible, these markets promote economic efficiency. When financial markets cease to function properly, resources are no longer channeled to their best possible use, and we all suffer.[6]

In this section, we will look at the role of financial markets and the economic justification for their existence. Next, we will examine the structure of the markets and how they are organized. Finally, we will look at the characteristics that are essential for the markets to work smoothly.

The Role of Financial Markets

Financial markets serve three roles in our economic system (see Table 3.3). They offer savers and borrowers *liquidity*; they pool and communicate *information*; and they allow *risk sharing*. We encountered the concept of liquidity in our discussion of money, where we defined it as the ease with which an asset can be turned into money without loss of value. Without financial markets and the institutional structure that supports them, selling the assets we own would be extremely difficult. Thus, we cannot overstate the importance of liquidity for the smooth operation of an economy. Just think what would happen if the stock market were open only one day a month. Stocks would surely become less attractive investments. If you had an emergency and needed

---

[5]An important exception is the common desire to borrow using future income as collateral. While young people with good career prospects might wish to spend their future earnings now, lenders worry that such loans will diminish the borrower's incentive to work and repay.

[6]An example demonstrates the point. Following the September 11, 2001, terrorist attacks, the New York Stock Exchange became inaccessible, and other markets were not functioning properly. Alarmed government officials took measures to ensure that markets would open as soon as possible so that trading could proceed. Without these efforts to get the financial markets up and running, the financial system might quickly have come to a standstill.

money immediately, you probably would not be able to sell your stocks in time. Liquidity is a crucial characteristic of financial markets.

Related to liquidity is the fact that financial markets need to be designed in a way that keeps transactions costs—the cost of buying and selling—low. If you want to buy or sell a stock, you have to hire someone to do it for you. The process is complex, and we need not go into it in detail, but you must pay a broker to complete the purchase or sale on your behalf. While this service can't be free, it is important to keep its cost relatively low. The trading volumes in global stock markets—several billion shares per day in the United States, over two billion per day in Tokyo, and a billion per day in London—is evidence that worldwide stock markets have low transactions costs and are liquid. (One market in which transactions costs are high is the market for housing. Once you add together everything you pay agents, bankers, and lawyers, you have spent almost 10 percent of the sale price of the house to complete the transaction. The housing market is not very liquid.)

Financial markets pool and communicate information about the issuers of financial instruments, summarizing it in the form of a price. Does a company have good prospects for future growth and profits? If so, its stock price will be high; if not, its stock price will be low. Is a borrower likely to repay a bond? The more likely repayment is, the higher the price of the bond. Obtaining the answers to these questions is time consuming and costly. Most of us just don't have the resources or know-how to do it. Instead, we turn to the financial markets to summarize the information for us so that we can look it up in the newspaper or on the Internet.

Finally, while financial instruments are the means for transferring risk, financial markets are the place where we can do it. The markets allow us to buy and sell risks, holding the ones we want and getting rid of the ones we don't want. As we will see in Chapter 5, a prudent investor holds a collection of assets called a portfolio, which includes a number of stocks and bonds as well as various forms of money. A well-designed portfolio has a lower overall risk than any individual stock or bond. An investor constructs it by buying and selling financial instruments in the marketplace. Without the market, we wouldn't be able to share risk.

Table 3.3	The Role of Financial Markets

Liquidity: Ensure that owners of financial instruments can buy and sell them cheaply and easily.

Information: Pool and communicate information about the issuer of a financial instrument.

Risk Sharing: Provide individuals with a place to buy and sell risks, sharing them with others.

The Structure of Financial Markets

There are lots of financial markets and many ways to categorize them. Just take a look at any source of business news. You will see charts and tables for domestic stocks, global stocks, bonds and interest rates, the dollar exchange rate, commodities, and more. Keep going and you will find references to stock markets, bond markets, credit markets, currency trading, options, futures, new securities, and on and on. Grasping the overall structure of all of these financial markets requires grouping them in some sort of meaningful way—but how?

There are three possibilities (see Table 3.4 on page 96). First, we can distinguish between markets where new financial instruments are sold and those where they are resold, or traded. Second, we can categorize the markets by the way they trade financial instruments—whether on a centralized exchange or not. And third, we can group them based on the type of instrument they trade—those that are used primarily as a store of value or those that are used to transfer risk. We'll use the vocabulary that is

TOOLS OF THE TRADE
Trading in Financial Markets

Trading is what makes financial markets work. No one would ever buy a stock or bond if he or she couldn't sell it. Let's take a brief look at how trading works. For this example, we will focus on the stock market.

Placing an order in a stock market is a bit like going to a fast-food restaurant or a coffee shop. You have to enter your order and wait to be served. Not only that, but the order can be very complicated, and how long you wait depends on both what you ordered and on how many other people are waiting to be served.

If you place an order, it will have a number of important characteristics.

- The stock you wish to trade.
- Whether you wish to buy or sell.
- The size of the order—how many shares you wish to trade.
- The price at which you would like to trade.

You can place either a *market order*, in which case your order is executed at the most favorable price currently available on the other side, or a *limit order*, which places a maximum on the price you wish to pay to buy or a minimum on the price you will accept to sell. Placing a market order means you value speed over price; you want the trade to occur as soon as possible and are willing to pay for the privilege. By contrast, you can specify a time at which the limit order is canceled if it hasn't been filled.

Executing the trade requires finding someone to take the other side. To do this, you can ask a broker to do it, or your broker can provide "direct access" to electronic trading networks. Even though IBM is traded on the New York Stock Exchange, you are not required to send an order to buy 100 shares of IBM to the floor of the exchange. Instead, you can request execution through an electronic communication network (ECN) like Arca (that is part of the NYSE) or Instinet (that is part of Nasdaq).

Electronic networks operate in a very simple way. If you want to buy, you enter a bid. If your bid is better than everyone else's, and there is someone willing to sell at or below the price you bid, then you trade immediately. Otherwise, your bid goes into an order book to wait for a seller. On a network like Arca or Instinet, customer orders interact automatically following a set of priority rules established by the network, but with no one acting as an intermediary in the transaction. The liquidity in the market is provided by the customers.

For a stock like IBM or GE, the New York Stock Exchange is an alternative place to send the order. A NYSE order may be satisfied electronically, through Arca. On the NYSE, liquidity provided by customer orders is supplemented by designated market makers (DMMs). A DMM is the person on the floor of the Stock Exchange charged with making a market, ensuring that it is liquid so that people can both buy and sell and that prices aren't overly volatile. Electronic mechanisms match the orders as they come in, keeping track of orders that are outstanding. To make the system work, DMMs often buy and sell on their own account.*

On the next page is a portion of the screen from an independent ECN known as BATS. The screen shows outstanding bids and offers for the common stock of General Electric (GE)

common as of this writing. Bear in mind that there are no hard and fast rules for the terminology used to describe these markets, so it may change.

Primary versus Secondary Markets   A primary financial market is one in which a borrower obtains funds from a lender by selling newly issued securities. Businesses use primary markets to raise the resources they need to grow. Governments use them to finance ongoing operations. Most of the action in primary markets occurs out of public view. While some companies that want to raise funds go directly to the financial markets themselves, most use an investment bank. The bank examines the company's financial health to determine whether the proposed issue is sound Assuming that it is, the bank will determine a price and then purchase the securities in preparation for resale to clients. This activity, called *underwriting*, is usually very profitable. Since small investors are not customers of large investment banks, most of us do not have access to these new securities.

◉ ◉ ◉	GE – BATS Exchange Book Viewer				

BATS   GE   Go

GENERAL ELECTRIC CO COM

Orders Accepted			Total Volume	
206,348			5,312,986	

TOP OF BOOK			LAST 10 TRADES	
SHARES	PRICE	TIME	PRICE	SHARES
17,600	15.90	12:59:39	15.85	100
25,000	15.89	12:59:39	15.85	1,000
26,604	15.88	12:59:39	15.85	100
25,539	15.87	12:59:39	15.85	100
23,065	15.86	12:59:39	15.85	200
17,303	15.85	12:59:39	15.85	100
21,941	15.84	12:59:39	15.85	700
21,905	15.83	12:59:39	15.85	100
21,043	15.82	12:59:39	15.85	100
20,760	15.81	12:59:39	15.85	100

SOURCE: *www.batstrading.com, 1:00 pm, November 9, 2009.*

at 1:00 pm on November 9, 2009. The system shows more than 100,000 limit orders on each side of the market (bids in blue; asks in pink) within a few cents of the most recent execution price ($15.85). The system combines the sell (buy) orders of different customers at each price, so we see the aggregate supply (demand) for the stock at that price. If a market sell order for 100 shares were to arrive, the system would match that order with the highest bid ($15.85). If a market buy order for 100 shares were to arrive, the system would match that order with the lowest offer ($15.86). More than 5,000,000 GE shares already had traded that day.

*For a description of designated market makers, see http://www.nyse.com/pdfs/fact_sheet_dmm.pdf.

Everyone knows about secondary financial markets. Those are the markets where people can buy and sell existing securities. If you want to buy a share of stock in IBM or Microsoft, you won't get it from the company itself. Instead, you'll buy it in a secondary market from another investor. The prices in the secondary markets are the ones we hear about in the news.

Centralized Exchanges, Over-the-Counter Markets, and Electronic Communication Networks

Buying a stock or bond is not like buying a new pair of shoes. You can't just go into a store, ask for the stock you want, pay for it with your credit card, and walk out with it in a bag. Instead, you can either ask a broker to buy the stock for you or you can do it yourself on an electronic exchange. In both cases, the transaction is in a secondary market. The organization of secondary financial markets is changing rapidly. Historically there have been two types. Some organizations, like the New York Stock Exchange and the large exchanges in London

Table 3.4	The Structure of Financial Markets

Primary versus Secondary Markets

Primary markets:	Markets where newly issued securities are sold.
Secondary markets:	Markets where existing securities are traded.

Centralized Exchanges versus Over-the-Counter Markets

Centralized exchanges:	Secondary markets where buyers and sellers meet in a central, physical location.
Over-the-counter markets:	Decentralized secondary markets where dealers stand ready to buy and sell securities electronically.
Electronic communication networks (ECNs):	An electronic system that brings buyers and sellers together for electronic execution of trades without the use of a broker or dealer.

Debt and Equity versus Derivatives Markets

Debt and equity markets:	Markets where financial claims are bought and sold for immediate cash payment.
Derivatives markets:	Markets where claims based on an underlying asset are traded for payment at a later date.

and Tokyo, are centralized exchanges. Others, like the Nasdaq, are over-the-counter (OTC) markets, which are merely a collection of dealers who trade with one another via computer from wherever they are sitting. Today, we can add electronic communication networks (ECNs) to the list of secondary-market types—Instinet and Archipelago (Arca) are the biggest. While all of these markets allow for the trading of existing (that is, already issued) financial instruments, they do it in different ways.

To understand how things work today, we need to start with how they worked a few years ago. Let's begin with the New York Stock Exchange (NYSE). The NYSE is a place with an address where trading takes place in person on the floor of the exchange. To get onto the floor and trade, a firm purchases one of the licenses issued by the exchange. For the year 2010, the price of a trading license was set at $40,000. Most licenses are purchased by brokerage firms that earn revenue from trading on behalf of their customers. Until recently, others were acquired by *specialists* who oversaw the trading of individual stocks. Every one of the roughly 3,500 stocks traded on the NYSE was assigned to a specialist whose job it was to maintain order in the market for that stock. While not all of the trading in stocks that are listed on the New York Stock Exchange actually takes place at the exchange itself, a significant fraction does. And all of that trading went through the specialists.

In the past, the only alternative to a centralized exchange was an over-the-counter (OTC) market. These dealer-based markets are best thought of as networks of physically dispersed dealers, each of whom has a computer screen on which buy and sell orders are posted. The dealers buy and sell various securities both for themselves and for their customers. With the exception of stocks that are sold on organized exchanges, financial instruments are sold in dealer-based markets. The biggest is the Nasdaq, which trades the stocks of roughly 4,000 companies, most of them small. The dealers use their computers to match the orders and execute the trades.

Compared with a physically centralized exchange, a financial market that is organized as an electronic network—such as an OTC market or an ECN—has both advantages and disadvantages. On the plus side, customers can see the orders (look at the Tools of the Trade: Trading in Financial Markets on page 94), orders are executed quickly, costs are low, and trading is 24 hours a day. But electronic networks are not perfect. When dealers are in a hurry or simply get tired, they can push the wrong button, turning a $3 million trade into a $30 million or $300 million trade. On the morning of December 8, 2005, an unlucky clerk for the Japanese firm Mizuho Securities discovered the risks. Instead of entering an order to sell one single share of J-Com, a small Japanese recruiting firm, at a price of ¥610,000 (about $5,200), the clerk placed an order to sell 610,000 shares at ¥1 (less than $0.01) apiece. The sell order was for 40 times the number of J-Com shares in existence! Because Mizuho was acting as a broker for a client, the mistake was theirs and the firm was financially responsible. What became known as the "fat-finger incident" eventually cost Mizuho $340 million. Such mistakes cannot occur on the floor of centralized exchanges where trades are executed face to face between two people who write them down for verification later.

On the other side, a clear advantage of electronic networks was evident on September 11, 2001. The NYSE building stands only a few blocks from the site of the World Trade Center. When the twin towers fell, the floor of the exchange became inaccessible. Because its operation depends on the ability of people to gather there, trading stopped and did not restart until Monday, September 17, 2001. Meanwhile, the Nasdaq could have continued functioning. The New York dealers shut down, but those located elsewhere in the country were able to continue. Networks are designed so that if one section shuts down, the rest of it can continue working, and that is what happened. In a dealer-based market, when one dealer can't trade, someone else is usually waiting to step in.

Returning to the structure of financial markets, in late 2005 the NYSE merged with Archipelago (now NYSE Arca), and Nasdaq merged with Instinet. That is, the largest centralized exchange and the largest over-the-counter dealer-based system each merged with one of the two largest ECNs. At the time, trading volume on the NYSE averaged a bit over 1.5 billion shares a day, and Nasdaq's average volume was about 1 billion shares daily. Meanwhile, trading on the two ECNs was between 600 and 800 million shares per day. For the Nasdaq, the merge wasn't much of a change, as it merged with a system that is similar to the one that it already had.

For the NYSE, the change was huge. The fact that the NYSE occupies a physical space is now much less important. Today, electronic mechanisms keep track of orders, and specialists have been replaced by designated market makers, who add their orders to the electronic flow to keep the market functioning smoothly. The rationale for having specialists was that they were necessary to maintain liquidity in the market—especially for small stocks that trade infrequently. But today, even individuals can enter and execute trades on their own, so one has to wonder if designated market makers and other NYSE liquidity suppliers are necessary. We'll have to wait and see.

The continuing globalization of finance is also altering exchanges. In 2007, for example, the NYSE merged with Paris-based Euronext, a pan-European stock exchange, to link major exchanges in Paris, Amsterdam, London, Brussels, and Lisbon. Nasdaq attempted to acquire the London Stock Exchange, but dropped its bid in 2007 shortly before the financial

The trading floor of a stock exchange.

IN THE NEWS
Lessons of the Financial Crisis—One Year Later

THE WALL STREET JOURNAL.
WSJ.com

by Gregory Zuckerman

August 30, 2009

The numbers hardly tell the story.

Today, the Dow Jones Industrial Average stands roughly 2000 points below where it was on this end-of-summer weekend one year ago. No one knew then, of course, but the U.S. stock market and the world economy were just days from historic calamity, unprecedented in the lives of anyone born in the last 80 years.

And today? We are nearly six months into one of the most impressive bull markets in memory. . . .

Go figure. It's been a year of horrors and opportunities for investors.

The troubles began in 2007 with rising defaults among "subprime" mortgage borrowers and a market slowly drifting downward from an all-time high set that October.

But then critical mass was reached over a stunning two-week period last September. The U.S. government rapidly took over mortgage-lending giants Fannie Mae and Freddie Mac, along with huge insurer American International Group.

Onetime Wall Street power Lehman Brothers filed for bankruptcy, wounded brokerage giant Merrill Lynch rushed into the arms of Bank of America, and federal regulators seized Washington Mutual in the largest bank failure in U.S. history.

At one point, panicked investors offered to buy U.S. Treasury bills without asking for any return on their investment, hoping to simply find somewhere safe to put their money.

By early 2009, when the stock market hit what looks like its post-crisis bottom, the collapse had vaporized more than $30 trillion, a decade's worth of investment gains.

Yet, almost as stunning as the fall, has been the stock market's recovery. Although still well below 2007 levels, the market has defied horrible levels of unemployment, a housing market that is still barely breathing, and an economy bound in recession.

There are ample signs that the worst is over, of course, and a recovery may already be under way. (Yes, but tell that to the millions who have lost jobs, business owners who have shut down their companies, or the legions whose retirement nest eggs may not recover in time. Their personal recessions may never be over.)

So what have investors learned from all this? With a full year of hindsight, here are some lessons of the crisis:

Diversification doesn't always work. Financial advisers have drilled into investors the need for diversification. But the past year has taught that spreading money around the globe and into different asset classes sometimes results in less safety than one would expect. The lesson isn't to put more eggs in a single basket, but to acknowledge the limits of diversification.

Markets are more interlocked than ever before. When the U.S. markets began to fall, investors pulled money from foreign stocks, almost every kind of bond and even investments that sometimes are sold as a way to protect a portfolio, such as commodities and hedge funds. Even gold, a traditional haven, experienced some rough periods as investors raised cash by selling almost anything they could get rid of.

Understand every investment. Even the most sophisticated investors can be fooled by complicated investments.

In October of last year, Chuck Prince, Citigroup's CEO [chief executive officer], said "we expect to return to a more normal earnings environment as the year progresses," while UBS CEO Marcel Rohner said "we expect positive investment bank performance." But Citigroup and UBS turned into two of the biggest losers from the crisis, as the seemingly safe collateralized debt obligations on their books led to billions of dollars in losses.

Just as banks need to make sure they understand the risks and downsides of their holdings, so do individual investors.

Make sure your portfolio is as liquid as you need it to be. Some of the biggest mistakes were made by investors who thought their holdings were more "liquid," or easy to exit without incurring big cost, than they actually were.

Even university endowments run by some of the most sophisticated investors were surprised to find that their hedge funds, private equity and other holdings were difficult to exit in the heat of the crisis. They've vowed to do a better job of matching their needs and their investments.

Government works. The aggressive steps by the government seem to have helped avert an even deeper recession, or even a depression, suggesting that big government can sometimes be a friend of business.

But questions remain about whether all the spending will eventually lead to inflation or other problems, making this a qualified lesson of the period.

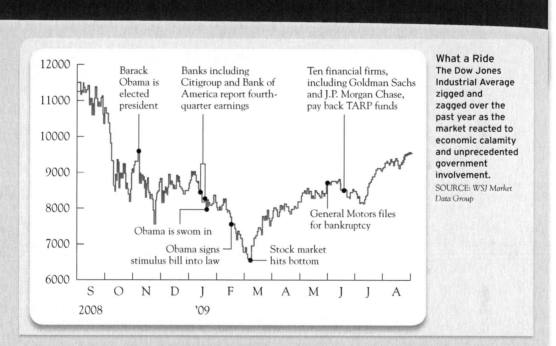

What a Ride
The Dow Jones Industrial Average zigged and zagged over the past year as the market reacted to economic calamity and unprecedented government involvement.

SOURCE: *WSJ Market Data Group*

Chart annotations:
- Barack Obama is elected president
- Banks including Citigroup and Bank of America report fourth-quarter earnings
- Ten financial firms, including Goldman Sachs and J.P. Morgan Chase, pay back TARP funds
- Obama is swom in
- Obama signs stimulus bill into law
- General Motors files for bankruptcy
- Stock market hits bottom

X-axis: S O N D J F M A M J J A
2008   '09

Y-axis: 6000, 7000, 8000, 9000, 10000, 11000, 12000

Don't let financial companies become too big to fail. It's not clear if regulators fully understand this lesson of the fiasco. For years, critics said companies like Fannie Mae and Freddie Mac had grown too large, and that firms like Lehman Brothers carried too much debt. Today, firms like Goldman Sachs and J.P. Morgan Chase are growing and might end up too big to be allowed to crumble, some analysts say.

Factor into any investment equation a worst-case scenario. Too many investors piled into housing-related investments, confident that real estate never had dropped on a national basis or that investment-grade mortgage investments never defaulted. They would have been better served to examine potential holes in their bullish stance.

Don't get too gloomy. Like the old saying goes, in every crisis is an opportunity. As nations around the globe confronted the crisis and pumped huge sums into their economies, the economy stabilized. And even as the recession looked its worst, the stock market began to sense that a recovery was coming.

SOURCE: *The Wall Street Journal Online*. "Lessons of the Financial Crisis—One Year Later" by Gregory Zuckerman, August 30, 2009. Copyright 2009 by Dow Jones & Company, Inc. Reproduced with permission of Dow Jones & Company, Inc. in the formats Textbook and Other Book via Copyright Clearance Center.

LESSONS OF THE ARTICLE

The article highlights the large swings in financial markets during the financial crisis of 2007-2009. Before the crisis, professional investors had made their own institutions and the overall financial system vulnerable by taking on too much risk (see Lessons from the Crisis: Leverage, earlier in this chapter). When the crisis hit, they faced a shortfall of liquidity (see Chapter 2, Lessons from the Crisis: Market Liquidity, Funding Liquidity, and Making Markets). At the height of the crisis, panic purchases of Treasury bills constituted a classic "flight to safety" by investors seeking the most liquid assets. Liquidity swings caused many financial markets—including the stock market—to plunge and rebound together.

crisis erupted. Exchanges seem inclined to take advantage of their technologies and customer relationships by linking across borders to lower costs and speed transactions. Whether these economies of scale and scope lead to further international consolidation will depend both on performance *and* on the attitudes of various governments toward foreign ownership and operation of national exchanges.

Debt and Equity versus Derivative Markets   A useful way to think of the structure of financial markets is to distinguish between markets where *debt and equity* are traded and those where *derivative instruments* are traded. Debt markets are the markets for loans, mortgages, and bonds—the instruments that allow for the transfer of resources from lenders to borrowers and at the same time give investors a store of value for their wealth. Equity markets are the markets for stocks. For the most part, stocks are traded in the countries where the companies are based. U.S. companies' stocks are traded in the United States, Japanese stocks in Japan, Chinese stocks in China, and so on. Derivative markets are the markets where investors trade instruments like futures and options, which are designed primarily to transfer risk. To put it another way, in debt and equity markets, actual claims are bought and sold for immediate cash payment; in derivative markets, investors make agreements that are settled later.

Looking at debt instruments in more detail, we can place them in one of two categories, depending on the length of time until the final payment, called the loan's maturity. Debt instruments that are completely repaid in less than a year (from their original issue date) are traded in money markets, while those with a maturity of more than a year are traded in bond markets. *Money market instruments* have different names and are treated somewhat differently from *bond market instruments*. For example, the United States Treasury issues Treasury bills, which have a maturity of less than one year when they are issued and are traded in the money market. U.S. Treasury bonds, which are repaid over 10 years or more, are traded in the bond markets. The same distinction can be made for large private corporations, which issue commercial paper when borrowing for short periods and corporate bonds when borrowing for long periods.

Characteristics of a Well-Run Financial Market

Well-run financial markets exhibit a few essential characteristics that are related to the role we ask them to play in our economies. First, these markets must be designed to keep transaction costs low. Second, the information the market pools and communicates must be both accurate and widely available. If analysts do not communicate accurate assessments of the firms they follow, the markets will not generate the correct prices for the firms' stocks. The prices of financial instruments reflect all the information that is available to market participants. Those prices are the link between the financial markets and the real economy, ensuring that resources are allocated to their most efficient uses. If the information that goes into the market is wrong, then the prices will be wrong, and the economy will not operate as effectively as it could.

INFORMATION

Finally, investors need protection. For the financial system to work at all, borrowers' promises to pay lenders must be credible. Individuals must be assured that their investments will not simply be stolen. In countries that have weak investor protections, firms can behave deceptively, borrowing when they have no intention of repaying the funds and going unpunished. The lack of proper safeguards dampens people's willingness to invest. Thus, governments are an essential part of financial markets,

LESSONS FROM THE CRISIS
INTERBANK LENDING

Interbank lending is a critical foundation of modern financial markets. In normal times, banks lend to each other in large volumes at low cost for periods ranging from overnight to a few months. These liquid, interbank loans are the marginal source of funds for many banks, and their cost guides other lending rates.

Interbank lending helps smooth the function of markets because it allows banks to satisfy temporary, localized excess demand for funding liquidity (see Chapter 2, Lessons from the Crisis: Market Liquidity, Funding Liquidity, and Making Markets). If a bank could not reliably borrow and lend each day to offset the random ebbs and flows of its deposits and loans, it would need to hold a larger volume of cash to insure itself against unanticipated payment outflows or loan demand. For the banking system as a whole, such extra cash holdings waste resources that could be lent profitably elsewhere.

Events occasionally strain the interbank market. For example, on September 11, 2001, physical disruptions and communication obstacles boosted banks' demand for funds. The Federal Reserve supplied extraordinary amounts of liquidity for a few days until efficient interbank lending was restored.

The financial crisis of 2007–2009 triggered much greater, and more prolonged, strains in interbank lending. Rather than lend out additional liquid assets, anxious banks preferred to hold them in case their own needs might rise. Banks also grew concerned about the safety of their trading partners as the level of trust and confidence plunged. The rising cost and reduced availability of interbank loans created a vicious circle of increased caution, greater demand for liquid assets, reduced willingness to lend, and higher loan rates.

The waves of the financial crisis may be seen in the accompanying figure that shows the extra cost (or *spread*) of an interbank loan over the expected federal funds rate (the interest rate that the U.S. Federal Reserve chooses to control as its primary policy tool—see Chapter 16). Beginning in August 2007, this spread jumped and remained elevated. When Lehman Brothers failed on September 15, 2008, the spread leapt above 350 basis points as panic dried up interbank lending.

Unprecedented actions by governments to add liquidity and guarantee bank debt eventually eased the record interbank lending strains in 2009, but these actions did not prevent extensive disruptions in the financial system and the global economy. The financial crisis made painfully clear to surviving financial institutions that they cannot always count on being able to borrow at a low cost when needed.

Strains in the Interbank Market: Interbank Lending Rate *Minus* Expected Federal Reserve Policy Interest Rate, 2007-2009

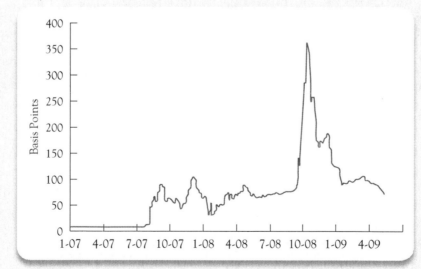

SOURCE: www.bloomberg.com

Note: The vertical scale is in basis points (a basis point is 0.01 percent). The figure shows the gap between two measures: (1) the cost of an interbank loan, represented by the three-month London Interbank Offered Rate (LIBOR, see Chapter 13) and (2) the expected federal funds rate (the Federal Reserve's policy interest rate), represented by a financial instrument called the overnight indexed swap (OIS). One party in an OIS pays a fixed interest rate in return for a payment from the other party equal to the average federal funds rate over the life of the swap. The OIS rate should closely reflect the expected federal funds rate.

because they set and enforce the rules of the game. While informal lending networks do develop and flourish spontaneously, they can accommodate only simple, small-scale transactions. Because modern financial markets require a legal structure that is designed and enforced by the government, countries with better investor protections have bigger and deeper financial markets than other countries.

Financial Institutions

Financial institutions are the firms that provide access to the financial markets, both to savers who wish to purchase financial instruments directly and to borrowers who want to issue them. Because financial institutions sit between savers and borrowers, they are also known as *financial intermediaries*, and what they do is known as intermediation. Banks, insurance companies, securities firms, and pension funds are all financial intermediaries. These institutions are essential; any disturbance to the services they provide will have severe adverse effects on the economy.

To understand the importance of financial institutions, think what the world would be like if they didn't exist. Without a bank, individuals and households wishing to save would either have to hold their wealth in cash or figure out some way to funnel it directly to companies or households that could put it to use. The assets of these household savers would be some combination of government liabilities and the equity and debt issued by corporations and other households. All finance would be direct, with borrowers obtaining funds straight from the lenders.

Such a system would be unlikely to work very well, for a number of reasons. First, individual transactions between saver-lenders and spender-borrowers would likely be extremely expensive. Not only would the two sides have difficulty finding each other, but even if they did, writing the contract to effect the transaction would be very costly. Second, lenders need to evaluate the creditworthiness of borrowers and then monitor them to ensure that they don't abscond with the funds. Individuals are not specialists in monitoring. Third, most borrowers want to borrow for the long term, while lenders favor more liquid short-term loans. Lenders would surely require compensation for the illiquidity of long-term loans, driving the price of borrowing up.

A financial market could be created in which the loans and other securities could be resold, but that would create the risk of price fluctuations. All these problems would restrict the flow of resources through the economy. Healthy financial institutions open up the flow, directing it to the most productive investments and increasing the system's efficiency.

The Role of Financial Institutions

Financial institutions reduce transactions costs by specializing in the issuance of standardized securities. They reduce the information costs of screening and monitoring borrowers to make sure they are creditworthy and they use the proceeds of a loan or security issue properly. In other words, financial institutions curb information asymmetries and the problems that go along with them, helping resources flow to their most productive uses.

At the same time that they make long-term loans, financial institutions also give savers ready access to their funds. That is, they issue short-term liabilities to lenders while making long-term loans to borrowers. By making loans to many different borrowers at once, financial institutions can provide savers with financial instruments

LESSONS FROM THE CRISIS
SHADOW BANKS

Over the past few decades, financial intermediation and leverage in the United States has shifted away from traditional banks* and toward other financial institutions that are less subject to government rules. These other intermediaries include brokerages, consumer and mortgage finance firms, insurers, money-market mutual funds (MMMFs) and investment firms (such as hedge funds and private equity firms†). There are also more exotic bank-created firms called special investment and special purpose vehicles (SIVs and SPVs) that may even be set up offshore for tax, regulatory, and/or legal purposes in places like the Cayman Islands and Bermuda.

These other intermediaries have come to be known as *shadow banks* because they provide services that compete with or substitute for those supplied by traditional banks. Unlike banks, however, shadow banks do not accept deposits. In addition, the leverage and risk taking of shadow banks can be greater than that of traditional banks while being less transparent.

Beginning in the 1970s, financial innovation sped the shift of intermediation to the shadow banks and was, in turn, stimulated by it. Broader markets, plunging information costs, new profit opportunities, and government practices all encouraged the development of new financial instruments and institutions to meet customer needs at lower cost.

Over time, the rise of highly leveraged shadow banks—combined with government relaxation of rules for traditional banks—permitted a rise of leverage in the financial system as a whole, making it more vulnerable to shocks (see Lessons from the Crisis: Leverage earlier in this chapter).

Rapid growth in some new financial instruments made it easier to conceal leverage and risk-taking. Derivatives—options, futures, and the like—allow investors to transfer risks at low cost (see Chapter 9). After 2000, the use of customized derivatives that do not trade in open markets (so-called over-the-counter, or OTC, derivatives) rose dramatically. Those derivatives permitted some large financial institutions to take risks that were unknown to their investors and trading partners and to the public officials who were supposed to monitor them. The spillover from the failure of these firms during the financial crisis nearly sank the entire system.

The financial crisis transformed shadow banking. During the fateful week that began with the failure of Lehman Brothers on Monday, September 15, 2008, the largest U.S. brokerages failed, merged, or converted themselves into traditional banks in order to gain access to funding. In the same month, the loss of confidence in MMMFs required a U.S. government guarantee to halt withdrawals. Over the past two years, many SIVs failed or were reabsorbed by the banks that created them. Many hedge funds chose to shrink or close as investors fled.

The future of shadow banking remains highly uncertain. The crisis has encouraged governments to scrutinize any financial institution that could, by its risk taking, pose a threat to the financial system. Partly as a result, the scope for leverage and risk taking is lower, at least for now.

*One traditional form of bank is a commercial bank, which is defined in Chapter 12 as accepting deposits from and making loans to businesses and individuals.

†Hedge funds (defined in Chapter 13) are private, largely unregulated investment partnerships that bring together small groups of wealthy people who meet certain financial requirements. Private equity funds are investment pools that typically invest directly in private companies.

that are both more liquid and less risky than the individual stocks and bonds they would purchase directly in financial markets.

Figure 3.2 is a schematic overview of the financial system. It shows that there are two types of financial institutions: those that provide brokerage services (top) and those that transform assets (bottom). Broker institutions give households and corporations access to financial markets and direct finance. Institutions that transform assets take deposits and issue insurance contracts to households. They use the proceeds to make loans and purchase stocks, bonds, and real estate. That is their transformation function. Figure 3.3 shows what the balance sheet for such an institution would include.

The Structure of the Financial Industry

In analyzing the structure of the financial industry, we can start by dividing intermediaries into two broad categories called depository and nondepository institutions. *Depository institutions* take deposits and make loans; they are what most people think of as banks, whether they are commercial banks, savings banks, or credit unions.

Figure 3.2   Flow of Funds through Financial Institutions

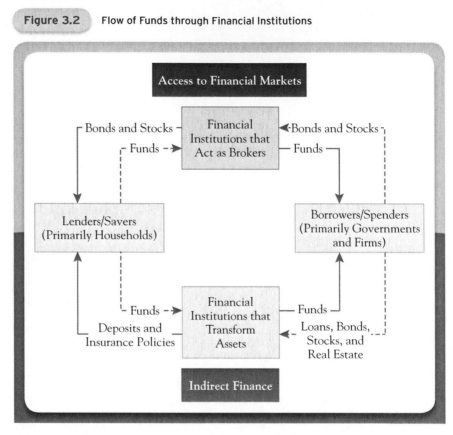

Financial institutions perform both brokerage and asset transformation services. As brokers, they provide access to financial markets, giving households and corporations access to indirect finance. Institutions transform assets by taking deposits and issuing insurance contracts to households at the same time that they make loans and purchase stocks, bonds, and real estate.

Figure 3.3   The Simplified Balance Sheet of a Financial Institution

Assets	Liabilities
Bonds	Deposits
Stocks	Insurance policies
Loans	
Real estate	

Nondepository institutions include insurance companies, securities firms, mutual fund companies, hedge funds, finance companies, and pension funds. Each of these serves a very different function from a bank. Some screen and monitor borrowers; others transfer and reduce risk. Still others are primarily brokers. Here is a list of the major groups of financial institutions, together with a brief description of what they do.

1. **Depository institutions** (commercial banks, savings banks, and credit unions) take deposits and make loans.
2. **Insurance companies** accept premiums, which they invest in securities and real estate (their assets) in return for promising compensation to policyholders should certain events occur (their liabilities). Life insurers protect against

YOUR FINANCIAL WORLD

Shop for a Mortgage

Everyone loves a bargain. There are people who will spend hours making sure they pay the lowest price they can for virtually anything they buy. Borrowing shouldn't be any different. When the time comes to buy a house, most of us need to borrow. That is, we need to get a mortgage. Because the mortgage payment will almost surely be your biggest monthly expense, getting the cheapest mortgage you can will save you more than a year's worth of bargain hunting in stores.

There are a number of ways to shop for a mortgage. Any real estate agent can hand you a list of mortgage providers in your area. You can also find Web sites that publish quotes for mortgages. As you look through these lists, you'll notice that many of the firms on them are not banks. Instead, they are *mortgage brokers*, firms that have access to pools of funds earmarked for use as mortgages.

Say, for instance, that a financial firm raises a large amount of financing to be used to make mortgages. A pool of $100 million can finance a thousand $100,000 mortgages. Shares in these pools are sold to investors. If you get a mortgage from one of these firms, it will go into the pool. In 2009, half of the nearly $15 trillion in mortgages in the United States was in these mortgage pools.

Should you care whether you get your mortgage from a traditional bank or a mortgage broker? Should you care if your mortgage is pooled and sold off? The answer is no; it should make no difference to you. In fact, chances are that regardless of which option you choose—bank or mortgage broker—you'll make your payments to a company that does nothing but collect them and monitor your compliance. From your point of view, a mortgage is a mortgage. Get the one that suits you best. But shop before you sign on the dotted line. And if you let the various brokers know that you are shopping around, they may start competing for your business and give you a better deal.

the risk of untimely death. Property and casualty insurers protect against personal injury loss and losses from theft, accidents, and fire.

3. **Pension funds** invest individual and company contributions in stocks, bonds, and real estate (their assets) in order to provide payments to retired workers (their liabilities).

4. **Securities firms** include brokers, investment banks, underwriters, and mutual-fund companies. Brokers and investment banks issue stocks and bonds for corporate customers, trade them, and advise customers. All these activities give customers access to the financial markets. Mutual-fund companies pool the resources of individuals and companies and invest them in portfolios of bonds, stocks, and real estate. Hedge funds do the same for small groups of wealthy investors. Customers own shares of the portfolios, so they face the risk that the assets will change in value. But portfolios are less risky than individual securities, and individual savers can purchase smaller units than they could if they went directly to the financial markets.

5. **Finance companies** raise funds directly in the financial markets in order to make loans to individuals and firms. Finance companies tend to specialize in particular types of loans, such as mortgage, automobile, or certain types of business equipment. While their assets are similar to a bank's, their liabilities are debt instruments that are traded in financial markets, not deposits.

6. **Government-sponsored enterprises** are federal credit agencies that provide loans directly for farmers and home mortgagors. They also guarantee programs that insure loans made by private lenders. The government also provides retirement income and medical care to the elderly through Social Security and Medicare. Pension funds and insurance companies perform these functions privately.

As we continue our study of the relationship between the financial system and the real economy, we will return to the importance of financial institutions, the conduits that channel resources from savers to investors. These intermediaries are absolutely essential to the operation of any economy. When they cease to function, so does everything else. Recall from Chapter 2 that the measures of money (M1 and M2) include checking deposits, savings deposits, and certificates of deposit, among other things. These are all important liabilities of banks. Because they are very liquid, they are accepted as a means of payment. Clearly, the financial structure is tied to the availability of money and credit. But we are getting ahead of ourselves. Before we study financial institutions, we need to look more closely at financial instruments and financial markets, the subjects of Part II of this book.

Terms

asset, 83
asset-backed security, 91
bond market, 100
centralized exchange, 96
collateral, 90
counterparty, 88
debt market, 100
derivative instrument, 89
direct finance, 83
electronic communications networks
  (ECNs), 96
equity market, 100
financial institutions, 102

financial instrument, 85
financial markets, 92
indirect finance, 83
liability, 83
money market, 100
mortgage-backed security, 91
over-the-counter (OTC) market, 96
portfolio, 93
primary financial market, 94
secondary financial market, 95
underlying instrument, 89

Chapter Lessons

1. Financial instruments are crucial to the operation of the economy.
   a. Financial arrangements can be either formal or informal. Industrial economies are dominated by formal arrangements.
   b. A financial instrument is the written legal obligation of one party to transfer something of value, usually money, to another party at some future date, under certain conditions.
   c. Financial instruments are used primarily as stores of value and means of trading risk. They are less likely to be used as means of payment, although many of them can be.
   d. Financial instruments are most useful when they are simple and standardized.

e. There are two basic classes of financial instruments: underlying and derivative.
   i. Underlying instruments are used to transfer resources directly from one party to another.
   ii. Derivative instruments derive their value from the behavior of an underlying instrument.
f. The payments promised by a financial instrument are more valuable
   i. The larger they are.
   ii. The sooner they are made.
   iii. The more likely they are to be made.
   iv. If they are made when they are needed most.
g. Common examples of financial instruments include
   i. Those that serve primarily as stores of value, including bank loans, bonds, mortgages, stocks, and asset-backed securities.
   ii. Those that are used primarily to transfer risk, including futures and options.

2. Financial markets are essential to the operation of our economic system.
   a. Financial markets
      i. Offer savers and borrowers liquidity so that they can buy and sell financial instruments easily.
      ii. Pool and communicate information through prices.
      iii. Allow for the sharing of risk.
   b. There are several ways to categorize financial markets.
      i. Primary markets that issue new securities versus secondary markets, where existing securities are bought and sold.
      ii. Physically centralized exchanges, dealer-based electronic systems (over-the-counter markets), or electronic networks.
      iii. Debt and equity markets (where instruments that are used primarily for financing are traded) versus derivative markets (where instruments that are used to transfer risk are traded).
   c. A well-functioning financial market is characterized by
      i. Low transactions costs and sufficient liquidity.
      ii. Accurate and widely available information.
      iii. Legal protection of investors against the arbitrary seizure of their property.

3. Financial institutions perform brokerage and asset transformation functions.
   a. In their role as brokers, they provide access to financial markets.
   b. In transforming assets, they provide indirect finance.
   c. Indirect finance reduces transaction and information costs.
   d. Financial institutions, also known as financial intermediaries, help individuals and firms to transfer and reduce risk.

Conceptual Problems

1. As the end of the month approaches, you realize that you probably will not be able to pay the next month's rent. Describe both an informal and a formal financial instrument that you might use to solve your dilemma.

2.* While we often associate informal financial arrangements with poorer countries where financial systems are less developed, informal arrangements often coexist

*Indicates more difficult problems

with even the most developed financial systems. What advantages might there be to engaging in informal arrangements rather than utilizing the formal financial sector?

3. If higher leverage is associated with greater risk, explain why the process of deleveraging (reducing leverage) can be destabilizing.

4. Consider a financial instrument based on the level of a river that occasionally floods. The contract could state that the seller, in return for an annual premium, would pay the buyer $1,000 if the river reaches flood stage at a particular city along the river during the year the contract was in force. Why would a market for this contract arise? How does the contract benefit both the buyer and the seller?

5. Consider an annuity that makes monthly payments for as long as someone lives. Describe what happens to the purchase price of the annuity as (1) the age of the purchaser goes up, (2) the size of the monthly payment rises, and (3) the health of the purchaser improves.

6. Consider the investment returns to holding stock. Which of the following would be more valuable to you: Stocks that rise in value when your income rises or stocks that rise in value when your income falls? Why?

7. Go to the website for the European Central Bank and find the most recent interest rates for (i) the main refinancing operations, (ii) the deposit facility, and (iii) the marginal lending facility. Explain what each of these means.

8. Advanced economies have highly developed financial systems, while less developed economies often do not. Do you think the link between the stage of development of the financial system and the level of economic development is a causal one, with financial development causing economic development? Explain why or why not. Could there be causality from economic development to financial development? Explain.

9. The design and function of financial instruments, markets, and institutions are tied to the importance of information. Describe the role played by information in each of these three pieces of the financial system.

10. How can a bank crisis spread across national borders?

11.* Advances in technology have facilitated the widespread use of credit scoring by financial institutions in making their lending decisions. Credit scoring can be defined broadly as the use of historical data and statistical techniques to rank the attractiveness of potential borrowers and guide lending decisions. In what ways might this practice enhance the efficiency of the financial system?

Analytical Problems

12. For each pair of financial instruments, can you say which has the highest value? Explain.
    a. A $1,000 bond issued by a country with a budget deficit of 10 percent of its GDP or a $1,000 bond issued by a country with a budget deficit of 1 percent of its GDP? Assume both bonds are due in one year.
    b. A bond that will pay $1,000 in three months or a bond by the same issuer that will pay $1,000 in six months?
    c. A bond paying $1,000 in six months or one paying $1,001 in one year?

13. By adopting technologically advanced methods, suppose that geologists find previously-unknown fault lines deep underground. What will happen to insurance rates for earthquake protection for houses in the area? If you think they will change, do you think it will be by a large or small amount?

14. When you apply for a loan, the loan officer gives you the option of posting collateral in return for a lower interest rate. What is the rationale of the loan officer?

15.* Everything else being equal, which would be more valuable to you—a derivative instrument whose value is derived from an underlying instrument with a very volatile price history or one derived from an underlying instrument with a very stable price history? Explain your choice.

16. Explain why a person starting up a small business is more likely to take out a bank loan than to issue bonds.

17. Splitland is a developing economy with two distinct regions. The northern region has great investment opportunities, but the people who live there need to consume all of their income to survive. Those living in the south are better off than their northern counterparts and save a significant portion of their income. The southern region, however, has few profitable investment opportunities and so most of the savings remain in shoeboxes and under mattresses. Explain how the development of the financial sector could benefit both regions and promote economic growth in Splitland.

18. Suppose that a government decides to regulate more heavily the issuance of financial securities, like stocks and bonds. Give an argument that this action will raise economic growth. Give an argument that this action will lower economic growth.

19. Before the financial crisis of 2007–2009, shadow banks were highly leveraged. Explain what this implied about their balance sheets.

20. Explain how a rise in interest rates makes a bank's balance sheet riskier.

21.* As the manager of a financial institution, what steps could you take to reduce the risks referred to in question 20?

www.mhhe.com/cecchetti3e

Appendix from:
Fundamentals of Corporate
Finance, European Edition
by Hillier-Clacher-Ross-
Westerfield-Jordan

APPENDIX A
MATHEMATICAL TABLES

Table A.1 Future value of £1 at the end of t periods = $(1 + r)^t$

Table A.2 Present value of £1 to be received after t periods = $1/(1 + r)^t$

Table A.3 Present value of an annuity of £1 per period for t periods = $[1 - 1/(1 + r)^t]/r$

Table A.4 Future value of an annuity of £1 per period for t periods = $[(1 + r)^t - 1]/r$

Table A.5 Cumulative normal distribution

TABLE
A.1

Period	1%	2%	3%	4%	5%	6%	7%	8%	9%	10%	12%	14%	15%	16%	18%	20%	24%	28%	32%	36%
1	1.0100	1.0200	1.0300	1.0400	1.0500	1.0600	1.0700	1.0800	1.0900	1.1000	1.1200	1.1400	1.1500	1.1600	1.1800	1.2000	1.2400	1.2800	1.3200	1.3600
2	1.0201	1.0404	1.0609	1.0816	1.1025	1.1236	1.1449	1.1664	1.1881	1.2100	1.2544	1.2996	1.3225	1.3456	1.3924	1.4400	1.5376	1.6384	1.7424	1.8496
3	1.0303	1.0612	1.0927	1.1249	1.1576	1.1910	1.2250	1.2597	1.2950	1.3310	1.4049	1.4815	1.5209	1.5609	1.6430	1.7280	1.9066	2.0972	2.3000	2.5155
4	1.0406	1.0824	1.1255	1.1699	1.2155	1.2625	1.3108	1.3605	1.4116	1.4641	1.5735	1.6890	1.7490	1.8106	1.9388	2.0736	2.3642	2.6844	3.0360	3.4210
5	1.0510	1.1041	1.1593	1.2167	1.2763	1.3382	1.4026	1.4693	1.5386	1.6105	1.7623	1.9254	2.0114	2.1003	2.2878	2.4883	2.9316	3.4360	4.0075	4.6526
6	1.0615	1.1262	1.1941	1.2653	1.3401	1.4185	1.5007	1.5869	1.6771	1.7716	1.9738	2.1950	2.3131	2.4364	2.6996	2.9860	3.6352	4.3980	5.2899	6.3275
7	1.0721	1.1487	1.2299	1.3159	1.4071	1.5036	1.6058	1.7138	1.8280	1.9487	2.2107	2.5023	2.6600	2.8262	3.1855	3.5832	4.5077	5.6295	6.9826	8.6054
8	1.0829	1.1717	1.2668	1.3686	1.4775	1.5938	1.7182	1.8509	1.9926	2.1436	2.4760	2.8526	3.0590	3.2784	3.7589	4.2998	5.5895	7.2058	9.2170	11.703
9	1.0937	1.1951	1.3048	1.4233	1.5513	1.6895	1.8385	1.9990	2.1719	2.3579	2.7731	3.2519	3.5179	3.8030	4.4355	5.1598	6.9310	9.2234	12.166	15.917
10	1.1046	1.2190	1.3439	1.4802	1.6289	1.7908	1.9672	2.1589	2.3674	2.5937	3.1058	3.7072	4.0456	4.4114	5.2338	6.1917	8.5944	11.806	16.060	21.647
11	1.1157	1.2434	1.3842	1.5395	1.7103	1.8983	2.1049	2.3316	2.5804	2.8531	3.4785	4.2262	4.6524	5.1173	6.1759	7.4301	10.657	15.112	21.199	29.439
12	1.1268	1.2682	1.4258	1.6010	1.7959	2.0122	2.2522	2.5182	2.8127	3.1384	3.8960	4.8179	5.3503	5.9360	7.2876	8.9161	13.215	19.343	27.983	40.037
13	1.1381	1.2936	1.4685	1.6651	1.8856	2.1329	2.4098	2.7196	3.0658	3.4523	4.3635	5.4924	6.1528	6.8858	8.5994	10.699	16.386	24.759	36.937	54.451
14	1.1495	1.3195	1.5126	1.7317	1.9799	2.2609	2.5785	2.9372	3.3417	3.7975	4.8871	6.2613	7.0757	7.9875	10.147	12.839	20.319	31.691	48.757	74.053
15	1.1610	1.3459	1.5580	1.8009	2.0789	2.3966	2.7590	3.1722	3.6425	4.1772	5.4736	7.1379	8.1371	9.2655	11.974	15.407	25.196	40.565	64.359	100.71
16	1.1726	1.3728	1.6047	1.8730	2.1829	2.5404	2.9522	3.4259	3.9703	4.5950	6.1304	8.1372	9.3576	10.748	14.129	18.488	31.243	51.923	84.954	136.97
17	1.1843	1.4002	1.6528	1.9479	2.2920	2.6928	3.1588	3.7000	4.3276	5.0545	6.8660	9.2765	10.761	12.468	16.672	22.186	38.741	66.461	112.14	186.28
18	1.1961	1.4282	1.7024	2.0258	2.4066	2.8543	3.3799	3.9960	4.7171	5.5599	7.6900	10.575	12.375	14.463	19.673	26.623	48.039	85.071	148.02	253.34
19	1.2081	1.4568	1.7535	2.1068	2.5270	3.0256	3.6165	4.3157	5.1417	6.1159	8.6128	12.056	14.232	16.777	23.214	31.948	59.568	108.89	195.39	344.54
20	1.2202	1.4859	1.8061	2.1911	2.6533	3.2071	3.8697	4.6610	5.6044	6.7275	9.6463	13.743	16.367	19.461	27.393	38.338	73.864	139.38	257.92	468.57
21	1.2324	1.5157	1.8603	2.2788	2.7860	3.3996	4.1406	5.0338	6.1088	7.4002	10.804	15.668	18.822	22.574	32.324	46.005	91.592	178.41	340.45	637.26
22	1.2447	1.5460	1.9161	2.3699	2.9253	3.6035	4.4304	5.4365	6.6586	8.1403	12.100	17.861	21.645	26.186	38.142	55.206	113.57	228.36	449.39	866.67
23	1.2572	1.5769	1.9736	2.4647	3.0715	3.8197	4.7405	5.8715	7.2579	8.9543	13.552	20.362	24.891	30.376	45.008	66.247	140.83	292.30	593.20	1178.7
24	1.2697	1.6084	2.0328	2.5633	3.2251	4.0489	5.0724	6.3412	7.9111	9.8497	15.179	23.212	28.625	35.236	53.109	79.497	174.63	374.14	783.02	1603.0
25	1.2824	1.6406	2.0938	2.6658	3.3864	4.2919	5.4274	6.8485	8.6231	10.835	17.000	26.462	32.919	40.874	62.669	95.396	216.54	478.90	1033.6	2180.1
30	1.3478	1.8114	2.4273	3.2434	4.3219	5.7435	7.6123	10.063	13.268	17.449	29.960	50.950	66.212	85.850	143.37	237.38	634.82	1645.5	4142.1	10143.
40	1.4889	2.2080	3.2620	4.8010	7.0400	10.286	14.974	21.725	31.409	45.259	93.051	188.88	267.86	378.72	750.38	1469.8	5455.9	19427.	66521.	*
50	1.6446	2.6916	4.3839	7.1067	11.467	18.420	29.457	46.902	74.358	117.39	289.00	700.23	1083.7	1670.7	3927.4	9100.4	46890.	*	*	*
60	1.8167	3.2810	5.8916	10.520	18.679	32.988	57.946	101.26	176.03	304.48	897.60	2595.9	4384.0	7370.2	20555.	56348.	*	*	*	*

Interest Rate

*The factor is greater than 99,999.

Table A.1 Future value of £1 at the end of t periods $= (1 + r)^t$

Interest Rate

Period	1%	2%	3%	4%	5%	6%	7%	8%	9%	10%	12%	14%	15%	16%	18%	20%	24%	28%	32%	36%
1	.9901	.9804	.9709	.9615	.9524	.9434	.9346	.9259	.9174	.9091	.8929	.8772	.8696	.8621	.8475	.8333	.8065	.7813	.7576	.7353
2	.9803	.9612	.9426	.9246	.9070	.8900	.8734	.8573	.8417	.8264	.7972	.7695	.7561	.7432	.7182	.6944	.6504	.6104	.5739	.5407
3	.9706	.9423	.9151	.8890	.8638	.8396	.8163	.7938	.7722	.7513	.7118	.6750	.6575	.6407	.6086	.5787	.5245	.4768	.4348	.3975
4	.9610	.9238	.8885	.8548	.8227	.7921	.7629	.7350	.7084	.6830	.6355	.5921	.5718	.5523	.5158	.4823	.4230	.3725	.3294	.2923
5	.9515	.9057	.8626	.8219	.7835	.7473	.7130	.6806	.6499	.6209	.5674	.5194	.4972	.4761	.4371	.4019	.3411	.2910	.2495	.2149
6	.9420	.8880	.8375	.7903	.7462	.7050	.6663	.6302	.5963	.5645	.5066	.4556	.4323	.4104	.3704	.3349	.2751	.2274	.1890	.1580
7	.9327	.8706	.8131	.7599	.7107	.6651	.6227	.5835	.5470	.5132	.4523	.3996	.3759	.3538	.3139	.2791	.2218	.1776	.1432	.1162
8	.9235	.8535	.7894	.7307	.6768	.6274	.5820	.5403	.5019	.4665	.4039	.3506	.3269	.3050	.2660	.2326	.1789	.1388	.1085	.0854
9	.9143	.8368	.7664	.7026	.6446	.5919	.5439	.5002	.4604	.4241	.3606	.3075	.2843	.2630	.2255	.1938	.1443	.1084	.0822	.0628
10	.9053	.8203	.7441	.6756	.6139	.5584	.5083	.4632	.4224	.3855	.3220	.2697	.2472	.2267	.1911	.1615	.1164	.0847	.0623	.0462
11	.8963	.8043	.7224	.6496	.5847	.5268	.4751	.4289	.3875	.3505	.2875	.2366	.2149	.1954	.1619	.1346	.0938	.0662	.0472	.0340
12	.8874	.7885	.7014	.6246	.5568	.4970	.4440	.3971	.3555	.3186	.2567	.2076	.1869	.1685	.1372	.1122	.0757	.0517	.0357	.0250
13	.8787	.7730	.6810	.6006	.5303	.4688	.4150	.3677	.3262	.2897	.2292	.1821	.1625	.1452	.1163	.0935	.0610	.0404	.0271	.0184
14	.8700	.7579	.6611	.5775	.5051	.4423	.3878	.3405	.2992	.2633	.2046	.1597	.1413	.1252	.0985	.0779	.0492	.0316	.0205	.0135
15	.8613	.7430	.6419	.5553	.4810	.4173	.3624	.3152	.2745	.2394	.1827	.1401	.1229	.1079	.0835	.0649	.0397	.0247	.0155	.0099
16	.8528	.7284	.6232	.5339	.4581	.3936	.3387	.2919	.2519	.2176	.1631	.1229	.1069	.0930	.0708	.0541	.0320	.0193	.0118	.0073
17	.8444	.7142	.6050	.5134	.4363	.3714	.3166	.2703	.2311	.1978	.1456	.1078	.0929	.0802	.0600	.0451	.0258	.0150	.0089	.0054
18	.8360	.7002	.5874	.4936	.4155	.3503	.2959	.2502	.2120	.1799	.1300	.0946	.0808	.0691	.0508	.0376	.0208	.0118	.0068	.0039
19	.8277	.6864	.5703	.4746	.3957	.3305	.2765	.2317	.1945	.1635	.1161	.0829	.0703	.0596	.0431	.0313	.0168	.0092	.0051	.0029
20	.8195	.6730	.5537	.4564	.3769	.3118	.2584	.2145	.1784	.1486	.1037	.0728	.0611	.0514	.0365	.0261	.0135	.0072	.0039	.0021
21	.8114	.6598	.5375	.4388	.3589	.2942	.2415	.1987	.1637	.1351	.0926	.0638	.0531	.0443	.0309	.0217	.0109	.0056	.0029	.0016
22	.8034	.6468	.5219	.4220	.3418	.2775	.2257	.1839	.1502	.1228	.0826	.0560	.0462	.0382	.0262	.0181	.0088	.0044	.0022	.0012
23	.7954	.6342	.5067	.4057	.3256	.2618	.2109	.1703	.1378	.1117	.0738	.0491	.0402	.0329	.0222	.0151	.0071	.0034	.0017	.0008
24	.7876	.6217	.4919	.3901	.3101	.2470	.1971	.1577	.1264	.1015	.0659	.0431	.0349	.0284	.0188	.0126	.0057	.0027	.0013	.0006
25	.7798	.6095	.4776	.3751	.2953	.2330	.1842	.1460	.1160	.0923	.0588	.0378	.0304	.0245	.0160	.0105	.0046	.0021	.0010	.0005
30	.7419	.5521	.4120	.3083	.2314	.1741	.1314	.0994	.0754	.0573	.0334	.0196	.0151	.0116	.0070	.0042	.0016	.0006	.0002	.0001
40	.6717	.4529	.3066	.2083	.1420	.0972	.0668	.0460	.0318	.0221	.0107	.0053	.0037	.0026	.0013	.0007	.0002	.0001	*	*
50	.6080	.3715	.2281	.1407	.0872	.0543	.0339	.0213	.0134	.0085	.0035	.0014	.0009	.0006	.0003	.0001	*	*	*	*

*The factor is zero to four decimal places.

Table A.2 Present value of £1 to be received after t periods $= 1/(1 + r)^t$

TABLE A.2

TABLE A.3

Number of Periods	Interest Rate																			
	1%	2%	3%	4%	5%	6%	7%	8%	9%	10%	12%	14%	15%	16%	18%	20%	24%	28%	32%	36%
1	.9901	.9804	.9709	.9615	.9524	.9434	.9346	.9259	.9174	.9091	.8929	.8772	.8696	.8621	.8475	.8333	.8065	.7813	.7576	.7353
2	1.9704	1.9416	1.9135	1.8861	1.8594	1.8334	1.8080	1.7833	1.7591	1.7355	1.6901	1.6467	1.6257	1.6052	1.5656	1.5278	1.4568	1.3916	1.3315	1.2760
3	2.9410	2.8839	2.8286	2.7751	2.7232	2.6730	2.6243	2.5771	2.5313	2.4869	2.4018	2.3216	2.2832	2.2459	2.1743	2.1065	1.9813	1.8684	1.7663	1.6735
4	3.9020	3.8077	3.7171	3.6299	3.5460	3.4651	3.3872	3.3121	3.2397	3.1699	3.0373	2.9137	2.8550	2.7982	2.6901	2.5887	2.4043	2.2410	2.0957	1.9658
5	4.8534	4.7135	4.5797	4.4518	4.3295	4.2124	4.1002	3.9927	3.8897	3.7908	3.6048	3.4331	3.3522	3.2743	3.1272	2.9906	2.7454	2.5320	2.3452	2.1807
6	5.7955	5.6014	5.4172	5.2421	5.0757	4.9173	4.7665	4.6229	4.4859	4.3553	4.1114	3.8887	3.7845	3.6847	3.4976	3.3255	3.0205	2.7594	2.5342	2.3388
7	6.7282	6.4720	6.2303	6.0021	5.7864	5.5824	5.3893	5.2064	5.0330	4.8684	4.5638	4.2883	4.1604	4.0386	3.8115	3.6046	3.2423	2.9370	2.6775	2.4550
8	7.6517	7.3255	7.0197	6.7327	6.4632	6.2098	5.9713	5.7466	5.5348	5.3349	4.9676	4.6389	4.4873	4.3436	4.0776	3.8372	3.4212	3.0758	2.7860	2.5404
9	8.5660	8.1622	7.7861	7.4353	7.1078	6.8017	6.5152	6.2469	5.9952	5.7590	5.3282	4.9464	4.7716	4.6065	4.3030	4.0310	3.5655	3.1842	2.8681	2.6033
10	9.4713	8.9826	8.5302	8.1109	7.7217	7.3601	7.0236	6.7101	6.4177	6.1446	5.6502	5.2161	5.0188	4.8332	4.4941	4.1925	3.6819	3.2689	2.9304	2.6495
11	10.3676	9.7868	9.2526	8.7605	8.3064	7.8869	7.4987	7.1390	6.8052	6.4951	5.9377	5.4527	5.2337	5.0286	4.6560	4.3271	3.7757	3.3351	2.9776	2.6834
12	11.2551	10.5753	9.9540	9.3851	8.8633	8.3838	7.9427	7.5361	7.1607	6.8137	6.1944	5.6603	5.4206	5.1971	4.7932	4.4392	3.8514	3.3868	3.0133	2.7084
13	12.1337	11.3484	10.6350	9.9856	9.3936	8.8527	8.3577	7.9038	7.4869	7.1034	6.4235	5.8424	5.5831	5.3423	4.9095	4.5327	3.9124	3.4272	3.0404	2.7268
14	13.0037	12.1062	11.2961	10.5631	9.8986	9.2950	8.7455	8.2442	7.7862	7.3667	6.6282	6.0021	5.7245	5.4675	5.0081	4.6106	3.9616	3.4587	3.0609	2.7403
15	13.8651	12.8493	11.9379	11.1184	10.3797	9.7122	9.1079	8.5595	8.0607	7.6061	6.8109	6.1422	5.8474	5.5755	5.0916	4.6755	4.0013	3.4834	3.0764	2.7502
16	14.7179	13.5777	12.5611	11.6523	10.8378	10.1059	9.4466	8.8514	8.3126	7.8237	6.9740	6.2651	5.9542	5.6685	5.1624	4.7296	4.0333	3.5026	3.0882	2.7575
17	15.5623	14.2919	13.1661	12.1657	11.2741	10.4773	9.7632	9.1216	8.5436	8.0216	7.1196	6.3729	6.0472	5.7487	5.2223	4.7746	4.0591	3.5177	3.0971	2.7629
18	16.3983	14.9920	13.7535	12.6593	11.6896	10.8276	10.0591	9.3719	8.7556	8.2014	7.2497	6.4674	6.1280	5.8178	5.2732	4.8122	4.0799	3.5294	3.1039	2.7668
19	17.2260	15.6785	14.3238	13.1339	12.0853	11.1581	10.3356	9.6036	8.9501	8.3649	7.3658	6.5504	6.1982	5.8775	5.3162	4.8435	4.0967	3.5386	3.1090	2.7697
20	18.0456	16.3514	14.8775	13.5903	12.4622	11.4699	10.5940	9.8181	9.1285	8.5136	7.4694	6.6231	6.2593	5.9288	5.3527	4.8696	4.1103	3.5458	3.1129	2.7718
21	18.8570	17.0112	15.4150	14.0292	12.8212	11.7641	10.8355	10.0168	9.2922	8.6487	7.5620	6.6870	6.3125	5.9731	5.3837	4.8913	4.1212	3.5514	3.1158	2.7734
22	19.6604	17.6580	15.9369	14.4511	13.1630	12.0416	11.0612	10.2007	9.4424	8.7715	7.6446	6.7429	6.3587	6.0113	5.4099	4.9094	4.1300	3.5558	3.1180	2.7746
23	20.4558	18.2922	16.4436	14.8568	13.4886	12.3034	11.2722	10.3741	9.5802	8.8832	7.7184	6.7921	6.3988	6.0442	5.4321	4.9245	4.1371	3.5592	3.1197	2.7754
24	21.2434	18.9139	16.9355	15.2470	13.7986	12.5504	11.4693	10.5288	9.7066	8.9847	7.7843	6.8351	6.4338	6.0726	5.4509	4.9371	4.1428	3.5619	3.1210	2.7760
25	22.0232	19.5235	17.4131	15.6221	14.0939	12.7834	11.6536	10.6748	9.8226	9.0770	7.8431	6.8729	6.4641	6.0971	5.4669	4.9476	4.1474	3.5640	3.1220	2.7765
30	25.8077	22.3965	19.6004	17.2920	15.3725	13.7648	12.4090	11.2578	10.2737	9.4269	8.0552	7.0027	6.5660	6.1772	5.5168	4.9789	4.1601	3.5693	3.1242	2.7775
40	32.8347	27.3555	23.1148	19.7928	17.1591	15.0463	13.3317	11.9246	10.7574	9.7791	8.2438	7.1050	6.6418	6.2335	5.5482	4.9966	4.1659	3.5712	3.1250	2.7778
50	39.1961	31.4236	25.7298	21.4822	18.2559	15.7619	13.8007	12.2335	10.9617	9.9148	8.3045	7.1327	6.6605	6.2463	5.5541	4.9995	4.1666	3.5714	3.1250	2.7778

Table A.3 Present value of an annuity of £1 per period for t periods $= [1 - 1/(1 + r)^t]/r$

TABLE A.4

Number of Periods	1%	2%	3%	4%	5%	6%	7%	8%	9%	10%	12%	14%	15%	16%	18%	20%	24%	28%	32%	36%
1	1.0000	1.0000	1.0000	1.0000	1.0000	1.0000	1.0000	1.0000	1.0000	1.0000	1.0000	1.0000	1.0000	1.0000	1.0000	1.0000	1.0000	1.0000	1.0000	1.0000
2	2.0100	2.0200	2.0300	2.0400	2.0500	2.0600	2.0700	2.0800	2.0900	2.1000	2.1200	2.1400	2.1500	2.1600	2.1800	2.2000	2.2400	2.2800	2.3200	2.3600
3	3.0301	3.0604	3.0909	3.1216	3.1525	3.1836	3.2149	3.2464	3.2781	3.3100	3.3744	3.4396	3.4725	3.5056	3.5724	3.6400	3.7776	3.9184	4.0624	4.2096
4	4.0604	4.1216	4.1836	4.2465	4.3101	4.3746	4.4399	4.5061	4.5731	4.6410	4.7793	4.9211	4.9934	5.0665	5.2154	5.3680	5.6842	6.0156	6.3624	6.7251
5	5.1010	5.2040	5.3091	5.4163	5.5256	5.6371	5.7507	5.8666	5.9847	6.1051	6.3528	6.6101	6.7424	6.8771	7.1542	7.4416	8.0484	8.6999	9.3983	10.146
6	6.1520	6.3081	6.4684	6.6330	6.8019	6.9753	7.1533	7.3359	7.5233	7.7156	8.1152	8.5355	8.7537	8.9775	9.4420	9.9299	10.980	12.136	13.406	14.799
7	7.2135	7.4343	7.6625	7.8983	8.1420	8.3938	8.6540	8.9228	9.2004	9.4872	10.089	10.730	11.067	11.414	12.142	12.916	14.615	16.534	18.696	21.126
8	8.2857	8.5830	8.8932	9.2142	9.5491	9.8975	10.260	10.637	11.028	11.436	12.300	13.233	13.727	14.240	15.327	16.499	19.123	22.163	25.678	29.732
9	9.3685	9.7546	10.159	10.583	11.027	11.491	11.978	12.488	13.021	13.579	14.776	16.085	16.786	17.519	19.086	20.799	24.712	29.369	34.895	41.435
10	10.462	10.950	11.464	12.006	12.578	13.181	13.816	14.487	15.193	15.937	17.549	19.337	20.304	21.321	23.521	25.959	31.643	38.593	47.062	57.352
11	11.567	12.169	12.808	13.486	14.207	14.972	15.784	16.645	17.560	18.531	20.655	23.045	24.349	25.733	28.755	32.150	40.238	50.398	63.122	78.998
12	12.683	13.412	14.192	15.026	15.917	16.870	17.888	18.977	20.141	21.384	24.133	27.271	29.002	30.850	34.931	39.581	50.895	65.510	84.320	108.44
13	13.809	14.680	15.618	16.627	17.713	18.882	20.141	21.495	22.953	24.523	28.029	32.089	34.352	36.786	42.219	48.497	64.110	84.853	112.30	148.47
14	14.947	15.974	17.086	18.292	19.599	21.015	22.550	24.215	26.019	27.975	32.393	37.581	40.505	43.672	50.818	59.196	80.496	109.61	149.24	202.93
15	16.097	17.293	18.599	20.024	21.579	23.276	25.129	27.152	29.361	31.772	37.280	43.842	47.580	51.660	60.965	72.035	100.82	141.30	198.00	276.98
16	17.258	18.639	20.157	21.825	23.657	25.673	27.888	30.324	33.003	35.950	42.753	50.980	55.717	60.925	72.939	87.442	126.01	181.87	262.36	377.69
17	18.430	20.012	21.762	23.698	25.840	28.213	30.840	33.750	36.974	40.545	48.884	59.118	65.075	71.673	87.068	105.93	157.25	233.79	347.31	514.66
18	19.615	21.412	23.414	25.645	28.132	30.906	33.999	37.450	41.301	45.599	55.750	68.394	75.836	84.141	103.74	128.12	195.99	300.25	459.45	700.94
19	20.811	22.841	25.117	27.671	30.539	33.760	37.379	41.446	46.018	51.159	63.440	78.969	88.212	98.603	123.41	154.74	244.03	385.32	607.47	954.28
20	22.019	24.297	26.870	29.778	33.066	36.786	40.995	45.762	51.160	57.275	72.052	91.025	102.44	115.38	146.63	186.69	303.60	494.21	802.86	1298.8
21	23.239	25.783	28.676	31.969	35.719	39.993	44.865	50.423	56.765	64.002	81.699	104.77	118.81	134.84	174.02	225.03	377.46	633.59	1060.8	1767.4
22	24.472	27.299	30.537	34.248	38.505	43.392	49.006	55.457	62.873	71.403	92.503	120.44	137.63	157.41	206.34	271.03	469.06	812.00	1401.2	2404.7
23	25.716	28.845	32.453	36.618	41.430	46.996	53.436	60.893	69.532	79.543	104.60	138.30	159.28	183.60	244.49	326.24	582.63	1040.4	1850.6	3271.3
24	26.973	30.422	34.426	39.083	44.502	50.816	58.177	66.765	76.790	88.497	118.16	158.66	184.17	213.98	289.49	392.48	723.46	1332.7	2443.8	4450.0
25	28.243	32.030	36.459	41.646	47.727	54.865	63.249	73.106	84.701	98.347	133.33	181.87	212.79	249.21	342.60	471.98	898.09	1706.8	3226.8	6053.0
30	34.785	40.568	47.575	56.085	66.439	79.058	94.461	113.28	136.31	164.49	241.33	356.79	434.75	530.31	790.95	1181.9	2640.9	5873.2	12941.	28172.
40	48.886	60.402	75.401	95.026	120.80	154.76	199.64	259.06	337.88	442.59	767.09	1342.0	1779.1	2360.8	4163.2	7343.9	22729.	69377.	*	*
50	64.463	84.579	112.80	152.67	209.35	290.34	406.53	573.77	815.08	1163.9	2400.0	4994.5	7217.7	10436.	21813.	45497.	*	*	*	*
60	81.670	114.05	163.05	237.99	353.58	533.13	813.52	1253.2	1944.8	3043.8	7471.6	18535.	29220.	46058.	*	*	*	*	*	*

Interest Rate

*The factor is greater than 99,999.

Table A.4 Future value of an annuity of £1 per period for t periods $= [(1 + r)^t - 1]/r$

TABLE A.5

d	N(d)	d	N(d)	d	N(d)	d	N(d)	d	N(d)	d	N(d)
−3.00	.0013	−1.58	.0571	−.76	.2236	.06	.5239	.86	.8051	1.66	.9515
−2.95	.0016	−1.56	.0594	−.74	.2297	.08	.5319	.88	.8106	1.68	.9535
−2.90	.0019	−1.54	.0618	−.72	.2358	.10	.5398	.90	.8159	1.70	.9554
−2.85	.0022	−1.52	.0643	−.70	.2420	.12	.5478	.92	.8212	1.72	.9573
−2.80	.0026	−1.50	.0668	−.68	.2483	.14	.5557	.94	.8264	1.74	.9591
−2.75	.0030	−1.48	.0694	−.66	.2546	.16	.5636	.96	.8315	1.76	.9608
−2.70	.0035	−1.46	.0721	−.64	.2611	.18	.5714	.98	.8365	1.78	.9625
−2.65	.0040	−1.44	.0749	−.62	.2676	.20	.5793	1.00	.8413	1.80	.9641
−2.60	.0047	−1.42	.0778	−.60	.2743	.22	.5871	1.02	.8461	1.82	.9656
−2.55	.0054	−1.40	.0808	−.58	.2810	.24	.5948	1.04	.8508	1.84	.9671
−2.50	.0062	−1.38	.0838	−.56	.2877	.26	.6026	1.06	.8554	1.86	.9686
−2.45	.0071	−1.36	.0869	−.54	.2946	.28	.6103	1.08	.8599	1.88	.9699
−2.40	.0082	−1.34	.0901	−.52	.3015	.30	.6179	1.10	.8643	1.90	.9713
−2.35	.0094	−1.32	.0934	−.50	.3085	.32	.6255	1.12	.8686	1.92	.9726
−2.30	.0107	−1.30	.0968	−.48	.3156	.34	.6331	1.14	.8729	1.94	.9738
−2.25	.0122	−1.28	.1003	−.46	.3228	.36	.6406	1.16	.8770	1.96	.9750
−2.20	.0139	−1.26	.1038	−.44	.3300	.38	.6480	1.18	.8810	1.98	.9761
−2.15	.0158	−1.24	.1075	−.42	.3372	.40	.6554	1.20	.8849	2.00	.9772
−2.10	.0179	−1.22	.1112	−.40	.3446	.42	.6628	1.22	.8888	2.05	.9798
−2.05	.0202	−1.20	.1151	−.38	.3520	.44	.6700	1.24	.8925	2.10	.9821
−2.00	.0228	−1.18	.1190	−.36	.3594	.46	.6772	1.26	.8962	2.15	.9842
−1.98	.0239	−1.16	.1230	−.34	.3669	.48	.6844	1.28	.8997	2.20	.9861
−1.96	.0250	−1.14	.1271	−.32	.3745	.50	.6915	1.30	.9032	2.25	.9878
−1.94	.0262	−1.12	.1314	−.30	.3821	.52	.6985	1.32	.9066	2.30	.9893
−1.92	.0274	−1.10	.1357	−.28	.3897	.54	.7054	1.34	.9099	2.35	.9906
−1.90	.0287	−1.08	.1401	−.26	.3974	.56	.7123	1.36	.9131	2.40	.9918
−1.88	.0301	−1.06	.1446	−.24	.4052	.58	.7190	1.38	.9162	2.45	.9929
−1.86	.0314	−1.04	.1492	−.22	.4129	.60	.7257	1.40	.9192	2.50	.9938
−1.84	.0329	−1.02	.1539	−.20	.4207	.62	.7324	1.42	.9222	2.55	.9946
−1.82	.0344	−1.00	.1587	−.18	.4286	.64	.7389	1.44	.9251	2.60	.9953
−1.80	.0359	−.98	.1635	−.16	.4364	.66	.7454	1.46	.9279	2.65	.9960
−1.78	.0375	−.96	.1685	−.14	.4443	.68	.7518	1.48	.9306	2.70	.9965
−1.76	.0392	−.94	.1736	−.12	.4522	.70	.7580	1.50	.9332	2.75	.9970
−1.74	.0409	−.92	.1788	−.10	.4602	.72	.7642	1.52	.9357	2.80	.9974
−1.72	.0427	−.90	.1841	−.08	.4681	.74	.7704	1.54	.9382	2.85	.9978
−1.70	.0446	−.88	.1894	−.06	.4761	.76	.7764	1.56	.9406	2.90	.9981
−1.68	.0465	−.86	.1949	−.04	.4840	.78	.7823	1.58	.9429	2.95	.9984
−1.66	.0485	−.84	.2005	−.02	.4920	.80	.7881	1.60	.9452	3.00	.9987
−1.64	.0505	−.82	.2061	.00	.5000	.82	.7939	1.62	.9474	3.05	.9989
−1.62	.0526	−.80	.2119	.02	.5080	.84	.7995	1.64	.9495		
−1.60	.0548	−.78	.2177	.04	.5160						

This table shows the probability [N(d)] of observing a value less than or equal to d. For example, as illustrated, if d is −.24, then N(d) is .4052.

Table A.5 Cumulative normal distribution